ALSO BY STEPHEN E. AMBROSE

Eisenhower and Berlin, 1945

The Supreme Commander

Rise to Globalism

Crazy Horse and Custer

Pegasus Bridge

Nixon: The Education of a Politician

Nixon: The Triumph of a Politician, 1962–72

Nixon: Ruin and Recovery, 1973–1990

Band of Brothers

Upton and the Army

D-Day

Halleck

Eisenhower

Citizen Soldiers

Americans at War

Duty, Honor, Country

Ike's Spies

The Victors

Comrades

Nothing Like It In The World

Wild Blue

To America

Stephen E. Ambrose

UNDAUNTED
COURAGE

*The Pioneering First Mission To Explore
America's Wild Frontier*

POCKET
BOOKS

LONDON • SYDNEY • NEW YORK • TOKYO • TORONTO

This edition published by Pocket Books, 2003
An imprint of Simon & Schuster UK Ltd
A Viacom Company

5 7 9 10 8 6 4

Simon & Schuster UK Ltd
Africa House
64-78 Kingsway
London WC2B 6AH

www.simonsays.co.uk

Simon & Schuster Australia
Sydney

A CIP catalogue record for this book is available from the British Library

ISBN 0-7434-7788-X

Typeset by M Rules
Printed and bound in Great Britain by
Cox & Wyman Ltd, Reading, Berks

For Bob Tubbs

"Of courage undaunted, possessing a firmness & perseverance of purpose which nothing but impossibilities could divert from it's direction, careful as a father of those committed to his charge, yet steady in the maintenance of order & discipline, intimate with the Indian character, customs & principles, habituated to the hunting life, guarded by exact observation of the vegetables & animals of his own country, against losing time in the description of objects already possessed, honest, disinterested, liberal, of sound understanding and a fidelity to truth so scrupulous that whatever he should report would be as certain as if seen by ourselves, with all these qualifications as if selected and implanted by nature in one body, for this express purpose, I could have no hesitation in confiding the enterprize to him."

—THOMAS JEFFERSON
on Meriwether Lewis

CONTENTS

INTRODUCTION   xiii

ACKNOWLEDGMENTS   xvii

1   Youth   1
1774–1792

2   Planter   13
1792–1794

3   Soldier   23
1794–1800

4   Thomas Jefferson's America   38
1801

5   The President's Secretary   46
1801–1802

6   The Origins of the Expedition   57
1750–1802

7   Preparing for the Expedition   71
January–June 1803

8   Washington to Pittsburgh   86
June–August 1803

9   Down the Ohio   103
September–November 1803

10   Up the Mississippi to Winter Camp   118
November 1803–March 1804

11   Ready to Depart   131
April–May 21, 1804

12   Up the Missouri   139
May–July 1804

13   Entering Indian Country   152
August 1804

14 Encounter with the Sioux   167
    September 1804

15 To the Mandans   180
    Fall 1804

16 Winter at Fort Mandan   196
    December 21, 1804–March 21, 1805

17 Report from Fort Mandan   207
    March 22–April 6, 1805

18 From Fort Mandan to Marias River   218
    April 7–June 2, 1805

19 From Marias River to the Great Falls   240
    June 3–June 20, 1805

20 The Great Portage   252
    June 16–July 14, 1805

21 Looking for the Shoshones   264
    July 15–August 12, 1805

22 Over the Continental Divide   283
    August 13–August 31, 1805

23 Lewis as Ethnographer   301
    The Shoshones

24 Over the Bitterroots   307
    September 1–October 6, 1805

25 Down the Columbia   322
    October 8–December 7, 1805

26 Fort Clatsop   339
    December 8, 1805–March 23, 1806

27 Lewis as Ethnographer   359
    The Clatsops and the Chinooks

28 Jefferson and the West   365
    1804–1806

29 Return to the Nez Percé   378
    March 23–June 9, 1806

30 The Lolo Trail   397
    June 10–July 2, 1806

31 The Marias Exploration   409
    July 3–July 28, 1806

32 The Last Leg 428
July 29–September 22, 1806

33 Reporting to the President 441
September 23–December 31, 1806

34 Washington 459
January–March 1807

35 Philadelphia 469
April–July 1807

36 Virginia 478
August 1806–March 1807

37 St. Louis 485
March–December 1808

38 St. Louis 503
January–August 1809

39 Last Voyage 515
September 3–October 11, 1809

40 Aftermath 522

NOTES 533

BIBLIOGRAPHY 556

INDEX 00

MAPS

The Lewis and Clark Expedition 74

Up the Missouri 142

Headwaters of the Missouri 222

Crossing the Bitterroot Mountains 316

Exploring the Mouth of the Columbia 344

Traveler's Rest 412

INTRODUCTION

On the nation's twenty-seventh birthday, July 4, 1803, President Thomas Jefferson proclaimed, in the pages of the Washington, D.C., *National Intelligencer*, that the United States had just purchased from Napoleon "Louisiana." It was not only New Orleans, but all the country drained from the west by the Mississippi River, most especially all the Missouri River drainage. That was 825,000 square miles, doubling the size of the country for a price of about fifteen million dollars—the best land bargain ever made.

That same July 4, the president gave to Meriwether Lewis a letter authorizing him to draw on any agency of the U.S. government anywhere in the world anything he wanted for an exploring expedition to the Pacific Ocean. He also authorized Lewis to call on "citizens of any nation to furnish you with those supplies which your necessities may call for" and signed "this letter of general credit for you with my own hand," thus pledging the faith of the United States government. This must be the most unlimited letter of credit ever issued by an American president.

The next day, July 5, 1803, Lewis set off. His purpose was to look for an all-water route across the western two-thirds of the continent, and to discover and describe what Jefferson had bought from Napoleon.

The Louisiana Purchase and the Lewis and Clark Expedition stretched the boundaries of the United States from sea to shining sea. Thus July 4, 1803, was the beginning of today's nation. The celebration in 1976 was designated as the Bicentennial, and that was appropriate for the original thirteen colonies, but it was with the Louisiana Purchase and the Lewis and Clark Expedition that the United States west of the Mississippi River became a part of the nation. Therefore July 4, 2003, can be regarded as the real Bicentennial.

The Louisiana Purchase in 1803 added everything west of the Mississippi River and east of the Continental Divide to the United States, including today's Louisiana, Arkansas, parts of northeastern Texas, Oklahoma, eastern Colorado, and Minnesota. In their exploration, Lewis and his partner, William Clark, described Missouri,

Kansas, Iowa, Nebraska, the Dakotas, and Montana, all a part of the Purchase. And the expedition made possible the American acquisition of the great Northwest Empire—Idaho, Washington, Oregon. Clark joined Lewis in October 1803, at Clarksville, Indiana Territory, across the Ohio River from Louisville, Kentucky. Thus it was Lewis who became the first man ever to cross the North American continent in today's United States. And it was Clark who, on November 7, 1805, wrote the immortal line, *"Ocian in view! O! the joy."*

Meriwether Lewis was present on March 9, 1804, as the official American witness, at St. Louis, when the first American flag was raised west of the Mississippi River. Later, he and William Clark raised the Stars and Stripes at their campsites along the Missouri River, in the Rocky Mountains, and on the Columbia River, also the first ever, capped by the one at the westernmost camp, near Astoria, Oregon, on the Pacific Ocean.

Thomas Jefferson did so many things of such magnitude that it would be foolish to declare that this or that action—the Declaration of Independence, religious freedom, the Northwest Ordinance of 1787, many others—was the greatest. In the Northwest Ordinance he made certain that when the population of Ohio, Indiana, Illinois, and Wisconsin was large enough these territories would come into the Union as fully equal states. They would have the same number of senators and representatives as the original thirteen states, they would elect their own governors, and so on. Jefferson was the first man who ever had such a thought. All previous empires had been run by the "mother country," with the king appointing the governors, and the legislature in the mother country's capital setting the laws. Jefferson said no: the territories would not be colonies, they would be states, and they would be equal to the original members of the Union. No one knows how things might have turned out if Washington, D.C., had tried to govern the territories west of the Appalachian Mountains.

Surely the best thing Jefferson ever did as president was the Louisiana Purchase. The Federalist Party opposed the Purchase, arguing that nowhere in the Constitution is power granted to the President to purchase additional lands and that in any case the United States should not pay money, of which it had too little, for land, of which it had too much. Jefferson rejoined that nowhere in the Constitution does it say that the president cannot purchase additional lands. And in making the argument that cheap lands in the West were the last things the United States should pay for, the Federalists dug their own grave.

Jefferson also applied the principles of the Northwest Ordinance to the Louisiana Purchase territories—and later, by extension, to the

Northwest Empire. Thus Jefferson, more than any other man, created an empire of liberty that stretched from sea to shining sea.

The next-best thing Jefferson did as president was to organize, set the objectives, and write the orders for an exploring expedition across the country. He then picked Meriwether Lewis to command it, and, at Lewis's insistence, William Clark became co-commander.

Since 1803 and the return of the expedition in 1806, every American everywhere has benefited from Jefferson's purchase of Louisiana and his setting in motion the Lewis and Clark Expedition. And we all live in a democracy and enjoy complete religious liberty, thanks to Jefferson.

I am often asked, "What is the secret to being a successful author?" My reply, always, is: "Marry an English major." Before suppertime, at cocktail hour, Moira listens to me reading whatever I've written in a day, then tells me how good it is (she has been married to a writer for a very long time and knows always what to say first), then says, "But," and tells me to make more of this, less of that, change this word or that image, whatever. She is also there for the research. She has sat beside me, looking at documents, at libraries ranging from the Eisenhower Library in Abilene, Kansas, to the Nixon Collection at Yorba Linda, California, to the Bancroft Library in Berkeley, California. Field research has taken us on a Union Pacific train from Omaha to Sacramento; to Normandy, London, Paris, Belgium, Germany; a couple of times to Italy; lately to the South, Central, and North Pacific.

We were together for every inch of the Lewis and Clark route. Once, in 1976, we were backpacking on the Lolo Trail in the Bitterroot Mountains. She was behind me (where else?) and said, "Walking in Lewis's footsteps makes my feet tingle." That is the kind of line you can get from an English major.

The second secret is: "Get a good editor." My editor for the past two decades and many books has been, and will always be, Alice Mayhew. She is famous, for good reason. When I first told her I wanted to write about Meriwether Lewis for my next book, she insisted that I put in as much Tom Jefferson as possible. Because, she said, people never get tired of reading about Jefferson. She was, as she almost always is, right.

It was Alice who came up with the title for this book. I wanted to call it *Of Courage Undaunted*, the opening phrase of Jefferson's marvelous one-sentence description of Lewis, the finest praise any member of the president's official family ever received from the man himself. Alice changed it to *Undaunted Courage*. That is not only an exact description of Lewis, but of Alice as well. She is the only editor in the whole world with the courage to edit Thomas Jefferson.

That was almost a decade ago. Much has happened since. Moira and I are getting close to the time when the realization of the dream we had then, described in the last paragraph of the Acknowledgments, will come true, for our grandchildren are now in high school.

The best thing that has happened is the number of people who canoe the Missouri and Columbia Rivers, who backpack over the Bitterroots, who visit Lewis and Clark sites all along the Trail. The Bicentennial years, 2003 to 2006, will see an upsurge in the visitation. We want every American to go see at least a part of the trail. It is your duty, your privilege, as an American. We urge you to take only photographs, leave only footprints, as you paddle in the wake of the Corps of Discovery or hike in their footsteps.

Bring along a copy of the Journals of Lewis and Clark. Either the Biddle edition, or the Moulton edition, or De Voto's one-volume abridgment, or any of the other abridgments. And at your campfire, whether on the Missouri River in Missouri or Kansas or Nebraska or Iowa or the Dakotas or Montana, or on Lemhi Pass, or in the Bitterroot Mountains in Idaho, or on the Columbia River in Washington and Oregon, read aloud from the journals. Often, in some stretches nearly always, your campfire will be at the site where Lewis or Clark wrote his account of what happened to the Corps of Discovery that day, describing territory you have just covered, telling about the adventures the men went through on that spot. I guarantee that if you practice you can learn to read well the run-on sentences the captains indulged themselves in, and that when you do, you will have your children or friends or parents or whoever is sitting around that campfire leaning forward just a bit, listening intently, so as not to miss a word. Like you, like me, like every American, they want to know: what happened next?

STEPHEN E. AMBROSE
August 2002

ACKNOWLEDGMENTS

For two decades, I have wanted to write about the Lewis and Clark Expedition. As a biographer, I was drawn to the two captains and wanted to do Lewis, but other projects intervened; besides, there already existed a good biography, written by Richard Dillon and published in 1965. Since I like Clark as much as I do Lewis, and since there was no biography of Clark, in 1992 I called my friend Harry Fritz of the History Department at the University of Montana to ask if he knew of anyone doing Clark. Harry said James Ronda was writing a biography. Since Ronda is one of the leading Lewis and Clark scholars in the country, a fine historian and writer, that was that for Clark.

But then Harry pointed out that in the thirty years since Dillon's biography there has been a tremendous amount of research and writing on Lewis and the expedition. Many new documents by and about Lewis have appeared since 1965, including those in the revised edition of Donald Jackson's great work, *Letters of the Lewis and Clark Expedition.* Further, there are scores of outstanding articles published in *We Proceeded On*, the quarterly journal of the Lewis and Clark Trail Heritage Foundation.* Best of all, there was the new edition of the journals edited by Gary Moulton and published by the University of Nebraska Press, and including among other gems Lewis's journal of his trip down the Ohio River in 1803. Using these new materials and others, Lewis and Clark historians have published more than twenty monographs with various university presses on different aspects of the expedition.

Harry urged me to do an updated biography of Lewis incorporating the new material. Thus this book.

I am grateful to all the Lewis and Clark scholars who have preceded me. I owe a special thanks to Arlen Large and Gary Moulton, who read the manuscript and saved me many errors, while providing innumerable insights.

---

* To join the Foundation and become a subscriber to *We Proceeded On*, write the Lewis and Clark Trail Heritage Foundation, Inc., P.O. Box 3434, Great Falls, MT 59403.

A special thanks to John Howard, Hans von Luck, and Dick Winters for teaching me what makes for a good company commander.

I give up on finding some new way to say what a wonderful editor Alice Mayhew is, but I must thank her for using her blue pencil to curb some of my boyish enthusiasm for Captain Lewis. Her combination assistant, chief of staff, and executive officer, Elizabeth Stein, is a model of efficiency, patience, and good humor. Without Liz, working with Alice would be impossible; with Liz, working with Alice and the entire production team at Simon and Schuster is a joy.

Obviously, WordPerfect Spell Check doesn't work with the imaginative spelling of Lewis and Clark. I had my son Hugh, who has his M.A. in history from the University of Montana (where Harry Fritz was one of his teachers), check each quotation against the Moulton edition of the journals—a demanding task which he carried out splendidly. And I incorporated almost all his suggestions, ranging from questionable word choice to matters of interpretation.

I thank all those who have joined us on one or another part of the Trail, sharing the trials, tribulations, and triumphs.

But most of all Moira and I owe more than can ever be repaid to our children and grandchildren, whose enthusiasm for our outings never flags. They make us so proud and give meaning to our lives. Together we have followed in the footsteps of Crazy Horse and Custer, Lewis and Clark—these were the best days of our lives. Without our children, there would have been no book.

It is our dream that someday they will be taking their grandchildren on horseback over the Lolo, or by canoe down the Missouri, or camping at Lemhi on the Fourth of July, and that for them it will be as it has been for us, the greatest experience of all, one that draws their families together as it has ours.

1

YOUTH

1774–1792

From the west-facing window of the room in which Meriwether Lewis was born on August 18, 1774, one could look out at Rockfish Gap, in the Blue Ridge Mountains, an opening to the West that invited exploration. The Virginia Piedmont of 1774 was not the frontier—that had extended beyond the Allegheny chain of mountains, and a cultured plantation life was nearly a generation old—but it wasn't far removed. Traces of the old buffalo trail that led up Rockfish River to the Gap still remained. Deer were exceedingly plentiful, black bear common. An exterminating war was being waged against wolves. Beaver were on every stream. Flocks of turkeys thronged the woods. In the fall and spring, ducks and geese darkened the rivers.[1]

Lewis was born in a place where the West invited exploration but the East could provide education and knowledge, where the hunting was magnificent but plantation society provided refinement and enlightenment, where he could learn wilderness skills while sharpening his wits about such matters as surveying, politics, natural history, and geography.

The West was very much on Virginians' minds in 1774, even though the big news that year was the Boston Tea Party, the introduction of resolutions in the House of Burgesses in support of Massachusetts, the dissolution of the Burgesses by the Royal Governor Lord Dunmore, and a subsequent meeting at Raleigh Tavern of the dissolved Burgesses, whose Committee of Correspondence sent out letters calling for a general congress of the American colonies. In September, the First

Continental Congress met in Philadelphia, and revolution was under way.

Lord Dunmore was a villain in the eyes of the revolutionaries. He was eventually forced to flee Virginia and take up residence on a British warship. But in January 1774, he had done Virginia a big favor by organizing an offensive into the Ohio country by Virginia militia. The Virginians goaded Shawnee, Ottawa, and other tribes into what became Lord Dunmore's War, which ended with the Indians defeated. They ceded hunting rights in Kentucky to the Virginians and agreed to unhindered access to and navigation on the Ohio River. Within six months, the Transylvania Company sent out Daniel Boone to blaze a trail through the Cumberland Gap to the bluegrass country of Kentucky.

Meanwhile, the British government, in the Quebec Act of 1774, moved to stem the flow of Virginians across the mountains, by extending the boundary of Canada south to the Ohio River. This cut off Virginia's western claims, threatened to spoil the hopes and schemes of innumerable land speculators, including George Washington, and established a highly centralized crown-controlled government with special privileges for the Catholic Church, provoking fear that French Canadians, rather than Protestant Virginians, would rule in the Ohio Valley. This was one of the so-called Intolerable Acts that spurred the revolution.

Meriwether Lewis was born on the eve of revolution into a world of conflict between Americans and the British government for control of the trans-Appalachian West in a colony whose western ambitions were limitless, a colony that was leading the surge of Americans over the mountains, and in a county that was a nursery of explorers.

His family had been a part of the western movement from the beginning. Thomas Jefferson described Lewis's forebears as "one of the distinguished families" of Virginia, and among the earliest. The first Lewis to come to America had been Robert, a Welshman and an officer in the British army. The family coat of arms was "Omne Solum Forti Patria Est," or "All Earth Is to a Brave Man His Country." (An alternate translation is "Everything the Brave Man Does Is for His Country.") Robert arrived in 1635 with a grant from the king for 33,333⅓ acres of Virginia land. He had numerous progeny, including Colonel Robert Lewis, who was wonderfully successful on the Virginia frontier of the eighteenth century, in Albemarle County. On his death, Colonel Lewis was wealthy enough to leave all nine of his children with substantial plantations. His fifth son, William, inherited 1,896 acres, and slaves, and a house, Locust Hill, a rather rustic log home, but very comfortable and filled with things of value, including much table silver. It was just seven miles west of Charlottesville, within sight of Monticello.[2]

One of the Lewis men, an uncle of Meriwether Lewis's father, was a member of the king's council; another, Fielding Lewis, married a sister of George Washington.[3] Still another relative, Thomas Lewis, accompanied Jefferson's father, Peter, on an expedition in 1746 into the Northern Neck, between the Potomac and the Rappahannock. Thomas was the first Lewis to keep a journal of exploration. He had a gift for vivid descriptions, of horses "tumbling over Rocks and precipices," of cold, rain, and near-starvation. He wrote of exultation over killing "one old Bair & three Cubs." He described a mountain area where they were so "often in the outmoust Danger this tirable place was Calld Purgatory." One river was so treacherous they named it Styx, "from the Dismal appearance of the place Being Sufficen to Strick terror in any human Creature."[4]

In 1769, William Lewis, then thirty-one years old, married his cousin, twenty-two-year-old Lucy Meriwether. The Meriwether family was also Welsh and also land-rich—by 1730, the family held a tract near Charlottesville of 17,952 acres. The coat of arms was "Vi et Consilio," or "Force and Counsel." George R. Gilmer, later a governor of Georgia, wrote of the family, "None ever looked at or talked with a Meriwether but he heard something which made him look or listen again." Jefferson said of Colonel Nicholas Meriwether, Lucy's father, "He was the most sensible man I ever knew."[5] He had served as commander of a Virginia regiment in Braddock's disastrous campaign of 1755.

The Lewis and Meriwether families had long been close-knit and interrelated. Indeed, there were eleven marriages joining Lewises and Meriwethers between 1725 and 1774. Nicholas Meriwether II, 1667–1744, was the great-grandfather of Lucy Meriwether and the grandfather of William Lewis. The marriage of Lucy and William combined two bloodlines of unusual strength—and some weaknesses. According to Jefferson, the family was "subject to hypocondriac affections. It was a constitutional disposition in all the nearer branches of the family."[6]

Despite William Lewis's tendency toward hypochondria—or what Jefferson at other times called melancholy and would later be called depression—Jefferson described his neighbor and friend as a man of "good sense, integrity, bravery, enterprize & remarkable bodily powers."[7]

A year after their marriage, William and Lucy Lewis had their first child, a daughter they named Jane. Meriwether Lewis was born in 1774. Three years later, a second son, Reuben, was born.

In 1775, war broke out. Jefferson noted that, when it came, William Lewis was "happily situated at home with a wife and young family, & a fortune placed him at ease." Nevertheless, "he left all to aid in the liberation of his country from foreign usurpations."[8] Like General Washington, he served without pay; going Washington one better, he bore his own expenses, as his patriotic contribution to his country.

Meriwether Lewis scarcely knew his father, for Lieutenant Lewis was away making war for most of the first five years of his son's life. He served as commander of one of the first regiments raised in Virginia, enlisting in July 1775. By September, he was a first lieutenant in the Albemarle County militia. When the unit integrated with the Continental Line, he became a lieutenant in the regulars.

In November 1779, Lieutenant Lewis spent a short leave with his family at Cloverfields, a Meriwether family plantation where his wife, Lucy, had grown up. He said his goodbyes, swung onto his horse, and rode to the Secretary's Ford of the Rivanna River, swollen in flood. Attempting to cross, his horse was swept away and drowned. Lewis managed to swim ashore and hiked back to Cloverfields, drenched. Pneumonia set in, and in two days he was dead.[9]

People in the late eighteenth century were helpless in matters of health. They lived in constant dread of sudden death from disease, plague, epidemic, pneumonia, or accident. Their letters always begin and usually end with assurances of the good health of the letter writer and a query about the health of the recipient. Painful as the death of an honored and admired father was to a son, it was a commonplace experience. What effect it may have had on Meriwether cannot be known. In any case, he was quickly swept up into his extended family.

Nicholas Lewis, William Lewis's older brother, became Meriwether's guardian. He was a heroic figure himself. He had commanded a regiment of militia in an expedition in 1776 against the Cherokee Indians, who had been stirred up and supported by the British. Jefferson paid tribute to his bravery and said that Nicholas Lewis "was endeared to all who knew him by his inflexible probity, courteous disposition, benevolent heart, & engaging modesty & manners. He was the umpire of all the private differences of his county, selected always by both parties."[10]

Less than six months after his father's death, another man came into Meriwether's life. On May 13, 1780, his mother married Captain John Marks. Virginia widows in those days commonly remarried as soon as possible, and family tradition has it that in marrying Captain Marks she was following the advice of her first husband, given as he lay dying.[11]

Lucy Meriwether Lewis Marks was a remarkable woman. She bore five children, two by John Marks (John Hastings, born 1785, and Mary Garland, born 1788). She had a strong constitution; she buried two husbands and lived to be almost eighty-six years old. Jefferson called her a "tender" mother. She was slim, fragile in appearance, with light brown hair and hazel-blue eyes, "a refined face and a masterful eye." A family history described her: "Her position as a head of a large family connection combined with the spartan ideas in those stirring times of discipline, developed in her a good deal of the autocrat. Yet she . . . had much sweetness of character, was a devoted Christian and full of sympathy for all sickness and trouble."

Known far and wide for her medicinal remedies, she grew a special crop of herbs which she dispensed to her children, her slaves, and her neighbors. She also knew the medicinal properties of wild plants. She took care to teach her son all that she had learned about herbal remedies.

Stern and spartan though she may have been, her son loved her dearly. Although he was scarcely ever with her from age fourteen on, he was a faithful and considerate correspondent.

On March 31, 1805, he wrote her from "Fort Mandan, 1609 miles above the entrance of the Missouri," to relate to her some of his various adventures in ascending the river so far and to inform her that he was about to set off into the unknown. "I feel the most perfect confidence that we shall reach the Pacific Ocean this summer." It was going to be easy, he wrote, because everyone in the party was in good health and "excellent sperits, are attached to the enterprise and anxious to proceed."

Still, mothers will worry, so he added: "You may expect me in Albemarle [County, Virginia] about the last of next September twelve months. I request that you will give yourself no uneasiness with rispect to my fate, for I assure you that I feel myself perfectly as safe as I should do in Albemarle; and the only difference between 3 or 4 thousands miles and 130, is that I can not have the pleasure of seeing you as often as I did while [I lived] at Washington."[12]

The woman who inspired such concern and love was also capable of leading an expedition of her own into the wilderness, of running a plantation, of supervising at hog-killing time. When some drunken British officers burst into Locust Hill one evening, she grabbed her rifle down from its peg and drove them off. Another time, a hunting party from Locust Hill and neighboring plantations got separated from the dogs. The hounds brought a buck to bay on the lawn at Locust Hill. Lucy grabbed her rifle, rushed out, and shot it. When the crestfallen hunters returned, empty-handed, the buck's hindquarters were already roasting over the fire.

She had a county-wide reputation for her culinary talents. Jefferson was especially fond of her cured Virginia hams. His overseer recorded, "every year I used to get a few for his special use." She had a small library, which she treasured. She valued it so much that she was careful to leave directions in her will for its equal division among her surviving children.

"Her person was perfect," said one of her male acquaintances, "and her activity beyond her sex." Even as an old lady, "Grandma Marks" was seen riding about Albemarle on horseback to attend the sick. According to a contemporary, in her mid-seventies she retained "refined features, a fragile figure, and a masterful eye."[13]

Georgia Governor George Gilmer described her: "She was sincere, truthful, industrious, and kind without limit." He added that "Meriwether Lewis inherited the energy, courage, activity, and good understanding of his admirable mother."[14]

As a child, Meriwether absorbed a strong anti-British sentiment. This came naturally to any son of a patriot growing up during the war; it was reinforced by seeing a British raiding party led by Colonel Banastre Tarleton sweep through Albemarle in 1781. Jefferson recorded: "He destroyed all my growing crops of corn and tobacco, he burned all my barns containing the same articles of last year, having first taken what he wanted; he used, as was to be expected, all my stocks of cattle, sheep and hogs for the sustenance of his army, and carried off all the horses capable of service; of those too young for service he cut the throats, and he burned all the fences on the plantation, so as to leave it an absolute waste. He carried off also about 30 slaves."[15]

Tarleton also ordered all the county court records burned. This wanton act was roundly and rightly condemned by Reverend Edgar Woods in his 1932 history of Albemarle County: "It is hard to conceive any conduct in an army more outrageous, more opposed to the true spirit of civilization, and withal more useless in a military point of view, than the destruction of public archives."[16]

When Meriwether was eight or nine years old, his stepfather, Captain Marks, migrated with a number of Virginians to a colony being developed by General John Matthews on the Broad River in northeastern Georgia. Few details of this trek into the wilderness survive, but it is easy enough to imagine a wide-eyed boy on the march with horses, cattle, oxen, pigs, dogs, wagons, slaves, other children, adults—making camp every night—hunting for deer, turkey, and possum; fishing in the streams running across the route of march; watching and perhaps helping with the cooking; packing up each morning and striking out again; crossing through the Carolinas along the eastern edge of the mountains; getting a sense of the vastness of the country, and growing comfortable with life in the wilderness.

Meriwether lived in Georgia for three, perhaps four years. It was frontier country, and he learned frontier skills. He gloried in the experience. Jefferson later wrote that he "was remarkable even in infancy for enterprize, boldness & discretion. When only 8 years of age, he habitually went out in the dead of night alone with his dogs, into the forest to hunt the raccoon & opossum. ... In this exercise no season or circumstance could obstruct his purpose, plunging thro' the winter's snows and frozen streams in pursuit of his object."[17]

At about this time, according to family legend, eight- or nine-year-old Meriwether was crossing a field with some friends, returning from a hunt. A vicious bull rushed him. His companions watched breathless as he calmly raised his gun and shot the bull dead.[18]

Another favorite family story about Meriwether at a young age concerned an Indian scare. When one of the cabins was attacked, the transplanted Virginians gathered at another for defense. Then they decided they were too few to defend it from a determined attack and fled for concealment to the forest. As dusk came on, one hungry, not very bright refugee started a fire to cook a meal. The fire attracted the Indians. A shot rang out. The women shouted alarms, men rushed for their rifles, something close to panic set in. In the general confusion and uproar, only ten-year-old Meriwether had sufficient presence of mind to throw a bucket of water over the fire to douse it, to prevent the Indians from seeing the whites silhouetted against the light of the fire.[19] A family friend commented, "He acquired in youth hardy habits and a firm constitution. He possessed in the highest degree self-possession in danger."[20]

Curious and inquisitive as well as coolheaded and courageous, he delighted his mother by asking questions about her herbs and about wild plants that she used as nostrums. He wanted to know the names and characteristics of the trees, bushes, shrubs, and grasses; of the animals, the fish, the birds, and the insects. He wanted to know the why as well as the way of things. He learned to read and write, and something of the natural world, from one of the adults in the Georgia community. An anecdote survived: when told that, despite what he saw, the sun did not revolve around the earth, Meriwether jumped as high into the air as he could, then asked his teacher, "If the earth turns, why did I come down in the same place?"[21]

He wanted more knowledge. He could not get it in Georgia. And he was a youngster of considerable substance and responsibility, for under Virginia's laws of primogeniture he had inherited his father's estate. This included a plantation of nearly 2,000 acres, 520 pounds in cash, 24 slaves, and 147 gallons of whiskey. Though it was being managed by Nicholas Meriwether, it would soon be Meriwether's to run. His mother agreed that he should return to Virginia, at about age thirteen, to obtain a formal education and prepare himself for his management responsibilities.

There were no public schools in eighteenth-century Virginia. Planters' sons got their education by boarding with teachers, almost always preachers or parsons, who would instruct them in Latin, mathematics, natural science, and English grammar. Jefferson biographer Dumas Malone notes that "the sons of the greater landowners had all the advantages and disadvantages that go with private instruction. The quality of this instruction was often high, but it naturally varied with the tutors who were available."[22] These men were all overworked, their "schools" too crowded. Finding a place was difficult. Even with his guardian, Nicholas Lewis, and his father's friend Thomas Jefferson to help him, it took Meriwether some months, perhaps as long as a year, to become a formal student.

His first extant letter, dated May 12, 1787, he addressed to his "Moste loving Mother." Apparently he had not yet found a place. He began by complaining that he had no letter from his mother, then confessed: "What Language can express the Anxiety I feel to be with you when I sit down to write but as it is now a thing impossible I shall quit the Subject, and say nothing more about it." He was glad to report that all the Lewises and Meriwethers in Albemarle were in good health. He passed on a rumor, that "Cousin Thomas Meriwether is marryed," and asked if she knew anything about it. He concluded, "I live in Hopes of recieving a letter from you by which as the only Means I may be informed of your Helth and Welfare. I enjoy my Health at present which I hope is your situation. I am your ever loving Sone."[23]

Meriwether's next surviving letter to his mother, undated, written from Cloverfields, related family news and the complications he was encountering in trying to get into school. His brother-in-law, Edmund Anderson, who had married his older sister, Jane, in 1785, when she was fifteen, was preparing to go into business in Richmond and "would have been there before this, had not the small-pox broke out in that City which rages with great violence and until this Disorder can be extirpated, they will continue where they are"—i.e., in Hanover. "Sister [Jane] and Children are well; the children have grown very much, but I see no appearance of another."

Parson Matthew Maury, son of one of Thomas Jefferson's teachers, was the man Meriwether wanted to study with, but so far he had not been able to get started. "I hope Reubin [his younger brother, still in Georgia] is at school tho I am not yet ingaged in that persuit myself," he wrote. "Robert Lewis and myself applied to Mr. Maury soon after my return [to Albemarle] who informed us that he could not take us by any means till next Spring and as what we would wish to learn would interfer so much with his Latin business that he had rather not take us at all."

Meriwether had therefore applied to Reverend James Waddell, but success was uncertain. "If we do not go to Mr. Waddle we shall certainly go to one Mr. Williamson a young Scochman who teaches in about ten Miles of this Place and who was earnestly recommended both by Mr. Maury and Waddle. In this situation I have now been waiting for this three Weaks past."[24]

In the fall of 1787, Reuben came to Cloverfields for a visit. As he was leaving, he asked Meriwether to come to Georgia the following fall. On March 7, 1788, Meriwether wrote Reuben to say he could not make the visit, "by Reason of my being at School. I set in with Parson Maury, soon afer you left me, with whom I continued till Christmas, and then I fully expected to have stayed six Months longer at least, if not another Year; but couzen William D. Meriwether then said he did not think it worth while, as I had got well acquainted with the English Grammer, and mite learn the Georgraphy at Home. Upon this, I concluded to stay at Uncle Peachy Gilmers, and go to school to a Master in the Neighbourhood in Order to get acquainted with Figurs, where I am now stationed."

He hated not being able to visit Georgia: "I should like very much to have some of your Sport, fishing, and hunting," he told Reuben. But he was determined to improve himself and said he must "be doing Something that will no Doubt be more to my advantag hereafter"— that is, getting an education.[25]

In June 1788, Meriwether's guardian paid seven pounds for room, board, and tuition. In January 1789, he paid thirteen pounds and in July another two pounds. That summer Meriwether was able to go to Georgia for a visit.

In the fall, he studied under Dr. Charles Everitt. His schoolmate and cousin Peachy Gilmer, five years younger than Meriwether, hated Dr. Everitt. According to Gilmer, he was "afflicted with very bad health, of an atrabilious and melancholy temperament: peevish, capricious, and every way disagreeable. . . . He invented cruel punishments for the scholars. . . . His method of teaching was as bad as anything could be. He was impatient of interruption. We seldom applied for assistance, said our lessons badly, made no proficiency, and acquired negligent and bad habits."

Young Gilmer described Meriwether as "always remarkable for persevereance, which in the early period of his life seemed nothing more than obstinacy in pursuing the trifles that employ that age; a martial temper; great steadiness of purpose, self-possession, and undaunted courage. His person was stiff and without grace, bow-legged, awkward, formal, and almost without flexibility. His face was comely and by many considered handsome."[26]

Meriwether loved to "ramble," as Jefferson put it. Into the mountains, or to visit Jane and other relatives, or down to Georgia, a trip he made at least once on his own. Later in his life he met his mother's half-joking complaints about his roving propensities with the laughing response that he had inherited this disposition from her.[27]

Albemarle County records show that Meriwether's guardian was meticulous. His accounts include the purchase of "1 pr Knee Buckls," "10 Vest buttons," "2 hanks Silk," "1 Pin Kniff." There are numerous entries for "poct Money." One arresting entry is for "1 quart Whiskey for Negroe Wench." Another covers "1 Quart Rum & 1 lb Sugar."[28]

Meriwether transferred in 1790 to Reverend James Waddell, who was a great contrast to the ill-tempered Everitt. Meriwether called Waddell "a very polite scholar." He wrote his mother in August, "I expect to continue [here] for eighteen months or two years. Every civility is here paid to me and leaves me without any reason to regret the loss of a home of nearer connection. As soon as I complete my education, you shall certainly see me."[29]

In October 1791, he wrote his mother to report that he had received a letter from Uncle Thomas Gilmer (Peachy's father) "which gives moste agreeable information of your welfare and my brothers assiduity and attention at School." He said he had just returned from a visit with his sister, Jane, who had shown him a letter their mother had written that summer. From it he learned that Captain Marks had died, leaving his mother once again a widow, with Reuben plus the two younger children to care for. Mrs. Marks wanted Meriwether to come to Georgia to organize a move back to Virginia for her and her dependents.

"I will with a great deal of cheerfullness do it," Meriwether wrote his mother, "but it will be out of my power soon[er] than eighteen Months or two years." He promised her she would always have a home at Locust Hill and "you may relie on my fidelity to render your situation as comfortable as it is in my power."[30]

In April 1792, Meriwether wrote his mother that he had learned from her letters to Jane that she was anxious to return to Virginia that spring. "This together with my sisters impatience to see you has induced me to quit school and prepare for setting out immediately." He had employed an artisan at Monticello to make a carriage for the trip; it would be ready by May 1. Meriwether needed to purchase horses and collect some money. "If I can not collect a sufficiency from the lands that are now due I shall dispose of my tobacco for cash in order to be detained as little time as possible. I shall set out about the 15th of May."[31]

He did as promised, and by fall he had gone to Georgia, organized the move of his mother and her children and the slaves, animals, and equipment, and brought the whole back to Virginia, where he set up at Locust Hill and began his life as a planter and head of household.

Thus ended Meriwether Lewis's scholarly career. What had he learned? Not enough Latin to use the language in his extensive later writings, nor any other foreign language. Not enough orthography ever to be comfortable or proficient with the spelling of English words—but, then, he lived in an age of freedom of spelling, a time when even so well read and learned a man as Jefferson had trouble maintaining consistency in his spelling. He did develop a strong, sprightly, and flowing writing style.

What he read can only be inferred from references in his writings, which indicate he read a little ancient history, some Milton and Shakespeare, and a smattering of recent British history. He was an avid reader of journals of exploration, especially those about the adventures of Captain James Cook.

He got his figures down pretty well, along with a solid base in botany and natural history. He picked up all he could about geography. He had achieved the educational level of the well-rounded Virginian, who was somewhat familiar with the classics, reasonably current with philosophy. Only in the field of plantation affairs was he expected to be a specialist, and to that end Lewis now set out.

He may have done so with some regret, for he valued education highly. All his life he kept after Reuben and his half-brother, John Marks, and half-sister, Mary Marks, to make every effort and meet every expense to further their educations. The last paragraph of his March 31, 1805, letter to his mother, written from Fort Mandan, far up the Missouri River, reads: "I must request of you before I conclude this letter, to send John Markes to the College at Williamsburgh, as soon as it shall be thought that his education has been sufficiently advanced to fit him for that ceminary; for you may rest assured that as you reguard his future prosperity you had better make any sacrefice of his property than suffer his education to be neglected or remain incomple[te]."[32]

Perhaps as an eighteen-year-old he wished to continue his education, to attend the "ceminary" at William and Mary, but it could not be. He was responsible for his mother, his brother, John and Mary Marks, the slaves at Locust Hill, his inheritance. Instead of book learning at William and Mary, he was destined to learn from the school of the plantation. At age eighteen, he was the head of a small community of about two dozen slaves and nearly two thousand acres of land. His lessons from now on would be in management, in soils, crops, distillery, carpentry, blacksmithing, shoemaking, weaving, coopering, timbering, in killing, dressing, and skinning cattle and sheep, preserving vegetables and meats, repairing plows, harrows, saws, and rifles, caring for horses and dogs, treating the sick, and the myriad of other tasks that went into running a plantation.

At eighteen years, he was on his own. He had traveled extensively across the southern part of the United States. He had shown himself to be a self-reliant, self-contained, self-confident teenager, and was a young man who took great pride in his "persevereance and steadiness of purpose," as Peachy Gilmer had put it. His health was excellent, his physical powers were outstanding, he was sensitive and caring about his mother and his family. He was started.

2

PLANTER

1792–1794

Foaled, not born, Virginia planters were said to be. They would go five miles to catch a horse in order to ride one mile afterward.

As one scholar put it, "In a country without large settlements and where plantation seats were far apart, riding was not a matter of occasional diversion but daily necessity, and good horsemanship was taken for granted among the gentry."[1] They had to be experts in the judging, feeding, breeding, and care of horses.

From the time he was able to sit astride a horse, Meriwether Lewis was a fine, fearless rider. He became an excellent judge of horses and an expert in their care. Jefferson, believing that the taming of the horse had resulted in the degeneracy of the human body, urged the young to walk for exercise. Lewis took his advice and became a great hiker, with feet as tough as his butt. As a boy and young man, he went barefoot, in the Virginia manner. Jefferson's grandson claimed not to have worn shoes until he was ten. According to Jefferson, the young Lewis hunted barefoot in the snow.[2]

Like riding and hiking, dancing was taken for granted. Indeed, dancing was little short of a social necessity. "Virginians are of genuine blood," said one traveler. "They will dance or die." Like Jefferson, Lewis learned to dance the minuet, reels, and country dances at Reverend Maury's school. One diarist wrote in the year of Lewis's birth, "Any young gentleman, travelling through the Colony . . . is presumed to be acquainted with dancing, boxing, playing the fiddle, and small sword, and cards."[3] There is no evidence that Lewis learned to fiddle, but he knew the rest of the list.

By no means were all Virginia planters or their sons paragons of virtue. If there was high-minded and learned political talk around the table, and much idealism and protestation of devotion to the common good, there also were temptations often too strong for healthy, wealthy young men to resist.

Jefferson's father died when he was a boy. Decades later, in a letter to his grandson, Jefferson wrote in a famous passage:

> When I recollect that at 14 years of age the whole care and direction of myself was thrown on my self entirely, without a relative or friend qualified to advise or guide me, and recollect the various sorts of bad company with which I associated from time to time, I am astonished I did not turn off with some of them, and become as worthless to society as they were. . . .
>
> From the circumstances of my position I was often thrown into the society of horseracers, cardplayers, Foxhunters, scientific and professional men, and of dignified men; and many a time I asked myself, in the enthusiastic moment of the death of a fox, the victory of a favorite horse, the issue of a question eloquently argued at the bar or in the great Council of the nation, well, which of these kinds of reputation should I prefer? That of a horse jockey? A foxhunter? An Orator? Or the honest advocate of my country's rights?[4]

Quite possibly Jefferson talked to Lewis in the same Polonius-like style in which he wrote his grandson. Certainly Lewis had thoughts similar to those expressed by Jefferson. On his thirty-first birthday, Lewis wrote, in a famous passage, "This day I completed my thirty first year. . . . I reflected that I had as yet done but little, very little indeed, to further the hapiness of the human race, or to advance the information of the succeeding generation. I viewed with regret the many hours I have spent in indolence, and now soarly feel the want of that information which those hours would have given me had they been judiciously expended." He resolved: "In future, to live for *mankind*, as I have heretofore lived *for myself*."[5]

Such high-blown, idealized language—and the sentiments it reflected, along with that heartfelt resolve to do better—was characteristic of the Virginia gentry. It was almost a convention, a part of the social standard, like good manners.

A Virginia gentleman was expected to be hospitable and generous, courteous in his relations with his peers, chivalrous toward women, and kind to his inferiors. There was a high standard of politeness; Jefferson once remarked that politeness was artificial good humor, a valuable preservative of peace and tranquillity. Wenching and other debauchery, heavy drinking, and similar personal vices were common enough, but as long as they did not interfere with relations between members of the gentry they were condoned. The unpardonable sins were lying and meanness of spirit.[6]

Along with his perseverance, all his life Lewis prided himself on his honesty. These qualities were important for his self-esteem. His word, written and spoken, was his bond.

A less admirable part of the code of the Virginia gentleman was the drinking, which could be excessive. One English traveler just after the revolution described his perception of the typical Albemarle planter. "He rises about eight o'clock, drinks what he calls a julep, which is a large glass of rum sweetened with sugar, then walks, or more generally rides, round his plantation, views his stock, inspects his crops, and returns about ten o'clock to breakfast on cold meat or ham, fried hominy, toast and cider. . . . About twelve or one he drinks a toddy to create him an appetite for dinner, which he sits down to at two o'clock. [He] commonly drinks toddy till bed time; during all this time he is neither drunk nor sober, but in a state of stupefaction. . . . [When] he attends the Court House or some horse race or cock fight he gets so egregiously drunk that his wife sends a couple of negroes to conduct him safe home."[7]

One may doubt that this planter was as typical as the Englishman asserted but still regret that such men were among the contemporaries of the teenaged master of Locust Hill.

Plantation management required attention to detail and sharp observation. In these areas, Lewis excelled. Jefferson described him as "an assiduous and attentive farmer, observing with minute attention all plants and insects he met with."[8]

Lewis did not plant or harvest with his own hands. No member of the Virginia gentry did. When Jefferson or Lewis or any other slaveowner said he had planted such-and-so, or that he had built this fence or that building, he did not mean to imply that he had done it with his own hands. His slaves did the work. "It is the poor negroes who alone work hard," one traveler commented, "and I am sorry to say, fare hard. Incredible is the fatigue which the poor wretches undergo, and it is wonderful that nature should be able to support it."[9]

Lewis was successful at adding land to his holdings, something also critical to a Virginia planter. He ran Locust Hill and in addition acquired an eight-hundred-acre tract on the Red River in Montgomery County, took title to 180 acres of land that had belonged to Captain Marks, and secured another parcel in Clarke County.

Such constant expansion was critical, because the Virginia plantation of the day was incredibly wasteful. The low ground or inferior bottomland was planted to corn, to provide food for slaves and animals. Fertile land—identified by hardwood growth—was saved for tobacco. The planters had their slaves gird large trees and leave the trees to die while plowing lightly around them. Slaves created hills for tobacco with a hoe, without bothering to remove the trees. After three annual crops of tobacco, these "fields" grew wheat for a year or so before being abandoned and allowed to revert to pine forest. The planters let their stock roam wild, made no use of animal manure, and practiced only the most rudimentary crop rotation. Meanwhile, the planters moved their slaves to virgin lands and repeated the process. The system allowed the planters to use to the maximum the two things in which they were really rich, land and slaves. Tobacco, their only cash crop, was dependent on an all-but-unlimited quantity of each.

The Virginians' lust for land and their resulting rage for speculation can only be marveled at. Before the revolution, George Washington owned tens of thousands of acres in the Tidewater and Piedmont and over sixty-three thousand acres of trans-Appalachia. He wanted more.[10] Jefferson inherited more than five thousand acres in the Piedmont from his father. He wanted more. From his wife he got another eleven thousand acres. And though he was a substantial landowner, he was not a great one by Virginia standards.[11]

Tobacco wore out land so fast there could never be enough, but tobacco never brought in enough money to allow planters to get ahead. Their speculation in land was done on credit and promises and warrants, not cash, so they were always land-rich and cash-poor. Small wonder Jefferson was obsessed with securing an empire for the United States.

Tobacco culture represented an all-out assault on the environment for the sake of a crop that did no good and much harm to people's health as well as to the land, not to mention the political and moral effects of relying on slavery for a labor force. But to Virginia's planters, even to so inventive a man as Jefferson, there appeared to be no alternative. In fact, an alternative existed right under their noses.

German immigrants, farming in the Shenandoah Valley, had a much different relationship with the land from that of the planters of English stock. The Germans had not received huge grants of land from the English king or the royal governor; they had bought their land, in relatively small holdings. Coming from a country with a tradition of keeping the farm in the same family for generations, even centuries, they were in it for the long haul, not for quick profit. They cleared their fields of all trees and stumps, plowed deep to arrest erosion, housed their cattle in great barns, used manure as fertilizer, and practiced a precise scheme of crop rotation. They worked with their own hands, and their help came from their sons and relatives. No overseer, indentured servant, or slave—men with little interest in the precious undertaking of making a family farm—was allowed near their fields.[12]

Although Jefferson did not comment on the German farmers in Virginia, he did compare the planters' practices to those of European farmers and explained that the Europeans were much superior in agriculture for a simple reason: "It [results] from our having such quantities of land to waste as we please. In Europe the object is to make the most of their land, labour being abundant: here it is to make the most of our labour, land being abundant."[13]

In the years following the revolution, life on the Virginia plantation had much to recommend it. There was the reality of political independence. There were the balls and dinners, the entertainment. There was freedom of religion. The political talk, about the nature of man and the role of government, has not been surpassed at any time or any place since, and at its best the talk could stand to be compared to the level in ancient Athens.

Life at Monticello in the years after the revolution was delightful to the eye, ear, taste, and intellect. Just imagine an evening as Thomas Jefferson's guest, following a day of riding magnificent horses over hedges, fields, and rivers, chasing fox or deer or bear. The entertainment would begin with toasts to the successful hunters. The table would be groaning under the weight of sweet potatoes, peas, corn, various breads, nuts, quail, ham, venison, bear, ducks, milk, and beer, all produced locally. The wines would come from France and be the best available in America, personally selected by Jefferson. If it was a large party, there would be conversations in French, Italian, and German as well as English. Jefferson would play the violin for the Virginia reel and other dances—when he wasn't talking.

Most guests found Jefferson to be the most delightful companion they ever met. He charmed and delighted his political enemies as well as his friends. "Spent the evening with Mr. Jefferson," John Quincy

Adams wrote in his diary in Paris in 1785, "whom I love to be with." He later added, "You can never be an hour in this man's company without something of the marvellous." Before the election of 1800, Abigail Adams wrote of Jefferson, "He is one of the choice ones of the earth."[14]

Jefferson's guests were also choice. Whether from Europe or America, they were men of the Enlightenment, well educated, intensely curious, avid readers, and pursuers of new knowledge of all kinds but especially about natural history and geography. They were politically active, thoughtful about matters of government, full of insight into the human condition, and also witty conversationalists, quick with a quip, full of hearty laughter even when the joke was on them.

Life on the Albemarle plantations after the revolution had something of a Garden of Eden quality to it, but there was a snake in the garden. The glittering social, intellectual, economic, and political life of Virginia rested on the backs of slaves. Those backs were crisscrossed with scars, because slavery relied on the lash. Not every master whipped his slaves—Jefferson almost surely never did; there is no evidence one way or another with Lewis—but every master had to allow his overseers to use the lash whenever the overseer saw fit, or felt like it. Slavery worked through terror and violence—there was no other way to force men to work without compensation.

This was the other side of the coin of one of the proudest boasts of the Virginia gentry. They claimed that they knew how to lead, that command came naturally to them. Edmund Burke spoke to this point. Although he disapproved of slavery, he observed that slaveowners were among the foremost in asserting the rights of man precisely because they were slaveowners. "Where there is a vast multitude of slaves as in Virginia," he observed, "those who are free, are by far the most proud and jealous of their freedom. ... To the masters of slaves, the haughtiness of domination combines with the spirit of freedom, fortified it, and renders it invincible."[15] Thus the sting in Dr. Samuel Johnson's embarrassing question: "How is it that we hear the loudest yelps for liberty from the drivers of Negroes?"[16]

No man did more for human liberty than Thomas Jefferson, author of the Declaration of Independence and of Virginia's Statute for Religious Freedom, among other gifts to mankind. Few men profited more from human slavery than Jefferson.

No man knew better than Jefferson the price Virginia paid for slavery, most of all in what the system did to young men. In *Notes on the State of Virginia*, he wrote: "The whole commerce between master and slave is a perpetual exercise of the most boisterous passions, the most unremitting despotism on the one part, and degrading submissions on the other. Our children see this, and learn to imitate it. . . . If a parent could find no motive either in his philanthropy or his self-love, for restraining the intemperance of passion towards his slave, it should always be a sufficient one that his children is present. But generally it is not sufficient. The parent storms, the child looks on, catches the lineaments of wrath, puts on the same airs in the circle of smaller slaves, gives a loose to his worst of passions, and thus nursed, educated, and daily exercised in tyranny, cannot but be stamped by it with odious peculiarities. The man must be a prodigy who can retain his manners and morals undepraved by such circumstances."[17]

Jefferson knew whereof he wrote, and he knew no prodigies in this matter.

Slavery was critical to tobacco planters because their agricultural practices were so wasteful and labor-intensive. Slavery prospered in the American South in the decades after the revolution because of technological progress. By the time Jefferson became president, the steam engines of James Watt had been applied in England to spinning, weaving, and printing cotton, which led to an immense demand for that staple. Simultaneously, Eli Whitney's cotton gin had made it practical to separate short upland cotton from its seeds. Slaves and land were necessary to grow cotton; the land was available in Alabama, Georgia, and Mississippi; the slaves were available from the excess on the Virginia plantations. These were the central economic facts in the life of the Virginia gentry, whose principal export soon became slaves.

Profitable as it was to him, Jefferson hated slavery. He regarded it as a curse to Virginia and wished to see it abolished throughout the United States. Not, however, in his lifetime. He said that his generation was not ready for such a step. He would leave that reform to the next generation of Virginians, and was sure they would make Virginia the first southern state to abolish slavery. He thought the young men coming of age in postwar Virginia were superbly qualified to bring the American Revolution to this triumphant conclusion because, as he said, these young men had "sucked in the principles of liberty as if it were their mother's milk."[18]

Of all the contradictions in Jefferson's contradictory life, none exceeded this one. He hoped and expected that the Virginians from the generation of Lewis and Clark would abolish slavery—even while recognizing that anyone brought up as a master of slaves would have to be a prodigy to be undepraved by the experience. And it should be noted that, as far as can be told, he said not a word about his dream that young Virginians would lead the way to emancipation to precisely those young Virginians he knew best, Meriwether Lewis and William Clark.

Jefferson did not marry until one year short of his thirtieth birthday; Lewis never married. In this they were unusual. As Jefferson noted, very few of the gentry pursued their studies to their twentieth year, for they commonly married very young and were soon encumbered with families. They had to give constant attention to the management of their plantations.

Attitudes toward and relations with women are central to every man's personality and character, but seldom discussed, especially among eighteenth-century Virginia gentry. Jefferson, who wrote about almost everything, wrote little about women in general and almost nothing about his mother or his wife. Lewis never wrote about his mother.

An exception in Jefferson's case was his remarks about the contrast between American and Parisian women. In America, Jefferson rejoiced, women knew their place, which was in the home and, more specifically, in the nursery. Instead of gadding frivolously about town as Frenchwomen did, chasing fashion or meddling in politics, American women were content with "the tender and tranquil amusements of domestic life" and never troubled their pretty heads about politics.[19]

Foreign travelers tended to agree, at least to the extent that they found Virginia women dull and insipid. Denied any role in politics or the management of the plantation, surrounded by a small circle of household slaves, the women of the Virginia plantation tended to become indolent, self-indulgent, frustrated, and unhappy. The great ornithologist Alexander Wilson, in an 1809 letter describing a southern trip, commented: "Nothing has surprised me more than the cold, melancholy reserve of the females, of the best families. . . . Old and young, single and married, all have that dull frigid insipidity, and reserve, which is attributed to solitary old maids. Even in their own houses they scarce utter anything to a stranger, but yes or no."

There were obvious exceptions: Jefferson's daughters, for example, and Lewis's mother. In general, however, it seems the men who ran Virginia plantations in the years after the revolution missed an essential part of the human experience by denying themselves, or by having denied to them, a full, open, mutually respecting relationship with women.

By contrast with the white women on the plantations, Wilson observed, "The negro wenches are all sprightliness and gayety." Winthrop Jordan, in his masterful study *White Over Black: American Attitudes Toward the Negro,* speculates that the dull frigidness of the white plantation women "was hardened by the utter necessity of avoiding any resemblance to women of the other race."[20]

Jordan further points out that, on the plantation, "The traditional European double standard for the sexes was subject to caricatural polarization. More sexual freedom for white men meant less for white women."[21] Whether Lewis indulged himself sexually with his female slaves or not is a subject on which no evidence of any kind exists. That many masters did so indulge themselves is a commonplace, with evidence aplenty in the form of mulattoes. Whether Jefferson so indulged himself is the subject of much speculation, argument, and controversy, all of it based on very little evidence. The most the scholar can say with confidence two centuries later is that the nature of Jefferson's and Lewis's relationships with women is almost unknown, and unknowable.

Jefferson wrote that, had Lewis stayed with it, "his talent for observation which had led him to an accurate knolege of the plants & animals of his own country, would have distinguished him as a farmer."[22] But, although he was good at it, Lewis ran Locust Hill only out of necessity, not desire. What he wanted to do was roam and explore.

On May 11, 1792, the American sea captain Robert Gray sailed into the estuary of a river he named for his ship *Columbia* and fixed its latitude and longitude. Jefferson, who had twice since the winning of independence tried to sponsor an American exploration across the continent, proposed to the American Philosophical Society of Philadelphia that a subscription be taken to engage a daring traveler to undertake an expedition to the Pacific. George Washington subscribed, as did Robert Morris and Alexander Hamilton.

On hearing of the project, Lewis approached Jefferson and, in Jefferson's words, "warmly sollicited me to obtain for him the execution of that object. I told him it was proposed that the person engaged should be attended by a single companion only, to avoid exciting alarm among the Indians. This did not deter him."[23]

Jefferson's high opinion of Lewis apparently did not extend that high. In any event, he passed over the teenage Lewis and chose instead a French botanist, André Michaux, who got started in June 1793. But he had scarcely reached Kentucky when Jefferson discovered that

Michaux was a secret agent of the French Republic, whose chief aim was not to explore or collect natural-history specimens but to raise an army of American militia to attack the Spanish possessions beyond the Mississippi. At Jefferson's insistence, the French government recalled Michaux.

Lewis, meanwhile, continued to toil on Locust Hill. But he was increasingly unhappy with the sedentary life of a planter. His mother was now well re-established in the family home, and she was fully capable of running the plantation. His desire to see new lands, to explore, to experience, to roam was insatiable. So, as Jefferson wrote, "At the age of 20, yielding to the ardor of youth and a passion for more dazzling pursuits, he engaged as a volunteer in the body of militia which were called out by Genl. Washington" to quell the Whiskey Rebellion.[24]

3

SOLDIER

1794–1800

The Whiskey Rebellion of 1794 was the greatest threat to national unity between the winning of independence and the outbreak of the Civil War. The North-South split over slavery had nothing to do with it; the struggle pitted West against East.

The precipitate cause was simple enough: a new tax. Secretary of the Treasury Alexander Hamilton wanted to increase the power and extend the reach of the federal government. In addition, the government needed money. Hamilton therefore laid an excise tax on whiskey, the principal product of the trans-Appalachian region.

Those at the frontier felt neglected, misunderstood, mistreated. There was little or no hard cash around, yet Hamilton demanded a tax paid in currency. A tax on whiskey was a tax on what the frontier made and sold, not on what it purchased—exactly the objection the Founding Fathers had raised against "internal" taxes imposed by England before the revolution. More generally, the frontiersmen complained that the government attempting to collect the tax neglected to provide western settlers with protection from the Indians, failed to build western roads or canals, and favored the rich absentee land speculators, the biggest and most important of whom was President Washington himself, over the simple, hardworking frontiersman who was trying to acquire land and build a home.

The frontier farmers revolted. They refused to pay the tax; they shot at revenue officers; they tarred and feathered revenue officers; they burned down the houses of revenue officers. President Washington, alarmed at these "symptoms of riot and violence," called out thirteen thousand militiamen from Virginia, New Jersey, Pennsylvania, and Maryland in August 1794 to quell the rebellion.

Washington needed volunteers because the regular army, with an authorized strength of 5,424 officers and men, was in the Ohio country, on an Indian campaign led by Major General Anthony Wayne, launched in response to two successive, humiliating, and costly defeats suffered by the army in Ohio—in 1790 under General Josiah Harmar, and in 1791 under General Arthur St. Clair. Those Indian victories had inspired widespread Indian attacks on frontier settlements, which in turn were among the causes of the Whiskey Rebellion. On the East Coast, men might fear a standing army; in the West, they clamored for one that could protect them.

On August 20, 1794, at the Battle of Fallen Timbers, at the rapids of the Maumee River in northwestern Ohio, Wayne won a decisive victory, thus meeting one of the chief complaints of the western rebels, which was that the army would not or could not provide protection. Word of that victory had not reached Pennsylvania, however, when Washington called out the militia. Nor did westerners know that Chief Justice John Jay was negotiating for a British withdrawal from the posts in the Northwest—another source of unhappiness, for the frontiersmen believed the British encouraged Indian massacres of American pioneers. Jay's Treaty would be signed in London in November 1794, but news did not reach the United States until March 1795.

There was a certain irony in the Whiskey Rebellion. Washington, Hamilton, and the other heroes of the American Revolution who were determined to put down this rebellion were espousing a policy that they had once risked their lives to oppose—taxation without representation. For there was no question about the truth of the complaints from the frontier, that this excise tax on whiskey was specific to the westerners and that they were not properly represented in the general government that imposed the tax.

Implicit in the rebellion was the idea of secession, a Second American Revolution. The rhetoric of the Whiskey Rebels was all but identical to the rhetoric of Sam and John Adams, Thomas Jefferson, and Patrick Henry. The logic of the rebellion was the logic of the revolution—just as the ocean that separated England from America dictated that they should be two nations, so did the mountains separate the East from the West and dictate two nations.

But what the West saw as simple political logic, the East saw as riot and rebellion. President Washington had not suffered the rigors of Valley Forge, or come out of retirement to serve as the first president, in order to preside over the dissolution of the nation or lose ownership of the tens of thousands of acres he owned in the West. Rumors of negotiations between rebels and representatives of England and Spain inspired Washington and eastern nationalists with military fervor. So determined was the president to put down the rebels that he took the field to review the troops who answered his call.[1]

Among those troops was Meriwether Lewis. He was one of the first to enlist, as a private in the Virginia volunteer corps. Surely a part of his motivation was his lust for adventure and his penchant for roving, but he told himself—and his mother—that he signed on for the campaign in order "to support the glorious cause of Liberty, and my country." He considered the rebels to be traitors and was delighted that "our leading men are determined entirely to consume every attuum of that turbulent and refractory sperit that exists among the Incergents."[2]

He was hardly alone. Thousands of young men from the Middle States volunteered. They had been children during the Revolutionary War. Throughout their teenage years they had heard war stories from their fathers and uncles. They envied the older generation its adventures and leaped at this chance to experience the camaraderie of the campfire, and the possibility of becoming a hero. They were also well aware that the government had rewarded the Revolutionary War veterans with land warrants in the West.

The volunteers, thirteen thousand of them, marched into Pennsylvania in two columns. The New Jersey and Pennsylvania troops gathered at Carlisle; the Virginians and Marylanders bivouacked at Cumberland. Washington, magnificently mounted and in his full-dress uniform, reviewed the troops in each camp, and marched with them as far as Bedford.

The roll of the drums, the cadence of the march, the glittering new uniforms, the eager young patriots, the thrilling sight of General/President Washington at the head of the column, was the way artists of the campaign saw it. The reality was different. As Washington bade farewell and Godspeed, the invasion of western Pennsylvania began. Crossing the mountains through rain and mud proved far more difficult than anyone had imagined. Disease, lack of discipline, insufficient rations, and squabbles about rank and command threatened to dissolve the force. Negotiations over rank, command, uniforms—color, design, and accoutrements—occupied far too much of the young officers' time and energy. Where egos and sartorial tastes went unsatisfied, anger welled up. In historian Thomas Slaughter's words, "Honor and ambition often supplanted patriotism as the highest priorities of both the resplendent dragoons riding west and those who petulantly stayed behind."[3]

Discipline and desertion were major problems, brought on by the vast gap between officers and privates, of which the most important was that officers could resign their commissions and take a walk, whereas the men were in for the duration. The officers got more and better rations, and usually managed to billet themselves in log homes; the men spent the nights in tents or on the open ground. Drunkenness was widespread in the whiskey country, as well as rampant gambling— both punished among the men, ignored among the officers. Each morning, senior officers sent out patrols to round up deserters, then had those who were caught brutally punished with a hundred lashes well laid on.

The men were inadequately clothed and fed. One month into the campaign, many were barefoot. On October 7, Hamilton lamented that "the troops are everywhere ahead of their supplies. Not a shoe, blanket, or ounce of ammunition is yet arrived." Food shortages led to plundering, which harmed relations with civilians along the army's path and was met with severe punishment. One of Lewis's fellow Virginia volunteers was caught taking a beehive. It cost him a hundred lashes. Nevertheless, the desperate men tore down fences for firewood, stole chickens and, when they could find them, cattle and sheep. Slaughter records, "The journals of officers often read like tourist guides to taverns and scenery along the route, while enlisted men's diaries recounted weeks of hunger and cold."[4]

Meriwether Lewis was an exception. Although only a private, he was a planter, a member of the gentry, welcomed into the company of the junior officers of the Virginia militia, who knew that his rank reflected his age, not his station in life. His letters to his mother read like those tourist guides Slaughter described.

On October 4, 1794, from the initial camp in Winchester, Virginia, Lewis wrote his mother. He had only recently arrived, whereas two regiments had been for ten days "at this school if I may term it so where they have been well equiped, tutured and now cut a moste martial figure." Lewis's company, he reported, "shall this day draw all our accutrements and receive our first lesson."

His first experience in camp was all he had hoped for, and more. "We have mountains of beef and oceans of Whiskey," he told his mother, "and I feel myself able to share it [with the] heartiest fellow in camp. I had last night the pleasure of suping with all my acquaintances in Capt. Randolphs company, they are all well except himself."

His spirits were soaring. He signed off, "Remember me to all the girls and tell them that they must give me joy today, as I am to be married to the heavest musquit in the Magazun tomorrow."[5]

A week later, on the march to Cumberland, he wrote: "I have retired from the hury and confusion of a camp with my constant companion Ensign Walker to write I know not what. . . . I am still blessed with a sufficiency of bodily strength and activity to support the glorious cause of Liberty, and my Country. . . . The lads from our neighbourhood are all harty. . . . Remind Rubin [sic] of the charge entrusted to him. . . . Ever believe me with sincerity your dutiful son."[6]

As the columns crossed the mountains and began to converge on Pittsburgh, the leaders of the rebellion fled down the Ohio River, headed for Spanish Louisiana. Two rebels were captured, marched east for trial, and found guilty of treason, but they were subsequently pardoned by President Washington. The show of force had worked; although the whiskey tax never was collected, land taxes, poll taxes, and tariffs on imported products were collected. Thanks to these, the victory at Fallen Timbers, and Jay's Treaty, the threat of a western secession receded; it did not, however, disappear.

In late October or early November, Lewis received a commission as an ensign in the Virginia militia. When that militia marched home, he volunteered to stay on with the small occupying force charged with patrolling and policing western Pennsylvania under the command of General Daniel Morgan. The enlistment was for six months. "I am situated on the Mongahale [Monongahela]," he told his mother, "about 15 miles above Pittsburg where we shall be forted in this winter. . . . I am in perfect health. I am quite delighted with a soldier's life." He was also feeling the responsibility of being older brother and head of the family: "I would wish Rubin to amuse himself with ucefull books. If he will pay attention he may be adiquate to the task [of running Locust Hill] the ensuing year."

There was more to his decision to stay in the army than his delight at the soldier's life. He informed his mother that, come spring and the end of his enlistment, he would "direct my cource down to Kentucky," where he intended to speculate in lands. He also planned to pay the taxes on "warrant land" his mother had inherited from Captain Marks, part of Marks's bonus for his service in the Revolutionary War, so as to prevent its forfeiture to the state as vacant or abandoned land.[7]

Two weeks later, he wrote to ask his mother to send money to pay the taxes on the warrant land, and papers proving ownership. He concluded, "I am in perfect health and constantly employed in building huts to secure us from the clemency of the approaching season.

Remember me to all the girls of the neighbourhood ... your affectionate son."

On Christmas Eve, 1794, he made his first complaint as an army officer. "I am a more confined overseer here than when at Locust Hill," he wrote, "having been ever since my last [letter] constantly confined to the huting department. There is no probability of a cessation of axes untill the middle of next month." He was learning one of the chief responsibilities of being an officer, concern for his men: "The situation of the soldairy is truly deplorable exposed to the inclemency of the winter which is about this time compleatly set in without any shelter more than what eight men can derive from a small tent. Many are sick but fortunately few have died as yet."

For himself, the best he could do for his Christmas feast was "a little stewed beef," but "to my great comfort I have this Day been so fortunate as for the price of one dollar to procure a quart of Rum for a chrismas dram."[8]

Sometime that winter, Reuben wrote Meriwether to inform him that their mother was uneasy about his long absence. On April 6, 1795, Meriwether wrote his mother to "press you by all the ties of parental affection not to give yurself any uneasiness [about me] as I can assure you I shall not undertake any enterprise more dangerous than being at Locust Hill." He admitted that "I have had a pretty severe touch of the disorder which has been so prevelent among the Troops," almost certainly diarrhea, "but have fortunately been restored to my usual state of health."

He was due to be discharged in mid-May, at which time he would go to Kentucky "to see to your land" and to take advantage of a "great opening for acquiring lands." Again he had advice and orders for Reuben: "Incourage Rubin to be industrious and be attentive to business. ... Remember me to Aunt and uncle Thomson and all the girls, and tell them that I shall bring an Insergiant girl to see them next fall bearing the title of Mrs. Lewis." That last cryptic line had no follow-up to it, but it may have caused Mrs. Marks considerable concern, or perhaps raised her hopes that her boy would soon settle down.[9]

If so, she was about to be disappointed. Instead of taking his discharge in mid-May and going to Kentucky, then home, on May 1, 1795, Lewis joined the regular army, with the rank of ensign. That same month, he was vaccinated for smallpox. He received a letter from Reuben, who again told him their mother wished his return to Locust Hill. He replied on May 22, in some wonderfully convoluted sentences: "So violently opposed is my governing passion for rambling to the wishes of all my friends that I am led intentionally to err and then have vanity enough to hope for forgiveness. I do not know how to account for this Quixottic disposition of mine in any other manner or its being affliected by any other cause than that of having inherited it [from] the Meriwether Family and it therfore more immediately calls on your charity to forgive those errors into which it may at any time lead me Tho all I shall ask at present is that you will not finally condemn me untill next fall at which time it will be my task personally to plead an excuse for my conduct."

In other words, it was all her fault. He signed off, "Your ever sincere tho wandering Son."[10]

Seldom would he spend more than a winter at one place for the rest of his life.

With the end of the Whiskey Rebellion, the ratification of Jay's Treaty and resulting better relations with the British, and the victory at Fallen Timbers, the army of 5,424 officers and men of 1794 was cut back to 3,359. Thus Lewis received his commission in the regular army at a time when that army was undergoing a sharp reduction, strong evidence that he had made a good impression on his seniors. Of course, they would have known his stepfather, and probably his father, and his lineage generally, which didn't hurt. The army he entered had many officers who were tied by blood or marriage to distinguished families. More than a third were sons of officers in the Continental Army or in the militia during the revolution.

The army's role was primarily to serve as a frontier constabulary, which caused it to be dispersed into small, isolated garrisons, most with fewer than a hundred officers and men. Historian William Skelton, in his authoritative *An American Profession of Arms: The Army Officer Corps, 1784–1861*, calls these tiny garrisons west of the Appalachian Mountains "an archipelago of tiny islets strung along thousands of miles of remote frontier."[11]

Discipline was imposed with shocking severity on the enlisted men. Flogging was commonplace; branding somewhat less so but still used as a disciplinary measure. A court-martial at Fort Defiance, in northwestern Ohio, found two soldiers guilty of laying their muskets aside and sitting down while on guard duty. They were sentenced to one hundred lashes well laid on. Theft of a blanket brought fifty lashes; striking a noncommissioned officer was a hundred-lash offense.

Desertion was a major problem, both because so many men gave in to the temptation to run off and lose themselves on the frontier, where they could establish squatters' rights and escape the harsh punishments common to eighteenth-century soldiers, and because the loss of just two or three men in the small garrisons would badly reduce fighting efficiency in the event of an Indian attack. So desertion was severely punished. When a private ran off from Fort Defiance in the fall of 1795, the officers offered two Shawnee Indians a reward of ten dollars for bringing him back alive and twenty dollars for his scalp. One of the warriors returned the following day with the soldier's scalp and collected the reward, along with "many compliments from the officers."[12]

On paper, the officer corps was also tightly disciplined. It was governed by Baron von Steuben's *Regulations for the Order and Discipline of the Troops of the United States*, usually called the Baron and the Rules and Articles of War. Among other things, officers were forbidden to use profanity, express disrespect for their commanding officer or federal or state officials, be drunk on duty or absent without leave, or in any way participate in duels. They were subject to dismissal if convicted of "behaving in a scandalous and infamous manner, such as is unbecoming an officer and a gentleman." They were further forbidden to keep mistresses, a habit "repugnant to the rules of society—burthensome to the service—ever pregnant with discord—always disgraceful and frequently destructive to men of merit."[13]

Most officers cultivated a flamboyant style of life, featuring heavy drinking and wenching. They were allowed at least one soldier from the line as a personal servant, or a slave maintained at the expense of the army. Second lieutenants were paid $402 in annual salary, with additional compensation for special assignments, but they had to purchase their uniforms, which were terrifically expensive on the frontier. Skelton comments: "Lower-ranking officers had only a precarious grip on middle-class respectability."[14] Many officers supplemented their pay by speculating in land, taking advantage of their location in the West; they speculated primarily in the bounty-land warrants issued to revolutionary veterans.

Skelton found that "one of the dominant characteristics of the officer corps was internal dissension; indeed, seldom has an army been led by a more refractory and contentious group of men. That officer was a rarity whose career was not punctuated by acts of indiscipline and acrimonious controversies with his comrades-in-arms, many of which led to courts-martial or duels."[15] One cause was the isolation and boredom of frontier posts. This was exacerbated because the officer corps was one of the few places in the early republic in which Americans from a variety of regional, religious, ethnic, educational, and social backgrounds mingled in close quarters. Probably more important was the over-blown sense of honor of the officers, especially those from the South.

Any officer who issued or accepted a challenge to a duel or served as a second or even upbraided a fellow officer for refusing a challenge was subject to immediate dismissal. In practice, neither the War Department nor senior officers made the slightest effort to enforce these regulations. General Anthony Wayne, in fact, urged his officers to duel, telling them to find "some other mode of settling their private disputes" than by troubling the army with courts-martial. There was a logic at work: duels avoided the expense and inconvenience of frequent courts-martial, and, in contrast to duels, courts-martial tended to perpetuate rather than resolve the frequent personal disputes.[16]

In the army of 1795, one officer declared, to be publicly insulted—denounced as not a gentleman in the presence of other officers—and not to seek redress in a duel would subject the insulted party "to the scoff and ridicule, and what is worse the contempt of his brothers in arms."[17]

Ensign Meriwether Lewis's first posting as an officer of the regular army was to the Second Sub-Legion, under General Wayne. Thus Lewis was present at Wayne's headquarters on August 3, 1795, when the humbled chiefs of the tribes of the Ohio region gave their assent to the Treaty of Greenville. In November, a fever swept through the camp; at one point some 300 of the 375 men at Greenville were sick. Lewis was one of the fortunate; he assured his mother, "I enjoy perfect health."[18]

Although there were as yet no formal political parties in the United States, most officers in the Second Sub-Legion, like the officer corps as a whole, were Federalists. One of the most contentious political issues of the day was attitudes toward the French Revolution. Federalists, led by Alexander Hamilton, despised it. Jeffersonians—soon to be known as Republicans—embraced it. Embraced it so thoroughly, in fact, that many of them copied the French and used the simple title "citizen" in addressing one another. Lewis was one of these; he addressed his May 22, 1795, letter to his mother: "Cittizen Lucy Markes, Albemarle, Virginia."

Lewis's views—and his drinking—soon got him into trouble. On November 6, 1795, he was brought before a General Courts Martial at Wayne's headquarters. Charges were brought against him by a Lieutenant Eliott. The first charge: "A direct, open & contemptuous Violation of the first & second Articles of the seventh section of the Rules and Articles of War." (Article one read, "No officer or soldier shall use any reproachful or provoking speeches or gestures to another." Article two forbade challenging to a duel.)

The specification in the proceeding charged Lewis with "abruptly, and in an Ungentleman like mannner, when intoxicated, entering his (Lieutenant Eliott's) House on the 24th of September last, and without provocation insulting him, and disturbing the peace and harmony of a Company of Officers whom he had invited there." They had argued politics; Lewis had apparently been thrown out; he then "presumed on the same day to send Lieutenant Eliott a Challenge to fight a duell."

When the charges were read to Lewis, he entered a plea of "Not Guilty." Testimony was taken, over a period of nearly a week. The officers of the court then rendered their judgment: "We are of opinion that Ensign Meriwether Lewis is not guilty of the charges exhibited against him, and sentence that he may be acquitted with honor." General Wayne, the court-martial report concluded,

> confirms the foregoing sentence and fondly hopes, as this is the first, that it also may be the last instance in [this command] of convening a Court for a trial of this nature—
> Ensign Meriwether Lewis is liberated from his Arrest.[19]

Quite obviously, Ensign Lewis could not continue to serve in the same outfit as Lieutenant Eliott. General Wayne transfered the twenty-one-year-old Lewis to the Chosen Rifle Company of elite riflemen-sharpshooters. The captain of that company had Albemarle ties—his family came from Charlottesville, although he had been born in Caroline County, Virginia, four years earlier than Lewis. His name was William Clark. His older brother was General George Rogers Clark, the conqueror of the Old Northwest during the revolution and a close friend of Jefferson. In the fall of 1795, William Clark had been in the army four years and taken part in the Battle of Fallen Timbers. In six months, he would resign his commission because of ill-health and the press of family business, but during that half-year he and Lewis became great friends, and admirers one of the other.

So the partnership of Lewis and Clark, destined to become the most famous in American history, began because General Wayne preferred to have his officers fight out their differences in a duel rather than in a court-martial and therefore found for the man who had issued the challenge rather than the one who had followed the law and brought charges.

Two weeks after his release from arrest, Lewis wrote his mother. He said his promised trip home for a visit had proved "impracticable." He issued instructions for his stepbrother: "I desire that Jack may be sent to Mr. Maury as soon as he shall have learnt to read tollerably well, being determaned that he shall receive a liberal education if at my own expense," certainly a generous gesture and another indication of how much he valued education.

As to his difficulties with the code of conduct of an officer, Lewis took them in his stride. "The general idea is that the army is the school of debauchery," he wrote, "but believe me it has ever proven the school of experience and prudence to your affectionate son." He was apparently learning to be less provocative in his politics, however: he addressed the letter to "Mrs. Lucy Marks," not "Cittizen Lucy Markes" (he never could decide how to spell "Marks").[20]

His army life over the next four years gave him enough travel to satisfy even his rambling nature. He covered vast chunks of the West, north and south of the Ohio River, beginning with a reconnaissance through Ohio in the spring of 1796. In October, he marched from Detroit to Pittsburgh with a small escort, delivering dispatches. He got lost, twice, and ran out of rations; he found some abandoned and rotting bear meat in an old Indian camp and pronounced it "very exceptable."

In November 1796, he transferred to the First U.S. Infantry Regiment. That month he made another march from Detroit to Pittsburgh, again carrying dispatches for General Wayne. This time he did not get lost, perhaps because he was accompanied by a Wyandot Indian who probably served as a guide; the Indian's name was Enos Coon, and Lewis paid his bill at a Pittsburgh inn.[21]

Following that journey, he took a furlough and rode home to Locust Hill, his first time there since he left in August 1794 promising his mother to return in six months. No anecdotes survive from the visit, but apparently he made the rounds of his old friends, after satisfying his mother's desire to know about his adventures and arranging his business affairs at the plantation. Invited to join the Virtue Lodge Number 44 of the Masonic Order, in Albemarle, he did so on January 28, 1797. He advanced through Masonic degrees with dizzying speed; by April 3 he was the recipient of the degree of Past Master Mason.

(Because his military duties kept him out of Albemarle most of the time over the following years, he attended few lodge meetings, although he was present in June and July 1798, while on furlough. He was an officer in the lodge and that summer made a motion to earmark a portion of lodge funds for charity. By October 1799, he was a Royal Arch Mason. He apparently took the ritual and idealism of the Masons quite seriously; he later gave names taken from Masonic ritual to western rivers—Philosophy, Wisdom, and Philanthropy. William Clark joined the Masons in St. Louis in 1809.)[22]

Lewis's furlough extended through the summer of 1797, during which time he settled "my domestick concerns." He made arrangements to bring some of his mother's slaves still in Georgia back to Virginia, made a trip to Kentucky to do some additional speculating in land—he bought twenty-six hundred acres for himself at twenty cents per acre, telling his mother, "I am much more pleased with this country than I supposed I should"—sold some of his Virginia land to his brother, Reuben, bought some of Captain Marks's land from his mother, and generally acted as Virginia planters did in those years, making himself land-rich and cash-poor.[23]

In an age of powdered wigs, lace, and ruffles, he was something of a fop. In a January 15, 1798, letter to a friend, Lieutenant Ferdinand Claiborne, he complained about his tailor. "Of all the damned pieces of work," he wrote, "my coat exceeds. It would take up three sheets of paper, written in shorthand, to point out its deficiences, or, I may even say, deformities. ... The lace is deficient. ... Could I have done without it I should have returned it."

In a postscript, he made a complaint about a military matter, a complaint that virtually every officer in every army in every age has made: "No doubt you have had forwarded to you the late regulation of our generous Congress relative to the delivery and distribution of fuel and straw to the garrisons. ... The allowance falling so far short of what is really necessary, I am at a loss to determine what steps to pursue. Do let me know what plan you adapt as I am confident the proportion of fuel is so small that the soldiers cannot subsist on it."[24]

In 1798, John Adams was president. Thanks to Jay's Treaty, relations with England were good, which meant that relations with France were bad. There was an undeclared war on the high seas. French Foreign Minister Talleyrand demanded a bribe from an American mission. Public opinion was outraged. Political parties were formed around these events, which ushered in one of the most bitterly partisan periods in American history. At the center of the disputes was the size of the army.

The High Federalists, led by Alexander Hamilton, hoped to use the crisis of a threatened war with France to build a classic European-style standing army, meaning one designed more to suppress internal dissent than to repel foreign invasion. Hamilton, and to a lesser extent Washington and Adams, who were not High Federalists, regarded the

Republican opposition to government policy, led by Jefferson, as illegitimate, even treasonous—an attitude that led to the Alien and Sedition Acts.

In July 1798, the Federalist-controlled Congress voted for a huge increase in the army, authorizing as many as ten thousand regulars and thirty thousand militia.[25] To President Adams and other Federalist leaders, the appointment of men of "sound" politics to the officer corps of the new army was crucial, if that army was to provide a reliable check on internal disorder. As active politicians, Adams and his friends were also aware of the vast patronage possibilities in the expansion of the army. But the Federalist Party was divided internally between Hamilton's High Federalist faction and Adams's supporters, so a struggle for power lay ahead.

Adams appointed Washington to command the new army, with the rank of lieutenant general. Washington, reluctant to end his retirement, did so only partially, for he insisted on remaining at Mount Vernon until war actually began. That decision meant that the second-in-command would have effective control of the new army. A series of Cabinet intrigues followed that soon embroiled Adams and Washington in a controversy over Hamilton. Eventually Washington forced Adams to make a humiliating concession, threatening to resign unless Adams agreed to make Hamilton the second in command.

The humiliation caused Adams to have second thoughts about the expansion of the army. As a consequence, it did not grow to anything remotely approaching the authorized strength. In practice, there was a rapid increase in the officer corps, but almost none in the enlisted ranks.

That meant that Adams still had many commissions to hand out, and they were eagerly sought. Federalists naturally got the lion's share. Washington established the criteria. He proposed giving first priority to active revolutionary veterans and the second to "young Gentlemen of good families, liberal education, and high sense of honour." In no case, Washington told Adams, should he appoint "any who are known enemies to their own government; for they will certainly attempt to create disturbances in the Militry."

Adams went so far in excluding applicants suspected of Republicanism that even Hamilton thought he had gone too far. Hamilton said that some at least of the junior officers should come from the opposition ranks. "It does not seem adviseable to exclude all hope & give to appointments too absolute a party feature. Military situations, on young minds particularly, are of all others best calculated to inspire a zeal for the service and the cause in which the Incumbants are employed."[26] In other words, young Republicans of promise and talent could be won over if given a commission.

Adams tended to ignore Hamilton; the vast majority of appointments went to Federalists. Even though they were officers without an army, their political orientation struck fear in the hearts of the Republicans, who talked, somewhat wildly, about the coming Federalist terror.

The involvement of the army in politics and the use of the officer corps as a major patronage source was destined to have a decisive impact on Meriwether Lewis. It began with a promotion. On March 3, 1799, he became a lieutenant and was posted to recruiting duty in Charlottesville, which must have pleased his mother.

After Adams made his decision to ignore the authorization to increase the enlisted ranks of the army by several thousand, Lewis's recruiting duties ran out. In 1800 he was posted to Detroit, where he joined a company commanded by his friend Captain Claiborne. It was a presidential-election year, with Jefferson challenging Adams. Lewis indulged in vigorous political argument, on at least one occasion exchanging hot words with a Federalist officer and overwhelming—at least to his own satisfaction—the "Fed" with his own Jeffersonian Republican arguments.[27]

He shortly became regimental paymaster. This was a new post, provided for by Congress in March 1799 as part of the expansion. He got the appointment, Jefferson later wrote, because he always attracted "the first attention where punctuality & fidelity were requisite."[28]

It was an ideal posting for Lewis, for two reasons. The first was personal—his duties gave him a veritable carte blanche for rambling. The second was political—the rambling gave him an opportunity to get to know the officers scattered throughout the West, and to assess their political views, thereby acquiring knowledge that soon became a great asset.

He roamed the West, up and down the Ohio River—Cincinnati, Fort Wayne, Limestone, Maysville, Chillicothe, Wheeling—on a twenty-one-foot bateau, or keelboat, and a pirogue. He learned the craft of a waterman on western rivers. He traveled by horseback to forts south of the Ohio, riding through the wilderness carrying large sums in banknotes—not hard currency, which was too bulky. He kept extensive records—transfers, AWOLs, deserters, recruits. He established a reputation for thoroughness, accuracy, and honesty.

On December 5, 1800, Lewis was promoted to captain. That month the states selected their delegates to the Electoral College. In February

1801, those delegates created a political crisis when the count came out seventy-three votes each for Jefferson and his running mate, Aaron Burr of New York, with sixty-five votes for Adams. The tie threw the election into the House of Representatives, where another deadlock followed, as the Federalist caucus decided to back Burr. In other words, the Federalists would not accept the outcome of the election, in which the people's choice of Jefferson was clear.

So intense was the partisanship of the day, so much did the Federalists hate and fear Jefferson, that they were ready to turn the country over to Aaron Burr. Had they succeeded and made Burr the president, there would almost certainly be no republic today. Fortunately for all, Hamilton was smart enough and honest enough to realize that Jefferson was the lesser evil. He used his influence to break the deadlock. On the thirty-sixth ballot, February 17, 1801, Jefferson was chosen president and Burr was elected vice-president.

It was an age marked by a certain extravagance of language. What the alarmists among the Federalists feared, they said, was "the general ascendancy of the worthless, the dishonest, the rapacious, the vile, the merciless and the ungodly."[29] Such sentiments emboldened Adams to radical measures. On March 3, hours before Jefferon's inaugural, Adams made his famous "midnight appointments," stuffing the federal courts with Federalist judges. Not so well known but equally outrageous—at least to the Republicans—was his commissioning of eighty-seven men to fill vacancies in the six regiments of the permanent military establishment. Virtually all were Federalists, thus guaranteeing that the army—like the courts—would remain predominantly Federalist for years to come.[30]

Or so, at least, Adams hoped. President Jefferson had other ideas. To implement them, he turned to his neighbor Captain Meriwether Lewis of the First Infantry.

4

THOMAS JEFFERSON'S
AMERICA

1801

When Thomas Jefferson took the Oath of Office as the third president of the United States on March 4, 1801, the nation contained 5,308,483 persons. Nearly one out of five was a Negro slave. Although the boundaries stretched from the Atlantic to the Mississippi River, from the Great Lakes nearly to the Gulf of Mexico (roughly a thousand miles by a thousand miles), only a relatively small area was occupied. Two-thirds of the people lived within fifty miles of tidewater. Only four roads crossed the Appalachian Mountains, one from Philadelphia to Pittsburgh, another from the Potomac to the Monongahela River, a third through Virginia southwestward to Knoxville, Tennessee, and the fourth through the Cumberland Gap into Kentucky.

The potential of the United States was, if not limitless, certainly vast—and vastly greater if the nation could add the trans-Mississippi portion of the continent to its territory. In 1801, however, it was not clear the country could hold on to its existing territory between the Appalachians and the Mississippi, much less add more western land.

As the famed chronicler of the nineteenth century Henry Adams noted, "The entire population, both free and slave, west of the mountains, reached not yet half a million; but already they were partly disposed to think themselves, and the old thirteen States were not altogether unwilling to consider them, the germ of an independent empire, which was to find its outlet, not through the Alleghenies to the seaboard, but by the Mississippi River to the Gulf."[1] This threat of secession was quite real. The United States was only eighteen years old, had itself come into existence by an act of rebellion and secession, had changed its form of government just twelve years earlier, and thus was in a fluid political situation.

In addition, it seemed unlikely that one nation could govern an entire continent. The distances were just too great. A critical fact in the world of 1801 was that nothing moved faster than the speed of a horse. No human being, no manufactured item, no bushel of wheat, no side of beef (or any beef on the hoof, for that matter), no letter, no information, no idea, order, or instruction of any kind moved faster. Nothing ever had moved any faster, and, as far as Jefferson's contemporaries were able to tell, nothing ever would.*

And except on a racetrack, no horse moved very fast. Road conditions in the United States ranged from bad to abominable, and there weren't very many of them. The best highway in the country ran from Boston to New York; it took a light stagecoach, carrying only passengers, their baggage, and the mail, changing horses at every way station, three full days to make the 175-mile journey. The hundred miles from New York to Philadelphia took two days. South of the new capital city of Washington, D.C., there were no roads suitable for a stagecoach; everything moved on horseback. "Of eight rivers between here [Monticello] and Washington," Jefferson wrote in 1801, "five have neither bridges nor boats." It took Jefferson ten days to go the 225 miles from Monticello to Philadelphia.[2]

To the west, beyond the mountains, there were no roads at all, only trails. To move men or mail from the Mississippi River to the Atlantic Seaboard took six weeks or more; anything heavier than a letter took two months at least. Bulky items, such as bushels of grain, bales of fur, barrels of whiskey, or kegs of gunpowder, could be moved only by horse-, ox-, or mule-drawn wagons, whose carrying capacity was severely limited, even where roads existed.

People took it for granted that things would always be this way. The idea of progress based on technological improvements or mechanics, the notion of a power source other than muscle, falling water, or wind, was utterly alien to virtually every American. Writing in the last decade of the nineteenth century about conditions in the year of Jefferson's inaugural, Henry Adams observed that "great as were the material obstacles in the path of the United States, the greatest obstacle

---

* The generalization stretches, obviously—light, sound, a lightning bolt, a few animals for very short distances, and even some man-made objects such as rifle bullets, cannonballs, or arrows (for extremely short distances) moved faster than the fastest horse—but it doesn't stretch by much.

of all was in the human mind. Down to the close of the eighteenth century no change had occurred in the world which warranted practical men in assuming that great changes were to come."[3]

Jefferson was an exception. He had a marvelous imagination; Monticello was stuffed with gadgets he had invented. He also had developed practical devices for the general good of mankind. Farmers in Europe and America up to the end of the eighteenth century had used wooden plows with straight moldboards that showed no improvement over those of the ancient Romans. It was Jefferson who developed the curved-moldboard plow.[4]

In 1793, he saw a hot-air balloon ascent. Though it was presented as an entertainment, he at once saw a potential practical application. "The security of the thing appeared so great," he wrote to his daughter Martha, "that I wish for one sincerely, to travel in, as instead of 10 days, I should be within 5 hours of home."[5]

With regard to travel by air, Jefferson was a full century ahead of the curve. With regard to travel by land, he imagined the possibility of locomotion by something other than horse power. He was attracted by the idea of using steam power to move carriages. In 1802 he predicted, "The introduction of so powerful an agent as steam [to a carriage on wheels] will make a great change in the situation of man." Jefferson was a hundred years ahead of the automobile, however powered. He never saw a train.[6]

With regard to travel by water, Jefferson in 1801 could not imagine any way to overcome the difficulties or to improve the advantages of this most essential means of transportation for commerce. At the beginning of the nineteenth century, all heavy items or items in any quantity moved over water, either in canoes powered by human muscle, or on rafts floating down rivers, or on barges on canals drawn by mules, or on sailing ships propelled by the wind.

Because the movement of commerce was by water, Americans of 1801 were constantly thinking about water. Their heads were full of schemes to build canals, using locks to advance upriver or to go around rapids. Jefferson wrote of "a people occupied as we are in opening rivers, digging navigable canals, making roads."[7]

Since the birth of civilization, there had been almost no changes in commerce or transportation. Americans lived in a free and democratic society, the first in the world since ancient Greece, a society that read Shakespeare and had produced George Washington and Thomas Jefferson, but a society whose technology was barely advanced over that of the Greeks. The Americans of 1801 had more gadgets, better weapons, a superior knowledge of geography, and other advantages over the ancients, but they could not move goods or themselves or information by land or water any faster than had the Greeks and Romans.

In Henry Adams's words, "Rip Van Winkle, who woke from his long slumber about the year 1800, saw little that was new to him, except the head of President Washington where that of King George had once hung." Describing the mind-set of the time, Adams wrote, "Experience forced on men's minds the conviction that what had ever been must ever be."[8]

But only sixty years later, when Abraham Lincoln took the Oath of Office as the sixteenth president of the United States, Americans could move bulky items in great quantity farther in an hour than Americans of 1801 could do in a day, whether by land (twenty-five miles per hour on railroads) or water (ten miles an hour upstream on a steamboat). This great leap forward in transportation—a factor of twenty or more— in so short a space of time must be reckoned as the greatest and most unexpected revolution of all—except for another technological revolution, the transmitting of information. In Jefferson's day, it took six weeks to move information from the Mississippi River to Washington, D.C. In Lincoln's, information moved over the same route by telegraph all but instantaneously.

Time and distance, mountains and rivers meant something entirely different to Thomas Jefferson from what they meant to Abraham Lincoln.

Rivers dominated Jefferson's thinking about North America. For the immediate future, he was determined to get control of New Orleans for the United States, so as to prevent the West from breaking away from the United States. Beyond that, he sought an all-water route through the unexplored western two-thirds of the continent.

When Robert Gray sailed *Columbia* into the estuary of the river he named for his ship and fixed its latitude and longitude, mankind knew for the first time how far the continent extended. Knowing the exact location of the mouth of the Columbia represented a great triumph of eighteenth-century science and exploration. Most closely associated with England's Captain James Cook, the Second Great Age of Discovery had used the sextant and other navigational devices to delineate the continents and the seacoasts of the world, the great harbors and the mouths of the great rivers, with precision on the map, and with descriptions of the landforms and native people.

What remained to be discovered on earth was the interior of Africa, Australia, the Arctic and Antarctic, and the western two-thirds of North America. The latter was most important to Europeans and Americans.

It was known to be vast, some two thousand miles from the Mississippi River to the mouth of the Columbia. It was known to contain a wealth of furs. It was presumed to contain immense quantities of coal, salt, iron, gold, and silver. It was assumed that the soil and rainfall conditions were similar to those in Kentucky, Ohio, and Tennessee—which is to say, ideal for agriculture.

But what was not known, or what was assumed but was badly wrong, was more important than what was known. Donald Jackson, the great Lewis and Clark scholar, points out that, although Jefferson had the most extensive library in the world on the geography, cartography, natural history, and ethnology of that awesome *terra incognita* west of the Mississippi, when he took the Oath of Office in 1801 he believed these things: "That the Blue Ridge Mountains of Virginia might be the highest on the continent; that the mammoth, the giant ground sloth, and other prehistoric creatures would be found along the upper Missouri; that a mountain of pure salt a mile long lay somewhere on the Great Plains; that volcanoes might still be erupting in the Badlands of the upper Missouri; that all the great rivers of the West—the Missouri, Columbia, Colorado, and Rio Grande—rose from a single 'height of land' and flowed off in their several directions to the seas of the hemisphere. Most important, he believed there might be a water connection, linked by a low portage across the mountains, that would lead to the Pacific."[9]

Louisiana in 1801—that part of North America lying between the Mississippi River and the Rocky Mountains—was up for grabs. The contestants were the British coming out of Canada, the Spanish coming up from Texas and California, the French coming up the Mississippi-Missouri from New Orleans, the Russians coming down from the northwest, and the Americans coming from the east. And, of course, there were already inhabitants who possessed the land and were determined to hold on to it.

There were scores of Indian tribes living across Louisiana, but, given their lack of effective political organization, their inability to combine forces into an alliance, their utter dependence on whites for rifles, and the experience of Americans east of the Appalachians in the seventeenth and eighteenth centuries and in Kentucky and Ohio in the 1790s, it could be taken for granted that the conquest of the Indian tribes would be bloody, costly, time-consuming, but certain.

Jefferson's attitude toward Indians was the exact opposite of his attitude toward Negroes. He thought of Indians as noble savages who could be civilized and brought into the body politic as full citizens. In

1785, he wrote, "I believe the Indian then to be in body and mind equal to the whiteman." He thought the only difference between Indians and white men was religion and the savage behavior of the Indians, which was caused by the environment in which the Indian lived. Never did he say that the perceived shortcomings of the Negro—such as laziness or thievery—were caused by their condition as slaves. Keenly interested in Indian ethnology, an avid collector of Indian vocabularies, he had not the slightest interest in African ethnology or African vocabularies.[10]

When Jefferson or young Virginians like Lewis and Clark looked at an Indian, they saw a noble savage ready to be transformed into a civilized citizen. When they looked at a Negro, they saw something less than a human, something more than an animal. Never in their lives did they imagine the possibility of a black man's becoming a full citizen. William Clark tried to adopt a part-Indian boy as his own son. He would not have dreamed of adopting a black boy as his own son.

Spain claimed to own Louisiana, which was roughly defined as that part of the interior of the continent drained by the Missouri River and the southwestern tributaries of the Mississippi River. But, except for a handful of weak garrisons scattered along the Mississippi and anchored by New Orleans in the south and St. Louis in the north, Spain had no effective force in the empire.

The British had fur-trading interests in upper Louisiana, and a claim of sorts to the Oregon country west of the Rockies. The Russians had interests in the area around and north of the mouth of the Columbia. The Spanish had some vague claims to the entire Pacific Coast. The French, who had once owned Louisiana and whose people (French Canadians) were the only white men to have much experience in Louisiana, were considering reasserting their position.

But European ambitions for the inland empire were more theoretical than real, partly because the chief concerns of the contestants were their wars with one another within Europe, even more because of time and distance, mountains and rivers. In 1801, the European nations were no more capable of exploring, conquering, settling, and exploiting the western two-thirds of North America than they had been in the preceding three centuries.

Nor was the United States—not immediately, anyway—but Mr. Jefferson's America had two great advantages over its European rivals. First, citizens of the United States were crossing the Appalachians and settling in the Ohio country, right up to the eastern bank of the Mississippi. Indeed, a handful of Americans had already crossed the Mississippi to settle, most of them illegally, in upper Louisiana.

Americans, in short, were beginning to take physical possession of lands to which the Europeans had only claims or hopes. The second great advantage was that the United States had Thomas Jefferson for its leader.

But on the day of Jefferson's inaugural, frontiersmen west of the mountains could move their bulky agricultural products to market only by river, which meant via the Ohio-Mississippi route. That economic fact dictated politics—the Americans of the West would join Spain, France, or Britain, or whoever controlled New Orleans, or create their own nation and take New Orleans for themselves. Vice-President Aaron Burr was full of plots and schemes and conspiracies to break the west loose from the United States and form a new nation.

Jefferson would have none of it. He believed in what he called an "Empire of Liberty." "Our confederacy must be viewed as the nest from which all America, North or South, is to be peopled," he wrote even before the Constitution was adopted, and as president he said that he awaited with impatience the day when the continent would be settled by a people "speaking the same language, governed in similar forms, and by similar laws."[11]

In an age of imperialism, he was the greatest empire builder of all. His mind encompassed the continent. From the beginning of the revolution, he thought of the United States as a nation stretching from sea to sea. More than any other man, he made that happen.

His motives were many. He sought greatness for himself and for his nation. He rejected the thought of North America's being divided up into nation-states on the European model. He wanted the principles of the American Revolution spread over the continent, shared equally by all. He was one of the principal authors of the Northwest Ordinance of 1787, as revolutionary a document as his Declaration of Independence. The Ordinance provided for the admission into the Union of from three to five states from the territory east of the Mississippi and north of the Ohio, when the territories had a large enough population. These states would be fully equal to the original thirteen. Thanks to Thomas Jefferson, the United States would be an empire without colonies, an empire of equals. The Ordinance helped bind the trans-Appalachian region to the United States; what mountains and rivers threatened to drive asunder, Jefferson helped to overcome through a political act.

But it was not just the largeness of his mind that made Jefferson an imperialist. One of his basic motives was land hunger. Jefferson and his fellow Virginia planters made their living through tobacco and slavery, and tobacco and slavery demanded the unending acquisition of new land.

Jefferson's actions as wartime governor of Virginia showed more clearly than anything else the centrality of western lands to his politics.

He was elected governor in 1779. The next year, the British invaded the Carolinas. Virginia was in no position to aid its beleaguered neighbor states to the south, because Jefferson had invested Virginia's military resources in George Rogers Clark's campaign to conquer British outposts in the region north of the Ohio River. Jefferson's passion to take full possession of western lands almost cost the United States their independence.

As a politician, Jefferson was keenly sensitive to the needs and dreams of his constituents. In Virginia his supporters were small farmers, men who after the revolution were apprehensive about the obvious trend to ever-larger plantations tilled by slave labor. They looked to the west for new and cheaper lands, especially in the rich virgin soil beyond the mountains. There they could raise bumper crops that could be sent quickly to the world market via the fabulous river system of the Ohio-Mississippi.

While the Northwest territories were being settled, in Jefferson's view the trans-Mississippi western empire could serve as a vast reservation for Indians displaced from east of the river. There they could learn to farm and become civilized, so that they could be incorporated into the body politic. Eventually, Louisiana would be available for farmers emigrating from the east or immigrating from Europe. There was land enough for all in a United States stretching from sea to sea, land enough to sustain the American dream for centuries to come. Henry Adams wrote: "Jefferson aspired beyond the ambition of a nationality, and embraced in his view the whole future of man. . . . He wished to bring a new era. . . . [In 1801] he set himself to the task of governing, with a golden age in view."[12]

The Spanish might have title to Louisiana, the French might have interests in Louisiana, the British might have designs on Louisiana; the Spanish and French and Russians and British might be contemplating exercising vague titles to or otherwise meddling in Oregon; but in Jefferson's mind it would all be part of the United States, in due course.

Most of his countrymen agreed with him. Like him, they thought big. Henry Adams described the American of 1801 in these words: "Stripped for the hardest work, every muscle firm and elastic, every ounce of brain ready for use, and not a trace of superfluous flesh on his nervous and supple body, the American stood in the world a new order of man."[13]

Adams was generalizing, but he could have been describing Meriwether Lewis.

5

THE PRESIDENT'S SECRETARY

1801–1802

On February 23, 1801, eleven days before his inauguration, President-elect Jefferson wrote Captain Lewis. He said he needed a secretary, "not only to aid in the private concerns of the household, but also to contribute to the mass of information which it is interesting for the administration to acquire. Your knolege of the Western country, of the army and of all it's interests & relations has rendered it desireable . . . that you should be engaged in that office."

The salary would be only five hundred dollars per year, scarcely more than the pay and rations that Lewis would have to relinquish, although Jefferson assured him that he would retain his rank and his right to promotion. Further, service as the president's secretary "would make you know & be known to characters of influence in the affairs of our country, and give you the advantage of their wisdom." He would live in the President's House* "as you would be one of my family."

Jefferson wrote a job description: "The office is more in the nature of that of an Aid de camp, than a mere Secretary. The writing is not considerable, because I write my own letters & copy them in a press. The care of our company, execution of some commissions in the town occasionally, messages to Congress, occasional conferences and explanations with particular members, with the offices, & inhabitants

---

* At 1600 Pennsylvania Avenue. Not until after it had been burned by the British during the raid on Washington in the War of 1812 and was repainted was it called the White House.

of the place where it cannot so well be done in writing, constitute the chief business."[1] The president's secretary would be paid from the president's private funds, and provided with a servant and a horse, also at the president's expense. The post "has been solicited by several, who will have no answer till I hear from you." He requested an immediate reply.[2]

It took almost two weeks for Jefferson's letter to reach Lewis in Pittsburgh. On March 7, Lewis expressed his joy in a letter to his company commander, tent mate, and fellow Virginian, Captain Ferdinand Claiborne: "I cannot withhold from you my friend the agreeable intelligence I received on my arrival at this place [Pittsburgh] by way of a very polite note from Thomas Jefferson, the newly elected President of the United States, signifying his wish that I should except the office of his private Secretary; this unbounded, as well as unexpected confidence, confered on me by a man whose virtue and talents I have ever adored, and always conceived second to none, I must confess did not fail to raise me somewhat in my own estimation, insomuch that I have almost prevailed on myself to believe that my abilities are equal to the task; however be that as it may I am resolved to except it, and shal therefore set forward to the City of Washington in a few days; I deem the prospect two flattering to be neglected by a man of my standing and prospects in life." He closed the euphoric letter with a hint of his instinct for politics, along with the air of self-importance that went with being the president's secretary: "I shal take the liberty of informing you of the most important political occurrences of our government or such of them as I may feel myself at liberty to give."[3]

The maddening delays and infrequency of the mails forced the eager young man to wait three days before he could post his reply to Jefferson. In a letter dated March 10, Lewis explained: "Not untill two late on friday last to answer by that days mail, did I recieve your's of the 23rd Ult. . . . [asking] that I accept the place of your private Secretary."

He immediately got to the point: "I most cordially acquiesce, and with pleasure accept the office." After profuse thanks for the honor, Lewis promised "to get forward to the City of Washington with all possible despatch: rest assured I shall not relax in my exertions. Receive I pray you Sir, the most undisembled assureance, of the attatchment and friendship of Your most obedient, & Very Humble Servt., Meriwether Lewis."[4]

He set off at once, but spring rains, a lame horse, and miserable roads conspired to slow his progress. It took him three weeks to get from Pittsburgh to Washington, where he arrived on the afternoon of

April 1. Shortly thereafter, he wrote his friend Thornton Gilmer of Albemarle: "I feel my situation in the President's family an extreemly pleasent one. I very little expected that I possessed the confidence of Mr. J. in so far as to have produced on his part, a voluntary offer of the office of his private secretary—however nothing is extraordinary in these days of revolution, and reform."[5]

He was active in reform. Jefferson had a specific mission in mind when he offered the post to Lewis, who became a key participant in one of the president's most important projects, one of the planks in his election campaign: reducing the size of the army.

In a letter of February 23, 1801, to General James Wilkinson, commanding general of the army, asking Wilkinson to release Captain Lewis from active service while allowing him to retain his rank and right to promotion, Jefferson had explained that he had chosen Lewis on the basis of "a personal acquaintance with him, owing from his being of my neighborhood."[6]

But the president had something more specific in mind. He knew Lewis not only as a neighbor but as a solid Republican and as an army officer who, because of his responsibilities as paymaster, had traveled extensively throughout the trans-Appalachian region visiting the various army posts, and thus a man who knew the officer corps well. Jefferson's somewhat cryptic reference to Lewis's "knolege of the Western country, of the army and of all it's interests & relations," was a reference not to an upcoming exploration of the Missouri River country but to politics. What Jefferson wanted first of all from Lewis was help in reducing the grip of the Federalists on the army officer corps.

Jefferson intended to reduce the size of the army by one-half. This was good Republican principle and sound policy. The undeclared war with France was over, and relations with the British were quiet. Money could be saved by the government—also solid Republican principle—if the number of officers was cut back, something that made sense in any event because of the way John Adams and the Federalists had swelled the ranks of the officer corps during the war scare of 1798, and again through Adams's midnight appointments in March 1801. If officers were going to be cut, Jefferson figured it should be done, at least to some extent, on the same basis according to which they had been given their commissions—partisan politics.

But Jefferson had never worn a uniform. He did not know even the senior, much less the junior officers in the army. He did not know which officers were competent, which were extreme Federalists, which were inferior, which superior. But his young friend Meriwether Lewis knew, and Jefferson could count on him to evaluate the officer corps with complete candor.

Thus Lewis's first task as Jefferson's secretary was to go through a roster from the War Department listing all commissioned officers. Using a simple code of symbols (+++, or 00, or #, etc.), Lewis passed a judgment on every officer in the army. There were eleven symbols in all. The first "denotes such officers as are of the 1st Class, so esteemed from a superiority of genius & Military proficiency." The second showed "officers of the second class, respectable." The third listed "the same. Republican." The fourth covered officers whose politics Lewis could not "positively ascertain." Fifth, officers without politics. Sixth, those "Opposed to the Administration, otherwise respectable." Seventh, "More decisively opposed to the Administration." Eighth, "Most violently opposed to the administration and still active in its vilification." Ninth, professional soldiers without a political creed. Tenth, "Unworthy of the commissions they bear." Finally, "Unknown to us."

Jefferson did not take a meat ax to the Federalists on Lewis's list. If one puts the list beside the names of the officers dismissed from the service, it is clear that in the winnowing process military qualifications were given much greater consideration than party preference. Federalist officers rated superior by Lewis retained their commissions; of those rated acceptable, seven of eighteen were retained. This was good politics as well as good military policy; Jefferson wanted to bring the country together, not make it more divided than it already was, and of course he hoped to win over at least some Federalists to his cause, so he had to keep some Federalists in the army. But all except one of those noted as "Most violently opposed to the administration" were dropped.[7]

Despite the purge, Federalist officers continued to outnumber Republicans by a majority of 140 to 38.[8] The only senior officer thought to be sympathetic to the Republicans was Wilkinson—and he was notorious for swimming with the tide. Jefferson had not gone as far as his more extreme supporters wished. Secretary of War Henry Dearborn complained, "We have been much more liberal towards them [the Federalists] than they would be towards us, and in future I think we ought to give them measure for measure."[9] Jefferson put it well when he commented, "The army is undergoing a chaste reformation."[10] Lewis had been invaluable in bringing it about on a fair rather then an excessively partisan basis.

Beyond his active role in the reduction of the army, Lewis's duties were varied and not particularly exciting. He spent long hours at the writing desk, performing menial tasks, such as drawing up a list of all U.S. postmasters, with their locations and compensation, a total of twenty pages. He copied many other routine documents, including a list of prisoners in the Washington jail as of March 29, 1802; an extract of a letter of March 6, 1802; four pages of a report on the cost of a naval arsenal on December 4, 1802; and so on. He delivered messages from Jefferson to Congress.[11] It was tedious work, but instructive.

Abigail Adams, the first resident of the President's House, called it the "great castle" and hated the place. It was too large—twenty-three rooms—and basically unfurnished and unfinished. Mrs. Adams complained that it took thirty servants to run the place. The roof leaked. The walls were unplastered. In the nearest stable, at Fourteenth and G Streets, John Adams told his successor, were seven horses and two carriages in the stables that were the property of the United States and available for the president's use.

Jefferson ran the place with only eleven servants, brought up from Monticello. There were no more powdered wigs, much less ceremony. Washington and Adams, according to Republican critics, had kept up almost a royal court. Jefferson substituted Republican simplicity—to a point. He had a French chef, and French wines he personally selected. His salary was $25,000 per year—a princely sum, but the expenses were also great. In 1801 Jefferson spent $6,500 for provisions and groceries, $2,700 for servants (some of whom were liveried), $500 for Lewis's salary, $3,000 for wine. And it turned out he had to buy his own horses; Congress, thinking it an outrage that the government should pay for the president's horses, ordered that the ones Adams had turned over to Jefferson be sold. Adams was so mortified over this action that he left town before the inauguration.[12]

Jefferson was a widower. His two daughters were married and had their husbands, children, and own affairs to look after. Secretary of State James Madison and his wife, Dolley, stayed with Jefferson in the President's House for several weeks in May 1801, and Dolley Madison often acted as hostess for dinner parties, but essentially the President's House was a bachelor house in the years Lewis lived there.[13] Other than the servants, Jefferson and Lewis were the only residents. On May 28, 1801, shortly after the Madisons took their own residence, Jefferson wrote his daughter Martha, "Capt. Lewis and myself are like two mice in a church."[14]

They ate together, spent the evenings together—usually with guests—and worked closely together, especially on matters concerning the army. Jefferson came to know Lewis as well as he knew any man.

He later praised Lewis for, among other attributes, "sound understanding and a fidelity to truth." But he also noted, "While he lived with me in Washington, I observed at times sensible depressions of mind." He had seen the same melancholy in Lewis's father, and felt it was a malady that ran in the family: "Knowing their constitutional source, I estimated their course by what I had seen in the family." Lewis's depressions, in other words, did not unduly alarm the president, or last long—but Jefferson could not help noticing them.[15]

Lewis's quarters were in what became the East Room. It contained almost no furniture and was damp, cold, drafty, and depressing. Abigail Adams had hung her wash in it. Life in the President's House, however, was as exciting and rewarding to Lewis as life in the White House has been to most of the young people lucky enough to live or work there in the following two centuries.

First of all, there was that daily association with Jefferson. No American has ever surpassed Jefferson, and fewer than a handful have ever equaled him, as friend, teacher, guide, model, leader, companion. Dumas Malone, author of the definitive multivolume biography, called Jefferson "this extraordinarily versatile and seemingly inexhaustible man."[16] For Lewis, left fatherless as a child, thirty-one years younger than Jefferson, the president was all that and a father figure as well.

Lewis took his meals with the president, and was almost always present when he entertained, which was four or five nights a week. The dinner parties were small affairs, usually two or three guests, sometimes six to eight, never more than a dozen.

One of the guests, Mahlon Dickerson, four years older than Lewis, was a lawyer from Philadelphia and a politician who later became governor of New Jersey and then a Cabinet officer. He noted in a letter that Jefferson "is accused of being very slovenly in his dress, & to be sure he is not very particular in that respect, but however he may neglect his person he takes good care of his table. No man in America keeps a better." "You drink as you please, and converse at your ease," another guest reported.[17]

The table was an oval one, encouraging a general conversation. The talk flowed freely, on any subject that interested Jefferson, which meant practically all subjects. But the concentration was on natural science, geography, natural philosophy, Indian affairs, and of course politics.

Jefferson had promised Lewis that if he accepted the appointment he would "know & be known to characters of influence in the affairs of our country, and give you the advantage of their wisdom," and that was exactly what happened. Lewis sat with the Republican high command, including such regulars as Madison, Dearborn, Secretary of the Treasury Albert Gallatin, and Attorney General Levi Lincoln. Nonpolitical guests included the poet and journalist Joel Barlow, the artist Charles Willson Peale, the author Thomas Paine, the poet Philip Freneau, and other writers, scientists, and travelers.

Lewis and Dickerson, who met at Jefferson's table, became good friends. Lewis visited him in Philadelphia, where young bachelor Dickerson moved in the highest social circles. Dickerson kept a diary, with such entries as "Frid. 14 [May 1802], A fine day—Capt. Lewis & others dined with me—went to see Rannie's deceptions—much pleased." Rannie was a magician and ventriloquist. "Wed. 19 [May], Cloudy & rainy part of the day—cold at evg.—spent the evg. at Madmoiselle Fries with Capt. L." "Frid. 21. Clear in Morng. rained very hard PM.—rode out with Capt. L. to Dr. Logans—diner there—retd. at eveng." George Logan was a physician and U.S. senator and a founder of the American Philosophical Society, in which Dickerson was active and Jefferson was a member.[18]

It was a feature of Jefferson's personality that he reached out to men older and younger than he, men with different life experiences who could bring to his table perspectives and information foreign to him. Henry Adams wrote, "Three more agreeable men than Jefferson, James Madison, and Albert Gallatin were never collected round the dinner-table of the White House; and their difference in age was enough to add zest to their friendship."[19] Jefferson was fifty-eight years of age in 1801, Madison fifty, Gallatin forty, and Lewis twenty-seven.

Lewis's activities with Dickerson added to the list of famous men with whom he visited. "Mon. 24. A charming day—rode with Capt. L. to Wilmington—on a visit to Jno Dickinson—he was from home—we put up at Craigs." John Dickinson was the revolutionary pamphleteer who wrote the Letters from a Farmer in Pennsylvania in 1768. That same week, Lewis and Dickerson dined with Pennsylvania Governor Thomas McKean, former member of the Continental Congress and signer of the Declaration of Independence. On a visit to Philadelphia a year later, Lewis joined Dickerson for dinner with Henry Sheaff, a merchant who had been the provider of wine and sundries for President Washington when the capital was in Philadelphia.[20] Clearly Captain Lewis was moving in elite circles.

In August 1802, Jefferson retired to Monticello for a two-month vacation. Lewis accompanied him and stayed at the clapboard house three miles east of Monticello on the estate called Franklin, home of Ben Franklin's grandson William Bache. Being there allowed Lewis to visit his mother, brothers, and sister at Locust Hill, and to attend dinners at Monticello. One Albemarle planter, Lewis's schoolboy friend Peachy Gilmer, called the company that gathered at Jefferson's table "the most accomplished and elegant society that has been anywhere, at any time, within my knowledge in Virginia. Meriwether Lewis was, too, sometimes with us, sometimes absent."[21]

In Washington, Lewis was on the move much of every day, carrying messages and invitations, gathering information for his boss. He had the honor of copying and then delivering Jefferson's first State of the Union Address to Congress. This broke the precedent set by Washington and Adams, who had delivered their speeches in person. Jefferson thought that practice a bit monarchical; besides, he disliked making public speeches.*

The summer of 1802 was marked by a juicy scandal full of invective and slander, leaks from men in high places, hush money, blackmail, and charges of immoral sexual conduct and miscegenation by Jefferson. Meriwether Lewis was involved, in his capacity as aide and messenger for the president.

The scandal had its origins in 1798, when Jefferson leaked some information on foreign affairs to a Richmond journalist named James Thomson Callender. It was not new or secret information, but it had received little publicity and Jefferson wanted it known, although he did not want his having supplied it to Callender to be known. He asked Callender to attribute what he had supplied to an unnamed source, which was done. Jefferson then read some of the page proof of a book Callender was writing, *The Prospect Before Us*, for the 1800 presidential campaign, and approved of what he saw. He wrote Callender, "Such papers cannot fail to produce the best effect. They inform the thinking part of the nation."

But the work as a whole turned out to be full of such spleen and scurrility that Jefferson disapproved of it and feared its extreme language would help the Federalists and hurt the Republicans. For example, Callender called Washington "the grand lama of Federal adoration, the immaculate divinity of Mt. Vernon," and described Adams as a "hideous hermaphroditical character which has neither the force and firmness of a man, nor the gentleness and sensibility of a woman."[22]

Callender was arrested for his words, tried before Supreme Court Justice and arch-Federalist Samuel Chase on charges of violating the

---

* Jefferson's precedent lasted until it was broken by another Virginian, Woodrow Wilson. Wilson, a professor, could not resist a captive audience.

Sedition Act of 1798, found guilty, fined two hundred dollars, and thrown into prison. By the time Jefferson became president, Callender had paid his fine and served his nine-month sentence. Jefferson gave him a pardon. He could do no other, not so much because Callender had been his supporter in the election as because he and his party had denounced the Sedition Act—along with the Alien Act—as unconstitutional in the Virginia and Kentucky Resolutions.

When he granted the pardon, Jefferson also ordered the fine returned to Callender, who was pleading poverty and simultaneously demanding the postmaster position in Richmond. But a series of red-tape delays held up the repayment.

Callender came to Washington in May 1801 to demand his money. He accused Jefferson of going back on his word and said among other things that it would have been advantageous to Jefferson's reputation if his head had been cut off five minutes before he began his inaugural address. In a letter of May 29 to James Monroe, the governor of Virginia who had suggested raising the two hundred dollars by private contributions in order to get Callender to shut up, Jefferson related what happened next: "Understanding he [Callender] was in distress I sent Captain Lewis to him with 50 D[ollars] to inform him we were making some inquiries as to his fine which would take a little time, and lest he should suffer in the meantime I had sent him, &c."

But Callender wanted that postmastership, not a paltry fifty dollars. Jefferson's report to Monroe continued, "His language to Captain Lewis was very high-toned. He intimated that he was in possession of things which he could and would make use of in a certain case: that he received the 50 D. not as a charity but a due, in fact as hush money; that I knew what he expected, viz. a certain office, and more to this effect. Such a misconstruction of my charities puts an end to them forever. . . . He knows nothing of me which I am not willing to declare to the world myself."

Jefferson absolutely refused to make the appointment or have anything further to do with Callender. Monroe regretted that Lewis had handed the money over to the man, although it is not clear whether Lewis did so before or after Callender made his threats. Callender went back to Richmond, where he switched political sides and began publishing scurrilous attacks on Jefferson in the Richmond *Recorder*. These were picked up by Federalist papers around the country, including Hamilton's organ, the New York *Evening Post*. In the summer of 1802, the vengeful campaign of the embittered Callender reached its crescendo. Jefferson was deeply hurt, not so much by what Callender charged as by the readiness of men he respected, including

Hamilton, to believe the slanders. "With the aid of a lying renegade from Republicanism," he wrote, "the Federalists have opened all their sluices of calumny."[23]

The charges were: Jefferson had a slave mistress, "Black Sally," who had borne him several children; Jefferson had approached another man's wife when the man was away; Jefferson had cheated on a debt. The first charge lives on. The second charge was true and was later admitted to by Jefferson. The third was false.

Within a year, Callender had fallen into a three-foot pool of water, dead drunk, and drowned. The Federalists tried to pound Jefferson with the charges in the election of 1804, without effect. By that time, Lewis had left Washington.

Beyond vicious partisanship and vile political journalism, what had Meriwether Lewis learned in the first two years of his life in Washington? A great deal about practical politics, including the politics of the U.S. Army. He was an insider's insider in Washington, privy to the president's hopes, plans, ambitions, and secrets. He got to know and be known to the elite of Washington and Philadelphia. His biographer Richard Dillon wrote that the President's House "served as an ideal finishing school for Lewis."[24]

Further, he advanced his scientific education. He was introduced to new instruments of navigation; he listened to discussions of the geography of North America and the world, and of the Indians of the United States; he heard experts on the birds and animals and plant life of the eastern United States, and speculation on what lay beyond the Mississippi River.

In addition to the school of the practical and scientific, he greatly expanded his understanding of philosophy, literature, and history. He read extensively in Jefferson's library. And somehow, from someone— who else could it have been but Jefferson?—he learned how to write.

A distinct difference is evident between Lewis's writing before 1800 and after 1802. His sense of pace, his timing, his word choice, his rhythm, his similes and analogies all improved. He sharpened his descriptive powers. He learned how to catch a reader up in his own response to events and places, to express his emotions naturally and effectively.

Though his sentences remained convoluted and cried out for punctuation, he managed to carry them off by retaining a flow of narrative interspersed with personal observations and reactions, all held together by using the right phrase at the precise moment in an arrangement of words that stands the ultimate test of being read aloud and making perfect sense while catching the sights and sounds and drama and emotion of the moment in a way that can be compared to the stream of consciousness of James Joyce or William Faulkner, or the run-on style of Gertrude Stein—only better, because he was not making anything up, but describing what he saw, heard, said, and did.

Lewis was able, through his writing, to take us, two centuries later, to the unexplored Missouri River, Rocky Mountain, and Oregon wilderness country of 1804–6, to meet Indian tribes untouched by European influence, to paint their portraits in words that capture the economic, political, and social conditions of their lives, along with their vibrancy, savagery, beliefs, habits, manners, and customs in a way never since surpassed and seldom matched. The journals he wrote are among his greatest achievements and constitute a priceless gift to the American people, all thanks, apparently, to lessons learned from Mr. Jefferson during his two years of intimate contact with the president in his house.

6

THE ORIGINS OF
THE EXPEDITION

1750–1802

Jefferson's interest in exploring the country between the Mississippi River and the Pacific Ocean ran back a full half-century. His father had been a member of the Loyal Land Company, which had been awarded by the crown some eight hundred thousand acres west of the Appalachian Mountains. In 1750 one member of the company, Thomas Walker, founder of the town of Charlottesville, led a small party over the mountains to locate lands. In his travels, he crossed the Cumberland Gap.

Three years later, ten-year-old Thomas Jefferson's teacher, the Reverend James Maury, made plans to explore farther west for the Loyal Company. In January 1756, Maury wrote, "Some persons were to be sent in search of that river Missouri in order to discover whether it had any communication with the Pacific Ocean; they were to follow the river if they found it, and exact reports of the country they passed through, the distances they traveled, what worth of navigation those rivers and lakes afforded, etc." Thomas Walker was once again chosen to lead the expedition, but the French and Indian War intervened before he could get started. Nothing came of the plan after the war.[1]

In the decade following the winning of independence, there were four American plans to explore the West. Jefferson was the instigator of three of them. Within weeks of the conclusion of the Revolutionary War, Jefferson wrote General George Rogers Clark, the man who had won the Old Northwest for the United States, to report that some British capitalists had subscribed a "very large sum of money for exploring the country from the Mississipi to California. They pretend it is only to promote knolege. I am afraid they have thoughts of colonising into that quarter. Some of us have been talking here in a feeble way of making the attempt to search that country. . . . How would you like to lead such a party?"[2]

General Clark replied, "It is what I think we ought to do." Not, however, the way Jefferson proposed to do it. Clark warned that sending a large party, as Jefferson intended, would be a mistake. "Large parties will never answer the purpose. They will allarm the Indian Nations they pass through. Three or four young Men well qualified for the Task might perhaps compleat your wishes at a very Trifling Expence." He thought it would take four or five years, and regretted that his own business affairs precluded his going.[3] Again nothing happened.

Two years later, in 1785, Jefferson was in Paris as minister to France. There he learned that Louis XVI was sending out an expedition to the Pacific Northwest under the command of Jean-François de Galaup, Comte de La Pérouse. The French government said the objective was strictly scientific, but Jefferson knew at once that La Pérouse was looking for something more than the Northwest Passage. He wrote on August 14, "They [the French] give out that the object is merely for the improvement of our knowledge. . . . Their loading and some other circumstances appear to me to indicate some other design; perhaps that of colonising on the West coast of America, or perhaps to establish one or more factories there for the fur trade." He added that the real question was whether the French were yet weaned from their desire to have colonies in North America. Admiral John Paul Jones reported to him that they were not, that the La Pérouse expedition was preparing the way for French fur trade and colonization on the northwestern coast.[4]

The following summer, 1786, Jefferson met John Ledyard, who had sailed with Captain Cook and as a consequence was the first American to set foot in the Pacific Northwest. A born wanderer, a great talker, intense, dynamic, he convinced Jefferson that he could travel by land from Moscow to easternmost Siberia, cross the Bering Sea on a Russian fur-trade vessel, then walk across the North American continent and eventually march into the Capitol to announce that he had arrived to report on the West. Ledyard proposed to do this with two dogs. Jefferson was supportive.

Ledyard set forth. He made it to Siberia, where the absurd idea died when Ledyard was arrested by Empress Catherine the Great and sent back to Poland.[5]

La Pérouse, meanwhile, had sailed around South America, come up to the northwestern coast, taken observations and scouted for trading posts, and set sail for home. In January 1788, he made port in Botany Bay, Australia. When he left Botany, he vanished. The wreckage of his vessels was found forty years later on an island north of the New Hebrides.

In 1790, United States Secretary of War Henry Knox tried to mount a secret Missouri River reconnaissance. In Knox's view, "An enterprising Officer with a non commissioned Officer well acquainted with living in the woods, and perfectly capable of describing rivers and countries, accompanied by four or five hardy indians would in my opinion be the best mode of obtaining the information requested." General Josiah Harmar nominated Lieutenant John Armstrong for the command of the expedition, but warned Knox that "it seems very much too adventrous." The governor of the Northwest Territory, Arthur St. Clair, was equally blunt. He told Knox, "It is, sir, I believe, at present, altogether impracticable."

Lieutenant Armstrong gave it a try, but by the time he reached the Mississippi he was ready to admit, "This is a business much easier planned than executed." Knox had said that the pocket compasses and pencils and papers would do for making maps and recording discoveries, a mark of how little he understood the problem. Armstrong, after reaching the Mississippi, made a list of items any exploring party would have to have, starting with oilcloth to secure the papers from the elements, and including proper writing instruments and scientific tools for measurements. A tent would also help. He sent in his expense account: "for himself & Servant, totaling one hundred and ten dollars and thirty nine ninetieths of a Dollar."[6] He never got to the west bank of the Mississippi.

In 1792, Jefferson had another idea on how to explore the West. On May 11 of that year, the American sea captain Robert Gray had sailed his *Columbia* into the estuary of the Columbia River. Later that month, he met and traded information with Captain George Vancouver, who was making an official voyage of discovery of the Pacific Coast for the British government. The discovery of the great river of the West established the mouth of the Columbia at 124 degrees of longitude, and the latitude at 46 degrees. From the results of James Cook's third voyage in 1780, Jefferson had a rough idea of the extent of the continent; with the Gray and Vancouver information, the knowledge was exact. The continent was about three thousand miles wide.

Jefferson was spurred, not depressed, by the information. He proposed to the American Philosophical Society of Philadelphia that a subscription be undertaken to engage an explorer to lead an overland expedition to the Pacific. Big donors, led by George Washington, Robert Morris, and Alexander Hamilton, came in on the subscription, ensuring its success. Washington's pledge came with a matching challenge: "I readily add my mite to the [project] and do authorise you to place me among & upon a footing with the respectable sums which may be Subscribed."[7] With such help, by January 23, 1793, the American Philosophical Society was in a position to offer one thousand pounds to the explorer who could make it to the Pacific and back and report on what he saw.

As noted, eighteen-year-old Meriwether Lewis volunteered to lead the expedition, but Jefferson passed him off as obviously too young and insufficiently trained. He chose instead the French botanist André Michaux.

Jefferson wrote the instructions for Michaux and went over them with Washington. Since Hamilton and other officials were also involved, the instructions can be said to represent the motives, expectations, and hopes of the Founding Fathers toward the North American West, ten years after independence was recognized in the Treaty of Paris and at the beginning of the second term of the Washington administration.

The instructions were dated April 30, 1793. The first purpose, Jefferson wrote, was "to find the shortest & most convenient route of communication between the U.S. & the Pacific ocean, within the temperate latitudes." Since that was almost certain to be the Missouri River, "It has therefore been declared as a fundamental object of the subscription, (not to be dispensed with) that this river should be considered & explored."

Because the country belonged to Spain, not the United States, Michaux should cross the Mississippi somewhere far enough north of the Spanish garrison in St. Louis to "avoid the risk of being stopped." He should then march west until he struck the Missouri, follow it to the mountains, get over them, and descend the Columbia River to the Pacific.

Beyond the search for the all-water route across the continent, Jefferson told Michaux that as he proceeded he should "take notice of the country you pass through, it's general face, soil, river, mountains, it's productions animal, vegetable, & mineral so far as they may be new to us & may also be useful; the latitude of places . . .; the names, numbers, & dwellings of the inhabitants, and such particularities as you can learn of them."

Jefferson had selected Michaux because he was a trained scientist; botany, astronomy, mineralogy, and ethnology were among the subjects he had studied. Throughout, the instructions emphasized practical, useful knowledge. There was no hint of encouraging exploration for its own sake or merely to satisfy curiosity about what was out there. This was a true Enlightenment venture.

Geography was what most interested the subscribers. "Ignorance of the country thro' which you are to pass and confidence in your judgment, zeal, & discretion," Jefferson wrote, "prevent the society from attempting more minute instructions, and even from exacting rigorous observance of those already given, except indeed what is the first of all objects, that you seek for & pursue that route which shall form the shortest & most convenient communication between the higher parts of the Missouri & the Pacific ocean."[8]

Beyond the fur trade and other commerce, beyond the acquisition of knowledge, Jefferson and the subscribers wanted to tie the two coasts together, using the Missouri-Columbia waterway to form the knot, in order to create a continent-wide empire for the United States. It was a breathtaking vision.

It had, however, an anticlimactic ending. Michaux got started in June 1793, but he had scarcely reached Kentucky when Jefferson discovered that he was a secret agent of the French Republic whose chief aim was to raise a western force to attack Spanish possessions beyond the Mississippi. At Jefferson's insistence, the French government recalled Michaux.

Over the following decade, Jefferson neither spoke nor wrote about the West. Partly this was because he was so busy with politics and his other duties, but it had also become obvious that the West could not be explored by private subscription, and that the federal government could not afford to sponsor an expedition. Further, conditions in the country to be explored were so totally unknown that there could be no agreement on how many men it would take, what they would need, how long it would last.

But there was no hurry, for, as long as Louisiana was in Spanish hands and Ohio River Valley pioneers had access to the wharves of New Orleans, the United States could afford to wait. Spain was old and decrepit, growing weaker each year. America was young and dynamic, growing stronger every day. The people who were going to transform the Mississippi Valley, from its source to New Orleans, into farms and villages would come from the United States, not from Spain. Time would come soon enough to take Louisiana from the hapless Spanish.

In the spring of 1801, however, Jefferson learned of the secret treaties between France (read Napoleon) and Spain (read Napoleon's brother) that had transferred Louisiana from Spain back to France. It was called a retrocession.

Jefferson was greatly alarmed. As he put it in one of his more famous passages, "There is on the globe one single spot, the possessor of which is our natural and habitual enemy. It is New Orleans, through which the produce of three eighths of our territory must pass to market."

As long as the Spanish were in possession, the United States was willing to wait before asserting sovereignty. But revolutionary France? Napoleonic France? Expansionist France? Never. Often derided as a hopelessly romantic Francophile, Jefferson was a hardheaded practitioner of realpolitik on this one. "The day that France takes possession of New Orleans fixes the sentence which is to restrain her forever within her low water mark," he warned, because "From that moment we must marry ourselves to the British fleet and nation."[9]

He let the French know of his resolve. He suggested that Napoleon cede Louisiana to the United States, to eliminate the possibility of war between the former allies, a war which Jefferson warned would "annihilate France on the ocean." And he flatly declared that his government would consider any attempt to land French troops in Louisiana a cause for war.[10]

That was the kind of blunt talk Americans liked to have their president use when it came to America's national interests in a clash with any foreign nation. Also persuasive was that it was based on facts. Napoleon's expeditionary force was being devastated in Santo Domingo. It was obvious France could not reconquer that colony, much less send an army to New Orleans. The British and Americans in combination would have sunk the French navy and merchant fleet. Napoleon could not defend what he owned; he could only lose in Louisiana; why not give it to the United States and be done with the problem, and in the process re-establish the alliance between the two countries?

But Napoleon had not become emperor of France by giving things away. Though he agreed with the logic, he would rather sell than give.

The Spanish, still in command in New Orleans, waiting for the French to arrive and take possession, had meanwhile withdrawn the right of deposit.* The immediate effect was minor. Americans could still offload directly from raft or keelboat to ships in the port, or pay fees. And the Spanish gave a solid reason: smuggling had gotten

---

* The right to offload goods at the piers in New Orleans, sell them, and then reload onto sailing vessels.

completely out of hand. But decisions about Louisiana could only be made by Napoleon. Jefferson instructed the American minister in Paris, Robert Livingston, to negotiate for a tract of land on the lower Mississippi for use as a port or, failing this, to obtain an irrevocable guarantee of the right of deposit.

To reinforce Livingston, Jefferson began working on a plan to send James Monroe over to Paris as a minister plenipotentiary with specific instructions for the purchase of New Orleans for two million dollars. As he talked this up among Republican leaders, Jefferson indicated he would be willing to ask Congress for up to ten million for New Orleans. And why not? It would be cheaper than a war, and quicker. It would keep America out of an alliance with the British—the very thought of which to these Revolutionary War veterans was mortifying. It would certainly be constitutional—there was no other single thing the federal government could do that would more exactly meet its charge to improve commerce.

The thought that Napoleon might be willing to sell all of Louisiana had not occurred to anyone.

It was not the French who got Jefferson to start another project for an exploring expedition across the West—the retrocession had nothing to do with it—but the British.

Alexander Mackenzie was a young Scotsman in the fur trade out of Montreal, working for the North West Company. In 1787, he was posted to a wild trading post on the west end of Lake Athabaska, in what is now northern Alberta, at sixty degrees of latitude. Though he imported enough of the comforts of civilization to Fort Chipewyan so that it was called "the Athens of the North," another part of him yearned not for what had been left behind but, rather, what lay ahead. In 1789, he led a small party to Great Slave Lake. On the river that now bears his name, he set out for the sea. But the river swung to the north, and Mackenzie made tidal water on the shores of the Arctic Ocean, not the Pacific.

Undeterred, the next year Mackenzie tried again. He wintered at the North West Company's westernmost post—Fort Fork, on the Peace River. From there, on May 9, 1793, he set out. Accompanying him was his fellow Scot Alexander Mackay, six French Canadian voyagers, and two Indians, plus a ton and a half of provisions. Within the month, he had crossed the Continental Divide at a place where it was just three thousand feet high, and easily portaged. Mackenzie reported to the governor general of Canada, "We carried over the height of Land (which is only 700 yards broad) that separates those Waters, the one empties into the Northern [Atlantic] Ocean, and the other into the Western."

Mackenzie got onto the Fraser River, which he mistakenly thought was the northern tributary of the Columbia, but abandoned it when it became impassable, and struck out overland for the coast. Thirteen days later, he made it to saltwater, in the northern reaches of the Strait of Georgia. He camped that night atop a steep, overhanging rock. Using a makeshift paint of vermilion and hot grease, he inscribed on the rock: "Alexander Mackenzie, from Canada, by land, the twenty-second of July, one thousand seven hundred and ninety-three." The British had their claim on the northwestern empire.

Mackenzie got the latitude and longitude of the place. He worked out the latitude using his sextant, which measured the height of the sun above the horizon. Knowing the moment the sun crossed the local meridian made it possible for him to compute how far north of the equator he was.

Longitude was much more difficult, although easy in theory. The earth turns 360 degrees every twenty-four hours, without variation, meaning that the passage of time is also a measure of distance from some arbitrary starting point. By 1793, Greenwich, England, down the Thames River from London, was becoming firmly established as a conventional marker for zero longitude. In four minutes, the turning earth moves one degree in longitude. It is relatively easy to calculate longitude if the explorer knows precisely when it is noon in Greenwich and what time it is where he is standing. But it is almost impossibly difficult to calculate longitude if you can't tell the time, in either Greenwich or the wilderness. Englishman John Harrison had invented a clock that was reliable and portable, making it possible to know both times. Captain James Cook had used the Harrison chronometer in the Pacific Ocean in 1775, proving its superiority. But the rigors of overland journeys were too much for such delicate instruments—they got banged around, they got dust in them—so land explorers relied on the telescope and astronomy.

Mackenzie picked out Jupiter with his telescope and noted the time when the moons Io and Ganymede disappeared behind the planet. From tables showing the times of the same events from Greenwich, Mackenzie computed a longitude of 128.2 degrees west, which was almost a degree, or sixty miles, off. He realized he had been "most fortunate. . . . a few cloudy days would have prevented me from ascertaining the final longitude of it." Clouds were always the bane of the navigator.

Back at Fort Chipewyan, Mackenzie tried to prepare his journal for publication, but he fell into a depression. His biographer writes that this was his second attempt to find a practical commercial route to the

Pacific, "and it was at least in part a failure. He had reached the Pacific, but he knew his route could not be used for trade." He left Canada that year, and never came back.[11]

Mackenzie's account was not published until 1801, in London. It was probably ghostwritten, for Mackenzie was not learned enough to have written the book in its published form.[12] The title was *Voyages from Montreal, on the River St. Lawrence, Through the Continent of North America, to the Frozen and Pacific Ocean*. Jefferson ordered a copy as soon as he heard of the book's existence, but did not have one in his hands until the summer of 1802. He was at Monticello, Lewis was with him, and when the book finally arrived, they devoured it.

If the news that the British were exploring overland to the Pacific was a bit of a shock and most unwelcome, it was more than balanced by Mackenzie's evidence that, although there was only a one-day portage over a low mountain pass to a westward-flowing river, that river was not navigable. But, then, Mackenzie had been five full degrees north of the Columbia when he struck the coast. If the mountains four hundred miles south were similar to those he crossed, the portage would also be similar.

In their minds Jefferson and Lewis saw the Rockies as resembling the Appalachians in height and breadth. That image was greatly reinforced by Mackenzie. Geographer-historian John Logan Allen, in his seminal work *Passage Through the Garden: Lewis and Clark and the Image of the American Northwest*, notes that Mackenzie said in effect that "The way to the Pacific lay open and easy." According to Professor Allen, "It was this simple fact of imaginary geography that gave birth to the Lewis and Clark expedition."[13]

Through those hot August days of 1802 at Monticello, Jefferson and Lewis read and talked about little else than Mackenzie. Although Mackenzie stressed that his had been a "long, painful and perilous journey," and although things had turned out badly for Mackenzie, Lewis saw a competitive challenge and an opportunity to act out his life's dream. Anything the British could do, he could do better.

It was easy to point to mistakes or shortcomings in the Mackenzie expedition. He had been on a strictly commercial venture with a single purpose only, to find a practicable route for the fur trade. He had collected few specimens, made few descriptions, in general did not advance knowledge of the plant, animal, mineral, or Indian life of the country.

Although nearly every sentence in the book was a magnet to Lewis, what struck hardest was the line: "Alexander Mackenzie, from Canada, by land." This raised the matter of national honor. The name painted on that rock on the Pacific Coast was a direct, open, irresistible challenge. It was also a warning that, if the United States did not get going, it would lose the western empire to the British before the game was well under way.

The sentences that most struck Jefferson were in Mackenzie's final "geographical review," in which he urged Great Britain to develop a land passage to the Pacific for trade with Asia. He knew it could not be the Fraser, or any other river north of the Columbia, which was "the most Northern situation fit for colonization, and suitable to the residence of a civilized people. By opening this intercourse between the Atlantic and Pacific Oceans, and forming regular establishments through the interior, and at both extremes, as well as along the coasts and islands, the entire command of the fur trade of North America might be obtained, from latitude 48. North to the pole, except that portion of it which the Russians have in the Pacific [in Alaska]. To this may be added the fishing in both seas, and the markets of the four quarters of the globe."[14]

No wonder the North West Company liked Mackenzie. He thought big and he thought like a businessman. The fire he lit, however, was not under the company, or the British government, but under Jefferson.

The news that the British were threatening to set up shop in the Northwest galvanized Jefferson into manic activity and changed Meriwether Lewis's life overnight.

Sometime late that summer or in the fall of 1802—it is impossible to tell even what week, much less the moment—President Jefferson informed Captain Lewis that he would command an expedition to the Pacific. Or Captain Lewis talked President Jefferson into giving him the command. We don't know when or how Jefferson made his decision that there would be an American answer to Mackenzie and that Lewis would lead it. Evidently he consulted no one, asked no one for advice, entertained no nominees or volunteers, other than Lewis. This was the most important and the most coveted command in the history of exploration of North America. Jefferson was confident that he had the right man under his roof.

Later, Jefferson explained why he chose Lewis rather than a qualified scientist: "It was impossible to find a character who to a compleat science in botany, natural history, mineralogy & astronomy, joined the firmness of constitution & character, prudence, habits adapted to the woods, & a familiarity with the Indian manners & character, requisite for this undertaking. All the latter qualifications Capt. Lewis has."[15]

That was not to say Lewis was ignorant of science. Further, Lewis had demonstrated a remarkable ability to learn, especially with Jefferson as his teacher. Jefferson's library at Monticello was the most extensive in the world on the subject of the geography of the North American continent. Lewis had the run of the library. He consulted maps and conferred with Jefferson over them. In Professor Allen's words, "It must be assumed that he and the President talked at great length about the nature of the country west of the Mississippi and the possible character of the speculative passage to Pacific waters."[16]

From his later journals, we know that Lewis read Captain James Cook's *A Voyage to the Pacific Ocean* (London, 1784), the account of Cook's third voyage, to the Pacific Northwest. It almost certainly was at this time that he read it. He also read Antoine Simor Le Page du Pratz's *The History of Louisiana, or of the Western Parts of Virginia and Carolina* (London, 1763), and took it with him on his expedition. He read other books and consulted more maps.

He took botany lessons from Jefferson, who taught as they walked through the gardens at Monticello or, later in the season, along the banks of the Potomac. Jefferson once said no country gentleman should be without "what amuses every step he takes into his fields," and he ranked botany with the most valuable of sciences, "whether we consider its subjects as furnishing the principal subsistence of life to man and beast, delicious varieties for our tables . . . the adornments of our flower borders . . . or medicaments for our bodies."[17] Jefferson introduced Lewis to the Linnaean system of affixing binomial Latin names, and taught him enough to use the system in the field. He taught Lewis how to use a sextant and tried to teach him the use of the equatorial theodolite.[18]

Lewis rightly believed that he had Jefferson's complete confidence. They had a cipher so that they could communicate secretly, which might be necessary, since Jefferson had told Lewis, privately, that he would be sending the expedition into foreign territory. The Spanish might protest. They talked about the Indians along the Missouri, of their attachment to the British trading posts north of the Missouri and of the possibility of bringing the tribes into the American orbit. They talked of finding the Welsh Indians on the Missouri. They talked flora and fauna, mountains and rivers. They talked about the size of the party, whether too many would alarm the Indians to the point of active war, whether too few would invite an Indian attack to seize the rifles and supplies. They agreed on the basic need to bring back accurate records, descriptions, and maps.

In short, between the time Mackenzie's book arrived at Monticello and December 1802, Jefferson gave Lewis a college undergraduate's introduction to the liberal arts, North American geography, botany, mineralogy, astronomy, and ethnology.

In the fall of 1802, back in the President's House, Jefferson and Lewis continued their preparations for the expedition. While Lewis drew up an estimate of expenses, to present to Congress as part of a request for an appropriation, Jefferson began to widen the circle of those who knew about the proposal.

The first outsider brought into the plan was Carlos Martínez de Yrujo, the Spanish minister to the United States. Martínez was married to the daughter of Governor Thomas McKean of Pennsylvania and was on friendly terms with Jefferson—in fact, had found a cook for the president. On December 2, Martínez reported to the minister of foreign affairs in Madrid that Jefferson had asked him, "in a frank and confident tone, if our Court would take it badly, that the congress decree the formation of a group of travelers, who would form a small caravan and go and explore the course of the Missouri River [with] no other view than the advancement of the geography."

Jefferson, Martínez reported, had explained that, as a strict constructionist of the Constitution, he could not ask Congress for an appropriation for a mere literary expenditure, so he intended to lie to Congress and pass the expedition off as one designed to promote commerce—which was a power given Congress by the Constitution.

At this point, Jefferson was into a third or fourth degree of indirection. Martínez cut him off: "I replied to him that making use of the same frankness with which he honored me, I would take the liberty of telling him, that . . . an expedition of this nature could not fail to give umbrage to our Government."

Jefferson could not see why. The only subject would be to fill in the map, which would benefit everyone.

Martínez did not believe him, any more than Jefferson had believed the British in 1783 about the purposes of their proposed exploration, or Louis XVI about the purposes of the La Pérouse expedition of 1785. Martínez told his government, "The President has been all his life a man of letters, very speculative and a lover of glory, and it would be possible he might attempt to perpetuate the fame of his administration . . . by discovering . . . the way by which the Americans may some day extend their population and their influence up to the coasts of the South Sea [Pacific Ocean]."[19] Martínez knew his man.

Undeterred by Martínez's negative reaction (and his refusal to give Captain Lewis a passport), Jefferson plunged ahead. In the late winter of 1802–3, he got a passport for Lewis from the British minister, and another from the French. Simultaneously he moved forward with the Monroe project to purchase New Orleans from Napoleon.

Lewis meanwhile completed his estimate. He based it on the costs for a party of one officer and ten to twelve soldiers—surely reflecting a decision he and Jefferson had made together about the ideal size—and kept it as low as possible, to avoid congressional criticism. With $696 for "Indian presents" as the largest expenditure, and other large sums for provisions, mathematical instruments, arms, medicines, and a boat, it came to twenty-five hundred dollars on the nose.[20]

Jefferson put a request for that amount into his first draft of his annual message to Congress in December 1802. When Treasury Secretary Gallatin saw the draft, he suggested that the request be confined to a separate, later, confidential message, "as it contemplates an expedition out of our own territory." Jefferson agreed and sent up a special, secret message to Congress on January 18, 1803. Even then he buried the request in a discourse on the Indian problem, couching it in terms of commerce.

"The river Missouri, & the Indians inhabiting it," he said, "are not as well known as is rendered desireable by their connection with the Mississippi, & consequently with us. It is however understood that the country on that river is inhabited by numerous tribes, who furnish great supplies of furs & pelts to the trade of another nation carried on in a high latitude, through an infinite number of portages and lakes, shut up by ice through a long season." The Missouri, traversing an area with a moderate climate, might offer a better source of transportation, "possibly with a single portage, from the Western ocean." Those congressmen who were listening hard got the clear message: we can steal the fur trade from the British.

It would not cost much. One officer and a dozen soldiers, who would have to be paid regardless, could explore "the whole line, even to the Western ocean." They could talk with the Indians, persuade them to accept American traders, agree on the sites for trading posts. They could do all of this in two summers, and for a pittance.

Jefferson concluded: "The interests of commerce place the principal object within the constitutional powers and care of Congress, and that it should incidentally advance the geographical knowledge of our own continent can not but be an additional gratification." He then asked for an appropriation of twenty-five hundred dollars "for the purpose of extending the external commerce of the U.S."[21] There was some muttering from the Federalists, who always resented and resisted spending money on the West, but they were too badly outnumbered to be effective. Congress approved the whole package.

The twenty-five hundred went down easy, compared with Jefferson's request the previous week, which had been for an open-ended (up to $9,375,000) appropriation for the purchase of New Orleans. The Federalists had protested, over the amount of money and because some of the High Federalists were clamoring for war against France. But the Republicans held firm, and the Congress made the appropriation. The president selected Monroe to go to Paris to join Livingston in the negotiations. If Jefferson saw the link between the January 12 and the January 18 appropriation bills, he never mentioned it to anyone, except perhaps Lewis.

As soon as the appropriation for western exploration passed, as Jefferson recalled it, "Captain Lewis immediately renewed his solicitations to have the direction of the party." Perhaps command really was still an open question; more likely Jefferson was pretending that until Congress had authorized the expedition he had made no choice of a leader.

Whatever his reason for the remark, Jefferson never hesitated to confirm Lewis's appointment. Jefferson by this time had spent two full years with Lewis on a daily basis, and had taught Lewis on an intense schedule for about four months. He later wrote that, by the beginning of 1803, "I had now had opportunities of knowing him intimately."

Jefferson gave his reasons for picking Lewis to Dr. Benjamin Rush of Philadelphia: "Capt. Lewis is brave, prudent, habituated to the woods, & familiar with Indian manners & character. He is not regularly educated, but he possesses a great mass of accurate observation on all the subjects of nature which present themseles here, & will therefore readily select those only in his new route which shall be new. He has qualified himself for those observations of longitude & latitude necessary to fix the points of the line he will go over."[22]

Lewis still had much to learn. To that end, Jefferson had plans for him to do graduate work in Philadelphia, with America's leading scientists. That Lewis would benefit, Jefferson had no doubt. That Lewis could simultaneously plan the expedition and begin putting it together, Jefferson had no doubts. Some of his advisers did; they considered Lewis not well educated and perhaps too strongheaded and too much of a risk-taker. But Jefferson was sure he had the right man.

7

PREPARING FOR THE EXPEDITION

January–June 1803

A week after Congress appropriated the funds for the expedition, Jefferson began writing his scientific friends. The message was the same in each case: the expedition has been authorized but is still confidential; I have chosen Captain Lewis to lead it; Lewis needs advice and instruction. The letters made it clear that Jefferson intended the recipients to provide advice and instruction without cost to the government.

Lewis's schooling began during the period from New Year's Day to the Ides of March. Lewis was still living in the President's House, conferring with Jefferson as often and for as long as Jefferson's schedule would allow. Beyond the conferences and the practical lessons in the use of the sextant and other measuring instruments, which took place on the lawn, Lewis studied maps in Jefferson's collection.

He also conferred with Albert Gallatin, a serious map-collector. Gallatin had a special map made up for Lewis showing North America from the Pacific Coast to the Mississippi, with details on what was known of the Missouri River up to the Mandan villages in the Great Bend of the river (today's Bismarck, North Dakota), and a few wild guesses as to what the Rockies might look like and the course of the Columbia. There were but three certain points on the map: the latitude and longitude of the mouth of the Columbia, of St. Louis, and of the Mandan villages (thanks to British fur traders).

By the time he finished studying with Jefferson and Gallatin, Lewis knew all that there was to know about the Missouri and what lay to the west of it.

The problem was that west of the Mandans nearly to the coast was *terra incognita*. And the best scientists in the world could not begin to fill in that map until someone had walked across the land, taking measurements, providing descriptions of the flora, fauna, rivers, mountains, and people, not failing to note the commercial and agricultural possibilities.

To make that journey required a frontiersman's expert knowledge combined with an understanding of technology and what it could do to make the passage easier and more fruitful. That was the positive side of Jefferson's choice of Lewis, who was in fact the perfect choice. Indeed, Lewis's career might almost have been dedicated to preparing him for this adventure. He knew the Old Northwest about as well as any man in the country, he knew lonely forest trails through Indian country, he knew hunting and fishing and canoes, he knew how to keep records, had adequate mathematical skills, and for two years had been privy to Mr. Jefferson's hopes and dreams, his curiosity and knowledge.

Jefferson told Patterson that Lewis had the required frontier skills, to which "he joins a great stock of accurate* observation on the subjects of the three kingdoms. ... He has been for some time qualifying himself for taking observations of longitude & latitude to fix the geographical points of the line he will pass over." But he needed help, and it was Patterson's and the other scientists in Philadelphia's privilege and—not stated but clearly implied—duty to supply that help. Of course they were all delighted to do so anyway.[1]

It was a favorite saying of one of President Jefferson's twentieth-century successors, Dwight Eisenhower, that in war, before the battle is joined, plans are everything, but once the shooting begins, plans are worthless. The same aphorism can be said about exploration. In battle, what cannot be predicted is the enemy's reaction; in exploration, what cannot be predicted is what is around the next bend in the river or on the other side of the hill. The planning process, therefore, is as much guesswork as it is intelligent forecasting of the physical needs of the expedition. It tends to be frustrating, because the planner carries with him a nagging sense that he is making some simple mistakes that could be easily corrected in the planning stage, but may cause a dead loss when the mistake is discovered midway through the voyage.

---

* Initially, Jefferson used the word "scientific" here, but crossed it out and substituted "accurate."

For this expedition, planning was going on at two levels. The president was working on the first draft of his instructions to Lewis. It was becoming a long, complex document, for Jefferson was making a list of the things he wanted to know about the West. Since there was so much he wanted to know, far more than a single expedition could answer, he had to make choices. There was no mention of looking for gold or silver in the draft Jefferson was circulating, for example, whereas soil conditions and climate were included. Trade possibilities were prominent.

Taken all together, the instructions represented a culmination and a triumph of the American Enlightenment. The expedition authorized by the popularly elected Congress would combine scientific, commercial, and agricultural concerns with geographical discovery and nation-building. All the pillars of Enlightenment thought, summed up with the phrase "useful knowledge," were gathering in the instructions.

While Jefferson worked on the instructions, Lewis had his own planning to do. Jefferson would set the objectives, but it was Captain Lewis who would get the expedition there and back. The responsibility was his for deciding the size of the expedition, how it would proceed up the Missouri River, what it would need to cross the Rocky Mountains and descend the Columbia to the Pacific Ocean and return. The team would have to do this as a self-contained unit. Once the expedition left St. Louis, Lewis would be stuck with the decisions he had made during the planning process.

How many men? With what skills? How big a boat? What design? What type of rifle? How much powder and lead? How many cooking pots? What tools? How much dry or salted rations could be carried? What medicines, in what quantity? What scientific instruments? What books? How many fishing hooks? How much salt? Tobacco? Whiskey?

Lewis and Jefferson talked into the late evening about such questions. Jefferson thought it would be a good idea to carry some cast-iron corn mills to give the Indians as presents. Lewis agreed.[2] They discussed the trade beads that were the currency of the western Indian tribes, and agreed that plenty would be needed. They made up lists of other items. Together, they concocted the idea of a collapsible iron-frame boat, one that could be carried past the falls of the Missouri, wherever that might be, and put together at the far end with animal skins to cover it, so that the expedition would be back in business on the water.

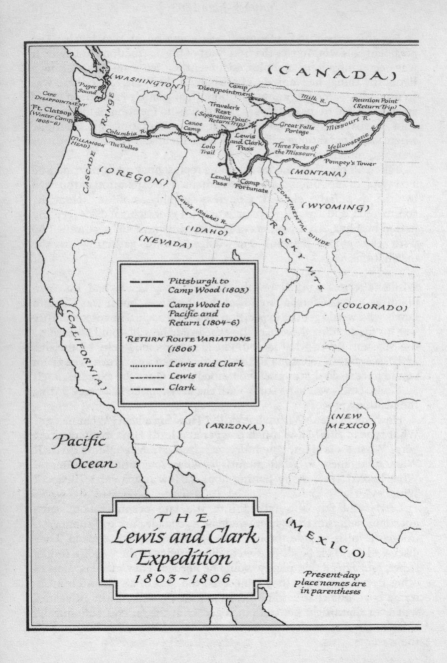

THE
Lewis and Clark
Expedition
1803~1806

Present-day
place names are
in parentheses

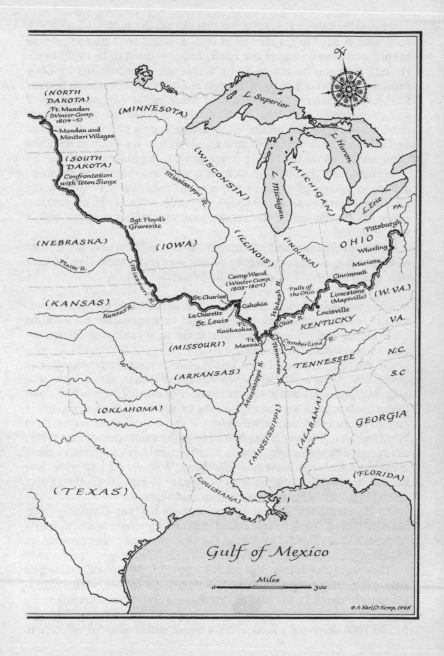

They talked about timing. Now that the appropriation was in hand, both men wanted to get started as soon as possible. With the coming of spring and the drying of the roads, Lewis wanted to be ready to go. He told Jefferson he hoped to be across the Appalachians by early summer. He intended to go to the post at South West Post, near present Kingston in eastern Tennessee, and there enlist his core group of soldier-explorers from the garrison. He planned to march them overland to Nashville, where he would pick up a previously ordered keelboat to float down the Cumberland River to its junction with the Ohio, not far above the Ohio's junction with the Mississippi.

He planned to be in St. Louis by August 1 and thought he might be able to proceed a good bit of the way up the Missouri before being forced into winter camp. In 1804, he expected to cross the mountains, reach the Pacific, make the return journey, and report back before winter set in.[3]

Lewis and Jefferson talked through January and February and on into March, trying to imagine what the trip was going to be like, so that they could be certain of what would be needed.

But that was only the half of it. The other half involved preparing Lewis for the scientific observations he would be responsible for making. That meant study. Hard, intensive study in a variety of disciplines under a severe time pressure.

On the Ides of March, Lewis left Washington for Harpers Ferry, site of the U.S. Army's arsenal. Lewis's purpose was to obtain arms and ammunition for his party. He could select from existing stock or order items made special for the expedition by the arsenal's craftsmen. He carried a letter to the superintendent of the arsenal from Secretary of War Dearborn: "You will be pleased to make such arms & Iron work, as requested by the bearer Captain Meriwether Lewis and to have them completed with the least possible delay."[4] When he had what was needed, he would arrange for it to be shipped to Pittsburgh, then hurry on to Philadelphia for more schooling and shopping.

At Harpers Ferry, he got fifteen muzzle-loading, flintlock, long-barreled rifles, sometimes called "Kentucky" but more properly "Pennsylvania rifles." They were the *sine qua non* of the expedition. On them depended the food supply and self-defense.

They were absolutely dependable—the U.S. Model 1803, the first rifle specifically designed for the U.S. Army, .54-caliber, with a thirty-three-inch barrel. Lewis referred to these weapons as short rifles, for they were considerably shorter than the civilian Pennsylvania rifle. The Model 1803 delivered a lead slug on target with sufficient velocity to kill a deer at a range of about a hundred yards. An expert could get off two aimed shots in one minute.[5] Lewis also selected pipe tomahawks and ordered the artisans at Harpers Ferry to make three dozen. He picked up fish gigs, knives, and so on.

Mainly, however, he supervised the construction of the iron boat frame. It was so important to him that he stayed on at Harpers Ferry for a month, instead of the week he had planned. This was cutting into the time Jefferson had wanted him to spend in Philadelphia.

On April 22, having heard nothing from Lewis since March 7, Jefferson learned in reports from others about Lewis's delay at Harpers Ferry. With Lewis gone, the president needed a secretary. He had selected a young man, Lewis Harvie of Virginia, but had put off announcing the appointment for reasons he explained in a letter to Harvie. Jefferson had been living in "in the daily expectation that the stage of the day would bring back Capt. Lewis, and that then within a few days he would set out on his Missisipi expedition."

Jefferson also said that he had put off writing "because my great regard for Capt. Lewis made me unwilling to show a haste to fill his place before he was gone, & to counteract also a malignant & unfounded report that I was parting with him from dissatisfaction, a thing impossible either from his conduct or my dispositions towards him."[6]

Washington will have its gossip. Jefferson was extremely sensitive to it. But far more important to him was Lewis's delay. He was almost desperate because of it, but he subdued his feelings and wrote Lewis with some care in his word choices: "I have no doubt you have used every possible exertion to get off, and therefore we have only to lament what cannot be helped, as the delay of a month now may lose a year in the end."[7]

Lewis might have read that as an expression of confidence, but on second reading wondered if it was a complaint. Most likely the former. In any case, he knew Jefferson would understand and would agree with his judgment on priorities. Jefferson's letter of complaint crossed Lewis's explanation for the delay, a frequent occurrence given the maddeningly slow mails.

Lewis described his activities. Besides arranging for the rifles, knives, and other equipment, he had written to the commander at South West Post to request help in getting suitable volunteers. The soldier volunteers could be promised their regular pay and a reward of land grants.

Lewis anticipated gathering his party as he made his way to St. Louis that summer, and strengthening it through personnel selection as the expedition proceeded, rejecting the weak, ignorant, and unmanageable for the strong, skilled, and eager volunteers. He told Jefferson he intended to be ruthless about it.

He had written to a congressman from Tennessee requesting that he find a boatbuilder in Nashville who could make a boat and a canoe for the expedition. These and other matters took longer than he had expected.

But by far the biggest cause of delay was Lewis's experimenting with the boat he and Jefferson had dreamed up. Every day he was at the work site, because he was convinced that without his personal attention the workmen would never understand the design. He carried out some sophisticated experiments with two different designs, one curved, the other "simicilindrical," the former for the stem and stern, the latter for the body of the boat. He triumphantly reported to Jefferson that the frame would weigh only forty-four pounds, whereas the boat when covered with hide would carry 1,770 pounds. Lewis told Jefferson, "I was induced from the result of this experiment to direct the iron frame of the canoe to be completed."[8]

He had made his first important independent decisions: where to spend his fast-disappearing time, and what boat to build. This was the beginning of a new relationship with Jefferson. Though Lewis was not yet quite out of the reach of the president's communiqués, he was not far short of it—witness his decision to stay three extra weeks at Harpers Ferry despite his knowledge that Jefferson desperately wanted him to get to Philadelphia to study, and then get on the road.

In mid-April, Lewis set off to the east. He stopped first in Frederickstown, where on April 15 he wrote General William Irvin, superintendent of military stores, with headquarters in Philadelphia. Lewis said he wanted Irvin to purchase for him some necessary articles. First on the list was "Portable-Soup," a dried soup of various beans and vegetables that Lewis may have used during his travels as an army paymaster. In any case, he was enthusiastic about it. He told Irvin, "Portable Soup, in my opinion, forms one of the most essential articles in the preparation [for the expedition], and fearing that it cannot be procured readily in such quantity as is requisite, I . . . take the liberty to request that you will procure two hundred pounds of it for me," or however much was available on the market. "I have supposed that the soup would cost about one dollar pr lb; should it however, come much higher then quantity must be limited by the sum of $250 as more cannot be expended."[9] In the end, Lewis spent $289.50 on 193 pounds of portable soup, by far the highest sum for any area of provisions. He spent as much for dried soup as he had originally estimated for his instruments, arms, and ammunition.[10]

On April 19, Lewis arrived in Lancaster. He went immediately to the home of Andrew Ellicott, America's leading astronomer and mathematician. Jefferson had earlier written Ellicott to ask him to teach Lewis to make celestial observations, and Ellicott had replied, "Mr. Lewis's first object must be to acquire a facility, and dexterity, in making the observations; which can only be obtained by practice."

Lewis and Ellicott wasted no time; on April 20, Lewis reported to Jefferson, "I have commenced, under his direction, my observations &c to perfect myself in the use and application of the instruments." He found Ellicott to be "extreemly friendly and attentive, and I am confident is disposed to render me every aid in his power: he thinks it will be necessary I should remain here ten or twelve days."[11]

While at Lancaster, Lewis picked up additional rifles. How many is not known, nor why he couldn't get all he wanted at Harpers Ferry. They may have been improved models, since Lancaster was the manufacturing center for long rifles. But his list of necessary items, and of quantities required, continued to grow, indicating that at Harpers Ferry he had decided the expedition had to be a party considerably larger than a dozen men.

Another thought had come into his head: that another officer would be required. No evidence exists as to when, or even if, he discussed either of these critical matters with Jefferson, but how could he have failed to do so?

Lewis's schooling in Lancaster in the use of sextant, chronometer, and other instruments took longer than Ellicott had anticipated. Not until May 7 was he ready to go to Philadelphia. The ride from Lancaster to Philadelphia took him over the most modern highway in America, completed in 1795, made of broken-stone, the country's first gravel road. Stage wagons were able to average five to seven miles per hour on it.[12] Going that fast in a stage was a new experience for Lewis.

In Philadelphia, he went to Patterson, who continued his instruction. With Patterson's help, he selected a chronometer. He bought it from Thomas Parker, a clock- and watchmaker on South Third Street, for $250, by far the largest sum expended for any single item carried on the expedition. Lewis sent it to Ellicott to be regulated, with this note: "I have at length been enabled to procure a Chronometer which you will receive . . . and you will also receive with her a screw-driver and kee, the inner cases of the Chronometer are confined by a screw. She is wound up and the works are stoped by inscerting a hog's bristle which you will discover by examination. She has been cleaned by Mr. Voit, and her rate of going ascertained by observation to be 14″ too slow in 24 h."[13]

Jefferson sent Lewis a current draft of his instructions, asking Lewis to comment, and to circulate the draft among the various savants in Philadelphia, for their comments and suggestions. Lewis worried about a phrase in the draft that indicated that the scientific instruments had already been provided. By whom? he wondered. What were they? He asked Jefferson for a list, so that he could consult with Patterson and Ellicott to make certain nothing had been omitted. He further informed Jefferson that his teachers "both disapprove of the Theodolite," which Jefferson had told Lewis would be his best instrument for accurate measurements. It was "a delicate instrument, difficult of transportation, and one that would be very liable to get out of order," and anyway it was "much more inacurate than the Sextant."

His teachers agreed on what instruments would be "indispensably necessary." They were "two Sextants, an artificial horizon or two; a good Arnold's watch or chronometer, a Surveyor's compass with a ball and socket and two pole chain, and a set of plotting instruments."[14]

There was just a hint of a reminder in the letter that the decision-making power for the expedition was coming into Lewis's hands. Jefferson acknowledged as much in his reply, regretting "the impression which has been misunderstood." The draft Lewis had of the instructions would not be dated until the day he departed; Jefferson had assumed that by then Lewis would have made *his* selections and purchases. As to the theodolite, Jefferson told Lewis to do whatever Patterson and Ellicott recommended.[15]

Lewis was in Philadelphia through much of May and the first week in June. He made the rounds of the city, the list he and Jefferson had drawn up in hand, making purchases: fishing tackle, lead canisters, medicines, dry goods, tobacco, shirts. He spent $2,324.

Herewith a sampling of the items he purchased: six papers of ink powder; sets of pencils; "Creyons"; two hundred pounds of "best rifle powder," and four hundred pounds of lead; "4 Groce fishing Hooks assorted"; twenty-five axes; woolen overalls and other clothing items, including "30 yds. Common flannel"; one hundred flints; "30 Steels for striking or making fire"; six large needles and six dozen large awls; three bushels of salt.

He bought oilskin bags to protect the instruments and journals. He got mosquito netting and field tables, and large, multipurpose sheets of oiled linen, each eight by twelve feet, for tents, and candles, so that he could write at night. The sheets of oiled linen could double up as sails by day.

For Indian presents, five pounds of "white Glass Beads mostly small," and twenty pounds of red assorted beads; 144 "small cheap Scizors"; "288 Common brass thimbles"; ten pounds of assorted sewing thread; silk; paint and vermilion; 288 knives; combs; arm bands; and ear trinkets. Lewis insisted on taking a preponderance of blue beads, because they were "far more valued than the white beads of the same manufacture and answer all the purposes of money." The emphasis was on the gay and gaudy rather than the useful. Although Lewis called them presents, they were trade goods. He did not intend to give them away; rather, he would use them to purchase goods and services from the Indians.

Lewis and Clark scholar Paul Russell Cutright writes, "It was no small task to anticipate all that he would need in the way of arms, food, clothing, camping paraphernalia, scientific instruments, and Indian presents for a party of still undetermined size that, for an indefinite period of time, would be out of touch with normal supply sources."[16]

How well he had done, only the event could tell. One small peek ahead is appropriate here, however, because it reveals so much about Lewis and the point of view he held. During the expedition, the party ran out of many useful or pleasure-giving items, including tobacco, whiskey, salt, and blue beads. A frontiersman could live without those things. The expedition ran short of, but never out of, many critical items. But when it got home, the expedition had sufficient powder and lead to repeat the journey, and plenty of rifles. (Lewis had arranged at Harpers Ferry for lead canisters that when melted down made exactly the right number of balls for the amount of powder in the canister.)

Lewis had the frontiersman's faith in his rifle. As long as a man had his rifle, ammunition, and powder, he would take on anything the wilderness could throw at him.

Lewis also had plenty of ink left when he got home, enough for another voyage. That ink wasn't critical to making the trip, but it was critical to making the expedition a success by recording its findings. Lewis had his priorities right.

The purchase of the soup was a serious cost overrun. Along with the extra rifles he purchased in Lancaster, the amount indicates that, the more he thought about what he might encounter, the larger the size of the party was becoming in his imagination. The amounts of medicine he purchased also indicate he now planned to take many more than a dozen men.

His medical adviser was Dr. Benjamin Rush, a member of the American Philosophical Society, a signer of the Declaration of Independence, and the most eminent American physician of the day. On May 17, Lewis called on him at his home on the corner of Walnut and Fourth Streets, bringing along Jefferson's draft instructions for Rush's comments.

They talked. Rush gave advice, beginning with: "When you feel the least indisposition, do not attempt to overcome it by labour or marching. *Rest* in a horizontal posture. Also fasting and diluting drinks for a day or two will generally prevent an attack of fever. To these preventatives of disease may be added a gentle sweat obtained by warm drinks, or gently opening the bowels by means of one, two, or more of the purging pills."

Those pills were under Dr. Rush's patent, known as "Rush's pills" but generally referred to as "Thunderclappers." As far as Rush was concerned, they were sovereign for nearly all mankind's ills. They were composed of calomel, a mixture of six parts mercury to one part chlorine, and jalap. Each drug was a purgative of explosive power; the combination was awesome. Mercury had an even more important role in Lewis's pharmacy: it was the treatment of choice for syphilis (and remained so until the advent of penicillin during World War II).

Another piece of advice from Dr. Rush: "After long marches, or much fatigue from any cause, you will be more refreshed by *lying down* in a horizontal posture for two hours, than by resting a much longer time in any other position of the body."[17] There is no evidence of Lewis's asking the good doctor what he thought they would be encountering out there.

Lewis reported to Jefferson, "Dr. Rush has favored me with some abstract queries under the several heads of *Physical History*, *medicine*, *Morals* and *Religeon* of the Indians, which I have no doubt will be servicable in directing my inquiries among that people."

Rush's questionnaire asked about the diseases of the Indians, and their "remidies," at what age menstruation began and ended, the age of marriage, how long they suckled their children, the state of the pulse in the morning, at noon, and at night, before and after eating. At what time did they rise? What about baths? Murder? Suicide? "Do they employ any substitute for ardent spirits to promote intoxication?" Any animal sacrifices in their religion? "What Affinity between their religious Ceremonies & those of the Jews?" (Here Rush was looking for the fabled Lost Tribe of Israel.) More realistically, "How do they dispose of their dead, and with what Ceremonies do they inter them?"[18]

It was an eclectic list of questions, some silly, some stunningly on the mark. They illustrated how little could even be guessed about the nature of the Indian tribes of the West, or their numbers.

In addition to the questionnaire, Rush prepared a medical list for Lewis. Amounting to $90.69 for drugs, lancets, forceps, syringes, and other supplies, it included fifty dozen (!) Rush's Pills along with thirty other kinds of drugs. Those most used were Peruvian bark, jalap, opium, Glauber salts, niter (i.e., potassium nitrate, or saltpeter), tartar emetic, laudanum, calomel, and mercurial ointment. The drugs Lewis bought contained thirteen hundred doses of physic, eleven hundred of emetic, thirty-five hundred of diaphoretic (sweat inducer), and more, including drugs for blistering, salivation, and increased kidney output, along with tourniquets and clyster syringes.

While at Harpers Ferry, Lewis had thought of bringing a doctor along, but by May he evidently had decided he himself would be the doctor. He had learned from his mother a great deal about herbs and simples and herb therapy, and wasn't afraid to experiment. Like all frontiersmen, he knew how to set a broken bone or remove an embedded bullet or arrow, how to cope with croup or dysentery.

Rush was impressed by Lewis. He wrote Jefferson, "His mission is truly interesting. I shall wait with great solicitude for its issue. Mr. Lewis appears admirably qualified for it. May its advantages prove no less honorable to your administration than to the interests of science."[19]

It wasn't all work. Lewis did a considerable amount of socializing in Philadelphia with his friend Mahlon Dickerson. They moved in the highest social circles: dinner one evening with Jefferson's great friend Dr. George Logan; another evening with Governor Thomas McKean at his mansion on the northeast corner of Third and Pine Streets.[20]

By day, Lewis expanded his studies. He went to Dr. Benjamin Smith Barton, professor at the University of Pennsylvania and author of the first textbook on botany in the United States, just published when Lewis came to him. Barton lived a few steps from Independence Hall, at 44 North Fifth Street. He had studied in England and Germany, and he had made fairly extensive field trips in Pennsylvania. He was mesmerized by the expedition. The thought of all that was waiting to be discovered tempted him so much that he talked with Lewis about the possibility of going along. Lewis was enthusiastic about the idea; Barton would certainly be an asset in collecting and describing. But he was thirty-seven years old, a scholar, not a soldier. "I fear the Dr. will not carry this design into effect," Lewis told Jefferson—rightly, as it turned out.[21]

Still, Barton made important contributions. He taught Lewis how to preserve specimens, either plant or bird- or animal skin. He taught Lewis the importance of specimen labels, including place and date of collection. Barton expanded Lewis's vocabulary and range of knowledge. In a painstaking study on the scientific writing of Lewis,

Elijah Criswell compiled a list of almost two hundred different technical terms the captain employed in describing new plants and animals, a quantity showing, in Criswell's words, "a remarkable knowledge for an amateur, of scientific, especially botanical, descriptive terminology."[22]

Dr. Caspar Wistar was the last of the Philadelphia savants Lewis turned to for education. Wistar held the chair of anatomy at the University of Pennsylvania and had published the first American textbook on anatomy. He was also a member of the American Philosophical Society and the foremost authority on fossils in America. He talked with Lewis about that anomalous beast the *Megalonyx*, which he and Jefferson had discovered, and about the mastodons he and Jefferson believed might still inhabit the prairies.[23]

One last thing Lewis got in Philadelphia—his traveling library. It included Barton's *Elements of Botany*, which was not a gift—Lewis paid six dollars for it. Lewis borrowed a book from Barton, Antoine Simor Le Page du Pratz's *History of Louisiana*. He had Richard Kirwan's *Elements of Mineralogy* (London, 1784), a two-volume edition of Linnaeus (the founder of the system of Latin classification of plants), and a four-volume dictionary, along with *A Practical Introduction to Spherics and Nautical Astronomy* and *The Nautical Almanac and Astronomical Ephemeris*, together with tables necessary to finding latitude and longitude.[24]

On May 29, Lewis sent a long-overdue report to Jefferson. He announced that on June 6 or 7 he would be able to depart for Washington for a final conference, then would be off. He would have all his preparations completed in a day or two, but wanted to stay on an extra few days for additional study with Patterson. He enclosed some tracings he had made of Vancouver's map of the northwestern coast. He explained why a tracing rather than the original: "The maps attached to Vancouver's voyage cannot be procured seperately from that work, which is both too costly, and too weighty, for me either to purchase or carry."[25]

Geographer John Logan Allen points out that it took considerable cartographic technique to copy the charts from Vancouver's work. Lewis, Allen writes, "was not simply a passive receptor of the geographical materials being assembled by Jefferson and Gallatin. It seems, rather, that he was active in gathering data for the purpose of taking it along on the expedition." Dr. Allen further speculates, on the basis of internal evidence, that Lewis made a copy of the David Thompson map of the Great Bend of the Missouri River, done late in the last century and in the possession of the British chargé d'affaires in Washington.[26]

During the second week in June, Lewis abandoned his original plan to go by South West Post. He had heard there were too few good men in the garrison, and that no boat would be waiting in Nashville. So he arranged transportation by the army, at the army's expense, for thirty-five hundred pounds of goods to be moved from Philadelphia to Pittsburgh. Because the "road which from necessaty they must travel is by no means good," Lewis ordered a five-horse team to pull the wagon.[27] Apparently it was also at this time that he entered into a contract with a boatbuilder in Pittsburgh.

Then he set off for Washington. Probably foremost in Lewis's mind was the size of the party, along with an inevitable need for a second officer. None had been mentioned, but Lewis wanted one. If Jefferson approved, Lewis had a candidate in mind, as well as a highly unusual command arrangement. The president and the captain also needed to go over the final instructions in detail. Jefferson needed to bring Lewis up-to-date on the status of the proposed purchase of New Orleans. The two men had a lot to talk about before Lewis headed west.

8

WASHINGTON TO PITTSBURGH

June–August 1803

When Lewis arrived in Washington, he and Jefferson went to work immediately on the instructions. Jefferson had circulated them among his Cabinet and had their replies to consider.

Secretary of State James Madison had wondered "if the laws give any authority at present beyond the limits of the U.S?"[1] That was a shorthand way of raising the point that this expedition was going into territory belonging to France and administered by Spain, whose governments might regard it as a military reconnaissance, or even an invasion.

Attorney General Levi Lincoln warned Jefferson that, "because of the perverse, hostile, and malignant state of the opposition, with their facility, of imposing on the public mind, & producing excitements, every measure originating with the executive will be attacked, with a virulence," including the expedition. For his part, Lincoln declared, "I consider the enterprise of national consequence."

But as a politician Lincoln knew that more justification was needed, to keep the Federalists from howling at the cost. He came up with a rationale that would appeal to the New England clergy: advertise the thing as a mission to elevate the religious beliefs of the heathen Indians. "If the enterprise appears to be, an attempt to advance them, it will by many people, on that account, be justified, however calamitous the issue." Jefferson bought the idea; in his final instructions he ordered Lewis to learn what he could about Indian religion, because it would help "those who may endeavor to civilize & instruct them."

Lincoln had another important suggestion. Jefferson had written that if Lewis were faced with certain destruction he should retreat rather than offer opposition. Lincoln commented, "From my ideas of Capt. Lewis he will be much more likely, in case of difficulty, to push to far, than to recede too soon. Would it not be well to change the term, '*certain* destruction' into *probable* destruction & to add—that these dangers are never to be encountered, which vigilance percaution & attention can secure against, at a reasonable expense."[2]

There is more than a hint here that Lincoln was one of the president's advisers who feared Lewis was a reckless risk-taker, one of those Virginia gentlemen who would overreact to any challenge to his honor or bravery. Jefferson may have agreed; in any event, he adopted the wording Lincoln suggested.

Treasury Secretary Albert Gallatin saw nothing in Jefferson's draft that needed changing, but he did want some things added. He wanted to know more about the Spanish posts in Louisiana and the British activities along the Missouri River. "The future destinies of the Missouri country are of vast importance to the U.S.," Gallatin wrote, "it being perhaps the only large tract of country and certainly the *first* which lying out of the boundaries of the Union will be settled by the people of the U. States." Therefore, he wanted as much information as possible on the Missouri drainage.

As the instructions indicated, Jefferson had a multitude of motives for sending off the expedition, but number one for him was the all-water route to the Pacific. Not for Gallatin. He flatly stated, "The great object is to ascertain whether from its extent & fertility the Missouri country is susceptible of a large population, in the same manner as the corresponding tract on the Ohio." He wanted Lewis enjoined to describe the soil and make judgments on its fertility by noticing the prevailing species of timber, to assess annual rainfall, temperature extremes, and other factors important to farmers.[3]

Jefferson adopted most of Gallatin's suggestions, but in its final form the instructions issued by Commander-in-Chief Jefferson to Captain Meriwether Lewis put exploration and commerce ahead of agriculture. "The object of your mission," Jefferson wrote, "is to explore the Missouri river, & such principal stream of it, as, by it's course and communication with the waters of the Pacific ocean, whether the Columbia, Oregan, Colorado or any other river may offer the most direct & practicable water communication across this continent for the purposes of commerce."

Commerce being the principal object, Jefferson naturally wanted Lewis to learn what he could about the routes used by the British traders coming down from Canada to trade with the Missouri River tribes, and about their trading methods and practice. He wanted Lewis to make suggestions as to how the fur trade, currently dominated by the British, could be taken over by Americans using the Missouri route.

Good maps were essential to commerce. So Jefferson's orders read, "Beginning at the mouth of the Missouri, you will take careful observations of latitude & longitude, at all remarkable points on the river, & especially at the mouths of rivers, at rapids, at islands, & other places & objects distinguished by such natural marks & characters of a durable kind." Jefferson admonished Lewis to write his figures and observations "distinctly & intelligibly" and to make multiple copies, one of these to be "on the paper of the birch, as less liable to injury from damp than common paper."

The fur trade would require knowledge of the Indian tribes. Jefferson instructed Lewis to learn the names of the nations, and their numbers, the extent of their possessions, their relations with other tribes, their languages, traditions, monuments, their occupations—whether agriculture or fishing or hunting or war—and the implements they used for those activities, their food, clothing, and housing, the diseases prevalent among them and the remedies they used, their laws and customs, and—last on the list but first in importance—"articles of commerce they may need or furnish, & to what extent." This was an ethnographer's dream-come-true set of marching orders.

"In all your intercourse with the natives," Jefferson went on, "treat them in the most friendly & conciliatory manner which their own conduct will admit." Lewis should "satisfy them of your journey's innocence," but simultaneously tell them of the size and strength of the United States. He should temper that implied threat by assuring the tribes of our wish to be "neighborly" and of our peaceful intentions: Americans only wished to trade with them. Lewis should invite a few chiefs to come to Washington for a visit, and arrange for some Indian children to come to the United States and be "brought up with us, & taught such arts as may be useful to them."

On the distinct possibility of an Indian attack, Jefferson was specific. If faced by a superior force determined to stop the expedition, "you must decline it's further pursuit, and return. In the loss of yourselves, we should lose also the information you will have acquired. . . . To you own discretion therefore must be left the degree of danger you may risk, and the point at which you should decline, only saying we wish you to err on the side of your safety, and to bring back your party safe even if it be with less information."

Jefferson told Lewis that, "on the accident of your death, you are hereby authorised to name the person who shall succeed to the command."

When Lewis reached the Pacific Coast, he should seek out a European trading vessel and possibly sail back to the United States on it. Or he could send back a copy of the journals with two men, if he wished, and return by the route he had come.

Taken all together, the military section of Jefferson's orders was all that a company commander setting off on an expedition could hope for. He had the authority he needed, including the specific permission from the commander-in-chief to make his judgments in the field.

Jefferson realized that, when Lewis reached the Pacific, "You will be without money, clothes or provisions." To deal with that situation, Jefferson provided a letter of credit for Lewis, authorizing him to draw on any agency of the U.S. government anywhere in the world, anything he wanted. "I also ask of the Consuls, agents, merchants & citizens of any nation to furnish you with those supplies which your necessities may call for. . . . And to give more entire satisfaction & confidence to those who may be disposed to aid you, I Thomas Jefferson, President of the United States of America, have written this letter of general credit for you with my own hand, and signed it with my name."

In its final version, dated July 4, 1803, this must be the most unlimited letter of credit ever issued by an American president.

Beyond commerce, the purpose of the expedition was to discover flora and fauna. The instructions ordered Lewis to notice and comment on the soil, the plant and animal life—especially plants not known in the United States—dinosaur bones, and volcanoes. Jefferson wanted to know about "mineral productions of every kind," but the ones he listed were limestone, pit coal, and salt.

There is no direct order to keep a daily journal. Jefferson did write about the possibility of sending Indians down the Missouri to St. Louis, carrying letters and "a copy of your journal, notes & observations," the only use of the word "journal" in the instructions, and he did tell Lewis to send "a copy of your notes" by sea if he could, but there is no order about journal keeping.[4] Perhaps it was a taken-for-granted matter; perhaps, in their many long discussions about the instructions, Jefferson made the order orally.

Donald Jackson's description of Jefferson's instructions cannot be bettered: "They embrace years of study and wonder, the collected wisdom of his government colleagues and his Philadelphia friends; they barely conceal his excitement at realizing that at last he would have facts, not vague guesses, about the Stony Mountains, the river courses, the wild Indian tribes, the flora and fauna of untrodden places."[5]

As they talked about the instructions, Lewis and Jefferson also discussed such matters as when Lewis could get going, what additional instruments and maps he would need, the size of the party and additional supplies, what the War Department could contribute to the expedition, and the negotiations over Louisiana. All these subjects were intermingled. They came together in the need for another officer.

Recognition of that need evidently came simultaneously; it certainly came naturally. The arguments for such an appointment were overwhelming. The instructions called for information in so many areas that one man could hardly provide it all and certainly could not do it all well. It was plain common sense to have two officers, so that if something happened to one the other could bring back the maps, scientific discoveries, descriptions of the Indians encountered, and all the rest. A second officer would be a help in enforcing discipline, and in fighting Indians if it came to that. There was no good reason *not* to take a second officer, except cost—and since Jefferson had just authorized spending millions of dollars for New Orleans, and he had his whole heart and mind invested in the Lewis expedition, he wasn't going to let cost be a factor.

Jefferson opened the coffers of the War Department for Lewis, acting in his capacity as commander-in-chief in support of an expedition sanctioned by Congress. In the process, he stretched the Constitution considerably, but penny-pinching the expedition was worse than bending his strict constructionist principles. He told the War Department to pay Lewis an eighteen-month advance in his salary, possibly for land speculation or to pay off debts; Lewis also borrowed $108 from Jefferson.[6] Secretary of War Henry Dearborn had sent an order to Harpers Ferry to supply anything Lewis requested in the way of arms and ironwork, "with the least possible delay." Jefferson saw to it that Lewis had unlimited purchasing power; the chief clerk of the War Department received orders to "purchase when requested by [Lewis] such articles as he may have occasion for, which he has not been able to obtain from the public Stores," and the Treasury Department was ordered to turn over a thousand dollars for Lewis's goods.[7] Even with some smoke-and-mirrors bookkeeping, the cost overrun was now at 100 percent, and growing daily.

Making the selections took time. Jefferson had hoped that Lewis would be off by June 28, or even earlier, but the day came and went and Lewis still had much to do. Nevertheless, Lewis expected to be on the

Missouri by September 1, which would give him two traveling months, during which he hoped to go seven or even eight hundred miles up the Missouri, before going into winter quarters.[8]

On June 29, Dearborn ordered the army paymaster to give Lewis $554, "being six Months pay for one Lieutenant, one Sergeant, one corporal, and ten Privates."[9]

That amounted to Lewis's official authorization to add an officer. Lewis had already acted on it, because Jefferson had agreed within a day or so of Lewis's arrival in Washington that it had to be done. On June 19, Lewis had written to William Clark. The letter contained what Donald Jackson described as "one of the most famous invitations to greatness the nation's archives can provide."[10]

It is a critical document. It launched one of the great friendships of all time and started the friends on one of the great adventures, and one of the great explorations, of all time.

It is also revealing. Lewis and Clark have become so entwined by history that for many Americans the name is Lewisandclark, but in 1803 they were not intimate friends. Although Clark was born in Virginia four years earlier than Lewis, he had moved to Kentucky as a small boy. They knew each other only in the army, for six months, when Lewis had served under Clark. No ancedotes survive, or any correspondence between them in the next decade except for a business letter from Lewis to Clark, asking him to make inquiries about land in Ohio.

But in that six months together they had taken each other's measure. That they liked what they saw is obvious from Lewis's letter to Clark, and Clark's response. They complemented each other. Clark was a tough woodsman accustomed to command; he had been a company commander and had led a party down the Mississippi as far as Natchez. He had a way with enlisted men, without ever getting familiar. He was a better terrestrial surveyor than Lewis, and a better waterman. Lewis apparently knew of his mapmaking ability. In general, in areas in which Lewis was shaky, Clark was strong, and vice versa.

Most of all, Lewis knew that Clark was competent to the task, that his word was his bond, that his back was steel. Clark knew the same about Lewis. Their trust in each other was complete, even before they took the first step west together. How this closeness came about cannot be known in any detail, but that it clearly was there long before the expedition cannot be doubted.

*

Clark had retired from the army in 1796, partly for reasons of health, partly to try his hand in business, mainly to do something to help straighten out the terribly tangled financial affairs of his older brother, General George Rogers Clark. He was living in Clarksville, Indiana Territory, when Lewis's letter arrived.

Lewis opened his invitation thus: "From the long and uninterupted friendship and confidence which has subsisted between us I feel no hesitation in making to you the following communication." He described the origins of the expedition, the congressional action, what he had done in Harpers Ferry and Philadelphia to get ready, and his intention to set out for Pittsburgh at the end of June. He thought he would be in Clarksville to meet Clark about August 10. On the way, he intended to "find and engage some good hunters, stout, healthy, unmarried men, accustomed to the woods, and capable of bearing bodily fatigue in a pretty considerable degree: should any young men answering this discription be found in your neighborhood I would think you to give information of them on my arivall at the falls of the Ohio."

Lewis described the expedition in matter-of-fact language that may well have left Clark breathless: "My plan is to descend the Ohio in a keeled boat thence up the Mississippi to the mouth of the Missourie, and up that river as far as it's navigation is practicable with a keeled boat, there to prepare canoes of bark or raw-hides, and proceed to it's [the Missouri's] source, and if practicable pass over to the waters of the Columbia or Origan River and by descending it reach the Western Ocean."

Lewis wrote that he would return to the United States on a trading vessel, if possible. He gave Clark a summary of his instructions from Jefferson, and described the instruments he had collected for making observations.

To carry out the mission, Lewis said he had authorization from Jefferson to pick noncommissioned officers and men, not to exceed twelve, from the western army posts. He added that he was also authorized "to engage any other man not soldiers that I may think useful in promoting the objects of succes of this expedition." He had in mind hunters, guides, and interpreters.

"Thus my friend," Lewis concluded, "you have a summary view of the plan, the means and the objects of this expedition. If therefore there is anything under those circumstances, in this enterprise, which would induce you to participate with me in it's fatiegues, it's dangers and it's honors, believe me there is no man on earth with whom I should feel equal pleasuure in sharing them as with yourself."

Lewis wrote that he had talked with Jefferson about the offer and that the president "expresses an anxious wish that you would consent to join me in this enterprise." There followed the most extraordinary offer. "He [Jefferson] has authorized me to say that in the event of your accepting this proposition he will grant you a Captain's commission which of course will intitle you to the pay and emoluments atached to that office and will equally with myself intitle you to such portion of land as was granted to officers of similar rank for their Revolutionary services; your situation if joined with me in this mission will in all respects be precisely such as my own."

It was remarkable for Lewis to propose a co-command. He did not even have to add a lieutenant to the party, and most certainly did not have to share the command. Divided command almost never works and is the bane of all military men, to whom the sanctity of the chain of command is basic and the idea of two disagreeing commanders in a critical situation is anathema. But Lewis did it anyway. It must have felt right to him. It had to have been based on what he knew about Clark, and what he felt for him.

Lewis wanted Clark along, even if not as an official member of the party. He closed his letter by saying that, if personal or business or any other affairs prevented Clark from accepting, Lewis hoped that he could "accompany me as a friend part of the way up the Missouri. I should be extremely happy in your company."[11]

It would take a month for Lewis's letter to reach Clark, another ten days for his reply to arrive. Meanwhile, a mystery. Ten days after Lewis made his offer of a shared command to Clark, he received from Secretary Dearborn the advance pay for the party to be recruited. It authorized one lieutenant only. Lewis made no known protest. Jefferson should have been alert enough to notice that Dearborn was thinking lieutenant while Lewis was offering captain, and he should have corrected the situation by telling Dearborn that Lewis's offer would prevail and Clark, if he accepted, would be a captain. But the commander-in-chief did nothing. It was uncharacteristic of Lewis and Jefferson to miss a detail of any kind, much less one fraught with such potential danger for embarrassment, misunderstanding, and bad feeling, but they missed this one.

Lewis spent the last week of June buying supplies and instruments, gathering more books, and going over maps. He made arrangements for a stand-in as his fellow officer, should Clark decline. He chose a man he had met in 1799 and served with, Lieutenant Moses Hooke, and assured Jefferson that Hooke was the best officer in the army, "endowed with a good constitution, possessing a sensible well informed mind, is industrious, prudent and persevering, and withall intrepid and enterprising." Lewis didn't hand out praise easily, and since it was clear that he was ready to cross the continent with Hooke, he obviously meant what he said about Hooke's superior abilities. But there was no hint of a promotion to captain and a co-command.[12] Good as Hooke was, he wasn't William Clark.

By July 2, Lewis was nearing completion of the preparations and about to set off for Pittsburgh. That day, he wrote his mother.

He opened with an apology for not having the time to come home for a visit before departing for the western country, a trip he expected to take about a year and a half. As boys setting off on an adventure are wont to do, he reassured his mother: "The nature of this expedition is by no means dangerous, my rout will be altogether thorugh tribes of Indians who are perfectly friendly to the United States, therefore consider the chances of life just as much in my favor on this trip as I should conceive them were I to remain at home."

After telling his mother not to worry, he wrote of what being Mr. Jefferson's choice meant to him: "The charge of this expedition is honorable to myself, as it is important to my Country."

Then it was back to reassurance: "I feel myself perfectly prepared, nor do I doubt my health and strength of constitution to bear me through it; I go with the most perfect preconviction in my own mind of returning safe and hope therefore that you will not suffer yourself to indulge any anxiety for my safety."

There followed a series of instructions on the education of Lewis's half-brother, John Marks. Lewis insisted that John go to the College of William and Mary at Williamsburg, even if land certificates had to be sold to pay the tuition. Given how deeply Virginia planters hated to sell land, Lewis's priorities show the high value he set on education. After the crash courses he had been put through in Philadelphia, he had reason to wish he had gone to college.

He closed with a wish to be remembered to various members of the family, especially the two youngsters, Mary and Jack. "Tell them I hope the progress they will make in their studies will be equal to my wishes."[13]

Also on July 2, Dearborn handed Lewis the authorization to select up to twelve noncommissioned officers and privates. He could pick them from the garrisons at the posts at Massac and Kaskaskia, the former on the lower Ohio and the latter on the Mississippi, above the mouth of the Ohio. In separate orders, Dearborn told the commanding officers at the posts to furnish Lewis with every assistance in "selecting and engaging suitable men to accompany him on an expedition to the Westward." That was a license to raid, sure to be resented by captains about to lose their best men, but Dearborn made it stick. "If any [man] in your Company should be disposed to join Capt. Lewis," and if Captain Lewis wanted the volunteer, "you *will* detach them accordingly."

In addition, Captain Russell Bissell at Kaskaskia was ordered to provide Lewis with the best boat on the post and with a sergeant and "eight good Men who understand rowing a boat." They would carry baggage for Lewis, to his winter quarters on the Missouri, then descend before the ice closed in. Bissell refused Sergeant Patrick Gass's request to join the expedition, presumably on the grounds that he couldn't afford to lose his best noncommissioned officer. Lewis used the authority given him by Dearborn to enlist Gass anyway.[14]

For the descent of the Ohio, Lieutenant Colonel Thomas Cushing provided Lewis with eight recruits from the post at Carlisle, Pennsylvania. In a pouch accompanying the order, Cushing included a couple of dozen letters for Lewis to deliver to officers at the western posts. He asked Lewis, after he reached St. Louis, to send the eight recruits down the Mississippi to Fort Adams. Cushing closed with a nice note: "That your expedition may be pleasant to yourself and advantageous to our Country; and when its toils and dangers are over, that you may enjoy many years of happiness, prosperity and honor, is the sincere wish of, Sir, Your most Obdt. Servt."[15]

July 4, 1803, the nation's twenty-seventh birthday, was a great day for Meriwether Lewis. He completed his preparations and was ready to depart in the morning. He got his letter of credit in its final form from President Jefferson. And the *National Intelligencer* of Washington reported in that day's issue that Napoleon had sold Louisiana to the United States.

It was stunning news of the most fundamental importance. Henry Adams put it best: "The annexation of Louisiana was an event so portentous as to defy measurement; it gave a new face to politics, and ranked in historical importance next to the Declaration of Independence and the adoption of the Constitution—events of which it was the logical outcome; but as a matter of diplomacy it was unparalleled, because it cost almost nothing."[16]

Napoleon's decision to sell not just New Orleans but all of Louisiana, and the negotiations that followed, and Jefferson's decision to waive his strict constructionist views in order to make the purchase, is a dramatic and well-known story. It is best described by Henry Adams in his *History of the United States in the Administrations of Thomas Jefferson*, one of the great classics of American history writing.

Napoleon was delighted, and rightly so. He had title to Louisiana, but no power to enforce it. The Americans were sure to overrun it long before he could get an army there—if he ever could. "Sixty million francs for an occupation that will not perhaps last a day!" he exulted. He knew what he was giving up and what the United States was getting—and the benefit to France, beyond the money: "The sale assures forever the power of the United States, and I have given England a rival who, sooner or later, will humble her pride."[17]

For Lewis, what mattered was not how Louisiana was acquired, a process in which he played no role, but that the territory he would be crossing from the Mississippi to the Continental Divide now belonged to the United States. As Jefferson nicely put it, the Louisiana Purchase "lessened the apprehensions of interruption from other powers."

The Purchase did more for the expedition than relieve it of threats from the Spanish, French, or British. As Jefferson noted, it "increased infinitely the interest we felt in the expedition."[18]

When Adams wrote that the Purchase "gave a new face to politics," he meant that it signified the end of the Federalist Party, which was so shortsighted and partisan that many of its representatives criticized the act. Alexander Hamilton was wise to content himself with remarking that Jefferson had just been lucky. The Purchase, he said, resulted from "the kind interpositions of an over-ruling Providence." But a Boston Federalist newspaper did not like the deal at all: it called Louisiana "a great waste, a wilderness unpeopled with any beings except wolves and wandering Indians. We are to give money of which we have too little for land of which we already have too much." Jefferson was risking national bankruptcy to buy a desert.[19]

Angry partisanship was the order of the day. Senator John Quincy Adams complained in his diary, "The country is so totally given up to the spirit of party, that not to follow blindfold the one or the other is an inexpiable offence." But the New England Federalists were putting themselves on the wrong side of history to oppose the Purchase. One denounced it as "a great curse," and another feared that the Purchase "threatens, at no very distant day, the subversion of our Union."[20]

Caspar Wistar of Philadelphia, Lewis's sometime tutor, got it right. He wrote to congratulate Jefferson "on the very happy acquisitions you have made for our Country. Altho no one here appears to know the extent or price of the cession, it is generally considered as the most important & beneficial transaction which has occurred since the declaration of Independence, & next to it, most like to influence or regulate the destinies of our Country."[21]

One immediate effect of the Purchase was to change Lewis's relationship with the Indian tribes he would encounter east of the Divide. The Indians were now on American territory. Lewis would be responsible for informing them that their Great Father was Jefferson rather than the Spanish and French rulers. Jefferson wanted Lewis to bring them into the trading net of the United States, which meant bringing peace among them and telling the British around the Mandan villages that they were on foreign soil.

By far the most important effect of the Purchase on the expedition was a negative that stemmed from the fact that no one knew what the boundaries of Louisiana were. Napoleon sold Louisiana "with the same extent that it now has in the hands of Spain, and that it had when France possessed it." The general belief was that Louisiana consisted of the western half of the Mississippi drainage. That meant from the Gulf of Mexico northward to the northernmost tributaries of the Missouri, and from the Mississippi westward to the Continental Divide. But no American, Spaniard, Frenchman, or Briton knew how far north that was. Jefferson, greatly excited by the prospect of adding more northern territory to the Purchase, at once began urging Lewis to explore those northern tributaries, where earlier, in the formal instructions, he had emphasized exploration of the southern tributaries.

Jefferson wanted land. He wanted empire. He reached out to seize what he wanted, first of all by continually expanding the boundaries of Louisiana. Diplomatic historian Thomas Maitland Marshall describes it well: "Starting with the idea that the purchase was confined to the western waters of the Mississippi Valley, Jefferson's conception had gradually expanded until [by 1808] it included West Florida, Texas, and the Oregon Country, a view which was to be the basis of a large part of American diplomacy for nearly half a century."[22]

Lewis started out for Pittsburgh on July 5, 1803, the day after the news of the Purchase arrived. Although he was in a good mood, he had a great deal to be worried about. Would Clark accept, or would his health or business commitments prevent him from joining? Had the wagonload of supplies gotten from Philadelphia to Pittsburgh? Had the weapons and other items selected at Harpers Ferry been sent to Pittsburgh? Had he selected the right items, in sufficient quantity? What kind of soldiers would be meeting him in Pittsburgh for the trip down the Ohio? Was the keelboat he had ordered made in Pittsburgh completed?

He had a sense of urgency. Having used up more than a month of good traveling weather, he knew the Ohio River would be falling as summer wore on, knew that he had to get going if he were to have any hope of making any significant distance up the Missouri before the weather closed in. But he still had a great deal to do, in Harpers Ferry and Pittsburgh.

So he could not have been altogether easy in his mind as he turned his horse's head west and started out. But he must have had a joy in his heart. He certainly had a determination: with that first step west, he intended never to look back until he had reached the Pacific.

Lewis got to Fredericktown (present Frederick), Maryland, the evening of July 5. There was good news: the wagon carrying supplies from Philadelphia had passed through Fredericktown ten days earlier. There was bad news: on arrival at Harpers Ferry, the driver had decided the arms and other weapons Lewis had ordered were too heavy for his team, so he had gone on to Pittsburgh without them. Lewis hired a teamster in Fredericktown, who promised he would be in Harpers Ferry by July 8. Lewis pushed on to Harpers Ferry, where "I shot my guns and examined the several articles which had been manufactered for me at this place; they appear to be well executed." What pleased him most was the completed iron-frame boat.

But good feelings gave way to worries—the teamster "disappointed me." Lewis hired another, locally; the man promised to load up the guns and the iron-frame and the rest and be on his way to Pittsburgh early the next morning. Lewis then set off for Pittsburgh, where he arrived at 2:00 p.m. on July 15.[23] He immediately wrote a report to Jefferson, so as to catch the 5:00 p.m. post. It had been hot and dry, the roads "extreemly dusty, yet I feel myself much benifitted by the exercise the journey has given me, and can with pleasure anounce, so far and *all is well*." Though the Ohio was low, it could be navigated if he could get a quick start. He had not yet had time to see the boat he had ordered.[24]

The boat contract called for completion on July 20, but, to Lewis's intense disappointment, the builder wasn't even close to done. The contractor claimed he had found it difficult to get the proper timber, but now it had arrived, and he promised to have the work completed by July 30. Lewis reported to Jefferson that he was "by no means sanguine" that he could meet that date; August 5 was more like it. "I visit him every day," Lewis wrote, "and endeavour by every means in my power to hasten the completion of the work, I have prevailed on him to engage more hands. . . . I shall embark immediately the boat is in readiness."

Some good news: the wagon from Harpers Ferry arrived on July 22. So had the party of seven recruits (the eighth recruit had pocketed his bounty for enlisting and promptly deserted) from Carlisle who would make the descent of the Ohio with the keelboat. But what nagged was the falling river. "The current of the Ohio is extreemly low and continues to decline," Lewis told Jefferson. "This may impede my progress but shall not prevent my proceeding, being determined to get forward though I should not be able to make a greater distance than a mile pr. day."[25]

The next week was agony for Lewis. The boatbuilder was a drinking man, so he seldom worked mornings, and sometimes not in the afternoons either. He had none of Lewis's sense of urgency. But there was no one else in Pittsburgh capable of doing the work. So Lewis fretted and fumed but did not fire the contractor.

On July 29, the mail brought in the best possible news. It was a letter from Clark. He had accepted! "The enterprise &c. is Such as I have long anticipated and am much pleased with," Clark wrote, "and as my situation in life will admit of my absence the length of time necessary to accomplish such an undertaking I will chearfully join you in an 'official Charrector' as mentioned in your letter,* and partake of the dangers, difficulties, and fatigues, and I anticipate the honors & rewards of the result of such an enterprise. . . . This is an undertaking fraited with many difeculties, but My friend I do assure you that no man lives with whome I would perfur to undertake Such a Trip &c. as yourself."

He asked Lewis to tell Jefferson to send his commission on to Louisville, across the river from Clarksville. He said he would try to find a few good men for the expedition, which he reported was the chief subject of conversation in Louisville.[26]

In a follow-up letter of July 24, Clark related that "several young men (Gentlemens sons) have applyed to accompany us—as they are not accustomed to labour and as that is a verry assential part of the services required of the party, I am causious in giveing them any encouragement." He told Lewis he would be ready to go as soon as the keelboat reached Louisville, for he too was eager to get as far up the

---

* Here Clark first wrote "on equal footing &c.," then crossed it out and substituted "as mentioned in your letter."

Missouri as possible that season. "My friend," he concluded, "I join you with hand & Heart."[27]

"I feel myself much gratifyed with your decision," Lewis told Clark by the next post, August 3, "for I could neither hope, wish, or expect from a union with any man on earth, more perfect support or further aid in the discharge of the several duties of my mission, than that, which I am confident I shall derive from being associated with yourself."

Lewis said he was pleased that Clark had engaged some men and reminded him that this was their most critical job. The enterprise "must depend on a judicious scelection of our men; their qualifycations should be such as perfectly fit them for the service, outherwise they will reather clog than further the objects in view; on this principle I am well pleased that you have not admitted or encouraged the young gentlemen you mention, we must set our faces against all such applications and get rid of them on the best terms we can. They will not answer our purposes."[28]

Clark absolutely agreed. On August 21, he informed Lewis that "I have had many aplications from stout likely fellows but have refused to retain some & put others off with a promis of giveing 'an answer after I see or hered from you.'" Lewis was simultaneously being pestered by young men in Pittsburgh who wanted to join up.

Clearly the word was out in the western country, and what young unmarried frontiersman—whether gentlemen's sons or the sons of whiskey-making corn farmers—could resist such an opportunity? It was the ultimate adventure. The reward for success would be a land grant, similar to those given the Revolutionary War veterans—a princely reward to frontiersmen.

So Lewis and Clark could be highly selective. Clark was an excellent judge of men. He had gathered seven of "the best young woodsmen & Hunters in this part of the Countrey"—these were the men awaiting Lewis's approval before being accepted. They included Charles Floyd, Nathaniel Pryor, William Bratton, Reubin Field, Joseph Field, George Gibson, and John Shields. Lewis was equally good as a judge; in Pittsburgh, he selected John Colter and George Shannon (at eighteen, the youngest of the group), subject to Clark's approval.

The boatbuilder was guilty of "unpardonable negligence," Lewis charged. August 5 came and went and only one side of the boat was partially planked. In desperation, Lewis thought of purchasing two or three pirogues. It is impossible to tell what he meant by this, as he used the words "pirogue" and "canoe" interchangeably. A pirogue is a flat-bottomed dugout, designed for marshes and shallow waters, most popular today among Louisiana duck-hunters. The pirogues Lewis had in mind, however, were much larger (and possibly not dugouts at all, but big flat-bottomed, masted rowboats built from planks). A canoe is a round- or curved-bottom craft, either dug out of the trunk of a large tree, or built to a frame and covered with bark or skins, most popular today for recreation on large, fast rivers. When Lewis said "canoe," however, what he meant was a round-bottomed dugout much larger than today's sporting canoes.

In his anxiety to get going, and with his doubts that the boatbuilder would ever complete the keelboat, Lewis was proposing to descend the Ohio River in pirogues until he could find a keelboat somewhere downriver to purchase. But when the local merchants told him there was no place to procure a boat below, and the boatbuilder promised to be done by August 13, Lewis abandoned the fantasy and waited and fumed.

Four days later, the builder got drunk and quarreled with his workmen, several of whom quit on the spot. Lewis threatened him with a canceled contract, but there wasn't much reality to the threat: the boatbuilder had no competition within hundreds of miles. The builder did give a promise of greater sobriety, but this lasted less than a week. Lewis charged that he was "continuing to be constantly either drunk or sick." Lewis spent most of his time at the work site, "alternately persuading and threatening." He soothed himself some by buying a dog and naming it Seaman. He paid twenty dollars for the Newfoundland, a large black dog.

Each day the river sank a bit lower. It got so bad that Lewis was told "the river is lower than it has ever been known by the oldest settler in this country."[29]

The delays all but drove him mad, but they had to be endured, because the job had to be done right. After all, Lewis was proposing to descend the Ohio, then ascend the Mississippi to the mouth of the Missouri, then ascend the Missouri to the Mandan villages in that boat. A lot of thought had gone into it, requiring skilled woodworking; the complexity of the thing must have been some part of the cause of the delay.*

Lewis had designed it, and he oversaw its construction and probably made modifications in the plans as the work progressed. It was

---

* It took a dozen or more volunteers in Onawa, Iowa, more than sixty working days to build a replica in the late 1980s, using power tools.

basically a galley, little resembling the classic keelboat of the West. It seems to have been the standard type of vessel for use on inland waters at the outset of the nineteenth century, especially for military purposes. Lewis probably had been on a similar keelboat on the Ohio when he was a paymaster.

It was fifty-five feet long, eight feet wide at midships, with a shallow draft. It had a thirty-two-foot-high mast that was jointed near the base so it could be lowered. The mast could support a large square sail and a foresail. A ten-foot-long deck at the bow provided a forecastle. An elevated deck of ten feet at the stern accommodated a cabin. The hold was thirty-one feet in length and could carry a cargo of about twelve tons. Crossing the deck were eleven benches, each three feet long, for use by two oarsmen.

The boat could be propelled by four methods: rowing, sailing, pushing, and pulling. In pushing, the crew set long poles in the river bottom and pushed on them as they walked front to rear on the boat. Men or horses or ox used ropes for pulling, sometimes from the water, sometimes from the shore.[30]

To hurry the builder along, Lewis tried getting on his knees, he tried shouting and cursing, "but neither threats, persuasion or any other means which I could devise were sufficient to procure the completion of the work sooner than the 31st of August."

He had hoped to be on his way on by July 20, at the latest by August 1. By the time the boat was ready, the river had fallen so low that "those who pretend to be acquainted with the navigation of the river declare it impracticable to descend it." Lewis was going anyway.[31]

How anxious he was to get going he demonstrated on the morning of August 31. The last nail went into the planking at 7:00 a.m. By 10:00 a.m., Lewis had the boat loaded. To keep it as high in the water as possible, he shipped a considerable quantity of goods by wagon to Wheeling. In addition, he purchased a pirogue to carry as much as possible, to further lighten the load. He intended to purchase another at Wheeling to carry the goods coming by land. Then he was on his way.

9

DOWN THE OHIO

September–November 1803

Lewis had proceeded only three miles when he pulled over at an island and at the request of the pioneers living on it gave a demonstration of his air gun, purchased from gunsmith Isaiah Lukens of Philadelphia. It was a pneumatic rifle. The stock was the reservoir, and it could be pumped full of air to a pressure of five to six hundred psi, at which point it was not much inferior in hitting power to the Kentucky rifle. That it produced no smoke or noise astonished the frontiersmen.[1]

Lewis fired seven times at fifty-five yards "with pretty good success." He passed the curiosity around for examination. It went off accidentally; the ball passed through the hat of a woman about forty yards off, "cuting her temple; she fell instantly and the blood gusing from her temple. we were all in the greatest consternation supposed she was dead but in a minute she revived to our enespressable satisfaction, and by examination we found the wound by no means mortal or even dangerous." Never again did he pass the air gun around when it was pumped up and loaded.

The expedition returned to the river. After a mile or so, "we were obledged to get out all hands and lift the boat over about thirty yards." Then another ripple. And another. The captain got out too, and pulled or lifted. Twice. A third time. Fortunately, the water was temperate, but when Lewis had the boat put ashore for the night, having gone only ten miles downstream, he "was much fatiegued after labouring with my men all day. Gave my men some whiskey and retired to rest at 8 OClock."[2]

*

That was the first entry in what became the journals of Lewis and Clark.* The journals are one of America's literary treasures. Throughout, they tell their story in fascinating detail. They have a driving narrative that is compelling, yet they pause for little asides and anecdotes that make them a delight to read. Their images are so sharp they all but force the reader to put down the book, close the eyes, and see what the captains saw, hear what they heard. The journals never flash back or forward. From start to finish, they stick to the present. The more closely they are read, the greater the reward.

Theodore Roosevelt, no stranger to adventure, said this about the journals: "Few explorers who saw and did so much that was absolutely new have written of their deeds with such quiet absence of boastfulness, and have drawn their descriptions with such complete freedom from exaggeration."[3]

It is not known when Lewis made entries in the journals. Not even the first entry. Did Lewis write it that night, before blowing out his candle? Or the next morning, on the boat? Or a week or so later, at a weather-enforced halt? There is an extensive literature on the subject, capped by an essay by Gary Moulton in the introduction to volume 2 of the modern edition of the journals. Moulton concludes, "Most of the material we now have was written by the captains in the course of the expedition." Not all, just most. Moulton adds that it cannot be said *when* during the expedition the entries were written, whether on the day of the event or a few days or even a few months later. Never mind: as Moulton remarks, in reading the journals "we are in a sense traveling with the captains and sharing their day-by-day experiences and uncertainties."[4]

There is another, more important and tantalizing mystery. Lewis began his journal the day he began the expedition, August 31, 1803. He was a faithful recorder of flora and fauna, weather, the difficulties of getting down the river, unusual occurrences, people encountered. The journal, a combination travelogue and record, a description of matters new to science and of geography, and much more, obviously meant a

---

* There are many editions of the journals. By far the best is Gary Moulton, ed., *The Journals of the Lewis & Clark Expedition*, published in eight volumes by the University of Nebraska Press between 1987 and 1993. My quotations are taken from the Moulton edition. I have not annotated quotations from the journals, because it is just as easy to look up the original by searching for the date of the entry as by searching for volume 3, page 76, or whatever. Also, relying on the date will allow those who wish to see the full entry to do so in the Reuben Gold Thwaites eight-volume edition, or the Biddle paraphrase, or any of the various other editions.

great deal to him, and he was well aware of its importance to the success of the expedition. And he clearly enjoyed writing, thinking through the events of the day and sorting them out and making sense out of them in very long, very complex sentences that often threatened to get completely out of control but were always rescued by the last verb. Geographer Paul Russell Cutright speaks of "Lewis's recurrent artistry in stringing apt words together colorfully," and notes that among his virtues as a writer were "his sizable working vocabulary, his quietly authoritative statements, his active unrestrained interest in all natural phenomena, his consistent adherence to truth and, above all, his wide command of adjectives, verbs and nouns which repeatedly give color to his sentences."[5]

Yet there are long periods—months at a time, nearly a year in one case—for which few and only sporadic journal entries by Lewis are known to exist. These gaps include September 19 to November 11, 1803; May 14, 1804, to April 7, 1805; August 26, 1805, to January 1, 1806; and from August 12 to the end of September 1806.

There is no explanation for the gaps. Possibly he was depressed, or maybe it was just a severe case of writer's block. Neither explanation seems likely, however. In any event, as Moulton warns, no one is ready to say that no Lewis journal exists for those gaps, because scholars are always discovering new documentation about the expedition.

So maybe the entries Lewis made for those dates are just lost. But that too seems unlikely, because of internal evidence and because there exists no known letter lamenting the loss of daily journals kept by Lewis, either at the time or after his death.[6] Meanwhile, we are grateful for what we do have.

On the morning of September 1, fog over the river kept Lewis and his party ashore until 8:00 a.m. Lewis took care to load as much as possible in the pirogue, to lighten the load in the boat, but nevertheless ripples and shoals forced him again and again to unload and then lift the empty boat over the obstacle. At the last ripple of the day, Lewis was forced to seek out a local pioneer and hire a team of oxen to pull the boat off. The expedition made but ten miles.

September 2 was a repeat performance. The water was the lowest ever seen on the Ohio, sometimes but six inches deep, so low and clear Lewis could see catfish, pike, bass, and "stergeon" swimming. Stuck again, Lewis went ashore to hire a horse and an ox. "Payd the man his charge which was one dollar," Lewis noted in his journal. Then he passed his judgment on the Ohio River pioneers, circa 1803: "The inhabitants who live ner these riffles live much by the distresed situation of the traveller

[They] are gnerally lazy charge extravegantly when they are called on for assistance and have no filantrophy or contience."

On the 3rd, at dawn, the air temperature was sixty-three, that of the river seventy-five. Lewis noted that "the fogg thus prodused is impenetrably thick at this moment" (one of the few times Lewis makes a reference to his precise time of writing). The party made six miles that day; Lewis discharged one of the men, for reasons unstated.

The following day, Lewis purchased another pirogue, for eleven dollars. He was cheated; it leaked badly. Goods got wet; guns began to rust. The party pulled over and spent the afternoon airing the articles, oiling the rifles, putting perishables into oilcloth bags, and otherwise repairing the damage. Lewis hired another hand, to replace the man dismissed.

On September 6, the wind came up strong from the north in a stretch of river free of ripples. Lewis hoisted the foresail on the mast and experienced the inexpressible joy of running downstream with a wind dead astern and a good sail to catch the power of that wind. "We run two miles in a few minutes," Lewis wrote, almost unbelieving. Unfortunately, the wind strengthened to the point where Lewis was obliged to haul in the sail lest it carry away the mast.

At the next ripple, the exhilaration gave way to consternation. Lewis hoisted the mainsail on the mast to run the stuck boat over the ripple, only to break the crosspiece. "My men woarn down by perpetual lifting," Lewis wrote, "I was obliged again to have recourse to horses or oxen." He went to "Stewbenville," on the Ohio bank of the river, and found it a "small well built thriving place has several respectable families residing in it, five yers since it was a wilderness." He got the oxen and soon was afloat again. He concluded his entry with the sad news that, on the day during which he had covered two miles in but a few minutes, his total mileage for the day was but ten.

On September 7, he reached Wheeling, Virginia, which he found to be "a pretty considerable Village of fifty houses." He dined that evening with Dr. William Patterson, son of the Robert Patterson of Philadelphia who had been one of Lewis's teachers. Young Patterson was enthusiastic about Lewis's expedition. "He expressed a great desire to go with me," Lewis recorded, and Lewis was receptive, at least in part because Patterson had the largest collection of medicines west of the mountains—a pharmacy worth one hundred pounds.

Lewis told Patterson that a doctor was not authorized, but if he went on to St. Louis, where Lewis expected to spend the winter, there would be an opportunity to get Jefferson's authorization for Patterson to join the party.

This was Lewis's first admission that he would not have time to ascend the Missouri River for any distance at all before winter set in. Progress down the Ohio was so excruciatingly slow, he had to adjust. But he was eager to get going. Lewis told Patterson to be ready by 3:00 p.m. on September 9 and they'd be off together. Wouldn't miss it for the world, the doctor replied.

In Wheeling, Lewis picked up the shipment of rifles and ammunition he had sent overland from Pittsburgh and found it in good order. To carry it, he purchased another pirogue. That took up the better part of the day on September 9. By midafternoon, everything was finally packed and ready to go—but no sign of Dr. Patterson.

Lewis shoved off. That night, he opened his journal entry on a laconic note: "The Dr. could not get ready I waited untill three this evening and then set out." Thus did Dr. Patterson miss the Lewis and Clark Expedition. It was undoubtedly just as well; his reputation was one of constant drunkenness, which may well have been the cause of his being late.

That night, the rain came down in torrents. Lewis covered the pirogues with oilcloth to no avail. He was up past midnight in a cold rain, wet to the skin. Finally, "I wrung out my saturated clothes, put on a dry shirt and turned into my birth." In the morning, he stopped at an Indian earth mound on the Virginia bank and described it in considerable detail. Even with the stop, he made his best distance to date, twenty-four miles, because the river below Wheeling was relatively free of ripples and other obstructions. The next day, September 11, it was twenty-six miles. The highlight of the day was a performance by Seaman, Lewis's Newfoundland, described by Lewis as "very active strong and docile."

Squirrels were migrating across the Ohio River, north to south, for reasons obscure to Lewis, since their principal food, hickory nuts, was in abundance on both banks.* Seaman started barking at them; Lewis let him go; Seaman swam out, grabbed a squirrel, killed him, and fetched him back to Lewis, who sent the dog out for repeated performances. Lewis had the squirrels fried and declared "they were fat and I thought a plesent food."

On the morning of September 13, Lewis saw another natural-history phenomenon: passenger pigeons flying over the river, north to south, on their migration. They flew in such great flocks they obscured the sun.

---

* The squirrel population today is much reduced, and the migrations Lewis saw are all but extinct.

The river he was descending continued to broaden and deepen. It still sparkled in the sunlight, especially as the angle of the sun on the water became more acute with the shorter days. The water was dark, almost black, after the recent heavy rains. The banks were lined with hardwoods, deep green, enclosing. All the sounds on the river, other than the splash of the oars, were from nature's chorus—frogs and birds mainly, and the wind through the trees.

Although clearings were rare and villages even rarer, this was not wilderness. Lewis and at least some of the men in the boat party had been down the river before, as had thousands of other Americans. It had been mapped, so Lewis had no reason to use his instruments to determine longitude and latitude. Still, it was wild enough to suit.

When Lewis pulled into Marietta at 2:00 p.m., he was in high spirits. He wrote a report to Jefferson, outlining his progress since Wheeling, describing his several methods for getting over obstructions, and indulging himself in a little joke: "Horses or oxen are the last resort; I find them the most efficient sailors in the [riffles], altho' they may be considered somewhat clumsey."[7]

Marietta, founded in 1788, was the oldest settlement in Ohio. Only a handful of children had been born there; indeed, only a few adult residents had been born in Ohio. Lewis spent a night there. He dismissed two of the men, for unstated reasons, reducing his party to a dozen. He had a visit with Colonel Griffin Greene, one of the founders of Marietta "and an excelant republican." That last qualification had gotten Greene the appointment as postmaster.

Two men got drunk in the village and failed to report back to the boat. In the morning, Lewis went looking for them, found them "so drunk that they were unable to help themselves," had them picked up and thrown into the boat, and set off.

As the expedition got lower on the river, it entered country in which, Lewis wrote on September 14, "the *fever* and *ague* and *bilious fevers* commence their banefull oppression and continue through the whole course of the river with increasing violence as you approach it's mouth."

Lewis was referring to malaria, which was endemic in the Ohio, Mississippi, and lower Missouri Valleys. He knew it well from his experiences on the Ohio during his travels as paymaster, and anticipated it. Malaria was the most common disease in the country, especially on the frontier, where it was so inescapable that many refused to regard it as a disease: like hard work, it was just a part of life. Jefferson had it. It may have been the illness that forced Clark to resign his commission in 1796.[8]

No one knew what caused malaria. Dr. Rush's opinion was bad air, rising from swamps. He was on the edge of seeing the mosquito as the culprit, but never quite got there. The good doctor was helping one of his University of Pennsylvania graduate students in his research. S. Ffirth was doing his thesis on causation of malaria. The general view was that epidemics resulted from "contagium," meaning the fevers were transmitted by direct contact between people. Ffirth wanted to see whether this was true.

Ffirth's research methods were crude, heroic, and reckless. They demonstrated the almost total ignorance that the best-trained specialists of the era wallowed in, with regard to disease; as in means of transportation, mankind had made virtually no progress in the previous two thousand years. Ffirth inhaled vapors from black vomit taken from malaria or yellow-fever patients. He injected the vomit into the stomachs and veins of cats and dogs, and into his own body. Neither the cats and dogs nor Ffirth got malaria. He completed his research in June 1804, and reported his conclusion: the "autumnal disease" (yet another name for malaria) was not contagious.[9]

Whether Lewis met Ffirth is unknown. That Lewis talked about malaria with Dr. Rush is apparent, because he spent one-third of his medical budget on the purchase of Peruvian bark for his "armamentarium." For the thirty dollars, Lewis got fifteen pounds of the Peruvian bark. It came from a South American tree and contained many alkaloids, the most important being quinine and quinidine. Lewis had it in a powder form. It was considered sovereign for malaria, and rightly so; later in the nineteenth century, quinine became the drug of choice for the disease. One medical historian calls it "the drug that changed the destinies of nations," because "it alone made possible the invasion and exploitation of tropical countries."[10]

Quinine copes with rather than completely cures the disease. Recurrences are common to sufferers. The best preventive was to avoid getting bitten by infected mosquitoes—easier said than done, of course; even had he known that it was the mosquitoes transmitting the malaria, Lewis could have done little about it.

He had armed himself for the war against mosquitoes. In Philadelphia, he had purchased "Muscatoe Curtains" and "8 ps. Cat Gut for Mosquito Curtains," and two hundred pounds of tallow mixed with fifty pounds of hog's lard. The lard served a double purpose: insect repellent and a base for pemmican.[11]

Lewis took mosquitoes seriously, but his preparations were entirely defensive. Neither he nor anyone else alive in 1803 had the slightest idea how to take the offensive against them. Nor did anyone understand how serious was the battle against them. Lewis thought of the mosquitoes as a pest, not a threat.

Nor did he ever learn how to spell his enemies' name. His usual spelling, repeated at least twenty-five times, was "musquetoe." Clark was more inventive: he had at least twenty variations, ranging from "mesquetors" through "misqutr" to "musquetors."[12]

In many ways, the trip down the Ohio was a shakedown voyage for the boat and pirogues. Getting the packing right, for example, was a constant learning process. On September 15, it rained hard for six hours. Lewis kept paddling, and made eighteen miles. The following day, it was nineteen miles, but by dusk "my men were very much fatigued." The next morning, the expedition came to a long sandbar. It was "a handsome clean place," so Lewis decided to spend the day opening and drying his goods, "which I had found were wet by the rain on the 15th," even though he had wrapped them securely in oilcloths and had the canoes constantly bailed during the course of the day. The guns, tomahawks, and knives were rusting. Lewis had them oiled and exposed to the sun. Clothing of "every discription also was opened and aired." All hands, including the captain's, were kept busy in this enterprise from 10:00 a.m. to sunset, when Lewis had the canoes reloaded, this time paying more attention to getting vulnerable items up off the canoe bottom.

From Marietta it was about one hundred miles southwest to the point where Ohio, Virginia, and Kentucky joined, then another hundred or so to Cincinnati. The river was deep, the weather fine; Lewis covered the two hundred miles in two weeks without incident.

He stayed in the Cincinnati area for a week, to rest his men, take on provisions, do some research for Jefferson, and write two letters. The first was to Clark in Louisville, in reply to a letter of August 21 which Lewis had just picked up.

Clark reported that he had many applicants for the expedition "from stout likely fellows," but he was putting them on hold until Lewis got to Louisville and could look them over. Clark pointed out what he knew Lewis already knew, that "a judicious choice of our party is of the greatest importance to the success of this vast enterprise."

On a more general note, Clark concluded, "I am happy to here of the Session of Louisiana to the united States, this is an inestimable treasure to the Western People, who appear to feel its value."[13]

Lewis responded by reporting his progress and discussing the selection of men for the voyage up the Missouri. He said he liked Clark's ideas on the need for "a judicious selection," and that he had two young men with him, "taken on trial, conditionally only, tho' I think they will answer tolerably well." Apparently he meant John Colter and George Shannon. Obviously he meant that Clark would have a veto over his choices, just as *he* would over Clark's.[14] Lewis and Clark had not been together in seven years, but even before they met their partnership was flourishing, their trust in each other's judgment complete. There were no perils in divided command for this pair.

The second letter was to Jefferson. Lewis reported on his visit to Big Bone Lick, Kentucky, some twenty miles southwest of Cincinnati. Earlier in the year, Dr. William Goforth had discovered there the bones of a mammoth. Evidently Jefferson had urged Lewis to visit the site. Lewis did, and sent in a mammoth report on the mammoth, including 2,064 words to describe "a tusk of an immence size," along with some specimens of bones.

Lewis asked the president to send him "some of the Vaxcine matter, as I have reason to believe from several experiments made with what I have, that it has lost it's virtue."[15] He intended to use it to vaccinate against the smallpox. This too was a favorite subject of Jefferson's, who had sponsored the use of the cowpox and had inoculated himself and his family. The wording of the letter indicates that it was Jefferson who had provided Lewis with cowpox to bring to the frontier and to the Indians, and instructed him in its use.[16] The big problem, as Lewis's request reflects, was keeping the vaccine alive. When no scab formed where Lewis scratched the cowpox vaccine into a patient's arm, Lewis knew it was no longer virile.

Lewis concluded his letter to Jefferson with a statement of intentions. "As this Session of Congress has commenced," he began, and as for a variety of reasons, his progress had been delayed, "and feeling as I do in the most anxious manner a wish to keep them [the politicians] in a good humour on the subject of the expedicion in which I am engaged, I have concluded to make a tour this winter on horseback of some hundred miles through the most interesting portion of the country adjoining my winter establishment."

He said he would go up the Kansas River toward Santa Fe, and he proposed to have Clark make his own "excurtion throgh some other portion of the country." That way, by the end of February, he would be able to send Jefferson "such information relative to that Country which, if it does not produce a conviction of the utility of this project, will at least procure the further toleration of the expedition."[17]

Here was the president's aide at work, a zealot protecting his boss from the Federalist jackels in Congress. Here was the partisan politician, trying to give his party a winning issue in the upcoming

(1804) presidential campaign. Here too was the young adventurer, resigned to having to build a winter camp near St. Louis rather than getting on up the Missouri a few hundred miles, his mind alive with possibilities during the brilliant fall afternoons on the Ohio, refusing to submit to the anticipated dullness of an army-camp life for five months. But, alive though his mind was, here was a young man who had not thought things through.

This was the first Jefferson knew that Lewis had abandoned hope of getting up the Missouri before winter. He accepted the decision—indeed, endorsed it heartily—because he wanted Lewis to spend the winter gathering information in St. Louis, not out on the Kansas prairie, and because the expedition could draw its rations from the U.S. Army posts on the Mississippi, thus not depleting the stores for the voyage. So, as commander-in-chief, Jefferson had said directly to Lewis, "I leave it to your own judgment" as to where to spend the winter.

Not that the president had a lot of choice. The mails moved so slowly there was not the slightest possibility of Jefferson's giving Lewis orders that could arrive in time to be acted on. Jefferson did not receive Lewis's letter until mid-November; his reply did not reach Lewis until January.

Still, Jefferson tried to take control, because he was so alarmed by Lewis's proposal to set off on a midwinter exploration toward Santa Fe, into the part of the continent clearly Spanish and, because of its gold and silver mines, a part about which the Spanish were extremely sensitive. The great danger involved led Jefferson to issue a direct order, hoping it would arrive in time: "You must not undertake the winter excursion which you propose in yours of Oct. 3."

Lewis's proposal caused Jefferson great worry, not just about the dangers, but about Lewis's judgment. Thus there is a note of suppressed alarm in his response. He could hardly remove Lewis from the command, but he could try to get Lewis to think of first things first. Jefferson wrote: "The object of your mission is single, the direct water communication from sea to sea formed by the bed of the Missouri & perhaps the Oregon."

That was the most succinct statement about the purpose of the expedition Jefferson ever wrote.

He explained that the dangers of a Santa Fe trip would be greater than those Lewis would face on the Missouri, because the Spanish armed forces would be almost certain to arrest and detain him if he went southwest, but leave him alone on the Missouri, since that was now American territory. As to Clark's proposed excursion, Jefferson wrote: "By having Mr. Clarke with you we consider the expedition double manned, & therefore the less liable to failure, for which reason neither of you should be exposed to risques by going off of your line."

The Louisiana Purchase had another impact on the goals of the expedition. Jefferson described the boundaries of Louisiana as "*the high lands inclosing all the waters which run into the Missisipi or Missouri directly or indirectly.*" That was stretching the boundaries a bit, perhaps—no one really knew—but, as Jefferson explained, "it therefore becomes interesting to fix with precision by celestial observations the longitude & latitude of the sources of those rivers."

What he meant, or hoped for, was that northern tributaries of the Missouri would extend well north of the forty-ninth parallel, deep into the fur-rich country of western Canada. If so, that territory wasn't western Canada; it was the property of the United States.* Jefferson didn't want to risk not finding out because his young captain had indulged himself in a joy ride. He concluded his letter by repeating his order that Lewis stick to his assigned missions, which were "not to be delayed or hazarded by any episodes whatever."[18]

On October 4 or 5, Lewis pushed his boat and pirogues back into the river and headed west for the falls of the Ohio, some one hundred miles downstream. On October 14, he was at the head of the falls, which were actually long rapids created by a twenty-four-foot drop of the river over a two-mile-long series of limestone ledges. At the foot of the rapids, on the north bank, was Clarksville, Indiana Territory. Louisville, Kentucky, was on the south bank. On October 15, Lewis hired local pilots, who took the boat and pirogues into the dangerous but passable passage on the north bank.[19] Safely through, Lewis tied up at Clarksville and set off to meet his partner, who was living with his older brother, General George Rogers Clark.

When they shook hands, the Lewis and Clark Expedition began.

Each man was about six feet tall and broad-shouldered. Each was rugged in the face, Clark somewhat more so than Lewis, who had a certain delicacy to his profile. Their bodies were rawboned and muscled, with no fat. Their hands—sunburned, like their faces, even this late in the season—were big, rough, strong, capable, confident.

---

* Complicating everything was the 1783 treaty between the United States and Britain. It ran a line west from the source of the Mississippi River relative to the Lake of the Woods, or latitude 49 degrees. It was not clear whether the Purchase or the treaty would prevail in setting the boundary.

Each man was long-legged. Just a glimpse of their stride across a porch, or at how they seated themselves, showed the physical coordination of an athlete. Each, probably, was dressed in fringed buckskin. And who can doubt that, as they stuck out their hands to each other, both men had smiles on their faces that were as broad as the Ohio River, as big as their ambitions and dreams.

Oh! To have been able to hear the talk on the porch that afternoon, and on into the evening, and through the night. There would have been whiskey—General Clark was the host, and General Clark was a heavy drinker. There would have been tables groaning under the weight of pork, beef, venison, duck, goose, fish, fresh bread, apples, fresh milk, and more.

There were the two would-be heroes with the authentic older hero, all three Virginians, all three soldiers, all three Republicans, all three great talkers, full of ideas and images and memories and practical matters and grand philosophy, of Indians and bears and mountains never before seen. Excitement and joy ran through their questions and answers, words coming out in a tumble.

Unfortunately, we don't have a single word of description of the meeting of Lewis and Clark.

Over the next two weeks, the captains selected the first enlisted members of the expedition. They did not lack for volunteers. Word had spread up and down the Ohio, and inland, and young men longing for adventure and ambitious for a piece of land of their own set out for Clarksville to sign up. Lewis and Clark sized them up, making judgments on their general hardiness, their shooting and hunting ability, their physical strength and general character, their suitability for a long journey in the wilderness. How many applied is not known, but one of those eventually selected, Private Alexander Willard, boasted in his old age that "his fine physique enable[d] him to pass the inspection for enlistment in the expedition" that more than one hundred others failed.[20]

Seven of the men the captains picked had previously been conditionally approved by Clark, two by Lewis. They made Charles Floyd and Nathaniel Pryor sergeants. Floyd was the son of Captain Charles Floyd, who had soldiered with George Rogers Clark.[21] When these nine men were sworn into the army, in solemn ceremony, in the presence of General Clark, the Corps of Discovery was born.

In addition to the enlisted men, the corps consisted of the captains—and Clark's slave, York. York was big, very dark, strong, agile, a natural athlete. About Clark's age or a bit younger, he had been Clark's lifelong companion, bequeathed to him by his father, whose companion had in turn been York's father.

Certainly the captains discussed the size of the expedition. Secretary of War Dearborn had authorized twelve enlisted men and an interpreter, but Jefferson had orally given Lewis authorization to engage "any other men not soldiers that I may think useful." Back in 1783, General Clark had advised Jefferson that, if the American Philosophical Society did send out an expedition to explore the Missouri country, they should keep it small—a dozen at most—because any larger party would arouse the Indians to hostile acts. In 1803, he may have repeated that advice to his younger brother and Captain Lewis, but if he did, they ignored it. They intended a much larger party. According to a locally written newspaper story, it was said around Louisville that "about 60 men will compose the party." How many of them would be soldiers attached to the Corps of Discovery, how many soldiers who would go only as far as the first winter camp, how many civilians hired to power the keelboat, was to be determined.[22]

In any event, the core of the Corps of Discovery had been formed, and the captains were pleased with the stout young fellows they had picked.

The keelboat and pirogues set off from Clarksville on October 26. There was plenty of water, and no obstacles. On November 11, the party arrived at Fort Massac, built ten years earlier on the Illinois bank of the Ohio, about thirty-five miles upstream from the junction of the Ohio and the Mississippi. There Lewis expected to find eight soldiers who had volunteered from the army camp at South West Post, Tennessee, but they hadn't been seen. Lewis immediately hired George Drouillard, a locally renowned woodsman, to go to Tennessee, pick up the missing soldiers, and bring them on to winter quarters, which he should look for on the east bank of the Mississippi, near St. Louis.

Although he never learned how to spell Drouillard's name—it usually came out "Drewyer"—Lewis was impressed by him from the start. Son of a French Canadian father and a Shawnee mother, Drouillard was a skilled frontiersman, hunter-trapper, and scout. He was an expert in Indian ways, fluent in a couple of Indian languages and in French and English, and master of the sign language. He exuded a calm confidence, giving the strong impression that, no matter what happened, he could handle it. Lewis signed him to a contract to serve as interpreter at twenty-five dollars per month, and arranged for the paymaster at Massac to advance him thirty dollars in coin.

Though Lewis was authorized to draw volunteers from the garrison at Fort Massac, he was disappointed in the quality of the men who stepped forward. Only two met his standards.

On November 13, the expedition set off from Massac. There was a heavy rain. "I was siezed with a violent ague," Lewis wrote in his journal, "which continued about four hours and as is usual was succeeded by a fever which however fortunately abated in some measure by sunrise."

He had malaria. When he woke, "I took a doze of Rush's pills, which operated extremly well." The fever passed.

That night, the party landed on the point at which the Ohio and Mississippi flowed together. For the following week, Lewis and Clark made measurements and conducted celestial observation. With his measuring chain and circumferentor, or surveying compass, Clark determined by triangulation that the width of the Ohio at the point just before junction was 1,274 yards, that of the Mississippi 1,435 yards, and of the combined rivers 2,002 yards.

During the encampment at the mouth of the Ohio, Lewis began to apply the lessons he had learned in Philadelphia on celestial observation, and simultaneously to teach Clark what he knew.

Establishing latitude was complicated, but doable in the field. Using the octant (in the summer) or the sextant (winter), Lewis would "shoot" the sun at noon and take its altitude. He would then consult a table to determine latitude. The angle of the sun at high noon, together with the date, would tell him for certain how far north of the equator he was.

Determining longitude was almost impossibly complicated. If Lewis knew it was high noon in Greenwich, and he knew exactly what time it was where he was, he could figure out his longitude. But to know the time in Greenwich required an accurate chronometer. Though Lewis had bought the best available in Philadelphia, it was not reliable.

The alternative was to note the regular movement of the moon, measured against the sun and stars. The method was to choose a bright star as a fixed point against which to measure the moon's easterly motion in its orbit around the earth. The stars that could be used for the measurement were Antares, Altair, Regulus, Spica, Pollux, Aldeberan, Formalhaut, Alphe, Arieties, and Alplo Pegas.

Lewis could identify those stars, and many others—a skill that he had absorbed in the course of his life. He had spent countless nights stretched out in the open, countless hours staring at the stars. He had enjoyed the privilege of walking the grounds after dark at the President's House and at Monticello with Thomas Jefferson for his guide to the skies. The skill also grew out of his character. His intense curiosity compelled him to study the world around him and the sky above him.

His crash course in Philadelphia enabled him to make the observations. It was complicated. With the sextant, every few minutes he would measure the angular distance between the moon and the target star. The figures obtained could be compared with tables showing how those distances appeared at the same clock time in Greenwich. Those tables were too heavy to carry on the expedition, and the work was too time-consuming. Since Lewis's job was to make the observations and bring them home, he did not try to do the calculations; he and Clark just gathered the figures.

It meant staying up till midnight, making observations every five minutes or so for an hour or more. It meant frustration on those nights—too frequent—when clouds came up to render observation impossible.[23] The sky over the dark, murmuring river was black and transparent, free of any pollutants, far from any glowing village. Behind the captains, the men slept in their tents, the quiet sleep of healthy young men exhausted from the day's labors. The private on guard duty kept a small fire burning. Lewis's dog sat beside him as he called out the numbers for Clark.

This was practice—the longitude and latitude of the mouth of the Ohio were known—but Lewis and Clark worked at it as if it were the real thing, because soon enough it would be.

Seaman was always with Lewis. On the afternoon of November 16, the captains crossed to the Spanish side of the Mississippi to make observations. They encountered a camp of Indians. One of them, "a respectable looking Indian," offered Lewis three beaver skins for Seaman. Lewis refused, with considerable indignation. He pointed out that he had paid twenty dollars in cash for the dog. Besides, Lewis wrote, "I prised [Seaman] much for his docility and qualifications generally for my journey."

On November 18, Lewis complained that the men had discovered a nearby illegal trading post, with whiskey as the main trade item. He issued orders to stay away, but a number of the men went anyway and got drunk. Whiskey and whiskey traders were the bane of frontier life; Lewis had to anticipate more trouble with drinking during the long winter nights coming up.

On November 20, the expedition set out for St. Louis. Now it was headed upstream—and would continue to labor upstream until it reached the Continental Divide somewhere in the Rocky Mountains.

10

UP THE MISSISSIPPI
TO WINTER CAMP

November 1803–March 1804

The expedition headed out into the Mississippi, then turned upstream. Lewis and Clark scholar Arlen Large speculates that this may have been the instant when the captains decided they needed more men.[1] The power of that river, with its boils and swirls and floating obstacles, awed them.

Back east, Robert Fulton was doing his first experiments with a steamboat, but on the Mississippi, the expedition was proceeding at a pace closer to that of the first century than to the age of steamboats. Lewis now was face-to-face with what would be his major problem almost until he reached the Continental Divide, moving relatively large craft upstream on a major river.

The pirogues were badly undermanned; the keelboat was woefully so. They had to cross the river, east to west, west to east, at every bend, because only in the relatively slack water downstream from a point of land could they make any significant progress north. In eight hours of constant rowing or paddling, the expedition made ten and a half miles. Much more muscle power was needed. In addition, one man would have to stay constantly at the bow of the keelboat, watching for huge uprooted trees rushing downstream on the boiling current. More men would require more supplies.

Lewis had a lot to think about while the men dug in for all they were worth as the tiny fleet slowly inched its way north. He and Clark were not men who made snap judgments, but in this case it is likely that Arlen Large got it right: they decided on the first day to expand the party by more than 100 percent.

Over the next few days, the men worked the craft upstream, seldom making more than one mile per hour. Even more maddening, the river twisted and turned to such an extent that the twenty-five air miles to Cape Girardeau were forty-eight river miles. It took four days to reach the cape.

The village had been founded by Louis Lorimier some twenty years earlier. A French Canadian, he had been a Loyalist during the revolution and had fought George Rogers Clark, who had burned down one of his establishments, worth twenty thousand dollars. "This broke him as a mercht," Lewis noted in his journal on November 25, but Lorimier was a high-risk-taking, fast-talking, hard-bargaining, vigorous, and ambitious frontier entrepreneur, a man who could recover from disaster.

After General Clark burned him out, Lorimier talked the Spanish into giving him a land grant on the west bank of the river. He built a trading post at Cape Girardeau. He encouraged American emigration into the area, which consequently flourished.

Lewis called on Lorimier and was told that the boss was at a horse race. Lewis went to the course. "The seane reminded me very much of their small raises in Kentucky among the uncivilized backwoodsmen, nor did the subquent disorder which took place in consequences of the decision of the judges of the rase at all lessen the resembleance. . . . it is not extrawdinary that these people should be disorderly. they are almost entirely emegrant from the fronteers of Kentuckey & Tennessee, and are the most dessolute and abandoned even among these people; they are men of desperate fortunes, but little to loose either character or property."

Lorimier, on the other hand, intrigued him. Nearly sixty years old, he could not read or write. He had a "remarkable suit of hair; . . . it touched the grond when he stood errect. . . . when cewed it is kept close to his back by means of a leather gerdle." Lorimier's wife was a Shawnee woman. He had many children by her, including a daughter who caught Lewis's eye: "She is remarkably handsome & dresses in a plain yet fashonable stile or such as is now Common in the Atlantic States among the respectable people of the middle class. she is an agreeable affible girl, & much the most descent looking feemale I have seen since I left Louisville."

On November 28, the expedition reached the army post at Kaskaskia, on the Illinois side, some sixty miles below St. Louis. It was home to

Captain Russell Bissell's infantry company and to Captain Amos Stoddard's artillery company. Lewis's first act was to show the captains his orders from Dearborn, authorizing him to raid their companies. Then he called for volunteers and made his selections. The exact number is not known; Arlen Large thinks it was something more than a dozen.[2] Not all would go all the way to the Pacific; Lewis was thinking of sending a detachment back to St. Louis from the Mandan villages, where he anticipated spending the winter of 1804–5. Lewis also requisitioned Stoddard for seventy-five pounds of powder and a cask to hold it.[3]

On December 4, Clark set out with the boat party, headed for the mouth of Wood River, upstream from St. Louis on the Illinois side, directly opposite the mouth of the Missouri. The word was that it was well timbered, with plenty of game and a nearby settlement of pioneers.

Lewis traveled up the Illinois bank by horseback. He arrived at the village of Cahokia, almost directly across from St. Louis, on December 7. The next morning, Lewis crossed the river to St. Louis, along with Nicholas Jarrot (a Cahokia fur trader) as interpreter to meet the Spanish lieutenant governor of Upper Louisiana, Colonel Carlos Dehault Delassus. The meeting had some rough spots. Delassus denied Lewis permission to go up the Missouri until the transfer of sovereignty had taken place in St. Louis. Lewis did not argue the point. It was too late in the season to press on anyway, and Lewis needed to be near St. Louis to purchase supplies for the extra men.

Lewis told Delassus that his objective was to explore the Missouri country, purely for scientific purposes. Delassus, in a report to his superiors, said he had heard different: "According to advices, I believe that his mission has no other object than to discover the Pacific Ocean, following the Missouri, and to make intelligent observations, beause he has the reputation of being a very well educated man and of many talents."[4]

Built on a bluff above the flood plain, St. Louis when Lewis arrived was four decades old, with a population of a little over a thousand, mainly French Canadians. For so young and so small a town, St. Louis had a critical role to play in a vast empire. It was the center of the fur trade for the huge region drained by the Missouri. Most of the trade goods came from across the ocean, then crossed the continent to reach St. Louis. From that central point, the goods fanned out via individual traders to the farthest reaches of the frontier. And the pirogues and keelboats that carried the trade goods to the Indians brought back stacks and stacks of beautiful furs that brought king's ransoms in Europe.

Business opportunities abounded, in short, and continued to expand, because of the American pioneers slipping across to the Spanish side and making farms on the pieces of ground they had cleared. When the formal transfer of Louisiana from Spain to France and then to the United States took place, expected sometime in the coming spring, Americans would be rushing into the Missouri country. They would need outfitting.

As if things weren't good enough for the St. Louis merchants, here came Meriwether Lewis, with only enough supplies in hand for a party of fifteen, instead of the amounts needed for a party of forty-five, and armed with an authorization from the president to buy whatever he might need and charge it to the army. The merchants of the day had suddenly become the first military contractors in St. Louis.

In addition to supplies, Lewis was going to need men, voyagers with strong backs who could paddle the pirogues up the Missouri to the Mandan villages. He would be spending a lot of time in the town, haggling with merchants, sizing up volunteers. Before Lewis left Washington, Jefferson had given him oral instructions to gather as much statistical information as possible on Upper Louisiana, which meant another job to do in St. Louis.

At the time he arrived in St. Louis, Lewis had not yet received Jefferson's direct orders to abandon his risky plan to ride to Santa Fe during the winter months, but he had put the foolish thought out of his mind anyway. His problem was going to be finding enough time to do all that needed to be done, not how to pass time.

First came winter camp. On December 9, Lewis crossed to the Illinois side and met Clark and the party at Cahokia. He reported that the Spanish would not allow a movement up the Missouri, but Jarrot had a claim to a four-hundred-acre tract at the mouth of Wood River and suggested Lewis would find it a good place to build huts for the winter, to get started on modifying the keelboat for the long haul up the Missouri, and to select and train the men for the permanent party. Clark went on to the site to look it over.

Lewis returned to St. Louis to get going on his tasks. He began by doing his research on Upper Louisiana. It was the first survey done by an American of any part of the Purchase. Lewis worked up a questionnaire, with such queries as the population, the number of immigrants from the United States into Louisiana, how much land had been granted to individuals, the value of the imports and exports to and from St. Louis, and so on. Then he set out to talk to the men in town who had some knowledge of the local and regional situation.

He turned first to Antoine Soulard, surveyor general of Upper Louisiana for the Spanish government. Soulard, a Frenchman, told Lewis that the 1800 census recorded a population of about ten thousand in Upper Louisiana, two thousand of whom were slaves. About two-thirds of the whites were Americans. That was three years ago. In 1803 alone, it was estimated that another hundred American families had crossed over into Upper Louisiana. Scouts from North Carolina and elsewhere had come to look over the Missouri country, "in serch of some eligible positions to form settlements as soon as the American government is in operation."

In reporting these and other matters to Jefferson, Lewis referred to an idea Jefferson had often expressed to him—that the American pioneers in Upper Louisiana could be persuaded to accept land in Illinois in exchange for their holdings. It was Jefferson's notion that the land west of the Mississippi could be turned into a vast Indian reservation, where the Indians could learn to farm and become good citizens. That way there could be an orderly progression of the frontier, across Ohio and Indiana and on to Illinois, and a frontier free from Indian troubles, since all the Indians would be removed to the far shore.

This absurd notion showed how little Jefferson knew about Americans living west of the Appalachians. With the Purchase, or even without the Purchase, there was no force on earth that could stop the flow of American pioneers westward. Good, cheap land was a magnet that reached all the way back to Europe. The pioneers were the cutting edge of an irresistible force. Rough and wild though they were, they were the advance agents of millions of Europeans, mostly peasants or younger sons of small farmers, who constituted the greatest mass migration in history.

When Lewis and Clark arrived on the Mississippi River, they were following the first American settlers in Missouri and were but a jump ahead of thousands of others who were thinking about or already on their way to Missouri. Napoleon had gotten it right: he might as well sell and get some money for the place, because the Americans were going to overrun it anyway.

Lewis must have known that the government couldn't get the pioneers to abandon the land they had cleared and cultivated, yet he wrote Jefferson, "I am fully persuaded, that your wishes to withdraw the inhabitants of Louisiana, may in every necessary degree be affected in the course of a few years." With a bit more realism, he added that the slaveholders might cause trouble—they would not want to cross into the free territory of Illinois.[5]

Lewis also did research for his tour. Soulard gave him a map that traced the Missouri to the mouth of the Osage River. Lewis got two other maps, one a general map of Upper Louisiana, and another, the so-called Mackay

map, made by Scottish trader and explorer James Mackay, which Lewis
sent Jefferson. In 1795, Mackay had gone as far up the Missouri as the
village of the Omahas, and the following year he had sent a young
assistant, John Evans, on a mission to the Pacific. Evans got no farther
than the Mandan villages, but at least that gave Mackay the information
he needed to extend his map of the Missouri as far up as the Mandans.

Mackay was living in St. Louis in 1803, and Lewis had profitable talks
with him. As historian Roy Appleman puts it, from Mackay and the
maps Lewis had available to him, Lewis knew "virtually everything that
was known to white men of the Missouri country as far as the Mandan
villages and some Indian information about the lands to their west."[6]

The most powerful and prominent St. Louis citizens were the French
fur traders Auguste Chouteau, Sr., a founder of the city, his half-brother
Pierre Chouteau, Sr., and their brother-in-law Charles Gratiot, who had
established the first trading post at Cahokia, in 1777. Gratiot had
helped supply George Rogers Clark during the revolution. William
Clark had stayed at Gratiot's house during a September 1797 business
trip to St. Louis, where he also hobnobbed with Auguste Chouteau and
"all the fine girls and buckish Gentlemen."[7]

The Chouteaus had prospered in St. Louis, thanks to a license that
gave them exclusive rights on trade, but much of their wealth was in
land, taken in payment for goods. Their need was the need of those on
the frontier everywhere: fluid capital, long-term credit, and cash. Money
was so scarce in St. Louis that beaver skins were the coin of the land.

The Chouteaus had a nice setup—a monopoly, in fact, of every
imported item needed, and many of those desired, on the frontier, from
nails to glass beads, from ironwork to ladies' dresses, from powder and
lead to imported wine. But it was too good to last. In 1798, Manuel Lisa
arrived in St. Louis and began to muscle his way into the fur trade. He
was as quick and sharp as the Chouteaus, having grown up in New
Orleans, where he had hustled a living on the teeming waterfront. He
moved upstream to St. Louis, where as a Spaniard he got preferential
treatment, including some generous land grants. But he had no
intention of becoming a farmer; he could see that the real opportunity
in St. Louis was in trade. He began agitating for economic liberty; his
biographer, Richard Oglesby, says his attack on monopolies "made him
sound as if he was one of Adam Smith's most ardent disciples." To shut
him up, the Spanish gave him a license to trade.[8]

From these merchants, Lewis began making his purchases. Corn,
flour, biscuits, barrels of salt, kegs of pork, boxes of candles, kegs of
hogs' lard, "600 lb Grees," twenty-one bales of Indian goods, tools of

every description.[9] He bought from the Chouteaus, he bought from Lisa. He asked questions and got more information for Jefferson. He studied his maps.

On December 16, Drouillard reported in. He had brought the eight soldiers from Tennessee with him. Delighted, Lewis quickly examined them. Disappointed, he wrote Clark he found them "not possessed of more of the requisite qualifications; there is not a hunter among them." Still, there were possibilities: one of the soldiers was a blacksmith and another was a house-joiner. Lewis sent them on to Clark at Wood River. Eventually, four of the eight passed muster.[10]

Through the winter, Lewis kept up an active correspondence with Jefferson. Many letters recorded by Jefferson as received from Lewis, and many letters Jefferson wrote and noted, are missing. Still, what is available is informative and suggestive. On January 13, 1804, Jefferson wrote Lewis, saying he had been able to follow Lewis's progress by newspaper accounts. He reported that the transfer of Louisiana to the United States had been scheduled for December 20, and he had no doubt it had occurred.

"The acquisition of the country through which you are to pass has inspired the public generally with a great deal of interest in your enterprize," Jefferson wrote. "The enquiries are perpetual as to your progress. The Feds, alone still treat it as philosophism, and would rejoice in it's failure. Their bitterness increases with the diminution of their numbers and despair of a resurrection. I hope you will take care of yourself, and be the living witness of their malice and folly."[11]

To put it another way, those misguided Federalists who had criticized the Purchase and derided the expedition were committing political suicide, so the president's aide need not worry about pleasing them by making a ride to Santa Fe. Avoiding unnecessary risks was the way Lewis could confound the Feds.

On January 22, Jefferson wrote Lewis to confirm that the transfer had happened in New Orleans on December 20, and to give him instructions on how to deal with the Indians now that the United States was sovereign throughout Louisiana. The instructions came down to: tell them they have a new father. Jefferson also wanted Lewis to offer the Osage chief a free trip to Washington, to meet the new father—and to be impressed by the power and numbers of the Americans.

Jefferson closed with the welcome news that the American Philosophical Society had elected Lewis to membership.[12]

He had earned it. Two years of study under Thomas Jefferson, followed by his crash course in Philadelphia, had made Lewis into exactly what Jefferson had hoped for in an explorer—a botanist with a good sense of what was known and what was unknown, a working vocabulary for description of flora and fauna, a mapmaker who could use celestial instruments properly, a scientist with keen powers of observation, all combined in a woodsman and an officer who could lead a party to the Pacific.

Now the payoff for the American Philosophical Society savants began. In March, and again in May, Lewis sent boxes of specimens to Jefferson. They constituted the first shipment of natural-history specimens by Lewis to Jefferson from west of the Mississippi, and thus the first ever. He included slips, or cuttings, from trees owned by Pierre Chouteau, who had gotten them from the Osage Indian village three hundred miles to the west. Lewis wrote three long paragraphs of detailed description. As a man of the Enlightenment, now officially signified by his membership in the APS, Lewis was interested in practical uses of the tree, which he named the "Osage apple" (now the "Osage orange"). The fruit was never eaten, but the wood was perfect for making bows: "So much do the savages esteem the wood of this tree for the purpose of making their bows, that they travel many hundred miles in quest of it." That was Lewis's first description of a plant unknown to science. He could anticipate making many more.[13]

There are trees growing in Philadelphia (at Fourth and Spruce Streets) and the University of Virginia (at Morea, a guest house) today that grew from the cuttings Lewis sent.[14] And as historian Michael Brodhead notes, this was the beginning of "a rich, almost uniquely American phenomenon: the military naturalist."[15]

Among Lewis's worries that winter was Clark's commission. Clark had been on active service since the previous summer, but by February 1804 his commission had still not arrived. On February 10, Lewis wrote Dearborn, and Jefferson, about the matter. Through to the end of April, he got no reply, nor did the commission arrive in the meantime. The matter continued to nag.[16]

The missing commission had no practical effect. Lewis called Clark "captain" and their relationship was one of a genuine joint command. Indeed, through the second part of December and all of January, Clark was the officer with the troops in the field. He planned and oversaw the construction of the huts. He made a number of improvements to the keelboat, including some cleverly devised lockers running along the sides of the boat, with lids that could be raised to form a breastwork, or shield. When the lids were down, they provided catwalks, or "passe-avants," for men with poles pushing the boat.

Crosswise between the lockers, Clark had eleven benches built, each three feet long for use by two oarsmen. He added center poles, to support an awning.

Clark worried about the Indians. The word among the Americans living near the mouth of the Missouri was that upriver the Sioux were hostile, numerous, well armed, and certain to demand a ransom for passage. Clark added a bronze cannon, probably purchased by Lewis in St. Louis. Mounted on a swivel that allowed it to be turned and fired in any direction, it was the expedition's heaviest armament and in 1804 would be the largest weapon to that date ever taken up the Missouri. It could fire a solid lead ball weighing about one pound, or sixteen musket balls with sufficient velocity to go through a man. At close range, a highly effective antipersonnel weapon.

In addition to the swivel cannon, Clark asked Lewis to get four smaller weapons, called blunderbusses—heavy shotguns that used buckshot. Lewis found them in St. Louis. Clark mounted them on swivels, two for the stern of the keelboat and one on each pirogue. They could be loaded with musket balls, scrap iron, or buckshot.[17] At close range, devastating.

In early February, Lewis crossed over to the camp at Wood River. He looked over the men—there were nearly forty of them—and listened as Clark explained what he had done to the keelboat. Clark then left to spend a few days in St. Louis, to make purchases and to attend a ball at the Chouteaus'. Lewis had intended to join him at the ball, but was obliged to stay in camp to meet with some visiting Kickapoo Indians. Having missed the ball, he wrote Clark, "and finding more to do when I began to look about me than I had previously thought of I determined it would be as well to go to work [here, at Wood River] and pospone my return to St. Louis a few days." He wanted Clark to talk to Pierre Chouteau about the possibility of his leading an expedition of Osage chiefs to Washington.

Clark's tasks in St. Louis included picking a crew of voyagers to paddle the canoes—the captains by now having decided to keep the permanent detachment, the Corps of Discovery, together as a unit on the keelboat. Clark, who had once descended the Mississippi to Memphis, and who had lived on the Ohio River for many years, was the better waterman of the two captains, and thus probably the better judge of the voyagers.

Clark talked to Manuel Lisa, who was ready to contract out a crew that he would select and organize. Lewis wrote Clark, "Engage them immediately, if you think from their appearance and characters they will answer the purpose."

Lisa was doing quite a lot of business with the expedition. He paid a visit to Wood River to see what the captains didn't have that he did. Lewis dined in his home, although he most often stayed with Auguste Chouteau in the finest house in town.[18]

On February 20, Lewis prepared to shove off for St. Louis. He issued his first detachment orders, putting Sergeant John Ordway in command during his and Clark's absence, and directing the sawyers to continue their work, the blacksmiths to continue their work (with an extra gill, or four ounces, of whiskey* and exemption from guard duty), the men making sugar to continue to do so, and so forth. To save powder and lead, he ordered only one round per man per day for target practice. Sergeant Ordway would give instructions in shooting off hand at a distance of fifty yards. There was a prize of an extra gill of whiskey for the winner each day. Except for hunters, no man was to absent himself from camp without Sergeant Ordway's knowledge and permission. Finally, no whiskey beyond the legal ration.

Lewis went off to St. Louis, conducted business, and returned a week later. Sergeant Ordway reported to him that Privates Reubin Field and John Shields had refused to mount guard duty as ordered because they would be damned if they would take orders from anyone other than the captains. Privates John Colter, John Boley, Peter Weiser, and John Robinson had gone off "hunting"—or so they had told Ordway, who had tried to stop them. In fact, they went to a neighboring whiskey shop on the edge of the nearby American settlement and got drunk.

To deal with these disciplinary matters, Lewis wrote another detachment order, dated March 3 in the journal: "The Commanding officer feels himself mortifyed and disappointed at the disorderly conduct" of Field and Shields, especially since he had thought of them as excellent soldiers and men of judgment. He went on: "A moments reflection must convince every man of our party" that the captains had to be in St. Louis, to gather the necessary supplies and equipment for the voyage. When they were gone, Sergeant Ordway was in command. Period. Lewis confined Colter, Boley, Weiser, and Robinson to quarters for ten days.

On March 7, Lewis returned to St. Louis, to be present at the ceremonies marking the formal transfer of Upper Louisiana to the United States.

---

* Four ounces is about the alcoholic content of four beers. For most people, it raises the blood-alcohol value to 0.10 percent, or about what police regard as driving under the influence.

Captain Stoddard, the official American representative, invited Lewis to serve as the chief official witness. There was a detachment from the First Infantry Regiment out of Fort Kaskaskia on hand.

The ceremony took place on March 9, in front of Government House, Spanish headquarters in the city. First a transfer was made from Spain to France. Colonel Delassus presided for Spain, while Stoddard acted as agent for the French. When the Spanish flag was struck, Delassus presented it to Stoddard, who then ran up the French Tricolor. The crowd, composed of nearly all the residents of St. Louis, most of them French, cheered. With tears in their eyes, Frenchmen asked Stoddard to let the Tricolor wave over St. Louis for one night. Stoddard agreed.

The next day, to the salute of guns and cheers from the soldiers, the Tricolor was lowered and the Stars and Stripes was raised, the documents were signed, and appropriate speeches were made. Stoddard assumed the post of military-civil governor of Upper Louisiana, pending the establishment of territorial government. After the ceremonies, Lewis and Clark accompanied Stoddard on an inspection of Spanish defenses.[19]

A few days later, Clark returned to Wood River to continue preparations. The days were getting noticeably longer, the first hints of opening buds were on the tree limbs, the great duck and geese migrations were just starting, the ice no longer ran in the river, spring was coming. And with the first warm days came an ominously unwelcome visitor. On March 25, Clark wrote in his journal, "The musquetors are verry bad this evening."

On March 28, Lewis drew three drafts, or checks, of five hundred dollars each on the secretary of war. He had already drawn $1,669, and drew an additional $159 a few days later. He was also drawing money to provide for the Osage chief and Pierre Chouteau on their trip to Washington. And he was signing chits for supplies. Altogether, signing his name to a draft on the government was becoming a commonplace experience for Lewis. Indeed, it was threatening to become habit-forming.

On the afternoon of the 29th, Lewis crossed over to Wood River. Clark had alarming news. There had been fights between the men. John Shields had opposed an order and had threatened Sergeant Ordway's life, and wished to return to Kentucky. John Colter had disobeyed orders and had loaded his gun, threatening to shoot Ordway.

The men had been at Wood River for the better part of four months. They never got to go to St. Louis. The only women they saw were the pioneers at the nearby settlements, and there weren't many of them, and mostly they were married. There was a whiskey seller around but he was expensive and hard to get to. Once the huts were completed and the keelboat's alterations were finished, the men had almost nothing to do. A little drilling on the parade ground, which they hated, a little target practice, which they loved but only got to do once a day, was about it.

These young heroes were in great shape, strong as bulls, eager to get going, full of energy and testosterone—and bored. So they fought, and drank—and drank, and fought. Clark recorded various serious fistfights, sometimes with delightful comment: "R. Field was in a mistake & repents." "Frazer. has don bad."

But fighting among themselves was one thing, threatening the sergeant quite another. On March 29, the captains put Shields and Colter on trial for mutiny. The privates "asked the forgivness &c & promised to doe better in future." The captains relented; no punishment was noted. And two days later, Shields and Colter were welcomed into the permanent party.

On March 31, after a full exchange of views between themselves, the captains held a ceremony in order to enlist the twenty-five men they had selected to be members of "the Detachment destined for the Expedition though the interior of the *Continent* of North America." Another group of five soldiers was designated to accompany the expedition to its winter quarters, then to return to St. Louis with communiqués and specimens. Corporal Richard Warfington would be its leader. The main detachment was divided into three squads. Charles Floyd and Nathaniel Pryor joined Ordway as sergeants commanding the squads.

Warfington, Floyd, and Pryor were not the only soldiers who had impressed the captains. Pryor was sick. In the Detachment Order recording the selections, Clark wrote: "Dureing the indisposition of Sergeant Pryor, George Shannon is appointed (protempor) to discharge his the Said Pryor's duty in his Squad." Since Shannon was not yet twenty years old, the youngest man in the party, that appointment was a genuine compliment.

The permanent party was now in place. Besides the twenty-two men and three sergeants, it included Lewis and Clark, Clark's slave, York; Drouillard; and Lewis's dog, Seaman. It was straining to get going. Every morning, the men looked across the Mississippi and saw the Missouri pouring into the main stream, so powerful its muddy waters drove clear across three-quarters of the width of the mighty Mississippi, the Missouri being the more powerful of the two.

Clark also recorded, "I send to the Missouries water for drinking water, it being much Cooler than the Mississippi."

In the evening, the men could watch the sun go down over the Missouri. Surely, as they sipped their whiskey ration at the end of the day, they stared at that river, and talked about it, and thought about it. They were not daunted by it. Rather, they were drawn to it. What adventures awaited, what sights they would see, they knew they couldn't even guess, which only made them all the more eager to get going—so they could find out.

Sergeant Gass wrote in his journal that the local inhabitants had warned that the party was "to pass through a country possessed by numerous, powerful and warlike nations of savages, of gigantic stature, fierce, treacherous and cruel; and particularly hostile to white men." But, he insisted, "the determined and resolute character" of the men and the confidence pervading all ranks "dispelled every emotion of fear."[20]

A week after the ceremony of enlistment, Ordway wrote his parents. He expressed determination and confidence:

We are to ascend the Missouri River with a boat as far as it is navigable and then to go by land, to the western ocean, if nothing prevents, &c.

This party consists of 25 picked Men of the armey & country and I am So happy as to be one of them pick'd Men. . . .

We are to Start in ten days [April 18] up the Missouri River. . . .
We expect to be gone 18 months or two years. We are to Receive a great Reward for this expedition, when we Return.

Ordway said he would be drawing fifteen dollars per month in pay and would receive a bonus of four hundred acres of prime land. Then he reported what may have been just another soldiers' rumor, or an expectation encouraged by the captains; whichever it was, it spoke to the spirit of the men and their captains: "If we make Great Discoveries as we expect, the united States, has promised to make us Great Rewards more than we are promised, &c."[21]

11

READY TO DEPART

April–May 21, 1804

As the April sun grew warmer, the banks of the Mississippi exploded into color. Green-gold, nature's first hue, predominated early in the month, but it had serious competition. The captains noted spicewood in full bloom on April 1, along with the white dogtooth violet and the mayapple. On the 5th, the buds of the peach, apple, and cherry trees—imported by the pioneers—appeared. By the 17th, they were in full bloom. Osage apple and Chickasaw plum were in flower, along with the violet, the doves foot, and the cowslip.

It was gorgeous weather, with afternoon temperatures climbing into the sixties and, by the last week of the month, into the low seventies. But on the 26th, a frost killed fruit at Cahokia; St. Louis escaped without damage. That afternoon, the temperature was up to sixty-six.

Let's go! one can almost hear the men of the Corps of Discovery crying out to the captains. Let's go, for God's sake.

Lewis decided no, not yet. Sometime between April 8, when Sergeant Ordway wrote that the expedition would be off on April 18, and mid-April, Lewis concluded that he needed far more in the way of provisions, and he needed more time to round them up. And Lewis needed time to arrange for the Osage chief's journey to Washington.

He put departure day, D-Day, back a month.

At 7:00 a.m. on Saturday, April 7, Lewis and Clark set out in a canoe, with York and a private to paddle them, for St. Louis. They arrived at half past ten. Captain Stoddard greeted them and made them his guests;

at his quarters Lewis and Clark dressed, then went to a dinner and ball. Stoddard was the host. He had invited some fifty gentlemen of the city, to thank them for their support and the courtesies shown to him. The ball lasted until 9:00 a.m. Sunday. "No business to day," Clark wrote in his journal on Sunday evening.

On Monday, Clark returned to Wood River, while Lewis began buying. Flags. Mosquito nets. Shirts. Food. Liquor. Indian trade goods. Among other things, he bought and had shipped to Wood River, where it was repacked for the expedition: 4,175 complete rations, at $.14 each; 5,555 rations of flour at $.04 each; 100 gallons of whiskey at $1.28 each; 20 gallons of whiskey at $1 each; 4,000 rations of salt pork at $.04 each; plus ground corn and much more.

Clark sent Lewis his shopping list—nails for hinges (200 sent, Lewis noted on the list), red oil paint for the lockers (not to be had, Lewis noted), red and blue ribbon (sent), and so forth. On May 2, Lewis wrote Clark to report that the Osage party would set out in about ten days and to ask Clark to send to him in St. Louis "the specimines of salt which you will find in my writing desk, on the shelves where our books are, or in the drawer of the Instrument case." The invitation to rummage through Lewis's writing desk spoke to the absolute trust between the two men, and the sentence also gives a tiny glimpse into what their quarters at Wood River were like.

Sunday, May 6, was a grand day for Captain Clark, a horrible one for Captain Lewis. At Wood River, several of the settlers came in to challenge the soldiers to a shooting match. Of the challengers, Clark wrote with some satisfaction, "all git beet and Lose their money."

In St. Louis, Lewis was frustrated because there were no more kegs to be had—he had bought out the entire stock. He was furious because Manuel Lisa had evidently not gotten enough of Lewis's business to satisfy him, and had therefore sent a petition to the authorities protesting Lewis's high-handedness and other shortcomings. On May 6, Lewis wrote Clark about Lisa's actions, and his reaction. He let it all out.

"Damn Manuel," Lewis exploded. "And triply Damn Mr. B. [Francis Benoit, Lisa's partner]. They give me more vexation and trouble than their lives are worth. I have dealt very plainly with these gentlemen, in short I have come to an open rupture with them; I think them both great scoundrels, and they have given me abundant proofs of their unfriendly dispositions towards our government and its measures."

His blood was up. "These gentlemen," he wrote, then stopped, crossed it out, and continued: "These puppies, are not unacquainted with my opinions. . . . strange indeed, that men to appearance in their senses, will manifest such strong sumptoms of insanity, as to be *wheting knives to cut their own throats."*

Lewis had reason to contemplate cutting his own throat. He had been forced to begin this letter with an awful piece of news: "I send you herewith inclosed your commission accompanyed by the Secretary of War's letter; it is not such as I wished, or had reason to expect; but so it is—a further explaneation when I join you."[1]

It was a lieutenant's commission—not a captain's, as Lewis had promised. Lewis was mortified, and apparently helpless.

His heart had sunk as he read Dearborn's reply to his letter of February 10 asking about Clark's commission. Dated March 26, Dearborn's letter began, "The peculiar situation, circumstances and organisation of the Corps of Engineers is such as would render the appointment of Mr. Clark a Captain in that Corps improper." The best Dearborn could do for Clark was a commission as a lieutenant in the Corps of Artillerists, which he enclosed. Clark's military grade would have no effect on his compensation for the expedition, Dearborn said, meaning Clark would still be paid as a captain.

On March 24, Dearborn had sent a list of nominations to Jefferson, including Clark's as a lieutenant in the artillery. That afternoon, Jefferson had endorsed the list and sent it on to the Senate for confirmation, which was done on March 26.

In a shifty little bureaucratic maneuver, Dearborn managed to make a bad situation worse. He dated Clark's commission as of the day he signed it, March 26, 1804. That hurt Clark on the seniority list and denied his service from the day he enlisted, and even denied his service from mid-October 1803 to March 26, 1804.[2]

As far as is known, Jefferson made no protest; whether because he failed to notice or because he approved Dearborn's decision cannot be said. It had always been clear that, if Clark turned down Lewis's invitation and Moses Hooke took his place, it would be as a lieutenant and he would be clearly second-in-command, but that, if Clark joined up, it would be as a captain and a co-commander. Jefferson knew that, and reports sent to him from St. Louis and Wood River also made it clear that Lewis and Clark had been functioning as co-commanders.

It may be that Jefferson wanted Lewis in sole command. Perhaps he reasoned that in such a long voyage it was inevitable that the two leaders would disagree, perhaps sharply enough to paralyze the command, or, even worse, to divide the Corps of Discovery into hostile factions.

Whatever Jefferson's intentions, Dearborn's action gave Lewis an opportunity to take sole command. But he felt not the slightest temptation to take advantage of the situation. He immediately wrote Clark: "I think it will be best to let none of our party or any other persons know any thing about the grade, you will observe that the grade has no effect upon your compensation, which by G——d, shall be equal to my own."[3]

For the next seven years, only Dearborn, Jefferson, a clerk or two in the War Department, and Meriwether Lewis and William Clark knew that, as far as the army was concerned, Captain Lewis was in command of the Corps of Discovery, with Lieutenant Clark as his second-in-command. For the men of the expedition, it was Captains Clark and Lewis, co-commanders. That was all that counted.

Whether Clark ever talked to Lewis about the matter is unknown. In 1811, when Nicholas Biddle was editing the journals for publication, he asked Clark to explain the "exact relation" between the two officers. *"Equal in every point of view,"* Clark wrote in reply. He said his feeling on learning that the promised captain's commission would not be forthcoming "was as might be expected." But Lewis's stratagem satisfied him, and since "I wished the expidetion suckcess . . . I proceeded." He told Biddle that in the published journals he wished to be placed "on equal footing with Cap. Lewis in every point of view without exposeing any thing or even mentioning the Commission at all."

Clark confessed to Biddle, "I did not think myself very well treated," but said he had never mentioned the case to anyone, not even Jefferson or Dearborn. He instructed Biddle to keep the whole thing to himself.[4]

On another appointment matter, Lewis was successful. Jefferson had just taken the lead in founding the United States Military Academy at West Point. Lewis suggested using the academy as part of the effort to win over to the American side the French businessmen in the Purchase territory. As historian Theodore Crackel puts it, Lewis's plan was simple: "The sons of the area's leading citizens should be made cadets and sent to West Point. What better way to bind these families to the new nation—and to the [Jefferson] administration?" Dearborn and Jefferson accepted without hesitation.

In April, Lewis and Stoddard recommended some young men for appointment to West Point, including Charles Gratiot and two sons of Auguste Chouteau. One of these, Lorimier, was half Indian. Stoddard would not go along with the recommendation for Lorimier, because "he exhibited too much of the Indian in his color. This circumstance may make his situation among the cadets at the school rather disagreeable." Lewis stuck with the recommendation, and all three got their appointments. Three others were added later. Of the six, five graduated and got commissions, including young Lorimier, who served three years and won two promotions.[5]

In St. Louis in the first week of May 1804, there were difficulties and postponements connected to the Osage chief's trip. In Wood River, Clark was having a hard time holding the young lions in. During the day, they were packing, unpacking, repacking, as Clark experimented with various possibilities. At night, too many of them got drunk and brought on Clark's displeasure—but not much more, because he recognized the cause of the problem and felt it would solve itself once they were under way.

On May 7, Clark loaded the keelboat. The following day, he and twenty oarsmen took it for a ride in the Mississippi, to check its balance. Back on shore, Clark shifted more gear to the stern. On May 11, Drouillard brought to camp seven voyagers, who had been recruited in the St. Louis area with help from the Chouteaus.*

On Sunday, May 13, Clark sent a message to Lewis in St. Louis: all was ready. The boat and pirogues were loaded. The boat would have twenty-two privates to row her, along with the three sergeants. One canoe would be paddled by six soldiers with Corporal Warfington. The other canoe would be paddled by eight French voyagers, who would be returning with Warfington's group. The craft were "Complete with Sails &c. &c. men Compe. with Powder Cartragies and 100 Balls each, all in health and readiness to Set out."

They had everything needed, they hoped. Clark entered an ominous note, saying they had enough of the necessary stores "as we thought ourselves autherised to precure." Not what the captains thought was needed, only what was authorized. In fact, Clark bluntly declared in his journal that the expedition did not have as many stores "as I think necssy for the multitud of Indians tho which we must pass on our road across the Continent & &c."

Nevertheless, the next morning, May 14, Clark wrote in his journal, "fixing for a Start." That afternoon he set off at four o'clock, "under a jentle brease," and made four miles up the Missouri; he camped on an island. He described the men as being "in high Spirits" and said they

---

* This may have been one of the causes of the rift between Lewis and Lisa. Earlier, Lewis had expected to contract for a canoe crew with Lisa. Apparently the deal fell through, perhaps with some charges of bad faith.

were "robust young Backwoodsmen of Character helthy hardy young men, recomended."

The next day, he set out for St. Charles, on the north bank of the Missouri, where he would shift the load again, having found that in the Missouri the concealed timber, either embedded in the river bottom or floating downstream almost completely submerged, was difficult to avoid and must be bumped into by the bow, rather than letting the bow ride up on the obstacles. That meant getting more goods in the bow, fewer in the stern. On May 16, the expedition pulled into St. Charles, there to reload and wait for Captain Lewis to come up.

Lewis was busy with the Osage party and with making arrangements for Captain Stoddard to act as his agent in St. Louis until he returned. On May 16, he signed an authorization that gave Stoddard power to act in his behalf, to draw bills of exchange on the secretary of war "to any amount, which the nature of the service may in your judgment and at your discretion be deemed necessary." More specifically, Lewis declared that Indians would soon be arriving in St. Louis from upriver. He intended to select the delegations and start them on their way to Washington, where they would meet their new father.

Lewis told Stoddard to spare no reasonable expense in getting these trans-Mississippi Indians to Washington, and see to their comfort and protection, especially if they were Sioux, the most numerous and warlike tribe on the Missouri and one Lewis especially wanted to impress.

Further, Stoddard should pay the French voyagers when they returned to St. Louis. And if anyone showed up in St. Louis with a chit from Lewis, Stoddard should pay in cash and notify the secretary of war. Any letters arriving for Lewis, "from whatever quarter they may come," should be sent to Jefferson, who would hold them.[6]

Over the following couple of days, Lewis made last-minute preparations for Chouteau's and the Osage chief's trip to Washington. He prepared a package for Chouteau to carry to Jefferson, including mineral specimens, a horned lizard, a chart of the Mississippi from St. Louis to New Orleans, and a map of Upper Louisiana done by Clark and Lewis, based on the Evans map and on what they had heard from French boatmen around St. Louis. This map has been identified by Donald Jackson as "the first cartographic product of the expedition."[7] On May 19, Chouteau's party set off for Washington.

At noon on May 20, Lewis set off by horseback for St. Charles, accompanied by Stoddard, two of his lieutenants, Auguste Chouteau,

Charles Gratiot, and a dozen or more of the substantial inhabitants of St. Louis. Lewis made a journal entry about the trip, almost the only one he wrote between November 1803 and April 1805. He noted: "The first 5 miles of our rout laid through a beautifull high leavel and fertile prarie which incircles the town of St. Louis." At 1:30 p.m., a violent thunderstorm forced the party to take shelter in a little cabin. The men remained an hour and a half "and regailed ourselves with a could collation which we had taken the precaution to bring with us from St. Louis."

After the picnic, the rain continued. Impatient, Lewis said to hell with it and started off for St. Charles. Most of his companions accompanied him. They arrived at half past six "and joined Capt Clark, found the party in good health and sperits." After a supper with the local officials, Lewis retired early to spend the night on the boat.

In the morning Clark said some of the men, twenty in all, wished to attend a final mass, and he had some rearrangements to make in the packing, so it would be midafternoon before the party could set off. Lewis took a look around St. Charles. Founded in 1769, it was a village of some one hundred families living in homes Lewis described as "small and but illy constructed." It had a chapel and a priest, and about 450 inhabitants, overwhelmingly French Canadians. "Not an inconsiderable proportion of them," Lewis noted, "can boast a small dash of the pure blood of the aboriginees of America."

Lewis hired two half-breeds, Pierre (Peter) Cruzatte and Francis Labiche. Cruzatte, son of a French father and an Omaha mother, was skilled in the sign language and spoke Omaha. Labiche spoke several native tongues. Lewis attached them to the permanent party after swearing them in as privates in the U.S. Army—a sure sign of his high approval of the two men.[8]

Clark had characterized the people of St. Charles as "pore, polite & harmonious." Lewis had a harsher judgment: he found them "miserably pour, illiterate and when at home excessively lazy." Still, he found qualities to admire: "They are polite hospitable and by no means deficient in point of natural genious, they live in a perfect state of harmony among each other." He regretted the influence of the Roman Catholic priest among them, a typical Virginia planter's prejudice, and regretted too that the men regarded the cultivation of the soil as a "degrading occupation."

To support their families, the men either undertook hunting trips to collect furs, or hired themselves out as voyagers to paddle traders up the Missouri, the Osage, and other rivers. They were gone from six to eighteen months at a time. Perhaps looking ahead to what faced him,

Lewis said that the voyagers were "always subjected to severe and incessant labour, exposed to the ferosity of the lawless savages, the vicissitudes of weather and climate, and dependant on chance or accident alone for food, raiment or relief in the event of malady."

Lewis had brought to Clark a letter from Clark's brother-in-law, William Croghan, which carried the welcome news that George Rogers Clark had revived from an illness that his family had feared would prove fatal. Just before setting out, Clark replied, giving the letter to Stoddard to take to St. Louis and post. He thanked Croghan for the news, which relieved him much, expressed the hope that he would be back in Clarksville in two years, and said, "I think it more than probable that Capt. Lewis or myself will return by sea, the other by the same rout we proceed." He concluded with a description of the rain, thunder, and lightning of the previous three days and admitted that it "discommodes me a little in sitting out."

Discommoded or not, at 3:30 p.m., to the cheers of a crowd on the bank, the expedition set out. Captain Stoddard was there. A couple of weeks later, he reported to Dearborn that, as Lewis and his party had begun the ascent of the Missouri, in the boat and two pirogues, "All of them were deeply laden, and well manned. *His men posses great resolution and they are in the best health and spirits.*"[9]

As the keelboat turned her bow into the stream, Lewis and his party cut themselves off from civilization. There would be no more incoming letters, no orders, no commissions, no fresh supplies, no reinforcements, nothing reaching them, until they returned.

The captains expected to be gone two years, perhaps more. In all that time, in whatever lay ahead of them, whatever decisions had to be made, they would receive no guidance from their superiors. This was an independent command, such as the U.S. Army had not previously seen and never would again. Lewis and Clark were as free as Columbus, Magellan, or Cook to make their mark on the sole basis of their own judgments and abilities.

Their first afternoon together on the Missouri, they made three and a quarter miles. They camped that night on the head of an island on the starboard side. Spring storms continued and a hard rain lasted through the night. At 6:00 a.m., May 22, they were on their way.

12

UP THE MISSOURI

May–July 1804

The current ran at five miles per hour usually, but it sped up when it encountered encroaching bluffs, islands, sandbars, and narrow channels. The level was springtime high, almost flood stage. Incredible to behold were the obstacles—whole trees, huge trees, oaks and maples and cottonwoods, that had been uprooted when a bank caved in; hundreds of large and thousands of smaller branches; sawyers, trees whose roots were stuck on the bottom and whose limbs sawed back and forth in the current, often out of sight; great piles of driftwood clumped together, racing downriver, threatening to tear holes in the sides of the boat; innumerable sandbars, always shifting; swirls and whirlpools beyond counting. This was worse than the Mississippi.

How in the world did they move that bulky boat, overladen in the bow, against the full force and power of the Missouri? Donald Jackson gives us a vivid description: "A keelboat was a useful but ungainly craft. Load it with ten or twenty tons of cargo and it was a faithful, wallowing drudge. Arm it with a swivel gun, set a guard with firearms at the gunwales, and it became a little warship. Navigating it downstream was easy if you kept an eye out for submerged logs, but going upstream there was no ideal way to keep it moving. If the wind was fair you ran up a sail. When the wind failed you broke out the iron-pointed setting poles and started pushing. If the bottom was deep enough, you could row. If the current was too swift for rowing you could bend a forty-fathom length of cordelling cable to the mast and put the crew ashore to haul on the line. Failing all this, you could tie up to the bank and wait for the wind to rise and blow fair."[1]

Despite everything, they made good time generally, and if the wind was astern they made excellent time, once or twice twenty miles in a day. But when the wind wasn't astern it required absolute vigilance and complete concentration by the captains and the sergeants, and total physical commitment from the men, to make every mile. The labor of the men was incredible, whether pulling at the oars, or pushing against their setting poles as they walked on top of the lockers from bow to stern.

For Warfington's party in the white pirogue, and for the voyagers in the red pirogue, it was somewhat easier. Their craft were lighter and rode higher in the water. They were more maneuverable, so it was easier to turn away from danger. On the keelboat, to help dodge obstacles, the crew had to rush to one side or the other again and again. In the pirogues, all they had to do was lean.

The privates on the keelboat were tough, alert, quick. On June 16, Clark reported a typical incident: "Sand Collecting &c forming Bars and Bars washg a way, the boat Struck and turned, She was near oversetting. We saved her by Some extrodany exeretions of our party [who are] ever ready to incounture any fatigue for the premotion of the enterprise."

On June 1, the party reached the Osage River and made camp on the point on the left side. The captains ordered all the trees in the area cut down, so that they could make observations, and stayed there through the next two days. They spent hours observing the time and distance from the sun to the nearest limb of the early-morning sliver of a moon. Between 6:22 and 8:28 a.m., they recorded two sets of three figures each a total of thirty-six times, or about one every three minutes.

When the expedition was under way, Clark was more often on the keelboat, Lewis on shore, because Clark was the better waterman, Lewis the better scientist ("more skilled [in zoology] than in botany," according to Jefferson, but good at both).[2]

Lewis took long, solitary walks, collecting specimens, animal and plant, noting the physical characteristics of the land, judging the fertility of the soil, the presence of springs of good water, likely sites for homesteads, trading posts, and fortifications. Alas, none of his notes for the spring and summer of 1804 are known to exist.

It makes a terrible gap in the records. His notes would have expressed his first reactions to the biomass west of the Mississippi. This was hardly unknown territory; by 1804, the lower reaches of the

Missouri had been much traveled. The creeks, islands, and prominent landforms all had names, mainly French. An accurate map existed through the mouth of the Kansas up to the entry of the Platte, and a pretty good map of the country from the Platte to the Mandan villages. But for Lewis it was all new, and he was seeing it with different eyes.

Up to the mouth of the Kansas, most of the flora and fauna were known to science. But there was more than enough of the new to keep Lewis happily busy, collecting and describing and preserving. After the hours at his instruments—squinting at the sky, calling out numbers for Clark to record—the hours he got to spend tramping around the prairie on the high ground up from the valley, doing what botanists like to do best—discovering new species—were surely welcome.

But we can't catch his joy and wonder through his own words, because we don't have his notes. Or any journal entry, even though, in Detachment Orders that Lewis wrote and he and Clark signed and proclaimed on May 26, Lewis ordered the sergeants, in addition to all other duties, "to keep a seperate journal from day to day of all passing occurences, and such other observations on the country &c. as shall appear to them worthy of notice."

It seems impossible that he could have issued such orders and not kept a daily journal himself. But if he did, we don't have it. Thus, as the keelboat makes its way west across the present state of Missouri, then turns north at the mouth of the Kansas toward the Platte and on into the Dakotas, we see Lewis only through the eyes of other men, principally William Clark.

Clark was a great writer about events in which he participated, and described the country he was passing through with a lovely lyric quality, but he could be disappointingly terse when writing about an event he had not seen with his own eyes. Thus, on the second day of the journey, May 23, he wrote, "Capt Lewis' assended the hill which has peninsulis projecting in raged pints to the river, and was near falling from a Peninsulia of rocks 300 feet, he caught at 20 foot. Saved himself by the assistance of his Knife."

Surely Lewis told Clark more than Clark recorded about such a life-threatening incident. As soldiers, who either learned lessons or died, they had a need to talk over incidents that threatened the expedition. They had to avoid unnecessary risks. So Lewis must have told Clark in some detail how he came to fall, and how he saved himself—but this didn't make it into Clark's journal entry.

There is another tantalizing item. The next day, the expedition passed Boone's Settlement. The village consisted of a colony of Kentuckians led by Daniel Boone, who had settled there in 1799 on a

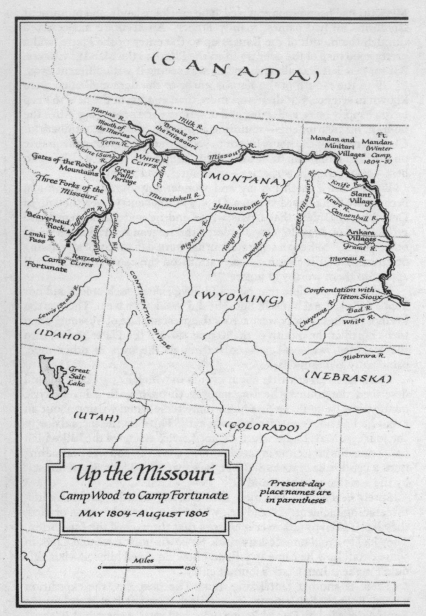

(CANADA)

(MONTANA)

Marias R.
Mouth of
the Marias
Teton R.
Milk R.
Breaks of
the Missouri
Missouri R.
Medicine (Sun) R.
Gates of the Rocky
Mountains
WHITE
CLIFFS
Great
Falls
Portage
Three Forks of the
Missouri
Musselshell R.
Beaverhead
Rock
Jefferson R.
Gallatin R.
Yellowstone R.
Lemhi
Pass
Madison R.
Camp
Fortunate
RATTLESNAKE
CLIFFS
Bighorn R.
Tongue R.
Powder R.

Mandan and
Minitari
Villages
Ft.
Mandan
(Winter
Camp,
1804-5)
Knife R.
Slant
Village
Heart R.
Cannonball R.
Little Missouri R.
Arikara
Villages
Grand R.
Moreau R.

CONTINENTAL DIVIDE

(WYOMING)

Confrontation with
Teton Sioux
Cheyenne R.
Bad R.
White R.

Lewis (Snake) R.

(IDAHO)

Great
Salt
Lake

Niobrara R.

(NEBRASKA)

(UTAH)

(COLORADO)

Present-day
place names are
in parentheses

Up the Missouri
Camp Wood to Camp Fortunate

MAY 1804–AUGUST 1805

0   Miles   150

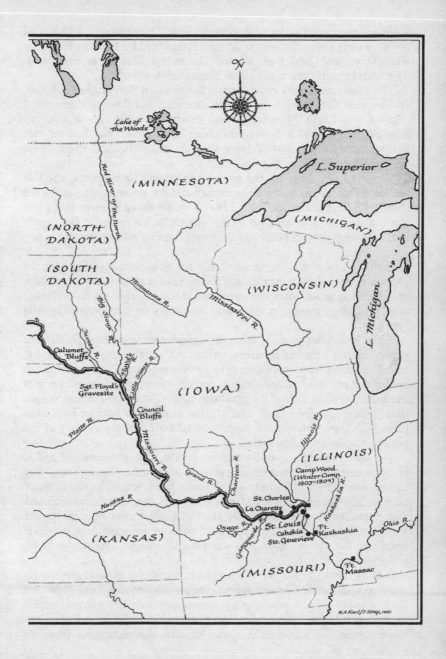

grant of land from the Spanish government. The man who had blazed the way into Kentucky was creating a farmstead for his family on the river. Lewis and Clark went ashore. The settlers flocked around them. The men bought corn and butter. Then they were off.

Did Lewis and Clark meet Daniel Boone? Did they shake his hand? Did he wish them luck, offer advice, or a drink? Did he pass the torch? "Lewis and Clark Meeting Daniel Boone" sounds like a Charley Russell painting, or a marvelous scene for a novel. But had he met Boone, surely Clark would have written about it. And there is no known Lewis entry for the day.

The next day, May 25, the expedition passed La Charette, the last settlement of whites on the river. French and American settlers had lived there for four or five years; Daniel Boone would move there in 1805. The site is gone now, washed away by the river. Clark recorded, "The people at this Village is pore, houses Small, they Sent us milk & eggs to eat."

The main Lewis document available for this period is his May 26 Detachment Orders. It established the routine, and serves as a reminder that this was much more than a bunch of the guys out on an exploring and collecting expedition. This was a military expedition into hostile territory.

From Jefferson's point of view, the captains were on an expedition to explore newly acquired territory, to find the water route to the Pacific, to extend commerce, to collect specimens for science, and to establish an American claim on the Oregon country. From the point of view of the various Indian tribes, the keelboat carried uninvited strangers into their midst and their land. The United States had bought Louisiana from Napoleon, but not the loyalty or alliance or subservience of the people who lived in Louisiana.

For Lewis and Clark, every strange Indian tribe encountered had to be considered belligerent until it proved otherwise. The Indians, they hoped, would be willing to talk and trade, but it would be the Indians' choice. They might decide to fight. Certainly they would be tempted. The expedition's arsenal was by far the biggest ever brought to the Missouri country, and any tribe able to take possession of it would dominate the region—no matter what the Louisiana Purchase said—for a long time to come.

The last thing Lewis wanted was an Indian fight. He was prepared— and was under orders—to do everything possible to avoid one. The best way to avoid a fight was to make sure one never got started, which meant in the first instance making certain that the expedition was never caught by surprise. A camp of sleeping men with weapons carelessly scattered around could well tempt a roving band of Indians into an attack. A well-regulated camp, with guards posted and calling out challenges, would not. Instead of a fight there would be a talk—which was what Lewis wanted most of all, because he believed the United States could bring more and better trade goods to the Missouri country from St. Louis than the British could bring down from Canada. Given a chance, Americans would win the fur trade.

To prevent surprise, Lewis's Detachment Orders of May 26 stressed alertness. The sergeant-of-the-guard had as part of his duty posting sentinels and ensuring the security of the camp. These were clear, direct orders, with no words wasted but all possibilities covered, and they signified that the expedition was now in a war zone and might be attacked at any time.

To add to nighttime security, the expedition camped on islands whenever feasible. There were daily inspections of the rifles, the blunderbusses, and the cannon, to be certain they were ready for action.

Lewis's May 26 order provides a series of images of life on the keelboat. He divided the permanent party into three squads, or "messes," which among other things would cook and eat together. Each evening, upon landing, Sergeant Ordway would hand out to each mess a day's provisions. It would be cooked at once, and a portion reserved for the following day. No cooking was allowed during the day. The regular ration was hominy and lard on one day, salt pork and flour the next, and cornmeal and pork the following day.

Eating hominy and lard cold on the day after it was cooked must have made fresh meat welcome. To provide it, Drouillard and two or three companions and two horses acquired in St. Charles went out every day to hunt. When they brought in deer or bear, no lard or pork was to be issued. From the third day of the expedition on, Lewis was conserving rations.

Lewis's Detachment Order was exact about the responsibilities of the sergeants on the boat as it moved upstream. One sergeant was stationed at the helm, another midships, and the third in the bow. The sergeant at the helm steered, saw to the baggage on the quarterdeck, and attended the compass. The sergeant midships commanded the guard, managed the sails, saw that the men at the oars did their duty, and kept a good lookout for the mouths of all rivers, creeks, islands, and other remarkable places. He also measured out the whiskey ration and served as the sergeant-of-the-guard at night. The sergeant at the bow was charged to keep a good lookout, and to report all pirogues or other craft in the river, and all hunting camps or parties of Indians.

Two of the privates had specified duty. They were Labiche and Cruzatte, the mixed-bloods who had joined up in St. Charles. They had been up the Missouri before and were the best rivermen in the enlisted ranks. Lewis ordered that they "man the larboard bow oar alternately, and the one not engaged at the oar will attend as the Bows-man, and when the attention of both these persons is necessary at the bow, their oar is to be maned by any idle hand on board." The bowman's tasks included warding off floating debris with his iron-tipped pole, calling out warnings of dangers ahead, looking for the best place to cross the river, and watching for sandbars, whirlpools, whatever.

On June 8, the bowman called out, "Pirogue ahead!" The boats tied up at a bank, and the two parties began to exchange information. The three downstream travelers explained that they had been hunting and trapping on the upper Missouri for the past year. Clark estimated that they had about nine hundred dollars' worth of pelts and furs. This was big money in the pre-industrial-revolution age, about as profitable a venture as any young ambitious entrepreneur could find, other than a gold or silver claim. Of course, as always, the men who did the hard part and took the greatest risks got the least reward. The nine hundred dollars the voyagers got in St. Louis would grow by a factor of ten by the time the furs reached New York. In China, they were worth ten times the New York price.

From the Indian point of view, the furs were *their* resources, taken without their permission and without payment. One had to doubt that they would continue to allow white men to trap their creeks and rivers. Even if they did, without trading posts scattered along the Missouri small parties could hardly hope to be successful. The three men the expedition met on June 8 were out of provisions and powder. Even with a handout from the captains, they were just going to make it back to St. Louis.

On June 12, the bowman again cried out, "Pirogues ahead!" This time, there were two pirogues. One contained furs, the other buffalo grease and tallow. Lewis bought three hundred pounds of "voyager's grease" from the trappers—whether for food or insect repellent, or both, is unclear. He paid with a chit that could be cashed with Stoddard in St. Louis.

The leader of the party was Pierre Dorion, Sr., a fifty-five-year-old Frenchman who had known George Rogers Clark back in Illinois during the Revolutionary War. In 1785, Dorion had settled down with the Yankton Sioux on the Missouri, above the Platte. He had a Yankton wife and spoke the language fluently, as well as French and English.

Such priceless skills could not be ignored; Lewis and Clark persuaded Dorion ("old Durioun" in Clark's journal) to return to the Sioux villages with them. They hoped that Dorion could persuade some Sioux chiefs to go to Washington to meet their new father.

On June 17, Clark complained, "The party is much aflicted with Boils and Several have the Decissentary, which I contribute to the water which is muddy." The next day, several men had "the Disentary, and two thirds of them with ulsers or Boils, Some with 8 or 10 of those Tumers."

Lewis agreed with Clark's diagnosis, that the water was to blame. The captains urged the men to dip their cups below the surface when they went for a drink of water. The surface water was full of scum, mud, and debris; if the men dipped deep, they would get cleaner water.

The captains were undoubtedly right about the bad effects of the water, but an equal culprit in bringing on the boils and other skin problems was their diet. Only on the rarest of occasions did the party get fresh vegetables, such as watercress, and there was no ripe fruit as yet. Roman legions put vinegar in their drinking water, but Lewis and Clark had taken no such precaution. They and their men were living on meat and cornmeal. The meat was contaminated with bacteria (of whose existence they were unaware). Infected mosquito bites also contributed to their ailments.

In camp, ticks and gnats were bad, mosquitoes a plague. They came up in droves, so thick that the men could not keep them out of their eyes, noses, ears, and throats. To escape, men stood in the smoke of the fire and coated their exposed limbs, neck, and face with voyager's grease.

On June 26, the expedition completed its westward trek of nearly 400 river miles across the present state of Missouri and arrived at the mouth of the Kansas River. There they spent nearly four days, making observations and airing, sunning, and repacking their goods. "The Countrey about the mouth of this river is verry fine," Clark wrote about the site of present-day Kansas City. He measured the width of the rivers; the Kansas was 230 yards wide, the Missouri 500. Lewis weighed the water of the two rivers and found the Missouri's to be heavier, meaning it carried more mud. Still, Clark found "the waters of the Kansas is verry disigreeably tasted to me."

On the evening of June 28, the party made ready to push back into the river at dawn. But that night there was a raid on the whiskey supply, serious enough to cause a delay.

Alcohol in any form has always been a curse and a necessity to military leaders. Drunkenness causes more discipline and personnel problems than any other cause, but soldiers must have their alcohol. Frederick the Great put it best: "If you contemplate some enterprise against the enemy, the commissary must scrape together all of the beer and brandy that can be found so that the Army does not lack either, at least during the first few days."[3]

In other words, don't run out of booze until there is no turning back.

Lewis had bought all the whiskey he felt could be carried without making an unacceptable sacrifice somewhere else—for example, in trade goods. The total figure is disputed, but about 120 gallons is generally accepted. The daily ration was one gill. Used at that rate, the whiskey would be gone in 104 days. That could be stretched by watering down the whiskey but it was still obvious that there was not enough to make it to the Pacific and back.[4]

No doubt every man in the party knew exactly how much whiskey was available, and how much of it was his by rights. They knew they would run out; it had happened to them before; they could handle it as long as everyone ran out at the same time and no man got a half-ounce more than his fair share.

Just after midnight, June 28–29, Private John Collins was on guard duty. He tapped a barrel. Just one little sip wouldn't hurt. Just one more. Another. Soon he was drunk. Private Hugh Hall came up; Collins offered him a drink; Hall accepted. Soon they were drunk together. At dawn, the sergeant-of-the-guard put them under arrest, and shortly thereafter Clark began drawing up court-martial papers.

While Clark prepared for the trial, Lewis took advantage of a clear sky and a morning moon. He measured the distance between the sun and the moon's nearest limb forty-eight times between 7:06 and 8:57 a.m. He faithfully recorded whatever he could whenever he could, leaving up to experts back east to work out the meaning of the figures.

At 11:00 a.m., the court convened agreeable to order. Sergeant Pryor presided, Private John Potts acted as judge advocate, and four privates were members.

Sergeant Ordway charged Collins with "getting drunk on his post this morning out of whiskey put under his Charge as a Sentinal and for Suffering *Hugh Hall* to draw whiskey out of the Said Barrel intended for the party."

Collins plead "Not guilty!"

The court deliberated, then concluded, "Guilty," and sentenced Collins to one hundred lashes on his bare back.

Hall was charged with "takeing whiskey out of a Keg this morning which was contrary to all order, rule or regulation."

Having seen what happened to Collins, Hall tried a bit of plea-bargaining: *"Guilty!"*

He was sentenced to receive fifty lashes well laid on.

Lewis and Clark approved the sentence and ordered it carried out at 3:30 p.m. It was, with vigor. Clark noted that "we have always found the men verry ready to punish Such Crimes."

Flogging was cruel, but not unusual. Slaveholders had seen it all their lives. Officers in the army saw it done on a regular basis to their own men. In this case, it fit the need perfectly. It allowed the men to let out their anger in a direct, physical way. It caused Collins and Hall great pain. But the expedition didn't lose their services; both men were at the oars—groaning, but at the oars—that afternoon. After a couple of sleepless nights of tossing and turning, they would be all right. Besides, there was no guardhouse on the boat to lock them up in.[5]

"Deer to be Seen in every direction and their tracks ar as plenty as Hogs about a *farm*," Clark wrote on June 30. Now headed north, the expedition was entering a near-paradise. Clark noted "rasberreis perple, ripe and abundant."

On July 4, the men ushered in the day with a firing of the cannon. Private Joseph Field got bitten by a snake. Captain Lewis treated him with a poultice, probably of Peruvian bark, that drew the poison. At noon, the party pulled ashore at the mouth of a creek of some fifteen yards wide, "coming out of an extensive Prarie" on the left (west) side. As they ate, the captains questioned the voyagers. No, they knew no name for the creek.

The captains thereupon named it, their second experience in bestowing a name.* They called it Independence Creek.

The expedition pulled over for the night at the site of an old Kansas Indian town. "We Camped in the plain," Clark wrote, "one of the most butifull Plains I ever Saw, open & butifully diversified with hills & vallies all presenting themselves to the river covered with grass and a few scattering trees, a handsom Creek meandering thro."

The captains ordered an extra gill distributed. As they sipped their portions, they took in their surroundings and were quite overwhelmed. The country was covered with a sweet and nourishing grass, interspersed

---

* Most of the rivers had French names; the first named by Clark was Cupboard Creek, on June 3, 1804.

with copses of trees "Spreding ther lofty branchs over Pools Springs or Brooks of fine water. Groops of Shrubs covered with the most delicious froot is to be seen in every direction, and nature appears to have exerted herself to butify the Senery by the variety of flours Delicately and highly flavered raised above the Grass, which Strikes and profumes the Sensation, and amuses the mind."

At sunset, the men again fired the cannon. It was the first-ever Fourth of July celebration west of the Mississippi River.

Perhaps the captains grew philosophical under the influence of the whiskey, as happens to earnest young men carrying heavy responsibilities who find themselves in the Garden of Eden as full dark comes on and the campfire burns down on their nation's birthday. Clark's last journal entry that day: "So magnificent a Senerey [here follow several words that Clark later crossed out] in a Contry thus Situated far removed from the Sivilised world to be enjoyed by nothing but the Buffalo Elk Deer & Bear in which it abounds & Savage Indians." Possibly the captains puzzled over why God had created such a place and failed to put Virginians in it, or put it in Virginia.

On July 8, there was an Indian scare—a fire on the east bank. All hands went on alert, but nothing came of it. On the night of July 11–12, Private Alexander Willard went to sleep on his post. Ordway found him and turned him in. The offense was one of the most serious possible—punishable by death, according to the regulations. The captains themselves constituted the court—rather than privates, as in Collins's case.

Ordway charged Willard with "*Lying down and Sleeping on his post whilst a Sentinal.*"

Willard pled, "*Guilty of Ly Down, and not Guilty, of Going to Sleep.*"

The captains conferred. After considering the evidence, they found Willard guilty on both counts. They sentenced him to one hundred lashes, each day for four days, beginning that evening at sunset. One shudders at the thought of Willard's back after the fourth day; one shudders at the thought of what might have happened had a roving band of Sioux come up while Willard was sleeping on guard duty.

On July 21, some six hundred miles and sixty-eight days upstream from Wood River, the expedition reached the mouth of the Platte River. This was a milestone. To go past the mouth of the Platte was the Missouri riverman's equivalent of crossing the equator. It also meant entering a new ecosystem—and Sioux territory. The expedition stopped so the captains could make the usual measurements.

Lewis wrote a five-hundred-word description of the Platte, that fabulous river that makes its way from the Rockies across modern Nebraska to the Missouri, running a mile wide and an inch deep, just bursting with animal and plant life. What most impressed Lewis was the immense quantity of sand the Platte emptied into the Missouri, and the velocity of the current. He measured, as he always did: whereas on the Mississippi below St. Louis a vessel would float at four miles an hour, and on the Missouri from five and a half to seven, depending, on the Platte that vessel would make at least eight miles an hour. Assuming it never ran aground, which it would at every bend or sandbar.

Lewis also made his celestial observations. The next morning, he wrote a thousand-word description of the instruments he was using, how he was using them, what he was measuring, and so forth. It seems Lewis wanted to be as sure as he could that someone someday would take all his figures and make some sense out of them.

On July 30, Clark recorded, "Capt. Lewis and my Self walked in the Prarie on the top of the Bluff and observed the most butifull prospects imagionable, this Prarie is Covered with grass about 10 or 12 Inch high." There were swans in a nearby pond. Great quantities of catfish were caught that evening.

Private Joseph Field killed and brought in to Lewis a badger. Lewis wrote that "this is a singular anamal not common to any part of the United States," and went on with a description of its weight, teeth, eyes, and so on. Then he skinned and stuffed the badger to send back to Jefferson. This was the first time he had put into practice the taxidermic skills Jefferson had taught him. The badger was not new to science: a specimen sent from Canada to Europe in 1778 had been technically described. (The expedition had already discovered and Lewis had described two animals new to science, the Eastern wood rat and the plains horned toad).[6]

So far, 640 miles up the river, the party had not seen an Indian. All the river tribes were out on the prairie, hunting buffalo.

13

ENTERING INDIAN COUNTRY

August 1804

August 1 was Clark's thirty-fourth birthday. To mark the occasion, "I order'd a Saddle of fat Vennison, an Elk fleece & a Bevertail to be cooked and a Desert of Cheries, Plumbs, Raspberries, Currents and grapes of a Supr. quallity." Taking note of the flora and fauna in this wonderland the expedition was entering, Clark noted, "What a field for a Botents [botanist] and a natirless [naturalist]."

No American, not even the professional naturalists such as John James Audubon and Alexander Wilson, had ever seen anything to surpass it.[1] Lewis was fully aware of the magnitude of the discoveries and greatly excited by the opportunity to be the one to note and describe plants and animals new to science. He spent hours examining and describing his finds. On August 5, for example, he killed a bull snake. He measured its length from nose to tail (five feet two inches), its "circumpherence" (four and a half inches), the number of scuta on its belly (221) and tail (53), its color, spots, and other distinctive markings.

That afternoon, he killed two aquatic birds he had previously observed but been unable to obtain. They were least terns. He used a thousand words to describe the specimens, including weight (an ounce and a half), length (seven and a half inches), markings, and so on. He recorded, "The tail has eleven feathers the outer of which are an inch longer than those in the center gradually tapering inwards. . . . the largest or outer feather is 2¾" that of the shortest 1¾". . . . This bird is very noysey when flying which it dose exttreemly swift. . . . It has two notes one like the squaking of a small pig only on reather a high kee, the other kit'-tee',-kit'tee' as near as letters can express the sound."

As the men laboriously moved the keelboat upriver, Lewis, in the cabin, weighed and measured and examined and recorded. He took his responsibilities seriously, but he had a lot of fun doing it, and he had a never-flagging sense of wonder and delight at seeing something new.

On August 8, one of the bowmen called back to Lewis, who was working in the cabin. The captain looked up to see a blanket of white coming down the river. He went to the bow to stare down into the water. The keelboat and the white whatever-it-was came together. On close examination it turned out to be a sea of white feathers, over three miles long and seventy yards wide.

The boat rounded a bend. Ahead was a large sandbar at the foot of a small island. It was entirely covered with white pelicans, preening themselves in their summer molt. To Lewis, the number of birds was "in credible; they apeared to cover several acres of ground." The mosquitoes were so thick that he could not keep them out of his eyes to take an aimed shot, so he fired his rifle at random into the mass and collected a specimen, which he then weighed, measured, and described. He was astonished to find that the pouch could hold five gallons of water.

The white pelican was not new to science. Lewis had not seen one before, but he knew enough about it to call it a "bird of clime" that wintered "on the coast of Floriday and the borders of the Gulph of mexico." That knowledge came from book learning; he had never been to Florida or the Gulf of Mexico.

On August 12, at 5:00 p.m., what Clark called a "Prarie Wolf" appeared on the bank and barked at the passing keelboat. The captains had not previously seen this animal, or read anything about it, so they went ashore to collect a specimen. But, Clark sadly noted, "we could not git him."

The animal was a coyote. Lewis and Clark were the first Americans to see one. The captains set a precedent; millions of Americans who came after have also failed in their attempt to kill the coyote.

On August 18, while waiting for an Indian delegation to approach, Lewis took twelve soldiers to a fishing pond used by the Otoes. The party caught 490 catfish and upward of three hundred fish of nine other species.

Beyond flora and fauna, Lewis studied and described the soil and minerals of the area. He was not so good a mineralogist as a botanist. One mineral experiment almost cost him his life. On August 22, along with some copperas and alum he found a substance that appeared to be arsenic or cobalt. Clark recorded, "Capt. Lewis in proveing the quality of those minerals was near poisoning himself by the fumes & taste" of the unknown substance. Lewis took some of Rush's pills to "work off the effects of the Arsenic."

By August 23, the expedition was almost at the ninety-eighth meridan, the generally agreed-upon eastern border of the Great Plains of North America. The sense of being in a Garden of Eden was strong. There were fat deer and elk and beaver and other species in numbers scarcely conceivable. That afternoon, Lewis sent Private Joseph Field on a hunt. A few hours later, Field came rushing down the bluff to the bank and hollered out to the boat to come ashore. When it did, he breathlessly announced that he had killed a buffalo.

The buffalo was the quintessential animal of the North American continent, the symbol of the Great Plains, more than any other animal save the beaver the magnet that drew men to the West. It was not new to science, but of the men of the expedition only the French voyagers had previously seen one. Lewis immediately detailed twelve men to accompany him to the site of the kill to bring the carcass back to the river. That night, for the first time, the party dined on buffalo hump, buffalo tongue, buffalo steaks. Next to the tail of the beaver, buffalo hump and tongue at once became the meat of choice.

In the Garden of Eden, man had but to reach out for his food. So too on the Great Plains, as Clark's birthday menu demonstrated. But this Garden of Eden was also a potential battlefield populated by numerous Indian tribes containing thousands of warriors. As a result, in addition to being a fabulous field for the botanist and naturalist, the Plains were also a challenging field for the soldier, the peacemaker, the ethnologist, and the businessman.

These tribes were virtually unknown except to a handful of British and French fur traders. There were many stories and rumors about them, most of all the Sioux, but little solid fact.

Jefferson and Lewis had talked at length about these tribes, on the basis of near-complete ignorance. They speculated that the lost tribe of Israel could be out there on the Plains, but it was more likely, in their minds, that the Mandans were a wandering tribe of Welshmen.[2] Because they subscribed to such odd ideas, Jefferson's instructions to Lewis on how to deal with the tribes were, in most particulars, hopelessly naïve and impossible to carry out. For example, Jefferson assumed that, although the Sioux were said to be the fiercest and greatest of the tribes, they were "very desirous of being on the most friendly terms with us." That bit of wishful thinking led to Jefferson's direct order to Lewis. "On that nation," he commanded, referring to the Sioux, "we wish most particulary to make a favorable impression."[3]

In general, Jefferson wanted Lewis to inform the tribes that the new father intended to embrace them into a commercial system that would benefit all involved, and that to make this happen the new father wished them to make peace with one another. Lewis's objectives, as given to him by Jefferson, were to establish American sovereignty, peace, and a trading empire in which the warriors would put down their weapons and take up traps.

Jefferson recognized that the possibility of resistance to this program existed, meaning there was a possibility that the Sioux, or some other, unknown tribe, would attempt to stop the expedition. Jefferson knew too that Lewis was, like other army officers of his day, extremely sensitive to perceived threats or slights, and he had reason to suspect that Lewis inclined more toward rashness than prudence. That was why Jefferson specifically ordered Lewis to avoid a fight if at all possible.

This brought back some realism to the commander-in-chief's orders. Relations with the Indians were important, establishing commercial ties with them was desirable, but the *sine qua non* of the expedition was to get to the Pacific and return with as much information as possible. Put more bluntly, Lewis's first objective was to get through, and whatever he had to sacrifice to do it would be sacrificed. That was why the standard of discipline was so high, why there was a cannon on a swivel on the bow of the keelboat, and blunderbusses on the stern and on the canoes. Jefferson, Lewis, Clark, everyone involved hoped to God that they would not be needed, but all were prepared to use them if necessary.

To avoid fighting and to promote commerce, Lewis had made a major effort to select gifts for the Indians. In Philadelphia in the spring of 1803 and in St. Louis in the winter of 1803–4, he had purchased beads, brass buttons, tomahawks, axes, moccasin awls, scissors, mirrors, and other wonders of the early industrial revolution, along with tobacco, vermilion face paint, and whiskey. On Jefferson's direct orders, he had lugged along two corn grinders, presumably to teach the tribes how to make grits.[4]

Lewis and Clark scholar James Ronda puts perspective on the Indian policy of the expedition: "These items, everything from ivory combs to calico shirts, represented what the United States offered to potential trading partners. As Jefferson repeated to every delegation of western

Indians, Americans sought commerce, not land. Lewis and Clark were on the road to show American wares. The expedition was the mercantile and hardware display case for a trade empire on the move. Moccasin awls and brass kettles were as much symbols of American power as the medals and flags destined for headmen and warriors. . . . Lewis and Clark, surrounded by bright mirrors and yards of red flannel, offered more than goods. They proposed membership in a system with well-established posts and dependable delivery schedules."[5]

The most desired items of all were rifles, balls, and powder. Most of the Indian-held guns on the Plains were cheap British shotguns. Lewis wanted to show the overall excellence of the American arms industry, but because of the bulk he could not carry along free samples. He could demonstrate what his men could do with a Kentucky long rifle, but he could only promise, not deliver, similar weapons for the Indians.

The presents, trade goods, certificates, medals, and the rest were packed into twenty-one bags, each containing a variety of items and each marked for one of the various tribes Lewis expected to encounter before going into winter camp. They began with the Poncas and Omahas, tribes of the lower Missouri, and went on to the Mandans. Five bales were stuffed with goods for the tribes beyond the Mandans.

Thus armed with his orders, guns, and goods, Lewis set out to meet the Indians of the Great Plains.

All the tribes of the lower Missouri had been out hunting buffalo as the expedition made its way west and north. It did not encounter a single Indian from St. Charles to past the Platte River. Then, at sunset on August 2, a party of Otos and a few Missouris arrived at camp, accompanied by a French trader and translator. After an exchange of greetings, the captains gave the Indians some tobacco, twisted together into what was called a carrot after its shape, and some pork, flour, and meal. "In return," Clark noted, "they Sent us Water millions [watermelons]."

The Indians said their band of combined Otoes and Missouris numbered 250. They were a farming as well as a hunting people, with semipermanent towns. The captains invited them to a council the next day, at their campsite, which they called Council Bluff (across and downriver from present Council Bluffs, Iowa). Clark recorded that he and Lewis also "put every man on his Guard & ready for any thing." The night was a restless one, marked by tension and anticipation instead of sleep.

In the morning, the expedition had its first meeting with Indians. Going into it, as James Ronda points out, the captains had expectations and actions that were deeply rooted in the history of white-red relations in North America, directly linked to generations of forest diplomats. They were preparing for exactly the kind of ritual Clark had seen at the council negotiating the Treaty of Greenville with General Anthony Wayne in 1795.[6]

On Friday morning, August 3, 1804, fog hung over the river. As he waited for it to lift and the Indians to come to the council, Lewis wrote out a long speech he intended to make. Clark supervised the preparation of the gifts. The voyagers opened bale number thirty and took out red leggings, fancy dress coats, and blue blankets, along with flags and medals. The sergeants put their squads through a close-order drill, then had some of the men use the mainsail to erect an awning to shield the diplomats from the August sun, while others put in place a flagstaff and ran the Stars and Stripes up it.

By 9:00 a.m., the sun had burned off the fog. An hour later, the Indian delegation arrived. The main chief of the Otos, Little Thief, was away hunting, but six or seven lesser chiefs were present. They joined the captains under the awning. Clark and Lewis were in full-dress uniform, complete with cocked hats. The sergeants put the men through a dress parade and passed in review. This must have been the first time the Otos had seen men march in step, turn as if one, shoulder arms in unison, fire a volley on command, and all the rest that goes into a well-run drill. But how the review impressed the Indians, no member of the expedition thought to record.

Lewis then stood to deliver his speech. It was some twenty-five hundred words, so it took him at least half an hour to deliver it, and the translator at least as long to put it into the Oto language. How accurately it was being translated, Lewis of course had no way to judge. Nor could he tell how much of what he was saying the Indians could understand, or how much of what they understood they accepted.

Lewis opened by advising the warriors to be wise and look to the true interests of their people. "Children," he continued, as Clark recorded his speech, "we have been sent by the great Chief of the Seventeen great nations of America to inform you . . . that a great council was lately held between this great chief and your old fathers the French and Spaniards." There it was decided that the Missouri River country now belonged to the United States, so that all those who lived in that country, whether white or red, "are bound to obey the commands of their great Chief the President who is now your only great father."

In a long, convoluted paragraph, Lewis told the Otos that the French and Spanish were gone "beyond the great lake towards the rising Sun, from whence they never intend returning to visit their former red children."

"Children," Lewis went on, the president was now "your only father; he is the only friend to whom you can now look for protection, or from whom you can ask favours, or receive good counciles, and he will take care to serve you, & not deceive you."

After giving out the good news about this wonderful new father the Otos had suddenly acquired, Lewis tried to explain the purposes of the expedition. No easy task, since the only white men the Plains Indians had ever seen were traders, whose purpose was obviously to do business. The expedition had more goods than any trader any Indian of the Plains had ever seen—yet the captains did not wish to trade. What on earth were they going to do with all those goods? The Indians had to wonder.

"Children," Lewis explained, the great chief "has sent us out to clear the road, remove every obstruction, and to make it the road of peace between himself and his red children residing there, to enquire into the Nature of their wants." When the expedition returned home, Lewis would tell the president what the Otos wanted, and the president would see that those wants were satisfied.

Lewis and Clark were advance men and traveling salesmen, in short, representing American business and the American people, whose numbers and skills were all but unlimited. In the seventeen great nations of America, Lewis declared, "cities are as numerous as the stars of the heavens."

What the Americans were doing, Lewis went on, was untainted by any base or self-serving motive. The great chief "has commanded us his war chiefs to undertake this long journey, which we have so far accomplished with great labour and much expence, in order to council with yourselves and his other red-children on the troubled waters, to give you his good advice; to point out to you the road in which you must walk to obtain happiness."

As a good father, the president told his children how to behave. They should not block or obstruct in any way the passage of any boat carrying white men, ever. They should make peace with all their neighbors.

Now came the threats. Lewis told the Otos that they must avoid the council of bad men "lest by one false step you should bring upon your nation the displeasure of your great father, who could consume you as the fire consumes the grass of the plains." The Great Father, "if you displease him," would stop all traders from coming up the river.

Do as we say, in other words, or no white man will come to you again, ever. That was an extreme threat, strange as it sounds to modern ears. Without contact with European trade goods, the Otos would suffer a severe setback in their living conditions and would be seriously vulnerable to their neighbors who had access to guns and powder.

But if the Otos did as Lewis advised them, he would see that a trading post was set up at the mouth of the Platte, where they could bring their furs to trade for "a store of goods in such quantities as will be equal to your necessities." Meanwhile, their old traders, whether French or British, could stay among them as long as they acknowledged the supremacy of the United States and gave good council. In short, after all that talk, Lewis told the Otos that nothing would be changing in the next year or two.

Next came an even bigger embarrassment. Because the expedition had such a long journey ahead of it, and therefore had to carry so many provisions, there were very few presents for the Otos.[7]

That was a flat ending. How Lewis's first oratorical experience went over with his audience cannot be said, although Private Gass recorded in his journal that the announcement about a new father was "well received."[8] Clark claimed, "Those people express great Satisfaction at the Speech Delivered," but he also noted that Lewis's speech consisted primarily of "Some advice to them and Directions how They were to Conduct themselves," words that would have served well as the title for the speech.

When Lewis concluded, the captains distributed presents. They weren't much. Each chief received a breech clout, a bit of paint, and a small medal with the new father's likeness on it or a comb.

The Oto chiefs spoke next. According to Sergeant Ordway, they were "very sensible," but Clark was unimpressed. In his opinion, "They are no Oreters." Still, they managed to make their point. The Oto chiefs acknowledged that they had heard what Lewis said, promised to follow his good advice, said they were happy that their new father could be depended on, and concluded by requesting some powder and whiskey.

Lewis was eager to please, because he wanted Little Thief and some other chiefs to go to Washington in the spring to meet the new father, so he met the request, providing a canister of powder, fifty balls, and a bottle of whiskey. He also shot off his air gun, to the astonishment of the Indians. He ended the council by giving the copy of his speech to one of the chiefs, to take back to Little Thief, along with a request that Little Thief come to the river to council.

The Indians departed, the expedition proceeded on. At camp that night, on a sandy point on the larboard side, the mosquitoes were excessively troublesome. Private Moses B. Reed told the captains that he had left his knife back at the council site. They gave him permission to go retrieve it—a simple act that illustrated how valuable knives were on the frontier.

Three days later, Reed had not returned. The captains talked it over and concluded that he had deserted. They selected a four-man detail, headed by Drouillard, to seek, find, and bring back "the Deserter reid with order if he did not give up Peaceibly to put him to Death, &c."

The orders were clear and logical, and met the situation perfectly. By making the orders a matter of record, the captains absolved Drouillard and the others in the event they had to kill Reed, and took the responsibility for his death onto themselves. The orders also highlighted the fact that the expedition was in a potential war zone and every rifle and paddle was needed.

The captains also instructed Drouillard to attempt to find Little Thief and bring him to camp on the river.

Drouillard was gone ten days. The captains moved upstream. By August 17, they were near present-day Sioux City, Iowa. Toward dusk, Private Francis Labiche, one of Drouillard's party, came into the camp. He reported success: Drouillard was bringing in Reed and also a delegation of chiefs from the Otos, including Little Thief. They would arrive in the morning.

When Drouillard came up at about 10:00 a.m. on August 18, the captains gave the Otos something to eat, then turned to the business immediately at hand, the trial of Private Reed.

The court-martial was formed; the charges were read. Reed confessed that he had deserted and stolen a public rifle, shot pouch, powder, and balls. He requested that the captains be as lenient with him as their oaths would allow. His manly behavior seemed to soften the captains; at least they didn't have him shot. Clark recorded that "we only Sentenced him to run the Gantlet four times through the Party & that each man with 9 Swichies Should punish him." That amounted to about five hundred lashes, well laid on. In addition, Reed was discharged from the permanent party. He had to give up his rifle and the privilege of standing guard. He would work with and be treated as if he were one of the voyagers, and would be sent back to St. Louis in the spring.

When these results were explained to Little Thief, he and the others "petitioned for Pardin for this man." Clark and Lewis explained to the chiefs the necessity for the beating. They must have been persuasive, for Clark recorded that the chiefs "were all Satisfied with the propriety of the Sentence & was witness to the punishment."

That evening, after eating, the expedition managed to rid itself of the bad taste from the day's principal event. It was Captain Lewis's thirtieth birthday. To celebrate, an extra dram of whiskey per man went round, and the fiddle came out, and the men danced about the campfire till nearly midnight.

In the morning, breakfast. Clark was astonished when one of the chiefs, Big Horse, showed up naked, to emphasize his poverty. After they had eaten, the awning went up and a council was held. Apparently Lewis read his speech, from the copy already held by Little Thief. The chief then asked the captains to act as honest brokers and negotiate a peace between the Otos and the Omahas. Lewis explained that, since the Omahas were out hunting and the expedition must press on, it would be impossible for him to arrange a peace.

Then the chiefs spoke. Big Horse pointed out the obvious, that he had come to the camp naked, and expressed his fear that he would return home naked. Peace was all very well, he said, but if there were peace where would the young men go to get their goods? If the captains wanted the Otos at peace, Big Horse pointed out, he could arrange it as long as he had something to give to his young men at home. Whiskey would be the most effective peacemaker.

The captains were not going to give Big Horse or any other Indian a barrel of whiskey. They did hand out tobacco, paint, and beads. These gifts made little impression on the chiefs or their warriors. The captains then tried handing around printed certificates proclaiming the bearer to be a "friend and ally" of the United States. These trifles did not answer either; one disgusted warrior disdainfully handed back his certificate. The captains, angered by this disrespect toward an official document, rebuked the man "very roughly."

There were bad feelings all around. To dissipate them and to impress the Indians with their powers, the captains gave the chiefs and warriors a dram of whiskey each and brought out their magic show, including the air gun, a magnifying glass that could concentrate the sun's rays to start a fire in a bit of dry grass, the telescope, and other items.

But the Otos had not come to be awed; they had come for goods. They had imagined wonderful giveaways of valuable items from the apparently endless supply on the keelboat, and what they got was some tobacco and a piece of paper. They went away unhappy. Still, Little Thief indicated that he would go to Washington in the spring, so Lewis's and Clark's first venture as frontier diplomats had some success.

The Otos were a tribe that had once been mighty but were now greatly reduced by the smallpox. Woefully inferior to the Sioux, in morale as well as numbers, they were not the Indians to try to use force to make the captains hand out the goods. With the Sioux, just upriver, things might well be different.

Sergeant Charles Floyd had been desperately ill the past few days. Lewis had diagnosed his disease as "Biliose Chorlick," or bilious colic, and had nothing effective to treat it with—but, then, neither did Dr. Rush back in Philadelphia.[9] On August 20, Floyd died, most likely from peritonitis resulting from an infected appendix that had perforated or ruptured.

Sergeant Floyd was the first U.S. soldier to die west of the Mississippi. The expedition carried his body to a high round hill overlooking an unnamed river. The captains had him buried with all the honors of war and fixed a red-cedar post over the grave with his name and title and the date. Captain Lewis read the funeral service over him. Clark provided a fitting epitaph in his journal: "This Man at all times gave us proofs of his firmness and Deturmined resolution to doe Service to his Countrey and honor to himself." The captains concluded the proceedings by naming the river Floyds River and the bluff Sergeant Floyds Bluff.

Two days and forty-one miles later, the captains ordered an election for Floyd's replacement. Private Patrick Gass got nineteen votes, while Privates William Bratton and George Gibson split the remainder. This was the first election ever held west of the Mississippi.

On August 26, Lewis issued general orders appointing Patrick Gass to the rank of "Sergeant in *the corps of volunteers for North Western Discovery*," the first time he used such a phrase. He praised Gass for his previous faithful service and concluded, "The commanding officers are still further confirmed in the high opinion they had previously formed of the capacity, deligence and integrety of Sergt. Gass, from the wish expressed by a large majority of his comrades for his appointment as Sergeant."

That same day, Private George Shannon, youngest member of the party, failed to come up after a day of hunting. Nor did he report in the next day, or the day after. The captains grew concerned, not about desertion—evidently Shannon gave them no uneasiness on that score—but about possible Indian trouble, or a hunting accident. They sent Private John Colter out looking for Shannon, but he had no luck. They sent Drouillard to look, but, after searching through the night of August 26–27, he too reported failure.

Reed dismissed in disgrace. Sergeant Floyd dead. Shannon missing. The expedition was almost 10 percent reduced in fighting strength as it moved toward the heart of Sioux territory.

*

But hope rather than fear was the main emotion felt by the captains as they entered Sioux country. This was the one tribe singled out for specific mention by Jefferson in his orders. It controlled the river, and had turned back previous traders coming up from St. Louis, and it was the largest of the tribes. Lewis hoped to make the Sioux the centerpiece of the vast American trading empire he was trying to establish, and he thought this was such a good deal for the Sioux that they couldn't say no.

On August 27, as the keelboat approached today's Yankton, South Dakota, old Dorion informed the captains that they were now in the territory of the Yankton Sioux, with whom he had lived for many years. Lewis ordered the prairie set afire as a signal to the Yanktons, inviting them to a council. A few hours later, as the boat passed the mouth of the James River, a teenage Yankton boy swam out to one of the pirogues. He gestured that he wished to talk.

The expedition put ashore. Two more teenagers appeared. Through Mr. Dorion, they said a large band of Yanktons were camped nearby. The captains delegated Sergeant Pryor, a voyager, and Mr. Dorion to go to the camp and invite the chiefs to come to council at Calumet Bluffs, near present Gavins Point Dam, on the Nebraska side.

On August 29, the expedition was in camp at Calumet Bluffs. As they waited for the Yanktons to come to council, they worked. Tracks along the riverbank had led Lewis to conclude that Shannon was ahead of them but thinking himself behind—so Shannon was pressing on to catch up to the expedition that was behind him. Lewis detailed a soldier to go look for Shannon. Reflecting his worry, Lewis told the private to take along some extra rations for Shannon, who might well be starving. He was not considered to be one of the expedition's better hunters.

Captain Clark put some men to work making a tow rope of elk skin, then sat at his field desk, dipped his quill into the inkstand, and began to write some remarks for the Yanktons. At 4:00 p.m., Mr. Dorion showed up on the opposite bank, at the head of a party of some seventy Yankton warriors. The Indians went into camp, while Dorion and Sergeant Pryor crossed over on a canoe sent by the captains.

Pryor reported that the Yanktons were extremely friendly, had even tried to carry him into their camp on a painted buffalo robe, thinking he was the leader of the expedition. He said the camp "was handsum made of Buffalow Skins Painted different Colour, all compact & handSomly arranged, their Camps formed of a Conic form Containing about 12 or 15 persons each and 40 in number."

Sergeant Pryor had just become the first American to describe the classic Plains tepee.

The Yanktons had cooked a fat dog for a feast; Pryor "thought it good & well flavored." They had provided him with a "Snug aptmt for to lodge." The Plains through which he had marched, Pryor said, were "covered with game."

The captains had presents packed into one of the canoes to send over to the Yanktons. They put in tobacco, corn, and some iron kettles and told Pryor and Dorion to ask the Indians to cross over in the morning for a council.

At 10:00 a.m., the captains sent a canoe to bring over the Indians. They had signified the importance of this first meeting with one of the Sioux bands by putting on their dress uniforms and putting up a flagstaff, near a large oak, running up the flag, and firing the bow swivel gun.

The Yanktons had a sense of drama too. They were in full regalia. As they came up from the riverbank, the chiefs were preceded by four musicians, singing and playing as they made their way to the flagstaff. The soldiers made ritual payments of tobacco to the musicians; the conferees shook hands and sat down.

With Dorion interpreting, Lewis gave his basic Indian speech. When he finished, the chiefs said they would respond in the morning—obviously they would need time to confer on this business of accepting a new father and becoming part of a new trade system. Lewis recognized that patience was not just a virtue in dealing with Indians, it was a necessity, and handed out medals to five chiefs. He pronounced a chief named Weuche the first chief—by what authority, on what basis, cannot be said—and gave him a red-laced military coat, a military cocked hat, and an American flag.

Lewis did all this with the utmost seriousness. It never occurred to him that his actions might be characterized as patronizing, dictatorial, ridiculous, and highly dangerous. From what he knew from old Dorion, these Yanktons were peaceable, at least compared with their neighbors and relatives, the Teton Sioux, farther upriver. But his idea of how to make them into allies was to give them worthless medals and wardrobe trappings rather than the guns and powder they needed. And to make one chief the big chief was to meddle in intertribal politics about which he knew nothing. In general, it would be impossible to say which side was more ignorant of the other.

The desire for friendship overrode ignorance. The men of the expedition had come to the Northern Plains as outsiders, but as James Ronda writes, "that night the explorers became part of a prairie community."[10] After the council, Indian boys showed off their skill with bows and arrows, to the delight of the soldiers, who handed out prizes of beads. At dusk, three fires were built in the center of camp. Indians in gaudy paint came leaping into the firelight, to sing of their great feats in battle and in the chase. They danced to music coming from deer-hoof rattles and a drum.

Sergeant Ordway recorded that the warriors began "with a houp and hollow and ended with the same." An individual would sing "of what he had done in his day and what warlike actions he had done. This they call merit. They would confess how many horses they had Stole." At Dorion's suggestion, the soldiers threw the dancers gifts of tobacco, knives, and bells.

Captain Clark was impressed. "The Souix," he wrote, "is a Stout bold looking people (the young men hand Som) & well made. The Warriors are Verry much deckerated with Pain Porcupin quils & feathers, large leagins & mockersons, all with buffalow roabs of Different Colours. The Squars wore Peticoats & and a white Buffalow roabes with the black hair turned back over their necks & Sholders."

That was the first American description of the ceremonial dress of the Plains Indians. The captains were doing pathbreaking ethnology. Clark wrote, "I will here remark a Society which I had never before this day heard was in any nation of Indains." It was a group of Indian warriors who had taken a vow "never to give back let the danger be what it may." That refusal to retreat had cost the society dreadfully; in the past year, eighteen of the twenty-two members had been killed. Clark was impressed by the survivors: "They stay by them Selves, fond of mirth and assume a degree of Superiority—Stout likely fellows."

Ethnology, however, was very much secondary to establishing the American system along the Missouri. What the Indians looked like was entertaining; what the chiefs said about Lewis's proposals was critical. In the morning, the chiefs gave their reply.

Weuche spoke first. His refrain was, "We are pore and have no powder and ball, our Women has got no cloathes." But if Mr. Dorion were with him, he would go to Washington in the spring—welcome news.

The other chiefs then spoke. They suffered from stage fright. "I am young and Cant Speek," Struck by the Pana confessed. "I am a young man and inexperienced, cannot say much," White Crane Man explained. But they all managed to make it clear that what they wanted was powder and ball, and perhaps some whiskey.

Clark and Lewis could not meet those needs. They could do one thing all the chiefs wanted: leave Mr. Dorion with them for the winter.

He could arrange peace with other tribes and organize an expedition of chiefs to go to Washington in the spring. The captains gave each chief a carrot of tobacco and Mr. Dorion a bottle of whiskey, and had the Indians ferried across the river to their camp on the other side. Thus the first encounter with a band of Sioux ended on a hopeful note, despite Yankton disappointment with the presents received.

The last chief to speak, Arcawechar, had also apologized: "I do not Speak verry well, I am a pore man." But if he did not speak well, he spoke with the voice of a prophet. It was all very well for the Yanktons to open their ears, he said, "and I think our old Friend Mr. Durion can open the ears of the other bands of Soux. But I fear those nations above will not open their ears, and you cannot I fear open them."

Arcawechar spoke not only prophetically but bluntly. He said the captains had given the Indians five medals. "I wish you to give five kegs of powder with them."

The captains did not, could not comply. As Arcawechar had warned them, where they were going they would need all their powder.

14

ENCOUNTER WITH THE SIOUX

September 1804

In the first two of weeks of September, the expedition gradually entered the country where the short-grass prairie of the drier High Plains predominated. The wildlife became even more abundant than below. There were herds of elk in every copse of woods along the riverbank. Deer were as plentiful as birds. Buffalo became a common sight. The men pointed out a "goat" which no one could identify but no one could catch either. Captain Clark pronounced the plums the "most delisious" he had ever tasted, the grapes "plenty and finely flavored."

On the 3rd, the captains sent Colter to chase Shannon again. Two days later, tracks along the riverbank indicated that Colter was still trying to catch up and that Shannon had lost one of the two horses he had with him. Private John Shields came in from a hunt to report another wonder, a deer with a black tail. Lewis saw more wild goats on a hill, but they ran off before he could even describe their color. The hunters brought in three bucks and two elk.

Moving the keelboat and pirogues upriver required a tremendous effort from each man; consequently, they ate prodigiously. In comparison with beef, the venison and elk were lean, even at this season. Each soldier consumed up to nine pounds of meat per day, along with whatever fruit the area afforded and some cornmeal, and still felt hungry.

On September 7, in present Boyd County, Nebraska, the captains took a stroll. To their astonishment, they found themselves in the middle of an extensive village of small mammals that lived in tunnels in the ground. Here, there, everywhere around them, the little mammals would pop up, sit up on their hind legs, and chatter.

The captains brought some men to the site and tried to dig to the bottom of one of the tunnels, but after digging six feet and running a pole down the rest they discovered they were not halfway to the animal's bed. They had five barrels of water fetched to the site and poured into a tunnel, which forced one animal out. He was killed and brought back to the keelboat so that a proper description could be written.

The voyagers informed the captains that these animals were "Petite Chien," or prairie dogs. The animal was new to science; the captains gave the prairie dog his first formal description.

On September 8, Clark went ashore to look for goats, with no success. Lewis went hunting, and on that day killed his first buffalo. All together, the hunters brought in that evening two buffalo, one large elk, one elk fawn, three deer, three wild turkeys, and a squirrel.

The following day, Lewis again went hunting, this time with Private Reubin Field along, and shot another buffalo. Field got one too, as did Clark. Drouillard killed three deer. York killed a buffalo, at the invitation of his master. The captains were amazed to see five hundred buffalo in one herd, grazing near the river.

On September 11, as the keelboat moved past a bend in the river, the bowman spotted Shannon sitting by the bank. The keelboat came to and Shannon came aboard. He was extremely weak—indeed, nearly starved to death. As his comrades gave him jerked meat, he related his story.

He had been sure the boat was ahead, so he had been chasing it for sixteen days. For the past twelve days, he had been without bullets. During that time, he had managed to kill one rabbit by shooting a long, hard, straight stick in place of a bullet. Otherwise, he had lived for nearly two weeks on grapes and plums. He had finally concluded that he was too weak ever to catch up with the keelboat and had decided to sit by the riverbank and hope for a trading boat coming down from the Mandan villages headed toward St. Louis. He had saved his horse as his last resort. Clark was astounded that "a man had like to have Starved to death in a land of Plenty for the want of Bulletes or Something to kill his meat."

On the 14th, Clark killed a goat. Lewis weighed, measured, and described it—the first scientific description of the pronghorn, or antelope, as it is usually but wrongly called. That afternoon, Private Shields brought in *"a hare of the prarie,"* giving Lewis a second opportunity in a single day to measure and describe a new species—in this case, the white-tailed jackrabbit. Intrigued by the animal, Lewis went looking for the jackrabbit in its native habitat a couple of days later. He found one, chased it, and made notes: "It resorts to the open plains, is extreemly fleet and never burrows or takes shelter in the ground when pursued. I measured the leaps of one which I surprised in the plains and found them 21 feet. They apear to run with more ease and to bound with greater agility than any anamal I ever saw."

That is one of three Lewis documents written between September 14 and 17, 1804. They constitute almost all of his known writings for a full year. This adds to the mystery of the lost (or never written?) journals of Meriwether Lewis. The passage quoted above comes from Lewis's field notes, which exist but in an obviously incomplete form. All his celestial measurements, hundreds and hundreds of them, are preserved. But there are only two journal entries, one on the 16th and the next on the 17th of September, 1804. The way they are written indicates that he almost had to have been writing regularly. There is no introduction, no "Sorry I've been away, here is what has happened since last I wrote" quality whatsoever to the entries. He picks up, apparently, at where he left off the previous evening and gives every sense at the conclusion of his second entry that more will follow in the morning. But until new journal entries are discovered, their existence remains speculative.

Writing as a biographer rather than an archivist or a historian—that is, on the basis of the internal evidence of the September entries—I am convinced that there once existed—and still may—an important body of Lewis journal entries. The pain of the loss is doubled by the quality of what Lewis wrote that September. He walks you through his day and lets you see through his eyes; what he saw no American had ever seen before and only a few would see in the future.

"This morning set out at an early hour," Lewis opened the entry for Sunday, September 16. "Come too at 1½ after 7 A.M. on the Lard. Shore 1¼ miles above the mouth of a small creek which we named *Corvus*, in consequence of having kiled a beautiful bird of that genus near it."*
The captains decided to lie by for two days, to dry the baggage and to lighten the keelboat by transferring a part of her load to one of the pirogues. "While some of the men were imployed in this necessary

---

* One of the few times Lewis used Latin. The bird was the black-billed magpie. In a later field note, he described it in a thousand-word entry.

labour," Lewis wrote, "others were dressing skins washing and mending their cloathes &c. Capt. Clark and myself killed each a buck immediately on landing, the deer were very gentle and in great numbers."

After a detailed description of the trees in the river bottom, he regretted that clouds during the day and night "prevented my making any observations." He reported on what had been related to him by scouts who had gone up Corvus Creek to have a look around. "Vast herds of Buffaloe deer Elk and Antilopes were seen feeding in every direction as far as the eye of the observer could reach."

Lewis went to see for himself. "Having for many days past confined myself to the boat," he opened his September 17 entry, "I determined to devote this day to amuse myself on shore with my gun and view the interior of the country." He set out before sunrise, accompanied by six hunters. They encountered a grove of plums. Lewis described the trees, then wrote, "This forrest of plumb trees garnish a plain about 20 feet lelivated." The whole of the plain—nearly three miles by three miles— was

intirely occupyed by the burrows of the *barking squril* [prairie dog]. This anamal appears here in infinite numbers. The shortness of the grass gave the plain the appearance throughout it's whole extent of beatifull bowlinggress in fine order.

This senery already rich pleasing and beatiful, was still farther hightened by immence herds of Buffaloe deer Elk an antelopes which we saw in every direction feeding on the hills and plains. I do not think I exagerate when I estimated the number of Buffaloe which could be comprehended at one view to amount to 3000."

At 8:00 a.m., Lewis and his companions "rested our selves about half an hour, and regailed ourselves on half a bisquit each and some jirk of Elk." Then they set off to kill a pronghorn. Lewis found the pronghorns to be "extreemly shye and watchfull insomuch that we had been unable to get a shot at them. . . . I had this day an opportunity of witnessing the agility and superior fleetness of this anamal which was to me really astonishing. I pursued a small herd of seven. . . . bad as the chance to approach them was, I made the best of my way towards them, frequently peeping over the ridge with which I took care to conceal myself from their view. . . . I got within about 200 paces of them when they smelt me and fled; I gained the top of the eminece as soon as possible from whence I had an extensive view of the counry.

The antilopes had disappeared in a steep revene now appeared at the distance of about three miles."

Lewis was struck by "the rapidity of their flight. . . . It appeared reather the rappid flight of birds than the motion of quadrupeds. I think I can safely venture the asscertion that the speed of this anamal is equal if not superior to that of the finest blooded courser."*

And with that, the entry suddenly breaks off. There is no ending describing the campfire that night, with the men talking of the strange and wonderful things they had seen. Either Lewis put down his quill, not to take it up again until April 1805—or what he wrote is lost.

Over the next week, in the southerly winds of early fall, the expedition sped ahead, making twenty-three, then twenty-five, then thirty-three miles in one day. The captains finally shot a coyote and added a mule deer to their list. On Sunday, September 23, they made twenty miles and camped on the starboard side in a cottonwood grove. As some men set up tents, others gathered firewood, and the cooks got their kettles ready, three teenage Teton Sioux swam across. With Drouillard exchanging messages with them via the sign language, they said there was a band of eighty lodges camped at the mouth of the next river, and a second band of sixty lodges a short distance above the first. The captains gave the boys two carrots of tobacco and told them to inform their chiefs that the expedition would come up tomorrow for a council.

The expedition proceeded in the morning past a two-mile-long island where Colter, with the last horse belonging to the expedition, had camped for the night and killed four elk. He had hung them on trees along the shore. Lewis sent a pirogue to pick up the meat. As it was being loaded, Colter ran up the bank to shout that Indians had stolen his horse. Soon after, the captains saw five Indians on the bank. They anchored the keelboat and "Spoke to them," either through signs flashed by Drouillard or by using "the old frenchman," Pierre Cruzatte, who could speak a bit of Sioux, as interpreter.

The captains were stern. They said they came as friends, but were ready to fight if need be, and warned that "they were not afraid of any Indians." They told a little lie, saying that the stolen horse had been

---

* Lewis was right, according to Joe Van Wormer in *The World of the Pronghorn*, p. 101: "It is generally conceded that the pronghorn is the fastest mammal in North America and second only to the cheetah in the world." Pronghorns can reach a speed of sixty miles per hour over a short distance; they can maintain fifty miles per hour for five miles; their cruising speed for long-distance running is between thirty and forty miles per hour.

sent by the new father of the red children as a present for the chief of the Tetons. They said they would not speak to any Tetons until the horse was returned.

The expedition arrived at the mouth of the next river, at the site of present Pierre, South Dakota,* late in the afternoon. As a defensive precaution, the party anchored the keelboat off the mouth of the river. The captains put the party on full alert, with one-third ashore on guard, the other two-thirds camping on board the boat and pirogues.

In the morning, the captains raised the flagstaff, set up the awning, and prepared for a council, taking the precaution to leave a majority of the party on board, with the keelboat anchored seventy yards off shore so that its swivel gun commanded the site. At 11:00 a.m., three chiefs and many warriors came in, bearing large quantities of buffalo meat as a gift. The captains offered some pork. Then it was time to talk.

To their dismay, the captains quickly discovered that Cruzatte could not speak the language beyond some simple words. Nor could Drouillard convey via the sign language the relatively complex thoughts and proposals Lewis was making in his basic Indian speech. Recognizing the difficulty, Lewis cut the speech short and began putting on the traveling medicine show. It started with a close-order drill by uniformed troops marching under the colors of the republic. Then came the air gun, magnifying glass, and the rest. Finally, Lewis handed out medals and gifts to the chiefs. He designated Black Buffalo as the leading chief present and gave him a medal, a red military coat, and a cocked hat. The other two chiefs, named the Partisan and Buffalo Medicine, got medals. As far as the captains were concerned, they had completed their part.

That's all? the Tetons demanded, unbelieving. Some worthless medals and a silly hat?

Sensing the discontent, especially from Black Buffalo's rivals the Partisan and Buffalo Medicine, the captains invited the chiefs on board the keelboat, where they gave each a quarter-glass of whiskey. The chiefs were "exceedingly fond of it, they took up an empty bottle, Smelted it, and made maney Simple jestures and Soon began to be troublesom."

Clark detailed a party of seven men to help him put the chiefs ashore. The chiefs resisted and had to be forced into the canoe. When it landed, three warriors seized the bowline while another hugged the

---

* Although the captains named it the Teton River, in honor of the tribe, on today's maps it appears as the Bad River.

mast. The Partisan "pretended drunkeness & staggered up against us, Declaring I should not go on, Stateing he had not recved presents Suffient from us." His insults became personal. He demanded a canoe load of presents before he would allow the expedition to go on.

Clark would take no more. He drew his sword and ordered all hands under arms. On the keelboat, Lewis ordered the men to prepare for action. The swivel gun was loaded with sixteen musket balls; the blunderbusses were loaded with buckshot; the men threw up the lockers as breastworks, loaded their rifles, and prepared to fire.

Up the bank, twenty yards from Clark and the pirogue, some warriors saw Lewis preparing the swivel gun and began to back away, but others strung their bows and took out their arrows from their quivers, or began to cock their shotguns.

It was a dramatic moment. Had Lewis cried "Fire!" and touched his lighted taper to the fuse of the swivel gun, the whole history of North America might have changed. Here is one possible scenario:

The cannon roared, spitting out sixteen musket balls. The blunderbusses roared, spitting out buckshot. The muskets roared, spitting out aimed lead bullets. Sioux warriors were mowed down in the dozens.

But there were still hundreds of warriors on the bank, and even as the smoke lifted they filled the air with arrows, and kept them coming, for they could reload and fire at a much faster pace than the American soldiers. Lewis and Clark, prime targets, went down. With the captains incapacitated or dead, Sergeant Ordway rallied the survivors, got into the keelboat, pushed off and retreated downriver.

In short, had that cannon fired, there might have been no Lewis and Clark Expedition. The exploration of the Missouri River country and Oregon would have had to be done by others, at a later time.

Meanwhile, the Sioux would have been implacable enemies of the Americans, and in possession of the biggest arsenal on the Great Plains. For some time to come, they would have had the numbers and the weapons to turn back any expedition the United States could send up the Missouri. They would have increased their trade with the British North West Company coming out of Canada. In the War of 1812, they would have been British allies, perhaps strong enough to wrest Upper Louisiana away from the Americans and make it part of Canada. Improbable, certainly. Impossible, almost certainly. Still . . .

Aside from the possible long-range consequences, the confrontation on the riverbank was threatening to make it impossible for Lewis to carry out his orders with regard to the Sioux: to make a good impression on them and make them into friends of the United States. This was the moment Jefferson had had in mind when he told Lewis in his formal orders to exercise caution.

If Lewis recalled that order, he ignored it. He refused to back down, and continued to hold the lighted taper over the swivel gun. Nor would Clark decline combat. He kept his sword out of its scabbard. Their blood was up. They were Virginia gentlemen who had been challenged. They were ready to fight.

So the white leaders pushed the moment to its crisis. Luckily for them, one of the red leaders stepped forward to avert hostilities. Black Buffalo seized the towline from the three warriors and motioned to the warrior hugging the mast to go ashore.

As they did so, the Partisan, sulking, joined his warriors on the bank, twenty yards off. The Indians kept their bows strung. Lewis remained at full alert, ready to fire. Disaster had been avoided, but the crisis continued.

Clark turned on the Indians. "I felt my Self warm & Spoke in verry positive terms," he wrote in his journal. He made dire threats. He said he had "more medicine on board his boat than would kill twenty such nations in one day." He told Black Buffalo that the expedition "must and would go on." He said his men "were not squaws but warriors."[1]

How much of the threat the Indians understood from Drouillard's sign language and Cruzatte's simple words cannot be known—but surely Clark's body language spoke plainly enough.

While he was haranguing the Indians, the crew took the pirogue back to the keelboat, where a dozen soldiers jumped in. When the reinforcements got to the bank, some warriors backed off. Then the three chiefs went into conference. Clark awaited the outcome, justifying his actions to himself: "Their treatment to me was verry rough," he wrote, "and I think justified roughness on my part." But then he managed to quiet his emotions sufficiently to walk over to the chiefs and offer his hand.

The chiefs refused to take it.

Clark turned on his heel, ordered his men to join him, and waded out to the pirogue. Before he could set off for the keelboat, Black Buffalo and two warriors waded after him. They indicated that they wanted to sleep aboard the boat. Clark nodded his consent.

"We proceeded on about 1 mile," Clark recorded, "and anchored out off a willow Island placed a guard on Shore to protect the Cooks & a guard in the boat, fastened the Perogues to the boat, I call this Island bad humered Island as we were in a bad humer."

The first meeting between the Sioux and the Americans had gone badly. Certainly Lewis and Clark had failed to make the favorable impression on the Sioux that Jefferson had ordered them to do. But, short of giving away almost a fifth of their total stock, the contents of one pirogue, there was nothing the captains could do to make that favorable impression. At least no shots had rung out, no arrows had been launched.

In the morning, the captains set out early and proceeded some four miles. The banks were lined with hundreds of curious but anxious Indians. At Black Buffalo's request, the expedition came to and anchored, near his village. The captains invited some men, women, and children to come aboard. Black Buffalo invited Lewis to visit his village. The chief "appeared disposed to make up and be friendly," so Lewis consented.

The village Lewis visited was a classic nomadic town, based on a buffalo-and-horse economy, numbering about a hundred tepees with a population of around nine hundred. These were the Brule band of the Tetons, and they were in high spirits, having only two weeks previously won a great battle against the Omahas. The Sioux had killed seventy-five Omaha warriors and taken forty-eight women and children prisoners. Cruzatte, who was with Lewis, could speak Omaha fluently; Lewis told him to find out what he could from the prisoners.

Black Buffalo was insistent on showing Lewis the greatest courtesies, including repeated invitations to take a squaw. The Indians made "frequent selicitations" for Lewis to remain one night longer so that they could "Show their good disposition towards us." Lewis agreed.

In the late afternoon, Clark and the entire party came to the village. Clark saw the Omaha prisoners and judged them "a retched and Dejected looking people. The Squars appear low & Corse but this is an unfavorable time to judge of them."

At dusk, Clark and Lewis were carried with much ceremony on a decorated buffalo robe to the great council lodge in the middle of the village. Fires glowed through translucent tepees as the women prepared a feast. Slabs of buffalo meat roasted over hot coals. Inside the council lodge, seventy elders and prominent warriors sat in a circle. The Americans sat beside Black Buffalo. In front of them a six-foot sacred circle had been cleared for holy pipes, pipe stands, and medicine bundles.

After smoking, Black Buffalo spoke with "Great Solemnity." The captains could not make out what he was saying, beyond that the

Sioux were poor and the Americans should have pity on them and give them something. Clark answered that the Sioux should make peace with the Omahas, and as a gesture of their good will release the prisoners they held. If Black Buffalo understood the translation of that idea, he must have thought Clark mad. Why should he give up valuable prisoners just to please the white man? And anyway, his people were about to hold a scalp dance, displaying those so recently acquired from the Omahas.

It was the first Sioux scalp dance ever seen by Americans. Clark described it: "A large fire made in the Center, about 10 musitions playing on tamberins made of hoops & skin stretched. long sticks with Deer & Goats Hoofs tied So as to make a gingling noise and many others of a Similer kind, those men began to Sing & Beet on the Temboren, the women Came forward highly Deckerated in theire way, with the Scalps an Trofies of war of ther father Husbands Brothers or near Connection & proceeded to Dance the war Dance. Women only dance—jump up & down. . . . Every now and then one of the men come out & repeat some exploit in a sort of song—this taken up by the young men and the women dance to it."

The Americans tossed presents of tobacco and beads to the dancers and singers. When one warrior thought he had not received his due, he flew into a rage and broke one drum, threw two others into the fire, then stormed out of the dance line. The drums were retrieved and the dancing went on. Sergeant Ordway found the music "delightful," and said it was done "with great Chearfullness."[2]

The dance broke up at midnight. Black Buffalo offered the captains young women as bed partners. Clark, who understood the meaning of the offering, wrote later that "a curious custom with the Sioux is to give handsom squars to those whome they wish to Show some acknowledgements to," but the captains said no. Black Buffalo and the Partisan then accompanied the captains to the boat, where they slept for the night.

During the night, Cruzatte came to the captains to report that the Omahas had told him that the Tetons intended to stop the expedition and rob it. The captains agreed they would show no sign of "a knowledge of there intentions," but they slept poorly. It apparently failed to occur to them that the Omaha prisoners had an obvious motive for stirring up the Americans, and might well be lying.

In the morning, Clark and Lewis went back to the village. They trod cautiously, suspecting treachery, and therefore "are at all times guarded & on our guard. They again offered me a young woman," Clark wrote, "and wish me to take her & not Dispise them, I wavered the Subject."

That evening, there was another scalp dance. It broke up about 11:00 p.m., with both captains scarcely able to stay awake. The Partisan and one of his warriors accompanied them back to the bank. Clark got into a pirogue, to be ferried out to the boat, while Lewis stayed on shore with a guard. Some clumsy steering brought Clark's pirogue slamming broadside into the keelboat's anchor cable. It broke. The boat began to swing dangerously.

Clark called out in a loud voice, "All hands up! All hands up and at their oars!"

The shouted orders and the hustle and bustle that immediately followed alarmed the Partisan. He began hollering that the Omahas were attacking. In ten minutes, the bank was lined with some two hundred warriors, led by Black Buffalo, prepared for anything but believing that the Omahas really were attacking, since they had genuine cause to want to make a surprise raid, and half-suspecting that the Americans were in an alliance with their enemies.

Misunderstanding cut both ways. Lewis, on shore with a small guard, was convinced that the Partisan's shouting was the signal for the intended treachery. He had his men on full alert, rifles primed.

Fortunately, the potentially explosive situation quickly resolved itself. When the warriors realized it was a false alarm, they returned to their beds. Lewis returned to the boat, which because of the lost anchor had to tie up to a tree under a falling bank, much more exposed than the captains would have liked. Clark concluded his journal entry for the day, "All prepared on board for any thing which might hapen, we kept a Strong guard all night in the boat. No Sleep."

In the morning, after a long fruitless search for the anchor, the expedition prepared to set out. At that moment, the Tetons appeared on the bank in great number, well armed. Black Buffalo came on board and asked the captains to stay one more day. Simultaneously, several warriors grabbed the bowline. Clark complained to Black Buffalo, who hurried forward to tell Lewis that the warriors only wanted some tobacco and then the expedition might proceed.

He wasn't asking for much—a carrot or two of tobacco was all, a trifle merely. But as a symbol, Black Buffalo was demanding what the captains thought of as a high price. It was an acknowledgment of the right of the Sioux to exact a toll from white men using their river.

Lewis's patience broke. He said he would not be forced into anything, ordered all hands ready for departure, had the sail hoisted, and detailed a man to untie the bow cable. As the soldier began to untie it, several warriors again grabbed the rope. The Partisan demanded a flag and some tobacco as the price of their letting go.

Clark threw a carrot of tobacco onto the bank, "saying to the chief you have told us you are a great man—have influence—take this tobacco and shew us your influence by taking the rope from your men and letting go without coming to hostilities."

Clark backed his sarcasm with action—he lit the firing taper for the swivel gun and moved toward it.

Black Buffalo stepped forward. He declared the expedition free to go, if only the captains would give some tobacco. Again the captains refused, Lewis saying they "did not mean to be trifled with."

It was Black Buffalo's turn for a bit of sarcasm. He said that "he was mad too, to see us stand so much for one carrot of tobacco." Perhaps stung by the remark, but still trying to retain his own sense of dignity and control, Lewis contemptuously threw some carrots of tobacco to the warriors holding the bowline. With that, Black Buffalo jerked the line from their hands and the boat cast off. The Teton confrontation was over.[3]

The expedition left breathing hard and breathing fire. Clark hollered out to a young Indian ashore to pass the word, "if they were for war or were Deturmined to Stop us we were ready to defend our Selves." But behind the bravado there was no sense of triumph. The captains had not made a favorable impression, they had just barely avoided a disastrous exchange of fire, they were exhausted and still nervous. They came to on "a verry Small Sand bar in the middle of the river & Stayed all night."

"I am Verry unwelle for want of Sleep," Clark concluded the day's entry. "Deturmined to Sleep to night if possible."

In the morning, September 29, the expedition got an early start. The Partisan and two warriors called out to the boat from the bank. They indicated they wanted to hitch a ride up to their village, not far distant. Captain Lewis absolutely refused, "Stateing verry Sufficint reasons and was plain with them on the Subject." Lewis said the party had already wasted two days with the Sioux and had to be getting on.

Given the hot tempers on both sides, it was just as well. No matter how long Lewis and Clark stayed with the Sioux, they were not going to make them into friends except by giving more than they could afford. Lewis and Clark had not initiated hostilities, but their insistence on standing their ground might well have led to bullets and arrows flying through the air.

Clark was defensive in writing his account; presumably Lewis also would have justified his actions. But to a superior officer looking over the report, he would have looked headstrong and rash. His orders to make every effort to establish good relations with the Sioux had been turned on their head. Lewis and Clark had managed to get past the Sioux, but the Sioux were still on the river, capable of blocking any later expeditions and in a rage at the Americans. And there was a good chance the expedition would have to pass the tribe again, on the return trip.

But for now, the Sioux were behind them. The wind was from the south. The men hoisted the sail and the boat made twenty miles that day. In the evening—once again on a sandbar island, the safest place to be—the captains refreshed the party with whiskey. It was a cold evening. Migrating geese flew downriver, honking, through the night. Fall was here. It was time to get on, as far north and west as possible, before winter set in.

15

TO THE MANDANS

Fall 1804

If there ever was a time in which the Lewis and Clark Expedition bore some resemblance to a bunch of guys out on a long camping trip, it was in the first part of October 1804.

Fall on the Missouri River in the Dakotas was a delight. On a cloudless day—and many were, in the first three weeks that October—the Great Plains of North America stretched out beyond the horizon under an infinity of bright-blue sky. The sun had gone past the equinox and was dropping lower in the sky each day, so the shadows were growing longer. On the Plains, the hills and bluffs, their grasses turned a golden brown, gleamed in the sunlight, or threw off long shadows up and down the valleys, creating a masterpiece of light and shade.

Nights were coming on sooner and lasting longer. They brought frost, which meant no more mosquitoes. The men built the fires up a little higher than in September, and gathered closer around as they talked about what they had done and seen that day and what they expected tomorrow. In the first two weeks of the month, the days started off cool but by midmorning the temperature was perfect and stayed so until an hour before sunset.

The great mammals of the Plains were gathering into herds. Many of them, including elk, pronghorn, and buffalo, began their mass migration to their wintering grounds. Sooner or later on their trek, most of the herds had to cross the river, thereby creating one of nature's greatest scenes.* Overhead, Canada geese, snow geese, brants, swans, mallards, and a variety of other ducks were on the move, honking and quacking as they descended the river. The fowl and mammals were in prime condition, which meant that the buffalo ribs, the venison haunches, the beaver tails, the mallard breasts all dripped fat into the fire as they were turned on the spit, causing a sizzle and a smell that sharpened already keen appetites.

For Meriwether Lewis it was a magical time. He spent most of it exploring, walking on shore, venturing out into the interior, catching up with the boat at night. Sometimes he went alone, save for his dog, Seaman; at other times he took a small party with him. He was a great walker, with long legs and a purposeful stride, capable of covering thirty miles in a day on the Plains. As he walked, he was constantly at full alert, his eyes sweeping across the horizon, then coming down with complete concentration on a stone or a plant or an animal den at his feet. He carried his field journal so that he could note down new plants, animals, minerals, the general lay of the land, the apparent fertility of the soil, the types and numbers of game animals around him, and more.

He wore moccasins of doubled-up buffalo hide, pants made of broadcloth, a fringed deerskin jacket, and a three-cornered leather hat. He carried a compass, a knife, a pistol, a powder horn and balls, some jerky, and his notebook in his knapsack. He had his rifle in one hand and his espontoon in the other. He was an excellent marksman, his skill even greater thanks to the espontoon—a sort of pike, about six feet in length, with a wooden shaft and a metal blade. It was a medieval weapon still in use as a symbol of authority for infantry officers in the U.S. Army, carried by Lewis because it was a most useful implement. Aside from being a walking stick and a weapon of last resort, the espontoon had a crosswise attachment at shoulder height that served as a rifle rest. Given the weight of his rifle, more than eight pounds, and the length of the barrel, more than four feet, he needed a support.

Lewis always had his rifle primed, with the bullet, wadding, and powder charge set in place, so that when he saw a target he had only to set his espontoon vertically on the ground, measure out the powder for the pan, swing his rifle up to the rifle rest, slip in his flint, bring the hammer to full cock, aim, and fire. If the target was within a hundred yards and bigger than a mouse, he usually got it.

---

* The migration of the great herds is a sight not seen, alas, by any living person for well over a hundred years, but imagined by Charley Russell in his painting *When the Land Belonged to God.*

He didn't always have to shoot to collect a specimen. On October 16, he glanced down and saw at his feet a sleeping bird. He didn't know the species but recorded that it was of the goatsucker family. He picked it up; it was alive but appeared to be in something approaching a dormant state. Lewis brought it back to the boat; two days later, when the morning temperature was thirty degrees, the bird could scarcely move. "I run my penknife into it's body under the wing and completely distroyed it's lungs and heart," Lewis reported, "yet it lived upwards of two hours. This fanominon I could not accfont for unless it proceeded from the want of circulation of the blood.*

A few days later, on October 20, in the vicinity of present Fort Lincoln State Park, across the river from Bismarck, North Dakota, Private Cruzatte was the first to encounter a grizzly bear, called a white bear by the Americans. They had heard about the grizzly, and knew the Indians were afraid of the bear, which according to rumor was gigantic in size (Clark had recently seen a footprint and pronounced it by far the biggest he had ever seen) and ferocious in behavior. The men of the expedition, naturally, were eager to get a look and a shot at it. Cruzatte was the lucky one—except, as Lewis dryly recorded in his field notes, "he wounded him, but being alarmed at the formidable appearance of the bear he left his tomahalk and gun."

Cruzatte returned to the scene an hour or so later to retrieve his tomahawk and rifle. "Soon after he shot a buffaloe cow," Lewis wrote, and "broke her thy, the cow pursued him he conceal himself in a small raviene." The little incident highlighted a major problem for the hunters. After they had fired their rifles, they were nearly helpless until they reloaded.

Beginning in October, as the expedition made its way through present northern South Dakota, it passed numerous abandoned villages, composed of earth-lodge dwellings and cultivated fields. Some of the fields, although unattended, still had squash and corn growing in them. These had once been home to the mighty Arikara tribe. About thirty thousand persons strong in the year the United States won its independence, the tribe had been reduced by smallpox epidemics in the 1780s to not much more than one-fifth that size. Another epidemic swept through in 1803–4, devastating the tribe. What had been

---

* The bird was the poorwill, a close relative of the whippoorwill. Lewis weighed and described it. Naturalist and Lewis and Clark scholar Raymond Burroughs notes that it was not until the 1940s that zoologists discovered the bird's tendency to hibernate.[1]

eighteen villages the previous year had been reduced to three by the time Lewis arrived.[2]

On October 8, the keelboat passed a three-mile-long island, near the mouth of the Grand River, home to the three villages of living Arikaras, about two thousand Indians all together. The island was one large garden, growing beans, corn, and squash. Arikaras lined the banks, watching the boat progress to the head of the island and then watching the men make camp on the starboard side. Lewis selected two voyagers who spoke the Arikara language and two soldiers, took a pirogue, and paddled across to meet the Indians on the island. Clark stayed in camp, posting guards on shore and sentinels on the boat and canoes, with "all things arranged both for Peace or War."

Lewis obviously did not know what kind of reception he was going to get, but he did have expectations. From what he knew, or thought he knew, the Arikaras were farmers oppressed by the Sioux. The reality was that the Sioux brought trade goods to exchange for Arikara crops in a mutually beneficial relationship. He knew the Arikaras were at war with the Mandans. He believed that they were the key to American diplomatic endeavors on the Missouri, because in Lewis's view, if the Arikaras could be broken away from the Sioux and if they made peace with the Mandans, the whole balance of power on the river would shift. The Sioux would be isolated and then frozen out of the coming American trade empire.

James Ronda comments that Lewis and Clark shared "a naive optimism typical of so much Euro-American frontier diplomacy. [They] believed they could easily reshape upper Missouri realities to fit their expectations. ... [But] to the surprise of the explorer-diplomats, virtually all Indian parties proved resistant to change and suspicious of American motives."[3]

So Lewis had cause for high hope as well as for apprehension as he paddled across to the island, and, finally, cause for relief as he received a warm welcome from the Arikaras. Best of all was meeting Joseph Gravelines, a trader who had been living with the Arikaras for thirteen years. He was an invaluable source of information on the upper-Missouri country, and his command of English, French, Sioux, and Arikara made it possible for Lewis to communicate swiftly and accurately with the Arikara. A large part of the problems with the Sioux had been the result of inadequate, incomplete, incompetent translation. With Gravelines's help, Lewis could expect to do much better with the Arikaras

Lewis pumped Gravelines for two or three hours, then asked him to bring a delegation to the expedition's camp in the morning for a council and hired him as interpreter.

In the morning, the wind was kicking up waves in the river higher than Clark had ever seen them. He was astonished to see bull boats brought to the bank—boats made each of a single buffalo hide stretched over a bowl-shaped willow frame—and five or six men get in, with three squaws to paddle them. The Indian women pushed off and despite the waves and wind crossed the river "quite uncomposed." They brought with them some chiefs, some warriors, and Pierre-Antoine Tabeau, the trader with another of the island villages.

Tabeau had been born near Montreal and educated in Quebec. In 1776, he had gone west as an engagé in the fur trade. He had lived in Illinois, then Missouri, and finally with the Arikaras. He too was an outstanding translator (Arikara, English, French, Sioux) and source of information. But even the best translators could not overcome the difficulties of the wind, which was whipping up sand and making a roar. The council was put off till the next day.

On October 10, Tabeau came over first. He warned the captains that there was some jealousy among the chiefs of the three villages. Then the chiefs themselves, and some of their warriors, came to the council. After smoking and an exchange of small presents, Lewis stood and began speaking, with Gravelines interpreting. It was his basic Indian speech, according to Clark providing the Indians with "good counsel," which was to accept American sovereignty, to make peace with the Mandans, to shun the Sioux, and to trade with American merchants. If they did as told, they would be protected by their new father, the chief of the seventeen great nations of America.

When Lewis finished, a detail fired three shots from the bow swivel gun. When the smoke cleared and the Indians recovered from their astonishment at the first cannon they had ever seen or heard, the captains brought out gift bale number fifteen, marked and prepared for the Arikaras' use months before at Wood River. There was vermilion paint, pewter looking glasses, four hundred needles, broadcloth, beads, combs, razors, nine pairs of scissors, knives, tomahawks, and more. (It is something of a puzzle why they were not so generous with the Sioux.)

No whiskey. The captains offered it, but the Arikaras not only said no thanks, they shamed Lewis and Clark by remarking that "they were surprised that their father should present to them a liquor which would make them act like fools."

For the chiefs there were military coats, cocked hats, medals, and American flags. Despite Tabeau's warning, the captains made Crow at Rest the first chief, on their unshakable assumption that every tribe had to have a single leader. They made Hawk's Feather and Chief Hay, leaders of the other two villages, as second chiefs. After the presents, Lewis shot off his air gun, to the by-now customary astonishment of the Indians. The council broke up, the chiefs promising to consult with their warriors and respond to Lewis's words the following morning.

That afternoon, the men visited the villages. York was a sensation. His size was impressive enough, but the Arikaras had never seen a black man and couldn't make out if he was man, beast, or spirit being. York played with the children, roaring at them, chasing them between lodges, bellowing that he was a wild beast caught and tamed by Captain Clark. The captains finally told him to stop, because "he Carried on the joke and made himself more turibal than we wished him to doe."

The soldiers, meanwhile, enjoyed the favors of the Arikara women, often encouraged to do so by the husbands, who believed that they would catch some of the power of the white men from such intercourse, transmitted to them through their wives. One warrior invited York to his lodge, offered him his wife, and guarded the entrance during the act. York was said to be "the big Medison." Whether the Indians got white or black power from the intercourse cannot be said, but what they had gotten for sure from their hospitality to previous white traders was venereal disease, which was rampant in the villages and passed on to the men of the expedition.

Still, Sergeant Gass pronounced the Arikara squaws to be "the most cleanly Indians I have ever seen . . . handsome . . . the best looking Indians I have ever seen." Sergeant Ordway agreed, noting that "some of their women are very handsome and clean."[4] Clark called the Arikara "Durtey, Kind, pore, & extravigent pursessing national pride. Not beggarley." They brought corn and squash and other welcome vegetables to the expedition, and quantities of a bean the Indians acquired by digging in the underground storage bins of the meadow mice. Clark called the bean "large and well flavoured and very nurishing." It was said that the Indians always left some other food in the place of that they had robbed from the mice.

The following day, October 11, Crow at Rest arrived to make his answer to Lewis's proposals. He said his heart was glad to have a new father, that the road was open to the expedition and would always be open. "Can you think any one Dare put their hands on your rope of your boat[?] No! Not one dare." He asked the captains to make a peace between his people and the Mandans.

The other two chiefs had not come into council, apparently put off by not having been made first chief, so the next day the captains went looking for them. They found Chief Hay first, surrounded by his warriors. After Lewis reminded the chief of "the magnitude and power of our country," Hay gave his own speech. He said his people had no hostility toward the whites, that he hoped the captains would help make a peace with the Mandans, that he might be willing to go to Washington to meet with President Jefferson in the spring, and other welcome words. But he concluded with a request that the captains were in no position to grant: "After you Set out," Hay said, "many nations in the open plains may Come to make war against us, we wish you to Stop their guns & provent it if possible. Finished."

Then it was on foot to the third village, where Hawk's Feather was chief. He too was ready with his reply to the American proposals. He too was thinking about a trip to Washington. He promised not to make war but said that he would believe a Mandan-Arikara peace only when he saw it with his own eyes. He gave two blunt warnings, "Mabie we [Arikara chiefs] will not tell the trooth," and "the Indians above [the Mandans] will not believe your word" about peace with the Arikaras.

One of the chiefs—unnamed—was willing to find out. He agreed to go on board and make the trip to the Mandans, to talk in council sponsored by the American peacekeeping delegation.

On October 13, Clark and Lewis were confronted with a severe disciplinary problem. Former Private Moses Reed, the erstwhile deserter, was a grousing, malcontented soldier who wanted to poison the mind of at least one member of the expedition. Anyone who has ever been in the army knows Reed's type. For some time past, he had been picking on Private John Newman, agitating him about those blankety-blank captains and how unfair they were and how arbitrary and worse.

Newman succumbed to the poison. He lashed out at the captains, who had him and Reed arrested. Reed was beyond their power to punish, but Newman was subject to the articles of war. The captains convened a court-martial, with Clark as president ("without giveing his opinion") and Sgt. Ordway head of the court.

Lewis read the charge, that Newman had "uttered repeated expressions of a highly criminal and mutinous nature; the same having a tendency not only to distroy every principle of military discipline, but also to alienate the affections of the individuals composing this Detachment to their officers, and disaffect them to the service for which they have been so sacredly and solemnly engaged."

Newman pled, "Not Guilty!"

Evidence was presented; Newman made his defense.

Whatever Newman said, his peers rejected. The ten men on the court "are unanimously of opinion that the prisonar John Newman is guilty of every part of the charge exhibited against him."

The sentence was seventy-five lashes on the bare back and "to be discarded from the perminent party engaged for North Western discovery." Not dismissed, not discharged, but *discarded*.

The captains approved the sentence and set noon the next day for the lashing. They further ordered that Newman join the Frenchmen in the canoes as a laboring hand.

On October 14, the keelboat set out early. At noon, it came to on the starboard side in order to carry out Newman's lashing. The Arikara chief with the boat watched the preparations. He was "allarmed verry much." When the whipping actually began, the chief "Cried aloud."

Clark explained the cause of the punishment. The chief, he recorded, "also thought exampls were necessary, & that he himself had made them by Death, but his nation never whiped even their Children."

By October 24, the expedition was well north of present Bismarck and approaching the Mandan villages. The captains knew from their research in St. Louis and from Mr. Gravelines that the Mandans (and their neighbors and allies the Hidatsas) were the center of the Northern Plains trade, attracting Indians from vast distances. At trading time, in the late summer, the river villages were crowded with Crows, Assiniboines, Cheyennes, Kiowas, Arapahoes, along with whites from the North West Company, the Hudson's Bay Company, and St. Louis businessmen.

Nowhere else could one see at a single glance the diversity and colorful life style of the Indians of the Plains. There were Spanish horses and mules to buy and sell, fancy Cheyenne leather clothing, English trade guns, baskets of produce, meat products, furs of all kinds, musical instruments, blankets, dressed buffalo hides, painted buffalo hides. During the fair, there was dancing until well into the night, and much visiting back and forth, and competition between the boys. It was a grand time in the five villages.

There were two Mandan villages. The lower one, on the west bank, was led by Big White and his second chief, Little Raven. Farther upriver, on the east bank, was the second village, led by Black Cat, with Raven Man Chief as his second-in-command. On the Knife River, coming in from the west, there were three Hidasta villages. One of these, forty lodges strong, was led by Black Moccasin. Another, with over 130 earth lodges, had 450 warriors who were led by Le Borgne, or

One Eye, a military chieftain of great reputation. The Mandans hunted buffalo on horseback, but they did not ride out on war parties ranging to the Rocky Mountains, whereas the Hidastas rode the whole way to the snow-covered peaks to make raids and capture horses and slaves.[5]

As it moved north, the expedition began seeing Mandan villages, but they were abandoned, because the tribe had been decimated by smallpox. As the expedition passed the mouth of the Heart River, center of the old Mandan homeland, the men saw a Mandan sun-dance post standing forlorn on the prairie, a silent witness to the past. In the earth lodges, the Americans found scattered bones of men and animals.

On the 24th, the captains met their first live Mandans, Chief Big White and a twenty-five-man hunting party. With Gravelines at his side, Lewis introduced Big White to the Arikara chief with "great Cordiallity & Sermony." They smoked a pipe. Lewis, Gravelines, and the Arikara chief accompanied Big White to his village. Peace between the Arikaras and the Mandans seemed possible. The captains were off to a good start with the Indians who would be their neighbors for the winter.

But even with all the good indications about relations with the Mandans, the captains were cautious. On October 26, the expedition was in camp just below the first Mandan village. Indians were all about them. Clark wrote, "Many men women & Children flocked down to See us." The captains discussed the situation and "Deturmined that both would not leave the boat at the Same time untill we Knew the Deposition of the Nativs." Lewis walked to the village with Big White and Gravelines, while Clark stayed on the boat and saw to security. There were over four thousand Indians in the five villages, about thirteen hundred of them warriors. Should they so choose, they could quite obviously overwhelm the Corps of Discovery. They would not so choose so long as the expedition could make it clear that the Indians would suffer grievously if they attacked, both in lives lost and future trade relations destroyed.

Fortunately, the Mandans understood all this and were friendly. Lewis received a warm welcome in Big White's village and was able to extend an invitation to the chiefs of all five villages to come to the expedition's camp for a council. Meanwhile, a trader from the second Mandan village, named René Jessaume, paid a visit to Clark. Jessaume had been living with the Mandans for fifteen years and participated fully in their ceremonial and social life. He had married a Mandan woman and was raising a family in the village. He claimed he had been a spy for General George Rogers Clark during the revolution, but apparently William Clark did not believe him; in any case, he wrote of

Jessaume, "Well to give my ideas as to the impression this man makes on me is a Cunin artfull an insoncear." But he was also useful, as interpreter and source of information, so Clark hired him on.

Relations with the Mandans continued to be excellent. The Indians were delighted that the expedition would spend the next five months as their neighbor.

On October 28, Black Cat, Lewis, Clark, and Jessaume walked up the river for some distance, looking for a place to build a fort for the winter—the Americans needed good trees and lots of them, and plenty of game. The country they examined that day would not answer.

On October 29, the first formal council was held. Lewis gave his basic Indian speech. To Clark's dismay, "the old Chief was restless before the Speech was half ended." Another chief "rebuked him for his uneasiness at Such a time." When Lewis finished, Clark introduced the Arikara chief, who smoked with the Mandans. Various promises were made, but Clark complained that the talk was "not much to the purpose," because "those nations know nothing of reagular Councils, and know not how to proceed in them, they are restless &c." Lewis was so busy with the Indians that he forgot to wind his chronometer, but he did find time to take a meridian altitude of the sun with his sextant, for latitude.

On the morning of the last day of October, Black Cat invited Clark to his lodge to "here what he had to Say." Since the captains regarded Black Cat as the first chief of all the Mandans, Clark readily went. Black Cat told Clark that it would fill his heart with joy if there could be a peace between the Arikaras and the Mandans, because if there were Mandan men could hunt without fear "and our womin Can work in the fields without looking every moment for the enimey."

Then came a rebuke: "When the Indians heard of your Coming up they all Came in from hunting to See, they expected Great presents. They were disapointed, and Some Dessatisfied." As for Black Cat, however, he was "not so much So but his Village was." Still, he would go to meet his Great Father in Washington in the spring.

Lewis, meanwhile, played host to Hugh McCracken, a British trader with the North West Company, who had just made a nine-day, 150-mile overland trip from the Assiniboine River post of the company.

McCracken was a regular in the village, as were other traders from the North West Company and its rival, the Hudson's Bay Company. The British in Canada were the primary suppliers of manufactured goods to the Mandans. This was a situation Lewis intended to change. His policy, Jefferson's policy, was to isolate the Sioux, open the river from St. Louis to the Mandans, and establish an American trading monopoly at this great emporium of the Northern Great Plains. But Lewis knew that he needed to be patient. Although he had the legal authority to throw the British traders out of Upper Louisiana, he didn't have the physical force to do so, not when the Indians outnumbered his party by fifty warriors to every soldier. He wouldn't have kicked the British traders out anyway, because they were providing a critically necessary service to the Indians that the Americans were not yet ready to replace.

McCracken was setting off on his return journey the next day, November 1, so Lewis seized the opportunity to establish contact with the British merchants in Canada and explain the new situation to them. While Clark talked to Black Cat, Lewis wrote a letter to McCracken's boss. He started off with a bit of a fib: "We have been sent by the government for the purpose of exploring the river Missouri, and the western parts of the continent, with a view to the promotion of general science." He added that his party had no intention of disrupting the trade relationship that existed, as long as the British acknowledged American sovereignty. Then, as a man who was about to go into a five-month winter camp surrounded by Indians and only Captain Clark to talk to as an equal, Lewis put in a heartfelt line: "As individuals, we feel everey disposition to cultivate the friendship of all well-disposed persons." More specifically, he said he would be grateful in the extreme for any "hints in relation to the geography of the country, its productions, etc. which you might conceive of utility to mankind." In short, he invited British traders to come on down for a visit.[6]

The British took him up on it. A number of them paid a call, including François-Antoine Larocque and Charles MacKenzie. Each man left a journal record of his visit. Larocque was twenty years old. Born in Quebec, he was educated in the United States. He wrote that he "was very politely received by Captains Lewis and Clarke and passed the night with them. Just as I arrived, they were dispatching a man for me, having heard that I intended giving flags and medals which they forbid me from giving in the name of the United States. . . . As I had neither flags nor medals, I ran no risk of disobeying those orders, of which I assured them."

Lewis told Larocque that "the object of our voyage is purely scientific and literary, and in no way concerns trade."

Lewis liked the young Canadian and "pressed me to remain a couple of days" for company. Larocque did. His compass was not working; the glass was broken and the needle would not point due north. He reported, "Capt. Lewis fixed my compass very well, which took him a whole day."

Larocque was out for adventure and recognized opportunity when he saw it. From his first meeting with the captains, he begged to be allowed to accompany them to the Pacific and back. But the captains were not about to give a clerk in the North West Company a free look at the commercial possibilities in the region and said no.[7]

MacKenzie's journal entries provide a sharp image of the American captains and the British traders lounging around a table in the captains' quarters, talking about a wide range of subjects. MacKenzie wrote, "Mr. Larocque and I having nothing very particular claiming attention, we lived contentedly and became intimate with the gentlemen of the American expedition, who on all occasions seemed happy to see us, and always treated us with civility and kindness."

But some subjects brought out Lewis's Anglophobia. MacKenzie wrote: "It is true, Captain Lewis could not make himself agreeable to us. He could speak fluently and learnedly on all subjects, but his inveterate disposition against the British stained, at least in our eyes, all his eloquence."[8]

The captains' quarters were in Fort Mandan, which was located on the north bank of the Missouri, some seven miles below the mouth of the Knife and directly opposite the lower Mandan village.* Work on it had begun on November 3. Private Joseph Whitehouse recorded in his journal that "all the men at Camp Ocepied their time dilligenently in Building their huts and got them Made comfortable to live in."[9] That same day, Lewis paid off in cash the Frenchmen who had paddled the pirogues upriver. Some of them built a pirogue and returned to St. Louis before the river froze; others stayed to spend the winter with the Indians and return in the spring with Corporal Warfington and the keelboat. Jessaume and his squaw moved into camp, providing instant translation capacity.

The fort consisted of two rows of huts, set at an angle, with a palisade on the river side, a gate and a sentry post, plus the swivel gun mounted. The outer walls were eighteen feet high. In the event of an Indian attack, it would answer, at least for a while. Larocque observed, "The fort is made so strong as to be almost cannon-ball proof."[10]

From the beginning of the work, Indians crossed the river to observe, mingle, and trade with the soldiers. Other visitors also came. On

---

* The site was about fourteen miles west of present Washburn, North Dakota. It has been washed away by the river and lies at least partially underwater.

November 4, Clark recorded that "a french man by Name Chabonah . . . visit us, he wished to hire & informed us his 2 Squars were Snake Indians."

His name was Toussaint Charbonneau. A French Canadian, about forty-five years old, he had once worked for the North West Company but was now living among the Hidatsas as an independent trader. His squaws, or "wives," were Shoshones, or Snakes, from a band that lived in the Rocky Mountains at the headwaters of the Missouri. They were teenagers who had been captured by a Hidatsa raiding party four years earlier at the place where three rivers came together to form the Missouri, called the Three Forks. Charbonneau had won them in a bet with the warriors who had captured them.

The captains eagerly accepted Charbonneau's offer to sign on as interpreter, not so much for his own sake as because his wives could speak the language of a mountain tribe. The wives could talk to Charbonneau in Hidatsa; he could then talk in French to Drouillard, who could pass it on to the captains in English. From their difficulties with the Sioux, the captains knew how hard it was to communicate with the Indians without a translator. So on the spot they signed up Charbonneau and one of his wives "to go on with us." He chose Sacagawea, who was about fifteen years old and six months pregnant.

MacKenzie got to know Charbonneau and was not much impressed. He noted that translation was more an art form than scientific at Fort Mandan. "Sacagawea spoke a little Hidatsa," he wrote, "in which she had to converse with her husband, who was a Canadian and did not understand English. A mulatto [Jessaume], who spoke bad French and worse English, served as interpreter to the Captains, so that a single word to be understood by the party required to pass from the natives to the woman, from the woman to the husband, from the husband to the mulatto, from the mulatto to the captains."

That might not have been so bad, except that Charbonneau and Jessaume argued about the meaning of every French word they used.[11]

Another visitor was Big White, the enormously fat, light-skinned Mandan chief.* On November 12, Clark recorded that "Big White Came Down, he packd about 100 W. of fine meet on his Squar for us," meaning his wife carried the hundred-pound load. Clark gave her some trinkets and a small ax for her labor.

---

* Gary Moulton points out (vol. 3, p. 201, n. 5) that the presence of unusually light-complexioned and fair-haired persons among the Mandans led to speculations about their being the fabled Welsh Indians, or somehow otherwise of European origin. There was nothing to the story.

On November 20, warriors from Black Cat's village came to inform the captains that the American peace policy was in danger. Two Arikara delegates who had gone to the Sioux with a peace offer had been roughed up, had their horses taken from them, and been generally made to realize how angry the Sioux were that the Arikaras had arranged through Clark and Lewis for a peace with the Mandans.

There were other meddlers, including the Mandans, who had filled the ears of the Hidatsas with lies. The Mandans had an obvious interest in keeping the Hidatsas away from Fort Mandan and thus having a monopoly on trade with the expedition, so they told the Hidatsas that the Americans had joined with the Sioux and intended to make war on the Hidatsas. They offered as proof such facts as Jessaume's moving into the fort, the strength of the fort, the constant presence of a sentry, and other military preparations.

Lewis realized how dangerous it was for the Americans to have the Hidatsas believing such things, so he reacted immediately. He set out on horseback for the Hidatsa villages, accompanied by Jessaume and Charbonneau as translators, to make the rounds of the principal men and assure them of the falsity of the Mandan stories.

But he was rebuffed. Later that day, he saw MacKenzie. "He observed to me," MacKenzie wrote, "that he was not very graciously received. 'I sent ahead,' said he, 'to inform Horned Weasel [the Hidasta chief] that I intended to take up my quarters at his lodge, he returned for an answer that "he was not at home." This conduct surprised me, it being common only among your English Lords, not to be "at home" when they did not wish to see strangers, but as I had felt no inclination of entering any house after being told the landlord would not be "at home", I looked out for another lodging, which I readily found.'"[12]

In the morning, Lewis and his men returned to Fort Mandan, accompanied by two lesser Hidatsa chiefs. From them, Lewis extracted a promise not to wage war on the Shoshones and Blackfeet, who resided north of the Shoshones, on the eastern edge of the Rocky Mountains. The promise was worthless; a day or two later, the leader of the Wolves, a society of young Hidatsa warriors, took a party of fifty on a raid into Blackfoot territory.

So it had always been and apparently would be. The terms "peace" and "war" as understood by the Americans had no meaning to the Indians. Hostilities could break out at any time, for no apparent cause other than the restlessness of the young warriors, spurred by their desire for honor and glory, which could only be won on raids, which always brought on revenge raids, in a regular cycle. The captains were hopelessly naïve on this point. Lewis was sure he had created a peace in the face of overwhelming evidence that his words were carried away by the wind. He told Larocque of his confidence in his "very grand plan," but Larocque had doubts, and rightly so.[13]

The truth was right in front of Lewis. He later recorded that, during this meeting with the Hidatsas, "I was pointing out to them the advantages of a state of peace with their neighbours. . . . The Chiefs who had already geathered their harvest of laurels and having forceably felt in many instances some of those inconveniences attending a state of war . . . readily agreed with me." That was easy enough; old men seldom want war. But "a young fellow . . . asked me if they were in a state of peace with all their neighbours what the nation would do for Chiefs?" The teenage warrior pointed out that the old chiefs must shortly die "and that the nation could not exist without chiefs," and the Hidatsas could not choose chiefs without witnessing the achievements of the contending warriors.[14]

Lewis had other difficulties with the Hidatsas. They may have believed his protestations that the Americans meant them no harm, but they resented the lack of presents, and resented even more what one of them called "the high-sounding language the American captains bestowed upon themselves and their nation, wishing to impress the Indians with an idea that they were great warriors, and a powerful people, who, if exasperated, could crush all the nations of the earth." Such boasting did not sit well with the proud Hidatsas.[15]

On the morning of November 30, a Mandan came to the fort with an alarming report. A raiding party of Sioux and Arikaras had attacked five Mandan hunters, killing one, wounding two others, and stealing nine horses. This was dismaying news to the peacemakers, for it indicated that the Arikaras had broken their promise and realigned themselves with the Sioux, and that those old allies were making war against the Mandans. This was welcome news too, however, because it provided the Americans with an opportunity to show their support of the Mandans and to display the kind of firepower they could bring to bear against tribes that displeased them.

The captains acted at once. Lewis took charge at Fort Mandan, while Clark marched across the frozen river at the head of a twenty-one-man detachment of soldiers to come to the aid of the Mandans.

The Mandans were not interested. They told Clark the snow was too deep, and anyway the Sioux had too much of a head start. Then they chastised the Americans for meddling in their affairs. The Mandans had believed Clark and Lewis and had gone out to hunt in small parties, thinking themselves safe, and now look what had happened. One chief said he had always known that the Arikaras were "liers, they were *liers*."

Clark was not ready to see the peace policy defeated by one small raid. He again proposed pursuit and was again turned down. Then he made a case for the Arikaras. He admitted that "some bad men [from the Arikaras] may have been with the Scioux [but] you know there is bad men in all nations, do not get mad with the racarees [Arikaras] untill we know if those bad men are Counternoncd. by their nation."

Clark could talk all he wanted. The Mandans knew what had happened and drew their own conclusions.

Clark and Lewis were meddling in affairs they did not understand, but the Mandans were patient with them. And protective too, although the captains hated to admit it. The expedition ate an enormous amount every day, and more every day as winter came on and it got colder, dipping down below zero frequently. To get through the winter, the Americans were going to need large quantities of Indian corn, beans, and squash, and they were going to have to find a regular supply of meat.

On December 7, a Mandan chief came to the fort to report that there were great numbers of buffalo on the hills a couple of miles or so away from the river. The chief offered horses for the soldiers and asked if the Americans would like to join the Mandans on a hunt.

Lewis gathered a party of fifteen men and, on the borrowed Mandan horses, went out to join the hunt. The Indians as riders put the Americans in the shade, even Americans from Virginia. Riding bareback at breakneck speed chasing the fleeing buffalo, they could guide their horses with their knees, leaving their hands free to shoot their arrows, which they did with such force that often an arrow would go right through the buffalo. Squaws came after, to butcher the animal before the wolves could get to the carcass.

Using rifles, Lewis and his men killed eleven buffalo that day. He enjoyed it so much he stayed out all night, apparently sleeping in a buffalo robe in below-zero weather. The next day, the Americans killed nine more buffalo. They ate only the tongues; the wolves got the rest. "We lived on the fat of the land," MacKenzie wrote. "Hunting and eating were the order of the day."[16]

That day, the temperature went down to forty-five below zero, the coldest it would get all winter. And winter was still thirteen days away.

16

WINTER AT FORT MANDAN

December 21, 1804–March 21, 1805

It was always cold, often brutally cold, sometimes so cold a man's penis would freeze if he wasn't quick about it.

Lewis kept a weather diary, in which he faithfully recorded the day's temperature at sunrise and at 4:00 p.m., as well as the conditions—fair, cloudy, snow, hail, and "c.a.r.s." to indicate "cloudy after rain and snow"—wind direction and force, and the rise and fall of the river. This was the first collection of weather data from west of the Mississippi River.

It recorded a somewhat colder winter than the norm during the thirty-year period 1951–80, when December, January, and February temperatures averaged 12.3 degrees above zero. In 1804–5, it averaged 4 degrees above zero for December, 3.4 degrees below for January, and 11.3 degrees above for February, or an average for the winter of 4 degrees above zero.[1]

The Indians could take it. On various occasions, the Americans would hear of or meet Indians who had spent the night out on the prairie, without a fire and with only a buffalo robe to cover them, and only thin moccasins and antelope leggings and shirt to wear, and hardly suffer from it. On January 10, 1805, Clark reported two such incidents and commented, "Customs & the habits of those people has ancered to beare more Cold than I thought it possible for man to indure."

The river was frozen solid enough so that great herds of buffalo could cross without breaking through. Lewis wanted to pull the keelboat on shore for repairs, but it was locked into the ice. Beginning on February 3, he tried various expedients to free it—chipping it out with axes, freeing it by means of boiling water and hot stones, or cutting it loose with "a parsel of Iron spikes." At each attempt, he had a windlass and a large rope of elk skin ready to haul her up on the bank when freed from the ice. But it took weeks to break her free. Not until February 26 did the party finally get the boat out of the water. Why they didn't pull the boat out before the river iced over neither of the captains ever bothered to explain.

Such extreme cold, one might have thought, would have induced the captains and the men to spend the winter in a state of semihibernation, seldom venturing away from their fires or out of their huts, which Ordway described as "warm and comfortable."[2] But the captains kept the men busy, both because there was lots of real work that had to be done and because they were good officers who knew for a certainty that an idle soldier is a bored soldier heading for trouble.

Larocque, MacKenzie, and other British traders could have told the captains about the troubles at Hudson's Bay Company and North West Company posts during the winter, the trappers shut up in their huts, small smoky rooms illuminated only by candlelight. Such conditions led to bad temper, fistfights, ill-will, and lack of discipline.

But the Corps of Discovery was not a wandering band of trappers; it was an infantry company of the U.S. Army. Still, Clark and Lewis had seen plenty of trouble at Wood River the previous winter, and, bad as the weather had been in Illinois, it was nothing compared with North Dakota.

Yet at Fort Mandan there were no fights, no desertions. The worst infraction was relatively minor. On February 9, Private Thomas Howard got back to the fort after dark. Rather than call out to the guard to have the gate opened, he scaled the wall. Unfortunately for Howard, an Indian was looking on and shortly thereafter climbed the wall himself. The guard reported these doings to Captain Lewis.

Lewis was much alarmed. Although relations with the Mandans were excellent, they were not so good with the Hidatsas, and in any case the Mandans might decide at any moment to take advantage of their overwhelming numbers, overpower the expedition, and help themselves to the treasure trove of rifles, kettles, trade goods, and the rest. Private Howard's thoughtless act had just revealed to the Indians how easy it was to scale the wall.

Lewis's first thought was to leave Howard until later and deal with the threat immediately, by convincing the Indian who had followed him over the wall that what he had done was a bad idea. He had the man brought to him. "I convinced him of the impropryety of his conduct," Lewis recorded, "and explained to him the riske he had run of being severely treated, the fellow appeared much allarmed, I gave him a small piece of tobacco and sent him away."

Then he turned to Private Howard. He had Howard put under arrest and ordered him tried by a court-martial. Lewis was not inclined to be lenient, because "this man is an old soldier which still hightens this offince."

In the morning, Howard was charged with "Setting a pernicious example to the Savages." He was found guilty and sentenced to fifty lashes, a heavy punishment for an offense that amounted simply to thoughtlessness. Perhaps for that reason, the court recommended mercy, and Lewis forgave Howard the lashing. That was the only court-martial held at Fort Mandan, and the last on the entire expedition.

The garrison at Fort Mandan maintained regular military security, with drills, sentry-posting, challenges, daily inspection of the weapons, and the rest. When the temperature went well below zero, sentries were replaced every half-hour. Aside from the possibility of a hostile move by Mandans and Hidatsas, the Sioux were definitely hostile and not so far away that they couldn't stage a raid, and the Arikaras might join them. So the expedition stayed constantly on guard.

The Sioux did make a raid, in mid-February. Clark had gone out on a nine-day hunt with a large party of men. The hunters killed more meat than they could transport. When Clark got back to Fort Mandan, he dispatched Drouillard with three men and three horse-drawn sleighs to retrieve the carcasses. A band of Sioux warriors spied the small party.

Clark's description of what happened next, based on Drouillard's testimony, tantalizes rather than satisfies our curiosity about how it went: "About 105 Indians rushed on them and Cut their horses from the Slays *two* of which they carried off in great hast, the 3rd horse was given up to the party [by the Indians, for] fear of some of the Indians being killed by our men who were not disposed to be Robed of all they had tamely."

However determined the party, the Indians got away with the two sleighs and two knives. However bold the Indians, they were forced to give back a tomahawk and one horse and sleigh. So the Americans didn't do too badly, given that the encounter pitted 105 warriors against four men—Drouillard, Privates Robert Frazier and Silas Goodrich, and Newman, who was not allowed to carry a weapon.

At the end of November, Clark had led a party to punish the Sioux and Arikaras for attacking the Mandans. This time it was Lewis's turn to go on the warpath. He set out at sunrise, February 15, at the head of twenty-four volunteers, including a few Mandan warriors coming along as allies, to find and punish the Sioux. But the weather was bad, the snow was deep, and the men soon had their feet cut and bleeding on the sharp ice. The Mandans told Lewis the trail was cold and the cause hopeless, and they abandoned the search.

Lewis, always persistent, doggedly kept on, covering thirty miles before he discovered two abandoned tepees. Thoroughly exhausted, the party slept in them. The next day, Lewis finally abandoned the search and instead went hunting. The party stayed out all week and brought back more than a ton of meat (thirty-six deer, fourteen elk).[3]

Encounters with the Mandans were altogether different. The neighbors got along just fine. The chiefs and captains, warriors and men called on one another, went hunting together, traded extensively, enjoyed sexual relations with the same women on a regular basis, joked, and talked—as best they could through the language barrier—about what they knew. They managed to describe wonders to one another, using their hands to illustrate their points, drawing maps, mountains, or wooden houses on the dirt floor of the lodge, educating one another. The Mandans and the Hidatsas knew something of the country to the west and were glad to share their knowledge with the captains; the Americans knew the country to the east of the Mississippi River and were eager to induce some Mandan and Hidatsa chiefs to make the journey to Washington.

Holidays and special occasions brought the red and white men closer together. On New Year's Day, 1805, half the detachment went to the lower Mandan village, at the particular request of the chief, to dance to the music of a tambourine, a sounding horn, and Private Cruzatte's fiddle. The Indians enjoyed the music and the dancing, especially the Frenchman, who danced on his hands.

Toward noon, Clark and York arrived at the village, where festivities were in full swing. Clark called on York to dance, "which amused the croud verry much, and Some what astonished them, that So large a man Should be so active."

The following day, it was Lewis's turn. He led the party of musicians and dancers to the second Mandan village, for more of what Sergeant Ordway called "frolicking."[4]

From January 3 to 5, the Mandans held a nightly dance of their own. They invited the garrison to join them. When the men arrived, they were ushered to the back of the communal earth lodge. The dance began. To the music of rattles and drums, the old men of the village, dressed in their finery, entered the lodge, gathered into a circle, sat down, and waited. Soon the young men and their wives filed in, to take their places at the back of the circle. They fixed pipes for the old men, and a smoking ceremony ensued.

As the drumbeat became more insistent and the chanting swelled, one of the youngsters would approach an old man and beg him to take his wife, who in her turn would appear naked before the elder. She would lead him by the hand and—but let Clark tell it, as only he can: "the Girl then takes the Old man (who verry often can Screcely walk) and leades him to a Convenient place for the business, after which they return to the lodge."

In the event that the old man failed to gratify the wife, the husband would offer her again and again, and throw a robe into the bargain, and beg the old man not to despise the couple.

"All this," Clark noted, "is to cause the buffalow to Come near So that They may kill them." In the winter, the herds migrated far and wide in search of windblown bare spots where they could get at the grass. The buffalo dance was thought to be a magnet to the wandering herds.

There was a second purpose to the dance. The Mandans believed that power—in this case, the hunting abilities of the old men—could be transferred from one man to another through sexual relations with the same woman. To the great good luck of the enlisted men, the Mandans attributed to the whites great powers and big medicine. So, throughout the three-day buffalo dance, the Americans were said to be "untiringly zealous in attracting the cow" and in transferring power. One unnamed private made four contributions.[5] Sure enough, there was a good buffalo hunt a few days later.

Much about the Mandans was curious or inexplicable. Lewis was especially struck by their treatment of their horses. When some Mandan ponies on loan to the Americans arrived at the fort late on February 12, they appeared "so much fatieged" that Lewis ordered them fed corn moistened with a little water, "but to my astonishment found that they would not eat it but prefered the bark of the cotton wood which forms the principall article of food usually given them by their Indian masters in the winter season."

The Mandans, according to Lewis, "are invariably severe riders, and frequently for many days in pursuing the Buffaloe they [the horses] are seldom suffered to tast food." After the hunt, the Indians brought their horses into their lodges for the night, where the animals were given what Lewis regarded as "a scanty allowance" of cottonwood ranging from the size of a man's finger to that of his arm. Lewis could hardly believe that a horse could exist long under such circumstances, but he had seen with his own eyes and knew it to be a fact that the Mandan horses "are seldom seen meager or unfit for service."

Lewis's long essay on Mandan horsemanship was the last in a series of ten journal entries he made beginning on February 3. That was the day Clark set out with sixteen men on a nine-day hunting expedition. In no way does Lewis indicate that because Clark was gone from Fort Mandan it had become his responsibility to keep up the journal, but since the Lewis journal stopped when Clark returned, it seems likely that is what happened. If so, Lewis was not keeping a regular journal in the winter of 1804–5, although he was doing a great deal of writing in the form of reports to Jefferson.

He was also doing a good deal of doctoring. On the first day of winter, a Mandan woman brought her child to Lewis, showed him an abscess on the child's back, and offered Lewis as much corn as she could carry for some medicine to cure the sore. Lewis complied. On January 10, a thirteen-year-old Mandan boy came to the fort with frozen feet. The captains used a standard treatment, soaking the feet in cold water. It appeared to work (it did with the men, who had frequent cases of frozen toes and fingers but always recovered). In this case, however, the boy was too far gone. On January 26, Clark recorded that "Capt. Lewis took off the Toes of one foot of the boy who got frost bit Some time ago."

Dr. E. G. Chuinard, whose medical history of the expedition all Lewis and Clark scholars turn to when the subject is doctoring, comments: "Probably the necrotic tissue had demarcated in the two weeks since his toes were frozen, and probably the amputations done by Lewis consisted of plucking loose the dead tissue, possibly disarticulating the joints, and possibly having to sever tendons."[6]

Five days later, the captains "sawed off the boys toes" from the other foot. How it was done, they don't say. Dr. Chuinard notes that a surgical saw was not listed in the medical kit and speculates that one of the two handsaws was used.[7] However it was done, more than three weeks later, on February 23, Clark reported, "The father of the Boy whose feet were frozed near this place, and nearly Cured by us, took him home in a Slay."

Aside from frozen skin and extremities, the most common medical problem the captains faced was syphilis. Few details come down in the journals, but it is possible that nearly every man suffered from the disease. As for the captains, they never mention taking the standard treatment themselves.

That treatment consisted of ingesting mercury, in the form of a pill called calomel (mercurous chloride). The side effects of mercury could be dangerous; the phrase "mad as a hatter" referred to hatmakers who used mercury in the process of their work and became a bit crazy from breathing in all those fumes. But it was sovereign for syphilis, and Lewis knew this and administered it routinely.[8]

The captains applied all their treatments on the principle that more is better. On January 26, one of the men was "taken violenty Bad with the Plurisee." How he survived the captains' treatment is a wonder. They bled him, purged him with Rush's pills, and greased his chest (which might actually have done some good). He was still suffering the next day, so Clark bled him again and then put him into a sweat lodge, where water was splashed onto hot rocks to produce a sauna—and that must have done some good, for the patient is not again mentioned.

Lewis's most unusual experience as a doctor came on February 11, when he was present at the labor of one of Charbonneau's wives, Sacagawea. Lewis noted that "this was the first child which this woman had boarn and as is common in such cases her labour was tedious and the pain violent." Lewis worried about her, because he was counting on her as a translator with the Shoshone Indians (known by Lewis to be rich in horses) when he got to the mountains. He consulted with Jessaume, who said that in such cases it was his practice to administer a small portion of the rattle of the rattlesnake. According to Jessaume, it always worked.

"Having the rattle of a snake by me," Lewis wrote in his journal, he broke the rattles into small pieces and mixed them with some water, which Sacagawea then drank. "Whether this medicine was truly the cause or not I shall not undertake to determine," Lewis said, "but she had not taken it more than ten minutes before she brought forth." In a sentence itself pregnant with hope but tempered by a skepticism befitting a scientist of the Enlightenment, Lewis wrote, "This remedy may be worthy of future experiements, but I must confess that I want faith as to it's efficacy."

The baby, a boy named Jean Baptiste Charbonneau, was healthy and active. The family had its own hut inside Fort Mandan, so the cries of a hungry infant rang through the parade ground and surely caused at least some pangs of homesickness among at least a few of the men, as they remembered their own families and their own little brothers or sisters. Siblings were very much on Lewis's mind. In a long letter to his mother about this time, he gave over a special section to his siblings.

Charbonneau, the new father, was all set up by what he had done and was coming to have a wholly new view of his own importance.

Quite probably this escalation in self-importance was fed by the conversations he translated through the winter between the captains and the Indians. From the captains' questions about what lay out west, and the Indians' answers, Charbonneau knew that Sacagawea was critical to dealing with the Shoshones. And without Charbonneau, no Sacagawea.

So, on March 11, when the captains sat down with Charbonneau to make a contract, it was Charbonneau who took the high ground and tried to dictate the terms. The captains said he would have to pitch in and do all the work the enlisted men had to do and would have to stand a regular guard. Charbonneau replied that "let our Situation be what it may he will not agree to work or Stand a guard." There was more: "If miffed with any man he wishes to return when he pleases, also have the disposial of as much provisions as he Chuses to Carry."

"In admissable," Clark and Lewis flatly declared. They told Charbonneau to move out of the fort, taking his family with him, and they hired Mr. Gravelines as interpreter.

After four days of living in the Mandan village, Charbonneau sent a message to the captains via one of the Frenchmen "to excuse his Simplicity and take him into the cirvise." Did he come to his senses on his own? Or did the Frenchmen tell him what a fool he was, what a once-in-a-lifetime opportunity he was passing up? Or was it Sacagawea who said she absolutely had to go see her people and participate in this great adventure? However it happened, Charbonneau was ready to crawl.

The captains sent word for him to come to the fort for a discussion. He showed up on March 17. "We called him in," Clark reported, "he agreed to our terms and we agreed that he might go on with us &c &c."

The roster for the expedition was complete. The permanent party that was getting ready to head west consisted of the three squads of enlisted men, each with its sergeant, plus the two captains, and five persons from outside the military establishment, namely Drouillard, York, Charbonneau, Sacagawea, and Jean Baptiste (nicknamed "Pomp" or "Pompey" by Clark).

By February 4, Lewis noted in his journal, the expedition had about run out of meat. That morning, Clark set out on his hunting expedition. The next day, Lewis reported that the immediate problem of scanty provisions had been overcome, although not with meat but with corn, and thanks to a bellows rather than a rifle.

Private John Shields was a skilled blacksmith. He had set up for business at the expedition's forge and bellows inside the fort. There he mended iron hoes, sharpened axes, and repaired firearms for the Indians in exchange for corn. But by the end of January, business was turning sour. The market for mending hoes had been satisfied. Shields needed some new product to attract business.

The arms trade was the obvious answer. Not in firearms—the captains turned away all requests for rifles or pistols—but in battle axes. There was a particular form of battle ax highly prized by the Indians and easily made by Shields. Lewis disapproved of the design, writing that it was "formed in a very inconvenient manner in my opinion." The blade was too thin and too long, the handle too short, the overall weight too little, all of which combined to make a weapon that made "an uncertain and easily avoided stroke."

But arms merchants give the customer what he wants. Shields went to work, getting his sheet iron from an all-but-burned-out stove. Some of the men were detailed to cutting timber to provide wood to make a charcoal kiln, to expand production capacity. Still, the Americans couldn't turn out battle axes fast enough.

The Indians were skilled traders who drove hard bargains. On February 6, Lewis had Shields cut up what was left of the stove into pieces of four inches square, which could then be worked into arrow points or buffalo-hide scrapers. After some haggling, a price was set: seven to eight gallons of corn for each piece of metal. Each side thought it had made a great bargain.*

In his February 6 journal entry, Lewis paid tribute to Shields and his helpers: "The blacksmiths take a considerable quantity of corn today in payment for their labour. the blacksmith's have proved a happy resoce to us in our present situation as I believe it would have been difficult to have devised any other method to have procured corn from the natives."

Lewis gave the full credit to Shields when he might well have split it, giving at least some to the Indians for having the corn available in the first place. Working as hard as they did in such extreme cold weather, the men ate prodigiously, six thousand calories or even more per day. A modern athlete seldom consumes more than five thousand, but the calories the men were getting in 1805 contained very little, if any, fat. Consequently, no matter how much they ate, the men were always

---

* How popular those axes were among the Indians, and consequently how far they traveled across the trade routes, Shields found out some fourteen months later, when he discovered axes he had made at Fort Mandan among the Nez Percé on the other side of the Rocky Mountains.

hungry.[9] It was Mandan corn that got the expedition through the winter. Had the Mandans not been there, or had they had no corn to spare, or had they been hostile, the Lewis and Clark Expedition might not have survived its first winter.

Lewis never put it that way and in fact probably never thought of it that way. Two days after writing the passage praising Shields for procuring corn, Lewis had a visit from the chief of the upper Mandan village, Black Cat. Lewis had been with him in Black Cat's village on January 2 and other occasions. This was Black Cat's seventeenth visit to Fort Mandan. He brought presents, including a fine bow. Lewis gave him some fishing hooks and some ribbon. Black Cat's squaw gave Lewis two pairs of handsome moccasins; he gave her a mirror and a couple of needles. Black Cat stayed to dine at the captains' quarters.

That evening, Lewis wrote in his journal, "This man possesses more integrety, firmness, inteligence and perspicuety of mind than any indian I have met with in this quarter, and I think with a little management he may be made a usefull agent in furthering the views of our government."

A remarkable sentence. In the first half, Lewis obviously was speaking from the heart. Clearly he enjoyed being with and greatly respected Black Cat. Yet, in the second half of the sentence, he blandly discusses his plans to manage and manipulate his friend for the benefit of the United States.

A further problem is this: what were the views of the Americans? On the one hand, peace. Lewis and Clark always preached peace to the Indians, giving them what the Americans thought of as overwhelmingly powerful reasons to avoid war. On the other hand, the Americans were arms merchants. As James Ronda puts it, "Typical of this dilemma was the request from a war chief who came to purchase an axe and obtain permission to attack Sioux and Arikara warriors. For the proper price in corn the axe was handed over but the request to use it was denied." The Hidatsa chief must have wondered what sort of man would sell arms to a warrior and then tell him not to engage the enemy.[10]

The winter at Fort Mandan involved hunting, trading, keeping fit, dealing with the cold, doing extensive repairs to old equipment and building new canoes, visiting the Indians, and much more. But for Meriwether Lewis it was primarily a winter of scholarship, of research and writing. For most of the day, most days, he was involved in gathering information or writing down what he had learned. He had endless discussions with the Indians about what lay out west, or what this or that faraway tribe was like. Or he bent over his writing desk in his smoky room, with a candle for illumination, dipped his quill into the inkstand, and wrote for hours on end.

His subject was America west of the Mississippi River. He wrote about what he had seen and learned, and what he had heard. He tried to think like Jefferson, to anticipate what the president would want to know or to guess how the president would present this or that subject.

And what of Jefferson, meanwhile? What did he know about where the expedition was, and how it was doing?

Precious little. He had no direct word from Lewis after the expedition left St. Charles. The Osage chiefs whose visit Lewis had arranged arrived in Washington in July 1804. In greeting them, Jefferson spoke of his "beloved man, Capt. Lewis."[11] On January 4, 1805, Jefferson wrote Lewis's brother, Reuben, to report that he had just learned (apparently by word-of-mouth via a trapper who had returned to St. Louis that fall) that on August 19 the expedition was near the mouth of the Platte. According to the report, "No accident had happened & he [Lewis] had been well received by all the Indians on his way. It was expected that he would winter with the Mandans, 1300 miles up the river."

Jefferson predicted that the expedition would reach the Pacific during the coming summer, then return to the Mandan villages for the winter of 1805–6. "If so," the president cheerfully concluded, "we may expect to see him in the fall of 1806."[12]

17

REPORT FROM
FORT MANDAN

March 22–April 6, 1805

New life was stirring. On the first day of spring, it rained—the first rain since fall. The river ice began to break up. Ducks, swans, and geese sometimes seemed to fill the sky. The Indians set fire to the dry grass to encourage new grass to come up, for the benefit of their horses and to attract the buffalo.

By the end of March, the ice was coming down in great chunks, along with drowned buffalo who had been on the ice when it gave way. "I observed extrodanary dexterity of the Indians in jumping from one Cake of ice to another," Clark wrote on the 30th, "for the purpose of Catching the buffalow as they float down."

The joy of spring was everywhere, and doubly welcome by the men of the expedition, who had just survived the coldest winter any of them had ever known. They worked with enthusiasm, eager to get going again. Teams of men were repairing the boat, while others were building canoes, packing, making moccasins, making jerky, pumping the bellows. They sang as they worked.

In the five months between May and October 1804, the captains and their men had traveled more miles than many of their contemporaries would do in a lifetime. In the five months between November 1804 and April 1805, they had stayed in one place. The anticipation of getting going on the river again was so keen it was almost unbearable.

On the last day of March, Clark wrote, "All the party in high Spirits, but fiew nights pass without a Dance. Possessing perfect harmony and good understanding towards each other. Generally healthy except venerials complains which is verry Commion. . . ."

On April 5, the keelboat and the two pirogues that had come down the Ohio and then up the Mississippi and Missouri to Fort Mandan, along with six new canoes, were put into the water. They would be packed the next day, then set off on April 7, the keelboat headed downstream for St. Louis while the two pirogues and the lighter and more maneuverable canoes headed upstream, where the river would gradually become shallower and swifter.

As the men went about their work, the captains wrote. So much writing did they do that Clark complained he had no time to write his family. Lewis managed to work in a letter to his mother, but most of it was unoriginal—he just copied passages from his report to Jefferson.

The captains worked with passion and dedication. For several weeks, Lewis did nothing but write, eat, and sleep. There was so much to say. He felt he needed to justify the expedition. He wanted to please Jefferson, to be able to report that they had discovered what he had hoped they would, to answer his questions, to promote his program for the development of Louisiana.

Even more, the captains wanted to be accurate in all their observations. They were men of the Enlightenment, dedicated to collecting facts and then putting the new knowledge to work for the good of mankind. So, in addition to describing the geography, the soils, the minerals, the climate, they had the responsibility of describing the tribes, and of making recommendations on the economic future of Louisiana. They needed to make available in permanent form as much as they could of what they had learned.

Lewis was determined to get these jobs done and done right. In his mind, everything that had happened since Jefferson put him in command was preliminary to the expedition, which was only now about to begin. On April 7, the Corps of Discovery would set out into territory no white man had entered. Thus far, as Gary Moulton writes, "All the men's efforts had been directed to reaching a point where other whites had ventured before them, on a route already mapped."[1]

But although the expedition had yet to do any exploring, the captains had managed to pick up a tremendous amount of new information on Upper Louisiana—its flora and fauna, its climate and fertility, its peoples and their wars and their economies. Put together correctly, and properly organized and labeled, all this information would constitute the first systematic survey of the trans-Mississippi West, and would thus provide an invaluable contribution to the world's knowledge—and equally invaluable to the United States government and American businessmen, frontier farmers, fur traders, and adventurers.

The captains collected information in two basic ways. First and foremost, from their own observations. Second, by making local inquiry. They asked questions about the surrounding country of every Indian and white trader they met. These information-gathering sessions sometimes lasted a full day, occasionally even longer.

Jefferson had a passion for Indian language, believing he would be able to trace the Indians' origins by discovering the basis of their language. So the gathering of vocabularies was an important charge on the captains. They put a major effort into attempting to render words from various Indian languages into an English spelling.

MacKenzie was present once to see the captains at work on their vocabularies. The language being recorded was Hidatsa. A native speaker would say a word to Sacagawea, who would pass it on in Hidasta to Charbonneau, who would pass it on in French to Jessaume, who would translate it into English for the captains. MacKenzie thought Jessaume's English ranged somewhere between inadequate and nonexistent, magnifying the chances for error.

On another occasion, MacKenzie wrote: "I was present when vocabularies were being made of the Mandans; the two Frenchmen [Charbonneau and Jessaume] had warm disputes upon the meaning of every word that was taken down by the captains. As the Indians could not well comprehend the intention of recording their words, they concluded that the Americans had a wicked design upon their country."[2] Despite the difficulties, Lewis kept at it. He put in immense amounts of time on the task. Whether he found the work interesting, or thought it important, cannot be said. It sufficed that Mr. Jefferson wanted it done.

Lewis was relatively uninterested in Indian mythology or spiritual life, but he was a skilled observer of some parts of Indian culture, especially how things were done. One of his contributions, for example, was a graphic and precise description of glass-bead-making among the Arikaras. As the expedition prepared to depart for the mountains, the captains purchased a buffalo-skin tepee to provide shelter for themselves, Charbonneau, Sacagawea, and Pomp. Lewis described it in his journal entry of April 7, 1805, in what James Ronda characterized as "one of the best descriptions yet drafted of that distinctive plains dwelling."[3]

In addition to their written descriptions, the captains gathered such objects as Arikara corn, tobacco seeds, mineral and botanical specimens, along with artifacts from Indian life, including bows, clothing, and painted robes, to be sent to Jefferson. Altogether, the amount of information they gathered, organized, and presented in a systematic fashion to Jefferson—and, beyond him, to the scientific world—was enough to justify the expedition, even if it made not a single further contribution.

The model for Lewis and Clark's report was Jefferson's *Notes on the State of Virginia*. Like that work, written a quarter-century earlier, Lewis's description of Upper Louisiana was part guidebook, part travelogue, part boosterlike promotion, part text to accompany the master map. Adding in Clark's contributions, the final report from Fort Mandan totaled something close to forty-five thousand words, almost book-length (Jefferson's *Notes* ran to some eighty thousand words).

Like Jefferson, Lewis began with a detailed account of the waterways, or, as he put it, "A Summary view of the rivers and Creeks, which discharge themselves into the Missouri . . . from the junction of that river with the Mississippi, to Fort Mandan."[4] As Jefferson had done for Virginia, Lewis described not only the tributaries but the people living along the rivers, whether the French at St. Charles, or the Otos, or the Sioux. He included information on the local economy, the soil, mineral deposits, climate, and more.

The report combined the captains' actual observations of the various rivers flowing into the Missouri with information received from traders and Indians about the upper reaches of those streams and their own principal tributaries. For example, Lewis saw only the mouth of the Platte River, but he described it up to its head in the mountains. From what he had been told, he said, the Platte ran "through immence level and fertile plains and meadows, in which, no timber is to be seen except on it's own borders." He named five major tributaries of the Platte, discussed the mineral deposits in its drainage, the soil, the people—Otos and Missouris—and more. Naturally, the farther west Lewis's report ventured, the more speculative it became. His conjecture about the Platte's relationship to Santa Fe and to the Black Hills was purely imaginative and badly wrong.

Lewis expected that Jefferson would have his work printed and distributed as a report to Congress, and he knew something about the audience for the work, so on occasion he sounded like a promoter writing a broadside: "This river [the Muddy, in eastern Missouri] waters a most delightfull country; the land lies well for cultivation, and is fertile in the extreem . . . covered with lofty and excellent timber, and supplyed with an abundance of fine bould springs of limestone water."

The Grand River, farther west, was also prime farm country. "The lands are extreemly fertile; consisting of a happy mixtuure of praries and groves, exhibiting one of the most beautifull and picteresk seens that I ever beheld."

Enthusiastic as he was in his report about the lower-Missouri country—he made it sound almost like heaven—he actually was holding back his emotions. In his letter to his mother, dated March 21, 1804, he allowed himself to rhapsodize about the country, writing not so much as son to mother as Virginia planter to Virginia planter. "This immence river so far as we have yet ascended," he wrote, "waters one of the farest portions of the globe, nor do I believe that there is in the universe a similar extent of country, equally fertile, well watered, and intersected by suuch a number of navigable streams." He added, "I had been led to believe that the open prarie contry was barren, steril and sandy; but on the contrary I found it fertile in the extreem, the soil being from one to 20 feet in debth, consisting of a fine black loam [that produces] a luxuriant growth of grass and other vegitables."

The Plains were not quite Eden, however; the absence of timber was a serious drawback, for it was almost unimaginable for any American in 1805 to live in a country without plenty of lumber and fuel. Indeed, in the eastern third of the United States, too much timber was the problem.[5]

In his report to Jefferson, Lewis took note of all the things that would spring to the mind of a frontier farmer hankering to move into Upper Louisiana. He pointed out "several rappids well situated for water-works"; he warned against areas that had tolerably fertile soil but no timber. Lewis was an advance man for the American fur trappers and traders as well as farmers. He noted the furs available and scouted likely spots for trading posts.

One of Lewis's responsibilities was to make recommendations on how to drive the British away from the Missouri so that American companies could take over the fur trade. His analysis of the economic-political situation on the river led him directly to his conclusion and recommendation.

"I am perfectly convinced that untill such measures are taken by our government as will effectually prohibit all intercourse or traffic with the Sioux" and the British fur companies, he reported to Jefferson, "the Citizens of the United States can never enjoy, but partially, those important advantages which the navigation of the Missouri now presents." He recommended establishing garrisons in places where the soldiers could stop the British from coming into Dakota from Canada or across today's Minnesota. If trade between the British and the Sioux was prohibited for a few years, he wrote, "the Sioux will be made to feel their dependance on the will of our government for their supplies of merchandize, and in the course of two or three years, they may most probably be reduced to order without the necessity of bloodshed." Given what happened in Sioux-American relations over the following seventy-one years, that was a hopelessly optimistic prediction.

Much of the report was a business prospectus, with the emphasis on the Indian as customer and supplier. In a separate section, written in Clark's hand but the product of both men's labor, entitled "Estimate of the Eastern Indians,"[6] the captains described no fewer than seventy-two different tribes and bands, with at least some information on where they lived, how they lived, who they were at war with, their numbers, their dwellings, and more. Of course the captains could only describe a few tribes from firsthand knowledge, but they made clear where their information was word-of-mouth.

Those they knew they did not hesitate to characterize, often in a heartfelt fashion. They wrote of their friends the Mandans, "These are the most friendly, well disposed Indians inhabiting the Missouri. They are brave, humane and hospitable." Of the Teton Sioux, the opposite: "These are the vilest miscreants of the savage race, and must ever remain the pirates of the Missouri, until such measures are pursued, by our government, as will make them feel a dependence on its will for their supply of merchandise."

Of the tribes living along the route they intended to follow, they wrote of the mountain-dwelling Flatheads: "They are a timid, inoffensive, and defenceless people. They are said to possess an abundance of horses."

Of the Shoshones, the captains' information indicated that they traded with the Spanish, who refused to give them firearms. Consequently, although the Shoshones were a very numerous and well-disposed people, "All the nations on the Missouries below make war on them & Steal their horses."

Of the Nez Percé: "Still less is known of these people, or their country. The water courses on which they reside, are supposed to be branches of the Columbia river."

Along with the written report, the captains sent back to Jefferson 108 botanical specimens, to add to the collections at the American Philosophical Society, all properly labeled as to where and when collected, and described. The first was "a species of Cress, taken at St. Louis May 10th 1804. It is common in the open growns on the

Mississippi bottomes, appears in the uncultivated parts of the lots gardens and orchards, the seed come to maturity by the 10th of May in most instances."

If medicinal properties were claimed for a plant, Lewis mentioned them. If the claim touched a common medical problem back in the States, Lewis emphasized it, none more so than a root known by the name of "white wood of the prairie" which was said to be sovereign for the bite of a mad wolf or a mad dog, and for the bite of the rattlesnake. Rabies and snakebite were common dangers in the early nineteenth century, so a cure was such an exciting prospect that Lewis made the root of the white wood the subject of a separate letter to Jefferson, in which he detailed how to prepare it as a poultice, how to apply it, and so forth. He concluded: "I have sent herewith a few pounds of this root, in order that experiments may be made by some skilfull person under the direction of the pilosophical society of Philadelphia."[7]

It was probably the purple coneflower, which was widely used by the Indians as an antidote for snakebite. Jefferson sent the root along to a doctor to experiment with it.[8]

Lewis also sent to Jefferson sixty-eight mineral specimens, all labeled as to where and when collected. He included such items as "sand of the Missouri," "one pint of Missouri water," "pebbles common to the Missouri," lead ore, quartz, Glauber salts, alum, pyrites, lime, lava and pumice stone, and fossils.

The plants and minerals were part of a larger shipment to Jefferson that included skeletons of a male and female pronghorn, the horns of two mule deer, insects and mice, skins of various animals, including a marten and a white weasel that came from beyond the mountains via the trade route, and more. There were live animals too, new to science: four magpies, a prairie dog, and a prairie grouse hen (only one magpie and the prairie dog reached Jefferson alive).

Included also in the shipment was Clark's map of the United States west of the Mississippi River. It was a masterpiece of the cartographer's art, and an invaluable contribution to knowledge. From St. Louis to Fort Mandan, Clark got it exactly right along the Missouri. His map became a bit sketchier as it moved west, naturally, because his depictions of the various tributaries was based on hearsay, often from people who did not claim to be eyewitnesses but knew someone who had been there. Lewis explained Clark's method: he would compare one Indian's description with another's, questioning them separately and at different times, and questioning as many as possible. Only when there was agreement on placement, distance, mountain passes, and so forth was the information put on Clark's map and into Lewis's report.

For all their concern with getting the specimens ready for shipment and with making their report and the map as complete as possible, in the first two weeks of spring what was uppermost in the captains' minds was what lay ahead. They pumped the Mandans, who never ventured very far west and thus could tell them little, and the Hidatsas, whose war parties ranged to the mountains and who thus could tell them a lot.

From the Hidatsas, Lewis had learned the names of rivers coming into the Missouri, and their connections with one another. He commented on his source: "I conceive [the Hidatsas] are entitled to some confidence."

Lewis expected to find, at 117 miles upriver from Fort Mandan, the White Earth River coming in on the north side. The prospect excited him greatly, because if the White Earth came in from as far north as the Indians indicated, it would mean that the boundary between Canada and the United States might be moved north by as much as a full degree of latitude, something Jefferson very much hoped for.

Three miles above the mouth of the White Earth, the Indians told Lewis he would come to the greatest of all the tributaries of the Missouri, the Yellowstone. The Hidatsas said that the Yellowstone "waters one of the fairest portions of Louisiana, a country not yet hunted, and abounding in animals of the fur kind." They thought the river navigable "at all seasons of the year for boats and perogues to the foot of the Rocky Mountains, near which place, it is said to be not more than 20 miles distant from the three forks of the Missouri."

The obvious importance of the Yellowstone led Lewis to recommend that the government build a trading post at the junction with the Missouri. It would "afford to our citizens the benefit of a most lucrative fur trade [and] might be made to hold in check the views of the British N. West Company," whose intention was "to panopolize" the Missouri River fur-trade business. "If this powerfull and ambitious company are suffered uninterruptedly to prosecute their trade," Lewis warned, the British might someday use their influence with the natives to block all American navigation on the Missouri.

Some 150 miles upstream from the mouth of the Yellowstone would come "The River Which Scolds at All Others," falling in on the north side. Then the Musselshell from the south. Another 120 miles and the expedition would be at the falls of the Missouri, "discribed by the Indians as a most tremendious Cataract. They state that the nois it makes can be heard at a great distance. . . . They also state that there is a fine open plain on the N. side of the falls, through which, canoes and baggage may be readily transported. this portage they assert is not greater than a half a mile."

Some fifteen miles beyond the falls, the Medicine River would fall in on the north side. Another sixty miles and the expedition would enter the first connected chain of the mountains. After another seventy-five miles, the Missouri would divide into three nearly equal branches, at the place called Three Forks, where Sacagawea had been captured some five years earlier. The most northern of the three rivers "is navigable to the foot of a chain of high mountains, being the ridge which divides the waters of the Atlantic from those of the Pacific ocean. The Indians assert that they can pass in half a day from the foot of this mountain on it's East side to a large river which washes it's Western base."

How Jefferson must have loved reading that line. The singular objective of the expedition was about to be realized.

The Divide was as far as the Hidatsas ever ventured. Lewis noted that "we have therefore been unable to acquire any information further West than the view from the top of these mountains."

But what the Hidatsas said they saw from the top of the mountain was exactly what Lewis and Jefferson hoped for and expected: "The Indians inform us that the country on the Western side of this river consists of open & level plains like those they themselves inhabit." The Flathead and Shoshone tribes lived on a river in that country. Their principal food was fish. "This river we suppose to be the S. fork of the Columbia," Lewis wrote, "and the fish the Salmon, with which we are informed the Columbia river abounds. This river is said to be rapid but as far as the Indian informants are acquainted with it is not intercepted with shoals."

What had been high expectations now soared, both at Fort Mandan and, some months later, in Washington, when the report arrived and Jefferson read it with what must have been the most intense satisfaction, feeling that, even as he was reading, the all-water route to the Pacific was being found and mapped.

Along with the report, Lewis sent back to St. Louis various letters, dispatches, and copies of the drafts and chits he had signed, what he called "my public accounts." In a covering letter to Jefferson dated April 7, but almost certainly written the previous day, Lewis confessed to considerable embarrassment about those accounts.[9] He had intended to put them in order and have them returned to St. Louis in the fall of

1804, but in the event it turned out that "the provision perogue and her crew could not have been dismissed ... without evedently in my opinion, hazarding the fate of the enterprise in which I am engaged, and I therefore did not hesitate to prefer the sensure that I may have incurred by the detention of these papers, to that of risking in any degree the success of the expedition."

Jefferson had instructed Lewis to be diligent about his accounts and to get his drafts back to the War Department with all possible speed. Lewis said his failure to do so had become "a serious source of disquiet and anxiety; and the recollection of your particular charge to me on this subject, has made it still more poignant."

Clearly, as an army officer, Lewis had made the correct decision. But as the president's protégé he felt terrible about it, because he hated disappointing Jefferson. Yet, however bad he felt about it, Lewis's casualness with his accounts and the chits he had signed was becoming habitual.

In the second half of his April 7 letter to Jefferson, Lewis told his commander-in-chief his plans. In the morning, he intended to send the keelboat and pirogues on their way. Accompanying Corporal Warfington would be four privates plus Newman* and Reed, Mr. Gravelines acting as pilot and interpreter, and four Frenchmen. They were well armed and adequately supplied. "I have but little doubt but they will be fired on by the Siouxs," Lewis wrote, "but they have pledged themselves to us that they will not yeald while there is a man of them living."

The expedition's six canoes and two pirogues were loaded, ready to go. They would shove off the instant Warfington turned the keelboat downstream. Lewis said he intended to leave the two pirogues at the falls of the Missouri. On the far side of the falls he intended to put his iron-frame boat together and cover it with skins.

Freed of the cumbersome keelboat, Lewis said he anticipated traveling at a rate of twenty to twenty-five miles per day until he reached the falls. After that, "any calculation with rispect to our daily progress, can be little more than bare conjecture." But his hopes were

---

* Newman had conducted himself admirably since his court-martial and discharge. He had volunteered for the toughest jobs and impressed the men so much that they urged Lewis to meet Newman's request that he be allowed to rejoin the expedition. Although he later had some words of praise for Newman, Lewis would not reinstate him, and he returned to St. Louis with the deserter Reed.

high: "The circumstance of the Snake Indians possessing large quantities of horses, is much in our favour, as by means of horses, the transportation of our baggage will be rendered easy and expeditious over land, from the Missouri to the Columbia river."

Supplies were adequate, Lewis said, thanks to the skills of the hunters, whose efforts made it possible to live on a diet of meat, thus saving the parched corn, portable soup, flour, and salt pork for the mountains. He put in not a word about Mandan corn, a glaring omission that left Jefferson with the entirely wrong impression that it was possible for white men to winter on the Plains without help from the Indians. Lewis did say that the Indians assured him the country ahead "abounds with a vast quantity of game."

Lewis predicted that the expedition would reach the Pacific Ocean that summer, then return as far as the head of the Missouri, or perhaps even as far as Fort Mandan, for the winter of 1805–6. He told Jefferson, "You may therefore expect me to meet you at Monachello in September 1806."

Lewis's concluding paragraph must be the most optimistic report from the field from an army officer about to set off on a great venture that any commander-in-chief ever received: "I can foresee no material or probable obstruction to our progress, and entertain therefore the most sanguine hopes of complete success. As to myself individually I never enjoyed a more perfect state of good health, than I have since we commenced our voyage. My inestimable friend and companion Capt. Clark has also enjoyed good health generally. At this moment, every individual of the party are in good health, and excellent sperits; zealously attatched to the enterprise, and anxious to proceed; not a whisper of discontent or murmur is to be heard among them; but all in unison, act with the most perfect harmoney. With such men I have everything to hope, and but little to fear."

18

FROM FORT MANDAN
TO MARIAS RIVER

April 7–June 2, 1805

In the morning and early part of the afternoon of April 7, 1805, Lewis was busy overseeing the last-minute wrapping of packages and their placement into the canoes that would head upriver to the mountains, or into the keelboat that was going downstream to St. Louis. He checked weapons, powder, food and medical stocks, trade goods, and implements. He gave last-minute instructions to Corporal Richard Warfington, in command of the keelboat—mainly to be on full alert in Sioux territory, to be prepared to shoot his way through the Sioux, and to make sure the plants, animals, and artifacts he had selected, and the letters, journals, and reports he and Clark had created, got through to President Jefferson.

At 4:00 p.m., the boat, pirogues, canoes, and crews were ready to shove off. The men of the permanent expedition called out goodbye, good luck, and Godspeed to the crew of the keelboat, then pushed their six small canoes and two larger pirogues, all heavily laden, into the current. They climbed in, took up their paddles, and began pulling upstream.

They quickly got into their stroke, all the blades on the six-man pirogues dipping into the Missouri in unison on both sides of the vessels as the men at the helm turned the craft upstream. How many strokes, and how much poling and pulling of the vessels remained before they reached the source of the Missouri, no man knew. But they all figured it would be a lot.

Lewis watched them go. For the past several weeks, he had been so busy writing he had taken no exercise. Feeling the want of it—and perhaps wanting to be alone on the occasion—he had decided to walk on shore that afternoon. He went up the north bank of the river some six miles, to the upper Mandan village, where he called on Chief Black Cat. When he found the chief not at home, he returned two miles downstream, where he joined Clark and the party.

Lewis took an early supper and went to bed. His bed was a buffalo-skin and a blanket placed inside a buffalo skin tepee, apparently put up (and taken down and packed the next morning) by Sacagawea, perhaps with some help from York. The men slept in the open. Joining Lewis in his lodge were Clark, Charbonneau, Drouillard, Sacagawea, and her baby. Putting her in the tent, surrounded by the two captains, the hunter and interpreter, her husband, and her son, removed temptation for the men. This sleeping arrangement persisted until Sacagawea and Charbonneau returned to the Mandan villages. It worked: there is not the slightest hint in the journals that having a young woman among those healthy, hearty soldiers ever caused a problem.

That night, or shortly thereafter, Lewis wrote his first journal entry since February 13* That entry is justly famous and deserves to be quoted at some length: "Our vessels consisted of six small canoes, and two large perogues. This little fleet altho' not quite so rispectable as those of Columbus or Capt. Cook, were still viewed by us with as much pleasure as those deservedly famed adventurers ever beheld theirs; and I dare say with quite as much anxiety for their safety and preservation. we were now about to penetrate a country at least two thousand miles in width, on which the foot of civillized man had never trodden; the good or evil it had in store for us was for experiment yet to determine, and these little vessells contained every article by which we were to expect to subsist or defend ourselves. however, as this the state of mind in which we are, generally gives the colouring to events, when the immagination is suffered to wander into futurity, the picture which now presented itself to me was a most pleasing one. entertaing as I do, the most confident hope of succeading in a voyage which had

---

* When Clark was gone on a hunting expedition from early February to the 13th, Lewis made daily journal entries—a strong indication that he was *not* writing in his journal when Clark was present. As to when Lewis wrote his April 7 entry, his verb tense is more tantalizing than conclusive. "We were now," he wrote at one point, not "we are now," making it seem he wrote it days or weeks or months later. But he also wrote (in what was a copy of a paragraph he had written to Jefferson, evidently that morning to give to Warfington), "The party are in excellent health and sperits, zealously atached to the enterprise, and anxious to proceed," which makes it seem he wrote it that night.

formed a darling project of mine for the last ten years, I could but esteem this moment of my departure as among the most happy of my life."

In the morning, Lewis again walked on shore. He came to the Mandan village after two miles, and there paid a farewell visit to Black Cat. They smoked a pipe together. At noon, he descended to the river, where he had to wait for the party to come up, since one of the canoes had filled with water. The men unloaded the craft and spread the contents to dry in the sun. That task completed, they made a few more miles in the late afternoon. In the evening, a Mandan man came up, bringing with him "a woman who was extreemly solicitous to accompany one of the men of our party, this however we positively refused to permit."

Lewis refused for an obvious reason: not because a woman would be an extra mouth to feed but, rather, because an unattached woman would be a source of jealousy and disruption. Sacagawea was already showing that she could make a contribution; Lewis noted on April 9 that "when we halted for dinner the squaw busied herself in serching for the wild artichokes which the mice collect and deposit in large hoards. this operation she performed by penetrating the earth with a sharp stick. . . . her labour soon proved successful, and she procurrd a good quantity of these roots." They were Jerusalem artichokes.

The roots were welcome, because the hunters were unable to kill anything. Hidatsa braves had frightened the game out of the river valley within two or three days' ride of the villages, reducing the party to subsisting on parched corn and jerky. But the Indians had assured Lewis that game would be plentiful once the expedition got beyond the range of the hunting parties, and meanwhile the little fleet was making excellent progress. On April 9, it covered twenty-three and a half miles, which was what Lewis hoped to make as an average, and was about double the distance the expedition had averaged on the river below the Mandans, when it had been encumbered by the clumsy, slow-moving keelboat.

The white pirogue was the flagship of the fleet. Slightly smaller than the red, the white pirogue was more stable, so it carried the astronomical instruments, the medicines, the best trade goods, the captains' writing desks, their journals and field notes, and several casks of gunpowder. It was propelled by six paddlers, including the three nonswimmers among the privates, who were on board for safety's sake. Sacagawea and her baby, riding all bundled up on her back in his cradleboard, joined Charbonneau, Drouillard, and the two captains (most of the time, one or the other of the captains walked on shore; their rule was that one of them should always be with the fleet).

The flat-bottomed pirogues were clumsy craft, but with experienced helmsmen they could be more or less controlled. The six canoes were round-bottomed dugouts, hewn from cottonwood trees, each with three paddlers. They were more difficult to maneuver and much more likely to ship water, especially when rounding a point into the wind. To overcome the wind, the men often got out and tugged the craft along, using elk-skin ropes and one hemp line per boat. Or they could use setting poles to propel the pirogues and canoes forward.

Best of all were the times when the wind was behind them. Then the men could raise their square sails and scoot along at a breathtaking three miles an hour.

Worst of all were the times when there was a strong head wind. This could force the party to stay in camp for an entire day. Of course the captains didn't waste the enforced layover; Lewis and Clark supervised drying damp articles, repairing the fleet, making moccasins and clothing, adding to the meat supply, writing in their journals, making observations.

During the first four days, the expedition covered ninety-three miles, to the mouth of the Little Missouri. In the process, it traversed the many-miles-long curve of the river called the Great Bend. That meant that, for the first time since Lewis left the mouth of the Kansas River, in July 1804, he was headed nearly straight west, instead of northwest or even straight north.

His journal entries were lyrical. On April 15, eight days out of Fort Mandan, the expedition passed the farthest point upstream on the Missouri known by Lewis to have been reached by white men. The previous voyagers were two French trappers, one of them now a member of the expedition, Private Baptiste Lepage.

Lewis was now stepping into the unknown. For all he had heard from the Hidatsas about what lay ahead, for all that he knew the distance to his destination—as the crow flies—he was as close to entering a completely unknown territory, nearly a half-continent wide, as any explorer ever was. His April 7 half-humorous comparison of his fleet to those of Columbus and Cook was on the mark.

He was entering a heart of darkness. Deserts, mountains, great cataracts, warlike Indian tribes—he could not imagine them, because no American had ever seen them. But, far from causing apprehension or depression, the prospect brought out his fullest talents. He knew that from now on, until he reached the Pacific and returned, he would be making history. He was exactly what Jefferson wanted him to be,

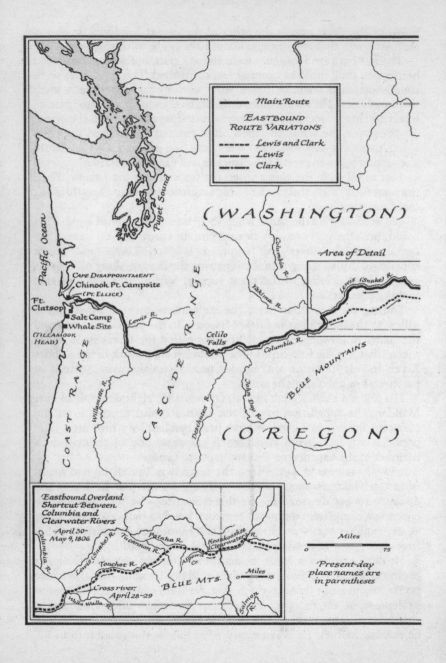

Main Route

EASTBOUND
ROUTE VARIATIONS

— — — Lewis and Clark
— ·· — Lewis
— · — Clark

(WASHINGTON)

Pacific Ocean

Puget Sound

Columbia R.

Area of Detail

CAPE DISAPPOINTMENT
Chinook Pt. Campsite
(PT. ELLICE)

Ft.
Clatsop

Salt Camp
Whale Site

(TILLAMOOK
HEAD)

Lewis R.

Yakima R.

Lewis (Snake) R.

CASCADE RANGE

Celilo
Falls

Columbia R.

COAST RANGE

Willamette R.

Deschutes R.

John Day R.

BLUE MOUNTAINS

(OREGON)

Eastbound Overland
Shortcut Between
Columbia and
Clearwater Rivers
-April 30-
May 4, 1806

Columbia R.

Lewis (Snake) R.

Touchet R.

Tucannon R.

Pataha R.

Alpowa
Cr.

Kooskooskie
(Clearwater) R.

Miles

0   75

Miles   15

Cross river,
April 28-29

BLUE MTS.

Walla Walla R.

Salmon R.

Present-day
place names are
in parentheses

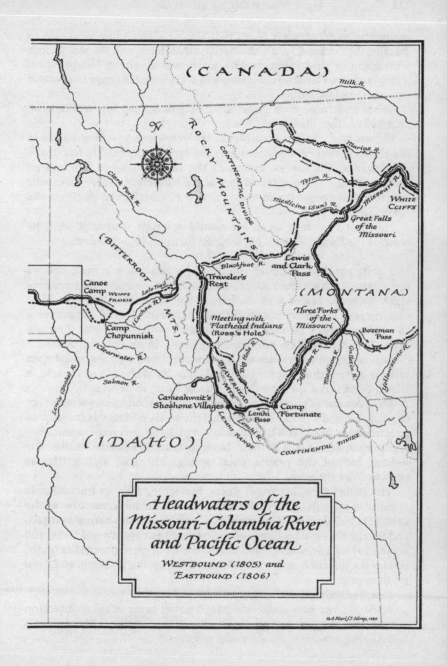

Headwaters of the
Missouri-Columbia River
and Pacific Ocean

WESTBOUND (1805) and
EASTBOUND (1806)

optimistic, prudent, alert to all that was new about him, and able to describe the flora and fauna, the native inhabitants, and the skies above with scientific measurement. His health was excellent. His ambition was boundless. His determination was complete. He could not, would not, contemplate failure.

Lewis had come to a point that he had longed for, worked for, dreamed of all of his life.

He was ready, intensely alive. Every nerve ending was sensitive to the slightest change, whether what the eye saw or the skin felt or the ears heard or the tongue tasted or the fingers touched. He had an endearing sense of wonder and awe at the marvels of nature that made him the nearly perfect man to be the first to describe the glories of the American West.

He turned his face west. He would not turn it around until he reached the Pacific Ocean. He stepped forward, into paradise.

Not quite paradise, although one would hardly know it from Lewis's descriptions, which were accurate enough but always given a positive slant. Overall, Lewis was enchanted by the Plains. May 5: "The country is as yesterday beatifull in the extreme." He did not mention the indications of average yearly rainfall, which was less than ten inches. He did mention one apparent result, in his entry of April 10: "The country on both sides of the missouri from the tops of the river hills, is one continued level fertile plain as far as the eye can reach, in which there is not even a solitary tree or shrub to be seen."

Most American pioneers believed that hardwood forests were a sign of good soil, and would have regarded the treeless Plains as unsuitable to agriculture, but Lewis had an easy—and, so far as it went, accurate— explanation for the lack of trees. No trees could get started because the Indians burned the prairie each spring. The soil was fertile, as evidenced by the grass.

The Plains grew luxuriant grass, enough to feed an uncountable number of animals. This really was paradise, for such creatures as the deer, elk, buffalo, sheep, pronghorns, and other grass-eating animals, and for the beaver who lived off the bark of the cottonwood trees, and for the coyote, fox, wolves, and bears who lived off the hoofed animals, and for the human hunters who declared war on the predators and lived off their prey.

Lewis exclaimed at the magnificance of it all.

April 17: "we saw immence quantities of game in every direction around us as we passed up the river; consisting of herds of Buffaloe, Elk, and Antelopes with some deer and woolves."

April 21: "We saw immence herds of buffaloe Elk deer & Antelopes."

April 22: "I asscended to the top of the cutt bluff this morning, from whence I had a most delightfull view of the country, the whole of which except the vally formed by the Missouri is void of timber or underbrush, exposing to the first glance of the spectator immence herds of Buffaloe, Elk, deer, & Antelopes feeding in one common and boundless pasture. . . . walking on shore this evening I met with a buffaloe calf which attatched itself to me and continued to follow close at my heels untill I embarked and left it."

April 27: "altho' game is very abundant and gentle, we only kill as much as is necessary for food. I believe that two good hunters could conveniently supply a regiment with provisions."

The men's labor was again such that each private ate as much as nine or ten pounds of meat per day. This meant that, when the captains went hunting (to free the hunters to help move the fleet forward), the two of them had to bring in three hundred pounds or so of meat.

May 6: "It is now only amusement for Capt. C. and myself to kill as much meat as the party can consum; I hope it may continue thus through our whole rout, but this I do not much expect."

On May 5, Lewis discovered and described the gray wolf. He noted that, unlike its larger relative, the wolf of the Atlantic states, the gray wolf never burrowed, but like the eastern species howled rather than barked. He marveled at the way the packs wore down buffalo, some wolves pursuing while others rested before taking up the chase in their turn. He noted, "we scarcely see a gang of buffaloe without observing a parsel of those faithfull shepherds on their skirts in readiness to take care of the mamed & wounded."

Of all the animals, the most prized was the beaver. In the immediate range, because the tail of the beaver was one of the most favored delicacies; in the longer term, because, if properly prepared, stacked, pressed, and aired once a month or so for moths, the beaver pelt could be gotten back to St. Louis, where it fetched a fair price, then to New York, and on to London, where it fetched a fabulous price. So some of the men became en-route beaver trappers, in the richest beaver country any white man had ever seen.

On the third day out, the expedition caught up with three French trappers, who accompanied it to the Little Missouri. These were the first beaver hunters west of Mandan, according to Lewis, and "the beaver these people have already taken is by far the best I have ever seen." He recorded on April 12 that, to his surprise, beaver were seen during the day, "proof that they have been but little hunted."

On the morning of April 18, Lewis came upon two of his privates engaged in a furious argument. It seemed that one beaver had gotten himself caught in two traps, belonging to the two different men. They were on the verge of blows when Lewis intervened.

Beaver was the greatest, most immediately exploitable wealth of the trans-Mississippi West. Beaver presence in such quality and quantity guaranteed an immediate penetration of Louisiana by American hunters. Lewis was their scout.

He characteristically thought of practical uses for other products of the Plains. On April 12, he took some cuttings from a creeping juniper (he called it "dwarf juniper") to send to Jefferson, and noted, "This plant would make very handsome edgings to the borders and walks of a garden . . . [and it is] easily propegated," advice that innumerable people living in suburbs in the American West ever since have followed.

Less successful was his suggestion that buffalo hair would produce a wonderful wool. He claimed it had "every appearance of the wool of the sheep, tho' much finer and more silkey and soft."

New birds always brought out his passion for detail. On May 1, Private George Shannon brought in "a bird of the plover kind." Lewis took more than five hundred words to describe it—length, weight, wingspan, number of feathers on the tail, and so on—and concluded with observations on its behavior ("it sometimes rests on the water and swims which I do not recollect having seen the plover do"). He named it the "Missouri plover"; actually it was the American avocet, already known to science but not to Lewis.

In April, he discovered and described for the first time the snow goose and the cackling goose. On April 13, Clark shot a Canada goose sitting on its nest in the top of a lofty cottonwood. Lewis climbed to inspect the nest and brought back an egg. He noted, "the wild gees frequently build their nests in this manner." That statement later was challenged by nineteenth-century ornithologists, because east of the Mississippi geese always nested on the ground. But Lewis was right; on the Plains, geese often nested in trees as a precaution against predators. So much so that on May 3 Lewis was surprised to find a nest among some driftwood, the first he had seen on the ground. He took three eggs from it.

Another description later challenged—indeed, dismissed as an inexplicable error—was of the grizzly bear. On April 29, Lewis and a party of hunters brought in their first grizzly. Lewis described it in some detail. Among other observations, he said the testicles were "suspended in seperate pouches from two to four inches asunder." He later described the same phenomenon on another bear. No one else has ever seen such a thing, but it is impossible to believe that Lewis made it up.

Lewis had seen the first grizzly sign on April 13. "The men as well as ourselves are anxious to meet with some of these bear," he then recorded. The Indians had given the white men "a very formidable account of the strengh and ferocity of this anamal," but Lewis had discounted the information, because the Indians had only bows and arrows or "the indifferent guns with which the traders furnish them, with these they shoot with such uncertainty and at so short a distance that they frequently mis their aim & fall a sacrefice to the bear." It gave him a bit of pause that the Indians, before attacking a grizzly, went through all the rituals they commonly used before going on a war party; still, he, Clark, and the men had faith in their long rifles and were eager to challenge the grizzly.

On April 29, Lewis was walking on shore with one man when they spotted two grizzlies. Each man fired and hit a bear. One of the wounded beasts escaped, but the other charged Lewis, pursuing him some eighty yards. Fortunately, the bear was badly enough wounded so that Lewis and the private had time to reload. They shot again and killed it. Though not full-grown, it weighed three hundred pounds. Lewis described it as a "much more furious and formidable anamal" than the black bear of the eastern United States. "It is asstonishing to see the wounds they will bear before they can be put to death," he admitted, but he remained cocky: the Indians "may well fear this anamal . . . but in the hands of skillfull riflemen [the bears] are by no means as formidable or dangerous" as the Indians indicated.

On May 5, his cockiness began to fade. Clark and Drouillard killed a grizzly. Lewis described it as "a most tremendious looking anamal, and extreemly hard to kill notwithstanding he had five balls through his lungs and five others in various parts he swam more than half the distance across the river to a sandbar & it was at least twenty minutes before he died; [he] made the most tremendous roaring from the moment he was shot."

The expedition had no equipment with which to weigh the bear. Clark thought he would go five hundred pounds; Lewis thought six. This was their first disagreement. They boiled the oil and put it in a cask; it was as hard as hog's lard.

A week later, the party saw a grizzly swim the river. He disappeared before an attack could be made on him. Lewis wrote, "I find that the curiossity of our party is pretty well satisfyed with rispect to this anamal." The size of the beast, and the difficulty in killing the bear, "has staggered the resolution [of] several of them, others however seem keen for action with the bear; I expect these gentlemen will give us some amusement shotly as they soon begin now to coppolate."

The first month of travel into the unknown was splendid all around. Progress was steady, if slower on the average than Lewis had hoped for, and it was generally straight west, directly toward the setting sun. No Indians, hostile or friendly, had been discovered—a good thing, Lewis thought, for he wanted to move as far west and as fast as possible. It is difficult to think of men who sometimes made but a few miles in one day, and never more than twenty-five, as being in a hurry, with no time to spend smoking pipes and explaining themselves to strange tribes, but this was so.

Cool or cold nights, mornings when the water froze on the paddles, gave way to warm, pleasant days—except for the wind.

There were enough adventures to satisfy everyone. On the fifth day out, Clark went walking while Lewis rode in the white pirogue. Lewis ordered the fleet to cross to the larboard (south) side in order to avoid a bank that was falling into the river on the starboard side, but although all the canoes saw his signal and crossed, the red pirogue did not. It was being pulled by the towline.

By the time Lewis noticed the failure of communications, it was too late to do anything about it. "I expected to have seen her carried under every instant," he wrote that night, but "it was too late for the men to reembark, and retreating is more dangerous than proceeding in such cases; they therefore continued their passage up this bank and much to my satisfaction arrived safe above it."

On April 13, there was another scare. The wind was from the east. Lewis ordered the square sail and the spritsail hoisted on the white pirogue, "which carried her at a pretty good gate." Charbonneau was at the helm. When a sudden squall of wind hit and rocked the boat, Charbonneau panicked. Instead of bringing the craft up into the wind, he laid her broadside to it, which came as close to "overseting the perogue as it was possible to have missed."

Lewis called out orders: Drouillard, take the helm and turn her into the wind! You men there, take in the sails! It was done and the pirogue righted.

On April 25, Lewis entered a wonderland. He decided to walk on ahead, knowing that the Yellowstone River could not be far distant, so that he could make his celestial observations and write a description of the country while the main party struggled up the Missouri against the wind. He took with him Sergeant Ordway, Drouillard, Private Joseph Field, and one other man. The party set out at 11:00 a.m., accompanied by Lewis's dog, Seaman, who had been out all night but had returned in the morning, to Lewis's delight. They were on the south bank of the Missouri. Shortly after noon, Lewis killed a buffalo calf. One of the men built a fire, and they enjoyed "a hearty meal" of excellent veal.

In the afternoon, Lewis ascended the hills, "from whence I had a most pleasing view of the country perticularly of the wide and fertile vallies formed by the missouri and the yellowstone rivers, which occasionally unmasked by the wood on their borders disclose their meanderings for many miles in their passage through these delightfull tracts of country. . . ."

The animal life added to the romantic quality of the place. "The whol face of the country was covered with herds of Buffaloe, Elk & Antelopes; deer are also abundant, but keep themselves more concealed in the woodland. the buffaloe Elk and Antelope are so gentle that we pass near them while feeding, without apearing to excite any alarm among them, and when we attract their attention, they frequently approach us more nearly to discover what we are."

That evening, Lewis and his men camped on the Yellowstone, two miles south of its junction with the Missouri. In the morning, Lewis sent Private Field up the Yellowstone with instructions to follow it as far as he could and still get back to base camp in a day.

Then Lewis set about examining the country. In the bottoms, he found redberry, serviceberry, redwoods, gooseberry, choke cherry, purple currant, and honeysuckle, intermixed with willow, a favorite winter food of the hoofed animals.

At 9:41, 9:42, and 9:43 a.m., he measured the altitude of the sun with his sextant and an artificial horizon. He was obtaining his local time, trying to establish the moment of high noon, against which to compare Greenwich time. He could figure out Greenwich time with a set of "lunar-distance" measurements that he could obtain by taking the sextant angle between the moon and the star Altair. What he wanted to fix was the longitude of the junction of the rivers.

Toward noon, he heard the discharge of several guns, indicating that Clark and the main party were at the mouth of the Yellowstone He sent Drouillard to tell Clark to send a canoe up the Yellowstone to collect the meat his party had killed and prepared. At 6:49, 6:50, and 6:52 p.m., he again measured the sun's altitude. Unfortunately, clouds came up and he was not able to make his nighttime observations.

Lewis walked down and joined the main party at the camp on the point of land formed by the junction of the rivers. He found the men "all in good health, and much pleased at having arrived at this long wished for spot, and in order to add in some measure to the general pleasure which seemed to pervade our little community, we ordered a dram to be issued to each person; this soon produced the fiddle, and they spent the evening with much hilarity, singing & dancing, and seemed as perfectly to forget their past toils, as they appeared regardless of those to come."

Private Field came in, to report that the Yellowstone wandered, had a gentle current, many sandbars, and a sand-and-mud bottom. Clark took measurements: the Missouri at the point of junction was 330 yards wide with a deep channel, whereas the Yellowstone was 297 yards wide and 12 feet deep at its deepest channel.

The Hidatsas had told Lewis that the Yellowstone was navigable for pirogues and canoes nearly to its source in the Rocky Mountains (at today's Yellowstone National Park), and that at one point it passed within less than a half-day's march of a navigable part of the Missouri. They also said that the sources of the Yellowstone were adjacent to those of the Missouri, Platte, and Columbia Rivers. They were right about the Missouri and Columbia, which do have their ultimate sources in the Yellowstone plateau, but wrong about the Platte, which rises in the Colorado and Wyoming Rockies.

The captains apparently never gave it a thought, but had they listened more closely to the Indians, and had Jefferson's instructions not been so contradictory (he wanted the explorers to follow the Missouri to its source, but he also wanted them to follow the shortest route across the continent; the president's assumption that these were one and the same was badly wrong), they might have abandoned the Missouri and ascended the Yellowstone. At today's Livingston, Montana, where the Yellowstone makes a sharp bend from a northerly to an easterly flow (or from west to south going upstream), the party could have abandoned the river and continued west to cross the divide between the rivers over a relatively low pass (today's Bozeman Pass) and gotten to Three Forks some weeks, maybe even two months, sooner.

But they continued upstream on the Missouri, as Jefferson had ordered. On May 3, Lewis, walking on the north bank among "vast quantities" of game, came to "a beatifull bold runing stream, 40 yards wide at its entrance; the water transparent." He called it Porcupine

River, from the unusual number of porcupines he spotted.* Clark named its first tributary "2,000 mile creek" (today's Red Water), since the expedition was now two thousand miles above the mouth of the Missouri. Lewis wrote of Porcupine River, "I have but little doubt that it takes it's source not far from the main body of the Suskashawan river, and that it is probably navigable 150 miles. . . . it would afford a very favorable communication to the Athebaskay country, from whence the British N[orth]-W[est] Company derive so large a portion of their valuable furs."

Lewis wrote something similar about every river flowing into the Missouri from the north (there are not very many of them). Jefferson wanted it so, because any stream coming in from the north that reached up into the Canadian prairie might extend the boundaries of Louisiana and would certainly give the Americans access to the most valuable portion of the British fur-trading country. But, as badly as Lewis wanted to please Jefferson, it was all wishful thinking; even for the smallest canoe, at the height of the spring runoff, Porcupine River would not be navigable much more than a couple of dozen miles, and its sources are south of the forty-ninth parallel.

On May 8, the expedition "nooned it" just above another river, coming in from the north. While the men ate, Lewis walked up it some three miles. "I have no doubt but it is navigable for boats perogues and canoes, for the latter probably a great distance," he wrote. "From the quantity of water furnised by this river it must water a large extent of country; perhaps this river also might furnish a practicable and advantageous communication with the Saskashiwan river."

The Hidatsas had told Lewis and Clark of this river, which they called "The River Which Scolds at All Others." Lewis named it Milk River, from the color of its water. It retains that name today. It rises in Glacier National Park, flows slightly north of west into southernmost Alberta, then bends back to a southwesterly flow to re-enter Montana. At no point does it come anywhere near the Saskatchewan.

That afternoon, Drouillard, Charbonneau, and Sacagawea went walking. She found some wild licorice and dug up a quantity of roots called the white apple. Lewis gave the root a full five-hundred-word

---

* Today's Poplar River. Lewis and Clark had been naming streams and creeks ever since they left Mandan, but few of their names appear on today's maps, because of the long delay in the publication of their journals. Early-nineteenth-century trappers and miners, not knowing what Lewis and Clark had called the rivers, gave them names.

description, concluding that, although it was "a tastless insippid food of itself . . . our epicures would admire this root very much, it would serve them in their ragouts and gravies in stead of the truffles morella." He never mentioned Sacagawea's contribution (Clark did), but he did write that it was a very healthy food.

It certainly was a welcome addition to the virtually all-meat diet. "We can send out at any time and obtain whatever species of meat the country affords in as large quantity as we wish," Lewis wrote. But all that meat, if not complemented by vegetables or fruit, might well lead to scurvy, and there are some indications that the men of the expedition at various times did suffer from scurvy. It was an age in which almost nothing was known about a balanced diet, making Lewis's comment on a "healthy food" notable. According to Dr. Eldon "Frenchy" Chuinard, the expert on medical aspects of the expedition, "malnutrition was an almost constant condition of all soldiers."[1]

Almost all American soldiers of the Revolutionary War and the War of 1812 suffered from malaria, dysentery, diarrhea, rheumatism, ophthalmia, and other scourges. So did the men of the expedition. Venereal disease, including syphilis, was so common it was scarcely commented upon. Lewis noted on April 24 that "soar eyes is a common complaint among the party." He attributed it to the fine sand driven by the wind: "so penitrating is this sand that we cannot keep any article free from it; in short we are compelled to eat, drink, and breath it very freely." Chuinard suggests that venereal disease may also have been a factor; Moulton posits the constant glare of the sun on the water as another.[2]

On May 4, Lewis, who did most of the doctoring, reported that Joseph Field was sick with dysentery and a high fever. Lewis treated him with Glauber salts (a strong laxative), "which operated very well," plus thirty drops of laudanum (a tincture of opium), which would have helped Field sleep. For sore eyes, he used a wash made of two parts white vitriol (zinc sulphate) and one part sugar of lead (lead acetate). For the "boils and imposthumes" that were common among the party and were probably caused by scurvy, he used "emmolient poltices," without specifying how he made the poultices.[3]

May 9 was a good day. The party made twenty-four and a half miles, and Lewis shot and described a willet, new to science. He was able to make astronomical observations after darkness fell. The buffalo had become "so gentle that the men frequently throw sticks and stones at them in order to drive them out of the way."

Lewis selected a fat buffalo and saved "the necessary materials for making what our wrighthand cook Charbono calls the *boudin blanc;* this white pudding we all esteem one of the gretest delicacies of the forrest." Lewis wrote a long, detailed recipe on the subject of Charbonneau's method of making the sausage. The recipe ended, "It is then baptised in the missouri with two dips and a flirt, and bobbed into the kettle; from whence after it be well boiled it is taken and fryed with bears oil untill it becomes brown, when it is ready to esswage the pangs of a keen appetite or such as travelers in the wilderness are seldom at a loss for."

Altogether, a perfect day and evening, except that the river was as broad here as at its mouth. Were it not much shallower, Lewis wrote, "I should begin to dispair of ever reaching it's source." And he confessed, if only to himself, "I begin to feel extreemly anxious to get in view of the rocky mountains."

At about 5:00 p.m. on May 11, Private William Bratton came running along the bank, shouting and making signs. Lewis ordered the pirogue to put to. Bratton was so out of breath when he came up that it was some minutes before he could explain that he had shot and wounded a grizzly, but the bear had turned on him and pursued him a considerable distance.

Lewis was not about to allow a bear to defeat one of his men so ignominiously or so completely. He ordered the crew of the white pirogue to join him on an expedition "in quest of this monster." Finding a trail of blood, they pursued the bear for a mile through thick brush before finding him concealed. They shot him through the head, twice. Examination disclosed that Bratton's shot had gone through the bear's lungs, "notwithstanding which he [the bear] had pursued him [Bratton] near half a mile and had returned more than double that distance."

Lewis concluded, "these bear being so hard to die reather intimedates us all; I must confess that I do not like the gentlemen and had reather fight two Indians than one bear."

Three days later, there was another battle between bear and party. The six men in the two rear canoes saw a bear on the bank. They put to shore and planned their attack in some detail. They sneaked up to within forty yards of the enemy without being spotted. Four men fired simultaneously, while two soldiers held their rifles in reserve. All four balls hit the mark, two passing through the lungs. The bear rose with a roar and launched an immediate counterattack, charging with open mouth. The two-man reserve force fired; one ball hit muscle only, but the other broke the bear's shoulder; this, however, only slowed him for an instant.

The men took to flight. The bear pursued down to the river, where two men got away in the canoe while the remainder took to hiding places in the willows, to reload and fire. They hit the bear several more times, but that only let him know where they were hidden. He routed two of the men, who threw away their rifles and pouches and dived into the river, from a perpendicular bank of near twenty feet.

The bear jumped in after them. He was about to reach one of the swimmers when a soldier on the bank finally shot him through the head and killed him. Examination revealed that eight balls had passed through the bear.

While that adventure was taking place, Lewis had one of his own, so dangerous to the enterprise that he later wrote, "I cannot recollect [it] but with the utmost trepidation and horror."

The incident took place while the two captains were on shore, contrary to their own orders and established routine, and for reasons neither ever explained. Charbonneau was at the helm of the white pirogue—despite his near-disaster on April 13, and despite Lewis's judgment of him as "perhaps the most timid waterman in the world." The pirogue was under sail when a sudden squall struck and turned her. Charbonneau, in a panic, instead of putting her bow into the wind, turned with it. The wind drew the brace of the sail out of the hands of the man attending it "and instantly upset the perogue and would have turned her completely topsaturva, had it not have been from the resistance made by the oarning against the water."

Watching from shore, the captains were in a state of near-panic themselves. They fired their rifles to attract the attention of the crew and hollered out to cut the halyards and haul in the sail—but the crew, on the far side of the river, could not hear either the shots or the shouts. Meanwhile, Cruzatte (perhaps the best waterman on the expedition) was shouting at Charbonneau to take up the rudder and turn the boat into the wind, but Charbonneau was crying to God for mercy and could not hear.

Before Charbonneau and the crew could recover their wits sufficiently to bring in the sail, the pirogue was filled to within an inch of the gunnels. Articles were floating away. Meriwether Lewis watched in the most awful agony and fearful anticipation.

Reacting instinctively, he dropped his rifle, threw aside his shot pouch, and began tearing off his coat. His idea was to swim unencumbered out to the pirogue to save what he could. But before he dived into the river, "I recollected the folly of the attempt I was about to make." The waves were high, the boat was three hundred yards away, the water was excessively cold, and the current strong. "There was a hundred to one but what I should have paid the forfit of my life for the madness of my project," he wrote that evening in his journal. But, considering that the white pirogue carried the journals, maps, instruments, and other invaluable items, "had the perogue been lost, I should have valued [my life] but little."

It all took but an instant. Prudence and common sense won out over rashness.[4] Fortunately, Cruzatte was able to force Charbonneau to do his duty by threatening to shoot him instantly if he did not. Charbonneau took up the tiller and the boat righted. Cruzatte put two men to work bailing with kettles, while with two others he paddled her toward shore, where she arrived scarcely floating.

All this time, Sacagawea was calm, collected, and invaluable. As Lewis put it the following day, "The Indian woman to whom I ascribe equal fortitude and resolution, with any person on board at the time of the accedent, caught and preserved most of the light articles which were washed overboard." Whether he praised her, or upbraided her husband, he did not say. He did record that, after the battle of the bear and the near-loss of the white pirogue, "we thought it a proper occasion to console ourselves and cheer the sperits of our men and accordingly took a drink of grog and gave each man a gill of sperits."

During the last week of May, the expedition entered a section of the river dominated by high, rugged bluffs composed of all shades of brown set off by the pure blue sky and blazing sun. It remains one of the most isolated parts of the United States, a stretch of almost 160 miles from the western end of today's Fort Peck Lake to today's Fort Benton, Montana, that has been designated a Wild and Scenic River by Congress and is the least changed part of the Missouri. The first (eastern) section is called the Missouri River Breaks, the second portion is designated the White Cliffs Area. The river continues to run mostly west-east through the breaks, then flows almost straight south and then southeast through the cliffs—for Lewis, that meant traveling west, then northwest, then north, and finally southwest.

Clark called the breaks "the Deserts of America" and declared, "I do not think it can ever be settled." Lewis spoke of "a desert, barren country," and for once he found no redeeming virtue. "The air of the open country is asstonishingly dry as well as pure," Lewis wrote.[5] A lifelong resident of the humid eastern third of the continent, he could scarcely believe how quickly his inkstand ran dry. By experiment, he discovered that a tablespoon of water would "avaporate in 36 hours."

On May 25, Lewis described at length the first specimen of the bighorn sheep the expedition had collected. Clark copied the entry, almost word for word. This was the first time Clark had done such a thing, but it quickly became habitual. As part of the small library Lewis had brought along, there was an edition of Linnaeus, and a four-volume set, *A New and Complete Dictionary of the Arts and Sciences*. In his May 25 entry, Clark for the first time indicates that he had been thumbing through what he called, in a marvelous spelling even for Clark, the "Deckinsery of arts an ciences."

Donald Jackson speculates that, when the white pirogue all but sank, some important papers were lost. (Private Joseph Whitehouse wrote in his journal, "Some of the papers and nearly all the books got wet, but not altogether spoiled.")[6] Jackson thinks it possible that the near-disaster made the captains more careful than they had been to have two sets of all written scientific descriptions.*

On the afternoon of May 26, at the eastern end of the breaks, Lewis climbed the surrounding bluffs, a "fortiegueing" task, but he thought himself "well repaid for any labour" when he reached the highest point in the neighborhood, because "from this point I beheld the Rocky Mountains for the first time."

Clark thought he had seen distant mountains the previous day; Lewis's confirmation made them the first two Americans to see the Rockies. "These points of the Rocky Mountains were covered with snow and the sun shone on it in such manner as to give me the most plain and satisfactory view."

The sight brought joy to his heart: "While I viewed these mountains I felt a secret pleasure in finding myself so near the head of the heretofore conceived boundless Missouri."

The sight also brought dismay: "when I reflected on the difficulties which this snowey barrier would most probably throw in my way to the Pacific, and the sufferings and hardships of myself and party in them, it in some measure counterballanced the joy I had felt in the first moments in which I gazed on them."

---

* Jackson's further speculation is more difficult to accept. He thinks it may be that, when the white pirogue almost went down, Lewis lost his journal for the period May 1804 through March 1805. But if Lewis kept a journal during that period, why didn't he send a copy of it to Jefferson with Corporal Warfington on the keelboat?

The sight brought forth his characteristic resolution and optimism: "As I have always held it a crime to anticipate evils I will believe it a good comfortable road untill I am conpelled to beleive differently."

With the mountains in view, the urge to get to them and over them became even greater, but, alas, progress was slower than ever, because of the numerous bends in the river, the way the bluffs came right down to the water's edge, the usually head-on wind, and the abundance of protruding rocks in the shallow water. For the most part, the men pulled the pirogues and canoes, using worn-out elk-skin ropes that were constantly getting wet, then drying in the sun, growing progressively weaker and rotting. Often they would snap; if they snapped when the men were working a craft through a rock garden, there was a great danger of the vessel's turning broadside and getting carried downstream out of control, to bump into a rock, which would surely overset her.

So progress was made, in Lewis's apt description, "with much labour and infinite risk." The water was cold on the men's legs, the sun hot on their bare backs. The footing was either slippery mud or sharp rocks that cut and bruised their feet.

They passed a point where rotten, stinking buffalo were piled up in incredible numbers. Lewis thought it was a pishkin, or buffalo jump. In one of his best-known passages, he described the way Indian boys wearing buffalo robes would lure the buffalo to their death as the tribe pressed from behind. He had his information from the Hidatsas, and he had it right—except that this place was not a buffalo jump, but a bend in the river where buffalo who had drowned in the river when the ice broke had piled up. Wolves were there in such number, and were so stuffed with putrid meat, that Clark walked up to one and killed it with his espontoon. Lewis named the nearby stream Slaughter Creek (later changed to Arrow Creek).

A couple of miles farther on, a stream came in on the south side. Clark walked up it and named it Judith's River, after his cousin Julia Hancock.

By May 31, the party was well into the White Cliffs Area. The river was worse than ever. For the men, that meant "their labour is incredibly painfull and great, yet those faithfull fellows bear it without a murmur." There was a terrible scare in the forenoon, when the tow rope of the white pirogue, the only rope made of hemp, broke at a bad place. The pirogue swung and just barely touched a rock, yet was near oversetting.

So relieved were the captains at the narrow escape, and so much did they feel for the men because of their incredible labor, that at noon they "came to for refreshment and gave the men a dram which they received with much cheerfullness, and well deserved." Lewis's heart was still thumping that night at the narrow escape of the white pirogue and her contents, which he valued as much as his own life. He wrote, "I fear her evil gennii will play so many pranks with her that she will go to the bottomm some of those days."

As for the White Cliffs themselves, Lewis's description is one of the classics of American travel literature: "The hills and river Clifts which we passed today exhibit a most romantic appearance," he began. They were two to three hundred feet high, nearly perpendicular, shining pure white in the sun. "The water in the course of time in decending from those hills . . . has trickled down the soft sand clifts and woarn it into a thousand grotesque figures, which with the help of a little immagination and an oblique view . . . are made to represent eligant ranges of lofty freestone buildings . . . statuary . . . long galleries . . . the remains or ruins of eligant buildings . . . some collumns standing . . . others lying prostrate an broken . . . nitches and alcoves of various forms and sizes. . . . as we passed on it seemed as if those seens of visionary inchantment would never had and end . . . vast ranges of walls of tolerable workmanship, so perfect indeed that I should have thought that nature had attempted herre to rival the human art of masonry had I not recollected that she had first began her work."*

There were swallows in uncountable numbers, nesting in the banks. After putting ashore, while the men made camp and cooked, Lewis went for a stroll. When he returned, he told Clark he had just seen "the most butifull fox in the world." Its colors were a fine orange, yellow, white, and black. Lewis shot at it but missed.[7]

On June 1, the river made a great bend, causing the expedition to change direction from a north-northwest course to southwest. Lewis spent most of the day walking on shore with hunters, looking for elk. He anticipated getting to the Great Falls of the Missouri any day now, based on the appearance of the mountains and on information gathered from the Hidatsas, and he was going to need elk skin to cover the iron-frame boat he had been hauling from Harpers Ferry the past two years. The party collected six elk, along with two buffalo, two mule deer, and

---

* It is today as Lewis saw it. The White Cliffs can be seen only from small boat or canoe. Put in at Fort Benton and take out three or four days later at Judith Landing. Missouri River Outfitters at Fort Benton, Montana, rents canoes or provides a guided tour by pontoon boat. Of all the historic and/or scenic sights we have visited in the world, this is number one. We have made the trip ten times.

a bear (the bear almost got Charbonneau, but Drouillard killed it with a shot to the head just in time).

At dusk, the party put in on the south shore. Across the water they could see a considerable river flowing into the Missouri. What was this? According to the Hidatsas, whose information had so far been more or less correct, they had passed already the last northern tributary of the Missouri. The Great Falls were supposed to be the next landmark after "The River Which Scolds at All Others," the one the captains had named the Milk River.

It was nearly dark, too late to examine the unexpected river that night. They would look it over in the morning.

19

FROM MARIAS RIVER TO THE GREAT FALLS

June 3–June 20, 1805

On the morning of June 3, the party crossed the Missouri and set up a camp on the point formed by the junction of the two large rivers. "An interesting question was now to be determined," Lewis wrote in his journal: "Which of these rivers was the Missouri?"

It was a difficult as well as a critical call. According to the Hidatsas, the Missouri ran deep into the Rocky Mountains to a place where it approached to within a half-day's portage of the waters of the Columbia River. So far, their description of the Missouri had been accurate. But they had said nothing about a river coming in from the north after passing Milk River. How could they have missed this one? But they had also said nothing about a great river coming into the Missouri from the south. That the Indians had not mentioned such a river "astonishes us a little," Lewis wrote.*

Jefferson's orders were explicit: "The object of your mission is to explore the Missouri river." The Hidatsas were explicit: the Missouri

---

* The explanation was simple, although it did not occur to Lewis or Clark, probably because their orientation was so completely centered on the river. When the Hidatsas raided to the west, they went on horseback. They could easily cut the big bends in the Missouri by riding overland. Up on the plains, they saved not only miles but the very rough country of the breaks and White Cliffs. Following that route, they would strike the Missouri again at or south of Fort Benton, and thus never see the river coming in from the northwest that so puzzled Lewis.

River had a Great Falls as it came out of the mountains, after which it penetrated those mountains almost to the Continental Divide, at which place lived the Shoshone Indians, who had horses, essential to getting over the Divide, and whose language Sacagawea spoke as her native tongue.

The right-hand or north fork came in on an almost straight west-east line, meaning that going up that river was heading directly toward the mountains. The left-hand or south fork came in from the southwest. The right fork was 200 yards wide, the left fork 372. The right fork was deeper, but the left fork's current was swifter. Lewis described the north fork as running "in the same boiling and roling manner which has uniformly characterized the Missouri throughout it's whole course so far; it's waters are of a whitish brown colour very thick and terbid, also characeristic of the Missouri." The water of the south fork "is perfectly transparent" and ran "with a smoth unriffled surface."

As Lewis suummed it up, "the air & character of this river [the north fork] is so precisely that of the missouri below that the party with very few exceptions have already pronounced the N. fork to be the Missouri; myself and Capt. C. not quite so precipitate have not yet decided but if we were to give our opinions I believe we should be in the minority."

Lewis reasoned that the north fork had to run an immense distance through the Plains to pick up enough sediment to make it so cloudy and turbid, whereas the south fork must come directly out of the mountains. The bed of the south fork was composed of smooth stones, "like most rivers issuing from a mountainous country," and the bed of the north fork was mainly mud. He and Clark talked it over, without reaching a precipitate conclusion. "Thus have our cogitating faculties been busily employed all day," Lewis wrote.*

The captains sent Sergeant Pryor up the north fork to scout; he returned in the evening to report that at ten miles the river's course turned from west to north. They sent Sergeant Gass up the south fork; he reported that at six and a half miles the river continued to bear southwest. "These accounts being by no means satisfactory as to the fundamental point," Lewis wrote, "Capt. C. and myself concluded to set out early the next morning with a small party each, and ascend these rivers untill we could perfectly satisfy ourselves. . . . it was agreed that I should ascend the right hand fork and he the left. . . . we agreed

---

* Sacagawea was of no help. She had not been on this part of the river.

to go up those rivers one day and a halfs march or further if it should appear necessary to satisfy us more fully of the point in question. . . . We took a drink of grog this evening and gave the men a dram."

Lewis packed his "happerst," or knapsack, and had it ready to swing on his back at dawn. He commented that this was "the first time in my life that I had ever prepared a burthen of this kind" (meaning, apparently, that since his childhood a slave, later an enlisted man or a servant, had carried his backpack), "and I am fully convinced that it will not be the last."

In the morning, he set off, accompanied by Sergeant Pryor; Privates Shields, Windsor, Cruzatte, and Lepage; and Drouillard. (Lewis was a great admirer of "Drewyer," calling him "this excellent man." Whenever Lewis led a small party on a scouting mission, Drouillard was almost always the first man chosen.)

The party ascended the river along its north bank. "The whole country in fact appears to be one continued plain to the foot of the mountains or as far as the eye can reach," Lewis wrote. The walking was difficult, partly because of the prickly pears, whose thorns readily penetrated the thin moccasins the men were wearing. These low cactus plants were so numerous "that it requires one half of the traveler's attention to avoid them." Further, the dry ravines were steep and numerous, so much so they caused Lewis to return to the river and travel through its bottoms. Despite the difficulties, he covered thirty-two and a half miles that day, most of it nearly straight north.

This was the most critical exploration Lewis had ever made. He was in country totally unknown except to the Blackfoot Indians, on a river he had never heard of that went he knew not where. Yet his eye for detail, for what was new, and for what was pleasing, was as sharp as always. He described the grass (short) and the distant mountains (the Bears Paw, the Highwoods, and Square Butte). He saw and wrote descriptions of two birds unknown to science, the long-billed curlew and McCown's longspur. He camped in a shelter of riverbank willows and got thoroughly soaked from a hard, cold rain, but still concluded his June 4 journal entry, "The river bottoms form one emence garden of roses, now in full bloe."

The following day, he made another thirty-plus miles upstream, or nearly to present-day Tiber Dam, on a course slightly north of west. He came to the conclusion, as he put it the next day, "that this branch of the Missouri had it's direction too much to the North for our rout to the Pacific." He made two discoveries: Richardson's ground squirrel and the sage grouse.

He decided to make camp, and at noon the next day make an observation of the sun in order to fix the latitude of the place, in the hope that he was north of forty-nine degrees of latitude. But at noon on June 6, the sky was overcast, "and I of course disappointed in making the observation which I much wished." His sense that he was at the northernmost point yet in the journey was correct, but he was not as far north as he hoped. Tiber Dam is about forty miles short of the forty-ninth parallel.

He had the men build two rafts to descend the river, but the craft proved too small for the task (one man almost lost his rifle), so "we again swung our packs" and set out over the plains. It was cold, rainy, miserable. The party made twenty-five miles that afternoon. Lewis closed his journal entry, "It continues to rain and we have no shelter, an uncomfortable nights rest is the natural consequence."

It rained all night, "and as I expected we had a most disagreable and wrestless night." At dawn "we left our watery beads" and proceeded downstream, but only with the greatest danger, because the wet clay was "precisely like walking over frozan grownd which is thawed to small debth and slips equally as bad."* In passing along the face of a bluff, Lewis slipped at a narrow walkway of some thirty yards in length across a bluff, made by the buffalo. He nearly went straight down a craggy precipice of ninety feet. He saved himself with his espontoon and just barely managed to reach a place where he could stand "with tolerable safety."

Before he could catch his breath, he heard Private Windsor call out, "God, God, Captain, what shall I do?"

Lewis turned and saw Windsor lying prostrate on his belly, with his right hand, arm, and leg over the precipice Lewis had just passed, holding on as best he could with his left arm and foot.

Windsor's fear was all but overwhelming him. His dangerous situation frightened Lewis considerably, "for I expected every instant to see him loose his strength and slip off." But, although alarmed, and still shaky from his own hairbreadth escape, Lewis managed to speak calmly.

He assured Windsor he was in no danger, then told him to take the knife out of his belt with his right hand and dig a hole with it in the face of the bluff to receive his right foot.

---

* A modern floater's guide to Montana states that the gravel roads in the area of the river are like "impassable grease" after a rain. Moulton, in his note to the June 7, 1805, entry, calls this clay a "gumbo," and writes, "Only a small amount of moisture is needed to make it extremely slippery."

Windsor did as instructed, and with his foot in the hole was able to raise himself to his knees. Lewis told him to take off his moccasins (the wet leather was more slippery than bare feet) and crawl forward on his hands and knees, taking care to hold the knife in one hand and his rifle in the other. "This he happily effected and escaped."

Their adrenaline used up, Lewis and Windsor joined the party to proceed. The plains were too slippery and too much intersected with ravines, so "we therefore continued our rout down the river sometimes in the mud and water of the bottom lands, at others in the river to our breasts and when the water became so deep that we could not wade we cut footsteps in the face of the steep bluffs with our knives and proceeded." They shot six deer, and after making camp at dark ate their first food of the day.

"I now laid myself down on some willow boughs to a comfortable nights rest, and felt indeed as if I was fully repaid for the toil and pain of the day, so much will a good shelter, a dry bed, and comfortable supper revive the sperits of the waryed, wet and hungry traveler."

His spirits may have been revived, but his worries remained. "The whole of my party to a man . . . were fully peswaided that this river was the Missouri." Lewis, however, was so certain it was not the Missouri that he named it Maria's River, after his cousin Maria Wood. "It is true that the hue of the waters of this turbulent and troubled stream but illy comport with the pure celestial virtues and amiable qualifications of that lovely fair one," he admitted, "but on the other hand it is a noble river . . . which passes through a rich fertile and one of the most beautifully picteresque countries that I ever beheld."

When the sun broke out around 10:00 a.m., the "innumerable litle birds" that inhabited the cottonwoods along the riverbanks "sung most inchantingly; I observed among them the brown thrush, Robbin, turtle dove, linnit goaldfinch, the large and small blackbird, wren and several other birds of less note."

At 5:00 p.m., "much fatigued," he arrived at camp at the junction of the Missouri and Maria's Rivers. Clark was relieved to see him come in, for he was two days later than expected. The captains conferred, studied the maps they had with them, especially the Arrowsmith 1796 map, and agreed that the south fork was the true Missouri.

The next morning, June 9, Lewis attempted to convince the men of the expedition that the south fork was the Missouri, without success. To a man they were "firm in the beleif that the N. Fork was the Missouri and that which we ought to take." Private Cruzatte, "who had been an old Missouri navigator and who from his integrity knowledge and skill as a waterman had acquired the confidence of every individual of the party declared it as his opinion that the N. fork was the true genuine Missouri and could be no other."

Despite Cruzatte's certainty, the captains would not change their minds, and so informed the men. In a magnificent tribute to the captains' leadership qualities, "they said very cheerfully that they were ready to follow us any wher we thought proper to direct but that they still thought that the other was the river."

Lewis and Clark were not taking a vote, but, "finding them so determined in this beleif, and wishing that if we were in an error to be able to detect it and rectify it as soon as possible it was agreed between Capt. C. and myself that one of us should set out with a small party by land up the South fork and continue our rout up it untill we found the falls or reached the snowy Mountains ... which should ... determine this question prety accurately."

Lewis rated Clark the better waterman and decided he should oversee the armada's progress up the river, while Lewis undertook the land expedition. Besides, Lewis liked to hike—and it may be that he wanted to be the first white man to see the Great Falls.

The captains determined to leave the red pirogue hidden and secured on an island at the mouth of Marias River. Lewis put his brand on several trees in the area.* The captains also decided to leave much of the heavy baggage in a cache—Cruzatte showed them how to make one. The purpose was to lighten the load, to have a supply depot available on the return journey (a strong indication that they intended to return overland and did not expect to meet a ship at the mouth of the Columbia River), and to provide seven more paddlers for the remaining pirogue and the canoes.

They buried the blacksmith's bellows and tools, beaver pelts, bear skins, some axes, an auger, some files, two kegs of parched corn, two kegs of pork, a keg of salt, some chisels, some tin cups, two rifles, and the beaver traps. They also buried twenty-four pounds of powder in lead kegs in two separate caches. To leave so much buried in the ground indicated either that the expedition had been grossly overloaded up to this point, or that it was setting off to conquer the Rocky Mountains and whatever lay beyond with inadequate supplies.

In choosing the south fork, the captains had made their most critical decision yet. It was not quite irrevocable, but, considering the lateness

---

* The branding iron bore the legend "U.S. Capt. M. Lewis." It is now in the Oregon Historical Society Museum, one of the few surviving authenticated articles associated with the expedition. It was found near Hood River, Oregon, in 1892, 1893, or 1894. See Moulton's note to the entry of June 10, 1805.

of the season, it was almost so.* Not one noncom, not one enlisted man, not Drouillard, presumably not York or Charbonneau or Sacagawea agreed with the decision. Yet such was the spirit of the Corps of Discovery that Lewis could conclude his June 9 journal entry, "In the evening Cruzatte gave us some music on the violin and the men passed the evening in dancing singing &c and were extreemly cheerfull."

The next day was spent in preparing the caches and making the deposits. Lewis saw and wrote the first description of the white-rumped shrike. He selected Drouillard and Privates Silas Goodrich, George Gibson, and Joseph Field to accompany him on his overland search for the Great Falls. Clark would come on with the remainder of the party in the white pirogue and six canoes.

During the night of June 10–11, Lewis suffered an attack of dysentery. He took some "salts," not otherwise described, for the malady. In the morning, he felt a bit better, but weak. Nevertheless, at 8:00 a.m., "I swung my pack and set forward with my little party." He was certain that he would discover the Great Falls. Drouillard, Goodrich, Gibson, and Field were sure he would not. They had covered some nine miles when they shot four elk, which they butchered and hung beside the river, for Clark and the party to use. Lewis directed that a feast of the marrowbones be made, but before it was ready "I was taken with such violent pain in the intestens that I was unable to partake." The pain increased, accompanied by a high fever. It got so bad Lewis could not proceed.

Having brought no medicines with him, he decided to experiment with some simples—exactly what his mother would have done and had taught him to do. He had the men gather some of the small twigs of the choke cherry, stripped them of their leaves, cut them into pieces of two

---

* Had the expedition gone up Marias River, at about one hundred miles it would have reached a fork, the junction of the Two Medicine and the Cut Bank Rivers. Had the party taken the left-hand fork, it would have arrived at Glacier National Park in the vicinity of present East Glacier. It would have gone over the Contintenal Divide at Marias Pass—the route that the Northern Pacific Railroad later used, and still uses today. That would have put the expedition in the Columbia River drainage—down the Middle Fork of the Flathead River to the Flathead, then south until eventually making a junction with the Clark's Fork, running north to the Columbia. As the crow flies, this would have been the shortest route, but it would have taken the party through an incredible jumble of mountains and whitewater, without horses. At the least, the odds would have been against the men and their captains.

inches, boiled them in water until "a strong black decoction of an astringent bitter tast was produced," and took a pint of it at sunset. An hour later, he forced down another pint, and within a half-hour "I was entirely releived from pain and in fact every symptom of the disorder forsook me; my fever abated, a gentle perspiration was produced and I had a comfortable and refreshing nights rest."

At sunrise, 4:30 a.m., Lewis rose feeling much revived. He took another pint of the choke-cherry decoction and set out. It was a glorious day. Despite his illness of the previous day, he made twenty-seven miles. The small party killed two bear. Lewis climbed to a height of land, from which

> "we had a most beatifull and picturesk view of the Rocky moiuntains which wer perfectly covered with Snow. . . . they appear to be formed of several ranges each succeeding range rising higher than the preceding one untill the most distant appear to loose their snowey tops in the clouds; this was an august spectacle and still rendered more formidable by the recollection that we had them to pass. . . .
>
> This evening I ate very heartily and after pening the transactions of the day amused myself catching those white fish [the sauger, unknown to science; another unknown species, caught by Goodrich on this stretch of the river, was the goldeye]. . . . I caught upwards of a douzen in a few minutes."

June 13 was an even better day. Lewis climbed to another height in the plains, where "I overlooked a most beatifull and level plain of great extent or at least 50 or sixty miles; in this there were infinitely more buffaloe than I had ever before witnessed at a view." He struck out for the river, with the men out to each side with orders to kill some meat and join him at the river for dinner.

"I had proceded on this course about two miles . . . whin my ears were saluted with the agreeable sound of a fall of water and advancing a little further I saw the spray arrise above the plain like a collumn of smoke. . . . [It] soon began to make a roaring too tremendious to be mistaken for any cause short of the great falls of the Missouri." He arrived at the river about noon and hurried down the two-hundred-foot bluff to a point on top of some rocks on an island, opposite the center of the falls, "to gaze on this sublimely grand specticle . . . the grandest sight I ever beheld."

He all but tripped over himself in attempting to describe the falls. After seven hundred words, he was "so much disgusted" with his "imperfect" description that he almost tore up the pages, "but then reflected that I could not perhaps succeed better than pening the first impressions of the mind." He wanted to "give to the enlightened world some just idea of this truly magnificent and sublimely grand object, which has from the commencement of time been concealed from the view of civilized man," a nice indication of just how seriously he took his role of being the first white man to see such sights and the resulting responsibility to describe them to "the enlighted world." He regretted that he did not have the "pencil of Salvator Rosa or the pen of Thompson." (Rosa was a seventeenth-century Italian landscape painter; James Thomson was an eighteenth-century Scottish poet.)

He did not neglect to describe his own feelings—the sight filled him with "pleasure and astonishment"—but he did not indicate that the sight gave him the satisfaction of having been right about the true Missouri River. Still, he must have felt it, not only as vindication of his thought process but even more because he now knew for certain that Clark and the expedition were coming the right way.

Drouillard and the privates met him on his island camp with plenty of prime buffalo meat. Goodrich caught some trout, unknown to science, described by Lewis, delicious to eat—they were cutthroats.

Sitting at his camp at the foot of the falls, Lewis concluded his entry for June 13: "My fare is really sumptuous this evening; buffaloe's humps, tongues and marrowbones, fine trout parched meal pepper and salt, and a good appetite; the last is not considered the least of the luxuries." A fine ending to a memorable day.

In the morning, Lewis sent Private Field with a letter to Clark, telling him of the discovery of the falls. He set the remainder of his party to work drying meat, then took his gun and espontoon and went for a walk. He thought he would go a few miles upstream to see where the rapids terminated. It couldn't be far—the Hidatsas had said the portage took half a day.

For the first five miles, however, it was one continuous rapid. Lewis came around a bend and to his surprise saw a second falls, this one of some nineteen feet, or about half as high as the first falls. He named this one Crooked Falls. He pushed on. "Hearing a tremendious roaring above me I continued my rout . . . and was again presented by one of the most beatifull objects in nature, a cascade of about fifty feet perpendicular streching at right angles across the river . . . a quarter-mile. . . . I now thought that if a skillfull painter had been asked to make a beautifull cascade that he would most probably have presented the precise immage of this one."

Inevitably, he compared this one with yesterday's discovery. "At length I determined between these two great rivals for glory that this was *pleasingly beautifull,* while the other was *sublimely grand."*

Then there was another fall, of fourteen feet, then another of twenty-six feet. Altogether, five separate falls made up the Great Falls of the Missouri. The Hidatsas had never mentioned more than one. It suddenly looked like a much longer and more difficult portage than Lewis had anticipated.

Finally, there was an end to the twelve-mile stretch of falls and rapids. Lewis arrived at a point where the Missouri "lies a smoth even and unruffled sheet of water of nearly a mile in width bearing on it's watry bosome vast flocks of geese which feed at pleasure in the delightfull pasture on either border."

He was quite beside himself with joy. He wrote of "feasting my eyes on this ravishing prospect and resting myself a few minutes." Then he decided to proceed as far as the river he had seen entering the Missouri from the northwest, a river the Hidatsas had mentioned and which they called Medicine River.

His walk took him past the biggest buffalo herd he ever saw—and therefore quite likely the biggest buffalo herd any white man ever saw. He thought he would kill a buffalo, then pick up the meat he needed for his dinner on his way back to camp from Medicine River. He shot a fat buffalo through the lungs, and watched as the blood spurted from its mouth and nostrils. Distracted by the sight, he forgot to reload his rifle.

At that moment, he became the hunted. Behind him, a grizzly had crept to within twenty steps of Lewis. Seeing the bear, Lewis brought up his rifle, but instantly realized she wasn't loaded, and further realized that he had not nearly enough time to reload before the bear—now briskly advancing—reached him.

Instinctively, he searched the terrain. Not a tree within three hundred yards. The riverbank was not more than three feet above the level of the water. In short, no place to hide in order to gain enough time to reload.

He started to walk faster. The bear pitched at him, "open mouthed and full speed, I ran about 80 yards and found he gained on me fast."

Lewis ran into the river, thinking that if he could get to waist-dccp water the bear would be obliged to swim. Lewis hoped he could then defend himself with his espontoon.

He got to the waist-deep water, turned on the bear, "and presented the point of my espontoon."

The bear took one look and "sudonly wheeled about as if frightened, declined the combat on such unequal ground, and retreated with quite as great precipiation as he had just pursued me."

Lewis learned a lesson: as soon as "I returned to the shore I charged my gun, which I had still retained in my hand throughout this curious adventure. . . . My gun reloaded I felt confidence once more in my strength . . . determined never again to suffer my peice to be longer empty than the time she necessarily required to charge her."

He got to, examined, and described Medicine River. By the time he was finished, it was 6:30 p.m. About three hours of daylight left, and twelve miles to hike back to camp.

He started down the level bottom of Medicine River. Just short of its junction with the Missouri, he spotted what he at first thought was a wolf; on getting to within sixty yards of it, he decided it was catlike. (It was probably a wolverine.) Lewis used his espontoon as a rest, took careful aim, and fired at it; the animal disappeared into its burrow. On examination, the tracks indicated the animal was some kind of tiger cat. Lewis saw no blood; apparently he had missed, which mortified him and bothered him not a little, since he absolutely depended on that rifle for his life (which was why he had had it with him, unloaded, in the river as the bear advanced on him; if he went down, it would be with his rifle in hand), and he was sure he had taken careful aim and that his rifle shot true.

He had not taken three hundred more steps when three buffalo bulls, feeding with a herd about half a mile away, separated from the others and ran full-speed at Lewis. He thought to give them some amusement at least and changed his direction to meet them head-on. At one hundred yards, they stopped, took a good look at Lewis, turned, and retreated as fast as they had come on.

"It now seemed to me that all the beasts of the neighbourhood had made a league to distroy me, or that some fortune was disposed to amuse herself at my expence," he wrote.

He returned to the carcass of the buffalo he had shot in the morning, where he had thought he might camp, but decided to go all the way to base camp at the foot of the first falls: he "did not think it prudent to remain all night at this place which really from the succession of curious adventures wore the impression on my mind of inchantment."

At times, walking over the plains as full darkness came on, he thought it was all a dream. But then he would step on a prickly pear.

In the morning, June 15, he spent hours writing in his journal (his entry covering his June 14 adventures is some twenty-four hundred words long; at twenty words a minute of stream-of-consciousness writing, with no pause for reflection, it would have taken him two hours minimum). Then "I amused myself in fishing, and sleeping away the fortiegues of yesterday."

The curious adventures that marked the week he discovered there were five great falls, not one, were not finished. When Lewis awoke from his nap, "I found a large rattlesnake coiled on the leaning trunk of a tree under the shade of which I had been lying at the distance of about ten feet from him." He killed the snake—he does not bother to tell how—and examined it (176 scuta on the abdomen and 17 on the tail).

Private Field returned, to report that Clark and the main party had stopped at the foot of a rapid about five miles below. Clark thought he had gone about as far upstream as possible, and that the portage should therefore begin from that place. Lewis needed to examine the ground. He had already decided there were too many ravines on the north bank, and that, because the river bent toward the southwest, a portage on the south side would be shorter.

Where and how he did not know. Or how long it would take. But it was obviously going to be a much greater task than he had anticipated, and far more time-consuming.

In a week, the days would start getting shorter. And always in the back of his mind, even as he wrestled with his immediate problems, were those tremendous mountains looming to the west, standing between him and his goal—mountains that he could only just see, but which he already realized were much greater, higher, deeper than anything he had seen in the Blue Ridge, or anywhere else. For a man who could never expect to travel more than twenty-five miles in one day, he was in a tremendous hurry.

He was eager to vault his energy over those mountains before winter set in, but he had to deal with the reality of a more-than-sixteen-mile portage over rough terrain, do it patiently, and use the time in as positive a way as possible.

20

THE GREAT PORTAGE

June 16–July 14, 1805

On Sunday morning, June 16, Lewis set out from his camp at the base of the first falls to rejoin Clark and the party at their camp, some six miles downstream. At 2:00 p.m., the captains were reunited. They had much to talk about—their experiences over the past few days, what they had seen, the meat supply, and most of all which side of the river to use to make the portage of the falls, and where to start the portage.

But before they could get into these immediate, pressing problems, Clark informed Lewis that there was an even more urgent matter. Sacagawea was ill, and had been for almost a week. Clark had tried bleeding her, which hadn't worked, and applying to her pelvic region a poultice of Peruvian bark and laudanum, also without success. He turned the patient over to Lewis, glad to be rid of the responsibility. In his journal, Clark wrote, "The Indian woman verry bad, & will take no medisin what ever, untill her husband finding her out of her Senses, easly provailed on her to take medison, if She dies it will be the fault of her husband as I am now convinced." (He did not explain why he blamed Charbonneau.)

Lewis's initial, cursory examination showed that Sacagawea was extremely ill, much reduced by her indisposition, with a high fever, a scarcely perceptible pulse, irregular breathing, and alarming twitching of the fingers and arms. "This gave me some concern," Lewis wrote, for Sacagawea and her baby boy, of course, but even more "from the consideration of her being our only dependence for a friendly negociation with the Snake Indians on whom we depend for horses to assist us in our portage from the Missouri to the columbia River."

Lewis gave Sacagawea a fuller examination and concluded that "her disorder originated principally from an obstruction of the mensis in consequence of taking could."* Apparently he wasn't far off in his diagnosis. His therapy was "two dozes of barks and opium," which soon produced an improvement in her pulse. She was thirsty. Lewis recalled a sulphur spring on the opposite (northwest) bank of the river; he sent a man over to bring him some. He figured it contained iron as well as sulphur and would be just what she needed. He was probably right; such symptoms as the twitching of the fingers and arms could have been due to loss of minerals resulting from Clark's bleeding her. For sure, his repeated bleeding had dehydrated her and stimulated her thirst.[1] She drank eagerly of the sulphur water, which was all the liquid Lewis would allow her to have. He continued the application of poultices to her pelvic region.

That evening, he was delighted with her progress. Her pulse had become regular, and much fuller; a gentle perspiration had come on; the twitching had in a great measure abated, "and she feels herself much freer from pain." Chuinard praises Lewis for his methods: "His recording of the patient's complaints, his physical examination of her, the medication employed, and his genuine concern about her probably would not be exceeded by any physician of his time."[2]

While Lewis was doing his doctoring, Clark took a party to a clump of cottonwoods about a mile below the entrance of a small creek (today's Belt Creek) to establish a base camp for the portage. This was the only place within miles in which there was enough wood for fuel. Lewis joined him in the afternoon. Clark had sent two men to examine the ground on the south side. Lewis told him that the portage was going to be at least sixteen miles long, a staggering piece of information. The captains decided they would have to leave the white pirogue at the base camp, and depend on Lewis's iron-frame boat for the upriver journey beyond the Great Falls. To further lighten the load, they also decided to make another cache of items they did not absolutely need.

At dusk, the two scouts came in "and made a very unfavourable report. They informed us that the creek just above us and two deep ravenes still higher up cut the plain between the river and mountain in

---

* Chuinard conjectures that Sacagawea may have suffered from chronic pelvic inflammatory disease, because of gonorrheal infection (*Only One Man Died*, pp.287–89).

such a manner, that in their opinions a portage for the canoes on this side was impracticable."

Another staggering piece of information. Lewis took it in stride. "Good or bad we must make the portage," he wrote with characteristic matter-of-fact realism. Besides, from what little he had seen with his own eyes, from the north bank, "I am still convinced . . . that a good portage may be had on this side."

The next morning, June 17, his conviction grew. Examination revealed that the small canoes could make it up the creek—which the captains named Portage Creek—almost two miles, from which point there was a gradual ascent to the top of the high plain. There the portage would begin. Clark set off with a small party to look over the route.

Lewis spotted a single cottonwood tree of some twenty-two inches in diameter just below the entrance of the creek, the only tree of such size within twenty miles. He put six men to work cutting it down and then sawing it crosswise to make wheels. He directed that the hardwood mast of the white pirogue be cut to make axles. The much softer cottonwood would serve for tongues, couplings, and bodies of the two wagons—or "trucks," as Lewis called them—which would transport the canoes and baggage.

Lewis's patient was much improved. She was free of pain, clear of fever, with a regular pulse and a healthy appetite. He continued the medication—sulphur water and poultices—and allowed her to eat broiled buffalo ("well seasoned with pepper and salt") and a soup of the same meat. With vast relief, he wrote in his journal that evening, "I think therefore that there is every rational hope of her recovery," an indication of how fearful he had been that she wouldn't make it.

He had other things to worry about, among them the covering for the iron-frame boat. He wanted elk skins, because he believed that they were more durable and stronger than buffalo skins and that they would not shrink so much in drying. But though there was an abundance of buffalo and deer around this part of the Missouri, elk were scarce. On the morning of June 19, he sent Drouillard and two of the enlisted men, Privates Reubin Field and George Shannon, to the north side of the Missouri with orders to proceed to the entrance of Medicine River and kill elk for their skins.

The wagons were ready; the baggage was sorted and prepared for the portage. The party was waiting only for Clark to return from his scouting mission. Lewis had a rare afternoon of genuine leisure; to amuse himself, he went fishing. The men mended their moccasins.

The Indian woman had been better in the morning. She had walked out onto the plains and gathered a considerable quantity of the white apples. She ate them raw—without telling Lewis—together with some dried fish.

Her fever returned. She felt awful. Lewis was furious: "I rebuked Sharbono severely for suffering her to indulge herself with such food he being privy to it and having been previously told what she must only eat. I now gave her broken dozes of diluted nitre [saltpeter, used as a diuretic and diaphoretic, for fevers and gonorrhea][3] untill it produced pespiration and at 10 P.M. 30 drops of laudanum which gave her a tolerable nights rest."

In the morning, she was "quite free from pain and fever and appears to be in a fair way for recovery, she has been walking about and fishing." His prognosis was correct; within a couple of days, she was well.

Lewis sent the men out hunting. He wanted to lay by as large a store of dried meat as possible, so that when the portage began he wouldn't have to detach men to hunt. That evening, Clark came into camp to report that the portage route was seventeen and three-quarters miles long.

The captains talked. They decided that Clark would oversee the portage while Lewis would go to the termination point, a group of islands that Clark had named White Bear Islands from the presence of so many grizzlies, where Lewis would oversee the preparation of his iron-frame boat. He would take the first load over the route, in a canoe carried on a wagon; the load would include the iron frame and the necessary tools. Sergeant Gass and Privates Joseph Field and John Shields would accompany him.

Clark told Lewis that there were no pines, only cottonwoods, in the area of the White Bear Islands. That gave Lewis something more to worry about: without pine pitch to pay the seams of the leather covering of his iron frame, he faced "a deficiency that I really know not how to surmount unless it be by means of tallow and pounded charcoal which mixture has answered a very good purpose on our wooden canoes."

The portage began shortly after sunrise on June 22. All the enlisted men, save two left behind to guard the baggage, joined the captains in moving the canoe over the plains. They had a multitude of problems, beginning with prickly pears and including numerous breakdowns. The axles broke. The tongues broke. Lewis renewed them with sweet-willow branches "and hope that they will answer better." Despite the difficulties, after dark they made it to the termination point. Along the way, Lewis discovered and described one of the best-loved birds of the Great Plains, the western meadowlark.

Over the next twelve days, Lewis stayed at the White Bear Islands camp, supervising the construction of the iron-frame boat (called "The Experiment" by the enlisted men), while Clark supervised the portage. The latter was the most difficult undertaking the expedition had yet experienced.

Let Clark describe it: "The men has to haul with all their Strength wate & art, maney times every man all catching the grass & knobes & Stones with their hands to give them more force in drawing on the Canoes & Loads, and notwithstanding the Coolness of the air in high presperation and every halt [the men] are asleep in a moment, maney limping from the Soreness of their feet Some become fant for a fiew moments, but no man Complains all go Chearfully on—to State the fatigues of this party would take up more of the journal than other notes which I find Scercely time to Set down."

They were assaulted by hail as big as apples, by "musquetoes," by hot sun and cold rain. The winds could be awesome. On June 25, Lewis noted that "the men informed me that they hoisted a sail in the canoe and the wind had driven her along on the truck wheels. this is really sailing on dry land."

To free up a man to help prepare elk skins for the boat covering, Lewis assigned himself the duty of cook. He collected the wood and water and in the biggest iron kettle boiled enough dried buffalo meat to feed thirty men, then made it into a suet dumpling by way of a treat for all the diners.

There were vast herds of buffalo in the neighborhood; Clark estimated he could see ten thousand in one view. The bulls kept Seaman up all night, barking at them. Grizzlies were also numerous, and, unlike the buffalo, they were dangerous; Lewis forbade any man to go alone on any errand that required passing through brush, and ordered all hands to sleep with their rifles close at hand. The bears came close around camp at night, Lewis wrote on June 28, "but have never yet ventured to attack us and our dog gives us timely notice of their visits, he keeps constantly padroling all night."

The bears often showed themselves at midday, which infuriated Lewis and his men. But "we are so much engaged that we could not spare the time to hunt them." Still, Lewis made a vow: "We will make a frolick of it" when the time came. He intended personally to direct an all-out attack on the enemy.

By June 30, the iron frame was put together and the skins—twenty-eight elk and four buffalo—had been prepared. In the morning, the sewing together of the skins over the frame would begin. Meanwhile, the portage was within two days of completion. Soon the expedition would be rolling up the river again.

Not soon enough to suit Lewis, who confessed in his journal, "I begin to be extremely impatient to be off as the season is now waisting a pace nearly three months have now elapsed since we left Fort Mandan and not yet reached the Rocky Mountains." He had given up any idea of getting to the Pacific and then back to the Mandans before winter set in, and had about concluded that he would not even be able to return from the ocean to join the Shoshone Indians for the winter.

Around this time, Lewis and Clark made a decision, later recorded in Lewis's journal of July 4. They had agreed before leaving Fort Mandan that, when they completed the Great Falls portage, they would send three men back to St. Louis, carrying specimens, artifacts, maps, journals, and other invaluable items. Now they changed their minds. They had made no contact with the Shoshone Indians, and even with Sacagawea along and in good health they could not count on those Indians' being friendly, or, even if friendly, disposed to trade horses for geegaws. As Lewis put it, "we conceived our party sufficiently small," meaning he wanted every rifle he could get.

The decision to keep the party at full strength has not drawn much commentary from Lewis and Clark scholars, but it deserves some consideration. Giving up 10 percent of the firepower and muscle power of the expedition might well have been fatal. But, then again, if the party ever got into a situation in which every rifle was needed, it might well not survive that situation, in which case all that had been discovered from April 7, 1805, to date, including the plants, birds, animals, rivers, lay of the land, the truth about the Great Falls, the latitude of the junction of the Yellowstone and Missouri Rivers would have been lost. To reduce the party by three men might endanger the others; but to send three men downriver to pass the Sioux would endanger them.

"We have never once hinted to any one of the party that we had such a scheme in contemplation," Lewis wrote. The passage illuminates the relationship between the captains and their men. In the first place, it indicates that at some times—around the campfire? while the men were eating?—the captains were able to talk without being overheard. It also speaks to the relative absence of rumors among the men. All soldiers love rumor—and this platoon-sized unit was coming upon rivers no one had ever heard of, finding five falls where they had been told to expect one, so it might be expected to do a lot of speculation on the captains' intentions. But it didn't, a tribute to the captains' leadership and discipline and the mark of how totally the men trusted them.

The passage indicates too how sensitive Lewis was to morale, for he goes on to say he feared that sending three men back "might possibly discourge those who would in such case remain." At that moment, the portage all but completed and the iron-frame boat about to be launched, morale was excellent. Lewis's description shows how strongly he had impressed his own personality and passion on the expedition. The men, he wrote, "all appear perfectly to have made up their minds to suceed in the expedition or purish in the attempt. we all believe that we are now about to enter on the most perilous and difficult part of our voyage, yet I see no one repining; all appear ready to met those difficulties which wait us with resolution and becoming fortitude."

The men of the expedition were linked together by uncommon experiences and by the certain knowledge that they were making history, the realization that they were in the middle of what would without question be the most exciting and important time of their lives, and the obvious fact that they were in all this together, that every man—and the Indian woman—was dependent on all the others, and they on him or her.

Together, under the leadership of the captains, they had become a family. They could recognize one another at night by a cough, or a gesture; they knew one another's skills, and weaknesses, and habits, and background: who liked salt, who preferred liver; who shot true, got the cooking fires going quickest; where they came from, what their parents were like, what dreams they had. Lewis would have hated to break them apart. He decided to hold them together. They would triumph, or die, as one.

On the morning of July 1, Lewis set two men to sewing the leather that would cover the boat, two men to preparing a pit to burn wood to try to make tar, and one man to making crosspieces for the boat, while he and Drouillard rendered the tallow, obtaining a hundred pounds. But the attempt to make tar failed, the sewing went slowly, and Lewis grew testy. The absence of pitch pine had forced him to experiment, and his experiments were terribly time-consuming because it was so difficult to obtain the necessary materials. Lewis found the work "extreemly tedious and troublesome." Everything about the boat was novel to the men, so "my constant attention was necessary to every part of the work; this together with the duties of cheif cook has kept me pretty well employed."

Lewis was fortunate to have at hand a worthy object for his frustration and pent-up energy. "The bear were about our camp all last night," he concluded his July 1 journal entry. "We have therefore determined to beat up their quarters tomorrow, and kill them or drive them from their haunts about this place."

At 8:15 a.m., after Lewis had measured the altitude of the sun, he and Clark led a twelve-man squad in an attack. They crossed to the largest of the islands and went through the brush in three-man teams. "We found only one," Lewis reported, "which made at Drewyer and he shot him in the brest at the distance of about 20 feet, the ball fortunately passed through his heart, the stroke knocked the bear down and gave Drewyer time to get out of his sight; the bear changed his course we pursued him about a hundred yards by the blood and found him dead." The soldiers were disappointed at finding only one of the enemy, but at least they had suffered no losses.

On returning to camp, the men, in moving some baggage, caught a large rat. Lewis examined and described the pack rat, previously unknown to science.

By July 3, as the boat neared completion, Lewis's doubts were assailing him. He nearly convinced himself that none of his experiments in finding a substitute for pitch was going to work. No matter what he tried, he could not produce tar. Without tar, "I fear the whole operation of my boat will be useless." There was something else: "I fear I have committed another blunder also in sewing the skins with a nedle which has sharp edges these have cut the skin and as it drys I discover that the throng does not fill the holes as I expected."

He and Clark and the men wanted to get going. "The current of the river looks so gentle and inviting that the men all seem anxious to be moving upward as well as ourselves."

That prospect brought Lewis's spirits back. His boat was done by evening, except for paying her (covering the skin with a composition that would make her watertight). Somehow he would find a way to do that. Meanwhile, he indulged himself in a bit of hubris about the design: "She has assumed her shape and looks extreemly well. She will be very light, more so than any vessel of her size that I ever saw."

The Fourth of July was a working day for the Corps of Discovery. Lewis had the men turn the boat and put her on a scaffold, then had small fires build underneath the craft to dry her.

That evening, the first Americans ever to enter Montana, the first ever to see the Yellowstone, the Milk, the Marias, and the Great Falls, the first Americans ever to kill a grizzly, celebrated their nation's twenty-ninth birthday. The captains gave the men a gill of whiskey—the last of the stock—"and some of them appeared a little sensible of it's effects." Cruzatte played the fiddle and the men danced "very merrily" until a 9:00 p.m. thunderstorm put an end to it. Even so, the men "continued their mirth with songs and festive jokes and were extreemly merry untill late at night."

As for the captains, "we had a very comfortable dinner, of bacon, beans, suit dumplings & buffaloe beaf &c. in short we had no just cause to covet the sumptuous feasts of our countrymen on this day."

That evening, Lewis described in his journal a phenomenon of the region, a repeated noise coming from the northwest at irregular intervals that resembled "precisely the discharge of a piece of ordinance of 6 pounds at the distance of three miles." The men had often mentioned the sound to him, but Lewis had been sure they had been hearing thunder, until "at length walking in the plains the other day I heard this noise very distictly, it was perfectly calm clear and not a cloud to be seen." He stopped and for an hour listened intently: he heard it twice more. "I have no doubt but if I had leasure I could find from whence it issued," he wrote. He would hear it again on July 11 and then recalled that the Hidatsas had mentioned such a noise. Clark also heard it; like Lewis, he was certain there was a rational explanation, although none came to mind.

No one since has explained it, but if Lewis and Clark said they heard it, it was there.*

On July 5, Lewis kept the fires going under the boat, and set some men to pounding charcoal to form a composition with beeswax and buffalo tallow. The boat was complete, except for paying her, and in every "rispect completely answers my most sanguine expectation." Eight men could carry her and she could carry four tons of goods. But Lewis feared that the charcoal-beeswax-tallow combination would not work, and, adding to his worries, "the stitches begin to gape very much since she has began to dry; I am now convinced this would not have been the case had the skins been sewed with a sharp point only and the leather not cut by the edges of a sharp nedle."

For two more days, the men kept the fires going, as the boat so slowly, ever so slowly, dried out, and more composition was produced. By 4:00 p.m. on July 7, Lewis was ready to pay the boat, but

---

* Ken Karsmizki, the archaeologist from the Museum of the Rockies in Bozeman who is directing the dig at the lower portage camp, has heard the boom several times.

a shower of rain attended by thunder and lightning prevented the operation.

It was done at noon the following day. Lewis was delighted with the result. After the first coat cooled, he put on a second: "This adds very much to her appearance whether it will be effectual or not. it gives her hull the appearance of being formed of one solid piece."

July 9 was launch day. Lewis had brought the frame of the Experiment all the way from Harpers Ferry. The frame had taken up space that could have been given to whiskey or trade goods or cornmeal or tools. Lewis had spent nearly two weeks getting her ready to launch, and had held up the entire expedition the past four or five days for the final preparations. He was counting on the boat to carry the bulky items to the Shoshone country at the source of the Missouri. He had a lot at stake.

Yet he began his journal entry describing the day with an account of the blackbirds that crowded the White Bear Islands. Only then did he record, "We launched the boat, she lay like a perfect cork on the water. five men would carry her with the greatest ease." Lewis directed the men to put the oars in place and load her up. He had others get the canoes ready to shove off. He was exultant.

But just as the expedition was about to become waterborne again, a violent wind came up, raising whitecaps on the river and wetting some of the baggage, forcing the men to unload the canoes.

It was late in the evening before the storm passed. When it did, Lewis discovered that the composition had separated from the skins and left the seams exposed. "She leaked in such manner that she would not answer."

Lewis was "mortifyed."

It turned out that the buffalo hides with a bit of hair left on them "answered much the best. . . . the parts which were well covered with hair about ⅛th of an inch in length retained the composition perfectly and remained sound and dry." Lewis felt certain that, if he had used all buffalo skins, and kept some hair on them, even with the composition he had the boat would have answered.

But, he said, "to make any further experiments in our present situation seemed to me madness." The season was advancing; the vast buffalo herds were moving downstream, away from the Great Falls. "I therefore relinquished all further hope of my favorite boat." He resigned himself to leaving her in a cache, but tortured himself with what-ifs. If he had only singed his elk skins, instead of shaving them, the composition would have worked. If he could have just kept her afloat for a couple of days, the expedition would have reached pine country, where pitch could be obtained. "But it was now too late to introduce a remidy and I bid a dieu to my boat, and her expected services." He never mentioned her again.*

Arlen Large indulges in a piece of imaginative speculation about the failure of the Experiment. He notes that, whereas Lewis's journal is stuffed with loving details about every step in preparing the Experiment for her launch, Clark's entries are brief, cold, distant, possibly indicating that he had no faith in the thing from the first. After the boat sank, Lewis wrote that he and Clark "recollected hving heard the hunters" mention some trees about eight miles upriver that would answer for canoes. Clark, however, in an 1810 interview with Nicholas Biddle, made it clear he had anticipated failure and had "previously" sent the hunters out to look for big trees. If Clark felt that the Experiment wasn't his baby and wouldn't work, he must have believed his friend's obsession with the boat had cost the expedition a lot of valuable time.

It may be, Large continues, that the Experiment caused a rift between the captains. If so, it was the only one. Lewis and Clark may have agreed on a period of separation to let things cool off. Clark took off the next morning to make canoes, and he stayed away from Lewis for most of the following two weeks.

The failure of the iron-frame boat left the expedition, despite the caches of so much material at Marias River and at Belt Creek, short of carrying capacity. Without the frame boat to substitute for the two pirogues hidden and secured downstream, more and larger canoes were needed. The hunters—acting at Clark's direction—had discovered a grove of cottonwood trees large enough for suitable canoes. The captains agreed that, in the morning, Lewis would oversee the transport of the baggage to the tree grove, while Clark would take ten men and proceed by land to the grove and begin to make canoes.

Stung so badly by the failure of his experiment, Lewis was gun-shy. He confessed in his journal that he would think it extremely fortunate if there were cottonwoods big enough to make into canoes at the grove, because he had not seen a single one in the past two months that would have been suitable.

But the hunters were right. Clark found two trees, one with twenty-five feet of usable length, another of thirty-three feet, each about three

---

* And no one bothered to pick her up on the return journey to take her back to Harpers Ferry.

feet wide. These answered nicely. It took five days to hollow them out and prepare them for the journey.

Anyone who has ever canoed on the upper Missouri River knows what a welcome sight a grove of cottonwoods can be. They provide shade, shelter, and fuel. For Indian ponies, they provided food. For the Corps of Discovery, they provided wheels, wagons, and canoes.

Pioneering Lewis and Clark scholar Paul Russell Cutright pays the cottonwoods an appropriate tribute: "Of all the western trees it contributed more to the success of the Expedition than any other. Lewis and Clark were men of great talent and resourcefulness, masters of ingenuity and improvisation. Though we think it probable that they would have successfully crossed the continent without the cottonwood, don't ask us how!"[4]

It had been a month since Lewis discovered the Great Falls, a month in which the total progress was about twenty-five miles, or less than a mile a day. On July 12, Lewis confessed, "I feel excessively anxious to be moving on." Two days later, everything was ready. With two large and six smaller canoes, and greatly reduced baggage, the expedition set out for the mountains. If the Hidatsas were right, the river would penetrate up to the Continental Divide, where Lewis and Clark would meet the Shoshone Indians, and where a half-day's portage would take the expedition over the Divide and into the Columbia River drainage.

Whatever lay ahead, and no one expected it to be easy, the captains and the men must have felt that it could not possibly be more arduous than the portage they had just completed. And for Lewis personally, nothing could be more heartbreaking than seeing his beloved boat go down. The worst had to be behind them.

21

LOOKING FOR
THE SHOSHONES

July 15–August 12, 1805

The captains were anxious to meet the Shoshones. The mosquitoes were troublesome. The prickly-pear thorns were painful. But for Lewis, despite these mental worries and physical problems, the second two weeks of July 1805 were a delight. He was keenly alive to sights and sounds, new birds and animals, the majesty of the western mountains and valleys. The first American ever to see such wonders, he took seriously his responsibility to provide the first report on what was out there. His descriptions of the things he saw are enchanting.

He had been a bit sour in the early-morning hours of departure day, July 15, because the canoes were overloaded. "We find it extreemly difficult to keep the baggage of many of our men within reasonable boundes," he wrote. "They will be adding bulky articles of but little use or value to them."

But at 10:00 a.m., when the loading was complete and the men began to push their canoes away from the shore and paddle upstream, his mood soared. "Much to my joy," Lewis wrote, "we once more saw ourselves fairly under way."

He walked on shore, with two privates, partly to lighten the load in the canoes, mainly because he loved to walk over new country. He was so pleased with life he even found something good to say about the prickly pear, which "is now in full blume and forms one of the beauties as well as the greatest pests of the plains." He described the abundant sunflowers in bloom, and how the Indians made bread of them. He noticed "lambsquarter, wild coucumber, sand rush and narrow dock." He saw a singular formation, a round, fortresslike mountain rising at the perpendicular one thousand feet above the plain with an extensive flat top. Lewis called it Fort Mountain (today's Square Butte, southwest of Great Falls, one of Charley Russell's favorite subjects).

The next day, Lewis decided to strike out ahead of the main body, so he could get to the place where the river came out of the mountains and make celestial observations. He brought along Drouillard and two privates. They walked through the morning; at noon, Lewis measured the sun's altitude and deduced his latitude as N. 46 degrees, 46' 50.2"—thirty-five miles too far north.

In the afternoon, he reached a spot where the mountains were crowding in on the river and made camp. He climbed to the summit of a rock he called "the tower . . . and from it there is a most pleasing view of the country we are now about to leave. from it I saw this evening immence herds of buffaloe in the plains below." He selected and killed a fat elk for supper.

As he began the ascent into the mountains, he encountered "a great abundance of red yellow perple & black currants, and service berries now ripe and in great perfection . . . vastly preferable to those of our gardens."

He was aware of passing from one ecological zone into another. On July 17, he noted that the broadleaf eastern cottonwood was giving way to the narrowleaf western cottonwood. The mosquitoes were troublesome. Just as he was ready to lie down, Lewis realized with a sharp pang that he had left his "bier," his mosquito netting, with the canoes. "Of course [I] suffered considerably," he wrote in his journal, "and promised in my wrath that I never will be guilty of a similar peice of negligence while on this voyage."

During the third week in July, Lewis had two new rivers to name. Previously he and Clark had used the names of the men, of Sacagawea, of relatives, or of unusual features or incidents. Now that they were past the Great Falls, they changed their references. It was as if they suddenly recalled that they had some political responsibility here, that no politician can ever be flattered too much or too brazenly, and that nothing quite matches having a river named for you.

Lewis named the first river coming in from the left Smith's River, for Robert Smith, Jefferson's secretary of the navy. Lewis described it as "a beautifull river. . . . the stream meanders through a most lovely valley. . . ." The first river coming in from the right he named

Dearborn's, for Henry Dearborn, the secretary of war. He called it a "handsome bold and clear stream."*

That morning, July 18, he noted "a large herd of the Bighorned anamals on the immencely high and nearly perpendicular clift opposite to us; on the fase of this clift they walked about and bounded from rock to rock with apparent unconcern where it appared to me that no quadruped could have stood, and from which had they made one false step they must have been precipitated at least a 500 feet."

Lewis's anxiety to meet the Shoshones increased. He talked with Clark; they agreed that one or the other of them would take a small party and proceed by land upriver, to get well ahead of the canoes, in order to find some Shoshones. Their idea was that the daily firing of the rifles by the hunters would frighten away the Shoshones, who would assume their enemy the Blackfeet were around. Of course the land party would also have to fire weapons to sustain itself—but not so many of them.

Clark led the party. It left at dawn on July 19. Lewis led the canoes up the river. It was hard going, whether using the cord, the setting poles, or the paddles. Whenever the mountains broke back to give a view, there was to their right the disheartening sight of lofty summits all covered with snow, standing between the expedition and its goal. Meanwhile, Lewis noted unhappily, "we are almost suffocated in this confined vally with heat."

That evening, "we entered much the most remarkable clifts that we have yet seen. these clifts rise from the waters edge on either side perpendicularly to the hight of 1200 feet. every object here wears a dark and gloomy aspect. the towering and projecting rocks in many places seem ready to tumble on us. . . . for the distance of 5¾ miles [the river is] deep from side to side nor is there in the 1st 3 miles of this distance a spot . . . on which a man could rest the soal of his foot. . . . it was late in the evening before I entered this place . . . obliged to continue my rout untill sometime after dark before I found a place sufficiently large to encamp my small party; at length such an one occurred on the lard. side. . . . from the singular appearance of this place I called it the *gates of the rocky mountains*."

In the morning, as the flotilla paddled its way out of the canyon, the mountains receded and a beautiful intermountain valley presented itself. But about 10:00 a.m., a distressing, worry-making sight appeared

---

* Had he traveled up the Dearborn, he would have come to today's Lewis and Clark Pass, a fairly low pass over the Divide with the Blackfoot River Valley on the other side, leading directly to today's Missoula, Montana, and the Clark Fork River, which flows into the Columbia.

in the sky: a column of smoke, coming out of a creek drainage some seven miles west, big enough to have been deliberately set. It had to have been done by Indians, all but certainly Shoshone, and almost surely because a single Indian or a small party had heard the discharge of a rifle and set fire to the grass to warn the rest of the tribe to retreat into the interior of the mountains.

That was about as bad as anything that could happen, but there was nothing to do but press on. The following day, the flotilla entered "a beautifull and extensive plain country of about 10 or 12 miles wide which extended upwards further than the eye could reach this valley is bounded by two nearly parallel ranges of high mountains which have their summits partially covered with snow."

Lewis was within a couple of hours' march from one of the great gold deposits, at Last Chance Gulch, in present Helena, Montana. But he wasn't looking for gold. His lack of interest in it was one of the things that distinguished his exploration from that of his Spanish predecessors (another was his lack of interest in converting Indians to Christianity). Interested in plants and animals, especially fur-bearing animals, he paid little attention to potential mineral deposits, especially after leaving the Mandans. He had noted lead deposits on the lower Missouri, but when he entered the Rockies he hardly ever commented on rocks or minerals.

Why should he? In the prerailroad age, there was no way to move heavy, bulky items—no matter how valuable—from the mountains back to the seaboard. In his final instructions to Lewis, Jefferson had ordered the explorer to take note of the mineral deposits, but he meant such minerals as lead, iron, and coal, valuable adjuncts to an agricultural economy, not export items.

Donald Jackson comments that this unconcern with minerals "was a blank spot in Lewis's thinking that he almost surely had acquired from Jefferson. The Rockies were too far away for mining, for any commerce but the fur trade, and so were not an object of study and speculation but only a wretchedly cold obstacle between men and the sea."[1] As far as Lewis and Jefferson were concerned, animals, not minerals, were the great wealth of the Rocky Mountains.

Ten days after passing Last Chance Gulch, the expedition made camp on a small creek entering today's Beaverhead River. The captains named it Willard's Creek, in honor of Private Alexander Willard. "Nothing remarkable happened," Donald Jackson writes. It would be sixty years before Willard's Creek was renamed Grasshopper Creek and the Beaverhead country teemed with gold miners.

Jackson speculates on what might have happened had the expedition brought back a handful of nuggets from Willard's Creek: "Nomadic fur traders, blazing trails in the years immediately following Lewis and Clark, might have been joined by adventurous miners. The finding of shorter and easier trails, such as the route across South Pass in southern Wyoming, would have occurred earlier. The timetable for western settlement would surely have been advanced by a generation, and that peculiar American invention, Indian removal, would have become standard government policy much earlier in the area west of the Mississippi."[2]

As the mountains began to close in again, toward evening on July 22, the expedition got a badly needed morale booster. The men were laboring mightily, often in the water pulling the canoes along, feet slipping (or getting cut on rocks), the river apparently having no end, the mountains crowding in, the great buffalo herds now left behind on the plains, no whiskey left, the days beginning to grow noticeably shorter. Sacagawea recognized this section of the river. She had been here as a girl; it was the river on which the Shoshones lived in the summer. The Three Forks were at no great distance ahead. "this peice of information has cheered the sperits of the party," Lewis duly noted.

At 4:00 p.m., the flotilla reached Clark, who had made camp on the starboard side. He had found no Indians, although he had seen signs that they were out there. He had left some presents, cloth and linen, "in order to inform the indians should they pursue his trale that we were not their enemies, but *white men* and their friends."

But the thing that stood out was Clark's physical condition, more specifically his feet. They were a raw, bleeding mass of flesh torn apart by prickly pears. "I opened the bruses & blisters of my feet which caused them to be painfull," Clark wrote, in his own get-to-the-point fashion. He spent the day resting, waiting for Lewis to come up with the canoes.

The captains talked. They agreed that another overland expedition was necessary. Clark wanted to lead it; he wanted another chance at finding Indians and overcoming prickly pears. One day of self-enforced idleness was all he could take; he itched to be back at work.

Lewis wrote, "altho' Capt. C. was much fatiegued his feet yet blistered and soar he insisted on pursuing his rout in the morning nor weould he consent willingly to my releiving him. ... finding him anxious I readily consented to remain with the canoes." Clark told the Field brothers and Private Robert Frazier to get ready to accompany him in the morning. Charbonneau asked if he could go along; Clark agreed.

This was about as close to a disagreement that the captains ever came, or at least ever wrote about, with regard to rank. In Lewis's version, "I readily consented." In Clark's version, "I deturmined to proceed on in pursute of the Snake Indians."

So insistent was Clark that he had determined, rather than Lewis's having consented, that years later, in editing the journals for publication, Clark had "I deturmined" substituted for Lewis's "he insisted."

As a dispute, that wasn't much, more a disagreement over the right word to describe the decision-making process than a fight over the question of who was in command. For Virginians, taught rank-consciousness from birth, sensitive to the slightest slight, concern about rank, status, and position was as much a part of life as breathing. Lewis's journal description of this little incident is written on an unspoken, probably unconscious, assumption: that he could order Clark to stay with the canoes while he took the scouts to look for Indians. Clark disagreed: in his view, this was a case of "I deturmined" rather than "you allowed."

There is a hint in the decision that the captains thought Clark was the better at approaching and dealing with Indians, but just a hint. The makeup of Clark's party is puzzling. Why did Charbonneau have to ask to come along, and why didn't Clark bring Sacagawea? The captains had brought her all this way so that she could to be the contact person with the Shoshones.

Instead, Clark was proposing to approach them with three other armed men, none of them proficient with the sign language (Drouillard was camped upriver a few miles that night; he had been hunting). The only Shoshone words Clark knew he had been taught by Sacagawea. He had asked her what was her people's word for "white man."

"*Tab-ba-bone*," she replied.

Actually, the Shoshones had no word for "white man," never having seen one. Scholars have guessed that *tab-ba-bone* might have meant "stranger," or "enemy."[3]

Certainly bringing along a recently ill young woman with a papoose on her back would have slowed the party, but, then, how fast was Clark going to go, with his feet in tatters? Anyway, proceeding slowly would have been preferable to blundering ahead hoping to bump into some Indians yet having no way to communicate with them.

When it came his turn to lead an overland search for Shoshones, Lewis followed Clark's example and did not ask Sacagawea to accompany him. The captains shared a hubris, that they could handle Indians. They believed they needed Sacagawea's interpreting ability only to trade for horses, not to establish contact. And they had no ability whatsoever to see the initial encounter from the Shoshones' point of view. Four-man parties, armed better even than the Blackfeet, approaching on foot, shouting something that sounded like "stranger," or "enemy"—did Clark really expect these Indians to come running to embrace him when they saw the American flag?

In this case, it would seem that the captains allowed their self-confidence, and perhaps their male chauvinism, to override their common sense.

Clark set out the next morning, July 23, in search of Indians. Lewis headed upriver. Conditions were awful. "Our trio of pests still invade and obstruct us on all occasions, these are the Musquetoes eye knats and prickley pears." It was hot. Progress was measured in yards, even feet. "The men complain of being much fortiegued, their labour is excessively great." So moved was Lewis by their effort—and so eager was he to get on—that "I occasionally encourage them by assisting in the labour of navigating the canoes, and have learned to *push a tolerable good pole* in their fraize."

He still had time for observation. Signs of beaver were noted, and otter. Cranes, geese, red-breasted mergansers, and curlews brought comment. He saw "a great number of snakes," killed one, examined its teeth to see if they were hollow and thus would carry poison, "and fund them innosent."

What excited wonder also caused worry. "The mountains they still continue high and seem to rise in some places like an amphatheater one rang above another as they receede from the river untill the most distant and lofty have their tops clad with snow." They loomed out there, every time Lewis looked to his right, waiting for him.

Another frustration—the river was now flowing from a southeasterly direction, so progress was taking the expedition in exactly the wrong direction.

Another worry—although Sacagawea insisted that there were no falls or obstructions in the river above, Lewis confessed, "I can scarcely form an idea of a river runing to great extent through such a rough mountainous country without having it's stream intersepted by some difficult and dangerous rappids or falls."

Another pest—needle grass, an invention of the devil, consisting of barbed seeds which "penetrate our mockersons and leather legings and give us great pain untill they are removed. my poor dog suffers with them excessively, he is constantly binting and scratching himself as if in a rack of pain."

Another day on the river. Making about eighteen miles per day. Endless. Exhausting.

July 27: "We set out at an early hour and proceeded on but slowly the current still so rapid that the men are in a continual state of their utmost exertion to get on, and they begin to weaken fast from this continual state of violent exertion." They had reached the breaking point.

Then fortune smiled. Just around the turn, at 9:00 a.m., Lewis in the lead canoe came to a junction with a river from the southeast. A quarter-mile or so upstream, two rivers came together, a southwest fork and a middle fork, making the Three Forks. As Lewis described it, "The country opens suddenly to extensive and beatifull plains and meadows which appear to be surrounded in every direction with distant and lofty mountains."

He came to shore on the larboard side. Telling the men to rest, he set out to climb a nearby high limestone cliff. At the top, "I commanded a most perfect view of the neighbouring country." Looking up the southeast fork, he saw "smoth extensive green meadow of fine grass. . . . a distant range of lofty mountains rose their snow-clad tops above the irregular and broken mountains which lie adjacent to this beautifull spot."

From the cliff Lewis stood on, the view today is still spectacular. There are modern intrusions—Interstate Highway 90, Montana Highway 287, and a few secondary roads run through it, and the little town of Three Forks is a few miles away—but the overall scene is as it was. There is a tremendous bowl, containing the linked valleys of the two rivers coming out of today's Yellowstone Park to the south and east, and the valley of the river to the southwest, coming down from the Madisons. The rivers are crowded with fish and waterfowl; the banks are crowded with deer. The mountains surround the bowl in a nearly complete circle of up to a hundred miles in diameter and are just as Lewis saw them, lofty and snow-covered.

After writing a description of the Three Forks area, Lewis returned to the canoes, ate breakfast, and led the flotilla upstream. At the junction of the middle and the southwest forks, he found a note Clark had written and stuck on a pole; it said he would rejoin Lewis here unless he fell in with some fresh sign of Indians, in which case he intended to follow the Indians and would count on Lewis to ascend the southwest (or right-hand) fork.

Lewis immediately agreed with Clark's judgment that the right-hand was the fork to take. He set up camp and made plans to stay awhile, because "beleiving this to be an essential point in the geography of this western part of the Continent I determined to remain at all events untill I obtained the necessary data for fixing it's latitude Longitude &c." And it wouldn't hurt to give the men a chance to rest.

Lewis set out to explore. Comparing the middle fork with the southwest fork, he could see no difference in character or size. "Therefore to call either of these streams the Missouri would be giving it a preference wich it's size dose not warrant as it is not larger than the other. They are each 90 yds wide."

Lewis named the southeast fork "Gallitin's river," in honor of Albert Gallatin, secretary of the treasury; the middle fork he called "Maddison's river," in honor of James Madison, secretary of state; the southwest fork, the one he intended to follow, he called "Jefferson's River in honor [of] that illustrious personage Thomas Jefferson President of the United States. . . ."*

At 3:00 p.m., Captain Clark came into camp. He was extremely sick, completely exhausted. He told Lewis he had been sick all night, with a high fever, frequent chills, and constant pains in his muscles. Nevertheless, in the morning, he had made a forced march of about eight miles up the middle fork but, finding no Indian sign, decided to return to Three Forks. He said he was "somewhat bilious and had not had a passage for several days."

Lewis convinced Clark that a dozen of Rush's pills would be sovereign in this case; he said it always worked. Clark agreed to take five. Lewis also convinced Clark to bathe his feet in warm water. Despite the treatment, Clark closed his short journal entry for the day, "I continue to be verry unwell fever verry high."

Lewis closed his journal that night with a worry. "We begin to feel considerable anxiety with rispect to the Snake Indians," he wrote. "If we do not find them . . . I fear the successfull issue of our voyage will be very doubtfull or at all events much more difficult in it's acomplishment." He believed the expedition would soon reach "the bosom of this wild and mountanous country," and realized that meant game would grow scarce, perhaps even nonexistent. Meanwhile, the expedition would be "without any information with rispect to the country not knowing how far these mountains continue, or wher to

---

* Usually the first captain to see a river named it, but not always. And often they saw a new river simultaneously. In this case, Clark had first seen the three rivers that merge to form the Missouri, but Lewis gave them their names. The following day, he solicited Clark's views; Clark said he agreed that no one could claim right of place and that therefore Jefferson, Gallatin, and Madison were appropriate names.

direct our course to pass them to advantage or intersept a navigable branch of the Columbia."

Without Shoshone horses, without Shoshone information, the expedition might as well turn around and go home, or so Lewis feared, although he was prepared to press on as long as it was possible. He consoled himself with the thought that the Jefferson River had to head with the tributaries of the Columbia. As to the lack of game, he figured that "if any Indians can subsist in the form of a nation in these mountains with the means they have of acquiring food we can also subsist."

The expedition spent two days at the Three Forks, the men making clothing or hunting, Lewis making celestial observations, Clark recuperating. Always the booster and developer, Lewis proposed the establishment of a fort at Three Forks, at the far-western limit of Louisiana, where the rivers and creeks teemed with beaver. That it was almost three thousand miles up the Missouri from St. Louis and the nearest civilization bothered him not a bit—there was plenty of timber, and "the grass is luxouriant and would afford a fine swarth of hay."

Sacagawea informed him that the expedition's camp was precisely on the spot where the Shoshones had been camped five years ago when a raiding party of Hidatsas discovered them. The Shoshones had retreated three miles upriver and hidden in a wood. But the Hidatsas had found and routed them, killing four men, four women, and a number of boys, and making prisoners of four boys and all the remaining women, including Sacagawea.

"I cannot discover that she shews any immotion of sorrow in recollecting this event," Lewis concluded his journal entry relating Sacagawea's story, "or of joy in being again restored to her native country; if she has enough to eat and a few trinkets to wear I believe she would be perfectly content anywhere."

One wonders if Lewis was comparing Sacagawea with the young black female slaves he had known, or with white women of his own class. One wonders too how the man who could be so observant about so many things, including the feelings and point of view of his men, could be so unobservant about Sacagawea's situation. A slave, one of only two in the party, she was also the only Indian, the only mother, the only woman, the only teenaged person. Small wonder she kept such a tight grip on her emotions.

Captain Clark had improved, somewhat. Though his fever was gone, he was "still very languid and complains of a general soarness in all his limbs." Lewis prescribed Peruvian bark (for the tonic effect of its quinine).

Over the next week, Lewis, with Drouillard and small parties of men (and once Sacagawea), marched ahead of the canoes, searching for Indians. The early-August sun beat down on the hikers; on the first day of the month, Lewis described himself as "much exhausted by the heat of the day the roughness of the road and the want of water." He nevertheless discovered and described the blue grouse and the pinyon jay. He found a profusion of berries, "now ripe and in full perfection, we feasted suptuously on our wild fruit." He saw more beaver signs than he had ever thought possible. He named two tributaries of the Jefferson River: "[We] called the bold rapid an clear stream *Wisdom* and the more mild and placid one *Philanthrophy*, in commemoration of two of those cardinal virtues, which have so eminently marked that deservedly selibrated character [Jefferson] through life."*

The junction of the Wisdom and the Jefferson presented a familiar problem. Which river to follow? Lewis decided on the Jefferson, not because it was bigger (it carried less water than the Wisdom) but because it was much warmer, "from which I concluded that it had it's source at a greater distance in the mountains." He wrote a note to Clark, recommending that he bring the canoes up the Jefferson if he got to the junction before Lewis returned from a two-day scout for Indians. He stuck the note on a pole at the fork of the river and set out with Drouillard, Charbonneau, and Sergeant Gass (who had disabled himself in an accident and was in great pain, too much so to work a canoe, though, according to Lewis, "he could march with convenience").

Two days later, August 6, Lewis returned to the area, empty-handed with regard to the Shoshones. Now he heard "the hooping of the party to my left." He marched toward the sound and found Clark and the canoes on the Wisdom River. They were a sorry mess. One canoe had just overset and all its baggage was wet, including the medicine box. Two other canoes had filled with water. Immediate action was necessary.

"The first object," Lewis wrote, was to examine, dry, and arrange the stores. They made a camp on a gravel bar at the mouth of the Wisdom and spread the stuff out to dry.

That job done, the captains talked. Why was Clark going up the Wisdom? Hadn't he seen Lewis's note? He had not. The captains

---

* The Wisdom is today's Big Hole; the Philanthropy is today's Ruby. The main stream the captains continued to call the Jefferson; on today's maps it is the Beaverhead.

puzzled over this, then concluded that Lewis had put the note on a green pole; a passing beaver had cut it down and carried it off, together with the note. "The possibility of such an occurrence never once occurred to me when I placed it on the green pole," Lewis confessed.

Clark had not agreed with Lewis on which river to take. He had gone up the Wisdom because he thought it went more directly in the direction the expedition wanted to go. But the Wisdom was much too narrow, willow-infested, rapid, and twisty. Clark said that he had met with Drouillard before Lewis came up, that Drouillard had informed him of the true state of the two rivers, and that he was in the process of turning around (which was what caused the canoe to upset) when Lewis arrived.

Another worry. Clark had sent Private Shannon ahead, up the Wisdom, to hunt. When Clark met Drouillard and decided to turn around, he told Drouillard to proceed upstream, catch up with Shannon, and bring him back. But toward dusk, Drouillard came in to report he could not find Shannon. Lewis ordered the trumpet sounded and had the men fire a couple of volleys, but Shannon made no appearance.

In the morning, August 7, the captains decided they had so far exhausted their supplies that they could proceed with one canoe less, so they hid and secured one in a thicket of brush. In the afternoon, they made seven miles up the Jefferson. Shannon failed to join the party. On the 8th, they made fourteen river miles, but, as Lewis noted, "altho' we travel briskly and a considerable distance yet it takes us only a few miles on our general curse or rout," because the river was "very crooked many short bends." Three days previously, Lewis had noted that "the men were so much fortiegued today that they wished much that navigation was at an end that they might go by land." Morale, and the energy level, were sinking fast.

The Corps of Discovery was becoming a walking hospital. Captain Clark's intestinal problems had disappeared, but he had developed a tumor on his ankle, which was much swollen and inflamed and gave him considerable pain. Sergeant Gass, Charbonneau, and four or five of the enlisted men had various indispositions. Everyone was more or less exhausted most of the time.

But that afternoon, Sacagawea again gave the men a much-needed lift. As Lewis put it, "The Indian woman recognized the point of a high plain to our right which she informed us was not very distant from the summer retreat of her nation on a river beyond the mountains which runs to the west." She said the Shoshones called the hill the "Beaver's Head," from a supposed resemblance of its shape to the head of a swimming beaver. "She assures us that we shall either find her people on this river or on the river immediately west of it's source."

So close. The men wanted to hide the canoes, put the baggage on their backs, and march to the dividing ridge. But if the captains let them do that, they would have to leave the greater part of the baggage as well as the canoes, and in Lewis's view, "we have a stock already sufficiently small for the length of the voyage before us." They had to have horses.

"As it is now all important with us to meet with those people [the Shoshones] as soon as possible," Lewis wrote, the captains decided to send out an overland party that would stay out until it located the Indians. Clark wanted to lead it, but "the rageing fury of a tumer on my anckle musle" made it impossible for him to walk.

Lewis's determination was absolute. His intention was "to proceed tomorrow with a small party to the source of the principal stream of this river and pass the mountains to the Columbia; and down that river untill I found the Indians; in short it is my resolusion to find them or some others, who have horses if it should cause me a trip of one month."

In the morning, before breakfast, Lewis did some "wrightings, which I conceived from the nature of my instructions necessary lest any accedent should befall me on the long and reather hazardous rout I was now about to take." What those writings consisted of, no one knows. It sounds as if they were written instructions to Clark in the event he did not return. Did he tell Clark to press on, whatever happened to him? Or to fall back to St. Louis and try again the next year, with a bigger party?

This was the first time he had done such a thing. Clearly he felt he had arrived at the critical moment and that he was in a do-or-die situation. He was a man whose mind never stopped working, and during his long walks on the plains or in the mountains he had plenty of time to think—even though his eyes were constantly picking up flora and fauna, geographical features, the distance to this or that spot, and registering them in his mind so he could write about them in his journal.

That was the naturalist/explorer in him, and his interest never flagged. But he was also an army officer operating under orders to go to the Pacific and return and report. And he was a company commander, responsible for the lives of thirty men. So what was the military-officer/explorer thinking?

In that capacity, Lewis was a worrier who took care to put his concerns down on paper. The question "Where is Shannon?" led to conjecture. Lewis's thought was that he must have shot an elk or two and was waiting beside the Wisdom for the expedition to come to him. Which river to take? Can we possibly make it without horses? Always he worried about the state of the men's health, and wondered how much more of this they could take.

As to what he thought lay ahead, on August 10 he wrote, "I do not believe that the world can furnish an example of a river runing to the extent which the Missouri and Jefferson's rivers do through such a mountainous country and at the same time so navigable as they are." His men were already questioning that word "navigable," but his optimism remained: "If the Columbia furnishes us such another example, a communication across the continent by water will be practicable and safe." This had to be the triumph of faith in Jefferson, at the expense of what he was seeing with his own eyes, the men at their uttermost limits and still so far to go.

His realism returned to him: "this [a short portage and an easy float to the Pacific] I can scarcely hope from a knowledge of its having in its comparitively short course to the ocean the same number of feet to decend which the Missouri and Mississippi have from this point to the Gulph of Mexico."

His mind covered the continent. If the Columbia had only one-fifth the course to run to get to sea level as the Missouri-Mississippi, and if they started out within a short hike of each other, then the Columbia was going to have lots more falls and rapids than anything they had so far encountered.

But his fixed rule was always to assume the road ahead was good, until proved otherwise.

Only a tiny number of people have ever had the experience of not knowing what they would see when they got to the top of the mountain or turned into the river or sailed around the tip of a continent. Lewis expected that, when he got up the mountain to the Divide, he would see something resembling the country he was traveling through—long, sweeping valleys dropping down to the broader valley of the Jefferson—only in this case the stream would be running to the south branch of the Columbia. Whatever he saw, he was either going to find horses on this trip, and get over the mountains and onto the Columbia, or die in the attempt.

Aside from his own calculation about the nature of the Columbia, he seldom wrote about what he expected to see. He did write about what the Hidatsas told him. Their information was awfully sketchy beyond Three Forks, and nonexistent on the western side of the Divide. Lewis's theoretical expectation, learned from Jefferson, was that the Rockies were a single chain of mountains, like the Appalachians. But, given that the Rockies were so much higher than anything east of the Mississippi, he really didn't know what he would see.

With regard to the Indians he was seeking, he neglected to think through his situation. He just blundered ahead on the unshakable and unacknowledged assumption that he was such an expert in handling Indians that when he met a Shoshone he would know instinctively what to do.

If he ever interviewed Sacagawea about her people, he didn't consider it important enough to put into his journal. If he ever asked her what the country beyond the Divide was like, he didn't write about it. Clark's asking her how to say "white man" in Shoshone was the full extent of the captains' interrogation of the most valuable intelligence source they had available to them. That Lewis did not bring her along on the most important mission of his life is inexplicable. She had made long marches before, and could again.

Also inexplicable was the failure of the captains to talk with each other, and to bring Drouillard and Charbonneau in on the discussion, about what to do when contact was made with a Shoshone. Furthermore, Lewis held no conference with Drouillard and Privates John Shields and Hugh McNeal, the men he had selected to go on the mission with him, to tell them what to do when an Indian was spotted—how to behave, what signs to use, what to say.

Lewis had good reason to believe the Shoshones would welcome the expedition. The tribe desperately needed contact with white traders, so that the braves could arm themselves and fight the Blackfeet, Hidatsas, and other enemies on more equal terms. Of course, Lewis wasn't bringing the hard-pressed Shoshones any guns—only the promise that if the Shoshones cooperated, American traders would come to their country. Short-term, Lewis needed the Shoshones far more than they needed him; long-term, their fate was tied up with the success of the expedition. But how to get them to recognize this would be a problem. So would getting past the initial moment of contact without anybody's firing or running away.

These problems required a plan and a strategy, but the captains never developed either one.

At breakfast on the morning of August 9, a good omen for Lewis's mission: Shannon came in, with three deer skins and an adventure story that had a happy ending.

"Immediately after breakfast," Lewis wrote that night, "I slung my pack and set out."

The first day, he covered sixteen miles. The second day, it was thirty miles, ending up in "one of the handsomest coves I ever saw, of about 16 or 18 miles in diameter."* He had followed an old Indian road, but it gave out on him. On the morning of the 11th, he met with his party and gave out the closest thing to a plan he could come up with. They would spread out across the valley, headed west, looking for the Indian road. Drouillard would go out to the right, Shields to the left; McNeal would stay with Lewis. If Drouillard or Shields should find the road, he would notify Lewis by placing a hat on the muzzle of his rifle and holding it aloft.

They marched abreast for five miles. No sign of a road. Suddenly Lewis squinted, looked again, took out his telescope, and saw for sure "an Indian on horse back about two miles distant coming down the plain toward us." His dress was Shoshone. "His arms were a bow and quiver of arrows, and was mounted on an eligant horse without a saddle."

"I was overjoyed at the sight of this stranger," Lewis wrote, "and had no doubt of obtaining a friendly introduction to his nation provided I could get near enough to him to convince him of our being whitemen."

Lewis hiked on at his usual pace. The Indian horseman came on. But when they were about a mile apart, the Indian stopped. So did Lewis. Lewis pulled his blanket from his pack, threw it into the air, and spread it on the ground, which he understood to be a signal of friendship. Unfortunately, "this signal had not the desired effect, he still kept his position." He was glancing from side to side. It seemed to Lewis that he was viewing Drouillard and Shields "with an air of suspicion."

Of course he was. The Indian was, probably, a teenager out on a scout, curious about these strangers but cautious, brought up to fear all strangers. Coming at him were four armed men. How could he not be suspicious? Especially since the Shoshones had just suffered a serious loss of people and horses from a Blackfoot raid.[4]

Lewis wanted to make Drouillard and Shields halt, but they were out of shouting range "and I feared to make any signal to them least it should increase the suspicion in the mind of the Indian of our having some unfriendly design upon him."

Lewis spread out the pitiful supply of trade goods he had brought with him—some beads, a looking glass, a few trinkets. Leaving his rifle and pouch with McNeal, he advanced toward the Indian.

---

* Shoshone Cove, now mostly covered by the Clark Canyon Reservoir.

The Indian sat his horse, and watched, until Lewis was within two hundred yards. At that point, he turned his horse and began to move off slowly.

Desperate, Lewis called in as loud a voice as he could command, "*tab-ba-bone*," repeatedly.

Instead of responding to Lewis, the Indian kept watching Drouillard and Shields as they advanced. Lewis was furious with them: "Neither of them haveing segacity enough to recollect the impropriety of advancing when they saw me thus in parley with the Indian." Finally, he broke his rule not to make signals—he signaled them to stop. Drouillard saw and obeyed; Shields ("who afterwards told me that he did not observe the signal") kept coming on.

At 150 yards, Lewis repeated "*tab-ba-bone*," and held up "the trinkits in my hands and striped up my shirt sleve to give him an opportunity of seeing the coulour of my skin."

At one hundred yards, the Indian "suddenly turned his hose about, gave him the whip, leaped the creek and disapeared in the willow brush in an instant and with him vanished all my hopes of obtaining horses for the preasent."

"I now felt quite as much mortification and disappointment as I had pleasure and expectation at the first sight of this indian." He was "soarly chargrined" by the conduct of the men, particularly Shields, whom he blamed for the failure.

"I now called the men to me," Lewis wrote, "and could not forbare abraiding them a little for their want of attention and imprudence on this occasion." Blaming them wasn't going to accomplish anything, however, and Lewis's refusal to assess his own mistakes in the encounter is noticeable. Surely he was just as guilty as they were, if not more so.

But he directed his anger at them. He had left his telescope with the blanket he had spread. McNeal had neglected to bring it along with the blanket, and Lewis seemed to take a bit of pleasure in ordering Drouillard and Shields to go back to search for it.

When they found it and returned, the party set off on the track of the horse, McNeal carrying a small U.S. flag attached to a pole. Thinking that the Indians might well be watching from the surrounding hills, and not wanting to give them the idea that an advance on them was being made, Lewis halted at an open place, built a fire, and cooked and ate breakfast. But just as he started out again, a heavy shower of rain raised the grass and wiped out the track. He saw several places where it appeared to him that the Indians had been digging roots that day, which meant the main village couldn't be far off. At twenty miles, he made camp.

*

On the morning of August 12, "we fell in with a large and plain Indian road. . . . it passed a stout stream. . . . Here we halted and brakfasted on the last of our venison, having yet a small peice of pork in reseve."

They hiked on, headed toward a pass, the stream growing small as they ascended the gentle slope. "At a distance of 4 miles further the road took us to the most distant fountain of the waters of the mighty Missouri in search of which we have spent so many toilsome days and wristless nights."

He assessed the impact on himself: "Thus far I had accomplished one of those great objects on which my mind has been unalterably fixed for many years, judge then of the pleasure I felt in allying my thirst with this pure and ice cold water."

Lewis was not alone in his rejoicing: "Two miles below McNeal had exultingly stood with a foot on each side of this little rivulet and thanked his god that he had lived to bestride the mighty & heretofore deemed endless Missouri."

Now was the moment to go to the top of the pass, to become the first American to look on Idaho and the great northwestern empire. Lewis described the moment: "We proceeded on to the top of the dividing ridge from which I discovered immence ranges of high mountains still to the West of us with their tops partially covered with snow."*

To what degree Lewis was surprised or disheartened by the sight, he never said. John Logan Allen asks us to "imagine the shock and the surprise—for from the top of that ridge were to be seen neither the great river that had been promised nor the open plains extending to the shores of the South Sea." What Allen calls "the geography of hope" had to give way to "the geography of reality."[5] With Lewis's last step to the top of the Divide went decades of theory about the nature of the Rocky Mountains, shattered by a single glance from a single man. Equally shattered were Lewis's hopes for an easy portage to a major branch of the Columbia.

But whatever Lewis felt as he first saw the Bitterroot Range of the Rocky Mountains, he never wrote about. Nor did he write about his feelings as he took his first step on the western side of the Divide, outside of Louisiana.

---

* He was at Lemhi Pass, on today's Montana-Idaho border. Except for a wooden fence along the border, a cattle guard at the crossing, and a logging road, the site is pristine. Along with the Missouri River from Fort Benton to Fort Peck Lake, and the Lolo Trail in Idaho, it is the closest we can come today to seeing a site as Lewis saw it in 1805. The U.S. Forest Service has done an excellent job of signposting the route Lewis traveled.

He descended the mountain, which was much steeper than the approach on the eastern side, about three-quarters of a mile, "to a handsome bold running Creek of cold Clear water. here I first tasted the water of the great Columbia river."

The party proceeded another ten miles or so before making camp. "As we had killed nothing during the day we now boiled and eat the remainder of our pork, having yet a little flour and parched meal."

Lewis was deep into Indian country with only three men, and his main body three or four days' march away. He had a few geegaws as his currency. He had a frightened Indian reporting back to the Shoshones that strangers were in the area. He had just been through enough experiences for an entire expedition, all in one day. He needed a good night's sleep, and lots of good luck in the morning.

22

OVER THE
CONTINENTAL DIVIDE

August 13–August 31, 1805

On Tuesday morning, August 13, 1805, Lewis set out early, headed west on a plain, heavily and recently used Indian trail that fell down a long, descending valley. Along the way, he saw and described the Rocky Mountain maple, the skunkbush sumac, and the common snowberry. He stopped to collect seeds of the snowberry for Mr. Jefferson.*

At nine miles, Lewis saw two Indian women, a man, and some dogs. When he had arrived within half a mile of them, he ordered Drouillard and the two privates to halt, unslung his pack and rifle and put them on the ground, unfurled a flag, and advanced alone at a steady pace toward the Indians. The women retreated, but the man stayed in place until Lewis was within a hundred yards.

Lewis called out *"tab-ba-bone,"* loudly and frequently. The man "absconded."

Lewis had his men join him and proceeded. The country was cut by some short and steep ravines. After less than a mile, topping a rise, they came on three Indian women, one a twelve-year-old, one a teen, and the third elderly, only thirty yards away. At the first sight, Lewis laid

---

* Jefferson later grew them in his garden and introduced them into Philadelphia gardens and the horticultural trade. Lewis compared the snowberry to the honeysuckle of the Missouri, or wolfberry; Gary Moulton notes, "Lewis's ability to distinguish between species based on leaf and fruit characteristics again demonstrates his remarkable botanical powers of observation" (*Journals*, vol. 5, p. 85).

down his rifle and advanced on the group. The teen ran off, but the old woman and the child remained. Seeing no chance to escape, they sat on the ground and held their heads down; to Lewis it looked as though they had reconciled themselves to die.

He approached and took the elderly woman by the hand, raised her up, said "*tab-ba-bone*," and rolled up his shirtsleeve to show her his white skin (his hands and face were so deeply tanned he might have been an Indian, and his clothes were entirely leather). Drouillard and the privates joined him. From their packs he gave the woman some beads, a few moccasin awls, a few mirrors, and some paint. His skin and the gifts, and his friendly attitude, were enough to calm her down.

Through Drouillard's sign language, he asked her to call the teen back, fearing that otherwise the girl might alarm the main body of Shoshones. The old woman did as asked, and the teen reappeared. Lewis gave her some trinkets and painted the "tawny cheeks" of the women with some vermilion. When the Indians were composed, Lewis told them, through Drouillard, that he "wished them to conduct us to their camp that we wer anxious to become acquainted with the chiefs and warriors of their nation." They did as requested, and the group set off, the Indians leading.

After two miles, the long-anticipated and eagerly sought contact took place. Sixty warriors, mounted on excellent horses and armed for war with bows and arrows plus three inferior rifles, came on at full speed. When they saw Lewis's party, they halted.

This was the first time an American had ever seen a Shoshone war party, and the first time this band of Shoshones had ever seen an American. The Indians were overwhelmingly superior. It would have been the work of only a moment for them to overwhelm Lewis's party, and they would have more than doubled their firepower in rifles and gathered as loot more knives, awls, looking glasses, and other trinkets than any Rocky Mountain Indian band had ever seen.

But rather than assuming a defensive position, Lewis laid down his rifle, picked up his flag, told his party to stay in place, and, following the old woman who was guiding, advanced slowly toward he knew not what.

A man Lewis assumed was the chief rode in the lead. He halted to speak to the old woman. She told him that these were white men "and exultingly shewed the presents which had been given." This broke the tension. The chief and then the warriors dismounted.

The chief advanced. Saying "*ah-hi-e, ah-hi-e*," which Lewis later learned meant "I am much pleased, I am much rejoiced," the chief put his left arm over Lewis's right shoulder and applied his left cheek to Lewis's right cheek, continuing "to frequently vociforate the word *ah-hi-e*."

The warriors and Lewis's men then came on, "and we wer all carresed and besmeared with their grease and paint till I was heartily tired of the national hug."

This first meeting between Shoshones and Americans went better than Lewis could have dared to hope. He had been exceedingly lucky. The war party had ridden out in response to the alarm given by the man who had fled earlier that day. The Shoshones expected to find Blackfeet and might have attacked without pause save for the old woman. Had Lewis not met her, and had she not responded so positively to his appeals and gifts, there might well have been a firefight.

Instead there was a parlay. Lewis brought out his pipe and sat, indicating to the Indians that they should do the same. They did, but not without removing their moccasins, a custom among the Shoshones to indicate sincerity in friendship, or, as Lewis put it, "which is as much as to say that they wish they may always go bearfoot if they are not sincere; a pretty heavy penalty if they are to march through the plains of their country."

Lewis lit and passed the pipe. After smoking several rounds, he distributed some presents. The Shoshones were "much pleased particularly with the blue beads and vermillion." Lewis learned that the chief's name was "Ca-me-ah-wait." Lewis told him that "the object of our visit was a friendly one," that after they reached Cameahwait's camp he would explain the expedition more fully, including "who we wer, from whence we had come and wither we were going." He gave Cameahwait an American flag, "which I informed him was an emblem of peace among whitemen [sic] . . . to be respected as the bond of union between us."

Cameahwait spoke to his warriors, and soon the entire party set out for the main camp. He sent some youngsters ahead to inform the others to prepare for their arrival. When they reached the camp, on the east bank of the Lemhi River, about seven miles north of today's Tendoy, Idaho, Lewis was ushered into an old leather tepee (the only one the band had left after the Blackfoot raid) and ceremoniously seated on green boughs and antelope skins.

After the ritual smoking, "I now explained to them the objects of our journey &c." How well the Shoshones could comprehend a trip across the continent—or if they could even conceive of the continent—Lewis did not say.

He was confident the sign language Drouillard was using was understood, even though he realized it was "imperfect and liable to error." Still, "The strong parts of the ideas are seldom mistaken."

Women and children crowded around, eager to see these "children of the Great Spirit." Lewis distributed the presents he had left, to the delight of the Shoshones. One Shoshone warrior later described the mirrors as "things like solid water, which were sometimes brilliant as the sun, and which sometimes showed us our faces."[1]

By this time, it was growing dark. Lewis and his men had not eaten in twenty-four hours. He mentioned this to Cameahwait, who said he was sorry but the band had nothing but berries to eat. He gave the white men some cakes of serviceberries and choke cherries. "Of these I made a hearty meal," Lewis wrote.

He strolled down to the Lemhi River and found it a rapid, clear stream about forty yards wide and three feet deep. Through Drouillard's signs, Lewis inquired about the course of the stream. Cameahwait replied that a half-day's march north it joined with another, twice as large, coming in from the southwest, forming today's Salmon River. On further questioning, Cameahwait said there was little timber along the river below, that the river was "confined between inacessable mountains, was very rapid and rocky insomuch that it was impossible for us to pass either by land or water down this river to the great lake where the white men lived as he had been informed."

Cameahwait was referring to the traders who called at the mouth of the Columbia River. His description of the Salmon was as accurate as it was unwelcome. It confirmed what Lewis must have feared when he first gazed on the Bitterroots from Lemhi Pass—there was no all-water route, or anything remotely resembling it, across the continent.

But Lewis dared to hope that this was untrue, suspecting that Cameahwait was only trying to detain the Americans for trading purposes.

In fact, as Lewis should have known from Sacagawea, it was time for Cameahwait's band to cross the Divide to meet other bands of Shoshones and Flatheads to go on a hunt in the Missouri River buffalo country. Having lied to the chief about the meaning of the flag, and being prepared to tell more lies if necessary to meet his aims, Lewis was ready to believe the worst about Cameahwait.

The distressing information about the Salmon was somewhat balanced for Lewis by the sight of "a great number of horses feeding in every direction around their camp." Drouillard later counted four hundred of them. Assuming he could trade for an adequate number of horses, Lewis had "little doubt but we shall be enable to . . . transport

Meriwether Lewis, oil (1807) by Charles Willson Peale. *(Courtesy Independence National Historical Park)*

William Clark, oil (1810) by Charles Willson Peale. *(Courtesy Independence National Historical Park)*

Thomas Jefferson, copy of the original oil (1791) by Charles Willson Peale. *(Courtesy Independence National Historical Park)*

George Catlin, Black Moccasin (1832). This Minitari chief was more than one hundred years old when Catlin portrayed him. This is one of the few drawings made from life of an Indian who knew Lewis and Clark. *(National Museum of American Art, Washington, D.C./Art Resource, N.Y.)*

York, watercolour (1908) by Charles M. Russell. A Mandan chief, suspicious of York's colour, is trying to rub it off. *(Montana Historical Society)*

George Catlin, *Bird's-Eye View of the Mandan River* (1837–39). *(National Museum of American Art, Washington, D.C./Art Resource, N.Y.)*

A. E. Mathews, *Three Forks* (1867).
(Montana Historical Society)

A. E. Mathews, *Gates of the Mountains* (1867).
(Montana Historical Society)

Charles M. Russell, *Lewis and Clark Expedition*. Meeting the Shoshones; to the right, Sacagawea is hugging her childhood friend Jumping Fish. *(From the collection of Gilcrease Museum, Tulsa)*

Charles M. Russell, *Indians at Ross' Hole*
(1912). *(Montana Historical Society)*

C. B. J. Févret de Saint-Mémin's portrait of Lewis in Indian dress, a watercolour on paper (1807). Lewis is wearing what may have been the white weasel tails Sacagawea gave Captain Clark for his Christmas present in 1806. *(Missouri Historical Society)*

our stores even if we are compelled to travel by land over these mountains."

His spirits were further raised when, on his return to his tepee, a warrior gave him a piece of fresh-roasted salmon, "which I eat with a very good relish. this was the first salmon I had seen and perfectly convinced me that we were on the waters of the Pacific Ocean." In other words, his positive assertion the previous day that he had first tasted the waters of the Columbia after crossing Lemhi Pass had been more an expression of hope than a certain fact; for all he knew, the Lemhi-Salmon River might have been a tributary of the Dearborn River.

That night, the Shoshones entertained Lewis and party with a dance. It lasted almost to dawn. At midnight, "I grew sleepy and retired to rest leaving the men to amuse themselves with the Indians. . . . I was several times awoke in the course of the night by their yells but was too much fortiegued to be deprived of a tolerable sound night's repose."

With contact made, Lewis now had to give Clark time to come up the Jefferson as far as the fork that marked the extreme limit of navigation—if that limit had not already been passed. Clark was making only four or five miles a day in the shallow, boulder-covered bed of the Jefferson, which was not much more than a large creek. Lewis decided to spend the morning of August 14 writing in his journal, the afternoon in procuring further information from Cameahwait about the country to the west.

He sent Drouillard and the privates out to hunt. The Indians furnished them with horses, and some twenty young braves joined them. Lewis was treated to a sight few white men ever saw, a chase on horseback by the young Indian hunters after ten pronghorns. "It lasted about 2 hours and considerable part of the chase in view from my tent. The hunters returned [they] had not killed a single Antelope, and their horses foaming with sweat."

When Drouillard returned, equally unsuccessful, Lewis used his sign-language ability to ask Cameahwait "to instruct me with rispect to the geogrphy of his country." The chief repeated what he had said the previous day, with more details. After drawing a waving line on the ground to represent the river, he piled sand on each side of it to represent "the vast mountains of rock eternally covered with snow through which the river passed." He spoke of "perpendicular and even juting rocks so closely hemned in the river that there was no possibilyte of passing along the shore. . . . the whole surface of the river was beat into perfect foam as far as the eye could reach. That the mountains were also inaccessible to man or horse."*

How, then, to cross those mountains? Cameahwait said he had never done it, but there was an old man in his band "who could probably give me some information of the country to the N.W." He added that "he had understood from the persed nosed Indians who inhabit this river below the rocky mountains that it ran a great way toward the seting sun and finally lost itself in a great lake of water which was illy taisted."

That sentence linked the continent. For the first time, a white man had a map, however imperfect and imprecise, to connect the great rivers of the western empire. Also for the first time, a white man heard of the Nez Percés, the major tribe living west of the mountains. Cameahwait added that the Nez Percés crossed to the Missouri River buffalo country to hunt each year.†

What route did they use? Lewis asked. It was to the north, the chief answered, "but added that the road was a very bad one as he had been informed by them and that they had suffered excessively with hunger on the rout being obliged to subsist for many days on berries alone as there was no game in that part of the mountains which were broken rockey and so thickly covered with timber that they could scarcely pass."

Far from being downcast by such a description, Lewis was encouraged. "My rout was instantly settled in my own mind," he wrote. "I felt perfectly satisfyed, that if the Indians could pass these mountains with their women and Children, that we could also pass them."

This is a wonderful sentence. It shows his complete confidence in himself, Captain Clark, and the men. He is not boasting, or challenging, just being matter-of-fact about it. If they can, we can.

It also shows Lewis's (and Clark's) ability to get more out of the men than the men ever thought they could give. Ascending the Missouri in the keelboat, the bitter cold winter at Mandan, the awful labor at the Great Falls portage, the incredible labor getting the canoes up the Jefferson—every time they had such an experience behind them, the men agreed that it had to be the worst, and that they could not possibly endure anything worse. Only to have it get worse.

---

* All this is nicely summed up in the modern nickname for the Salmon, River of No Return.

† "Nez Percé" meant "Pierced-Nosed" Indians. Whether they actually pierced their noses is a subject of dispute. See Moulton, ed., *Journals*, vol. 5, p. 94.

But well-led men working together can do far more than they ever thought they could. Especially if they are in life-threatening situations—which was exactly where Lewis intended to lead them. He dared to do so because he knew they had more in them than they thought, and he knew how to bring out the best in them.

Cameahwait had more information. He said there were no buffalo west of the mountains, that the Indians who lived there subsisted on salmon and roots. He complained about the Spanish policy of never selling guns to Indians, whereas the English sold guns to the Blackfeet, Hidatsas, and other enemies of the Shoshones. With that advantage in firepower, the Plains Indians were continually harassing the Shoshones, who were forced to hide in the interior of the mountains most of the year. But, Cameahwait added, "with his ferce eyes and lank jaws grown meager for the want of food, [such] would not be the case if we had guns, we could then live in the country of buffaloe and eat as our enimies do."

Here was the opening Lewis sought, here was the opportunity to make promises that would induce Cameahwait to help with the portage over the Continental Divide and to trade for horses that could get the expedition over the Bitterroots on the Nez Percé route. Lewis said that he had already induced the Hidatsas to promise that they would no longer raid against the Shoshones or make war on any of their neighbors (even though he knew that the Hidatsas had sent out a war party that spring), and that, when the expedition got to the Pacific and then returned to the United States, "whitemen would come to them [the Shoshones] with an abundance of guns and every other article necessary to their defence and comfort."

Since the expedition was now more than three thousand river miles from St. Louis, that was a promise for an uncertain future. He made it anyway.

Lewis told Cameahwait that he wanted the band to cross Lemhi Pass with him in the morning, bringing thirty horses, to meet with Clark and the main party at the forks of Jefferson River and help bring the baggage over the pass and down to the Indian camp on the Lemhi River, where "we would then remain sometime among them and trade with them for horses."

Cameahwait agreed. He "made a lengthey harrangue to his village," then told Lewis that everything was settled—they would start in the morning. Lewis was overjoyed. The Shoshone horses, he wrote, were excellent: "Indeed many of them would make a figure on the South side of James River or the land of fine horses." Even better, they had some surefooted mules. Lewis went to his tepee to sleep in a happy mood; as for the Indians, "they were very merry they danced again this evening untill midnight."

Lewis woke on the morning of Thursday, August 15, "as hungary as a wolf." The previous day, he had nothing to eat save a scant meal of flour and berries, which had not satisfied him as it "appeared to do my Indian friends." He had two pounds of flour left. He told McNeal to divide the flour into two equal parts and to cook one half mixed with berries. "On this new fashoned pudding four of us breakfasted, giving a pretty good allowance also to the Chief who declared it the best thing he had taisted for a long time."

After breakfast, a crisis. The warriors would not move, despite Cameahwait's urging. Lewis asked after the cause and was told "that some foolish persons among them had suggested the idea that we were in league with the Pahkees [the Shoshone word for Atsinas] and had come on in order to decoy them into an ambuscade where their enemies were waiting to receive them."

Lewis told Cameahwait that he forgave the warriors their suspicion: "I knew they were not acquainted with whitemen ... that among whitemen it was considered disgracefull to lye or entrap an enimy by falsehood." After that stretcher, Lewis threatened that, if the Shoshones did not help with the portage, no white man would come to bring them arms and ammunition.

Then he challenged their manhood, saying, "I still hope that there were some among them that were not affraid to die." The challenge "touched on the right string; to doubt the bravery of a savage is at once to put him on his metal."

Cameahwait mounted his horse and gave a speech to his people, saying he would go with the white men to convince himself of the truth of what Lewis said. He added that he hoped some at least of the warriors would join him. Six mounted their horses. The small party set out, even though "several of the old women were crying and imploring the great sperit to protect their warriors as if they were going to inevitable distruction."

The Indians rode on anyway, and soon enough another half-dozen men and three women joined them, making all together a party of sixteen Indians and four white men. Lewis was struck by the "capricious disposition of those people who never act but from the impulse of the moment. they were now very cheerfull and gay, and two hours ago they looked as sirly as so many imps of satturn."

They crossed Lemhi Pass and descended to Shoshone Cove, where they camped on the creek* and had their second meal of the day: "I now cooked and among six of us eat the remaining pound of flour stired in a little boiling water." The Shoshones, save Cameahwait and an unnamed warrior, had nothing to eat that day.

The next morning, August 16, Lewis sent Drouillard and Shields out to kill some meat. He asked Cameahwait to keep his young men in camp so that they would not alarm the game. That was a mistake, for it reawakened the suspicions of the Shoshones. They feared the white men were trying to make contact with the Blackfeet, so two parties of warriors set out on each side of the valley to spy on Drouillard and Shields.

Lewis, McNeal, and the remainder of the Shoshones followed. After about an hour, "when we saw one of the spies comeing up the level plain under whip, the chief pawsed a little and seemed somewhat concerned. I felt a good deel so myself." Lewis's fear was that by "some unfortunate accedent" the Blackfeet really were in the neighborhood. But when the scout arrived, breathless, he had good news—Drouillard had killed a deer.

"In an instant they all gave their horses the whip." Lewis was riding double with a young warrior. The Indian was whipping the horse "at every jump for a mile fearing he should loose a part of the feast. . . . As I was without tirrups . . . the jostling was disagreeable." Lewis reined in his horse and forbade the young man to use the lash. The Indian jumped off and ran on foot at full speed for a whole mile.

At the site of the kill, "the seen when I arrived was such that had I not have had a pretty keen appetite myself I am confident I should not have taisted any part of the vension. . . . each [Indian] had a peice of some discription and all eating most ravenously. Some were eating the kidnies the melt [the spleen] and liver and the blood running from the corners of their mouths, others were in a similar situation with the paunch and guts. . . . one of the last [to arrive] had provided himself with about nine feet of the small guts one end of which he was chewing on while with his hands he was squezzing the contents out at the other. I really did not untill now think that human nature ever presented itself in a shape so nearly allyed to the brute creation. I viewed these poor starved divils with pity and compassion."

However heartfelt, his pity and compassion did not extend far enough for him to note that, if the Indians appeared savage with the blood running down their cheeks, they had taken only the parts of the

_____
* Today's Horse Prairie Creek.

deer Drouillard had thrown away when he dressed the kill. They had not touched the meat.

Lewis saved a hindquarter for himself and his men and gave the balance to Cameahwait to divide among his people. They devoured it without bothering to start a fire to cook it. The party then moved on. Soon word came that Drouillard had killed a second deer. "Here nearly the same seene was encored." Lewis started a fire to cook his meat; Drouillard came in with a third deer, of which Lewis saved a quarter and gave the rest to the Indians, who were finally full and thus "in a good humour." Shields then killed a pronghorn; the problem of food was solved for that day.

As the party approached the forks, where Lewis had told the Indians they would meet Clark, Cameahwait insisted on halting. With much ceremony, he put tippets such as the Shoshones were wearing around the necks of the white men. Lewis realized that the chief's suspicions were still strong, that he wanted to make the white men look like Indians in case it was Blackfeet and not Clark waiting at the forks. Realizing this, Lewis took off his cocked hat and put it on Cameahwait. The men followed his example, "and we were son completely metamorphosed."

The entire party moved downstream to the forks. Lewis had a warrior carry the flag, so that "our own party should know who we were." But when they got to within a couple of miles of the forks, "I discovered to my mortification" that Clark had not arrived.

"I now scarcely new what to do," Lewis confessed, "and feared every moment when they would halt altogether."

Desperate, he gave Cameahwait his rifle and told him that if the Blackfeet were around he could use it to defend himself, "that for my own part I was not affraid to die and if I deceived him he might make what uce of the gun he thought proper or in other words that he might shoot me." Lewis had his men give up their rifles too, "which seemed to inspire them [the Indians] with more confidence."

This bold move bought Lewis enough time to think of a plan. Recalling that he had left a note for Clark at the forks, "I now had recource to a stratagem in which I thought myself justifyed by the occasion, but which I must confess set a little awkward." He sent Drouillard, accompanied by a warrior, to pick up the note. When Drouillard returned with the note and the warrior's confirmation that he had picked it up at the forks, Lewis told Cameahwait that Clark had written it and that it said he, Clark, was just below, coming on, and that Lewis should wait for him at the forks.

Lewis had told a lie that the Indians would never discover, but he was by no means through the crisis. Though his confidence in Clark was very great, in truth he did not know where Clark was. Clark might very well have found navigation impossible and be in camp many miles below, waiting for Lewis.

Lewis came up with another "stratagem." He told Cameahwait that in the morning he would send Drouillard ahead to meet Clark, and proposed that a warrior accompany Drouillard to see the truth of his words. Lewis, Shields, and McNeal would remain with the main party of the Shoshones. "This plan was readily adopted and one of the young men offered his services; I promised him a knife and some beads as a reward for his confidence in us."

He was taking a huge gamble. Several of the warriors were already complaining of Cameahwait's exposing them to danger unnecessarily "and said that we told different stories." The Indians held the rifles. If Clark was not coming up the Jefferson, they could easily kill the white men, and almost certainly would, although the only fear Lewis expressed was that the Indians "would immediately disperse and secrete themselves in the mountains."

He could hardly bear to think about it. At the least, "we should be disappointed in obtaining horses, which would vastly retart and increase the labour of our voyage and I feared might so discourage the men as to defeat the expedition altogether."

To hold the Shoshones, Lewis told them that Sacagawea was with Clark, and that there was also a man with Clark "who was black and had short curling hair." The Indians expressed great eagerness to see such a curiosity.

Nevertheless, that night Lewis wrote in his journal, "my mind was in reality quite as gloomy ... as the most affrighted indian but I affected cheerfullness." He lay down to sleep, Cameahwait beside him. "I slept but little as might be well expected, my mind dwelling on the state of the expedition which I have ever held in equal estimation with my own existence, and the fait of which appeared at this moment to depend in a great measure upon the caprice of a few savages who are ever as fickle as the wind."

In the morning, Lewis sent Drouillard and the warrior off at first light. The leftover meat from the previous day provided a scant breakfast. At about 9:00 a.m., an Indian who had gone down the creek for a mile or so returned and reported "that the whitemen were coming." The Shoshones "all appeared transported with joy." Lewis confessed, "I felt quite as much gratifyed at this information as the Indians appeared to be."

Shortly thereafter, Clark arrived, accompanied by Charbonneau and Sacagawea. Cameahwait gave Clark the national hug and festooned his hair with shells. In the midst of the excitement, one of the Shoshone women recognized Sacagawea. Her name, Jumping Fish, she had acquired on the day Sacagawea was taken prisoner, because of the way she had jumped through a stream in escaping the Hidatsas.[2] The reunited teens hugged and cried and talked, all at once.

Lewis had a camp set up just below the forks.* He had a canopy formed from one of the large sails. At 4:00 p.m., he called a conference. Dispensing with Drouillard and the sign language, he decided to use a translation chain that ran from Sacagawea, speaking Shoshone to the Indians and translating it into Hidatsa, to Charbonneau, who translated her Hidatsa into French, to Private Francis Labiche, who translated from French to English.

Scarcely had they begun the cumbersome process when Sacagawea began to stare at Cameahwait. Suddenly recognizing him as her brother, "she jumped up, ran & embraced him, & threw her blanket over him and cried profusely."[3]

What a piece of luck that was. No novelist would dare invent such a scene. As James Ronda writes, "the stars had danced for Lewis and Clark."[4]

Lewis wrote that the reunion was "really affecting." He wrote not a word to indicate that he was surprised by the show of so much emotion from Sacagawea, whom he had characterized a couple of weeks earlier as someone who never showed the slightest emotion.

When Sacagawea recovered herself, the council began—although it was frequently interrupted by her tears. The captains expanded on what Lewis had already told Cameahwait. They explained "the objects which had brought us into this distant part of the country," in the process making it appear that the number-one object was to help the Shoshones by finding a more direct way to bring arms to them. In the process, "we made them sensible of their dependance on the will of our government for every species of merchandize as well for their defence & comfort." But this could not be accomplished without Shoshone horses, or without a guide to take them over the Nez Percé trail.

In reply, Cameahwait "declared his wish to serve us in every rispect; that he was sorry to find that it must yet be some time before they could be furnished with firearms but said they could live as they had

---

* The site, later known as Camp Fortunate, is now under Clark Canyon Reservoir, just beside Interstate 15, twenty miles south of Dillon, Montana.

done heretofore untill we brought them as we had promised." Though he had insufficient horses to carry the baggage over Lemhi Pass, he would return to his village in the morning and encourage his band to come and help.

The captains were satisfied—indeed, they could hardly have dared hope for so much cooperation. They asked Cameahwait to indicate who were the lesser chiefs among his men. He pointed to two others. The captains gave Cameahwait a medal with Jefferson's likeness on one side and the clasped hands of an Indian and a white man on the other, and gave a smaller medal with George Washington's likeness to the two inferior chiefs. Next they presented Cameahwait with a uniform coat, a pair of scarlet leggings, a carrot of tobacco, and some geegaws. The lesser chiefs got a shirt, leggings, a handkerchief, a knife, and some tobacco. The captains distributed paint, awls, knives, beads, mirrors, and other items to the remaining Indians.

"Every article about us appeared to excite astonishment in ther minds," Lewis wrote: the appearance of the men, their arms, the canoes, York, "the segacity of my dog"—all were objects of admiration. Lewis shot his air gun, which the Indians immediately pronounced "great medicine."

Adding to the joyous mood, the hunters brought in four deer and a pronghorn. After the feast, the captains asked Cameahwait for more information "with rispect to the country." He repeated what he had already told Lewis, who by now was convinced of the truth of his description.

Even though he regarded Cameahwait as "a man of Influence Sence & easey & reserved manners, appears to possess a great deel of Cincerity," Clark wanted to see for himself before accepting Cameahwait's alarming description of the Salmon River route. He and Lewis conferred. Lewis agreed that in the morning Clark should set out with eleven men carrying axes and other necessary tools for making canoes. They would make a reconnaissance of the Salmon, accompanied by Charbonneau and Sacagawea. They would stay the first night at the Shoshone village, to hasten the return of the band to Camp Fortunate to make the portage.

If Clark found the river navigable, he would set to making canoes. Lewis, meanwhile, would bring on the remaining eighteen members of the party and the baggage to the Lemhi River. He figured the move would take a week or more, enough time for Clark to make his reconnaissance and determine whether the expedition was to proceed by land or water. If by land, "we should want all the horses which we could perchase."

Whatever the route, Lewis had cause for satisfaction. The expedition was once more united and would soon be on the move. He slept better than the previous night.

In the morning, August 18, while Clark prepared for his reconnaissance, Lewis traded for some horses. He intended to provide Clark with two, to transport his baggage, and keep one for his hunters, to transport whatever meat they obtained. He got what he wanted: three very good horses in exchange for a uniform coat, a pair of leggings, a few handkerchiefs, three knives, and some trinkets "the whole of which did not cost more than about 20$ in the U'States." (Not counting in the transportation costs!) "The Indians seemed quite as well pleased with their bargin as I was." One of the privates also purchased a horse, for an old checked shirt, a pair of old leggings, and a knife. At such prices, Lewis could count on obtaining quite a herd from the main village on the Lemhi River.

A problem emerged. The two lesser chiefs were "a little displeased" at not getting more presents. Clark thereupon gave them a couple of his old coats, and Lewis promised that "if they wer active in assisting me over the mountains . . . I would give them an additional present." With that, at 10:00 a.m., Clark set off, accompanied by all the Indians save the two lesser chiefs, Jumping Fish, and another woman.

Lewis prepared for the portage. He had all stores and baggage opened and aired, and had the men begin the process of forming packages into proper parcels for transport over Lemhi Pass. He had rawhides put in the water in order to cut them into thongs proper for lashing the packages, "a business which I fortunately had not to learn on this occasion."

Drouillard brought in a deer. One of the men caught a beaver. Lewis had a net arranged and set to catch some trout. He brought his journal up-to-date.

He concluded his August 18 journal entry with an oft-quoted passage of introspection and self-criticism. "This day I completed my thirty first year," he began. He figured he was halfway through his life's journey. "I reflected that I had as yet done but little, very little indeed, to further the hapiness of the human race, or to advance the information of the succeeding generation. I viewed with regret the many hours I have spent in indolence, and now soarly feel the want of that information which those hours would have given me had they been judiciously expended."

He shook the mood, writing that, since the past could not be recalled, "I dash from me the gloomy thought and resolved in future, to redouble my exertions and at least indeavour to promote those two primary objects of human existence, by giving them the aid of that portion of talents which nature and fortune have bestoed on me . . ." and here he seems to have lost his train of thought. Whatever the cause, he forgot to name those "two primary objects of human existence," and instead ended, "in future, to live for mankind, as I have heretofore lived *for myself*."

Much has been made of this remarkable passage, perhaps too much. It was not unusual for men of the Enlightenment to write such stuff— come to that, a thirtieth or thirty-first birthday leads to such thoughts for men of the late twentieth century—and Jefferson sometimes wrote in a similar mood and vein.

Among other things, the passage is a reminder of how young Lewis was to be carrying so heavy a burden of command. Physically tired and emotionally exhausted after the tension of the past few days, he was in what is still today one of the most remote places on the continent, with only eighteen enlisted men, Drouillard, and four Indians as companions. He had reached the source of the Missouri River, but he still had those tremendous mountains to cross and was dependent on the whims of Cameahwait and his people to make that crossing.

If he was halfway through his life's journey—always a gloomy thought for a young man—he was also only halfway through his journey of exploration from the Mandan village to the Pacific Coast, and the season was getting on. To him it seemed natural at this point to rededicate himself to doing better.

Lewis spent six days at Camp Fortunate. It gave him an opportunity to write some extended descriptions of the Shoshones. In addition, he oversaw the breaking up of boxes and the cutting off of the paddle blades to make enough boards for twenty wooden saddles. He established another cache, to lighten the burden of the portage. He made some celestial observations.

On August 22, an hour before noon, Cameahwait, Charbonneau, Sacagawea, and some fifty Shoshone men accompanied by women and children arrived at Camp Fortunate. After they set up camp, Lewis held a council. He distributed presents, especially to the second and third chiefs. Noting "these poor devils half starved," Lewis had the men prepare a meal of corn and beans, which he served after the council.

Cameahwait said he "wished that his nation could live in a country where they could provide such food." Lewis gave him a few dried squashes. He had them boiled "and declared them to be the best thing he had ever tasted except sugar, a small lump of which it seems his sister Sah-cah-gar Wea had given him."

The trout net yielded 528 fish, most of which Lewis distributed among the Indians. He purchased five good horses for six dollars in trade goods each. Though he wanted to get going first thing in the morning, Cameahwait requested that he wait another day, so that a friendly band of Shoshones could join them.

Lewis realized that he had no choice, but it brought on a new worry. The Shoshones were gathering for their annual excursion onto the buffalo plains, and Cameahwait's band showed "a good deel of anxiety" to get going. When the other group came in, during the afternoon, Lewis managed to trade with them for three horses and a mule.

On the morning of August 24, Lewis was once again on the road, this time with eighteen of his own men, Charbonneau, Sacagawea and Drouillard, nine horses and a mule, and Cameahwait's band. He gave Charbonneau some articles to trade for a horse for Sacagawea, which was done. He was going to need still more horses; much of the baggage was being carried by Shoshone women.

But, notwithstanding future problems, he was happy, because "I had now the inexpressible satisfaction to find myself once more under way with all my baggage and party."

His joy didn't last long. On August 25, when the hunters brought in three deer and the party stopped for a noon meal, Charbonneau casually mentioned to Lewis that he expected to meet the whole of Cameahwait's band coming over Lemhi Pass on the way to the buffalo country.

Why? Lewis asked.

Charbonneau explained that Sacagawea had overheard Cameahwait say to some of his young men to tell the band to meet him the next day, so that together the reunited band could go to the Missouri River.

If that happened, Lewis and his men would be left literally high and dry, halfway up Lemhi Pass, with only a dozen or so horses, and no guide for the Nez Percé trail.

Another gut-tightening crisis. Lewis's temper flared, but he was too good a diplomat to direct it at the cause, Cameahwait. Instead he cussed Charbonneau, who had been in possession of the information for some hours before divulging it to Lewis. Then he called Cameahwait and the two lesser chiefs for a smoke and a talk.

"I asked them if they had not promised to assist me with my baggage to their camp. . . . They acknowledged that they had." Then why were they preparing to abandon him to go to the buffalo country? The Indians hung their heads.

Lewis said that, had they not promised to help with the portage, "I should not have attempted to pass the mountains but would have returned down the river and that in that case they would never have seen anymore white men in their country."

In truth, he was going to try to get over those mountains come hell or high water, a resolution he frequently put into his journal. Still, he took the high moral ground, instructing the chiefs that "they must never promis us anything which they did not mean to perform." He concluded by directing the chiefs to send a young man over the pass to the village to tell the people to stay where they were until Lewis, Cameahwait, and the others arrived.

The two lesser chiefs spoke up. They wanted to help and be as good as their word, they said, and it was not they who had instructed the band to cross to the Missouri River side of the Divide. Cameahwait had done it, and they had not approved. This was a handsome payoff for Lewis's seeing their unhappiness a couple of days earlier and distributing more presents to them.

"Cameahwait remained silent for some time," Lewis wrote; "at length he told me that he knew he had done wrong but that he had been induced to that measure from seeing all his people hungary, but as he had promised to give me his assistance he would not in future be worse than his word."

His people were starving. The buffalo country was not much more than a day's march away. Other bands of Shoshones were already meeting with Flathead villages to go on the hunt. But he had given his word, and Lewis shamed him into keeping it. A pity that Lewis never showed the slightest gratitude, or gave any indication that he understood what a difficult position Cameahwait was in.

He did realize that the Shoshones had to eat. In the afternoon, the party marched almost to the pass. The hunters brought in but one deer. Lewis ordered it distributed to the women and children "and for my own part remained supperless."

At dawn on August 26, the temperature was at the freezing point, a sharp reminder where none was needed that the season was getting along. During the day's march, Lewis saw the women collecting roots "and feeding their poor starved children; it is really distressing to witness the situation of those poor wretches."

That evening, Lewis and his men and baggage made it to the camp on the Lemhi River. Private John Colter was already there, with a letter from Clark (who was in camp downstream) in which Clark described the Salmon River route as impassable.

Lewis was not surprised. He told Cameahwait that in the morning he wished to purchase twenty additional horses. Cameahwait pointed

out that his people had lost a great number of their horses to the
Blackfeet, but said he would see what he could do. He also said he
thought the old man who had once crossed the mountains with the
Nez Percé would be willing to guide Lewis and Clark.

"Matters being thus far arranged," Lewis ended his journal entry for
the day, "I directed the fiddle to be played and the party danced very
merrily much to the amusement and gratification of the natives, though
I must confess that the state of my own mind at this moment did not
well accord with the prevailing mirth as I somewhat feared that the
caprice of the indians might suddenly induce them to withhold their
horses from us without which my hopes of prosicuting my voyage to
advantage was lost."

The Indians were ready to sell, but the captains discovered over the
next few days that the price had gone up considerably. The Shoshones
had a captive, desperate market. It was perfectly clear to them that the
white men had to have horses, come what may. On August 29, Clark
found that he had to offer his pistol, a knife, and one hundred rounds
of ammunition for one horse. The captains had tried to make it a strict
rule never to reduce their arsenal, but now they had no choice.

Eventually, the captains bought twenty-nine horses, but, as James
Ronda puts it, "The Shoshonis had proven to be better Yankee traders
than the Americans." When Clark examined the horses in his corral,
he found them to be "nearly all Sore Backs [and] several Pore, &
young." The captains had bought the castoffs of the Shoshone herd.[5]

23

LEWIS AS ETHNOGRAPHER

The Shoshones

If the Shoshones were fascinated by the men and equipment of the expedition, Lewis was no less fascinated by them. The first Indians he had seen since the Mandans, they were about as close to being untouched by contact with white men as it was possible for any tribe to be at the beginning of the nineteenth century. Cameahwait's people had perhaps seen a Spaniard or two; they had some trade goods of European manufacture, not much; they had three indifferent rifles.

The biggest change the white man effected among the Shoshones was the introduction of horses, brought to the New World by the Spanish. Next came rifles, provided by the English and French to their trading partners on the Plains, the Blackfeet, Hidatsas, and some others. As Cameahwait so movingly noted, the arms trade with the enemies of the Shoshones put his people at a terrible disadvantage and regulated their lives. They had to sneak onto the Plains, make their hunt as fast as possible, and retreat into their mountain hideaway, or, as Lewis put it, "alternately obtaining their food at the risk of their lives and retiring to the mountains."

The civilized world knew nothing about the Shoshones. In describing them, Lewis was breaking entirely new scientific ground. His account, written during his stay at Camp Fortunate, is therefore invaluable as the first description ever of a Rocky Mountain tribe, in an almost precontact stage.

Lewis's ethnography, if not up to the standards of academic ethnographers of the late twentieth century, was wide-ranging. His curiosity, his catholic interests, and his responsibility for reporting to Jefferson on the tribes he met combined to create an informative, invaluable, and altogether enchanting picture of Cameahwait's people. Lewis covered their appearance, personal characteristics, customs, population, clothing, health, economy, the relations between the sexes, and politics. The richness of detail can only be hinted at here; interested readers are urged to go to the original journals for the full account.

The Shoshones were "deminutive in stature, thick ankles, crooked legs, thick flat feet and in short but illy formed, at least much more so in general than any nation of Indians I ever saw." Their complexion was darker than that of the Hidatsas or the Mandans. As a consequence of the losses they had suffered in the spring to the Blackfeet, men and women alike had their hair cut at the neck: "This constitutes their cerimony of morning for their deceased relations." Cameahwait had his hair cut close all over his head.

As to their demeanor, "notwithstanding their extreem poverty they are not only cheerfull but even gay, fond of gaudy dress and amusements; like most other Indians they are great egotists and frequently boast of heroic acts which they never performed." They loved to gamble. "They are frank, communicative, fair in dealing, generous with the little they possess, extreemly honest, and by no means beggarly."

Cameahwait's band numbered about one hundred warriors, three hundred women and children. There were few old people among them, and so far as Lewis could tell the elderly were not treated with much tenderness or respect. As to relations between the sexes, "the man is the sole propryetor of his wives and daughters, and can barter or dispose of either as he thinks proper." Most men had two or three wives, usually purchased as infant girls for horses or mules. At age thirteen or fourteen, the girls were surrendered to their "soverign lord and husband."

Sacagawea had been thus disposed of before she was taken prisoner, and her betrothed was still alive and living with this band. He was in his thirties and had two other wives. He claimed Sacagawea as his wife "but said that as she had had a child by another man, who was Charbono, that he did not want her."

That was lucky, because Sacagawea was accompanying the expedition to the Pacific. Neither Captain Lewis nor Captain Clark ever thought to discuss the matter in his journal, so it is unclear whether she chose to leave her people after a reunion of less than a month, or Charbonneau forced her to come along. Since she had never been in the territory they were entering, and so could recognize no landmarks, and since her linguistic abilities would be of little help with the Nez Percé or any other tribe west of the mountains, the captains had no pressing need to bring her along. One would like to think that the question whether she should stay with the expedition never came up, that she was by now so integral a member of the party that it was taken for granted that she would remain with it.

Lewis noted, with disapproval, that the Shoshones "treat their women but with little rispect, and compel them to perform every species of drudgery. They collect the wild fruits and roots, attend to the horses or assist in that duty, cook dreess the skins and make all their apparal, collect wood and make their fires, arrange and form their lodges, and when they travel pack the horses and take charge of all the baggage; in short the man dose little else except attend his horses hunt and fish."

Lewis failed to note that the warriors had to be always prepared to defend the village, which required them to be constantly on the alert, with their hands free. He did point out that each man had his best war horse tied to a stake near his lodge at night.

"The man considers himself degraded if he is compelled to walk any distance," Lewis noted. He did not add that in this they were very like Virginia gentlemen. The literal translation of Cameahwait, as best Lewis could make it out, was "One Who Never Walks."

"The chastity of their women is not held in high estimation," Lewis wrote. The men would barter their wives' services for a night or longer, if the reward was sufficient, "tho' they are not so importunate that we should caress their women as the siouxs were and some of their women appear to be held more sacred than in any nation we have seen." Lewis ordered his men to give the Shoshone braves "no cause of jealousy" by having sexual relationships with their women without the husbands' knowledge and consent. To prevent such affairs altogether, he recognized, would be "impossible to effect, particularly on the part of our young men whom some months abstance have made very polite to those tawney damsels."

Knowing that the Shoshones had no contact with whites, Lewis wrote that "I was anxious to learn whether these people had the venerial." His purpose was immediate—he had the health of his men in mind—but also scholarly. One of the oldest questions in medical history, still a subject of debate today, was whether syphilis originated in the Americas and spread to Europe after 1492, or was native to Europe and spread to the North American Indians by Europeans.

Through Sacagawea, Lewis made inquiries as to the presence of venereal disease among the Shoshones. He learned that it was a problem, "but I could not learn their remedy; they most usually die with it's effects." As far as he was concerned, "this seems a strong proof that these disorders bothe gonaroehah and Louis venerae are native disorders of America."*

But it was not conclusive, as Lewis realized, because the Shoshones had suffered much from the smallpox, "which is known to be imported," so they must have contracted it from other tribes that did have intercourse with white men. They might have contracted venereal disease in the same manner. Still, the Shoshones were "so much detached from all communication with the whites that I think it most probable that those disorders are original with them."

One part of Shoshone culture Lewis could observe and describe without having to go through a translation chain or Drouillard's sign language was clothing and general appearance. He wrote at great length about the Shoshone shirts, leggings, robes, chemises, and other items, about their use of seashells, beads, arm bands, leather collars, porcupine quills dyed various colors, earrings, and so forth.

Lewis pronounced the tippet of the Shoshones "the most elegant peice of Indian dress I ever saw." It was a sort of cloak made of dressed otter skin to which 100 to 250 rolls of ermine skin were attached. Cameahwait gave him one, which he prized.† Footwear could also be ornamental. "Some of the dressy young men," Lewis noted, "orniment the tops of their mockersons with the skins of polecats [skunks] and trale the tail of that animal on the ground at their heels as they walk."

For all that he wrote on clothing and customs, Lewis was most interested in Shoshone economics and politics. Here his goal was specific, to integrate the tribe into the trading empire the United States was going to create in Louisiana and beyond the mountains. The first requirement was a general peace along the Missouri River and in the mountains, but of course the Shoshones needed no prodding in that direction. They were victims, not aggressors.

What the Shoshones could contribute to the overall goal was ermine, otter, and other exotic skins of the mountain animals—if they could be taught to trap, and if they could be made dependent on a steady flow of the white man's goods. The Shoshones were so

---

* *Lues venera* is Latin for "syphilis." Gonorrhea was often confused with syphilis at the beginning of the nineteenth century, but Lewis here made a clear distinction. (Moulton, ed., *Journals*, vol. 5, p. 125.)

desperately poor that they had almost no economy to speak of. In the spring and summer, they lived on salmon; in the fall and winter, on buffalo.

That they could successfully hunt buffalo was thanks to their horses, the sole source of wealth among them. Having few to no rifles, without horses they would have been indifferent hunters at best. On August 23, Lewis watched a dozen young warriors pursuing mule deer from horseback. The chase covered four miles and "was really entertaining."

Shortly after noon, the hunters came in with two deer and three pronghorns. To Lewis's surprise, there was no division of the meat among the hunters. Instead, the families of the men who had made the kill took it all. "This is not customary among the nations of Indians with whom I have hitherto been acquainted," Lewis wrote. "I asked Cameahwait the reason why the hunters did not divide the meat; he said that meat was so scarce with them that the men who killed it reserved it for themselves and their own families."

Their implements for preparing food and eating were primitive. They had neither ax nor hatchet to cut wood; they used stone or elk horn. Their utensils consisted of earthen jars and buffalo-horn spoons. Lewis did an inventory of the metal objects possessed by Cameahwait's people: "a few indifferent knives, a few brass kettles, some arm bands of iron and brass, a few buttons, worn as ornaments in their hair, a spear or two of a foot in length and some iron and brass arrow points which they informed me they obtained in exchange for horses from the Crow or Rocky Mountains Indians." Any people so primitive that they were forced to trade horses for a few metal arrowheads obviously needed to get into a more extensive trading system.

What the Shoshones valued above all else, and depended on absolutely, was the bravery of their young men. Their childrearing system was designed to produce brave warriors. "They seldom correct their children," Lewis wrote, "particularly the boys who soon became masters of their own acts. They give as a reason that it cows and breaks the Sperit of the boy to whip him, and that he never recovers his independence of mind after he is grown."

In politics, they followed not the oldest or wisest or the best talker, but the bravest man. They had customs, but no laws or regulations. "Each individual man is his own soveriegn master," Lewis wrote, "and acts from the dictates of his own mind."

From this fact sprang the principle of political leadership: "The authority of the Cheif [is] nothing more than mere admonition supported by the influence which the propiety of his own examplery conduct may have acquired him in the minds of the individuals who compose the band, the title of cheif is not hereditary, nor can I learn that there is any cerimony of instalment, or other epoh in the life of a Cheif from which his title as such can be dated. in fact every man is a chief, but all have not an equal influence on the minds of the other members of the community, and he who happens to enjoy the greatest share of confidence is the principal Chief."

Since bravery was the primary virtue, no man could become eminent among the Shoshones "who has not at some period of his life given proofs of his possessing [it]." There could be no prominence without some warlike achievement, a principle basic to the entire structure of Shoshone politics.

These observations led Lewis to an insight into the problems the Americans were going to have in integrating not just the language but all the Indians west of the Mississippi River into their trading empire. He recalled the day at Fort Mandan when he was explaining to the Hidatsa chiefs the advantages that would flow to them from a general state of peace among the nations of the Missouri. The old men agreed with him, but only because they "had already geathered their havest of larals, and having forceably felt in many instances some of those inconveniences attending a state of war." But a young warrior put to Lewis a question that Lewis could not answer: "[He] asked me if they were in a state of peace with all their neighbours what the nation would do for Cheifs?"

The warrior went on to make a fundamental point: "The chiefs were now oald and must shortly die and the nation could not exist without chiefs."

In two sentences, the Hidatsa brave had exposed the hopelessness of the American policy of inducing the Missouri River and Rocky Mountain Indians to become trappers and traders. They would have to be conquered and cowed before they could be made to abandon war. Jefferson's dream of establishing through persuasion and trade a peaceable kingdom among the western Indians was as much an illusion as his dream of an all-water route to the Pacific.

This was a great disappointment, but it could not be helped. It was characteristic of the men of the Enlightenment to face facts. Lewis's ethnology helped establish the facts. It was therefore a great contribution to general knowledge—exactly the kind of contribution Lewis berated himself for not making in his thirty-first-birthday musings.

24

OVER THE BITTERROOTS

September 1–October 6, 1805

The party set out early on September 1, traveling cross-country over high, rugged hills, to today's North Fork of the Salmon River (Fish Creek to Lewis and Clark), following the Shoshone guide, whom the captains called Old Toby. They were headed almost due north and climbing toward the Continental Divide (on their right, to the east) in rough, seldom-traveled mountainous country, with no Indian trail or any other sign of human presence.

They were entering mountains far more difficult to pass than any American had ever attempted. The country is so remote and rugged that nearly two full centuries later it remains basically uninhabited. The confusion of creeks and ravines cutting through the steep mountainsides has made the route the expedition used one of the most disputed of the entire journey. One expert, Harry Majors, calls the route "the single most obscure and enigmatic of the entire Lewis and Clark expedition."[1]

Clark described the route: "thro' thickets in which we were obliged to Cut a road, over rockey hill Sides where our horses were in [perpetual] danger of Slipping to Ther certain distruction & up & Down Steep hills . . . with the greatest dificuelty risque &c. we made 7½ miles."

As the party ascended toward the Divide, the going grew worse. On September 3, it snowed. The last thermometer broke. Clark summed up the misery of the day: "We passed over emence hils and Some of the worst roade that ever horses passed our horses frequently fell." There was no game in the mountains, save grouse. The expedition consumed the last of its salt pork. At least they got to the Divide (whether at Lost Trail Pass or Chief Joseph Pass is disputed), which they followed for some miles, along the present Idaho-Montana border, before beginning their descent to the Bitterroot Valley, west of the Divide.

There was a hard freeze that night. On September 4, the party fell down a very steep descent to a north-flowing river that Lewis named "Clark's River" (today's Bitterroot River). There, at today's Ross's Hole, the captains encountered a band of the Salish Indians some four hundred people strong, with at least five hundred horses.

The Salish, whom the captains called Flatheads (a generic term with them, loosely used to signify all Northwest Indians, even though they did not deform their heads as Indians on the Columbia did), were friendly. The presence of Old Toby undoubtedly helped ease the way for the Americans, for the Salish were allies of the Shoshones; indeed, this band was on its way to join Cameahwait's people at the Three Forks.

Communication was possible if cumbersome. A Shoshone boy lived with the Flatheads; he could speak with the captains through the usual translation channels.

As he habitually did with previously unknown Indians, Lewis made a vocabulary of the Salish language, taking special care in this instance because the Indians' throaty, guttural speech led him to conjecture that they were descendants of Prince Madoc and the Welsh Indians. Like many others, Jefferson believed that this persistent myth might well be true, and had instructed Lewis to look for the tribe.

The Salish were not Welsh, but they were—in Private Joseph Whitehouse's words—"the likelyest and honestst Savages we have ever yet Seen."[2] They were also generous. Although their stock of provisions was as low as that of the expedition, they shared their berries and roots. And they traded for horses at much better prices than the Shoshones demanded, perhaps not aware of how desperate Lewis and Clark were. The captains bought thirteen horses for "a fiew articles of merchendize," and the Salish were kind enough to exchange seven of the run-down Shoshone ponies for what Clark called "elle-gant horses." The expedition now had approximately thirty-nine horses, three colts, and one mule—for packing, riding, or food in the last extreme.[3]

On the morning of September 6, the captains directed the men to lighten the loads on the Shoshone horses and pack the excess on the Salish horses. By midafternoon, that task was completed and the party set off down the Bitterroot River (north) while the Salish galloped out for Three Forks and the buffalo hunt. The expedition made ten miles and camped, with nothing to eat but two grouse and some berries. The captains were out of flour and had in the larder only a little corn and the portable soup Lewis had purchased in Philadelphia.

For the next three days, the descent of the wide and beautiful Bitterroot Valley was relatively easy. The expedition made twenty-two miles on the 7th, twenty-three on the 8th, and twenty-one on the 9th. But as they marched, the captains and their men kept looking to their left (west) at the snow-covered Bitterroot Mountains, described by Sergeant Patrick Gass as "the most terrible mountains I ever beheld."[4] The barrier would have to be crossed; how, they could hardly imagine.

The Bitterroot was wide enough to be floated in canoes, but the captains never thought of stopping to make the craft and becoming waterborne again. When they asked Old Toby about its course, he could only inform them that it continued to flow north as far as he knew it and he did not know whether it joined the Columbia River or not (it did, but far to the north). In any case, the absence of salmon on the river told the captains that there had to be a great falls downstream.

Making further geographical inquiries of Old Toby, Lewis learned that a few miles downstream (just west of today's Missoula, Montana) the Bitterroot was joined by another river (today's Clark Fork) that flowed from the Continental Divide through an extensive valley. If a party went up the Clark Fork to its source, it could cross the Divide over a low pass and would then descend down a gentle road to the Missouri River near the Gates of the Rocky Mountains. According to Old Toby, "a man might pass to the missouri from hence by that rout in four days."

Four days! It had taken the expedition fifty-three days to travel from the Gates of the Rocky Mountains to its present location. Whatever emotions Lewis felt when he learned that the party might have saved seven weeks he kept to himself.*

The party camped the night of September 9 at the junction of a stream coming in from the west (today's Lolo Creek, some ten miles south-southwest of Missoula). Old Toby informed Lewis that at this place the party would leave the Bitterroot River and head almost straight west, up Lolo Creek, and then over the mountains. The ordeal that every man had dreaded every time he looked left was about to begin. Lewis wrote of "those unknown formidable snow clad

---

* Of course, Old Toby meant it could be done in four days with horses, and Lewis and Clark had no horses when they ascended the Missouri above Great Falls.

Mountains," which the party was about to attempt "on the bare word of a Savage [Old Toby], while ⁹⁹⁄₁₀₀th of his Countrymen assured us that a passage was impracticable."[5]

"The weather appearing settled and fair," Lewis wrote, "I determined to halt the next day rest our horses and take some scelestial Observations." He called the campground *Travellers rest.*

On the morning of September 10, Lewis sent out all the hunters. They returned with four deer, a beaver, and three grouse. Even more welcome, if possible, Private John Colter brought in three Indians from a tribe that lived across the mountains. The captains called them Flatheads, but they were almost surely Nez Percé. They were in pursuit of a band of Shoshones that had stolen twenty-one horses—proof that the mountains could be crossed. One of the three agreed to remain with the Americans "to introduce us to his relations whom he informed us were numerous and resided in the plain below the mountains on the columbia river, from whence he said the water was good and capable of being navigated to the sea." He also told Lewis that "some of his relation were at the sea last fall and saw an old whiteman who resided there by himself." The best news of all, Lewis recorded, was that the Indian said "it would require five sleeps wich is six days travel, to reach his relations."

Six days' travel wasn't so bad. Perhaps those mountains were not so formidable as they appeared.

Further inquiry revealed that the river that flowed into the Bitterroot a few miles north (today's Clark Fork) received a smaller stream (today's Blackfoot) some little distance to the east (near the site of today's Missoula), and that it was this stream the Nez Percé followed to get to a low pass over the Continental Divide, bringing them to the buffalo country in the vicinity of either the Dearborn or the Medicine (today's Sun) River.

That news confirmed that there were two mountain crossings required to get to the Missouri drainage from the Nez Percé country west of the Bitterroot Mountains. And it told the captains that there were at least two better routes across the Continental Divide than the one they had taken—one via today's Clark Fork to today's MacDonald Pass (6,320 feet) down to today's Helena, a second via the Blackfoot River to today's Lewis and Clark Pass (elevation 6,000 feet exactly) down to the Great Falls, and a possible third, via Gibbons Pass (6,941 feet), down the Wisdom River to the Jefferson River.

Which of these answered Jefferson's order to find "the most direct & practicable water communication across this continent," only exploration would tell. It was much too late in the season to contemplate side journeys at this time—the entire party had to press on to the west, to the Pacific. Come next summer, on the return trip, they could examine the alternate routes; for now, the requirement was to get over the Bitterroots before the fall snows began.

During the night of September 10–11, two horses strayed. Not until 3:00 p.m. were they caught and brought in so the expedition could get started up Lolo Creek on the Nez Percé trail across the mountains (called today the Lolo Trail). It was an expensive delay. The Indian who had volunteered to guide the expedition to his people got impatient and took off. The party made seven miles and camped.

In the morning, Lewis found that his horse had strayed. He remained behind to search for it while Clark proceeded. On arrival at a hot springs that "Spouted from the rocks" and which was "nearly boiling hot" (today's Lolo Hot Springs), Clark waited for Lewis to come up. When he arrived, the party followed what Clark called a "tolerabl rout" that crossed the Divide, separating the Bitterroot drainage from the waters flowing west. A couple of miles east of today's Lolo Pass, they came to a beautiful open glade (today's Packer Meadows). Continuing, the expedition fell down today's Pack Creek (Glade Creek to Lewis and Clark) and camped.

Clark described the road west of the Divide as "verry fine leavel open & firm." Although the mountains stretched to the west as far as the eye could see, hopes were high. If the Indian informant was right, and if the road continued fine, in four days the expedition would be through the Bitterroots.

But on September 14, it rained, hailed, and snowed. Worse, Old Toby got lost. The Nez Percé trail followed the ridge line, north of the river the captains called the Kooskooskee (today's Lochsa), but Old Toby led the party down the drainage to a fishing camp on the Kooskooskee. Indians had recently been there, and their ponies had eaten all the grass—bad luck for the expedition. The road was "much worst than yesterday . . . excessively bad & Thickly Strowed with falling timber . . . Steep & Stoney."

By the time the men made camp (near today's Powell Ranger Station), they and the horses were "much fatigued" and famished. Since the hunters had been unsuccessful, "we wer compelled to kill a Colt . . . to eat . . . and named the South fork Colt killed Creek."

On the 15th, the party followed the Kooskooskee downstream four miles, where Old Toby recognized his mistake and led the men up today's Wendover Ridge, on the north side of the river, toward the ridge line. The going was incredibly difficult. It was a steep ascent made worse by "the emence quantity of falling timber." Several of the horses slipped and crashed down the hills. The horse carrying Clark's field desk rolled down the mountain for forty yards until it lodged against a tree; the desk was smashed, but the horse was unhurt. When the party reached the ridge line (at some seven thousand feet of elevation), there was no water. Using snow, the men made a soup out of the remains of the colt killed the previous day.

The expedition had made only twelve miles, despite "the greatest exertion." Even more discouraging, Clark wrote that "from this mountain I could observe high ruged mountains in every direction as far as I could See." There was no way the party was going to cross them in two more days.

September 16 was the worst day the expedition had experienced to date. It began to snow three hours before dawn and continued all day, piling up to from six to eight inches deep. Clark walked in front to find the trail "and found great dificuelty in keeping it" because of the snow. The pine trees were covered with snow that fell on the men as they passed and brushed the limbs. Clark wrote in his journal, "I have been wet and as cold in every part as I ever was in my life." The party made but thirteen miles, "passing emince Dificuelt Knobs Stones much falling timber and emencely Steep." The captains ordered a second colt killed, "which we all Suped hartily on and thought it fine meat."

The horses, in a near-starvation situation, strayed during the night, searching for grass. It took the whole morning to find and bring them in. Not until 1:00 p.m. did the expedition set out. The road was "excessively bad" and the party made only ten miles. It camped at a "Sinque hole full of water." The hunters had managed to kill only a few grouse, insufficient for supper. This "compelled us to kill Something. a coalt being the most useless part of our Stock he fell a Prey to our appetites." That was the last of the colts.

The captains talked. The men's spirits were low. They were approaching the limits of physical endurance. The food supply was all but gone, and there was no hope of finding game.* Lewis and Clark realized that the men—and they themselves—had reached a breaking point.

---

* They were in what is today prime big-game country: out-of-state hunters pay hundreds of dollars for a license and an outfitter to hunt elk and bear in these mountains. But in 1805, such animals were down on the plains and meadows; they were driven into the mountains by the coming of ranchers and farmers.

But to retreat was unthinkable—they would rather die than quit—and in any case impractical, for the five-day journey back to the Bitterroot River was probably beyond their capabilities. They had to go on. But to do so required desperate measures.

The captains concluded that in the morning Clark would go ahead with six hunters—in Lewis's words, to "hurry on to the leavel country a head and there hunt and provide some provision" to send back to the main party, which would follow under Lewis's leadership. They hated to split up—in the past seventeen months, they had done so only during the Marias River exploration and in the search for the Shoshones—especially in these god-awful mountains, with no firm idea as to how far ahead the "leavel country" might be.

On the morning of September 18, Clark struck out at first light. That day, Lewis resumed writing in his journal (he had done so only twice in the past three weeks, for unknown reasons; evidently he did so now to maintain a full record of the journey). He ordered the horses brought in early, "to force my march as much as the abilities of our horses would permit." Unfortunately, Private Alexander Willard allowed his horse to stray. Lewis sent him to search for it while the men ate what was left of the colt for breakfast. At 8:30 a.m., the party got started (Willard rejoined the men late that afternoon, without his horse). Lewis made eighteen miles that day and camped on the side of a steep mountain. He broke out "a skant proportion" of the portable soup, "a few canesters of which, a little bears oil and about 20 lbs. of candles form our stock of provision."

The situation was critical, Lewis wrote, "the only recourses being our guns & packhorses." Killing the packhorses would mean abandoning most of the baggage they were carrying, unthinkable with the Pacific still so far away, not to mention the return trip, and the rifles were "but a poor dependance [in a country] where there is nothing upon earth exept ourselves and a few small pheasants [grouse], small grey Squirrels, and a blue bird of the vulter kind [either the pinyon jay or Steller's jay]."

There was nothing for it but to proceed. In the morning, Lewis got the party going shortly after sunrise. At six miles, "the ridge terminated [at today's Sherman Peak] and we to our inexpressable joy discovered a large tract of Prairie country lying to the S.W. and widening as it appeared to extend to the W."

There was an end to the mountains, after all. The plain appeared to be sixty miles distant, but Old Toby assured Lewis "that we should reach it's borders tomorrow. the appearnace of this country, our only hope for subsistance greately revived the sperits of the party already reduced and much weakened for the want of food."

Lewis pressed on. "The road was excessively dangerous . . . being a narrow rockey path generally on the side of steep precipice, from which in many places if ether man or horse were precipitated they would inevitably be dashed in pieces." Late that afternoon, one horse did fall, "and roled with his load near a hundred yards into the Creek. we all expected that the horse was killed but to our astonishment when the load was taken off him he arose to his feet & appeared to be but little injured." Lewis commented that "this was the most wonderfull escape I ever witnessed." The expedition's luck was changing.

Only just in time. In addition to all the other problems, several of the men were sick with dysentery, and nearly all of them suffered from "brakings out, or irruptions of the Skin," probably caused by venereal disease contracted from the Shoshone women.

The following day, after proceeding two miles, Lewis saw a most welcome sight—"the greater part of a horse which Capt Clark had met with and killed for us." Clark had also left a note saying he intended to proceed as fast as possible to the plains, where he intended to hunt until Lewis came up. The party "made a hearty meal on our horse beef much to the comfort of our hungry stomachs."

But as Lewis ate, he got more bad news. One of the packhorses, with his load, was missing. That load was particularly valuable to Lewis, for it contained his stock of winter clothing. He sent Private Lepage—who was responsible for the horse—back to search for it, but Lepage returned at 3:00 p.m. without it. Lewis then sent "two of my best woodsmen in surch of him" and proceeded. The road was bad, as usual, with much deadfall.

That night, the party finished the horse Clark had provided. It wasn't much. But, sitting around the campfire, cold, hungry, exhausted, and miserable, Lewis summoned the energy to make significant additions to scientific knowledge (if he could get his journals back to civilization). He described the varied thrush, Steller's jay, the gray jay, the black woodpecker (known today as Lewis's woodpecker), the blue grouse, the spruce grouse, and the Oregon ruffed grouse, as well as the mountain huckleberry, the Sitka alder, and the western red cedar (called "arborvitae" by Lewis). All but the thrush were unknown to science.

On September 21, Lewis didn't get started until 11:00 a.m., because he had to wait for the horses to be collected, and his own packhorse to be brought in. He traveled down the heavily timbered bottom of a creek where the deadfall was so bad that "it was almost impracticable to proceed." At five miles, he came to Clark's campsite on what Clark had named "Hungery Creek as at that place we had nothing to eate." After six more miles, Lewis came to a small, open bottom "where there was tolerable food for our horses" and camped.

"I directed the horses to be hubbled to prevent delay in the morning," he wrote. He was "determined to make a forced march tomorrow in order to reach if possible the open country." The hunters killed a few grouse. Lewis "killd a prarie woolf [coyote]," which, with the leftover horsemeat and some crayfish, provided "one more hearty meal, not knowing where the next was to be found. . . . I find myself growing weak for the want of food and most of the men complain of a similar deficiency and have fallen off very much."

In the morning, to Lewis's chagrin, one of the men had "neglected to comply" with the order to hobble his horse. "He plead ignorance of the order." Not until 11:30 a.m. did the party get started. It had proceeded some two and a half miles when it met Private Reubin Field, a member of Clark's party, whom Clark had sent to meet Lewis with some dried fish and roots obtained from the Nez Percé. Field said that there was an Indian village some seven miles farther west, that Clark had made a friendly contact with the Nez Percé and had been able to procure food from them. This was great news, as welcome as the fish and roots, which were sufficient "to satisfy compleatly all our appetits."

After eating, the party proceeded to a village of eighteen lodges, which it reached at 5:00 p.m. The expedition had made 160 miles since it left Traveler's Rest eleven days ago. It was one of the great forced marches in American history.

Lewis tried to describe his emotions: "the pleasure I now felt in having tryumphed over the rocky Mountains and decending once more to a level and fertile country where there was every rational hope of finding a comfortable subsistence for myself and party can be more readily conceived than expressed, nor was the flattering prospect of the final success of the expedition less pleasing."

Outstanding leadership made possible the triumph over the Rocky Mountains. Lewis and Clark had welded the Corps of Discovery into a tough, superbly disciplined family. They had built an unquestioning trust in themselves, and knew the strengths and skills of each of their men intimately. They had taken a calculated risk in trusting Old Toby, but their judgment that he knew what he was talking about (even though the talking was in sign language) proved to be justified. In extremely trying conditions—"We suffered everything Cold, Hunger & Fatigue could impart," Lewis later wrote, as well as "the Keenest Anxiety excited for the fate of [our] Expedition in which our whole

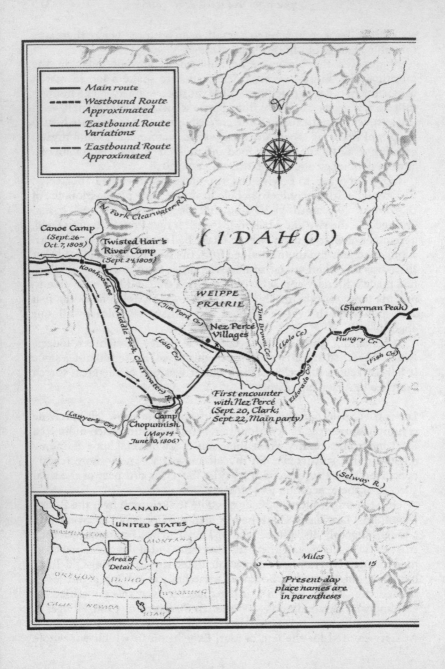

Legend:

— Main route
--- Westbound Route Approximated
— Eastbound Route Variations
- - - Eastbound Route Approximated

N

(IDAHO)

N. Fork Clearwater R.

Canoe Camp
(Sept. 26–
Oct. 7, 1805)

Twisted Hair's
River Camp
(Sept. 24, 1805)

Kooskooskee (Middle Fork Clearwater)

WEIPPE
PRAIRIE

(Jim Ford Cr.)

(Jim Brown Cr.)

(Sherman Peak)

Nez Percé
Villages

(Lolo Cr.)

(Lolo Cr.)

Hungry Cr.

(Fish Cr.)

(Lawyer's Cr.)

Eldorado Cr.

First encounter
with Nez Percé
(Sept. 20, Clark;
Sept. 22, Main party)

Camp
Chopunnish
(May 14–
June 10, 1806)

(Selway R.)

CANADA

UNITED STATES

WASHINGTON

MONTANA

Area of
Detail

OREGON

IDAHO

WYOMING

CALIF.

NEVADA

UTAH

Miles

0 — 15

Present-day
place names are
in parentheses

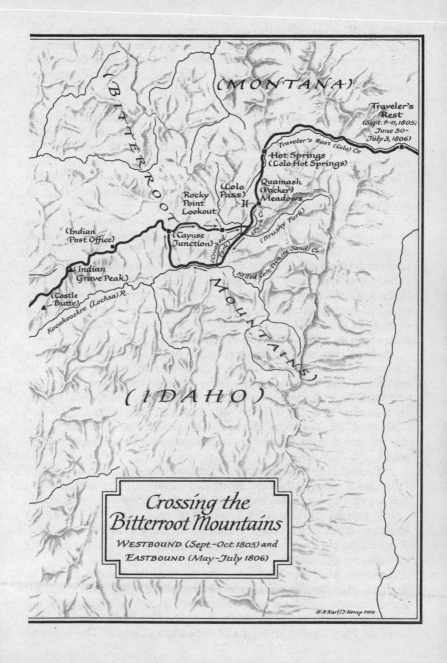

(BITTERROOT

(MONTANA)

Traveler's
Rest
(Sept. 9–11, 1805;
June 30–
July 3, 1806)

Traveler's Rest (Lolo) Cr.

Hot Springs
(Lolo Hot Springs)

Quamash
(Packer)
Meadows

(Lolo
Pass)

Rocky
Point
Lookout

(Pack Cr.)

(Brushy Fork)

(Indian
Post Office)

(Cayuse
Junction)

(Crooked Fork)

(Indian
Grave Peak)

(Killed Colt (White Sand) Cr.

MOUNTAINS)

(Castle
Butte)

Kooskooskee (Lochsa) R.

(IDAHO)

Crossing the Bitterroot Mountains

WESTBOUND (Sept.–Oct. 1805) and
EASTBOUND (May–July 1806)

© A. Karl / J. Kemp 1995

Souls were embarked"—the captains managed to keep morale from collapsing.[6] The men never sulked, lashed out, demanded to retreat, or insisted on some alternative route. When the captains decided to take the great risk of separating, with Clark going on ahead, no man protested.

Private Field told Lewis that Clark was at a second village, gathering information from the Nez Percé. At dark, Clark returned and joined Lewis. "I found Capt Lewis & the party Encamped," he wrote, "much fatigued, & hungery, much rejoiced to find something to eate of which They appeared to partake plentifully." Clark's experience was that too many roots had made his hunters violently ill, so "I cautioned them of the Consequences of eateing too much &c."

Clark was accompanied by Twisted Hair, a Nez Percé chief in his mid-sixties whom Clark described as a "Chearfull man with apparant Siencerity." Clark was the first white man most of the Nez Percé had ever seen. He informed Lewis that there were two villages in the area, called by the captains the "quawmash flats" or the "camas flats" (today's Weippe Prairie, near Weippe, Idaho), where the Indian women gathered great quantities of camas roots which they made into a kind of bread or cake. He said that at his request Twisted Hair had drawn him a map on a white elk skin of the country to the west.

Twisted Hair showed the creek they were on emptying into the Clearwater River, which was soon joined by a river coming in from the northeast (the North Fork of the Clearwater) and then flowing west to join with the Columbia. It was a five-sleep journey to the Columbia, then another five sleeps to the falls of the Columbia. "At the falls," Clark said, Twisted Hair "places Establishments of white people &c. and informs that great numbers of Indians reside on all those forks as well as the main river."

If Twisted Hair was right, the expedition was within ten days of the falls, and a couple of weeks from the ocean. But the captains had learned that either Indian estimates of distances were too optimistic, or the Indians traveled a lot faster than the white men. And that business about white people living at the falls sounded suspicious. Anyway, the expedition wasn't going anywhere until it found trees big enough to make canoes.

Over the next couple of days, the captains handed out medals to Twisted Hair and three lesser chiefs, along with shirts, knifes, handkerchiefs, and tobacco. These trifles (except for the knives) did not satisfy. At the end of the second day, the Nez Percé indicated they were no longer going to feed the expedition for free. The captains traded from their diminishing supply of goods for more roots, berries, and dried fish.

Clark's warning about overeating was easier given than followed. Lewis and his men gorged themselves and got sick, Lewis especially so. Most of the party were violently ill for a week, their dysentery producing acute diarrhea and vomiting.

"All Complain of a *Lax* & heaviness at the Stomack," Clark wrote, so "I gave rushes Pills." That was probably the worst thing he could have done; in any case, the following day, September 24, Lewis was so sick he was "Scercely able to ride on a jentle horse. . . . Several men So unwell that they were Compelled to lie on the Side of the road for Some time." Clark was nothing if not persistent; he handed out more of Rush's pills.

The sickness was presumably the result of the change of diet, from all meat to all roots and dried fish. Bacteria on the salmon may have contributed.[7]

On the 25th, Lewis was still suffering from severe gastrointestinal distress. Clark tried giving him some salts and "Tarter emetic," another laxative, which hurt more than helped. The next day, Clark tried "Salts Pils Galip [jalap, another purgative] Tarter emetic &c." again with unhappy results. By the 27th, most of the men were still sick, including Lewis; on the 28th, Clark opened his journal entry, "Our men nearly all Complaining of ther bowels, a heaviness at the Stomach & Lax." Not until the 30th could Clark report "the men recruiting a little." But they were still on a fish-and-roots diet, which "the men complain of as working them as much as a dost of Salts."

In short, for over a week the expedition resembled a hospital ward for the critically ill more than it did a platoon of fighting men. Herein lies one of the great stories of American history, even though it is a tale of what didn't happen rather than what did.

It would have been the work of a few moments only for the Nez Percé to kill the white men and take for themselves all the expedition's goods. Had the Indians done so, they would have come into possession of by far the biggest arsenal not just west of the Rocky Mountains but west of the Mississippi River, along with priceless kettles, axes, hatchets, beads, and other trade items in quantities greater than any of them would cver sec in their lifetimes.

Like the Shoshones, the Nez Percé had had no contact with whites, other than some cheap trade goods that had reached them from Columbia River tribes. They had only one or two inferior rifles. They were constantly harassed by their neighbors who did have guns, especially by the Blackfeet when the Nez Percé made their annual trip over the mountains to the buffalo country.

The Nez Percé were hardly oblivious to their once-in-a-lifetime opportunity. According to their oral-history tradition, when they first met Clark and his six hunters—who had also gorged themselves on roots and fish and gotten dysentery—they considered killing them for their weapons. They were dissuaded by a woman named Watkuweis (meaning "Returned from a Far Country"). She had been captured by Blackfeet some six or seven years earlier, taken into Canada, and sold to a white trader. She lived with him, among other traders, for several years before somehow finding her way home. The traders had treated her much better than the Blackfeet had done, so when Clark arrived she told the warriors, "These are the people who helped me. Do them no hurt."[8]

First Sacagawea, now Watkuweis. The expedition owed more to Indian women than either captain ever acknowledged. And the United States owed more to the Nez Percé for their restraint than it ever acknowledged. When, in 1877, the army, carrying out government policy, drove Chief Joseph and the Nez Percé from their Idaho home, there were in the band old men and women who had as children been in Twisted Hair's village.

During the week Lewis was on his back, Clark moved camp to the junction of the North Fork of the Clearwater with the main stream, where there were Ponderosa pines of sufficient size to make canoes. With only a few healthy men and inadequate axes, Clark resorted to the Indian method of canoe-making. Instead of hewing out the trunks, he put them over a slow-burning fire trench and burned them out. Apparently Twisted Hair showed him how to do it. It took ten days to complete four large and one small canoe.

Twisted Hair also promised to look after the expedition's herd of thirty-eight horses until the Americans came back in the spring on their return journey—Clark had the horses branded with Lewis's branding iron—and to accompany the party to serve as an intermediary with Indians downstream.

The captains had assumed that when they got out of the mountains they would be in a country with an ample supply of deer and elk. They were wrong. The hunters—those still on their feet—were unsuccessful. Fish and roots purchased from the Nez Percé remained the diet. On October 4, Lewis was still sick. The next day, Clark reported, "Capt

Lewis & my Self eate a Supper of roots boiled, which filled us So full of wind, that we were Scercely able to Breathe all night felt the effects of it."

On October 6, the canoes were finished. Clark made a cache for the saddles and a canister of powder. "I am verry Sick all night," he recorded, "pane in Stomach & the bowels." The next day, he opened his journal entry, "I continu verry unwell but obliged to attend every thing." Evidently Lewis was still so sick he couldn't even supervise the men's work. Lewis later wrote, "for my own part I suffered a severe Indisposition for 10 or 12 days, sick feeble & emiciated."[9]

Clark had the canoes put into the water and loaded. At 3:00 p.m., the party set out. The river was swift, with many bad rapids. Nevertheless, they made twenty miles. The expedition was once again waterborne, going downstream for the first time since Lewis had turned the keelboat from the Ohio into the Mississippi River, two years earlier. Ahead lay the Pacific.

25

DOWN THE COLUMBIA

October 8–December 7, 1805

As the expedition sped down the Clearwater toward its junction with the Snake, Lewis recuperated from his two-week bout with dysentery. On October 9, Clark recorded, "Capt Lewis recovring fast." Soon he was as active as always. On October 13, the party came to a "verry bad place . . . a long bad rapid in which the water is Confined in a Channel of about 20 yards between rugid rocks for the distance of a mile." It cried out for portaging, but the captains and the men wanted to get on. They were on the last leg and finally had gravity working for them. So, Clark recorded, "Capt Lewis with two Canoes Set out & passed down the rapid. The others Soon followed and we passed over this bad rapid safe."

The dugout canoes were cumbersome. They overturned or grounded on rocks. They swamped. They sprung leaks. Supplies were damaged, trade goods lost. Men's lives were endangered. The captains ran the rapids anyway, as many as fifteen in a day.

Old Toby was so frightened by the running of the rapids that he took off that night, without waiting for his pay. He was last seen running eastward along the riverbank. The captains asked Twisted Hair to send a horseman after Old Toby to ask him to come back to be paid, but Twisted Hair advised against such a course; the Nez Percé, he pointed out, would only take it from him as he passed their camps. Old Toby did pick up two of the expedition's horses to ride back over the Lolo Trail and then to Cameahwait's village on the Lemhi.*

On October 10, the expedition reached the Snake River, coming in from the left (south). The party camped that night near the site of present Lewiston, Idaho. The men bought dogs and dried fish from local Indians. "All the Party have greatly the advantage of me," Clark reported, "in as much as they all relish the flesh of the dogs." On the 14th, the unhappy Clark shot some ducks and was able to record, "for the first time for three weeks past I had a good dinner of Blue wing Teel."

The expedition swept on toward the junction of the Snake and the Columbia, passing through the canyon-lined Snake on into present Washington State, where the Great Columbian Plain offered a barren landscape in stark contrast to the wooded mountains the party was leaving behind. Along the way, the expedition passed innumerable Indian villages. The natives were members of the extended Nez Percé nation, by far the largest and most powerful of the tribes of the Pacific Northwest. They had more horses than any tribe on the continent and were the only North American Indians to practice selective breeding. They scorned eating horse flesh; their diet was primarily deer and elk, supplemented by large quantities of fish. The Columbia and Snake River system, on which they lived, produced more salmon than any other river in the world. Their catches were incredible; one man could kill a hundred salmon on a good day, a full ton or more of fish.[1]

The Indians were hospitable, partly because Twisted Hair and another Nez Percé chief, named Tetoharsky, went ahead of the party to reassure their relatives that the white men were friendly, partly because—in Clark's words—"the wife of Shabono our interpetr we find reconsiles all the Indians, as to our friendly intentions. a woman with a party of men is a token of peace."

Lewis was torn between his desire to keep moving and the need to bring the Nez Percé into the American orbit. He was not in American territory. Neither the United States nor Great Britain had established sovereignty over the Pacific Northwest. Both countries wanted it and had some sort of claim, as did the Russians and the Spanish. But Lewis and Clark were the first white men to enter present Idaho, Washington, and Oregon by land. Although they never planted a flag to make a formal claim on the territory for the United States, they acted as if it were already theirs.

---

* With that he rode out of history, but he will never be forgotten as the man who guided the Corps of Discovery over the Bitterroot Mountains.

Lewis took a vocabulary of the different bands as they were encountered. He found variations in words but correctly concluded that they had a common origin. Twisted Hair could understand them. The Yakimas, Wanapams, Wallawallas, and others all belonged to the same Shahaptian-language family. They practiced a similar economy. They were all rich in dogs as well as horses. Not wanting to waste time sending out hunters, the captains continued to purchase dogs to have some meat to supplement their fish and roots.

To bring the various branches of the Nez Percé into active participation in the American trading system, Lewis practiced his usual Indian diplomacy. Around the campfires on the banks of the rivers, he gave his speech expressing his joy "in Seeing those of our Children around us" and handed out medals with Jefferson's likeness on them. He urged the Indians to make peace with their neighbors and promised them trade goods, and he began to form in his mind a grand scheme involving the Nez Percé that would cut the British out of the fur trade with the Orient.

But long-term plans for an American takeover could be arranged in the spring, when the expedition could take its time going back upstream, since there was no point arriving on the western base of the Bitterroots before the snow had melted sufficiently to make a crossing practicable. That figured to be June at best, mid-July at worst. So, when Chief Yellept of the Wallawalla band asked Lewis to stay longer so that his people might come to see the white men, the captain excused himself—he wanted to keep moving. He promised instead that the party would spend a few days with Yellept's people in the spring.

No matter how badly Lewis and Clark wanted good relations with the natives, sometimes they put daily needs first. "We have made it a point at all times not to take any thing belonging to the Indians even their wood," Clark noted on October 14, but since there was no timber on the island where the party camped that night, "we are Compelled to violate that rule and take a part of the Split timber we find here." The next night, "we were obliged for the first time [sic] to take the property of the Indians without the consent or approbation of the owner. the night was cold & we made use of a part of those boards and Split logs for fire wood."

Stealing from the natives was as easy as it was tempting. The captains hated having it done to them, which was beginning to happen with increasing frequency as they made their way west. The articles taken were small, but, because the trade goods were the captains' capital and diminishing fast, their anger was large.

Still, their spirits were soaring. At night, around the fire, Private Cruzatte brought out his violin, to the delight of the men, who danced to the music, and to the Indian guests, who watched and then did their own dancing. On October 15, Lewis took a walk on the plains about the river and saw in the distance a mountain range that could only be the Cascades.

The next day, the party reached the junction with the Columbia, the first white men to be on the river east of the Cascades. They camped for two days; Clark investigated the Columbia for about ten miles upstream. The men were astonished at the numbers of salmon in the river, mostly dying after the spawn and therefore inedible. The water was so clear that, no matter how deep the river, the bottom was plainly visible.

By now, signs that the Pacific could not be far distant were everywhere. The nearness of the trading emporium at the mouth of the Columbia was apparent from items possessed by the natives, including scarlet-and-blue cloth blankets and a sailor's jacket. On October 19, Clark climbed a cliff and saw a snow-covered mountain which he deduced "must be one of the mountains laid down by Vancouver, as Seen from the mouth of the Columbia River." He thought it was Mount St. Helens; actually it was Mount Adams. But his essential point was right. Lewis's and Clark's sightings of the Cascades made the first connection, the first transcontinental linking, of what would become the United States.

Lewis had long realized that the Columbia had to have many rapids and some major falls on it as it descended from the Rockies to the Pacific. On October 23, the expedition came to the beginning of a spectacular but dangerous stretch of the river that extended some fifty-five miles. It contained four major barriers (all inundated today by dam reservoirs), beginning with the Celilo, or Great Falls. In one short stretch of violent, roaring cataracts, the river dropped thirty-eight feet through several narrow channels between cliffs as high as three thousand feet.

Today's Deschutes River came into the Columbia from the left just above the falls. At the mouth of the Deschutes, Lewis and Clark went off in different directions to examine the surrounding countryside and study the falls. Clark got to the falls first, Lewis having delayed on his exploration to examine a root, the wapato, that the natives dug in great quantities in the bottom of the Deschutes. After studying the falls and conferring, the captains decided that only the twenty-foot drop had to be portaged. They were able to hire local Indians and their horses to help portage the heavier articles. At other places, they managed to lower the canoes through the rapids, using strong ropes of elk skin, while packing the baggage on a portage.

Indians gathered on the riverbanks to watch the white men. Their presence was often a blessing. They had dogs and dried fish to sell, they provided information on the state of the river downstream, and they had a technology that the captains could use. Lewis visited a village where he had observed his first Chinookan canoe, made of pine, remarkably light, wide in the middle and tapering at each end, with crosspieces at the gunnels that made the craft surprisingly strong, and skillfully carved animal figures on the bow. Clark wrote that "these Canoes are neeter made than any I have ever Seen and Calculated to ride the waves, and carry emence burthens." Lewis was able to exchange the expedition's smallest canoe for one of the Indian craft, after he agreed to throw in a hatchet and a few trinkets.*

As the expedition prepared to make its way through the falls downstream, the captains learned that they would be passing into the country of a people with a different culture and language from any they had previously encountered. They were Chinookan, and the Nez Percé were at war with the Chinooks. On the night of October 23, Twisted Hair said he had heard from his relatives among the local Indians that the Chinookan people living farther down the river intended to kill the Americans when they arrived. The captains examined the rifles and made certain every man had a hundred rounds of ammunition, but that was a daily routine anyway. Clark commented, "as we are at all times & places on our guard, [we] are under no greater apprehention than is common."

The following day, Twisted Hair and Tetoharsky said they had decided to return home. They explained that the Chinooks would surely kill them if they had a chance; besides, they could not speak the language, so they could no longer serve as interpreters. The captains persuaded the chiefs to stay with them for two more days, until the expedition had gotten below the next falls, which were but two miles downstream, to give the captains an opportunity to bring about a peace between the warring nations.

The next set of falls, called The Dalles, began with the Short Narrows, a quarter-mile-long stretch in which the river was constricted to a mere forty-five yards in width. Clark was appalled by "the horrid

---

* On January 11, 1806, Lewis described the canoe: "she is so light that four men can carry heer on their sholders a mile or more without resting; and will carry three men and from 12 to 15 hundred lbs."

appearance of this agitated gut Swelling [water], boiling & whorling in every direction."

The captains explored the banks. Agreeing that no portage for the heavy canoes was possible over the rocky ledges, they decided to send by land the men who could not swim, carrying the most valuable articles with them, while they and the swimmers ran the fall in the canoes, bringing the heavy and less valuable baggage with them.

In selecting the items to be portaged, the captains showed their priorities. First of all, the journals, field notes, and other papers, including Jefferson's letter of credit to Lewis, which would become invaluable if they chanced to meet a trading ship at the mouth of the Columbia. Second, the rifles and ammunition (this was taking a chance—for the first time, the bulk of the party would be defenseless in the presence of Indians—but that risk was more acceptable than risking the rifles in the falls). Finally, the scientific instruments.

By the standards of today's canoeists, this was a Class V rapid, meaning it could not be run even in a modern canoe specially designed for whitewater. The natives, expert canoeists themselves, did not believe Lewis and Clark could do it in their big, heavy dugouts. They gathered by the hundreds along the banks to watch the white men drown themselves, and to be ready to help themselves to the abandoned equipment afterward. But, to the astonishment of the Indians, the Americans made the run without incident.

Below the Short Narrows was a relatively calm three-mile stretch. Along the bank there was an Indian village of wooden houses, the first wooden homes the captains had seen since they left St. Charles seventeen months earlier. There were stacks of dried, pounded fish on scaffolds, at least five tons by the captains' estimate. The principal chief from the village below paid a visit, which in Clark's words "afforded a favourable oppertunity of bringing about a Piece and good understanding between this chief and his people and the two Chiefs [Twisted Hair and Tetoharsky] which we have the Satisfaction to Say we have accomplished, as we have every reason to believe, and that those two bands of nations are and will be on the most friendly terms with each other." That was wishful thinking, and how the captains could have been so sure of themselves and so satisfied is a mystery: neither side could understand a word the other side said, and the sign language of the Plains Indians that Drouillard used was imperfectly understood by the Chinooks.

The next river obstacle was the Long Narrows, where the river narrowed to fifty to a hundred yards for some three miles. As at the

Short Narrows, the captains decided to have the nonswimmers portage the most valuable items while they ran the river in the canoes. Again Indians gathered on the banks to await the inevitable disaster; again the canoes made the passage safely.

Below the narrows, where the river widened, the party made camp on a high point of rocks. The captains chose the site because it formed a kind of fortification. Clark explained, "this Situation we Concieve well Calculated for defence." They called it "Fort Rock Camp" (on the site of today's city named The Dalles, Oregon). There they stayed for three days to make repairs to the canoes, dry the baggage, and do some hunting. Lewis took the opportunity to make some celestial observations for longitude and compass variation. They had a parting smoke with Twisted Hair and Tetoharsky.

The local Indians were proving troublesome because of their proclivity for petty theft: any object laid aside for a moment vanished. The captains' greatest concern became not the Indians' arrows but "the protection of our Stores from thieft." It got so bad that the men muttered they were "well disposed to kill a few of them." On at least one occasion, the captains had to restrain the men.[2] As Clark pointed out, "it [is] necessary at this time to treat those people verry friendly & ingratiate our Selves with them, to insure us a kind & friendly reception on our return."

On the night of October 26, two chiefs and fifteen men crossed the river in a canoe, bringing presents of deer meat and cakes of bread made of roots. The captains gave medals to the chiefs, trinkets to the men. Private Cruzatte brought out his violin. York danced for the Indians, to their delight. The hunters had brought in five deer that day, so there was plenty of meat. One of the men gigged a steelhead trout, which he fried in some bear oil given him by one of the Indians. Clark pronounced it "one of the most delicious fish I have ever tasted." The visiting chiefs spent the night. Altogether, it was a good start for U.S.-Chinookan relations.

As always, Lewis took a vocabulary of the Indians, although how he accomplished it without a translator is unclear. On October 30, the party set out again, to a point two miles above the last great drop, the Cascades of the Columbia (the "Great Shute" to Lewis and Clark), where it made camp in anticipation of a reconnaissance in the morning.

Lewis took a party of five men to visit a nearby Indian town. Along the way, he shot unsuccessfully at a California condor, which he correctly judged to be the largest bird in North America. At the village, he got a friendly reception. The Indians gave him berries, nuts, and fish to eat. But, he told Clark, "he could get nothing from them in the way of Information," because of the language barrier.

The reconnaissance revealed a section of river some four miles long filled with rapids passing through a series of chutes and falls, "the water passing with great velocity forming & boiling in a most horriable manner." But beyond the Great Shute the river widened "and had everry appearance of being effected by the tide," which was great news.

On November 1–2, the party made its way through this final barrier. At times the men had to portage the canoes and the baggage; at other places it was possible to run the canoes through, using elk-skin ropes to lower them. The following day, moving downstream, the party came to Beacon Rock, the beginning of tidewater.

The expedition had entered a much-changed world. The banks were covered with fir, spruce, ash, and alder, contrasting sharply with the treeless semidesert country upstream. Migrating waterfowl were everywhere. Fog was frequent and often thick; many days, the party could not set out until afternoon. Indian villages dotted the banks. Indian visits were frequent. The natives made a poor impression on Lewis and his party, except as canoeists, where their superiority over the white men was obvious and duly acknowledged. Otherwise, they were judged to be "low and ill-shaped . . . badly clad and illy made," petty thieves and objects of suspicion.

James Ronda points out that one reason for the overwhelmingly negative view the captains and their men had of the Indians near the mouth of the river was that the natives were "accustomed to hard bargaining with whites in the sea otter trade," and therefore "expected to drive equally hard bargains with the hungry explorers." Clark's journal is full of complaints about the inflated prices charged for roots and fish.[3]

The captains did not look forward to wintering with or near these Indians. They recalled, with nostalgia, the winter with the Mandans. They would have gladly traded the rainy weather for the bitter cold of Fort Mandan, especially if they could also have the honest and friendly Mandans for their winter companions, and buffalo to eat. But it was not to be, and they determined to make the best of their situation.

Their immediate concern was getting to the ocean. Not until that was accomplished could they begin to decide where to spend the winter. On November 2, the expedition passed the mouth of Sandy River, which had been the highest point upriver reached by European or American explorers.* The following day, it reached present Vancouver, Washington, and camped opposite the mouth of the Willamette River (although they did not know it, since the mouth was hidden by an island and they were on the north bank). For the first time since April 1805, the expedition was in country previously explored and mapped by whites. Here the maps from west and from east came together.

The party camped on an island. Lewis borrowed a small canoe from local Indians and with four men took her to a lake on the island, where they enjoyed an after-dark hunt. The lake was teeming with swans, brants, geese, and ducks. Lewis's party killed three swans, eight brants, and five ducks.

On the night of November 4, several canoe-loads of Indians from the village upstream came down for a visit. They were colorful, with scarlet-and-blue blankets, sailor's jackets, shirts, and hats, and apparently friendly. But they also brought along a show of weaponry that included war axes, spears, bows at the ready, quivers of arrows at their sides, some muskets and pistols.

It was a situation fraught with danger. Two groups of armed young men, from different cultures, unable to communicate with words, facing each other. The captains were up to the challenge. Even though "Those fellows we found assumeing and disagreeable," Clark wrote, "we Smoked with them and treated them with every attention & friendship."

But the atmosphere changed when Clark discovered that one of those fellows had "Stold my pipe Tomahawk which They were Smoking with." Though Clark searched every man and the Indians' canoes, he could not find his pipe. To add to the injury, while the search was being carried out, an Indian stole Drouillard's capote (a long blanket coat, hooded, made of heavy wool, long popular in the Canadian fur trade). More angry words, and another search. The capote was found, but not the pipe.

The captains showed their contempt and outrage, or, as Clark so nicely put it, "we became much displeased with those fellows, which they discovered and moved off."

At this time, the expedition was making better than thirty miles a day down the lower Columbia. On November 5, it met the first coastal canoes, a flotilla of four of different sizes. The largest had a bear's image carved into the bow and a man's image on the stern. The design so

---

* Lieutenant William Broughton of George Vancouver's 1792 expedition had gone this far up the Columbia.

impressed Clark that he did a sketch of the craft. On the 6th, another flotilla came out from a village, bringing roots, trout, and furs for sale at bargain prices. Clark bought two beaver skins for five small fishhooks. The Indians said there was a white man living below, with whom they traded. Encouraging news, and a good day.

But that night, the campground was scarcely sufficient. The men had to move large stones to make a place among the smaller stones where they could lie down on the level. All was wet and disagreeable.

In the morning, fog. As it slowly lifted, the expedition set off. By midafternoon, the sky was clear.

A shout went up. In his field notes, William Clark scribbled his immortal line, *"Ocian in view! O! the joy."*

The men dug in, putting everything they had into the race to the ocean. The canoes sped along; they made thirty-four miles that day. Once again, the campsite was barely sufficient to lie on and composed of small stones. It was raining. Despite the conditions, Clark wrote, "Great joy in camp we are in *view* of the *Ocian*, this great Pacific Octean which we been So long anxious to See." They could distinctly hear waves breaking on rocks.

Without comment (but there must have been some pride in it), Clark added up the miles since the first falls (Celilo, 190 miles upriver). Then he wrote, "Ocian 4142 Miles from the Mouth of *Missouri* R."

There was no celebration: it was raining too hard for Cruzatte to bring out his violin. But in their ragged, all-but-rotten clothes, and under their good-for-nothing covers, each man's heart must have been warm with satisfaction, each man's mind soaring with a sense of triumph.

One longs for Lewis's emotional reaction to the triumph of crossing the continent. He had been at it for two and a half years, ever since he left Washington, D.C., in the spring of 1803. One supposes that he shared that "Great Joy in camp" that Clark wrote of, but he never expressed it himself. He had not written in his journal since meeting the Nez Percé in September, and with minor exceptions would not again until the New Year.

For the biographer, Lewis's silence is a frustrating and tantalizing mystery. It was not that he didn't have time, or example—every day he saw Clark writing in his journal. Yet he did not lift his quill.

Except for his severe illness when he first met the Nez Percé, Lewis had been active, coping successfully with the various challenges the party had to face. There is no hint in Clark's journal, or in the journals of the enlisted men, that he was depressed, downcast, muttering to himself, or otherwise showing symptoms of the melancholia

Jefferson had observed in Lewis's father and in Lewis when they lived together in the President's House.

He was in a world filled with people, bays, weather, flora and fauna all new to him, a situation that usually sent his quill flying over the pages, but he did not write.

Was he depressed? Not so depressed as to neglect his duties, but enough to keep him from taking quill in hand to set down the day's events? If so, what caused the depression?

With manic-depressives, there is no agreement as to the cause of the disorder—whether biological or psychological—or what triggers either a manic or a depressed state. In many if not most cases, a wave of euphoria, a surge of energy, and a feeling that "I can do anything" just comes on, followed by a wave of nausea, a draining of energy, and a feeling that "I can't do anything." How long each state lasts depends on the individual—weeks, months, years.

In many cases, patients in a depressed state are almost incapable of acting. They have no energy, no sense of self-worth. They feel that nothing they do will matter to anyone.

Lewis would come to such a point, but he certainly didn't feel that way in the fall of 1805—he knew the importance of what he was doing, and he had the willpower to summon up the energy to operate at peak efficiency. Jefferson later commented that he thought Lewis's voyage helped him ward off depression. There is nothing like daily decision-making to get the brain functioning and the body moving. From personal experience, Jefferson knew what he was talking about.

But writing was another matter. Lewis couldn't summon the energy to be reflective.

Of course, he had some real problems, of which the most distasteful was having to inform Jefferson that there was no all-water route or anything remotely like it across the continent, a fact reinforced by those terrible falls on the Columbia. Did the prospect of having to cross the Bitterroots again weigh on his mind?

His worries were many. He feared that the expedition would not be able to rely on its rifles for subsistence until it got back to the Great Plains and the buffalo herds. He feared that the dwindling supply of trade goods was insufficient to purchase provisions in the quantity needed. Despite having reached the ocean, the expedition would not be a success unless and until the captains got their journals back to civilization.

Was the triumph of reaching the ocean only a reminder of how much remained to be done, and how little he had to do it with? Did he doubt that it could be done?

It cannot be that he was simply too tired. He had too often demonstrated an ability to forget his aching muscles and his nearly overwhelming need to sleep in order to describe the day's activities and discoveries. It cannot be that he felt he had nothing to say beyond what Clark had written, for he often went on side explorations and saw what Clark did not. It cannot be that he regarded his journal as unimportant: he took too good care of it at all times for that to be the case.

Yet he was a professional soldier ignoring direct orders from his commander-in-chief. There must be an explanation—but we can only guess.

My guess is that he was a manic-depressive. The disorder ran in his family. If this is true, then it was his special triumph that he seldom let his emotional state take over, and then only momentarily. Whether he was high or low, his emotional state played no role in daily decision-making for two and a half years.

Whatever Lewis's emotional state, it was strongly affected by his drinking habits.

It had been a long time since Meriwether Lewis had had a drink. And the certainty was that it would be a long time before he had another.

He had been a hard-drinking youth. In St. Louis during the winter of 1803–4, he attended a good many balls and private parties, where it seems likely he indulged in pretty heavy drinking. It went with the territory; frontier officers and traders drank a lot of whiskey.

For the first year of the expedition, Lewis had limited himself to the same ration of whiskey the men received, hardly enough to sustain a serious alcoholic, but enough to keep a habit, perhaps even a need, alive. On July 5, 1805, he had been forced to quit cold turkey. No one can say what, if any, effect Lewis's abstinence had on his mood.

Whatever the reason, the scene that so moved Clark, who gave us such a memorable phrase as he let his emotions burst forth, was not described by Lewis.

It is through Lewis's eyes and words that we see the White Cliffs, the Great Falls before the dams, the Gates of the Mountains, Three Forks, the Shoshones. Wonderful portraits, all. Vivid. Immediate. Detailed. They set the standard.

But we don't have his description of what he saw and how he felt in this moment of triumph.

Clark had been a bit premature: what he had seen was the Columbian estuary, not the ocean. Actually, they were too close to the ocean for their own good anyway. For the next week and more, they were pinned down by the tide, the waves, the wind, at Point Ellice. They were unable to go forward, to retreat, to climb out of their campsite because of the overhanging rocks and hills, to do anything except endure pure misery. It rained for eleven days. At high tide, gigantic waterborne trees of cedar, fir, and spruce, some of them almost two hundred feet long and up to seven feet in diameter, crashed into the camp. Fires were hard to start, difficult to maintain.

The captains and men of the expedition looked more like survivors from a shipwreck praying for rescue than the triumphant members of the Corps of Discovery. For a while, spirits remained high: "For Several days past," Clark wrote on the 9th, "not withstanding the disagreeable time of the Party, they are all Chearfull."

But it didn't last. Never one to suffer silently, Clark wrote on November 12, "It would be distressing to a feeling person to See our Situation at this time all wet and cold with our bedding &c. also wet, in a Cove Scercely large enough to Contain us . . . canoes at the mercy of the waves & driftwood . . . robes & leather Clothes are rotten."

November 22: "The wind increased to a Storm . . . blew with violence throwing the water of the river with emence waves out of its banks almost over whelming us in water, O! how horriable is the day."

November 27: "The wind blew with Such violence that I expected every moment to See trees taken up by the roots, Some were . . .! O how Tremendious is the day."

Since May 1804, the expedition had stopped only for winter or because the captains decided to take a couple of days' rest. They hated being immobilized by a force they could not fight. They had to be rescued by Clatsop Indians, the Chinookan people living on the south bank of the estuary, who were able to cross the estuary easily in their coastal canoes, in conditions that absolutely defeated every effort the Americans made to get out of their bad spot.* The Clatsops saved them by selling roots and fish.

On November 13, the desperate captains sent Privates Colter, Willard, and Shannon in the Indian canoe, which rode the swells better, to explore the shoreline beyond Point Ellice to see if a better campsite could be found. The next day, Colter returned, by land, to report that there was a sandy beach in the bay beyond the point, and a way inland from it, and game in the area. The captains agreed that Lewis would lead an advance party to the site while Clark arranged to move the entire camp as soon as the weather permitted.

---

* "Certain it is they are the best canoe navigators I ever Saw," Clark wrote.

The following afternoon, Lewis took advantage of a head-on wind to have five men take himself, Drouillard, and three privates around the point. The paddlers put Lewis and his party ashore on the beach and returned to the main camp, their canoe nearly swamped by the following waves breaking over it.

Finally, the impatient Lewis could do some exploring at the mouth of the river. He had a specific and immediate goal: he wanted to see if there really were some white men living on the coast. If so, and he could find their trading post, he figured to be able to use Jefferson's letter of credit to provide the expedition with ample trading goods for the return trip, and start a copy of the journals to Washington via a visiting sea captain. And of course he wanted to see the ocean.

When he set out in the morning, he found Privates Shannon and Willard in a precarious position. After separating from Colter, they had gone hunting and exploring. They had spent the night with five Chinooks, members of the tribe living on the north bank. While they slept, the Indians stole their rifles. In the morning, discovering the theft, they informed the Indians with crude but emphatic signs that a larger party of white men was about to join them and would surely shoot the thieves.

At that moment, Lewis and his small party appeared on the scene. His presence, and perhaps some threatening motions, convinced the thieves to repent. They handed back the rifles.

Lewis sent Shannon back to the sandy beach, which he correctly surmised Clark would have reached by now. The chastised Indians went with Shannon, virtual prisoners. When Clark heard Shannon's story, he exploded. "I told those Indians . . . they Should not Come near us, and if any one of their nation Stold anything from us, I would have him Shot, which they understoot verry well . . . and if any of their womin or bad boys took any thing to return it imediately and Chastise them for it."

Lewis, meanwhile, continued his exploration, rounding Cape Disappointment and going up the coastline for several miles. No trading post, no ship. He kept no journal. But he did carve his name into a tree at the extremity of Cape Disappointment with a certain sense of pride—enough, anyway, to tell Captain Clark later that he had recorded his presence.

At 1:30 p.m. on November 17, Lewis joined Clark at the camp on the sandy beach that the party would occupy for the next week (in present-day Fort Canby State Park, near McKenzie Head). It was a much-superior campsite, and the hunters could get out and bring in some meat.

On November 18, it was Clark's turn to ramble. He set out with York and ten men on a reconnaissance to Cape Disappointment, where he found Lewis's name carved in the tree. Together with the men, Clark followed Lewis's example but greatly improved on it by adding to his name and the date the magnificent line: "By Land from the U. States in 1804 & 1805."

On his return from his reconnaissance, Clark found Lewis with a group of Chinooks, including two chiefs. They all sat for a smoke. The captains handed medals and an American flag to the chiefs. Some trading was done.

One of the chiefs had on a robe made of sea-otter skins that Clark declared "more butifull than any fur I had ever Seen." Lewis agreed. In his turn, each captain tried to strike a bargain for the robe, offering different articles.

No, said the chief. He pointed at Sacagawea's belt of blue beads, the most highly prized beads of all. The captains looked at her, questioningly. She made it clear that if she had to turn over the belt she wanted something in return. One of the captains brought her a coat of blue cloth, and she handed over the belt. Clark's journal fails to say who ended up with the fur coat, but it surely wasn't Sacagawea.

The next day, an old Chinook woman appeared with six of her daughters and nieces in tow. She was selling their favors. Clark remarked, "Those people appear to view Sensuality as a Necessary evile. . . . The young females are fond of the attention of our men."

At this, their westernmost campsite, the captains again felt the urge to mark their presence. Lewis used his branding iron to mark a tree; Clark and all the men carved their names into the surrounding trees.

Meanwhile, the word had gotten out among the Clatsops that the captains would pay almost any price for sea-otter furs. That night, a group came over the estuary with two robes to sell. The captains wanted them, but the price was too high. Clark was astonished when one owner turned down the offer of a watch, a handkerchief, a bunch of red beads, and a dollar in American coin. The Indians wanted blue beads, and the captains were all but out of them. Still, the captains found they liked the Clatsops much better than their relatives the Chinooks, mainly because the Clatsops were not thieves.

That became a factor in the decision that now had to be made: where to spend the winter. The obvious requirements were good water, plenty of game, and some shelter. They had three choices: to stay where they were, to cross to the south bank to see if there was a better site there, or to go back upstream to the falls.

The Clatsops informed them that elk were plentiful on the south side. The captains were certain that their supply of beads and trinkets was so inadequate, and the Chinooks' prices were so high, that they could not get through the winter buying their food. They needed a continuing source of meat.

Lewis said that upriver the winter would be more severe, and this location would not really help them get started on the homeward voyage. They would have to wait for the snow to melt in the Bitterroots anyway, so there was plenty of time to go back up the Columbia-Snake in the spring. He wanted to get closer to the ocean, which was easier done on the south side, so that he could put men to making salt from the seawater. He and all the men craved salt.

Not Clark. He heartily disapproved, writing that he was indifferent to whether or not he had salt; anyway, "Salt water I view as an evil in as much as it is not helthy."

Lewis had a better reason than his taste buds for wanting to stay near the coast. There was at least a good chance that a trading vessel would arrive during the winter; if one did, it would solve major supply problems. Clark agreed. He also pointed out that, with elk more abundant on the south shore and deer on the north, the choice was easy: elk were bigger and easier to kill, and their skins were better for clothing.

So the captains made up their own minds, but on this occasion they decided to let everyone participate in the decision. They put it to a vote. They never explained why. Perhaps they felt that, since they were all going to be in this together, they should all have a say; maybe they just wanted to involve everyone so that none would have a right to complain.

The choices were to stay, to proceed to the falls, or to cross to and examine the other side before deciding. Naturally, the third alternative won, overwhelmingly—only Private John Shields voted against it. If the sites on the south side were unsatisfactory, about half the voters wanted to go up to the falls, half to stay at the mouth. York's vote was counted and recorded. Using Sacagawea's nickname, Clark noted, "Janey in favour of a place where there is plenty of Potas."*

This was the first vote ever held in the Pacific Northwest. It was the first time in American history that a black slave had voted, the first time a woman had voted.

On November 26, after going upriver for two days to find a shorter crossing, the party crossed to the south shore. They camped on the east

---

* Apparently she meant roots.

bank of the John Day River, and were again pinned down by bad weather. By the 29th, Lewis had had enough. He told Clark he would take their Indian canoe and round Tongue Point to examine the country where the Clatsops said there were elk. He hand-picked the men he wanted with him—Drouillard, of course, along with Privates Reubin Field, Shannon, Colter, and Labiche.

They set out early in the morning, got around the point, and made camp that night near the site of present-day Astoria, Oregon. Lewis sent out the hunters. They returned with four deer and some geese and ducks, a haul as encouraging as it was welcome. Lewis made a short journal entry, providing a bare outline of his activities, as he would do the next two days as well. Clark wrote on the last page of Lewis's writings, "Capt. Lewis rough notes when he left Capt. Clark near the mouth of Columbia for a few days to examine the S.W. side."[4]

Lewis set out at sunrise to explore Youngs Bay (so named by Lieutenant Broughton of Vancouver's expedition). Finding nothing satisfactory at the outlet of Youngs River, he went up today's Lewis and Clark River about a mile, and was discouraged. Lewis returned to the bay, hoping to find some Clatsops, "who have tantilized us with there being much game in their neighbourhood," to ask them where that game was. All about him, they might have answered—there were great numbers of brants, geese, sandhill cranes, and blue herons, and a large variety and immense number of ducks in the bay. But of course Lewis wanted elk. In his field notes that night, he recorded botanical data.

Over the next couple of days, he explored, this time going farther up the Lewis and Clark River, where he found his spot. He told Clark it was on a small bluff rising some thirty feet higher than the high-tide mark, some two hundred feet back from the river, and about three miles up from its mouth. It was near a spring, and there were plenty of big trees that could be used to make shelter and a fort. It was but a few miles to the open ocean, where salt could be made. Best of all, it promised good hunting: Drouillard and another hunter had killed six elk and five deer.

Clark reported that "this was verry Satisfactory information to all the party." The expedition made ready to move to its winter quarters as soon as the wind would allow it to round the point to get into the bay and then up the river. On December 6 the wind was too high, but the following morning Lewis guided the expedition to the site of what the captains would call Fort Clatsop. Clark took one look and pronounced it a "most eligable Situation."

26

FORT CLATSOP

December 8, 1805–March 23, 1806

On the morning of December 8, Clark set out to find the best route to the ocean and to find a place for a salt-making camp.* Lewis sent out the hunters and put the remainder of the party to work cutting down trees (probably grand fir) to make huts and a palisade. When Clark returned from a successful reconnaissance three days later, Lewis was still cutting trees. Not until December 14 did he have enough for the men to start splitting logs. They found that the wood split beautifully, even to the width of two feet and more. The first hut they commenced building was a smokehouse; they were finding that the preservation of meat in that rainy climate required extraordinary measures.

The work went slowly. It always rained, sometimes worse than others. On December 16, Clark recorded, "The winds violent. Trees falling in every derection, whorl winds, with gusts of rain Hail & Thunder, this kind of weather lasted all day. Certainly one of the worst days that ever was!"

Many of the men were sick or injured. Some had tumors. Private William Werner had a strained knee. Private Joseph Field had boils. Private George Gibson had dysentery. Sergeant Nathaniel Pryor had a dislocated shoulder. York suffered from "Cholick & gripeing." And the

---

* The method was to boil seawater in five large kettles until it evaporated, then scrape the sides for the salt. The requirements were a place where the salt-makers had ready access to saltwater and to wood for the fires, as well as enough game in the area to sustain them.

fleas, picked up from the Indians and inescapable, tormented their nights and prevented a sound sleep.

Entertaining and trading with visiting Indians took time. On December 12, the chief of a neighboring Clatsop village, named Coboway, paid a visit. The captains gave him the usual medal and traded for roots. Lewis purchased two lynx skins, Clark two otter skins. Prices were reasonable one day, outrageous the next. On December 23, Clark purchased a panther skin nearly eight feet long for six small fishhooks, a worn-out file, and some spoiled fish. The next day, a young chief named Cuscalah came with his brother and two women. They wanted to sell a parcel of roots but demanded two files for them, which the captains decided was too high a price.

Cuscalah then offered a woman to each captain, "which we also declined axcpting," Clark wrote, "which also displeased them. . . . the female part appeared to be highly disgusted at our refuseing of their favours &c."

Despite the daily interruptions, the work went forward. By December 17, enough of the walls of the huts were up so some of the men could begin filling the chinks between the logs. A week later, they were putting on the roofs. The captains moved into their unfinished hut on December 23; the next day, Private Joseph Field made writing tables for them, and the men moved into their as-yet-unroofed huts.

Fort Clatsop was about fifty feet square. It had two long, facing structures joined on the sides by palisaded walls. There was a main gate at the front and a smaller one at the rear that provided easy access to a spring some thirty yards distant. Between the buildings there was a parade ground about fifty feet by twenty feet. One of the structures was divided into three rooms, or huts, which served as enlisted men's quarters. The other contained four rooms: one for the captains; one for Charbonneau, Sacagawea, and their son, Jean Baptiste; one to serve as an orderly room; and the fourth the smokehouse. *

At first light on Christmas morning, 1805, the men woke the captains with a volley, a shout, and a song. They exchanged presents—Private Whitehouse gave Captain Clark a pair of moccasins he had made, Private Silas Goodrich gave him a woven basket, Sacagawea gave him two dozen white weasel tails, and Captain Lewis gave him a vest, drawers, and socks. The captains divided the small quantity of tobacco they had left, keeping one part for use with the Indians and dividing the

---

* The fort has been re-created today by the National Park Service, on the site.

other among the men who smoked. The eight nonsmokers each got a handkerchief.

The celebration didn't last long. It was a wet and disagreeable day, and, as Clark recorded, "We would have Spent this day the nativity of Christ in feasting, had we any thing either to raise our Sperits or even gratify our appetites, our Diner concisted of pore Elk, So much Spoiled that we eate it thro' mear necessity, Some Spoiled pounded fish and a fiew roots."

Three days later, the captains decided they could spare a small party of salt-makers. The party left for the camp just south of present-day Seaside, Oregon,* and went to work. On December 29, the Clatsops informed the captains that a whale had foundered on the coast near Tillamook Head. Lewis at once determined to go there by water to get some oil and blubber. He prepared a party to take the canoes to fetch it, but for the next week the wind was too high to risk setting out.

On December 30, the fort was completed. At sunset, the captains told the Clatsops that from now on, when darkness fell, the gates would be shut and they must all get out of the fort. "Those people who are verry foward and disegreeable," Clark reported, "left the huts with reluctiance." But on New Year's Eve, he was happy to record that the Indians were much better behaved. "The Sight of our Sentinal who walks on his post, has made this reform in those people who but yesterday was verry impertenant and disagreeable to all."

At dawn on New Year's Day, 1806, the men woke the captains with a volley and shouts of "Happy New Year!" There was no other celebration, and no feast. Lewis wrote that "we were content with eating our boiled Elk and wappetoe [roots], and solacing our thirst with our only bevereage *pure water.*"

During the more than three weeks the party had been building Fort Clatsop, Lewis wrote but two field notes, describing in some detail Steller's jay. But on January 1, he resumed making daily entries in his journal. He opened with a complaint, that the volley fired by the men to usher in the New Year "was the only mark of rispect which we had it in our power to pay this celebrated day, our repast of this day [was no] better than that of Christmass."

But after the first sentence, he wrote with a zest that seemed to indicate that a great weight had been lifted from him. It was 1806—he would be home this year. A year wasn't such a long time.

---

* The camp today has a small marker and a replica of the kettles and fireplaces. It usually had a three-man crew and over the winter produced three or four bushels of salt.

Evidently not until he began writing about getting home did Lewis realize how much he missed civilization. He had spent 1801–3 living with Thomas Jefferson in the President's House. His daily conversational fare had ranged from practical politics to the nature of man, from zoology to botany, geography to medicine, literature to history, all in the company of the leading cultural, intellectual, scientific, and political figures in the United States (and not a few from Europe). For two years, he had danced to the best music, dined at the finest table, drunk the choicest wine.

He had spent 1804–5 on the frontier and beyond. His daily conversational fare had been about immediate, practical problems, mostly with enlisted men who had little if any formal education. With Clark he could discuss scientific matters, natural history, geography, and other subjects, but Clark was more a Kentuckian than a Virginian, more a frontier soldier than a polished member of the president's staff. Even with Clark the flow of the talk had its limits.

Now, with the coming of the New Year, Lewis could dream of returning to Washington, Charlottesville, Philadelphia, civilization. The thought released him from his lethargy. He wrote with enthusiasm about how much he anticipated "the 1st day of January 1807, when in the bosom of our friends we hope to participate in the mirth and hilarity of the day. . . . We shall completely, both mentally and corporally, enjoy the repast which the hand of civilization has prepared for us." The anticipation was made all the keener by the thought that he would be able to draw on "the recollection of the present" to be the center of attention, telling around the table the story of the crossing of the continent. It was a prospect delicious to dream about.

So, on January 1, 1806, with winter quarters completed, his face and his mind turned east.

But first he had to get through the winter. After recording that the men had given him and Clark fresh elk marrowbone and tongue for a New Year's dinner, and noting his worry about two missing enlisted men who had apparently lost their way returning from the salt-making site, and with the fortification completed, he wrote out a detailed order "for the more exact and uniform dicipline and government of the garrison."

The order was precise. It was based on principles established at U.S. Army frontier fortifications over the past thirty years, principles that had been learned by the experience of living as a platoon-sized party in the midst of potentially hostile Indians. First, as was habitual with the expedition, there would be a sergeant-of-the-guard and three privates always on duty in the orderly room. Second, "the centinel shall be posted, both day and night, on the parade [ground] in front of the commanding offercers quarters." If at any time the sentinel thought it necessary to go to any other part of the fort "in order the better to inform himself of the desighns or approach of any party of savages, he is not only at liberty, but is hereby required to do so." It was also his duty to inform the sergeant-of-the-guard of the arrival of any party of Indians, and the sergeant's duty to report the same to the captains immediately.

Lewis ordered the men "to treat the natives in a friendly manner." Nor were they "permitted at any time, to abuse, assault or strike them," unless the natives started a fight. The soldiers were allowed to put out of his room "any native who may become troublesome to him." If the Indian refused to go, or made trouble, the sergeant-of-the-guard should take over. He was authorized to "imploy such coercive measures (not extending to the taking of life) as shall at his discretion be deemed necessary."

If an Indian was caught stealing, the sergeant should immediately inform the captains, who would take it from there. In this, as elsewhere, Lewis made certain that the lines of authority and the decision-making power were absolutely fixed.

All Indians were to be out of the fort at sunset except those the captains might specially permit to spend the night. Both gates should be shut and secured overnight.

The sergeant-of-the-guard would keep the key to the meat house, and see that regular fires burned as needed. He should visit the canoes each day to make sure they were safely secured. He should report to the captains in person upon being relieved.

The huts had their own cooks, kettles, and fires. The captains furnished each mess with an ax to provide firewood. All other "public tools" deposited in the captains' quarters could only be taken with their permission, and must be returned immediately after they were used. This was to prevent the men from falling into temptation and trading an awl or a file for sexual favors or furs. Lewis was explicit on the point: "Any individual selling or disposing of any tool or iron or steel instrument, arms, accoutrements or ammunicion, shall be deemed guilty of a breach of this order, and shall be tryed and punished accordingly." He exempted gunsmith John Shields from the restriction.

Discipline, order, regularity. Security. Peace with the neighbors if at all possible. These were Lewis's goals, as they have been the goals of

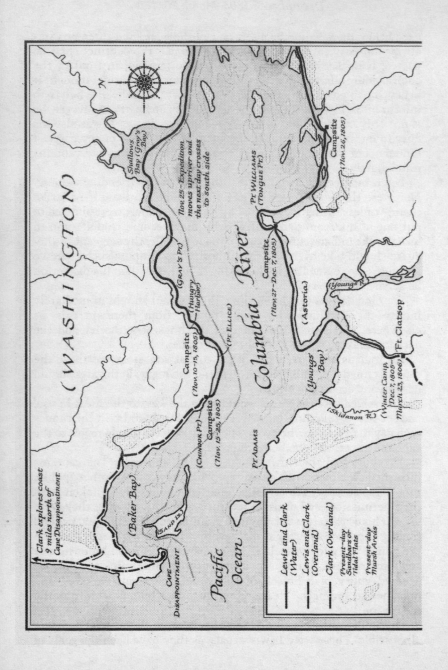

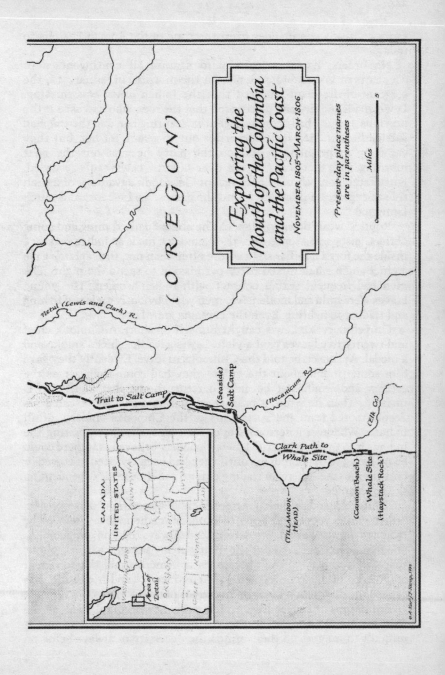

Exploring the
Mouth of the Columbia
and the Pacific Coast

NOVEMBER 1805–MARCH 1806

Present-day place names
are in parentheses

Miles

(OREGON)

Netul (Lewis and Clark) R.

Trail to Salt Camp

(Seaside)
Salt Camp

(Necanicum R.)

Clark Path to
Whale Site

(TILLAMOOK
HEAD)

(Cannon Beach)

Whale Site

(Haystack Rock)

(Elk Cr.)

CANADA
UNITED STATES

Area of Detail

every company commander from the time of the Roman Legions to today.

No orders, however, can guard against all contingencies or accidents or just stupid actions. On the morning of January 11, the sergeant-of-the-guard reported that the Indian canoe was missing. Lewis made inquiry and discovered that the men who had used it the previous evening had been negligent in securing her, and the tide had carried her off. He sent two parties out to search for her, but they came up empty-handed. So too the party he sent out the next morning. "We therefore give her over as lost," Lewis sadly recorded. Fortunately, on February 5, Sergeant Gass took advantage of a high tide to explore an inlet and found the canoe, "so long lost and much lamented."

Routine wears down vigilance. The almost daily coming and going of the Clatsops, and sometimes the Chinooks, made an Indian presence inside the fort a familiar sight. More often than not, the captains gave a chief and a small mixed party permission to spend the night. The men had frequent sexual contact with Indian women. The young braves were mild and inoffensive, men who obviously preferred fishing and trading to fighting. Even the captains grew lax.

On February 20, Lewis caught himself up short. A Chinook chief and twenty-five braves paid a visit. Lewis gave the chief a smoke and a medal. At sunset, he told the Chinooks to leave. Evidently they gave him some trouble about the order—they had come from across the estuary and would not be able to return home that night. Lewis insisted. Then he wrote a passage of justification that revealed his deeply rooted fears and suspicions of the Chinooks—indeed, of all Indians. Whatever Jefferson's hopes for eventually incorporating the Indians into the body politic, Lewis obviously believed that there could be no living with the Indians until they had been civilized or cowed or brought into the American trading empire and thus made dependent on the government.[1]

"Notwithstanding their apparent friendly disposition," Lewis wrote, "their great averice and hope of plunder might induce them to be treacherous. at all events we determined allways to be on our guard . . . and never place our selves at the mercy of any savages. we well know, that the treachery of the aborigenes of America and the too great confidence of our countrymen in their sincerity and friendship, has caused the distruction of many hundreds of us."

But despite the clear lesson of history, Lewis complained, as the men became accustomed to the visiting coastal Indians, "we find it difficult to impress on their minds the necessity of always being on their guard." Lewis believed that "the well known treachery of the natives by no means entitle them to such confidence," and caught himself up short with the realization that he too had become lax. So, he told himself, as for confidence in the peaceful intentions of the Indian visitors, "we must check it's growth in our own minds, as well as those of our men, by recollecting ourselves, and repeating to our men, that our preservation depends on never loosing sight of this trait [treachery] in their character, and being always prepared to meet it in whatever shape it may present itself."

James Ronda protests that Lewis was too extreme. He writes that Lewis's attitude, with its familiar themes of native treachery and brutality, was more suited to the Kentucky and Ohio frontier of the 1790s than to the coastal Indians of 1806.[2] Perhaps so. And perhaps the captains could have done more to establish good relations with the Chinooks, as Ronda suggests. But had Lewis heard such criticism he could have replied, We encouraged our suspicions, did security by the book, and had no trouble.

As in many frontier fortifications, life at Fort Clatsop was almost unbearably dull. Unlike most frontier garrisons, the fort suffered only one minor breach of discipline. Partly this was because the garrison was so small, partly because the men had been through so much together (and had so much more coming up), partly because they had no whiskey. No fistfights or similar troubles relieved the routine.

"Nothing worthy of note today," Lewis wrote in his journal, day after day. With one or two exceptions, his entries recorded the comings and goings and successes or failures of the hunters, the health of the men, the diet, trading sessions with the Clatsops—more often than not unsuccessful—and nothing else.

The weather was depressing at best. Fixing latitude and longitude exactly would have provided some diversion and a sense of accomplishment, but it couldn't be done. For the entire first month in the fort, Lewis was unable to make a single observation. "I am mortifyed," he wrote on February 25, 1806, "at not having it in my power to make more celestial observations since we have been at Fort Clatsop, but such has been the state of the weather that I have found it utterly impracticable."

The men had sex for diversion, but from all the evidence the captains did not. The men paid the price for their activity, not only in beads or trinkets but also by contracting venereal disease. Lewis was their doctor. "Goodrich has recovered from the Louis veneri [syphilis] which he contracted from an amorous contact with a Chinook damsel," Lewis wrote on January 27. "I cured him as I did Gibson last winter by the uce of murcury."*

Lewis was an attentive doctor. When Private Gibson came down with a violent cold, so severe it incapacitated him, Lewis first listed the cause (the constant rain, wading through streams and marshes, always wet), second the patient's condition ("nearly free from pain"), third the patient's appearance ("a gooddeel reduced and very languid"), and fourth the drug and physical therapy he prescribed ("broken dozes of diluted nitre [saltpeter] and made him drink plentifully of sage tea, had his feet bathed in warm water and at 9 P.M. gave him 35 drops of laudanum").

At Fort Mandan, the men's health had been a minor problem. At Fort Clatsop, the men's health was a major worry. There was always someone down with a cold or a flu or a venereal-disease attack or a strained muscle. On February 22, Lewis noted that there were five men in the sick bay—17 percent of the total strength—and commented, "We have not had as many sick at any one time since we left Wood River. The general complaint seams to be bad colds and fevers, something I beleive of the influenza."

On March 20, as the party was preparing to leave, Lewis noted, "many of our men are still complaining of being unwell; [they] remain weak, principally I beleive for the want of proper food." He rightly figured that, along with the diet, the weather was the cause. Unfortunately, there was nothing that Dr. Lewis could do for his patients to improve their food or the climate.

For the Clatsops and Chinooks, neither the weather nor the diet had an adverse effect. To the contrary. They were thriving tribes before the smallpox hit them, still vibrant when Lewis and Clark came to spend the winter. With few enemies and fewer wars, they were rich, enjoying an abundance of fish and furs and first access to European trade goods. They loved the food and the climate, had perfectly adjusted to them, and rightly thought of the Pacific Northwest as a bountiful provider, almost paradise.

To the captains and the men, it was a miserable place that they

---

* Gary Moulton points out that Lewis's apparent cure was temporary only. Six months later, Goodrich and McNeal were exhibiting symptoms of the secondary stage of the disease. Both men died young, as did many of the expedition veterans. It is possible that Lewis's heroic doses of mercury, dispensed so freely at the first sign of venereal disease, contributed to or even caused those early deaths—although Moulton declares it would be "unwise" to make such a conclusion. (*Journals*, vol. 6, p. 242.)

couldn't wait to get out of. Lewis expressed one major reason for that point of view: "I expect when we get under way we shall be much more healthy. it has always had that effect on us heretofore."

Fort Clatsop was almost more a prison than a fortification. The men not out hunting spent their days at hard labor, scraping elk hides and making moccasins (ten per man for the return trip), keeping the fire going in the smokehouse (difficult at best, because the timber was wet and only smoldered instead of smoking properly), and carrying out other tasks that they regarded as women's work and resented or even hated.

Lewis supervised the work. He made no recorded excursion from the fort. His boredom is evident in some of his journal entries.

February 2: "Not any occurrence today worthy of notice; but all are pleased, that one month of the time which binds us to Fort Clatsop and which seperates us from our friends has now elapsed."

March 3: "every thing moves on in the old way and we are counting the days which seperate us from the 1st of April [the scheduled departure date] and which bind us to fort Clatsop."

The food at Fort Clatsop contributed to the monotony. Getting enough of it was a daily worry for Lewis, getting some variety into the diet almost impossible. The expedition lived on elk. Over their more than three months on the coast the hunters killed 131 elk, along with 20 deer, a few beaver and otter, and a raccoon.[3] Drouillard was the most productive, sometimes killing a half-dozen or more elk in a day. On January 12, Lewis wrote that Drouillard had killed seven elk that day and commented, "I scarcely know how we should subsist were it not for the exertions of this excellent hunter."

Despite Drouillard's success, not enough game was coming in to feed the party. The captains supplemented the meat with dried fish and roots purchased from the Clatsops. It is odd that the captains, after their experience of doing so well fishing in the Missouri River, seldom if ever sent out fishermen. And apparently, despite the high prices charged by the Indians and the nearly spent supply of trade goods, no man—nor Sacagawea—ever went out to dig roots. Hunters sometimes brought back berries.

Occasionally the captains were able to purchase dogs. A good thing too, Lewis believed: "while we lived principally on the flesh of this anamal we were much more healthy strong and more fleshey than we had been since we left the Buffaloe country." Fortunately, the men were extremely fond of the dog meat; "for my own part," Lewis commented, "I have become so perfectly reconciled to the dog that I think it an agreeable food and would prefer it vastly to lean Venison or Elk."

Within a day of Lewis's resumption of journal writing, Clark had established a practice of copying Lewis's journal verbatim. He continued that practice as long as Lewis kept writing. But on this entry, of January 3, Clark made one change: "as for my own part," he concluded the entry on dog meat, "I have not become reconsiled to the taste of this animal as yet."

One of the captains' other differences of opinion also concerned food. On January 5, the salt-makers brought in a sample of their product. "We found it excellent, fine, strong, & white," Lewis wrote. "This was a great treat to myself and most of the party. . . . I say most of the party, for my friend Capt. Clark declares it to be a mear matter of indifference with him whether he uses it or not; for myself I must confess I felt a considerable inconvenience from the want of it."

Clark copied the passage, then added as an explanation, "I care but little [about salt] . . . haveing from habit become entirely cearless about my diat."

Lewis remarked that he didn't care what kind of meat he got, whether elk or dog or horse or wolf, so long as it was fat. "I have learned to think," he wrote, "that if the chord be sufficiently strong, which binds the soul and body together, it does not so much matter about the materials which compose it."

The cord that bound body and soul together at Fort Clatsop was made of elk. At breakfast and supper, day after day, it was boiled elk, dried and jerked elk, leftover elk from the previous meal, more elk. When there was fresh elk that could be roasted, the men gorged themselves.

But the meat was seldom fresh, because the hunters had to extend their range though the winter, and by mid-January the kills were taking place miles from the fort. Men had to go out to bring in the meat, which sometimes took days.

There often wasn't enough meat at all. Because the men devoured the fresh meat so prodigiously, Lewis worried about a steady supply. He ordered that all the meat would hereafter be jerked, then was surprised when it turned out they ate the jerky at a prodigious rate also. On January 20, there was only three days' supply on hand. But, he wrote, "no one seems much concerned about the state of the stores; so much for habit. we have latterly so frequently had our stock of provisions reduced to a minimum and sometimes taken a small touch of fasting that three days full allowance excites no concern."

Anyway, Lewis wrote, "our skill as hunters afford us some

consolation, for if there is any game of any discription in our neighbourhood we can track it up and kill it."

Lewis tried to be charitable to elk. He noted on January 29 that he was enjoying "the most perfect health . . . on this food." And after all it wasn't so bad: "a keen appetite supplys in a great degree the want of more luxurious sauses or dishes, and still render my ordinary meals not uninteresting to me, for I find myself sometimes enquiring of the cook whether dinner or breakfast is ready."

One welcome change in diet came on January 10. Four days earlier, Clark had set out in canoes with a party of eleven to find the whale that had washed ashore south of the salt camp. (Lewis had proposed to lead a party himself, earlier; why Clark took over, Lewis doesn't say.) Among the party was Sacagawea. In a charming passage, Lewis explained how she got to go along: "The Indian woman was very impotunate to be permited to go, and was therefore indulged; she observed that she had traveled a long way with us to see the great waters, and that now that monstrous fish was also to be seen, she thought it very hard she could not be permitted to see either. . . ."

When Clark returned, he brought back three hundred pounds of blubber and a few gallons of rendered oil. He had hoped for much more, but the carcass had been stripped by the time he arrived, and he had to buy what he got from the natives.

Despite Clark's disappointment, Lewis was more than satisfied. After eating, he felt so good he ventured a small joke.

"Small as the store is," he wrote, "we prize it highly, and thank the hand of providence for directing the whale to us, and think him much more kind to us than he was to jonah, having sent this monster to be *swallowed by us* in stead of *swallowing of us* as jona's did."

But soon the whale blubber and oil were gone. It was back to elk. Lewis wrote on February 7: "This evening we had what I call an excellent supper it consisted of a marrowbone a piece and a brisket of boiled Elk that had the appearance of a little fat on it. this for Fort Clatsop is living in high stile."

Toward the end of February, the eulachon, or candlefish, began to run in immense numbers. The Clatsops netted them and sold them to the expedition, after showing them how to prepare the fish (which Lewis called "anchovy"). Each eulachon was about seven inches long; the Clatsop method was to string them together on a wooden spit and roast them. "They are so fat," Lewis found, "they require no additional sauce, and I think them superior to any fish I ever tasted."

From then until they left, the captains bought all the eulachon they could afford.

Supervising the men's work and trading with the Indians took up only a part of Lewis's time. He spent much of each day at his desk, in his damp, chilly, smoky quarters, with only a candle for illumination, writing in his journal. It was an almost monklike existence. But he thrived on scholarship, and most of what he wrote was scientific. The subjects were botany, zoology, geography, and ethnology. Lewis's great outpouring during the Fort Clatsop winter constituted an invaluable contribution to knowledge.

Botany was the subject he wrote the most about, partly because of the astonishing growth of trees and plants on the Northwest Pacific Coast, partly because it was Jefferson's favorite scientific study.

Jefferson considered Lewis a better zoologist than botanist. Lewis agreed with that judgment. On February 4, 1806, writing about the fir trees in the vicinity of Fort Clatsop, he apologized by saying, "I shall discribe [them] as well as my slender botanicall skil will enable me." But he was skillful enough in both fields to provide descriptions of dozens of previously unknown plants and animals so accurate and complete that modern-day botanists and zoologists have little difficulty in recognizing the species.

Only rarely did Lewis use Latin-derived taxonomic botanical words, but his range of knowledge included at least two hundred technical botanical terms in English. At Fort Clatsop, he discovered and described in great detail (often hundreds of words) ten new plants and trees, including the magnificent Sitka spruce. He collected, labeled, and preserved to bring home to Jefferson dozens of plants, leaves, and cones. He demonstrated familiarity with their eastern counterparts by consistently comparing what he was seeing on the West Coast with what he remembered from the East Coast.[4]

Jefferson had ordered Lewis to observe "the animals of the country generally, & especially those not known in the U.S." Lewis faithfully obeyed. During that winter, he wrote about some hundred animals altogether—thirty-five mammals, fifty birds, ten reptiles and fish, and five invertebrates. Of these, eleven birds, two fish, and eleven mammals were new to science. In his classic study *Lewis and Clark: Pioneering Naturalists*, Paul Russell Cutright points out that, though Lewis used a minimum of technical words in his description of new birds, "he nevertheless supplied adequate data on color, shape of wings, number and length of tail feathers, color of iris, and note."[5]

Lewis also provided detailed descriptions of how things were done, ranging from Indian methods of preparing fish and roots to the making of canoes. On January 7, when Drouillard brought in a fat beaver (most welcome as food), Lewis asked him how the castor, or bait, was prepared for the traps. He used over five hundred words to describe the process as Drouillard explained it to him. You could prepare castor and place it correctly on a trap today from Lewis's description.

Some of Lewis's portraits were of animals he had encountered in the mountains, not native to the lower Columbia; for example, he wrote about Franklin's grouse, which, he said, he had not seen since leaving the mountains. This was another indication that he had not written in his journal while crossing the Nez Percé trail.

Jefferson has been criticized for not sending a trained naturalist on the expedition. Donald Jackson will have none of that. "If a botanist," he asks, "why not also a zoologist and perhaps a geologist? Later the government could send out such specialists; now the problem was to get a few men to the Pacific and back, encumbered no more than necessary by equipment, and intelligent enough to recognize and collect—but not necessarily to evaluate—the natural resources of the region."[6]

Cutright goes further. "Lewis was blessed with capabilities often missing in naturalists, particularly an outstanding, inherent observational competence, an all-inclusive interest, and an objective, systematic, philosophical approach to understanding the natural world. Nothing refutes Lewis's self-appraisal [as a botanist], and deprecating remarks of others, more eloquently than his own abundant writing. . . . In the context of the day, Lewis was an unusually capable naturalist, one with an attitude more consistent with scientists of the twentieth century than with those of his own."[7]

While Lewis described birds, plants, animals, and methods, Clark worked on his map, covering the country from Fort Mandan to Fort Clatsop. On February 11, he finished the work, an invaluable contribution to the world's knowledge. Together with his previous map of the lower Missouri, it brought the American West together for the first time.

The map was Clark's work, but the implications of it were a subject of intense discussion between the captains. For two months, they talked about what they had seen for themselves and learned from the Indians. The result, in the opinion of geographer John Logan Allen, was "the most important product of their winter on the Pacific."[8]

"We now discover," Lewis wrote on February 14, after three days of going over the completed map with Clark, "that we have found the most practicable and navigable passage across the Continent of North America."

That note, almost triumphant, hid a deep disappointment. The real headline news from the Lewis and Clark Expedition was that there was no all-water route across the continent. The short portage from the Missouri to the Columbia did not exist. "This negation of the Passage to India," Allen writes, "the feature of all images of the American Northwest since Marquette, was the greatest single transformation of geographical lore for which the journey of Lewis and Clark was responsible."[9]

The best route fell far short of Jefferson's hopes. That was the answer Lewis was going to have to give to the first question Jefferson would ask when they met next year.

Beyond his personal feelings, Jefferson would have to pay a political price. With the Sioux blocking the Missouri, and with no all-water route across the continent, the Federalists would have a peg upon which to ridicule the Louisiana Purchase.

At Fort Clatsop, Lewis started practicing how he would present the news. That business about the best route made for a positive start. He went on to claim that, just as Jefferson had anticipated, the best route was up the Missouri and down the Columbia, the route the expedition had followed (except for the two shortcuts from the Missouri, at the Gates of the Mountains and at the Great Falls, which the Shoshones and Nez Percé had told the captains about; these they intended to explore on the return trip). As for crossing the Bitterroot Mountains, Lewis explained that Indian information convinced him it would not be possible to go north or south to find a better passage than the Nez Percé trail. He recorded without comment that it was a distance of 184 miles.

Not much of a best route, but the reality of geography could not be wished away. In a little-known letter dated September 29, 1806,* Lewis came a bit closer to recognizing that reality than he had in his Fort Clatsop entry. In it he wrote that he had "no hesitation to say & declar" that the expedition had been "completely successful" in

---

* Written by Lewis in the form of a summary report, apparently given by Lewis to Mr. John Hay for copying and distribution. Hay was a businessman and minor civil official in St. Louis who had been of considerable help in packing for the expedition. Lewis liked and respected him and later recommended him for a federal post. It appears that Hay made several copies of the long document, and they got a wide distribution. For details, see Jackson, *Letters*, vol. I, pp. 156–57, 343.

discovering "the most practicable Route," but then added the crucial qualifier, "such as Nature has permitted."[10]

For the men of the Enlightenment, there was no arguing with nature. Surely Jefferson would be unhappy with the end of his dream, but still glad to know the truth. And the truth was that Jefferson would have to put out of his mind forever any comparison between the Rocky Mountains and the Appalachians.

Sitting on his rough-hewn stool at his rough-hewn desk at Fort Clatsop, Lewis could imagine sitting in the drawing room at the President's House, reporting to Jefferson. He could imagine Jefferson taking in the news, nodding, accepting the fact, and already beginning to think of how to deal with the newly discovered reality.

Lewis could suppose that, after getting some details, Jefferson might well ask about the commercial possibilities. Could Americans establish a trading post at the mouth of the Columbia and take over from the British the fabulously profitable fur trade with the Orient? Lewis was working on a plan to bring that about, but it had not yet matured. He revealed one part of it, however, by noting that the abundance and cheapness of horses among the natives on both sides of the mountains "will be extremely advantageous to those who may hereafter attemt the fir trade to the East Indies by way of the Columbia river and the Pacific Ocean."

The length and difficulty of the portage over that route could be overcome with readily available horses from tribes that had no contact with the British. He gave a census of the horse holdings of the Shoshone, the Nez Percé, and other tribes, "all of whom enjoy the bennefit of that docile, generous and valuable anamal the horse."

The British had to take their furs out the St. Lawrence and on to London before they could begin the voyage to the Indies. If only a man could figure out how to get a trading post established on the Columbia, and a way to get the furs from the Canadian and the American Great Plains to it, American businessmen would have a one-year advantage over their British rivals. Lewis continued to think about that larger problem.

But there would be no person-to-person report to Jefferson if Lewis did not get himself and his party home. He prepared accordingly. He checked the supplies, especially the rifles and ammunition, "now our only hope for subsistence and defence in a rout of 4000 miles through a country exclusively inhabited by savages." He found there was more than enough and congratulated himself on having come up with "that happy expedient which I devised of securing the powder by means of the lead." The lead canisters had been through many adventures but were "little dammaged." The powder was dry. Moccasins were being made. The rifles were all in order, thanks to John Shields's skills.

Lewis had determined to stay at Fort Clatsop until April 1, but on March 5 he indicated he wanted to move the date forward. For one thing, like everyone else, he wanted to get out of the place. For another, the elk were farther away than ever, making life even more difficult.

By mid-March, Lewis had fixed March 20 as departure day. It came and went—the wind blew so violently the Americans dared not attempt the river in their canoes. Still, Lewis used the occasion to say goodbye to Fort Clatsop. His statement was objective and philosophical, and had just a bit of nostalgia to it: "Altho' we have not fared sumptuously this winter at Fort Clatsop, we have lived quite as comfortably as we had any reason to expect we should; and have accomplished every object which induced our remaining at this place. . . ."

In making the preparations for departure, Lewis set out to purchase a couple of native canoes to use in going up the river as far as the lowest falls. On March 14, he bargained with a Clatsop over "an indifferent canoe," but Lewis thought the price was "more than our stock of merchandize would lisence us. I offered him my laced uniform coat but he would not exchange."

The expedition was desperately poor, almost broke. "Two handkercheifs would not contain all the small articles of merchandize which we possess," Lewis lamented on March 16. "The ballance of the stock consists of 6 blue robes . . . one uniform artillerists's coat and hat, five robes made of our large flag," and a bit of ribbon.

"On this stock," he realized, "we have wholy to depend for the purchase of horses and such portion of our subsistence from the Indians as it will be in our powers to obtain."

Thinking it over, he added, "A scant dependence indeed, for a tour of the distance of that before us."

But there wouldn't be any crossing of the mountains if the party couldn't get to the falls of the Columbia first, and to get there Lewis needed Indian canoes. On March 17, he sent Drouillard with his prized coat to pay the price demanded by the Indian owner of the canoe he wanted. He complained in his journal that the Indians valued their canoes too highly, and noted, "I think the U' States are indebted to me another Uniform coat, for that of which I have disposed on this occasion was but little woarn."

His poverty and his great need for another canoe put him in a foul and desperate mood. He made a decision and came up with a rationalization to justify it: "We yet want another canoe, and as the Clatsops will not sell us one at a price which we can afford to give we will take one of them in lue of the six Elk which they stole from us in the winter." He did not point out that the Clatsops had paid for the stolen elk, with dogs.

On March 18, the deed was done. Lewis did not record it, but Sergeant Ordway noted in his journal that four men went "over to the prarie near the coast" and took a canoe, "as we are in want of it." When they got it back to the fort, they found that Chief Coboway was visiting, so they hid it. Lewis admitted that the deception of Coboway "set a little awkward," but he covered his crime by giving the chief "a cirtificate of his good conduct and the friendly intercourse which he has maintained with us during our residence at this place."

James Ronda rightly characterizes this as "a particularly sordid tale of deception and friendship betrayed . . . at worst criminal and at best a terrible lapse of judgment. . . . The essential honesty that distinguished Lewis and Clark from explorers like Hernando DeSoto and Francisco Pizarro had been tarnished."[11]

Lewis felt he had no choice. Perhaps he was right. Perhaps the expedition's poverty did preclude purchase. Surely the Clatsops would have taken a rifle and some ammunition and powder for a canoe, but giving a rifle to a native would have involved a violation of an absolute rule—just as stealing a canoe did. Lewis chose to steal.

During Coboway's March 18 visit, Lewis had given him (with copies to other chiefs who visited that day) a list of the names of the men in the Corps of Discovery. He posted another copy in his quarters, explaining in a preamble that "the object of this list is, that through the medium of some civilized person who may see the same, it may be made known to the informed world, that the party consisting of the persons [named], and who were sent out by the government of the U' States in May 1804 to explore the interior of the Continent of North America, did penetrate the same . . . [to] the Pacific Ocean." On the back of the lists Clark added a sketched map of the Missouri and Columbia.

Lewis felt that the chances that a copy of the journals would get from the Clatsops to a trading vessel and then on to Washington were too small to take the risk. Likewise Jefferson's idea of sending one or two men home on a trading vessel with a copy of the journals and reports. "Our party are also too small to think of leaving any of them to return to the U'States by sea," Lewis wrote, "particularly as we shall be necessarily divided into three or four parties on our return in order to accomplish the objects [exploration of alternative routes] we have in view." Anyway, it was highly unlikely that a trader who had to go around the world to reach the East Coast of the United States could get there before the captains arrived. And there were no ships in the area; leaving two men to wait on the chance that one would arrive soon was not practical.

On March 22, the storm began to slack off, and the party prepared to push off in the morning. That day, Coboway paid a parting visit. Lewis gave him "our houses and funiture," a generous gesture even if he had no other option. He wrote of Coboway, in whose canoe he was about to depart, "He has been much more kind an hospitable to us than any other indian in this neighbourhood."

Then came the last words he wrote during his long wet winter at Fort Clatsop. Appropriately, they were botanical: "The leafing of the hucklebury riminds us of spring." Spring in Virginia, that is, where he intended to be when the leaves started to come out in 1807.

27

LEWIS AS ETHNOGRAPHER

The Clatsops and the Chinooks

Important as Lewis's biological and Clark's geographical work at Fort Clatsop was, Lewis's ethnological studies were even more valuable, because the plants and animals and the rivers and mountains they described in such painstaking detail are, mostly, still with us, but the coastal Indians are not. Badly depleted by two smallpox epidemics in the decades before Lewis and Clark arrived, the Clatsops and Chinooks and their relatives were decimated by an epidemic of malaria in 1825–26. The handful of survivors mingled with whites and lost much of their culture. Within a generation of the winter of 1805–6, the once-flourishing Chinookan family had almost ceased to exist. Lewis gave the world the first and by far the fullest description of this tribe.[1]

He did his ethnology on a daily basis, using his ears, eyes, and tongue. He made a vocabulary. He described what he saw. And he spent hours interviewing Clatsops and Chinooks about their way of life.

The conversations were difficult. The sign language of the Plains Indians was inadequate on the Pacific Coast, the Americans learned few Chinookan words, and the natives had only some bits and pieces of English. Lewis recorded on January 9, 1806, that they used such words as "musquit, powder, shot, nife, file, damned rascal, sun of a bitch &c." That wasn't much. There was no Chinookan Sacagawea to translate for him.

Under the circumstances Lewis did his best, and although he complained about his inability to get into depth on such subjects as religion or politics, his portrait of the coastal Indians was rich and fascinating, if not complete.

They were unlike any Indians that Americans (other than sea captains and their crews) had ever encountered. They were "a mild inoffensive people," Lewis wrote on January 4, in his first set of observations, "but will pilfer." They were "great higlers in trade," a consequence of their regular contact with trading vessels. But if a buyer walked away from an Indian seller, the Indian would be back the next day with a much-reduced price. And sometimes they would sell a valuable article "for a bauble which pleases their fancy."

Lewis did not at all approve of these practices, but he had to endure them while trying to profit from them. In his view, the cause was "an avaricious all grasping disposition" (January 6). But there were redeeming features. Also on January 6, Lewis described the Indians as "very loquacious and inquisitive; they possess good memories and have repeated to us the names [of the] captains of the vessels &c of many traders." That was potentially useful information for the captains, who made a list of the ships and their skippers who traded regularly at the mouth of the Columbia.*

Physically Lewis found the natives "generally low in stature, proportionably small . . . and much more illy formed than the Indians of the Missouri." They had "thick broad flat feet, thick ankles, crooked legs wide mouths thick lips nose moderately large, fleshey, wide at the extremity with large nostrils, black eyes and black coarse hair" (March 19). They bound their women's ankles, to produce swollen legs, a mark of beauty with them. They squatted rather then sat, which helped swell the legs. They practiced head-flattening by compressing the infant's head between two boards.

They were always barefoot, and women as well as men covered themselves only from the waist up, for the good reason—as Lewis took care to note—that they lived in a damp but mild climate and were in and out of their canoes in waist-deep water much of the time. Lewis remarked that he could do a visual examination for venereal disease on every man who came to the fort. He described their cloaks, furs, hats, and ornaments in considerable detail, then rendered his final, scathing judgment: "I think the most disgusting sight I have ever beheld is these dirty naked wenches" (March 19).

*

---

* It is used today by historians of the fur trade.

Disconcerting as it was to a Virginia gentleman to have fully exposed men and women squatting in front of him, Lewis was able to overcome his disgust and point out various positive attributes of the Clatsops and Chinooks. They built solid wood houses, twenty feet wide and up to sixty feet in length, divided into rooms where extended families lived. They had a fire in the center, slept on boards raised from the ground, and dried their fish and meat in the smoke. They had wooden bowls and spoons for eating, and woven baskets to store food.

Their bows were short, only two and a half feet, but "extreamly neat and very elastic." They were good for small game and fish, but not very effective with elk. "Maney of the Elk we have killed since we have been here," Lewis noted on January 15, "have been wounded with these arrows, the short piece with the barb remaining in the animal and grown up in the flesh."

They had no rifles, their only firearms "being oald refuse American and brittish Musquits which have been repared for this trade ... invariably in bad order" (January 30). Therefore, their principal method of getting elk was to trap them in deadfalls and pits.

Their hats were a masterpiece of design. They were conic in shape, made of the bark of cedar and bear grass (obtained in trade with upriver Indians) woven tightly together, and held in place by a chin strap. The shape "casts the rain most effectually," Lewis noted on January 30. He and Clark found these hats so attractive and practical that they ordered two made-to-measure hats from a Clatsop woman. When the work was done, Lewis reported that they "fit us very well" and satisfied so completely that the captains bought hats for each of the men. Lewis remarked that the style of the hat "is that which was in vogue in the Ued States and great Britain in the years 1800 & 1801."

The canoes beat anything Lewis or Clark had ever seen. "I have seen the natives near the coast riding waves in these canoes with safety and apparently without concern where I should have thought it impossible for any vessel of the same size to live a minute," Lewis wrote on February 1. Some of the larger canoes were up to fifty feet long and could carry five tons or thirty people. They were "waxed painted and ornimented with curious images at bough and Stern." Their paddles too were of a superior design. They chiseled out a canoe using only old files embedded in a block of wood as a handle. "A person would suppose that the forming of a large canoe with an instrument like this was the work of several years," Lewis wrote, but, to his astonishment, "these people make them in a few weeks."

So impressed was Lewis that he came as close as he ever did to praising the Clatsops and Chinooks. The canoes, he wrote on February

22, along with "the woodwork and sculpture of these people as well as these hats and their waterproof baskets evince an ingenuity by no means common among the Aborigenes of America."

"They are generally cheerfull but never gay," Lewis observed. He described their games and their gambling proclivities, but apparently saw no dances or celebrations. For pleasure, he found that they were "excessively fond of smoking tobacco." They inhaled deeply, swallowing the smoke from many draws "untill they become surcharged with this vapour when they puff it out to a great distance through their nostils and mouth." Lewis had no doubt that smoking in this manner made the tobacco "much more intoxicating." He was convinced that "they do possess themselves of all it's [tobacco's] virtues in their fullest extent."

To Lewis's approval, "these people do not appear to know the uce of sperituous liquors, they never having once asked us for it." He assumed that the captains on the trading vessels never paid for furs with whiskey, "a very fortunate occurrence, as well for the natives themselves, as for the quiet and safety of thos whites who visit them."

They were peaceful people who fought neither among themselves nor against others. "The greatest harmoney appears to exist among them," Lewis wrote on January 19. Their chiefs were not hereditary. A chief's "authority or the deference paid him is in exact equilibrio with the popularity or voluntary esteem he has acquired among the individuals of his band." His power "does not extend further than a mear repremand for any improper act of an individual." Their laws consisted of "a set of customs which have grown out of their local situations."

The Chinookan Indians at the mouth of the Columbia were at the center of a vast trade empire that ran from the Rocky Mountains to the Hawaiian Islands and on to the Orient. Lewis was keenly interested in how it worked and made such inquiries as he could.

"There is a trade continually carryed on by the natives of this river," he learned, "each trading some article or other with their neighbours above and below them; and thus articles which are vended by the whites at the entrance of this river, find their way to the most distant nations enhabiting it's water" (January 11).

The trading ships came to the Columbia in April and remained until October. The whites did not come ashore to establish trading posts; instead, the natives would visit them in their canoes, bringing furs and other items to barter. The ships anchored in today's Baker Bay, which was "spacious and commodious, and perfectly secure from all except the S. and S.E. winds. . . . fresh water and wood are very convenient and excellent timber for refiting and repairing vessels" (January 13).

No sailing vessel could possibly come to the Pacific Northwest from London or Boston in one year, which led Lewis to speculate that there had to be a trading post down the coast to the southwest, or perhaps on some island in the Pacific. He was wrong about the trading post, right about the island. Although he never knew of its existence, the trading base was Hawaii.

Lewis was always interested in how Indian tribes treated their women. His comparisons were between one tribe and another, never between Indian male-female relations and those of Virginia planters and their women, much less slaveowners and female slaves.

He noted first that the Indians had no compunctions about discussing their women even in their presence, "and of their every part, and of the most formiliar connection." They did not hold their virtue in high estimation "and will even prostitute their wives and daughters for a fishinghook or a stran of beads." As with other Indians, the women did every kind of domestic work, but, unlike other tribes, Chinookan men shared the drudgery. Even more surprising to Lewis, "notwithstanding the survile manner in which they treat their women [the men] pay much more rispect to their judgment and oppinions in many rispects than most indian nations; their women are permitted to speak freely before them, and sometimes appear to command with a tone of authority."

Old people were treated with rather more deference and respect than among the Plains Indians, in Lewis's judgment because the old-timers among the Chinooks made a contribution to obtaining a livelihood. That observation got him off on a philosophical point. "It appears to me that nature has been much more deficient in her filial tie than in any other of the strong affections of the human heart," he wrote. As far as he could tell, the Americans' practice of seeing to the ease and comfort of their old folks was a product of civilization, not human nature.

As for the Plains Indians, when their men or women got too old to keep up on a hunt or journey, it was the practice of their children "to leave them without compunction or remose; on those occasions they usually place within their reach a small peace of meat and a platter of water, telling the poor old supcrannuated wretch for his consolation, that he or she had lived long enough, that it was time they should dye and go to their relations who can afford to take care of them much better than they could" (January 6).

When Clark copied that passage, it reminded him of an experience he had had the previous winter among the Mandans. An old man had asked him for something to ease the pain in his back. "His grand Son a Young man rebuked the old man and Said it was not worth while, that it was time for the old man to die."

The Chinookan people buried their dead in canoes. The craft were placed on a scaffold, with a paddle, furs, eating implements, and other articles. A larger canoe was then lifted over the canoe-casket and secured with cords. "I cannot understand them sufficiently to make any enquiries relitive to their religeous opinions," Lewis lamented, "but presume from their depositing various articles with their dead, that they believe in a state of future existence."

Although Lewis never acknowledged it, obviously the Corps of Discovery could not have gotten through the winter on the coast without the Clatsops and Chinooks. They provided priceless information—where the elk were, where the whale had come ashore, who the ships' captains were and when they came—along with critical food supplies. It was only thanks to the natives' skills as fishermen and root collectors that the Americans were able to survive.

Lewis called them savages, even though they never threatened— much less committed—acts of violence, however great their numerical advantage. Their physical appearance disgusted him. He condemned their petty thievery and sexual morals, and their sharp trading practices. Except for their skill as canoe-builders, hatmakers, and woodworkers, he found nothing to admire in his winter neighbors.

And yet the Clatsops and Chinooks, without rifles, managed to live much better than the Americans on the coast of the Pacific Northwest. They had mastered the environment far better than the men of the expedition managed to do. The resources they drew on were renewable, whereas the Americans had shot out all the elk in the vicinity in just three months. With the coming of spring, the Corps of Discovery had no choice but to move on. The natives stayed, living prosperous lives on the riches of the Pacific Northwest, until the white man's diseases got them.

28

JEFFERSON AND THE WEST

1804–1806

From the spring of 1804 until the summer of the following year, President Jefferson had no direct communication with Lewis. People of that era accepted such anxiety. Much as he wanted to know about the safety, progress, and discoveries of the expedition, there was nothing Jefferson could do. He could not issue any orders, provide any warnings, consult on any decisions. He could only wait and hope.

In July 1804, Jefferson got his first return on the investment in the Corps of Discovery. A delegation of fourteen Osage Indians, from present-day Missouri, whom Lewis had convinced to make the journey in April, arrived in Washington.

Captain Stoddard made the final arrangements. Horses, food, shelter, and soldiers for guides and security made it an expensive trip, but the often penny-pinching president considered it a good investment. "The truth is," he wrote Secretary of War Dearborn, "the [Osages] are the great nation South of the Missouri, their possession extending from thence to the Red river, as the Sioux are great North of that river. With these two powerful nations we must stand well, because in their quarter we are miserably weak."

The representatives of the Osage nation arrived on July 11—which chanced to be the day of the Burr-Hamilton duel at Weehawken. The Osage men impressed Jefferson mightily: "They are the finest men we have ever seen." They were gigantic, he said, and noted with high approval that they were unused to spirituous liquor.

He intended to win their loyalty through a combination of bribes and threats, the traditional American Indian policy. "We shall endeavor to impress them strongly not only with our justice & liberality," he wrote, "but with our power."[1]

St. Louis businessman and friend of Lewis Pierre Chouteau accompanied the Osages as interpreter and general manager of the tour. Chouteau had his eye on the main chance; he met with Secretary of the Treasury Albert Gallatin, who sized him up thus: "He seems well disposed, but what he wants is power and money." He asked for a monopoly on the Indian trade west of the Mississippi. "I told him this was inadmissable, and his last demand was the exclusive trade with the Osage. . . . As he may be either useful or dangerous I gave no flat denial. . . ."[2]

Thus did the intense competition between frontier businessmen for the Indian trade continue under new management. The Chouteau family, along with Manuel Lisa, Joseph Robidoux, and others were adept at currying favor with corrupt Spanish bureaucrats for precious trading licenses with the western tribes. And no wonder: it was the most immediate and by far the most profitable source of wealth in the trans-Mississippi West.

There was a ritual to the Indians' visits: they were taken to the cities (Philadelphia, New York, Boston), some cannon were fired for their edification, troops paraded, and then they called on the president.

Jefferson's speech to the Osages, given in the President's House, was typical: "You have furs and peltries which we want," he said after announcing that he was their new father, "and we have useful things which you want." But a mutually beneficial commerce could not begin until the United States knew more about the Osages and their country. "For this purpose I sent a beloved man, Capt. Lewis, one of my own household to learn something of the people with whom we are now united, to let you know we were your friends, to invite you to come and see us, and to tell us how we can be useful to you."

When Lewis returned, "we shall hear what he has seen & learnt, & proceed to establish trading houses where our red brethren shall think best, & to exchange commodities with them."

Jefferson went on, in a passage that is almost poetry: "It is so long since our forefathers came from beyond the great water, that we have lost the memory of it, and seem to have grown out of this land, as you have done. . . . We are all now of one family, born in the same land, & bound to live as brothers; & the strangers from beyond the great water are gone from among us. The great Spirit has given you strength, and has given us strength; not that we might hurt one another, but to do each other all the good in our power." He concluded, "No wrong will ever be done you by our nation."[3]

(Two weeks later and more than a thousand miles west, Lewis made the same points in his speech to the Otos, and persuaded Chief Little Thief, two other Otos, three Pawnees, and a Missouri Indian to visit the president.)

In the fall of 1804, the Osages returned to St. Louis, thence on to their homes on the Osage River. According to Major James Bruff, who had replaced Captain Stoddard as commandant of the newly created Department of Upper Louisiana, they were "puffed up with ideas of their great superiority to other nations" because of all the presents they had been given and the attention lavished on them.[4]

That same fall, Jefferson began to get garbled reports on Lewis's progress. On November 6, he wrote Reuben Lewis, "I have the pleasure to inform you that we have lately received thro a channel meriting entire confidence,* advice that on the 4th of Aug. he [Lewis] was at the mouth of the river Plate, 600 miles up the Missouri. . . . Two of his men had deserted from him." According to the informant, Lewis's plans were to send one of his boats and half the men back to St. Louis before winter set in. In the spring, he would leave half the remaining men with the Mandans, to make corn for his return, and would proceed with the rest to cross the mountains and journey to the Pacific.

That was sketchy, and only about half true, but it was something. Jefferson, typically thoughtful, sent it on to Lewis's brother so that Reuben might inform his mother that her oldest son was safe so far.[5]

On November 5, Major Bruff passed on an even more garbled report that he got in St. Louis from some French trappers who had been on the Missouri River that summer. They told Bruff that "two of [Lewis's] boatmen deserted . . . that the others were much dissatisfied & complained of too regid a discipline. I am not, however, disposed to give *full* credit to their story, as they report other unfavourable circumstances that cannot be true:—Such as a difference between the Captains &c."[6]

That was awfully thin, and we may suppose that Jefferson joined Bruff in doubting the possibility of trouble between the captains, but it was the only news Jefferson was to get until the summer of 1805, following Corporal Warfington's arrival in St. Louis with the keelboat

---

* What that channel was, is a mystery. Donald Jackson suggests that an interpreter for the Oto tribe (to whom Lewis had just spoken) had come down to St. Louis with the news.

and the dispatch from there of the captains' reports, maps, and specimens to Washington.

For practical purposes, Lewis and Clark were almost as out of touch with the civilized world as Columbus had been. Even parties of experienced soldiers sent out to find them, couldn't.

The search for Lewis came about because the commanding general of the U.S. Army was secretly a Spanish spy, code name "Agent 13." General James Wilkinson (born in 1757) was a fabulous if despicable character. As an officer in the revolution, he had entered into the Conway Cabal (a group trying to supplant General Washington), and from then until his death in 1825 he never met a conspiracy he didn't embrace. Charming, amoral, shrewd, a high risk-taker, and a survivor, he was a double agent. As Donald Jackson writes, "One never really knows at any given time whether Wilkinson is acting on behalf of the United States, Spain, or—as was often the case—his own arcane greed for power and money."[7]

He had betrayed Washington; he betrayed his superior, General Anthony Wayne, intriguing against him for his job; he betrayed George Rogers Clark, his rival for popular leadership in the West, spreading rumors and telling lies about him; he betrayed his country when he swore to Spain in 1787 that he would work for the secession of the western states from the Union.

He further betrayed his country in a March 1804 message to Madrid. At the time, he was in New Orleans. He reported that Lewis's expedition was about to depart from St. Louis to ascend the Missouri River, and that its objective was to cross to the Pacific. In New Orleans, the established French and the newly arrived Americans were making bets on how long it would be before the United States established a seaport on the Pacific. Wilkinson told Madrid the big money was saying five years.*

Madrid was full of fear that an avalanche of Americans was about to cross the Mississippi and begin to descend on their gold and silver mines. Wilkinson therefore touched a raw nerve when he reported on the Lewis expedition, and so he got an immediate response to his suggestion: "An express ought immediately to be sent to the governor of Santa Fe, and another to the captain-general of Chihuaga, in order that they may detach a sufficient body of chasseurs to intercept

---

* A good estimate: in mid-April 1811, John Jacob Astor's trading house at Astoria on the Oregon coast was established.

Captain Lewis and his party, who are on the Missouri River, and force them to retire or take them prisoners."[8]

Nemesio Salcedo, commandant general of the Internal Provinces of New Spain, with headquarters in Chihuahua, read Wilkinson's advice and tried to act on it. He feared that "Captain Merry" intended to "penetrate the Missouri River in order to fulfill the commission which he has of making discoveries and observations." Those discoveries, he further feared, would be of gold and silver mines that were on Spanish territory. "The only means which presents itself is to arrest Captain Merry Weather and his party."[9]

The governor of New Mexico tried. Over the next two years he dispatched at least four armed parties from Santa Fe to search for Lewis. He was realistic enough to write, "Even though I realize it is not an easy undertaking, chance might proportion things in such a way that it might be successful."[10]

None of the four parties had any luck. They didn't even come close enough for the Indian grapevine to pass on word to Lewis that the Spanish were looking for him. Like Jefferson, the Spanish were going to have to wait for Lewis to get back to St. Louis to learn what he had done and discovered.

In the spring of 1805, in response to Lewis's entreaties the previous summer, Oto chiefs and warriors, as well as Indians from other tribes living along the Missouri, began descending on St. Louis. They wanted that grand tour at government expense Lewis had promised them. General Wilkinson—in St. Louis, about to assume the governorship of Louisiana Territory—complained to Secretary Dearborn. There were too many Indians, it was too expensive to send them to Washington, and the lines of authority were unclear.

Wilkinson charged that there had been a collision between Lewis, Stoddard, Bruff, and Chouteau. Lewis, he said, had given Stoddard authority to make all the arrangements for Indian delegations to proceed to Washington, with a blank check to draw on the War Department. But Bruff claimed the sole right to issue passports, "and Mr. Shoto has contended for the entire controul in all Indian relations."

Wilkinson believed out that "such conflicts produce pernicious animosities, & disgrace the Publick Service, and by confounding authorities destroy all responsibility." He asked Dearborn to put one man in command.[11] Later, he complained that Indians kept coming to St. Louis demanding their free trip to Washington and lots of presents. He held the delegates through the summer, on the grounds that it was too hot for them to travel. Costs for keeping them happy in St. Louis were escalating, as were expenses for the tour. He had to pay fifteen hundred dollars for horses (because "these Personages will not walk on an Embassy to their Father"); some of this he would recover for the government by selling the horses in Louisville, where he intended putting the Indians on a boat to Wheeling, making them march to Pittsburgh, then putting them on a stage to Washington.

Stoddard would be in charge of the tour. Wikinson ordered him to see to "the comfort and accommodation of our red Bretheren," but held him strictly accountable to an expense allowance: "Every unnecessary expense should be carefully avoided. You must guard against Tavern rates, by the purchase of your provision or by encamping and cooking, and by every others means in your power." Sleeping on the ground certainly saved the government money, and the event showed that Wilkinson was realistic about how much it would cost to feed the Indians at taverns—Stoddard later reported that these hearty travelers consumed nearly twelve pounds of beef a day during the journey. Each.[12]

Jefferson didn't mind the expense of courting the Indians. As he later explained to Congress, good relations with the tribes on the Missouri were "indispensable to the policy of governing those Indians by commerce rather than by arms," and the cost of the former was much less than the cost of the latter.[13]

Lewis was the advance agent of Jefferson's Indian policy. He was able to do exactly what Jefferson wanted, because he knew Jefferson's thinking so well. In his dealings with the Missouri River tribes, Lewis had represented the American government. He had announced that Jefferson was the new father of the red children, had served as mediator to establish peace, had warned the natives of the power of the United States, had promised that American trading posts would soon be set up in their country, had offered them steady jobs and a secure income if they would go to work instead of war, take furs rather than scalps.

If the policy succeeded, commerce would rule in Upper Louisiana. Happy red warriors would dance around the campfire with their good friends the white agents; guns and other manufactured goods would come up the Missouri; prime furs would float down to St. Louis.

The policy Lewis was establishing represented, in Jefferson's thinking, only a first phase. Jefferson knew that such a system of commerce could not last long. For one thing, the beaver east of the Rocky Mountains were not a renewable resource; the whole history of the fur trade in North America was one of overtrapping the beaver and moving west.* For another, immigration and emigration—the most important factors in shaping the United States—precluded leaving Louisiana to its current inhabitants. Americans, whether U.S. citizens or recent immigrants, would push west. No power on earth could stop them, certainly not the feeble U.S. Army or the distant government.

In the process of moving through Indiana, Illinois, Tennessee, and Kentucky, these emigrants and immigrants would push the natives westward. In the immediate future, Jefferson proposed to deal with that problem in three ways. As he put it in February 1803 in a directive to Governor William Henry Harrison of Indiana Territory, he first proposed to remove the white population of Upper Louisiana across to the east side of the river (giving them equal or larger holdings) and forbid emigrants access to Upper Louisiana. Second, he hoped to civilize at least some of the Indians living east of the Mississippi. Third, those Indians who remained uncivilized could be sent west of the river, into what would be a vast reservation. Jefferson told Harrison his hope was that the Indians would "incorporate with us as citizens of the United States," or, failing this, "remove beyond the Mississippi."[14]

From the government's perspective, that made perfect sense. The frontier would move forward at a regular pace, but only after the Indians had been civilized or removed. Pioneers would have to purchase regular deeds and titles to the land they farmed, rather than just squatting on it. Frontier clashes between red and white men would be reduced if not eliminated. There would be law and order, bureaucratic regularity, taxes collected, and a reduced need for the U.S. Army.

But it was all a pipe dream. As well try to stop an avalanche as to stop the moving frontier. American immigrants and emigrants wanted their share of land—free land—a farm in the family—the dream of European peasants for hundreds of years—the New World's great gift to the old. Moving west with the tide were the hucksters, the lawyers, merchants, and other men on the make looking for the main chance, men who could manufacture a land warrant in the wink of an eye.

This had been the experience in Virginia, and it was currently being acted out in Indiana Territory. And within a year of the day Lewis and Clark set out up the Missouri River on their expedition, it was taking place in Upper Louisiana. Wilkinson had his orders to block any movement into Upper Louisiana, but, as he told Secretary Dearborn,

---

* There is an exact parallel with the Virginia planters who grew tobacco for three years and then moved west.

"No opposition can be given to the bands of migrants who are crossing the Mississippi, because almost the whole Country is covered by Grants real or fictitious, and it would be hazardous in a publick office to remove a settler, until the merits of the title under which he *Squats* is ascertained."[15]

He had no clerks or officials to conduct such examinations of the titles. His situation was impossible. It was an experience he shared with every frontier governor in American history.

Jefferson was as responsible for this mad rush west as any man. He had purchased Louisiana. He had sent out his "beloved man" Lewis to explore and publicize it. He had printed and widely distributed the captains' glowing descriptions of the land along the lower Missouri. He was thus encouraging what he said he wanted to restrain.

Hypocrisy ran through his Indian policy, as it did through the policies of his predecessors and successors. Join us or get out of the way, the Americans said to the Indians, but in fact the Indians could do neither. By pushing them ever west, the Americans made it impossible for the Indians to become civilized as they meant the term, and it turned out there was almost no place where the Indians would be out of the way of the onrushing pioneers.

Jefferson said he believed the Indian was almost as capable as the European, and although not ready for assimilation soon would be (in contrast, blacks would never be ready). In this he differed from other presidents, yet only in theory, not in action. In fact, he stole all the land he could from Indians east of the Mississippi while preparing those west of the river for the same fate, after the beaver were trapped out.

How could the greatest champion of human rights in American history do such a thing? Jefferson (and his contemporaries) would not have regarded the question as valid. In their view, Indian ideas about land ownership were a lot of foolishness. As one historian observed, "A band of Sauks, say, rode twice a year through a tract as big as a couple of eastern states and claimed it as their own."[16] That same land could support thousands of farms, tens of thousands of settlers.

Anyway, no matter how much compassion Jefferson felt toward the Indians, however badly he wanted law and order and bureaucratic regularity on the frontier, on this question the people, not the government, ruled. Americans had but one Indian policy—get out of the way or get killed—and it was nonnegotiable.

The only thing that separated Jefferson from the settlers was that he wanted to buy the Indians out rather than drive them out. But that too was more rhetoric than reality. He wrote Harrison that the policy was "to exchange lands which they [the Indians] have to spare and we want for necessaries, which we have to spare and they want." Trading posts should be established among them, and the agents should extend credit. Soon the Indians would "run into debt." When their debts mounted, "they become willing to lop them off by a cession of lands."

Jefferson concluded, "In the whole course of this, it is essential to cultivate their love. As to their fear, we presume that our strength and their weakness is now so visible that they must see we have only to shut our hand to crush them. . . ."[17]

Keep the peace. Civilize the tribes, trade with them, and get title to their lands. As Donald Jackson comments, "These ends could be accomplished by fair or foul means, and fair was better, especially if it cost less. 'The Indians can be kept in order only by commerce or war,' Jefferson said. 'The former is the cheapest.'"[18]

However cynical Jefferson's long-term policy, his short-term decision to establish an American trading empire on the Missouri was eminently practical—if the Sioux could be brought into it. The immediate payoff on the Louisiana Purchase, he wrote Dearborn, was that it gave "us a perfect title [and thus] strengthens our means of retaining exclusive commerce with the Indians, on the western side of the Mississippi."[19] In other words, we can kick the British out of one of their most profitable markets—certainly something that would give the author of the Declaration of Independence satisfaction. As a bonus, it would be profitable to the United States and its citizens, and begin the process of extending American power to the Pacific.

Jefferson's Indian policy, with which Lewis would be associated all his adult life as advance agent, was subsidiary to his overall western policy, with which Lewis was also associated as advance agent. That policy was to make the United States into a continental power stretching from sea to sea. The first step was to find the Northwest Passage, if it existed, and in the process map and describe Upper Louisiana. The next steps were to map and describe the other parts of the Louisiana Purchase, which meant sending similar expeditions up the southern tributaries of the Mississippi and up the Mississippi itself to discover its sources. Government-sponsored explorations could only feed the frenzy of the frontiersmen, but that was a price Jefferson was willing (eager?) to pay.

As Lewis and Clark were preparing to shove off from Wood River in the spring of 1804, Jefferson was setting up other expeditions. One was designed to go up the Arkansas River to the mountains, march to the headwaters of the Red River, and descend it back to the Mississippi.

Another was to find the sources of the Mississippi. A third would explore the Ouachita. None was completely successful: the one going up the Red River was turned back by the Spanish; the one going up the Mississippi failed to find the source, as did the one going up the Ouachita. They all got started in 1806, after Lewis and Clark had reached the Pacific. Their failure illustrates how lucky, how good, and how well led the Corps of Discovery had been.

Jefferson's first goal was good maps—he wanted to know what he had bought. He explained his purpose to naturalist William Dunbar: "The work we are now doing is, I trust, done for posterity, in such a way that they need not repeat it. ... We shall delineate with correctness the great arteries of this great country: those who come after us will extend the ramifications as they become acquainted with them, and fill up the canvas we begin."[20] That the maps thus produced, once published and distributed, would encourage more westward movement, was a risk Jefferson was willing to take. That the westward movement might someday bring American settlers to the Pacific Coast was another risk he accepted. Indeed, it was his policy. Through the winter of 1805–6, Lewis was thinking of ways it could be implemented.

In May 1805, as Wilkinson was making the arrangements for the Indian delegations to go to Washington, Corporal Warfington brought the expedition's keelboat into St. Louis. News moved fastest by the newspapers, which copied articles from one another. On June 24, via that route, Jefferson got word of the keelboat's arrival and some information on the expedition. "We have just heard from Capt. Lewis," he wrote his daughter, "who wintered 1600 miles up the Missouri: all well." He expected to soon receive reports, maps, and specimens. That was all the news he had. Jefferson added that forty-five chiefs from six different nations "are forwarded by him to St. Louis on their way to this place."[21]

Because of the agonizing slowness of the mails, it wasn't until three weeks later that Jefferson learned that documents and boxes were on their way from St. Louis, the documents by land and the boxes via New Orleans. He was also told to expect a letter from Lewis by the next mail.

The next mail, however, wouldn't come for nearly two weeks. Jefferson postponed his annual trip to Monticello from July 15 to July 17 to wait for "the Western mail" to come in.[22] Jefferson was philosophical about the delay. On July 10, 1805, he wrote Reuben Lewis, "It is probable they are coming on by a special messenger who travels slow." He enclosed a newspaper account of the progress of the expedition to the Mandans.[23]

Three days later, Jefferson received the documents, including Lewis's letter of April 7, 1805, Clark's journal covering the period May 1804–March 1805, Clark's map of the lower Missouri, and an invoice from Lewis listing the items coming in boxes from New Orleans. Jefferson biographer Dumas Malone notes that "the invoice from Lewis could not have failed to arouse the eager anticipation of such an enthusiast for natural history as Jefferson." It listed animal skins, horns, and skeletons; specimens of plants and minerals; cages holding four live magpies, a prairie dog, and a grouse.

It was August before the boxes arrived in Washington. Jefferson was in Monticello. He sent instructions to have the furs dried and brushed and then done up in strong linen. The grouse and three of the magpies were dead, all killed by the survivor. Jefferson ordered that special care be given the remaining magpie and the prairie dog so that he might see them on his return to the capital.[24]

On October 4, Jefferson got back to the President's House, where he reveled in the specimens from the trans-Mississippi. He sent some to the American Philosophical Society, some to Charles Willson Peale for his museum in Philadelphia, some seeds to his botanist friends, and kept some articles for his Indian Hall at Monticello, where some horns and Indian artifacts are on display today. He entered into a long correspondence with his fellow naturalists about the discoveries, which, Malone writes, "gave him greater satisfaction than he gained from politics."[25]

But politics was his business, and the political payoff of the expedition was not curious animals and plants but maps and solid information about the trans-Mississippi Indians. These were contained in Clark's map of the Missouri and Lewis's statistical report on the tribes. The map would later be superseded by the much more accurate one Clark made at Fort Clatsop, but it was a great step forward in geographical knowledge. Lewis's statistical view of the Plains Indians, running to some sixty printed pages, provided a description of the tribes, their location, population, and activities, along with his glowing account of the fur trade and other commercial possibilities.

Together, the map and report surpassed both in scope and reliability anything hitherto available to the American government on the American West. By themselves, they justified the expense of the expedition. With considerable pride, Jefferson reported to the Congress on the achievements to date, and ordered the map and the statistical view to be printed and distributed as a part of his annual message.[26]

They were the first printed fruit of the expedition. There was an impatient audience for them. Publishers in Washington, New York, Natchez, and London printed editions in book form.[27]

In his message of transmittal of the Lewis and Clark documents to Congress, Jefferson mentioned the command structure of the expedition—the only time he did so. He reported that "Capt. Meriwether Lewis, of the 1st regiment of infantry was appointed with a party of men, to explore the river Missouri from it's mouth to it's source, and crossing the highlands by the shortest portage, to seek the best water communication thence to the Pacific ocean; and Lieut. Clarke* was appointed second in command."[28] As far as the president was concerned, it was the Lewis expedition.

In October 1805, Stoddard's tour left St. Louis, including forty-five Indians from eleven tribes. They arrived in Washington in January 1806. Jefferson gave them the standard Great Father talk: "We are become as numerous as the leaves of the trees, and, tho' we do not boast, we do not fear any nation. . . . My children, we are strong, we are numerous as the stars in the heavens, & we are all gun-men." He followed the threat with the carrot: if they would be at peace with one another and trade with the Americans, they could be happy.

(In reply, one of the chiefs said he was glad the Americans were as numerous as the stars in the skies, and powerful as well. So much the better, in fact, for that meant the government should be strong enough to keep white squatters off Indian lands.)[29]

How much good these tours did for Jefferson's Indian policy is questionable. Surely the visitors were impressed, but they had their own constituencies at home, who were not likely to embrace the program no matter what tales the returning warriors told about American power. Further, as almost always happened when trans-Mississippi Indians traveled to Washington, a number of the chiefs died from diseases picked up along the way, which created considerable resentment and mistrust back in the villages.

The Indian delegates brought with them grapevine news of Lewis's progress. On January 12, 1806, Jefferson wrote William Dunbar: "We have no certain information of Capt. Lewis since he left Fort Mandan. But we have through Indians an account of his having entered on the

---

* Jefferson consistently misspelled Clark's name.

passage over the high lands dividing the Missouri from the waters of the Pacific."

The next day, he wrote Reuben Lewis that he had a letter from Pierre Chouteau in St. Louis informing him that two Otos had said that "Capt. Lewis & his party had reached that part of the Missouri near the mountains where the Indian tract [road] leads across (in 8 days march) to the Columbia, that he had there procured horses and had, with his whole party entered on the tract." He did not expect to hear from Lewis again until he returned to St. Louis, but, "Knowing the anxiety of a mother in such a case, I mention this information praying you to present her my respects."[30]

Although his original orders gave Lewis permission to return by sea if it was possible and if he thought it best, obviously Jefferson expected the expedition to return overland. Why he was so certain is unclear. In 1805, he informed various sea captains headed around the Horn and onto the mouth of the Columbia of Lewis's possible presence there.[31]

Lewis and Clark hoped to find a trading vessel to replenish their supplies, but never did. Jefferson has been severely criticized, by historians Bernard De Voto and David Lavender and editor Elliott Coues among others, for failing to send a U.S. Navy vessel to pick up the explorers. The criticism ignores some fundamental factors.

In 1805, the navy was fighting a war in the Mediterranean against the Tripoli pirates. It had half its strength stationed there—six frigates, four brigs, two schooners, one sloop, two bomb vessels, and sixteen gunboats—or under orders to go there. All the remainder of the fleet was laid up for repairs and refitting. There were no vessels to send.

Even had there been, Jefferson couldn't be sure the expedition had reached the mouth of the Columbia, or would still be there when a ship showed up (indefinite at best, since it could take from one to three weeks to round the Horn, depending on the winds). Arlen Large's conclusion seems inescapable: "Jefferson's non-action seems justified by so many 'what ifs.'"[32]

The president could only wait, hope, conjecture. In February 1806, he told a correspondent that he guessed Lewis "has reached the Pacific, & is now wintering on the head of the Missouri, & will be here next autumn."[33] He was right about the first point, wrong about the second. Whether he had gotten the third point right or not remained to be seen. It depended on the captains.

29

RETURN TO THE NEZ PERCÉ

March 23–June 9, 1806

"At 1 P.M. we bid a final adieu to Fort Clatsop," Lewis wrote in his journal the night of March 23. The party had hardly proceeded a mile before it met a Chinook band of twenty or so. The chief said he had heard the expedition wanted to buy a canoe; he had brought with him an elegant one he wished to sell. But, Lewis wrote (whether with satisfaction or shame), "being already supplied we did not puchase it." The next day, an Indian guided them among some islands, then claimed the stolen canoe as his. Lewis offered him a dressed elk skin for it. Surrounded by thirty-two riflemen in five canoes, and without a clear title in his possession, the Indian accepted.

Maybe this "payment" assuaged Lewis's conscience. It didn't alter his act. The theft of the canoe showed how desperate he was.

As the party set out from Fort Clatsop, it cut a much less impressive figure than it had on April 7, 1805, as it set out from Fort Mandan. In 1805, the canoes were jammed with boxes, canisters, kettles, bales of trade goods, blankets, tobacco, whiskey, flour, salt pork, corn, dried squash and beans, writing desks, tents, scientific instruments, tools of many descriptions, knives, rifles, and more. In 1806, the party set out with canisters of powder, scientific instruments, kettles, dried fish and roots, the clothes on their backs, and rifles. They were only halfway through their journey, but they had spent 95 percent of their budget.

On the other hand, in 1805, they didn't know what was ahead. In 1806; they did know, and they had put supplies into caches stretching from the Nez Perce country to Great Falls, so they would be able to replenish as they moved east.

Knowing the lay of the land ahead was a mixed blessing, however, for part of that land was the Bitterroots. From the moment the men left Fort Clatsop, the rigors of those mountains were on their minds. "That wretched portion of our journy," Lewis called it in his June 2 journal entry, "the Rocky Mountain, where hungar and cold in their most rigorous forms assail the waried traveller; not any of us have yet forgotten our sufferings in those mountains in September last, and I think it probable we never shall."

Going up the Columbia was hard work. The current was always strong; in rapids, the canoes had to be towed; falls had to be portaged. Food was a constant problem, as were the multitudes of curious Indians. On April 1, Lewis learned from some natives along the Columbia that there was a "great scarcity of food" on the river, that the people upstream were starving, and that the salmon run wouldn't begin for a month.

This news "gave us much uneasiness," Lewis wrote. In the country above The Dalles, through the plains to the Nez Percé camps at the base of the mountains, there were no deer, pronghorns, or elk. Lewis conferred with Clark. They agreed that to wait for the salmon would keep them from getting onto and down the Missouri River before it froze. Delay would also cost their horse herd, being held by Twisted Hair, because he had told them the Nez Percé would cross the mountains at the beginning of May, and without Nez Percé help Lewis doubted the men could round up the expedition's horses.

On April 2, the captains decided, not surprisingly, "to loose as little time as possible in geting to the Chopunnish Village."* They would stay below The Dalles long enough for the hunters to kill and dry sufficient meat to sustain them until they reached the Nez Percé. Lewis figured that the party could live on horse meat as it crossed the Bitterroots. He explained, "we now view the horses as our only certain resource for food, nor do we look forward to it with any detestation or horrow, so soon is the mind which is occupied with any intcresting object reconciled to it's situation."

But there were no horses below The Dalles. There were dogs, which were purchased whenever possible and were a favorite food of nearly all the party.

---

* Chopunnish was the captains' name for the Nez Percé.

On the 3rd, Indians descending the river in search of food paid a visit. "These poor people appeared to be almost starved," Lewis noted. "They picked up the bones and little pieces of refuse meat which had been thrown away by the party."

Clark was off on a side expedition, probing the Willamette River, some ten miles upstream to the site of the present-day city of Portland. Lewis supervised the preparation of the jerky for the trip over the plains. Never one to waste time, while the men kept the fires going under the strips of elk and deer, he looked for and described new plants and animals. "I took a walk today of three miles," he wrote on April 8, "in the course of which I had an opportunity to correct an errow which I have heretofore made with rispect to the shrub I have hithertoo called the large leafed thorn." He was referring to the salmon-berry, which he had confused with the thimbleberry. He made amends for his error with a remarkably detailed description of the salmonberry,* including an attempt to classify it using the Linnaean system.

On the human side, he had Indians to deal with. They came in from the small villages up and down the river to see and steal from the white men. "These people are constantly hanging about us," Lewis complained on April 6. "I detected one of them in steeling a peice of lead," he wrote the next day. Back in Virginia, a plantation owner would have a slave whipped for petty theft, and perhaps Lewis felt the impulse to do just that, but these were Chinookan Indians with whom he wanted good relations. Instead of beating the thief, "I sent him from camp." But he also inspected the rifles and held a target practice in front of a group of Indians, who shortly "departed for their village."

The following night, April 8, the sentinel detected an old man trying to sneak into the expedition's campsite. The soldier threatened the intruder with his rifle, and "gave the fellow a few stripes with a switch and sent him off." As with Lewis, tempers were running high among the men; never before had they whipped an Indian.

But never before had they been so provoked. One party of warriors tried to wrest a tomahawk from Private John Colter, but they had picked the wrong man. "He retained it," Lewis dryly recorded. Still, as the expedition worked its way upriver, whether dragging the canoes through the rapids or portaging them, the Indians were always there, ready to grab anything left unguarded for an instant. At the Cascades, on April 11, Lewis had to detail guard parties to watch the baggage, because "these

---

* A sample: "Of the stamens the filaments are subulate, inserted into the recepticle, unequal and bent inwards concealing the pistillum." His description covers most of a printed page.

are the greatest theives and scoundrels we have met with. . . . One of them had the insolence to cast stones down the bank at two of the men." Others threatened Shields, who had to pull his knife to drive them off.

In the evening, three Indians stole Lewis's dog, Seaman, which sent him into a rage. He called three men and snapped out orders to follow and find those theives and "if they made the least resistence or difficulty in surrendering the dog to fire on them." The soldiers set out; when the thieves realized they were being pursued, they let Seaman go and fled. Lewis may have been ready to kill to get Seaman back, but the Indians weren't ready to die for the dog.

Back at camp, meanwhile, an Indian stole an ax, got caught, and after a tussle gave it up and fled. Lewis told a group hanging out at the camp that "if they made any further attempts to steal our property or insulted our men we should put them to instant death."

Lewis and his men were right up to the edge of serious violence. They had no patience left, and the temptation to use their rifles was very strong, especially since they felt surrounded. "I am convinced that no other consideration but our number at this moment protects us," Lewis wrote.

He and the party were in so foul a mood that they could entertain the thought of a first strike: one quick volley would drive the Indians away. But that was dangerous thinking. Giving in to temper would be risking not just good relations with the natives but the expedition itself. Lewis had to keep a check on himself, without allowing the Indians to pilfer the pantry of the expedition or run off with his dog. He controlled his breathing and began talking, through the sign language, with the chief.

The chief responded to Lewis's charges about Indian behavior by laying all the trouble at the feet of two bad men in his nation. They alone had been responsible for "these seenes of outradge of which we complained." The village as a whole wished for peace and good relations. So did Lewis, who concluded his account, "I hope that the friendly interposition of this chief may prevent our being compelled to use some violence with these people; our men seem well disposed to kill a few of them."

Of course, some young warriors in the Indian village were equally well disposed to kill a few of the whites. Knowing that, and determined to prevent it, Lewis recorded, "We keep ourselves perefectly on our guard."

The captains decided that, once they got onto the open plain country above The Dalles, they would go overland to the mountains. To do that, they needed as many horses as they could purchase. Clark went ahead beyond The Dalles to set up an advance camp and begin buying horses. Lewis stayed behind to oversee the portage of the baggage. After the first day of haggling, Clark sent a runner to tell Lewis the Indians would not sell at the price being offered. Lewis sent back a note telling Clark to double the price. He wanted at least five horses, and wanted them badly, for he wanted to get out of there, to shake these Indians from his heels. In addition, the longer the expedition stayed in the area, the more chances the Indians would have "to execute any hostile designh should they meditate any against us."

The Indians knew a seller's market when they saw one. They kept saying no to whatever Clark offered, which in truth wasn't much. What made it so maddening was that the natives beyond The Dalles, as Lewis complained on April 17, "have a great abundance of horses but will not dispose of them." On April 18 and 19, Lewis broke down and paid the price of two large kettles for four horses. Never before had he been willing to part with a kettle. The expedition was reduced to four small kettles to do its cooking, one per mess.

The night of the 19th, Lewis directed the horses be hobbled and allowed to graze, with orders that the man who was responsible for each horse stay with him and watch him. But Private Willard "was negligent in his attention to his horse and suffered it to ramble off." Lewis's temper again flared, this time at one of his men. "This in addition to the other difficulties under which I laboured was truly provoking," he explained in his journal. "I repremanded [Willard] more severely for this peice of negligence than had been usual with me."

As Lewis and the men with him made their way up the Columbia, the Indians continued to torment them. Tomahawks and knives disappeared during the night. On April 20, Lewis had once again to warn the local inhabitants "that if I caught them attempting to perloin any article from us I would beat them severely." That remonstrance had to be repeated at every village.

When the party got above The Dalles, Lewis decided to abandon the canoes—getting them past Celilo Falls appeared to be impossible—join Clark at his upriver camp, obtain as many packhorses as possible, and march to the mountains.

That decision made, on April 21 Lewis had all the spare poles and paddles placed on the canoes. Then he set fire to the pile. He was determined to make certain that "not a particle should be left for the benefit of the indians."

While the fire burned, Lewis caught an Indian stealing an iron socket that had been tossed aside from one of the poles. His pent-up fury burst forth. He caught the man, cursed him, beat him severely, and then "made the men kick him out of camp."

His blood was hot. He informed the Indians standing around that "I would shoot the first of them that attempted to steal an article from us. That we were not affraid to fight them, that I had it in my power at that moment to kill them all and set fire to their houses. . . ."

The release that came with the physical satisfaction of beating the thief and the psychological pleasure of shouting threats at the young hang-abouts who were gawking at him, drained some of Lewis's emotion. He breathed deeply and got control of his temper.

He told the Indians "it was not my wish to treat them with severity provided they would let my property alone." He could easily take some horses, he said, the horses of the men who had stolen knives and tomahawks, but since he did not know who the thieves were he would "reather loose the property altogether than take the hose of an inosent person." The Indians "hung their heads and said nothing."

That afternoon, Lewis set off, with nine horses carrying baggage and one being ridden by Private William Bratton, who had a severe back condition and could not walk. Lewis was in a better mood—he always was happiest when proceeding—and looking forward to getting out of the Chinookan country and back in the land of the Nez Percé, where he expected that the natives "will treat us with much more hospitality than those we are now with."

But the next morning, April 22, local Chinookans stole a saddle and robe. Lewis's blood rose past a danger point. He swore he would either get the stolen goods back or "birn their houses. they have vexed me in such a manner by such repeated acts of villany that I am quite disposed to treat them with every severyty, their defenseless state pleads forgivness so far as rispects their lives." He ordered a thorough search of the village and marched there himself, resolved to burn the place down if he didn't get the saddle and robe back.

That was the closest Lewis came to applying the principle of collective guilt. Fortunately, the men found the stolen goods hidden in a corner of one of the houses before Lewis reached the village.

He had been wonderfully lucky. Had those goods not been recovered, he might have given the order to put the houses to the torch. The resulting conflagration would have been a gross overreaction, unpardonably unjust, and a permanent blot on his honor. It would have turned every Chinookan village on the lower Columbia against the Americans and thus made impossible the fulfillment of the plan Lewis was developing for a transcontinental, American-run trading empire. He had a lot at stake, but he had been ready to allow his anger to override his judgment.

To modern eyes, this looks suspiciously like racism, just as Lewis's resolve to burn down the village raises images of the U.S. Army in the Indian wars and in Vietnam. But if one means by racism a blind prejudice toward native Americans, based on false but fully believed stereotypes, Lewis was no racist. When he talked about Indian "nations" he meant the word just as he applied it to European peoples. He was keenly aware of differences between tribes, a subject he wrote about at length and with insight. He liked some Indians, admired others extravagantly, pitied some, despised a few.

His response to native Americans was based on what he saw and was completely different from his response to African Americans. With regard to blacks, he made no distinctions between them, made no study of them, had no thought that they could be of benefit to America in any capacity other than slave labor.

But, despite his cold-blooded words and resolutions, and his hatred of the Chinooks, what stands out about his journey up the lower Columbia in the spring of 1806 is that he got through it without ever once ordering a man to put a torch to an Indian home, and no man ever fired a rifle at a native.

He had, however, four times lost his temper and twice threatened to kill. His behavior was erratic and threatening to the future of the expedition. There would be other tribes to encounter, other forms of provocation. Lewis would be tested on his self-control, not his strongest character trait.

On April 24, the expedition marched overland. "Most of the party complain of the soarness of their feet and legs this evening," Lewis recorded. "My left ankle gives me much pain." A cold-water footbath helped. By the 27th, the party reached the country of Chief Yellept and the Wallawallas, relatives of the Nez Percé. The chief rode up with six men and was delighted to see the white men, as they were to see him. Yellept was chief of a village of some fifteen lodges, with perhaps 150 men, and many horses. It was currently set up about twelve miles below the junction of the Columbia and the Snake, on the north bank.

The captains had promised Yellept the previous October that they would stay a day or two with him on the return journey. He now invited the captains to bring the expedition to his village, where he promised food and horses.

A three-day visit ensued. Yellept set an example for his people by personally bringing wood and fish to the white men. On the second morning, he presented Clark with "a very eligant white horse," an act of generosity that lost some of its luster when Yellept indicated he would like a kettle in return. No kettle, the captains said. Then whatever they thought proper, Yellept replied. Clark gave him his sword, plus a hundred balls and powder. Yellept was satisfied.

What Yellept did genuinely give away was information. For the first time since they had left the Shoshones, the captains had an interpretive route that allowed them to go beyond the sign language. There was a captive Shoshone woman with the Wallawallas who could speak to Sacagawea, who could pass it on to Charbonneau, who could communicate with Drouillard or Labiche, who, finally, could speak to the captains in English. "We conversed with them for several hours," Lewis wrote, "and fully satisfyed all their enquiries with rispect to ourselves and the objects of our pursuit." In return, Yellept told Lewis of a shortcut to the western end of the Lolo Trail.

That evening, Yellept's relatives and neighbors the Yakimas came in at his invitation to see the white men and have a party. There were about one hundred men and a few women. Together with the Wallawallas, they surrounded the white men and waited patiently to see them dance. Cruzatte brought out the fiddle and for an hour the men danced, to the delight of the Indians. Then the Indians, some 550 men, women, and children, "sung and danced at the same time. most of them stood in the same place and merely jumped up to the time of their music," but the bravest men went into the center of the circle "and danced in a circular manner sidewise." To the Indians' gratification, some of the white men joined in the dance. This was much different from evenings on the lower Columbia.

On the morning of April 29, two inferior chiefs presented each of the captains with a horse. The gift was welcome, but the return present was expensive. Lewis wrote, "we gave them sundry articles and among others one of my case pistols and several hundred rounds of ammunition." That pistol was a highest-quality, custom-made weapon, a so-called dueling pistol, kept in a case with accessories, and it was Lewis's personal property, not government issue.[1]

The following day, "we took leave of these friendly honest people the Wollahwollahs and departed at 11 A.M." The shortcut Yellept told them about took them across the base of the northern bend of the Snake, saving some eighty miles. Thanks to the Wallawallas, the party had twenty-three horses, "most of them excellent young horses, but much the greater portion of them have soar backs. These indians are cruell horse-masters; they ride hard, and their saddles are so ill constructed. . . . reguardless of this they ride them when the backs of those poor annimals are in a horrid condition."

The second night out, three teenage Wallawalla boys rode into camp. They were returning a steel trap that "had been neglegently left behind." Lewis called this "an act of integrity rarely witnessed among indians" (without adding that it was also rare among whites), but he praised the Wallawallas for returning knives "carelessly lossed by the men."

Lewis paid a final tribute to the Wallawallas: "I think we can justly affirm to the honor of these people that they are the most hospitable, honest, and sincere people that we have met with in our voyage."

The march the next two days was god-awful. The weather was miserable: rain, hail, and snow with high winds. At dinner on May 3, the captains divided the last of the dried meat and the balance of the dogs. "We made but a scant supper and had not anything for tomorrow."

Their luck held. The next day, the party encountered a band of roving Nez Percé, led by Chief Tetoharsky, the man who had helped Twisted Hair as a guide the previous autumn. He offered to take them to Twisted Hair's village and sold them some roots and fuel. They set off together in the morning. When they reached a village, they tried to purchase provisions, without much success. But they discovered that Captain Clark had quite a reputation with these natives as a doctor.

It seemed that the previous fall Clark had washed and then rubbed some liniment on an old Indian man's sore knee and thigh, accompanying the doctoring with what Clark called "much seremony." The man had not walked for months, but recovered with Clark's therapy. Since then, Lewis wrote, this band "has never ceased to extol the virtues of our medecines." Together with the effectiveness of the eye-water, the Nez Percé had "an exalted opinion of our medicine. my friend Capt. C. is their favorite phisician and has already received many applications."

The captains could pay for their keep by establishing a hospital. Lewis was a bit disturbed at thus fooling the Indians. He doubted there was much that could be done for most of the complaints, and he was embarrassed to be practicing psychosomatic medicine. He rationalized his way to a justification: "In our present situation I think it pardonable to continue this deseption for they will not give us any provision without compensation. . . . we take care to give them no article which can possibly oinjure them."

In fact, Clark did much good for the Nez Percé. The Indians kept coming because they were benefiting from his therapy; there was no need for Lewis to feel embarrassment. The Indians paid for the therapy with roots and dogs.

The dogs were another source of potential embarrassment. The Nez Percé ate horsemeat only to ward off starvation, and never ate dog. On May 3, Lewis related a dog-meat anecdote in a piece of concise storytelling: "While at dinner an indian fellow verry impertinently threw a poor half starved puppy nearly into my plait by way of derision for our eating dogs and laughed very heartily at his own impertinence; I was so provoked at his insolence that I caught the puppy and threw it with great violence at him and struk him in the breast and face, siezed my tomahawk and shewed him by signs if he repeated his insolence I would tommahawk him, the fellow withdrew apparently much mortifyed and I continued my repast *on dog* without further molestation."

Generally, relations with the Nez Percé were excellent. On May 7, an Indian rode in with two canisters of powder. His dog had dug them up at the cache the expedition had made in October. The captains rewarded his honesty with a piece of fire-making steel.

That day, the Bitterroot Mountains came into view. They "were perfectly covered with snow." The Nez Percé gave the captains unfortunate news: the winter snows had been heavy, the snow was yet deep in the mountains, so no passage was possible until early June, at best. "To men confined to a diet of horsebeef and roots," Lewis wrote, "and who are as anxious as we are to return to the fat plains of the Missouri and thence to our native homes," this was "unwelcom inteligence."

The party hated to be stopped. Every day, other than those in winter camp, the men tried to make some progress. Furthermore, beyond those mountains there was tobacco, tools, kettles. On the Missouri Plains there were the calves, providing unlimited quantities of tender veal, supplemented by buffalo hump and buffalo tongue, with sausage made by Charbonneau. The captains and their men had been thinking about the upcoming feast for weeks. Now they learned that they would have to stay where they were for three weeks, possibly longer, with nothing to eat but dried fish and roots and, when they were lucky, lean elk and deer, or horsemeat, or dog.

Morale sank. On the morning of May 8, some of the men ordered out to hunt instead lay about the camp, "without our permission or knoledge." The captains found it necessary to "chid them severely for their indolence and inattention."

That day, the Americans chanced on Chief Cut Nose with a party of six. Cut Nose had been off on a raid the previous fall, but Lewis had heard of him and knew he was regarded as a greater chief than Twisted Hair. The Indians and white men rode on together, and soon encountered Twisted Hair with a half-dozen warriors.

It was Twisted Hair who had agreed to keep the Americans' horses through the winter—he had been promised two guns and ammunition as his reward—and guided the expedition as far down the Snake-Columbia as The Dalles. The captains were naturally delighted to see him. But he greeted the white men very coolly. Lewis found this "as unexpected as it was unaccountable."

Twisted Hair turned to Cut Nose and began shouting and making angry gestures.

Cut Nose answered in kind. This continued for some twenty minutes.

The captains had no idea what was going on, but clearly they had to break it up. They needed the friendship of both chiefs if they were to get through the next three weeks, and they needed their horses if they were to have any chance of getting over the mountains. They informed the chiefs that the expedition was proceeding.

The Indians fell in behind, keeping a distance from each other. When the expedition made camp, "the two chiefs with their little bands formed seperate camps at a short distance, they all appeared to be in an ill humour."

The captains called for a council. They relied on a Shoshone boy with Cut Nose to interpret for them, but he "refused to speak, he aledged it was a quarrel between two Cheifs and that he had no business with it." For the next hour, the captains could make no sense out of the "violet quarrel." They were in an agony of suspense, anxious to reunite with their horses and to keep the Nez Percé as friends.

The captains pleaded with the Shoshone boy, but "he remained obstenately silent." The chiefs departed for their respective camps, still angry with each other. An hour later, Drouillard returned from hunting. The captains invited Twisted Hair for a smoke. He accepted, and through Drouillard explained that when he had returned from The Dalles the previous fall he had collected the expedition's horses and taken charge of them. Cut Nose then returned from his war party and, according to Twisted Hair, asserted his primacy among the Nez Percé. He said Twisted Hair shouldn't have accepted the responsibility, that it was he, Cut Nose, who should be in charge. Twisted Hair said he got so sick of hearing this stuff that he paid no further attention to the horses, who consequently scattered. But most of them were around, many of them with Chief Broken Arm, who lived upriver and was "a Cheif of great emenence."

The captains invited Cut Nose to join the campfire. He came and "told us in the presents of the Twisted hair that he the twisted hair was a bad old man that he woar two faces." Cut Nose charged that Twisted Hair had never taken care of the horses but had allowed his young men to ride them and misuse them, and that was the reason Cut Nose and Broken Arm had forbidden him to retain responsibility for the animals.

The captains said they would proceed to Broken Arm's camp in the morning, and see how many horses and saddles they could collect. This was satisfactory to Twisted Hair and Cut Nose, who had calmed down considerably after being allowed to tell their sides of the story.

The next day, everyone moved to Broken Arm's lodge, which was some 150 feet long, built of sticks, mats, and grass. There the expedition recovered twenty-one horses, about half the saddles, and some ammunition that had been cached. Lewis paid Twisted Hair one gun, a hundred balls, and two pounds of powder for his services, and said the other promised gun would be delivered when the balance of the horses were brought in. The gun he gave Twisted Hair was an old, beat-up British trading musket, for which he had paid a Chinook two elk skins.

When the captains explained their supply situation, and asked if the Indians would exchange a good but lean horse of theirs for a fat young horse, with a view to slaughter the colt for food, Broken Arm said he was "revolted at the aydea of an exchange." His people had a great abundance of colts, however, and the white men could have as many as they wanted. He soon produced two fat colts and demanded nothing in return. Lewis commented that this was "the only act which deserves the appellation of hospitallity which we have witnessed in this quarter."*

Over the next couple of days, various other chiefs joined Cut Nose and Twisted Hair at Broken Arm's lodge. All together, the Nez Percé were some four thousand strong, living in their separate bands, and had by far the largest horse herd on the continent. These chiefs had a constituency that demanded attention.

The captains seized their opportunity and held a conference of all the leading men of the Nez Percé. Lewis made a speech. It took nearly half a day for him to get his main points across, because the interpretation had to pass through French, Hidatsa, and Shoshone to get to Nez Percé.

---

* Clark later commented that those Indians who had had no contact with whites until the expedition arrived were much more hospitable than those who had, such as the Chinooks (Moulton, ed., *Journals*, vol. 7, p. 241).

The main points were: peace and harmony among the natives on each side of the Rocky Mountains; the strength and power of the United States; the trading posts that were coming. The captains did not refer to the Nez Percé as their children, or to Jefferson as the Indians' new father, but, as James Ronda writes, "thoughts of sovereignty were not far from the Americans' minds."[2]

Beyond the American claim to lands west of the Louisiana Purchase, Lewis and Clark had other goals. One was to persuade the Nez Percé to send some guides and diplomats with the expedition to the Blackfoot country. The captains said they would make a peace between the two tribes, so that the Nez Percé could come live on the buffalo side of the Continental Divide and, not incidentally, bring all those horses with them. The captains also wanted one, two, or three chiefs to accompany them back to Washington, to meet the president.

The chiefs "appeared highly pleased" with the presentation, but said that they would have to consult among themselves before replying.

After the conference, the captains held a magic show, displaying the latest in European and American technology, including a magnet, a spy glass, a compass, a watch, and "sundry other articles equally novel and incomprehensible to them." Lewis shot his air gun. The Nez Percé were astonished and impressed. The chiefs then withdrew for their consultation.

The next morning, May 12, the chiefs informed the captains that they had "resolved to pusue our advise." To get the power of the people behind the decision, Broken Arm held a sort of plebiscite. He made up a dish of pounded roots and soup, then gave a speech. He announced the decision to do as the Americans wished, then asked all those who were ready to abide by that decision to come forward and eat; those who opposed would show their sentiments by not eating. "There was not a dissenting voice on this great national question," Lewis wrote, "but all swallowed their objections if any they had, very cheerfully with their mush."

It turned out, however, that what the Nez Percé nation had agreed to do was far short of what the captains had asked. The chiefs said the people were willing to move east of the mountains, but only after the United States Army had a fort on the Missouri, where they could trade for arms and ammunition to defend themselves. As for a delegate to the Blackfeet, they rather thought not. And as for a delegate to the president, perhaps, maybe, sometime, later.

The Nez Percé concluded by warning the captains it was too early even to think about crossing the mountains. The captains could think of little else. "We are anxious to procure some guides to accompany us on the different routs we mean to take from Travellers rest," Lewis wrote.*

Lewis did most of the smoking and talking with the chiefs, while Clark practiced medicine. Every morning, his patients lined up for treatment. He used eyewash, hot rubdowns, and simples for sore eyes, scrofula (tuberculosis of the lymph glands), ulcers, rheumatism, and other ailments. One case was particularly difficult. An old chief had been suffering from paralysis for three years. He was "incapable of moving a single limb," Lewis reported, "but lies like a corps in whatever position he is placed, yet he eats heartily, digests his food perfectly, injoys his understanding, his pulse are good, and has retained his flesh almost perfectly." Nothing Clark tried on him seemed to do any good.

Among the party, Bratton was still suffering from his bad back; Sacagawea's son, Jean Baptiste, in addition to teething, had a high fever and a swollen neck and throat. The captains gave him some tartar and sulphur and applied a poultice of boiled onions to his neck, as hot as he could stand it.† The therapy did no good; a few days later, Lewis wrote that the boy "was very wrestless last night; it's jaw and the back of it's neck are much more swolen. . . . we gave it a doze of creem of tartar and applyed a fresh poltice of onions."

Clark had better results with Bratton. At Private John Shields's suggestion, Clark prescribed a sweat bath for Bratton. A sweat lodge was built, stones were heated up and placed inside, Bratton went in naked with a vessel of water to sprinkle on the stones to make steam, and after twenty minutes he was taken out and plunged into cold water. Then back to the sweat lodge. Within a day, Bratton was walking, free from pain for the first time in months.

Sacagawea's boy slowly recovered, but the paralyzed chief showed no improvement. Lewis regretted that he was not back in Philadelphia, where Benjamin Franklin had experimented with electricity to treat paralytic cases. "I am confident that this [chief] would be an excellent subject for electricity," Lewis wrote on May 27.

Instead of shock therapy, the captains decided on heat therapy. They built a sweat lodge for the chief and put him in, fortified with thirty drops of laudanum for relaxation. It worked. The chief regained the use

---

* This was his first mention of a decision he and Clark had made sometime earlier, probably at Fort Clatsop.

† It has been suggested that the boy had mumps, or perhaps it was tonsillitis. Dr. Chuinard thinks it was an external abscess on the neck. (*Only One Man Died*, pp. 370–75.)

of his hands and arms, and soon his leg and toes. "He seems highly delighted with his recovery," Lewis wrote on May 30. "I begin to entertain strong hope of his restoration by these sweats."

The medical practice was critical to maintaining a continuing food supply, but by itself insufficient: the men needed more food than Clark's fees could provide. They had nothing in the way of trade goods, so it was down to the clothes off their backs, the buttons off their coats and pants. When the men discovered that brass buttons were "an article of which these people are tolerably fond," the men cut off all their buttons to trade for roots.

Never ask your men to do something you won't do yourself, is time-honored advice to company commanders. In this case, the captains cut the buttons from their dress coats a few days later, which brought in three bushels of roots. "A successful voyage," Lewis said of the trading venture, "not much less pleasing to us than the return of a good cargo to an East India Merchant."

On May 21, the captains took a drastic step. They decided that each man should make his own deal for roots sufficient to get him over the Bitterroots. Each man got "one awl, one Kniting pin, a half an ounce of vermillion, two nedles, a few scanes of thead and about a yard of ribbon." Lewis called it "a slender stock indeed with which to lay in a store of provision for that dreary wilderness." He comforted himself with the thought that they could fall back on horsemeat. The expedition's herd was growing, thanks to Clark's doctoring, and by the beginning of June was up to sixty-five horses.

The long wait with the Nez Percé gave Lewis an opportunity to do more ethnography. He described the tribes' dress and ornaments at some length. He judged the Nez Percé to be "cheerfull but not gay."

Their young men were fond of gambling and games. So were Lewis's young men. In addition, Lewis had the problem of idle hands. Like most company commanders with that problem, he turned to athletics as a way to keep up morale and strength and reach out to the natives.

The result was a tournament. There was a shooting match, which Lewis won with two hits of a mark at a distance of 220 yards, something even more impressive to the Indians than his air gun. On horseback, the Nez Percé put the American soldiers to shame. Lewis was amazed at how accurate they were with the arrow, even when firing at a rolling target from the back of a galloping horse.

There were frequent horse races, among the Indians or between Indians and whites. Lewis remarked, "several of those horses would be thought fleet in the U States." The Indians could do feats that the whites could only watch: "It is astonishing," Lewis wrote, "to see these people ride down those steep hills which they do at full speed."

The stallions in the expedition's herd were so troublesome the captains offered to trade two of them for one of the Indians' geldings. The Indians refused. The captains decided they would have to take the risk of castration and began the operation. A young man interrupted to show the whites how the Indians did it. His method was to let the wound bleed, rather than tying off the scrotum. As an experiment, the captains had him operate on two stallions in the Indian way, while Drouillard gelded two in the white way. Two weeks later, Lewis wrote, "I have no hesitation in declaring my beleif that the indian method of gelding is preferable to that practiced by ourselves."

Horse care, horse trading, horse racing brought the white and red men together. On the evening of May 13, "we tryed the speed of several of our horses," in races against one another and Indians. It is an irresistible scene: the young braves, red and white, racing from point to point over that beautiful valley with the snow-topped mountains looming behind, whooping and whipping their horses, digging in their heels, while crowds of onlookers, also mounted and also a mix of red and white, cheered them on. Wherever one looked, there were horses, Appaloosas mostly, selectively bred, "active strong and well formed," according to Lewis.

They were present in "immence numbers," a phrase Lewis hadn't used to describe a herd of animals since he left the buffalo country. "50, 60 or a hundred hed is not unusual for an individual to possess."

That herd was by far the Nez Percés' greatest asset. It also represented a potential solution to one of the major transportation problems facing the proposed American trading empire stretching from St. Louis to the mouth of the Columbia. The trick would be to get the Nez Percé herd over to the other side of the mountains, which in turn depended on making a peace between the Blackfeet and the Nez Percé, which was hardly likely as long as the Blackfeet had guns and the Nez Percé did not.

Still, Lewis was resolved to try. As he gazed at the magnificent herd, he began to imagine two long strings of Indian packhorses passing each other on this prairie. One was headed east, carrying spices and other fabulous goods from the Indies; the other headed west, carrying furs from the Missouri River country and trade goods from Europe. In the image, Nez Percé horses would make up for the lack of an all-water route across the continent.

It was an idea Lewis had started working on back at Fort Clatsop.

His first attempts to begin creating the conditions that would make the plan workable had failed—he couldn't get a Nez Percé delegate to go with him to meet with the Blackfeet, or a chief to come to Washington with him. But he stayed with the idea, and continued to try to think it through.

There were frequent footraces. Lewis was impressed by one Indian who proved to be as fleet as the expedition's best runners, Drouillard and Reubin Field. There were games of prison base (an Indian game in which each side tries to make prisoners of those who run out of their base area), and pitching quoits (a white man's game of throwing flattened rings at a pin).[3] Lewis encouraged the games, for they gave the men who were not hunters some badly needed exercise. They "have had so little to do that they are geting reather lazy and slouthfull."

Mainly what they did was look at the Bitterroots to see how much snow was left. The expedition's energy was as tight as a coiled spring, ready to vault itself over those mountains, in an agony of anticipation of being released.

Waiting for snow to melt is rather like watching grass grow. The first discernible sign of progress is greeted with the greatest joy. Thus Lewis on May 17: "I am pleased at finding the river rise so rapidly, it no doubt is attributeable to the meting snows of the mountains."

Still they had to wait. The mountains remained: "That icy barier which seperates me from my friends and Country, from all which makes life esteemable."

"Patience, patience," Lewis advised himself as he concluded his journal entry and closed the elk-skin-covered volume.

Not until May 26 did he let a little optimism into his journal. "The river still rising fast and snows of the mountains visibly diminish," he wrote.

Ethnography and nature studies helped him get his mind off the snow. On May 27, one of the men brought him a "black woodpecker," which Lewis had already seen and noted but not held in his hand. He now gave it a five-hundred-word description ("the throat is of a fine crimson red," "the belly and breast is a curious mixture of white and blood red," "wings and tail are of a sooty black," "top of the head black . . . with a glossey tint of green in a certain exposure," and so on).

The bird is now named Lewis's woodpecker. Lewis preserved the skin, which ended up at Harvard University. It is his only surviving zoological specimen.[4]

On June 6, "we meet with a beautifull little bird," also described in charming detail. It was the western tanager.

Lewis also collected, described, and preserved close to fifty new plants, including camas, yellow bells, Lewis's syringa, purple trillium, ragged robin, and mariposa lily. Paul Cutright calls this his most productive period as a botanist.[5]

Every day, the Nez Percé told the captains they would have to wait. As May turned into June, the waiting got harder. Twisted Hair had told them that the tribe would cross the mountains in May, but that was before the winter snows began. It had snowed and snowed and snowed, far beyond an average year, to such an extent that some of the Indians were warning the captains they would have to wait until July.

But on June 3, Lewis was surprised and pleased to learn that "today the Indians dispatched an express over the mountains to travellers rest." The "express" was a teenage boy who went seeking information from the Flatheads about "the occurrences that have taken place on the East side of the mountains" during the winter.

If the Indians could send a boy over the Lolo Trail just to pick up some gossip, Lewis "thought it probable that we could also pass." He told the Nez Percé he was going to try, but they replied that, although their boys could make the trip, Lewis's men could not: the creeks were too high, there was no grass, and the snow was deep over the roads, which were extremely slippery. They told Lewis to have patience. In twelve to fourteen days, he could set out.

On June 4, Lewis met with some of the chiefs. He repeated his request for guides to accompany his party to the falls of the Missouri, then up to the Blackfoot country in search of a truce. The chiefs stalled.

Lewis checked the men's packs and was pleased to "find that our whole party have an ample store of bread and roots for our voyage." All around the campsite, the men were "much engaged in preparing their saddles arranging their loads provisions &c for our departure."

The captains planned to move camp eastward, from the banks of the Clearwater to higher ground at the western terminus of the Lolo Trail, on the southern end of Weippe Prairie, where they had first met the Nez Percé the preceding September. There they would make camp and begin the final preparations for the assault on the mountains.

On June 8, two days before the move, there was a sort of farewell party at the campsite they had occupied on the banks of the Clearwater for nearly a month. The afternoon featured horse- and footracing and game-playing. In the evening, Cruzatte brought out the fiddle and dancing began.

But as the festivities went on, an Indian told the captains that the snow was still deep and they would not be able to cross until the beginning of July. He warned that if they tried it sooner the horses would be at least three days without food.

"This information is disagreable," Lewis admitted. "It causes some doubt as to the time at which it will be most proper for us to set out." But not enough doubt to deter the captains. Lewis explained, "as we have no time to loose we will wrisk the chanches and set out as early as the indians generally think it practicable or the middle of this month."

By midday, June 9, everything was in readiness for the move to Weippe Prairie. The mood was exuberant. "Our party seem much elated with the idea of moving on towards their friends and country," Lewis happily noted. "They all seem allirt in their movements today." Notwithstanding the thoughts of what lay ahead, they were "amusing themselves very merrily today in runing footraces pitching quites, prison basse &c."

The expedition was about to resume its march.

30

THE LOLO TRAIL

June 10–July 2, 1806

On the morning of June 10, just before the expedition set off for Weippe Prairie, Cut Nose sent word that two of his young men would overtake the party in a day or so, guide it through the mountains, then lead Lewis to the falls of the Missouri. Welcome news, the best possible. The party moved out in high spirits.

Each man—and presumably Sacagawea—was mounted and leading a packhorse. In addition, there were several spare horses. "We therefore feel ourselves perfectly equiped for the mountains," Lewis wrote. He established camp at the quawmash flats. "Quawmash" was camas, the root that had stood off starvation for the men in September and then damn near killed them. Stomachs had adjusted; the men could eat it now without violent consequences. The plant was so central to the lives of the Nez Percé that Lewis wrote a fifteen-hundred-word description of camas and the Indian methods of preparing it for food. His concluding sentence was: "This root is pallateable but disagrees with me in every shape I have ever used it."

He enjoyed its appearance: "The quawmash is now in blume and from the colour of its bloom at a short distance it resembles lakes of fine clear water, so complete is this deseption that on first sight I could have swoarn it was water."

By June 13, the pressure on the captains—from both within and without—to get going was all but irresistible. But Cut Nose's young men had not shown up. Lewis gave them one more day. Meanwhile, he sent two hunters ahead, to a prairie eight miles east, to lay in a stock of meat.

The Indians did not show that day, or the next, and Lewis gave up on the guides. On the evening of June 14, he ordered the horses hobbled, in anticipation of an early start.

"From hence to traveller's rest," Lewis wrote that night, "we shall make a forsed march."

With the decision to go without guides, Lewis had allowed impatience to cloud his judgment. He was taking chances and violating Jefferson's orders to be always prudent so that he could carry out his number-one objective, to get to the Pacific and back with a report on the main features of the country. And for what was he taking such a risk? To get home a little earlier?

If the expedition could get to Traveler's Rest by early August, and if it then took the Nez Percé route to the buffalo country, it would be at Great Falls by the middle of August. There it could dig up its caches and then speed downstream, with two good traveling months to get to St. Louis.

But Lewis felt a pressing need to get going. Besides just giving in to impatience, he had some genuine objectives in mind, primarily further exploring. He and Clark had agreed to divide at Traveler's Rest. Clark would go to the Jefferson River and on to Three Forks, where he would cross to the Yellowstone Valley and proceed down the Yellowstone to the Missouri, mapping and describing new country every step of the way.

Lewis would follow the Nez Percé buffalo route to Great Falls, then conduct an exploration of the Marias River to its sources. He hoped that those sources would be well north of forty-nine degrees. That would be good news to bring to the president.

To make these side explorations, the captains needed to get over the mountains by the beginning of July. That was why Lewis felt time pressing. But, although the expeditions to the Marias and the Yellowstone were interesting and important, they were not significant enough to merit risking everything.

Lewis's usual good judgment had left him. Previously he had made his decisions on the basis of what needed to be done next to make the expedition succeed, not what might be done in two months if such-or-so were done now. Previously he had been a mature, responsible senior commander (except with the Sioux, where he had allowed himself to be provoked into taking excess risks); now he was an impatient junior officer acting more on impulse than on judgment.

He had always been self-confident; now he was cocksure. He remarked at Lemhi Pass in 1805 that anything Indians could do, he and his men could do. Even after seeing the Clatsops and Chinooks in their canoes, after seeing the Nez Percé ride their horses, he retained that notion of white superiority. Even when the Indian boy who set out to cross the mountains a couple of weeks earlier showed up to report that he had been forced back by the heavy snow, Lewis insisted on going.

The Nez Percé told him it couldn't be done. At first he discounted them; eventually he ignored them. He proposed to be the first to cross the Lolo Trail, in 1806, and without guides.

In his journal on June 14, Lewis admitted to apprehension. The snow and the lack of grass for the horses "will prove a serious imbarrassment to us as at least four days journey of our rout in these mountains lies over hights and along a ledge of mountains never intirely destitute of snow." Clark wrote that evening, "Even now I Shudder with the expectation with great dificuelties in passing those Mountains."

Lewis rationalized the decision. "We have now been detained near five weeks in consequence of the snows," he wrote, "a serious loss of time at this delightfull season for traveling."

Whatever the risk and apprehension, there is no doubt the decision to move out was a popular one. "Every body seems anxious to be in motion," Lewis wrote, "convinced that we have not now any time to delay if the calculation is to reach the United States this season; this I am detirmined to accomplish if within the compass of human power."

On the morning of June 15, in a cold, driving rain, the party set out. At eight miles, they found two deer the hunters had killed and hung. At noon, they halted at a creek and dined while the horses grazed. Through the afternoon, they marched. The going was difficult, because of fallen timber crisscrossing the trail and the slippery pathway, caused by the rain. Still, they made twenty-two miles. Lewis did a bird count, and found a hummingbird nest. So far so good. No snow yet, so the trail was easy to follow.

June 16, an early start. The party ascended a ridge and nooned it at a "handsome little glade" where there was grass for the horses. The glade was bursting with life. Lewis noted the dogtooth violet, the bluebells, the yellow flowering pea and the columbine in bloom, and the honeysuckle, huckleberry, and white maple putting out their first leaves, along with other signs of spring in the mountains.

But within a couple of hours of resuming the march, the party found itself in winter conditions. The snow was eight to ten feet deep. Fortunately, it was firm enough to bear the horses—indeed, it improved the traveling, for it covered the fallen timber—but it also covered the trail. They made fifteen miles during the day and camped at the small glade where Captain Clark had killed a horse the previous September and hung it for Lewis and his men. There was insufficient grass for the horses, and it was obvious that as they continued to gain altitude there would be even less grass.

In the morning, the going was "difficult and dangerous." The climb toward the ridge was steep, the elevation gain dramatic. After three miles of climbing, "we found ourselves invelloped in snow from 12 to 15 feet deep even on the south sides of the hills with the fairest exposure to the sun."

Lewis thought he had prepared himself for the worst, but he hadn't. "Here was winter with all it's rigors," he wrote that evening.

The party was six or seven days' march from Traveler's Rest, provided it was fortunate enough not to lose the way, and "of this Drewyer our principal dependance as a woods-man and guide was entirely doubtfull."

In an analysis that would have been better written five days earlier, Lewis admitted, "If we proceeded and should get bewildered in these mountains the certainty was that we should loose all our horses and consequently our baggage instruments perhaps our papers and thus eminently wrisk the loss of the discoveries which we had already made if we should be so fortunate as to escape with life."

He consulted with Clark. They reached an obvious conclusion: "We conceived it madnes in this stage of the expedition to proceed without a guide." This led to a resolution: "To return with our horses while they were yet strong" to an encampment with sufficient grass. Drouillard and Private Shannon would hurry on back to the Nez Percé villages to hire a guide. The party would wait for them and subsist on hunting, preserving their roots.

That resolution made, "we ordered the party to make a deposit for all the baggage which we had not immediate use for." In the deposit, the men put the roots they had brought, depending on the hunters for the next few days for food. In addition, Lewis put in the instruments and journals.

The journals were by far the most precious of all the expedition's possessions. The reason Lewis left them in the deposit illuminates what a risk he had taken in starting too soon: he wrote that they "are safer here than to wrisk them on horseback over the roads and creeks which we had passed."

The deposit was laid on scaffolds and well covered. At 1:00 p.m., the party started down the mountain.

Lewis hated to turn around. So did the men. "The party were a good deel dejected," Lewis wrote. "This is the first time since we have been on this long tour that we have ever been compelled to retreat or make a retrograde march." Sergeant Gass added that most of the men were "melancholy and disappointed."[1]

On June 18, Drouillard and Shannon struck out for the village to procure a guide. The price Lewis was ready to pay for a guide was unprecedented. He gave Drouillard an army rifle to be offered as reward for leading the party to Traveler's Rest, and authorized him to promise two additional army rifles and ten horses to any man who would lead the party to the falls of the Missouri.

The next evening, the party made camp in a meadow on the edge of the mountains. There was plenty of grass; the horses could fatten up here while the men waited for a guide. One of the men found some black morel mushrooms, which Lewis "roasted and eat without salt pepper or grease in this way I had for the first time the true taist of the morell which is truly an insippid taistless food."

On neither that day nor the next two was there any sign of Drouillard and Shannon. The captains worried about them, and talked about what they would do if they couldn't get a guide.

The plan they agreed on showed the depth of their desperation. "We have determined to wrisk a passage" without a guide, Lewis wrote. "Capt. C. or myself shall take four of our most expert woodsmen with three or four of our best horses and proceed two days in advance taking a plentifull supply of provision." The party would find the Lolo Trail by the marks on the sides of the pine trees, marks made over the decades by Indian horses and baggage rubbing against the trunks, and by tomahawks.

At the end of the second day, two men from the reconnaissance party would march back down the mountain to inform the main party whether to come right on or to give the scouts more time to locate the trail.

If the trail could be found, Lewis was confident he could get through, because the snow was firm, so the horses got good footing without having to step over or around fallen timber every few yards. If the trail could not be found, Lewis proposed to move far to the south in search of an alternate route over the Bitterroots.

On June 21, the party fell back to the quawmash flats, where the hunting was better. During the march, two young Indians, probably teenage boys, were encountered. They informed the captains that they were headed up the mountain to visit their friends on the other side. Lewis's eyes lit up at this news, but without Drouillard he found it difficult to understand the flashing hands of the warriors. Apparently the Indians were saying that Drouillard and Shannon would not be returning for two more days, but Lewis could not make out a reason for the delay. Lewis pressed the Indians to stay with his party until Drouillard and Shannon returned, and then to serve as guides for the crossing. They agreed to delay two days, no longer, at their own camp, closer to the mountains.

Two days later, still no sign of Drouillard and Shannon. Lewis was fearful that the two young Indians would set off that morning, so he sent four men to detain them, with Sergeant Gass in command. If the Indians insisted on going, Gass and his squad should accompany the Indians to Traveler's Rest, blazing the trees as they proceeded along the Lolo Trail.

That afternoon, to the relief of all, Drouillard and Shannon returned. The delay had been caused by bargaining, but it was well worth the time: they had with them three guides. One was a brother of Cut Nose, and the other two were men who had each given the captains a horse. Lewis described them as "all young men of good character and much respected by their nation." He was overjoyed to have them, even at the price of two rifles.

In the morning, the expedition was off at first light. The party made it back to the campsite of June 19–20, where it met with Gass, his squad, and the two Indians. The grass was good.

After dark, the Indians set some fir trees on fire, telling Lewis it was "to bring fair weather for our journey." This made a spectacular sight. "They have a great number of dry lims near their bodies," Lewis explained, "which when set on fire creates a very suddon and immence blaze from bottom to top. ... They are a beatifull object in this situation at night. This exhibition reminded me of a display of fireworks."

They were off at 6:00 a.m. In midmorning, they got to the deposit they had left nine days earlier. Everything was in good order. The snow had subsided from eleven feet to seven. As some men rearranged baggage, others cooked a meal of boiled venison.

The Indians urged haste. They said it was a considerable distance to the place they had to reach before dark, the only spot where there was grass for the horses. In two hours, everything was ready.

"We set out," Lewis wrote, "with our guides who lead us over and along the steep sides of tremendious mountains entirely covered with snow. . . . We ascended and decended severall lofty and steep hights . . . late in the evening much to the satisfaction of ourselves and the comfort of our horses we arrived at the desired spot and encamped on the steep side of a mountain convenient to a good spring. Here we found an abundance of fine grass for our horses."

They had reached the untimbered south side of Bald Mountain. The grass was ten days old, lush and green. The next grass, according to the Indians, was a day and a half's march away.

On June 27, another early start. After eight miles, the guides reached an elevated point where there was a conic mound of stones eight feet high.* The Indians stopped for a ceremonial smoke.

"From this place we had an extensive view of these stupendous mountains," Lewis wrote. The sight filled him with awe, dread, and an even greater respect for the Indian guides. "We were entirely surrounded by those mountains," he commented, "from which to one unacquainted with them it would have seemed impossible ever to have escaped; in short without the assistance of our guides I doubt much whether we who had once passed them could find our way to Travellers rest." The "marked trees" on which he had counted so heavily when he thought the party would have to go without guides turned out to be very few and far between.

But he had confidence in the guides. "These fellows are most admireable pilots," he explained. Whenever the snow was melted away, the party found themselves on the trail.

After smoking with the Indians and "contemplating this seene sufficient to have damp the sperits of any except such hardy travellers as we have become, we continued our march."

That day, they made twenty-eight miles and camped on the side of Spring Mountain. At Bald Mountain they had been at six thousand feet; at Spring Mountain they were five hundred feet higher. There was no grass for the horses, and the men had exhausted the meat supply. The captains distributed a pint of bear oil to go into each of the four kettles, there to be mixed with boiled roots. Lewis judged it "an agreeable dish."

In the morning, Lewis cast his eye over the herd and was disturbed to see the horses looking "extreemly gant." The guides reassured him: they would be at good grass by noon. Sure enough, after thirteen miles, at 11:00 a.m., "we arrived at an untimbered side of a mountain with a Southern aspect. . . . Here we found an abundance of grass."

---

* It is still there, reduced to about half its size since 1806, just west of Indian Grave Peak and just off Forest Service Road 500.

As the horses grazed, Lewis asked the guides how far to the next grass. Farther than the party could march in the afternoon, the Indians replied. "As our horses were very hungary and much fatiegued," Lewis decided to make camp right there.*

In the morning, after a march of five miles took them to Rocky Point, the guides led the party down the mountain to the Lochsa River, then up the trail to the quawmash flats (today's Packer Meadows, a couple of miles south of Lolo Pass), on the Divide between the Clearwater and the Bitterroot Rivers. They were at fifty-two hundred feet and there was plenty of grass. The horses grazed and the men ate.

There was still plenty of daylight left, so after dinner the party set off down the valley toward the Bitterroot River. At seven miles, the men reached today's Lolo Hot Springs and went into camp.

As soon as camp was set up, the men, red and white, plunged into the pools created by the Nez Percé over the decades by the use of rocks. The Indians would stay in the hot bath as long as they could stand it, then leap out and run to the creek, which was ice cold, and jump in, whooping and hollering and splashing. When they were too cold, they ran back to the hot bath.

Lewis took a hot bath only. He stayed in nineteen minutes. It was only "with dificulty" that he could remain that long. "It caused a profuse sweat."

On June 30, the party marched down the valley. The men were well out of the snow, but the trail was often difficult, sometimes dangerous. At one steep hillside, Lewis's horse slipped "with both his hinder feet out of the road and fell." Lewis fell off backward and slid forty feet before he could grab a branch to stop himself. "The horse was near falling on me" as he slid, he wrote, "but fortunately recovers and we both escaped unhirt."

Just before sunset, the party rode into Traveler's Rest. They had covered 156 miles in six days. The previous fall, the expedition had been slowed by Old Toby's losing the way and by the fallen timber, and it had taken eleven days to cover the distance.

On this crossing, the horses had grass every day but one. To Lewis's delight, they had stood the journey surprisingly well. Most of them were in fine order "and only want a few days rest to restore them perfectly."

---

* The site is accessible by foot or four-wheel-drive vehicle from Forest Road 500, which generally follows the Lolo Trail from near Lolo Pass to Weippe Prairie. The U.S. Forest Service has done an excellent job of locating and marking campsites.

This was thanks to the skill of the guides. Their sense of distance and timing, not to mention their sense of direction and ability to follow a trail buried under ten feet of snow, was a superb feat of woodsmanship. Most of the trail was in dense forest, and the guides were young men, not yet twenty years of age.

The expedition had been as lucky in its guides as Lewis had been in his fall from the horse, as Lewis knew. When he wrote that not even Drouillard could find his way in these mountains, he was giving his guides an extraordinary compliment.

The party stayed at Traveler's Rest for three days. The captains put the final details into the plan for exploration they had been discussing through the winter at Fort Clatsop. In its final version, the plan went like this:

Lewis, with nine men and seventeen horses, would follow the Nez Percé route to the falls of the Missouri. At the falls, he would drop off three men to dig up the cache and prepare to help in a portage. With the remaining six volunteers, Lewis would ascend the Marias "with a view to explore the country and ascertain whether any branch of that river lies as far north as Latd. 50." He also hoped to meet with the Blackfeet so that he could deliver his peace-and-trade speech. Those missions completed, he would go to the mouth of the Marias to meet the men coming down the Missouri.

Those men would be led by Sergeant Ordway. He was to proceed with Captain Clark to the head of the Jefferson River, where the expedition had left its canoes before crossing Lemhi Pass with the Shoshones. Ordway and a party of ten men would descend the Jefferson and the Missouri in the canoes. They would get help in the portage around the falls from the three men left there by Lewis. Once around the falls, the combined force of fourteen would proceed to the mouth of the Marias, there to pick up Lewis and his party. Reunited, they would descend to the mouth of the Yellowstone, where they would meet Clark and his group.

Clark's independent exploration would start at the Three Forks. After dispatching Sergeant Ordway's party, Clark and the remaining ten men, and Sacagawea and her boy, would cross the Divide between the Missouri and the Yellowstone. When they reached the river, they would build canoes. Clark and five of the men, plus Charbonneau and his family, plus York, would descend the Yellowstone in the canoes to its junction with the Missouri, where almost the entire expedition would come together again.

Missing would be Sergeant Pryor and two privates. They were

assigned an independent mission. When Clark set off in the canoes, they were to take the horses to the Mandan villages, to use as gifts, with strings attached, for the Mandans. They had a second charge: to deliver a letter from Lewis to the North West Company agent Hugh Heney, whether at the Mandans or, if necessary, at Heney's post in Canada.

It was a highly ambitious plan, exceedingly complex, full of promise about what could be learned, dependent on tight timing. It certainly showed how confident the captains were about their men. For the first time, they were dividing the party to pursue different missions. They were giving large responsibilities to sergeants and privates, counting on their men to be able to handle independent operations without a hitch.

It was also an excessively dangerous plan. The captains were taking chances they should have avoided. In the heart of the country that the war parties of Crows, Blackfeet, Hidatsas, and other tribes passed through regularly, the captains were dividing their platoon into five squads, so widely separated they were not in supporting distance of one another.

Lewis took the risk of dividing his command because he wanted the expedition to be as successful as possible, to bring back as much information as possible, to make every conceivable effort to broker peace among the tribes, to begin the process of creating the American trading empire. These were important objectives, but not important enough to justify having squads as small as three men, and none larger than ten, roving about independently.

The captains were underestimating the Indians. They had perhaps spent too long with the easily dominated Clatsops and Chinooks, too long with the always friendly Nez Percé. Although they knew more about the native peoples west of the Mississippi River than any man alive, they had no direct knowledge of the Blackfeet. They did know that all the other Indians feared the Blackfeet.

Lewis and Clark didn't know enough to fear the Blackfeet, nor did the men. Since Lewis was leading his squad to the heart of Blackfoot country, his was the most dangerous mission. Nevertheless, when he called for volunteers on July 1, "many turned out, from whom I scelected Drewyer the two Feildses, Werner, Frazier and Sergt Gass."

That afternoon, Lewis wrote a fifteen-hundred-word letter to Heney, to be carried to him by Sergeant Pryor. It represented his first step toward bringing about an American trade empire stretching from St. Louis to the mouth of the Columbia.

Lewis had met Heney the previous winter and been impressed by him, despite his being an agent for the North West Company. Heney had told Lewis that, if there was anything he could do for the Americans, he was ready to do it. Apparently he talked as if he was ready to drop his North West Company connection and go to work for the Americans. Lewis must have thought so, for he made Heney an offer to do just that.

If Heney could convince the influential chiefs of the Sioux to visit their new father in Washington, and go along with them to serve as interpreter, Lewis would pay him a dollar a day, from the date of the receipt of the letter, plus expenses. Lewis further promised that Heney would be first in line for the post of U.S. agent to the Sioux, which paid seventy-five dollars per month plus six rations per day.

Lewis was straightforward about his motives: he wanted the Sioux to "have an ample view of our population and resourses, and on their return convince their nations of the futility of an attempt to oppose the will of our government." Lewis provided Heney with arguments to convince the Sioux to make the journey, the chief being that the Sioux had no means of resisting the American plans for building posts and fortifications along the Missouri, and, in any case, "their acquiescence will be productive of greater advantages than their most sanguine hopes could lead them to expect from oppersition."

Lewis stressed a central point for Heney to pass onto the Sioux: the United States "will not long suffer her citizens to be deprived of the free navigation of the Missouri by a few comparitively feeble bands of Savages." But he should also tell the Sioux about the friendly views of the United States government toward them and the plan to establish trading posts in their neighborhood.

Through Heney, Lewis was trying to talk to the Sioux—and the British. He told Heney that the Corps of Discovery had gone to the Pacific Ocean by way of the Missouri and Columbia Rivers, and that he was about to explore the Marias. He obviously hoped that Heney would pass this information on to his superiors in the company, who would inform government officials in Montreal, who would thus learn of Lewis's explorations and the potential American claim on the Oregon country, and possibly on southern Alberta, Saskatchewan, and Manitoba.

Lewis said he hoped to arrive at the Mandan villages about the beginning of September. Heney should meet him there, with a party not to exceed twelve persons, the largest that the expedition could accommodate.[2]

A good idea. If it worked, Sioux chiefs would go to Washington, they would be mightily impressed, they would come home and make peace, renounce their British loyalties, welcome American trading posts on the Missouri, and become full-fledged partners in the grand enterprise of building the American empire.

If it worked, and if Lewis found a Blackfoot band and spread the good news of the coming of the Americans and persuaded the Blackfeet to join the enterprise, within a couple of years the Americans would take over the fur trade from the Mississippi to the mouth of the Columbia.

That was a big dream, an empire builder's dream. Lewis was thinking on a worldwide scale. He was proposing to set up and execute one of the biggest business takeover deals of the century, and add the northwestern empire to the United States in the bargain.

Sitting beside Lolo Creek, near the place where it flows into the Bitterroot River, in a wide, beautiful, extensive valley, at least a thousand miles from the nearest white outpost, in command of a platoon-sized force in a country teeming with war parties, utterly destitute of equipment (except for rifles and kettles and a few remaining knives—exactly the manufactured items the Indians most wanted), Meriwether Lewis got started on making his dream come true, in his letter to Heney.

What a many-faceted man was Lewis. On the day he put the final touches to the plan for separate explorations, informed the men of what he and Clark intended, picked the volunteers to accompany him, and wrote that long letter to Heney, he also found time to do a bird count and write a five-hundred-word essay on the prairie dog.

The next day, July 2, he spent much of his time in conversation with the Indians, using sign language, trying to get a better fix on the lay of the land ahead. In the evening, "the indians run their horses, and we had several foot races betwen the natives and our party with various success." He concluded with a handsome tribute to the five young Indians who had guided him over the Lolo Trail and thus saved the expedition: "These are a race of hardy strong athletic active men."

31

THE MARIAS EXPLORATION

July 3–July 28, 1806

On the morning of July 3, Lewis wrote, "I took leave of my worthy friend and companion Capt. Clark and the party that accompanyed him." As the captains and men shook hands and said their goodbyes, there must have been a question in every man's mind—I wonder if I'll ever see you again.

The proposed rendezvous at the Missouri-Yellowstone junction was a full five hundred miles east of Traveler's Rest, as the crow flies. Clark's proposed route would cover nearly a thousand miles, Lewis's nearly eight hundred.

Both captains would be in country they had not seen before, facing they knew not what dangers from the weather, the terrain, and the natives. Except for their rifles, scientific instruments, and journals, the men were no better equipped than the Indians, and none of the five detachments of the Corps of Discovery would have enough firepower to drive off a determined attack from even a moderate-sized war party. But such confident travelers had the captains become that what they said to each other as they parted was, See you at the junction in five or six weeks.

Whether their confidence in themselves and their men had swelled past all reason, was theirs to discover. That Lewis felt at least a tinge of apprehension is clear from his comment on the parting: "I could not avoid feeling much concern on this occasion although I hoped this seperation was only momentary."

Lewis, nine men, five Nez Percé guides, and seventeen horses set out northward, down the Bitterroot River. At ten miles, they crossed the river by raft and continued their march eastward along today's Clark Fork River to within a couple of miles of today's Missoula, Montana.

At sunset, they made camp. Hunters brought in three deer, which Lewis split with the Indians. He tried to persuade them to stay with his party until they got over the Continental Divide and down to the falls of the Missouri, but they said he didn't need them: the road was such a well-beaten track even a white man couldn't miss the way. Besides, they were afraid of meeting with a Hidatsa raiding party.

Just before lying down on his elk skin, Lewis ordered the hunters to turn out early in the morning to kill some meat for the guides, "whom I was unwilling to leave without giving them a good supply of provisions after their having been so obliging as to conduct us through those tremendious mountains."

They parted at noon the following day, July 4. Independence Day drew no comment from Lewis, no mention of the men firing their rifles. If anything, it was a sad day, the last contact with the Nez Percé, among whom the party had been living for two months.

The Nez Percé had seen the white soldiers hungry and fed them; seen them cold and provided fuel; seen them without horses and put them on mounts; seen them confused and provided good advice; seen them make fools of themselves trying to cross mountains ten feet deep in snow and not snickered; seen them lost and guided them. They had ridden together, eaten together, slept together, played together, and crossed the Lolo Trail together. Although they could communicate only with the sign language, they had an abundance of shared experiences that drew them together. They had managed to cross communication and cultural barriers to become genuine friends.

"These affectionate people our guides betrayed every emmotion of unfeigned regret at seperating from us," Lewis wrote. The Nez Percé could not hide their anxiety about their new friends: "They said that they were confidint that the Pahkees* . . . would cut us off."

As the Indians set off to the north, Lewis and his men headed east. They passed through present-day Missoula, up today's Broadway Street

---

* The term probably means "enemies," not a specific tribe (Moulton, ed., *Journals*, vol. 7, p. 90).

across the river from the University of Montana. At five miles, they came to today's Blackfoot River, called River of the Road to Buffalo by the Nez Percé, coming in from the east, and headed up it, through a heavily timbered country of high and rocky mountains. The next day, they made thirty-one miles.

The place they camped that night had been a Hidatsa war-party camp a couple of months earlier. On July 6, the Indian sign included fresh tracks along the trail. Lewis was concerned: "They have a large pasel of horses," he commented. He expected to meet with either the Hidatsas or another hunting party at any time, so he and the men were "much on our guard both day and night."

His luck held. There were no encounters with Indians, friendly or hostile. His trip up the Blackfoot River, through one of the most beautiful valleys in Montana, was happily uneventful. What caught Lewis's eye was "*much sign* of beaver in this extensive bottom."

On July 7, the party turned in a more northerly direction to follow the Nez Percé trail up today's Alice Creek. There were many beaver dams, many deer. Reubin Field wounded a moose. "My dog much worried," Lewis wrote, without giving any detail but apparently referring to the wounded moose. At about eleven miles, the creek was not much more than a trickle, coming from a spring on the side of a low, untimbered mountain. The trail wound up the north side of the creek, then switched back a couple of times before disappearing over the top of the pass.*

The party wound its way up the gentle slope. At the top, it reached "the dividing ridge betwen the waters of the Columbia and Missouri rivers." To the east, Lewis could see Square Butte, near the falls of the Missouri, not far from where he stood. The Great Plains of North America stretched out in front of him, apparently without limit, under an infinity of bright-blue sky. He took a step—and he was back in U.S. territory.

The descent was easy, through hills and hollows. The men could talk only of buffalo, but none were encountered, although tantalizing signs were all about them. The next day, the party crossed the Dearborn River and closed on the Medicine (today's Sun) River, where they camped.

---

* The trail is plainly evident today, including travois marks from the thousands of Nez Percé who used it. It can be reached by driving up Alice Creek Road, off Montana Highway 200 some ten miles East of Lincoln, Montana. The pass is called Lewis and Clark Pass (6,284 feet)—somewhat misnamed, since Clark never saw it.

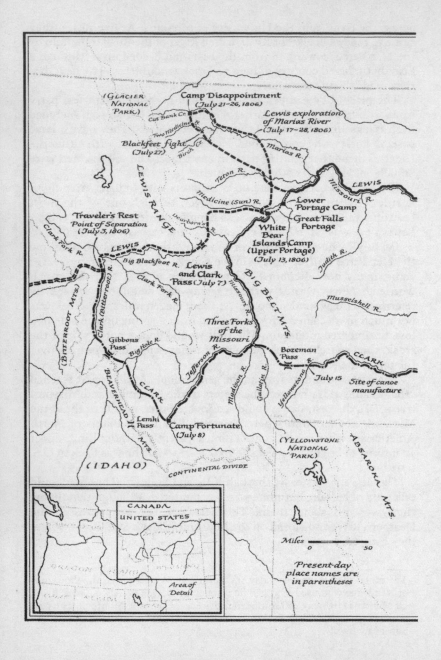

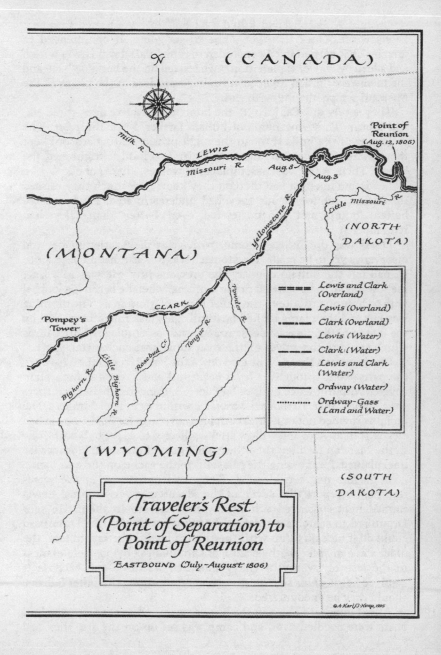

(CANADA)

N

Milk R.

LEWIS

Missouri R.   Aug. 8

Aug. 3

Point of
Reunion
(Aug. 12, 1806)

Little Missouri R.

(NORTH
DAKOTA)

Yellowstone R.

(MONTANA)

CLARK

Powder R.

Pompey's
Tower

Bighorn R.

Little Bighorn R.

Rosebud Cr.

Tongue R.

Legend:
- - - - - Lewis and Clark (Overland)
- - - - Lewis (Overland)
- - - Clark (Overland)
——— Lewis (Water)
——— Clark (Water)
═══ Lewis and Clark (Water)
——— Ordway (Water)
·········· Ordway-Gass (Land and Water)

(WYOMING)

(SOUTH
DAKOTA)

Traveler's Rest
(Point of Separation) to
Point of Reunion

EASTBOUND (July–August 1806)

© A. Karl / J. Kemp, 1995

On July 9, Joseph Field killed a fat buffalo. "We halted to dine," Lewis wrote. Once they got some roasts going, it commenced to drizzle. That settled it. "I concluded to remain all day," Lewis wrote, and added by way of explanation, "we feasted on the buffaloe." He and the men were "much rejoiced at finding ourselves in the plains of the Missouri which abound with game."

They surely did. On July 10, the hunters killed five deer, three elk, and a bear. They saw herds of buffalo farther down the river. The bellowing of the bulls through the night (it was mating season) kept them awake. It was "one continual roar," so loud it frightened the horses. There were "vast assemblages of wolves," herds of elk.

Lewis and his men had thought they knew how much they missed the Plains, but found out they had underestimated. Fresh roasted buffalo hump and tongue tasted even better than they had remembered.

Lewis was on his way home, with great discoveries made, and discoveries yet to be made. His stomach was full as it hadn't been since he had left the buffalo country the previous July. He was in a fine, mellow mood, as he showed in the morning, when he began his journal with a charming tribute to the Great Plains of Montana: "The morning was fair and the plains looked beatifull. the grass much improved by the late rain. the air was pleasant and a vast assemblage of little birds which croud to the groves on the river sung most enchantingly."

On the march that day, headed down the Sun River to the Missouri, the party went through "a level beautifull and extensive high plain covered with immence hirds of buffaloe. . . . I sincerely belief that there were not less than 10 thousand buffaloe within a circle of 2 miles." The buffalo provided not only meat but also coverings for boats. Lewis had eleven of them shot and willow sticks collected to make bull boats, one in the Mandan fashion, the other "on a plan of our own," (otherwise unexplained) for crossing the Missouri to the cache on the east bank.

In the morning, terrible news. The men sent to round up the horses returned to report that seven of the seventeen were missing. Lewis immediately suspected a hunting party had stolen them. He sent Drouillard to search for them, although what he thought Drouillard could do if he caught up with the thieves he did not say. In fact, the order was a mistake, both because of Drouillard's obvious helplessness in the face of twenty or thirty mounted warriors, and because it deprived Lewis of his sole means of communication with other Indians, should they be encountered.

After Drouillard rode off, the horses swam across the river, the bull boats were paddled over, and camp was set up on the site they had occupied during the great portage of 1805. The cache was opened; high water during the spring runoff had gotten into it; Lewis's plant specimens were all lost, but fortunately the papers and maps were okay.

The loss of the specimens was a terrible blow. They had been collected painstakingly, labeled, carefully dried (requiring daily attention) and preserved. Paul Russell Cutright writes, "Such losses were more than minor catastrophes, resulting as they did in the defeat of prime scientific objectives and the complete vitiation of weeks and months of dedicated effort and inquiry."[1]

That night, Lewis found that he had forgotten something else about life on the Missouri River. "Musquetoes excessively troublesome," he wrote, "insomuch that without the protection of my musquetoe bier I should have found it impossible to wright a moment."

On July 14, Lewis had the men prepare the baggage for the upcoming portage. He sent his trunks containing his papers and journals to one of the islands, to be put on a scaffold in thick brush, and covered with skins. "I take this precaution," he explained, "lest some indians may visit the men I leave here before the arrival of the main party and rob them."

In the aftermath of losing nearly half of his horses to a roving band of warriors, he was beginning to fear that perhaps he was dividing the Corps of Discovery in too many parts. But his fear was not so strong as to cause him to call off his exploration of the Marias, even though the loss of the horses meant he had to reduce the size of his party from six to three men. At least that would leave six men at the falls, perhaps enough for self-defense.

Drouillard didn't come in that day, which worried Lewis. Nor did he return the following day. Lewis began to fear that a grizzly had killed him. He explained his reasoning: "I knew that if he met with a bear in the plains even he would attack him. and that if any accedent should happen to seperate him from his horse in that situation the chances in favour of his being killed would be as 9 to 10."

At 1:00 p.m., July 15, Drouillard returned. He reported that he had searched for two days before discovering where the thieves had run the stolen horses over the Dearborn River. He pursued their tracks, but they had a two-day start, so he gave it up. He figured the strength of the party at fifteen lodges.

Lewis assumed it was a hunting party, looking for buffalo. He had seen that day how much roving it took to find the herds; there was not a buffalo in sight, where the previous day they covered the earth. Such huge herds had to keep moving to find grass, which meant that those who hunted them had to keep moving. Which meant that the Corps of Discovery had been exceedingly lucky the previous year to have avoided all contact with the natives until they got to the Shoshone village.

With Drouillard returned, Lewis was ready to set out in the morning for the Marias exploration. He had selected Drouillard and the Field brothers. He would take six horses, leaving two of the best and two of the worst with the party at the falls, to assist in the portage. He closed his journal, "The musquetoes continue to infest us in such manner that we can scarcely exist. . . . my dog even howls with the torture he experiences. . . . they are almost insupportable."

On July 16, the exploring party set out, stopping first at the falls where Lewis made a drawing. Then it was out of the river valley and up onto the high plains. To Lewis's eye, the plains "have somewhat the appearance of an ocean, not a tree nor a shrub to be seen." He was back in wonderland. "The whole face of the country as far as the eye can reach looks like a well shaved bowlinggreen, in which immence and numerous herds of buffaloe were seen feeding attended by their scarcely less numerous sheepherds the Wolves."

The enchantment of the place did not prevent Lewis from worrying. His expressed desire to meet the Blackfeet had given way to fear. When he was planning this exploration, he had hoped to have with him some leading Nez Percé men, so that he could make a peace between the Nez Percé and the Blackfeet. That motive was now gone. Further, he had planned to explore with a party of seven; now he was down to four. Finally, what the Nez Percé said about the Blackfeet—"they are a vicious lawless and reather an abandoned set of wretches"—had its effect on Lewis. His conclusion: "I wish to avoid an interview with them if possible," because he had no doubt that "finding us weak should they happen to be numerous [the Blackfeet] wil most probably attempt to rob us of our arms and baggage." He vowed to "take every possible precaution to avoid them if possible."

The ride through wonderland continued. On July 18, "we passed immence herds of buffaloe. . . . in short for about 12 miles it appeared as one herd only the whole plains being covered with them." Indians never left his mind. At camp that night, on the Marias River, he noted: "I keep a strict lookout every night. I take my tour of watch with the men."

For three more days, Lewis followed the Marias upstream. On the afternoon of July 21, the river forked into two branches, today's Cut

Bank Creek coming from the north and Two Medicine River flowing from the south. Since Lewis's whole purpose was to find the northernmost branch of the Marias, he did not hesitate to follow up Cut Bank Creek. But because the Marias had been leading him on an almost straight westward route, he confessed that "the most northern point . . . I now fear will not be as far north as I wished and expected."

On Tuesday, July 22, Lewis got to within twenty miles of the Rocky Mountains, in sight of the Continental Divide in today's Glacier National Park. About twenty miles northwest of the modern town of Cut Bank, he set up camp "in a beautifull and extensive bottom of the river," in a clump of large cottonwoods. From the bluff overhanging the bottom, Lewis could see where the creek came out of the mountains, and it was southwest, not northwest, of his position. He had reached the northernmost point of Cut Bank Creek.

He decided to stay there for a couple of days, to rest the men and horses and to make celestial observations. "I now have lost all hope of the waters of this river ever extending to N Latitude 50 degrees," he admitted, but he was not one to give up easily: "I still hope and think it more than probable that both *white earth* river and milk river extend as far north as latd. 50 degrees."

Arlen Large explains his methods and results:

> Lewis measured the sun's noon altitude on July 23, getting a raw octant reading of 62 degrees 00' 00". He didn't record any conversion of that suspiciously round number into a latitude. Using an 1806 Nautical Almanac and Lewis's usual method of computation, that octant reading would have produced a latitude of 48 degrees, 10', or some 30' too far south.
>
> I think it's very possible he didn't compute a latitude here because he wasn't carrying an 1806 almanac; my surmise is that the expedition's three almanacs covered 1803, 1804 and 1805 only. His conclusion that Cut Bank Creek didn't reach as high as 50 degrees probably was based on dead reckoning. Using as a benchmark the previous year's calculation of 47 degrees, 25' 17" as the latitude of the Marias-Missouri junction, he could have seen from his compass courses and distances on the way to Cut Bank Creek that it was well short of the 170-odd miles needed to reach the 50th parallel.[2]

What Lewis needed to know was the time, and that he got from his equal altitudes of the sun. He set his chronometer at high noon. If he could make a sextant measurement of a daytime sun-moon distance, he could figure the time in Greenwich. Then he would know his longitude.

The following day, Drouillard returned from a scouting mission to report that there was much sign of Indians in the area. Lewis's attempts to make his observations were frustrated by cloud cover, both that day and the next—and the next. The men went out to hunt, without success—a sure sign Indians had been hunting in the area in considerable numbers. The men reported various signs of Indians, some of them large campsites with many, many horses. "We consider ourselves extreemly fortunate in not having met with these people," Lewis wrote.

He decided he would leave in the morning, July 26, unless the sun came out so that he could make observations. He was "apprehensive that I shall not reach the United States within this season unless I make every exertion in my power which I shall certainly not omit."

The morning of Saturday, July 26, was cloudy. Lewis waited until 9:00 a.m. before giving up, "which I do with much reluctance." He had the horses caught, and "we set out biding a lasting adieu to this place which I now call camp disappointment." The party rode south, toward Two Medicine River, which it struck around midday. After eating and grazing the horses, the party resumed its march, with Drouillard ahead in the river bottom, hunting. As the hills closed in on the south bank of the river, Lewis and the Field brothers ascended them to the high plain above, while Drouillard continued to ride down the valley.

When Lewis got to the top and looked about, he was alarmed to see, at the distance of a mile or so, a herd of thirty horses. He brought out his telescope and discovered several Indians sitting their horses, staring intently into the valley. Lewis surmised they were watching Drouillard.

"This was a very unpleasant sight," Lewis admitted. If there were as many Indians as there were horses, which he assumed would be the case, he was overwhelmingly outnumbered. He thought they were Atsinas or Blackfeet; in either case, "from their known character I expected that we were to have some difficulty with them." He thought of flight and immediately gave it up. To run was to invite pursuit, and the Indians' horses looked better than his. Further, if he and the Field brothers ran, Drouillard "would most probably fall a sacrefice."

Lewis resolved "to make the best of our situation." He ordered Joseph Field to display the flag which Lewis had brought for just this purpose. When it was unfurled, the party advanced slowly on the

Indians, who were running about "in a very confused manner as if much allarmed."

Suddenly a single Indian broke out of the milling pack and whipped his horse full-speed toward the party. He was probably on a dare, trying to count coup. Lewis dismounted and stood, waiting for the onrushing horse and rider. The Indian was disarmed by Lewis's reaction. He halted, some hundred yards from the party. Lewis held out his hand. The Indian wheeled his horse around, gave it the whip, and galloped back to his companions.

Lewis could count them by now; there were eight teenage boys and young men. He suspected there were others hidden behind the bluffs, for there were several other horses saddled. He ordered the Field brothers to advance with him, slowly.

His heart pounded. His life and the lives of his men were at stake. So were his papers, dearer to him even than his life.

He told the Field brothers that, no matter how many Indians there were, he was resolved to resist "to the last extremity prefering death to . . . being deprived of my papers instruments and gun." He hoped they would form the same resolution. When they nodded a grim-faced assent, Lewis told them to be alert and on their guard.

James Ronda writes that Lewis's words were "filled with more swagger than wisdom."[3] There is a bit of melodrama in this mutual pledge to fight to the last breath. And asking the Field brothers to swear was hardly necessary—it was not as if they had a lot of choice. If the Indians wanted to fight, there would be a fight.

This was the pickle Lewis's leadership had brought them to. Four men alone (and one of them separated from the rest) in the heart of Blackfoot country had run into a roving band of young Indian braves. Two parties of armed young men, each suspicious of the other, were attempting to occupy the same space at the same time. That always meant trouble.

The red war party outnumbered the white war party by at least two to one, and possibly much more. The natives figured to have reinforcements close at hand; the whites had no reinforcements within two hundred miles.

It was Lewis's fault. He was the one who had dreamed up this exploration, the one who had decided to make it with a party of four only, the one who had delayed two full days at Camp Disappointment even though he knew that every additional hour in Blackfoot country raised the risks of an unwelcome encounter and that Clark would soon be waiting for him at the Yellowstone, and even though he wanted to get back to St. Louis as soon as possible.

But there were positive possibilities in the situation. If a friendly—or at least a nonviolent—initial contact could be made, Lewis would have a chance to bring these Indians into the American trading empire. That would justify the risks he had taken.

When he got to within a hundred yards of the Indians, Lewis had the Field brothers stop while he advanced singly to meet an Indian who had ridden out ahead of his group. The two men met and cautiously shook hands; then both passed on to shake hands with the others in their respective parties.

Lewis dismounted. So did the Indians, who asked for pipes and smoke. Using his limited sign-language skills, Lewis told them that the pipe was with his hunter—down below, in the valley. He proposed that an Indian ride down with Reubin Field to find Drouillard and bring him back. This was done.

Lewis asked who they were. He thought they replied that they were Atsinas, a tribe known to Lewis as "the Minnetares of the North." Actually, they were Piegans, members of one of the three main divisions of the Blackfeet.

Lewis asked who was the chief; three men stepped forward. Lewis thought they were too young and too many to be chiefs, but he also thought it best to please them. He handed out a medal, a flag, and a handkerchief.

By now Lewis had concluded that there were no more than eight Blackfeet in the immediate area, and he was "convinced that we could mannage that number should they attempt any hostile measures."

The late-July sun was starting to sink in the west. Lewis proposed that they camp together. That was agreed to. On the way down the steep bluff, they picked up Drouillard, Field, and the Indian. They came to a delightful spot on a bend in the river, a bowl-shaped bottomland with three large cottonwoods in the center and excellent grass. The Blackfeet made a rough dome with willow branches, threw some dressed buffalo skins over it, and invited the whites to join them in the shelter. Drouillard and Lewis accepted; the Field brothers lay near the fire in front of the shelter.

Lewis went to work. With Drouillard flashing the signs, he asked question after question.

The Blackfeet said they were part of a large band that was one day's march away, near the foot of the mountains. They said there was a whiteman in their band. Another large band of their nation was hunting buffalo on its way to the mouth of Maria's River where it would be in a few days.

Lewis had no way to judge how much of this was meant to intimidate him, how much was true. If it was all true, it meant he was in the middle of the Blackfeet nation, and that a Canadian trader was living with one band, which meant that they surely had many firearms. This group of eight had two muskets.

Lewis asked about the trading patterns of the Blackfeet. The boys informed him that they rode six days' easy march to reach a British post on the North Saskatchewan River, and that from the traders there "they obtain arms amunition sperituous liquor blankets &c in exchange for wolves and some beaver skins."

This was unwelcome news. It reinforced Jefferson's worst fears: that agents of the Hudson's Bay Company and the North West Company were firmly entrenched on the Northern Plains, and were rapidly extending their monopoly.

But it gave Lewis an opportunity, which he characteristically seized. He told the Blackfeet in great detail how much better a deal they would get from the Americans, once the Americans arrived on the high plains. He gave his peace speech. He said he had come from the rising sun and gone to where the sun set and had made peace between warring nations on both sides of the mountains. He said he had come to their country to invite the Blackfeet to join the American empire. To all of this, as he understood them, "they readily gave their assent."

The braves were willing to talk the sign language as long as the smoking continued. They were extremely fond of tobacco, so Lewis "plyed them with the pipe untill late at night." He let them know he had reinforcements in the area, a party of soldiers he would be meeting at the mouth of the Marias. He asked them to send two messengers to the nearby bands of Blackfeet to ask them to meet in three days at the mouth of the Marias River, for a council about peace and trade. Perhaps a few chiefs would be willing to accompany the expedition to St. Louis and go on to visit their new father in Washington.

Lewis concluded by asking the other six warriors to accompany him to the mouth of the Marias, and promised them ten horses and some tobacco if they would do these things.

"To this proposition they made no reply," Lewis recorded.

Lewis had just made a serious political mistake. He had told these youngsters that he had organized their traditional enemies—the Nez Percé, the Shoshones, others—into an American-led alliance. Worse, he had indicated that the Americans intended to supply these enemies with rifles. The Blackfoot monopoly on firearms, based on their exclusive access to British suppliers, would be broken.

As James Ronda puts it, "the clash of empires had come to the Blackfeet." After more than twenty years of being the bully boys of the high-plains country, they were being challenged, as were their British friends.[4]

Lewis took the first watch. He wrote in his journal, two thousand words about the day. He covered it from start to finish, with frequent interruptions to the narrative. In one paragraph he compared the quality of water in Cut Bank Creek and Two Medicine River. He made an astute ecological observation, here in the eastern foothills of the Rocky Mountains was the only place that the three major cottonwood species grew together.

Mainly, though, he described what had happened in an after-action report. At half past eleven, he roused Reubin Field. He ordered Field to watch the movements of the Indians and if one of them left camp to awake the party, lest the Indians attempt to steal the detachment's horses. Then he lay down and immediately fell into a profound sleep.

"Damn you! Let go my gun!"

Drouillard's shout woke Lewis. It was a few moments past first light. Lewis jumped up. He saw Drouillard scuffling with an Indian over a rifle. Lewis reached for his rifle but found it gone. He drew his horse pistol from its holster, looked up, and saw a second Indian running off with his rifle. Lewis ran at him and signaled to him when he turned that he would either lay down that rifle or get shot.

As the Indian started to lay the rifle down, the Field brothers came running up, in a state of the highest excitement. They aimed their rifles at the Indian, but, before they could shoot, Lewis called out to stop them: the Indian was complying with his order.

Drouillard came up, breathless and excited, asking permission to kill the Indian. Lewis forbade it. The party had recovered its rifles, the Indians were falling back.

What happened? Lewis demanded.

The explanation came in a rush of words. Joseph Field had carelessly laid down his rifle beside his sleeping brother at absolutely the worst possible moment, first light. A watching Indian had seized his opportunity to grab it and Reubin Field's rifle and run off.

At the same instant, Drouillard said, he woke to see two Indians stealing his rifle and Lewis's. He chased the Indian, caught him, and took back his own rifle, while Lewis was recovering *his*.

The Field brothers, meanwhile, had dashed after the Indian carrying off their rifles. At fifty yards, they caught him and wrestled the rifles out of his hands. Reubin pulled his knife and plunged it into the young warrior's heart. The Indian, Field later said, "drew but one breath and the wind of his breath followed the knife and he fell dead."

But Lewis didn't have an opportunity to hear this report, because, before the brothers finished, he noticed that the Indians were attempting to drive off his horses.

Lewis called out orders: Shoot those Indians if they try to steal our horses! The Field brothers ran after the main party of Indians, who were driving four of their horses up the river. Lewis ran after two men who were driving off the remainder of the horses, including Lewis's.

He sprinted for some three hundred yards, at which point the Indians had reached the almost vertical bluff. They hid in a niche, a sort of alcove, in the bluff, driving the horses before them.

Lewis, breathless, could pursue no farther. He shouted to them, as he had done several times already, that he would shoot them if they did not give back his horse.

How much if any of this the Blackfeet understood cannot be said. What happened was that an Indian jumped behind a rock and said something to his companion. That man was armed, with a British musket loader. He turned toward Lewis.

Lewis brought his rifle to his shoulder, aimed, and fired. He shot the warrior through the belly.

But the Blackfoot was not finished. He raised himself to his knee, took a quick aim, and fired at Lewis.

"Being bearheaded," as Lewis commented, "I felt the wind of his bullet very distinctly."

Since there were two Indians—one badly wounded—and they were armed and behind good shelters, and he wanted to get out of there, and his shot pouch was back at camp so he could not reload, Lewis decided to retreat. He made his way back to camp.

There he told Drouillard to run and call the Field brothers back: they had enough horses. Drouillard tried, but they were too far away to hear. Lewis and Drouillard went to work saddling the horses. The Field brothers returned with four of the party's original horses. Lewis cast his eye over the herd and selected four Indian horses and three of his original bunch.

As the men arranged saddles and the placement of the baggage on the packhorses, Lewis started burning the articles the Indians had left behind. Onto the fire went four shields, two bows, two quivers of arrows, sundry other articles. Only the musket the warriors had abandoned and the flag Lewis had given an Indian the previous evening escaped the fire; those he took with him.

Enraged at the Indian treachery, he left the medal he had given out at last night's campfire hanging around the neck of the dead Indian, "that they might be informed who we were." But, excited as he was, Lewis wasn't about to take a scalp, though he did cut off the amulets from the shields before throwing the shields on the fire, and put them in his pack as a war souvenir.

An after-action analysis of Lewis's first-ever Indian fight indicates that he and his men made many mistakes. The first and most important was Joseph Field's. It was inexcusable for the sentinel ever to lay down his rifle, immeasurably more so when in the presence of young Indians. One would have thought that, after two years in the wilderness, Lewis would have had that pounded into the head of every enlisted man.

Lewis's failure to give orders that he and the other sleeping men should be woken at first light was a grave error. It was his clear duty and responsibility to be up, alert, and in full command at this most dangerous moment in the day.

Once awake, he made a number of snap judgments, some of them showing restraint and good sense, others demonstrating his sometimes impetuous nature. His first order was exactly right—get the rifles back. However dangerous it might be to chase an Indian carrying a rifle, those rifles were indispensable.

His second order, forbidding the Field brothers and Drouillard to kill a retreating Indian who had laid down the stolen rifle, was also exactly right. Next to getting the rifles back and not losing the horses, avoiding bloodshed was clearly Lewis's first responsibility—and of course it was his commander-in-chief's direct order. (At this time in the fight, Lewis did not yet know that Private Field had stabbed an Indian to death.)

When the Blackfeet started running off the horses, they were again attempting to steal what was indispensable to life on the Plains. It is not so clear this time, however, that Lewis's immediate order to chase the Indians and get those horses back was necessary. There were forty horses in the bottom, milling about in little groups. The thieves were never going to get them together into a herd and drive it off; while they were gathering horses, Lewis could have had his men doing the same. He later admitted that the Indian horse he took "carried me very well in short much better than my own would have done and leaves me with but little reason to complain of the robery." But at the time, he didn't feel that way at all.

He held the campsite, which contained all the equipment from both parties. The Indians were in full retreat. Lewis might have decided,

Let's get some horses for ourselves, and let the Blackfeet go and get out of here.

Instead, he ordered pursuit. The Field brothers took off after the main party, which had crossed the river; Lewis was fortunate that the young men, with their adrenaline pumping, didn't kill one or two more warriors.

His decision to leave the campsite himself to pursue two Indians leading away one of his horses and three or four of theirs was questionable. He left his command post and exposed himself to harm for what was not indispensable. But his blood was up—three hundred yards is a long way to sprint when wearing tight leather leggings and carrying a rifle—over the thieving Indians.

Whether he had to shoot the warrior or not is unclear. Lewis's narrative of this fight is one of his best pieces of writing, with lots of drama and detail. One detail we don't get, however: what was the Indian doing just before Lewis shot him? Lewis does not say. If he was taking aim at Lewis, obviously Lewis had to fire. But if his musket wasn't at his shoulder, Lewis should not have fired.

Another missing detail: sometime before he fired his rifle, Lewis fired his pistol, but he does not say when. It seems most likely that he fired at the backs of the Indians as they were driving the horses toward the bluff.

Another blunder: leaving the medal "that they might be informed who we were" was an act of taunting and boasting that put into serious jeopardy the entire American-empire scheme Lewis was concocting. To turn the most powerful tribe on the upper Missouri into enemies of the United States was Lewis's biggest mistake.

Lewis made no analysis of his actions. He was content to describe them, with his characteristic honesty. He wasn't in the habit of justifying his decisions, although he usually explained his reasons for them.

In this case, the only thing he felt needed explaining was why he didn't have his shot pouch with him when he fired. He was very defensive about this, almost as if he felt it was the only thing he had done wrong and he wanted to make sure everyone understood it couldn't have been helped (because he had no time to return to camp after recovering his rifle before he started chasing the Indians driving off the horses).

One Indian boy killed, another with a presumably fatal wound. Four whites in the middle of a land with hundreds of Blackfoot warriors who would seek revenge the instant they heard the news. It was imperative that Lewis get himself and his men out of there. Immediately.

Off they rode, up the bluff to "a beatiful level plain," and on toward the mouth of the Marias. Lewis knew he had to get there as soon as possible "in the hope of meeting with the canoes and party at that place," because he had no doubt the Blackfoot party would ride at top speed to the nearest band to report. He anticipated that, on hearing the news, a large party of warriors would immediately set out to kill any white men they could find. He feared there was a band of Blackfeet between him and the Marias, a band already headed toward the mouth of the river. If they discovered Sergeant Ordway's canoe party coming down from the falls, the soldiers would not be alert to their danger and might well be overwhelmed.

The party retreated at a trot, covering about eight miles per hour. Fortunately, recent rains had left "little reservoirs" scattered about, the prickly pears were few, and there were not many rocks and stones.

They rode through the morning and midday, not stopping until 3:00 p.m., when they "suffered our horses to graze . . . [and] took some refreshment." They had covered sixty-three miles.

After an hour-and-a-half break, they mounted up and rode off, to cover seventeen more miles by dark. Then they killed a buffalo and ate, mounted up again and set off, this time at a walk.

It was a night to remember. The tension was high, so too the concentration. The setting was magical. The plains were as flat as a bowling green. There were thunderclouds and lightning "on every quarter but that from which the moon gave us light." Throughout the night, "we continued to pass immence herds of buffaloe."

At 2:00 a.m. on July 28, Lewis finally ordered a halt. The day had begun for the party at first light, about 3:30 a.m., on July 27. The captain and his men had had an Indian fight to start the day, followed by a hundred-mile ride. "We now turned out our horses," Lewis concluded his journal description of the day, "and laid ourselves down to rest in the plain very much fatigued as may be readily conceived."

Inexcusably and inexplicably, he did not post a sentinel. Lewis slept soundly, but only briefly. He woke at first light, to find he was so stiff he could scarcely stand. He woke the men and told them to saddle up so they could get going. They too complained of stiffness, and asked for more rest. "I encouraged them by telling them that our own lives as well as those of our friends and fellow travellers depended on our exertions at this moment."

That worked. They came alert, and the march was resumed. As they rode, Lewis exhorted. "I now told them that . . . we must wrisk our lives on this occasion. . . . I told them that it was my determination that if we were attacked in the plains . . . that the bridles of the horses should be tied together and we would stand and defend them, or sell our lives as dear as we could."

That proved unnecessary. At twelve miles they came to the Missouri, rode down it another eight miles, and "heared the report of several rifles very distinctly. ... we quickly repared to this joyfull sound and on arriving at the bank of the river had the unspeakable satisfaction to see our canoes coming down."

Lewis's party joined Sergeant Ordway's. The combined force consisted of sixteen men. There were heartfelt greetings, but brief: Lewis explained the need for haste. The men quickly took the baggage from the horses and put it in the canoes, turned the horses loose, and set off.

They went down the river to the mouth of the Marias, where they opened the caches from the previous summer. Some skins and furs were badly damaged, but the gunpowder, corn, flour, pork, and salt were in fairly good order. Back into the canoes—the white pirogue and five small canoes—and downstream as fast as possible. At fifteen miles, Lewis reckoned that they had left the Blackfeet safely behind and made camp—prudently, on the south bank, across the river from any Blackfeet. That night, there was a thunderstorm that lasted for hours. Lewis had no shelter of any kind; he just lay in the water all night.

Lewis's exploration of the Marias was over. All in all, it had been a big mistake from the start. Many things went wrong, and nothing had been accomplished.

32

THE LAST LEG

July 29–September 22, 1806

The job now was to reunite with Clark and his party and head on to the Mandan villages. In the morning, Lewis got an early start. "The currant being strong and the men anxious to get on they plyed their oars faithfully and we went at the rate of about seven miles an hour."

Progress continued to be good over the next five days. Game was so plentiful that at one stop the men killed twenty-nine deer. Lewis gave instructions to cook enough meat in the evening to last through the next day, so that no stops need be made for a noon meal; "by this means we forward our journey at least 12 or 15 miles Pr. day."

By August 7, they had reached the mouth of the Yellowstone. Clark wasn't there, but signs of an encampment indicated he had been a week earlier. Lewis found a piece of paper stuck on a pole; it had his name in the handwriting of Captain Clark. Only a fragment could be read, but from it Lewis learned that at this site game was scarce and mosquitoes were plentiful, so Clark had gone on and would be waiting for Lewis downstream.

"I instantly reimbarked," Lewis wrote, "and decended the river in the hope of reaching Capt. C's camp before night." He was so anxious to reunite that he wouldn't take the day or so necessary to fix the longitude of the junction, as he had promised to do the previous year, when clouds had made observations impossible.

He didn't catch Clark anyway. Clark had moved on. In the morning, Lewis followed. He didn't catch up that day, or the next.

On the morning of August 11, seeing some elk on a thick willow bar, he put in and set out with Private Cruzatte to replenish the meat supply. After Lewis killed one and Cruzatte wounded one, they reloaded and plunged into the willow to pursue more elk.

Lewis saw an elk some yards ahead. He raised his rifle to his shoulder, took aim, and was about to pull the trigger when he was hit in the buttocks by a rifle bullet. This severe blow spun him around.

The bullet had hit him an inch below his hip joint on his left side and passed through his buttocks to come out on the right side, leaving a three-inch gash the width of the ball. No bone had been hit. The spent ball lodged in Lewis's leather breeches.

Cruzatte was nearsighted in his only good eye, and Lewis was wearing brown leather, so his first thought was that Cruzatte had mistaken him for an elk.

"Damn you," Lewis shouted. "You have shot me."

There was no answer. Lewis called to Cruzatte several times, still with no response. The shot had come from less than forty yards away; if Cruzatte couldn't hear him, it must not have been Cruzatte who shot him. It must have been an Indian. In the thick willow, it was impossible to know if it was just one warrior or a war party.

Lewis called to Cruzatte to retreat, then retreated himself. He ran the first hundred paces, until his wound forced him to slow down. When he got in sight of the canoes, he called the men to their arms, "to which they flew in an instant." Lewis informed them of what had happened, told them he intended to return and give battle and save Cruzatte, and ordered them to follow him.

They did. But after a hundred yards, their captain collapsed. His wounds had become so painful and his thigh was so stiff he could not press on. He told the men to continue without him; if they encountered a superior force they should retreat, keeping up a fire.

Lewis struggled back to the canoes. He laid his pistol on one side of him, his rifle on the other, and his air gun close at hand. He was "determined to sell my life as deerly as possible."

He was alone for about twenty minutes, in a state of anxiety and suspense. Finally the party returned, with Cruzatte, who absolutely denied having shot the captain and swore he had never heard Lewis call to him.

"I do not beleive that the fellow did it intentionally," Lewis wrote, but neither did he believe Cruzatte's denials. He had the bullet in his hand; it was a .54 caliber, from a U.S. Army Model 1803, not a weapon any Indian was likely to have. He conjectured that, after shooting his captain in the ass, Cruzatte decided to deny everything. (Sergeants Ordway and Gass, who were with the party when it met Cruzatte, wrote in their journals that, as far as they could tell, Cruzatte was entirely ignorant of having shot Lewis.)

Sergeant Gass helped Lewis get out of his clothes. Lewis dressed his wounds himself as best he could, introducing rolls of lint into the holes on each side of his buttocks (so that the wound would stay open and new tissue could grow from the inside out).[1]

The party proceeded downriver, Lewis lying on his stomach in the pirogue. At 4:00 p.m., they passed Clark's campsite of the previous night; there one of the men found and brought to Lewis a note Clark had left on a post.

Bad news. Clark wrote that the reason Lewis had found only a fragment of the letter at the Yellowstone was that Sergeant Pryor and his small party had passed that place after Clark left and before Lewis arrived, and Pryor had torn off part of the note. Pryor and his three men were traveling in bull boats, which they had made after losing all their horses to Indian thieves.

Losing the horses wasn't so bad, especially since Pryor had been resourceful enough to build bull boats and rejoin Clark, but it was a serious blow in that Pryor had not been able to deliver to Mr. Heney of the North West Company the letter asking his help in getting some Sioux chiefs to come to Washington. Heney had been Lewis's only hope for pacifying the Sioux and making them a part of the American system.

Lewis's entire Indian policy was coming apart. He had hostile Blackfeet behind him and hostile Sioux in front of him; between them, they could block the entire middle section of the Missouri River to traders.

Along with the bad news, Lewis's wounds grew so painful that when the party made camp he found he could not bear to be moved. He had a poultice of Peruvian bark applied to the wounds, and spent the night stretched out on his belly on board the pirogue. He had a high fever and a restless night.

In the morning, he was stiff and sore, but the fever had receded, probably thanks to the Peruvian bark, a standard remedy for fevers with the captains. The pain remained.

The party set out. At 8:00 a.m., it encountered two white men coming upriver. They were Joseph Dickson of Illinois and Forrest Hancock of Boone's Settlement in Missouri, fur trappers out on their own. They had started in August 1804, spent the winter in Iowa, been robbed by Indians who also wounded Hancock, but were nevertheless proceeding upriver to get to the Yellowstone and trap beaver.

*

In other words, the Lewis and Clark Expedition had been only three months ahead of private trappers in exploring the Louisiana Purchase. Dickson and Hancock were the cutting edge of what might be called the fur rush. It could be taken for granted that there would be many others coming close behind them. However much Jefferson might want to reserve Upper Louisiana for displaced Indians from east of the Mississippi, no power on earth, and certainly no laws written in Washington, could stop the American frontiersmen. They were lured up the Missouri River by a spirit of adventure, by a cockiness and bravado that were not entirely without foundation, by a love of the wilderness, and by greed. Powerful motives in young men, the kind that can't be denied.

Lewis was eager to help establish an American presence in Upper Louisiana. He gave Dickson and Hancock information on what lay ahead of them, provided them with some sketch maps, and told them where they could find beaver in abundance. He also gave them a file and some lead and powder.

The party set out again. At 1:00 p.m., it overtook Captain Clark and his party. The joy of reunion was a bit dampened by Lewis's condition. Informed that his friend had been wounded, Clark dashed to his pirogue. He was much alarmed to see Lewis lying on his belly, but Lewis raised his head to assure him that the wound was slight and would be healed in three or four weeks. "This information relieved me very much," Clark wrote.

News was exchanged. The first was the best: everyone was present and, except for Lewis, in good health. Clark described the passage through today's Bozeman Pass to the Yellowstone, where Sacagawea was his guide. A party of Crows had stolen twenty-four of his fifty horses. He built two dugout canoes, each twenty-eight feet long, and lashed them together for stability. His trip down the river was comparatively uneventful. It had an important payoff, in the form of Clark's map.

Late in the afternoon, Dickson and Hancock came into camp. For some unknown reason they had decided to put off their trip to the Yellowstone for a while and join the party for the two-day trip to the Mandan villages.

That evening, Captain Clark washed Captain Lewis's wounds, which remained sore.* When Clark finished, Lewis wrote in his

---

* For sure he didn't wash them in water that had been boiled first: it was just plain Missouri River water. Lewis was lucky his wounds did not become infected.

journal. After describing the day, he declared that "as wrighting in my present situation is extreemly painfull to me I shall desist untill I recover and leave to my frind Capt. C. the continuation of our journal."

That was his last entry in the journals of Lewis and Clark. Fittingly, he did not end it right there, but felt compelled to go on to write one last botanical description.

"I must notice a singular Cherry," he wrote. It was the pin, or bird, cherry. Despite his pain and his "situation," he gave it a complete going over. He measured and examined and described: for example, "The leaf is peteolate, oval accutely pointed at it's apex, from one and a ¼ to 1½ inches in length and from ½ to ¾ of an inch in width, finely or minutely serrate, pale green and free from bubessence."

In the morning, the reunited expedition set off. Two days later, on August 14, the Mandan villages came into view.

"Those people were extreamly pleased to See us," Clark reported. There were reunions with such old friends as the Mandan chiefs Black Cat and Sheheke ("Big White") and the Hidatsa Le Borgne ("One-Eye"), and others. Hugs and small presents and a smoking ceremony marked the occasion. Then there were councils, with René Jessaume serving as translator. How much of a role Lewis played is unclear, but apparently it was a minor one (he had fainted that day when Clark was changing his dressing).

The news from the chiefs was all bad. The Arikaras and the Mandans had been fighting. The Hidatsas had sent a war party into the Rockies and killed some Shoshones—possibly from Cameahwait's band. The Sioux had raided the Mandans. And the Mandans were divided by internal quarrels.

This was dreadful. The American peace policy had failed within days of the departure of Lewis and Clark. The whole middle and upper Missouri River was at war. It was as if Lewis and Clark had never come, never made promises, never extracted pledges to be good.

Making matters worse, the chiefs turned down Clark's invitation to come to Washington. Black Cat said he wished to visit the United States and meet his Great Father, but he was afraid of the Sioux below and would not go. Clark promised protection and lots of presents. He said, if the chiefs would come to Washington, an American trading post would be built among the Mandans much sooner than otherwise. The chiefs still said no.

Eventually, after much pleading from Jessaume, who had his interpreter's fee at stake, Big White agreed to accompany the expedition to St. Louis and go on to Washington—if the captains would take his wife and son, Jessaume, and Jessaume's Indian wife and two sons. This was dangerously overloading the canoes, but the captains were desperate to bring chiefs to Washington, so Clark reluctantly agreed. When Big White and his entourage walked through the village past his people on the way to the canoes, Clark noticed that "Maney of them Cried out aloud." Few expected to see him return.

On August 17, just before departing, Clark settled with Charbonneau. He received $500.33⅓ for his horse, his tepee, and his services. Sacagawea got nothing.* The Charbonneaus stayed with the Mandans.

Another member of the expedition left the party that day. Dickson and Hancock had asked Private John Colter to join them in their Yellowstone venture. He accepted, subject to the captains' approval. They gave it, on the condition that no other man ask for a similar change in the conditions of his enlistment (Colter's enlistment would not expire until October 10, 1806). None did, and when the expedition set off downstream, Colter turned back upstream, back to the wilderness, back to the mountains, on his way into the history books as America's first mountain man and the discoverer of Yellowstone National Park.

Whether the men watched him depart, whether they thought, "What a fool!" or felt envy, Clark did not record. But his conditional approval of Colter's request indicates that Clark thought that at least some others might well be tempted to return to the Yellowstone country.

As the expedition began the final run for St. Louis, Captain Lewis was still on his belly. His wounds were healing but still so painful that he could not walk.

On the fourth day out, the Americans encountered three French trappers headed for the Yellowstone country. The news they had was another blow to Lewis's and Clark's Indian policy: the Arikara chief who in April 1805 had accompanied Corporal Warfington to St. Louis

---

* Clark offered to take her son, Jean Baptiste (called "Pomp" by Clark and the men, and described by Clark as "a butifull promising Child") to St. Louis and bring him up as if he were his own boy; she said maybe next summer, after he has been weaned. In a letter of August 20, 1806, to Charbonneau, Clark paid tribute to Sacagawea, referring to her as " Your woman who accompanied you that long dangerous and fatigueing rout to the Pacific Ocian and back diserved a greater reward for her attention and services on that rout than we had in our power to give her." (Jackson, *Letters*, vol. I, p. 315.)

and then went on to Washington, had died. The Arikaras did not yet know this.

That afternoon, the expedition reached the Arikara village. There was a council (whether Lewis attended is not known); Clark asked the chiefs to send a delegation to Washington; several said they were eager to "See their great father but wished to see the Chief who went down last sumer return first."

On August 22, Clark wrote a medical report: "I am happy to have it in my power to Say that my worthy friend Capt Lewis is recovering fast, he walked a little to day for the first time. I have discontinud the tent [lint] in the hole the ball came out." The next day, the report read: "My Friend Capt Lewis is recoverig fast the hole in his thy where the Ball passed out is Closed and appears to be nearly well. the one where the ball entered discharges very well."

On August 27, at the Big Bend of the Missouri River in present-day South Dakota, Clark put in to do some buffalo hunting. While he was gone, "My friend Capt Lewis hurt himself very much by takeing a longer walk on the Sand bar in my absence than he had Strength to undergo, which Caused him to remain very unwell all night." In the morning, Clark opened his journal, "Capt Lewis had a bad nights rest and is not very well this morning."

Four days later, the party passed the mouth of today's Niobrara River. This was Sioux country, requiring full alertness. Two miles below the Niobrara, nine warriors appeared on the bank. They signed for the expedition to come ashore. Clark assumed they were Tetons, the band that had been so troublesome in the fall of 1804. He wanted nothing to do with them and paid no attention to them, but since one of the canoes was behind and out of sight around a bend, he decided to put ashore as soon as he was around the next bend and wait for the canoe to come up.

About a quarter-hour after the party put ashore, several shots rang out. Clark figured it was the Sioux shooting at the three men in the trailing canoe.

Clark called out fifteen men, more than half the expedition's strength, and ran toward the sound of the guns. He was determined to provide cover for the men under attack, "let the number of the indians be what they might."

As Clark set off, Lewis hobbled up out of his pirogue, reached the bank, and formed the remainder of the men into a defensive line "in a Situation well calculated to defend themselves and the Canoes &c."

After running 250 yards, Clark rounded the bend and saw the canoe coming on, but still a full mile upriver. The Indians were just above him, shooting at targets. They turned out to be Yankton Sioux, the band that had been so friendly two years earlier. It also turned out that one of their chiefs had gone to Washington. That was the first good Indian news the captains had heard since they parted from the Nez Percé.

By September 1806, the captains and their men were real-life Rip Van Winkles, even if their period of absence was not twenty years but two years and five months.

The captains were starved for news. The health of their loved ones first of all, but no one in St. Louis would know about that. Politics next: there had been a presidential election. Who won? Was the nation at war? What was going on in St. Louis? Who was in command in Louisiana? All these questions, which they had put out of their minds as far as possible, were critically important to the captains—to their immediate futures as army officers, to their reception in Washington, to the publication and dissemination of their journals, to everything that mattered to them.

Their chance to start asking questions came at 4:00 p.m. on September 3, when they encountered a trading party of two canoes and several men coming upriver. The leader was James Aird, a Scotsman from Prairie du Chien in today's Wisconsin, who had a license to trade with the Sioux. A large, friendly man, he greeted the captains warmly and took them into his tent during a thunderstorm to talk (by this time, Lewis had recovered sufficiently to walk about with ease).

"Our first enquirey," Clark recorded, "was after the President of our country [well, and safely re-elected] and then our friends and the State of the politicks of our country &c. and the State [of] Indian affairs to all of which enquireys Mr. Aires gave us as Satisfactory information as he had it in his power to have Collected in the Illinois which was not a great deel."

Of course Aird knew nothing about Lewis's mother or Clark's brothers, but he did know a little about a lot of things of great concern or interest to the captains.

There had been a fire at the house of their warm friend and host in St. Louis, Jean-Pierre Chouteau. The home had burned to the ground.

General Wilkinson was the governor of Louisiana Territory, with headquarters in St. Louis. He had sent three hundred American troops to the disputed area between western Louisiana and eastern Texas, to oppose Spanish pretensions. Spanish gunboats had fired on the U.S. frigate *President* near Algeciras, Spain, in the fall of 1804. The British warship *Leander* had fired on the American merchant ship *Richard* off New York in April 1806.

There were other items. Two Indians had been hanged in St. Louis for murder; several others were in jail. Aaron Burr and Alexander Hamilton had fought a duel (July 14, 1804); Hamilton was dead.

The captains had not realized how starved they were for news until they got this appetizer. Their already high anxiety to get on with the greatest dispatch increased.

In the morning, Aird gave each man enough tobacco to last until St. Louis, and insisted that the captains accept a barrel of flour. At 8:00 a.m., Aird headed upriver and the captains started down. Three hours later, they stopped at Floyds Bluff and climbed the hill to pay their respects at Sergeant Floyd's grave. They found it disturbed by the natives and covered it over.

Apparently the climb was too much for Lewis: the next day, Clark reported that his friend was "still in a Convelesent State."

On September 6, the party encountered another trading boat, this one owned by Auguste Chouteau of St. Louis. The captains purchased a gallon of whiskey from the party and gave each man a dram, "the first Spiritious licquor which had been tasted by any of them Since the 4 of July 1805." Several men exchanged their leather tunics and beaver hats with traders for linen shirts and cloth hats.

But of what the captains most wanted, an update on the news from civilization, Chouteau's crew didn't have much. They were able to report only that General Wilkinson was preparing to leave St. Louis to follow the detachment to the Texas border.

On September 9, the expedition passed the mouth of the Platte River. It was making seventy to eighty miles a day. As it passed the Platte, it passed out of the Great Plains. It was on the home stretch.

"Our party appears extreamly anxious to get on," Clark wrote, "and every day appears [to] produce new anxieties in them to get to their Country and friends. My worthy friend Cap Lewis has entirely recovered his wounds are heeled up and he Can walk and even run nearly as well as ever he Could. the parts are yet tender &c. &."

On September 10, the expedition met a four-man trading party that had an update on General Wilkinson, who had set out with the troops for Texas, and news that Captain Zebulon Pike had left St. Louis to explore the Red and Arkansas Rivers.

Two days later, it was a two-canoe party under another of the Chouteau family, then a larger party led by former army captain Robert McClellan, an old friend of Clark's. With him were Joseph Gravelines and Pierre Dorion, interpreters who had accompanied the Arikara chief to Washington, returning with instructions from Jefferson.

Their first charge from the president was to make inquiries about Lewis and Clark. Gravelines had the difficult task of expressing to the Arikaras Jefferson's regret for the death of their chief. Dorion's charge was to get Gravelines safely past the Teton Sioux, and to persuade some chiefs of that tribe to visit Washington.

In the morning, McClellan gave a dram to each man on the expedition. The party set off just after sunrise in a merry mood. The next day, another party sent out by the Chouteaus was encountered; the traders gave the men whiskey, biscuit, pork, and onions, all most welcome. At camp that night, the men got a dram "and Sung Songs untill 11 oClock at night in the greatest harmoney."

On September 15, Lewis and Clark came to the mouth of the Kansas River. They landed and climbed a hill "which appeared to have a Commanding Situation for a fort, the Shore is bold and rocky imediately at the foot of the hill, from the top of the hill you have a perfect Command of the river." They were standing in what is today's downtown Kansas City, Missouri.

They were meeting trading parties daily. On September 17, it was John McClallen, an old army friend of Lewis's, on a large boat. He had resigned his commission in January 1806 to lead a venture that may have involved General Wilkinson. He intended to go up the Platte to the mountains, then overland to the Rio Grande and on to Santa Fe. There he proposed to bribe Spanish officials into allowing him to engage in trade with the Indians, using packhorse trains to get the goods to them, and bring the furs out.

Clark pronounced this "a very good [plan] if strictly prosued &c."

McClallen handed out biscuits, chocolate, sugar, and whiskey—and news. Perhaps the most interesting was that the American people were feeling a deep concern for the expedition. Among the rumors McClallen passed along was that the captain and men had all been killed, and that the Spanish had captured them and were working them as slave labor in the mines.

"We had been long Since given out by the people of the U.S. Generally and almost forgotton," Clark reported McClallen as saying. "The President of the U. States had yet hopes of us." That last should have gladdened the hearts of the leaders of the expedition.

McClallen said he himself had believed the worst. He had been astonished to see the expedition and was rejoiced to find his friend Lewis and the others all safe and sound.

By September 18, the party was within 150 miles of the settlements. It had run entirely out of provisions and trade goods. Other than the cooking kettles, the scientific instruments, and some tools, it had no manufactured goods—except rifles. It had plenty of those, and powder and lead, and there was game in the neighborhood, but the almost daily passage of traders' boats had caused the deer and bear to move back from the river, which meant that gathering in meat required sending out hunters on foot; this slowed the party down considerably.

There were plenty of ripe plums, which the men called "pawpaws." Gathering a few bushels was the work of a few minutes only. The men told the captains they could "live very well on the pappaws." The captains were even more anxious than the men to get on, so there were no halts to hunt.

"The party being extreemly anxious to get down ply their ores very well," Clark recorded on September 20. That afternoon, the men saw cows on the bank, a sight that brought out spontaneous shouts of joy. When the captains put in at the village of La Charette, the men asked permission to fire a salute. It was granted, and they fired three rounds, which were answered by three rounds from five trading boats on the riverbank.

The citizens rushed to them. "Every person," Clark wrote, "both French and americans Seem to express great pleasure at our return, and acknowledged them selves much astonished in Seeing us return. they informed us that we were Supposed to have been lost long Since."

The next day, the scene was repeated at St. Charles, where "the inhabitants of this village appear much delighted at our return and seem to vie with each other in their politeness to us all." On September 22, it was on to Fort Bellefontaine, established in 1805 by General Wilkinson, the first U.S. Army fort west of the Mississippi. The captains took Big White and his family to the public store at the fort and furnished them with clothes.

In the morning, the expedition set off for their last day's voyage. In less than an hour, it was swinging into the Mississippi River, past the old camp at Wood River, last seen twenty-eight months and eight thousand miles ago.

As the men paddled the last few miles to St. Louis, Lewis had cause to feel deep satisfaction, and could be forgiven a sense of hubris. He had completed the epic voyage. By itself that was enough to place him and his partner-friend in the pantheon of explorers.

Lewis had planned and organized and with Clark's help carried out a voyage of discovery that had been his dream for what seemed like all of his life. Indeed, it seemed he had been born for it, and had been training himself for it since childhood. His success was due to that training, and to his character, well suited to the challenge.

His leadership had been outstanding. He and Clark had taken thirty-odd unruly soldiers and molded them into the Corps of Discovery, an elite platoon of tough, hardy, resourceful, well-disciplined men. They had earned the men's absolute trust.

At most critical moments, Lewis and Clark had made the right decision—at the mouth of the Marias River in June 1805; in the dealings with the Shoshones in August 1805; in trusting in Old Toby to get them across the Lolo Trail in September 1805; in retreating from the Lolo in June 1806 and waiting for Nez Percé guides before trying again.

Lewis's biggest mistake had been the decision to split the expedition into five parts and make the Marias exploration. Otherwise, in his most important role, that of military commander, he had done a superlative job.

Jefferson had charged him with numerous nonmilitary goals. He had carried them out faithfully. He was certain he had accomplished the number-one objective of the expedition, to find the most direct and convenient route across the continent. He had brought back a treasure of scientific information. His discoveries in the fields of zoology, botany, ethnology, and geography were beyond any value.[*] He introduced new approaches to exploration and established a model for future expeditions by systematically recording abundant data on what he had seen, from weather to rocks to people.

On the more personal side, he had seen wonderful things. He had traveled through a hunter's paradise beyond anything any American had ever before known. He had crossed mountains that were greater than had ever before been seen by any American, save the handful who had visited the Alps. He had seen falls and cataracts and raging rivers, thunderstorms all but beyond belief, trees of a size never before conceived of, Indian tribes uncorrupted by contact with white men, canyons and cliffs and other scenes of visionary enchantment.

A brave new world.

And he had been first. Everyone who has ever paddled a canoe on the Missouri, or the Columbia, does so in the wake of the Lewis and Clark Expedition. Everyone who crosses the Lolo Trail walks in their footsteps.

---

[*] He had discovered and described 178 new plants, more than two-thirds of them from west of the Continental Divide, and 122 species and subspecies of animals (Cutright, *Lewis and Clark: Pioneering Naturalists*, pp. 423, 447).

Furthermore, the journals of Lewis and Clark provided the introduction to and serve as the model for all subsequent writing on the American West.

For all Lewis's accomplishments, however, there were some big disappointments, and as St. Louis came into view, he had reason for worry. His Indian diplomacy had so far been a failure. The Sioux and the Blackfeet, the strongest and most warlike tribes in Upper Louisiana, were enemies of the United States. Nevertheless, Lewis had some policies to recommend to the president that he hoped would force the Sioux, Blackfeet, and all other Plains tribes to recognize American sovereignty.

He was enthusiastic about the prospects for an American commercial empire stretching from St. Louis to the Pacific, and he had some specific schemes in mind to make it happen. God knew there were plenty of beaver out there. His task now was to get the journals published, to spread the word about the wonders of the Upper Louisiana and the Oregon country, and about the abundance of beaver, and to make his discoveries known to the scientific world.

The sad news he had to tell could not be helped: it was simple geographical fact. There was no all-water route, or anything close to it, and the Missouri River drainage did not extend beyond forty-nine degrees north latitude.

Lewis realized that Jefferson would want the news as soon as possible. So, as his canoe put in at St. Louis, it was the president who was on his mind. The men had fired a salute to the town when they saw all one thousand residents on the bank, waiting for them. The citizens gave them three cheers and a hearty welcome. A resident reported, "They really have the appearance of Robinson Crusoes— dressed entirely in buckskins."[2]

As Lewis scrambled out of his canoe, his first question was, When does the post leave?

It had just left, was the answer. Lewis quickly wrote a note to the postmaster at Cahokia, Illinois Territory, and sent it on by messenger: hold the post until the next day. He took a room at the home of Pierre Chouteau and began to write the president.

33

REPORTING TO
THE PRESIDENT

September 23–December 31, 1806

On September 23, 1806, Meriwether Lewis completed the first part of the work that had been his "darling project," and on which he had concentrated with single-minded intensity for the past four years. The second part of this great work, reporting on the results of his exploration to the president—and beyond him, to the people of America and of the world—would require a similar level of dedication. What he knew, and what he and Clark had recorded in their journals, papers, and maps, was invaluable—but of no value at all unless it was disseminated.

Lewis had gotten started on the process of making what he had learned available to the president and the public back at Fort Mandan, in the winter of 1804–5, with his reports to Jefferson on his discoveries during the first leg of his voyage. The president had ordered those reports and Clark's map published; they were widely copied and distributed. All across America, and in Britain and Europe as well, adventuresome young men and older entrepreneurs were making plans to go west—indeed, some had already started. But the real news was still to come.

Even before finishing the voyage, Lewis got started on his task of informing the public and the scientists of what he had found. As his canoe descended the last miles to St. Louis, he began writing a first draft of his report to the president.

Lewis opened his report by announcing his safe arrival in St. Louis, along with "our papers and baggage." Those words assured Jefferson that the expedition had brought back its scientific discoveries.

The second sentence went to the heart of the matter, as far as Jefferson was concerned: "In obedience to your orders we have penitrated the Continent of North America to the Pacific Ocean, and sufficiently explored the interior of the country to affirm with confidence that we have discovered the most practicable rout which does exist across the continent by means of the navigable branches of the Missouri and Columbia Rivers."

In the long paragraph that followed, Lewis was as positive about what he had found as reality allowed him to be. He said the navigation of the Missouri was "safe and good," so too the Clearwater-Snake-Columbia system, at least down to The Dalles. But the passage by land from the Missouri to the Columbia's waters was another matter altogether.

It was Lewis's unhappy task to tell the president that his hope for an all-water route linking the Atlantic and Pacific was gone. So, even as he pulled into St. Louis in triumph, he carried the burden of knowing that the headline news to come out of the expedition was bad. Never would he hide the truth—Jefferson was above all a man of facts—but if he felt a bit embarrassed by them, or defensive about them, if he went to great lengths to put the best possible face on what he was reporting, it was perhaps understandable.

In any case, Lewis was straightforward about the portage from the Missouri waters to the Columbia waters: it was a passage of 340 miles, 200 along a good road, the other 140 "the most formidable part of the tract . . . [over] tremendious mountains which for 60 mls. are covered with eternal snows."

With those words, Lewis put an end to the search for the Northwest Passage.

After outlining the difficulties of the portage, he shifted to the positive. "We view this passage across the Continent," he wrote, "as affording immence advantages to the fur trade." He went on to describe in detail the plan for the American fur-trading empire in Upper Louisiana and Oregon that he had been working on in his mind ever since he crossed the Rocky Mountains.

It was a breathtaking proposal, continent-wide in scope. The scheme involved nothing less than gathering all the furs collected in the whole of the Northwest, from the northern reaches of the Mississippi River to the Pacific Ocean, and transporting them to the mouth of the Columbia, whence they could be shipped to the Canton market to be exchanged for goods from the Orient.

The plan was based on the Shoshone and Nez Percé horse herds. The mountains could be passed, Lewis told Jefferson, from late June to the end of September, "and the cheep rate at which horses are to be obtained . . . reduces the expences of transportation over this portage to a mere trifle."

The British could be cut out of the trade almost entirely, because American furs could be sent direct to the great Canton market, whereas British mercantile laws required that all furs from the British Empire must be shipped first of all to London before being sent on to their market.[1] Americans could cut the distance and cost, their furs would arrive earlier and be in better condition and thus command a premium price, and British import and export duties, as well as profits for the East India Company, could be avoided.[*]

The route Lewis proposed was so far superior to the present one— from the Canadian west to Montreal and down the St. Lawrence and across the Atlantic to London, then on around Africa to the Orient— that Lewis thought it possible the North West Company would want to ship their furs via the Columbia.

In making this report, Lewis was attempting to create government policy. And as an adviser, he did not hesitate to reverse Jefferson's original idea, that furs from the Pacific Coast be sent to the Missouri, then brought on down to St. Louis.

To the objection that in Lewis's scheme the flow of goods from Canton to the mouth of the Columbia, over the mountains, down the Missouri to St. Louis, then up the Ohio and over the Appalachians, and finally down the Potomac to market, was too long and difficult for imports from the Orient, Lewis had a reply. "Many articles not bulky [or] brittle nor of a very perishable nature may be conveyed to the United States by this rout with more facility and at less expense" than by going around the Cape of Good Hope.

The exchange of furs for oriental goods could take place at a great trade fair to be held each year in July at the Nez Percé camp. And there would have to be a permanent trading establishment set up at the mouth of the Columbia.

Lewis obviously knew the intricacies of the fur trade, and about business practices, costs, profits, requirements. He also knew his countrymen. Thus he opened the third paragraph of his report to Jefferson with a sentence that became the most frequently quoted one he ever wrote: "The Missouri and all it's branches from the Cheyenne upwards abound more in beaver and Common Otter, than any other

---

[*] Canadian furs destined for the New York market had first to go to London, so that a tax could be paid.

streams on earth, particularly that proportion of them lying within the Rocky Mountains."[2] It was certain to set off a rush for the mountains.

Then he wrote a paragraph that reached considerably in its promises of what might be. "If the government will only aid, even in a very limited manner, the enterprize of her Citizens," he wrote, "I am fully convinced that we shall shortly derive the benifits of a most lucrative trade from this source, and that in the course of ten or twelve years a tour across the Continent by the rout mentioned will be undertaken by individuals with as little concern as a voyage across the Atlantic is at present."

It would take government action, at considerable expense to the public. It would take an expanded army, acting aggressively against hostile Indians on the Missouri. Neither proposition was part of Jefferson's overall philosophical position on the role of government. Never mind. Neither was the purchase of Louisiana. Whatever his philosophical musings, Jefferson was a man of the West, just as the Republican Party was a party of the West. Whenever the Constitution was silent, Jefferson, when in power, was willing to abandon a strict construction of the document in order to promote western expansion. His vision of the United States stretched from sea to sea—and more than any other individual, he made that happen.

That Lewis envisioned himself as a part of this vast enterprise he made clear over the next two years by his actions. Having discovered the American West, he wanted to be in on the first wave of Americans to exploit it. He knew that he would achieve worldwide fame after the president received his report; now he wanted riches. And there was no faster way to make a big profit on a small investment in the first decade of the nineteenth century than the fur trade to the Orient.

On his first day back in St. Louis, Captain Lewis got started on a career as both a lobbyist and publicist for, and a participant in, the development of the empire. He polished his report for the president and wrote another long letter for the newspapers. In both he called for "the earliest attention of our government." The immediate need, he told Jefferson, was to deal with "the unfriendly dispositions" of the Sioux, Blackfeet, and other tribes along the Missouri.

In the next section, Lewis apologized to Jefferson for not sending a report to him from the falls of the Missouri, as he had promised. He knew Jefferson had been terribly worried about him and the expedition—indeed, he knew that most Americans had given up on them—so he really did owe an explanation. He said he and Clark had "conceived it inexpedient to reduce the party" by sending back two soldiers with a report, "lest by doing so we should lessen the ardor of those who remained and thus hazard the fate of the expedition. [We decided that it was] better to let the government as well as our friends for a moment feel some anxiety for our fate than to wrisk so much." The subsequent difficulties the expedition encountered in crossing the Rockies, descending to the Pacific, and returning to St. Louis "proved the justice of our dicision, for we have more than once owed our lives and the fate of the expedition to our number which consisted of 31 men."

He next gave an inventory of the furs he was bringing back, along with the "pretty extensive collection of plants" and nine new Indian vocabularies. In addition, he had Big White with him, and the Mandan chief was "in good health and sperits, and very anxioius to proceede." Lewis knew his man. He gave no more details, no elaboration, counting on Jefferson to be greatly excited by the unadorned paragraph.

But this was a big mistake. He would have been wiser to write two or three pages on his discoveries. As it was, the early accounts available to readers said little or nothing about the first American scientific survey on a continental scale. As far as contemporaries could tell, the only contributions to knowledge made by the expedition were in the field of geography.

Lewis knew the value of what he had found, but he apparently felt it would be better to await the publication of his discoveries in book form (he was already planning to publish in three volumes, with the third containing the scientific material). He knew he needed help; before giving any publicity to the scientific studies, he wanted to get to Philadelphia, where he could turn over his raw materials to professionals, who in turn would prepare them for publication.

He was certain to get a warm welcome in Philadelphia, where there were so many leading scholars who had helped him prepare for the expedition and would be eager to hear his account of how this pill or that sextant had worked out. Also, Jefferson had arranged for Lewis's election to the American Philosophical Society, an incredibly prestigious honor.* Jefferson, full of pride in Lewis, described him as "a valuable member of our fraternity, [just returned] from a journey of uncommon length & peril." The president promised that Lewis would soon join the members to give them an account "of the geography & natural history of our country, from the Missisippi to the Pacific."[3]

That had to have been the most welcome announcement of a lecture ever received by the Philadelphia scientists. They were about to have two-thirds of a continent, previously almost unknown,

---

* Lewis learned of his election while in St. Louis.

revealed to them. They would get the first account of the discoveries and have entirely new paths of research to follow. These were scholars who had spent their lives discovering and describing the country, men who lived by facts who had been forced to rely on conjecture in delineating the mountains and rivers of the West. There was so much to learn about, examine, study, draw. Not since Columbus and Cook had there been so much that was new.

Given the time it would take to make the journals available to the public, however, Lewis's decision to postpone publishing his discoveries ran the risk of exposing the expedition to ridicule as little more than an adventure. And, indeed, that was done. Federalists, John Quincy Adams among them, expressed their scorn. Adams was not ready to accept the president's word for it that important discoveries had been made. "Mr. Jefferson tells large stories," he wrote in his diary on one occasion after dinner in the President's House. On another, he recorded that Jefferson had told him that once, for six weeks in Paris, the temperature never went above the zero mark Fahrenheit; Adams commented, "He knows better than all this; but he loves to excite wonder."[4]

Ridiculing the expedition became a tradition with the Federalists and their progeny. Nine decades later, Adams's grandson Henry Adams wrote a classic history of the Jefferson administration in which he scarcely found room for the expedition. He characterized it as "creditable to American energy and enterprise," but dismissed it as adding "little to the stock of science or wealth. . . . The crossing of the continent was a great feat, but was nothing more." The real news from the period 1804–6, Adams wrote, wasn't Lewis struggling against the current but Robert Fulton beginning to construct the hull of his new steamboat.*[5]

East versus West, technology versus human endeavor, partisanship versus patriotism. These are permanent themes in American politics. Lewis had been private secretary to the president, a Washington insider. He should have protected Jefferson, and his expedition, by providing information that could build anticipation and justify the costs.

Lewis said he would be in Washington shortly and would then provide Jefferson with additional details about his plan; he explained that until Jefferson had seen the map he could not understand what Lewis had in mind in dealing with the Indians, and there was but one copy of Clark's map, which "I am unwilling to wrisk by the Mail." He would come as

---

* In Adams's defense, he wrote before the Thwaites edition of the journals was published, so he had no way of knowing how much had been discovered.

soon as he could wrap up his business in St. Louis, but would go to Charlottesville before proceeding to Washington, because "I am very anxious to learn the state of my friends in Albemarle particularly whether my mother is yet living."

Before closing, Lewis added a paragraph that began with a splendid tribute to his dearest friend and closest companion, followed by a typically generous gesture: "With rispect to the exertions and services rendereed by that esteemable man Capt. William Clark in the course of [our] late voyage I cannot say too much; if sir any credit be due for the success of the arduous enterprise in which we have been mutually engaged, he is equally with myself entitled to your consideration and that of our common country."

That put it directly before the president: whatever rank Clark carried on the War Department rolls, Lewis wanted him treated as captain and co-commander. This was what he had promised, what Clark had earned. To Lewis, any other action was unthinkable.

The declaration was politically necessary and wise on Lewis's part. No matter what he said, on the army rolls Clark was a lieutenant, Lewis the captain. Worse, among the politicians (and the people, come to that), Clark was much less known than Lewis. Lewis counted on Jefferson to make the paragraph public (he did), and hoped that it would squash any inclination on the part of Congress to give less to Clark than to himself.[6]

In his last paragraph, Lewis asked Jefferson's pardon for "this haisty communication." He explained he had no time to write more, for he had already detained the post for a day. Still, he was sorry to "have been so laconic."

He signed, thought a moment, then added a postscript that showed what a good officer and fine man he was: "The whole of the party who accompanyed me from the Mandans have returned in good health, which is not, I assure you, to me one of the least pleasing considerations of the Voyage."[7]

In sum, Lewis's first communication with Jefferson in a year and a half answered the president's most pressing questions while holding out hope for an American empire stretching from sea to sea. Although written in haste, with critical material missing, it was a model of how to write a report that disposes of the bad news first, then draws attention to the good.

In addition to his praise of Clark, Lewis took care to provide each enlisted man with a handwritten testimonial. For instance, he praised Sergeant Gass's "ample support . . . manly firmness . . . the fortitude with which he bore the fatigues and painful sufferings," and said he had Lewis's "highest confidence." Gass was entitled to "the consideration and respect of his fellow citizens."[8] In a later recommendation to Secretary Dearborn, Lewis said he hoped that each and every man would "meet a just reward in an ample remuneration on the part of our Government."[9]

A good company commander looks after his men.

Lewis and Clark knew that news in the United States traveled fastest via the newspapers, which copied articles from one another. The nearest newspaper was in Frankfort, Kentucky. The captains knew that letters to their family members would be published and then copied, and that George Rogers Clark would get his letter more than two weeks earlier than Lewis's family in Virginia. But Clark felt Lewis was a better writer than he. No problem for these two: Lewis drafted the letter for Clark, who copied it, signed it, and sent it off to Kentucky.* The captains had George Drouillard take the report and letters across the Mississippi to the post on the Illinois side.

Donald Jackson comments that "the initial fame of the expedition rests largely upon this communication, which spread throughout the country as rapidly as the means of the day would allow." The Frankfort *Western World* ran it on October 11; the Pittsburgh *Gazette* had it on October 28; the Washington *National Intelligencer* put it into its November 3 edition; soon thereafter, it had been reprinted scores of times.[10]

The letter covered many of the points made in the report to Jefferson, but added considerable details on some of the difficulties and risks involved. Here Lewis may have had a pecuniary motive—for himself, for Clark, and for their men. He knew the politicians and their constituents. He knew how an adventure story filled with tremendous mountains and terrible portages and turbulent rapids and near-starvation and various Indian encounters would stir their hearts. And he knew it was Congress that would be responsible for the size of the reward he, Clark, and the men would receive from a grateful nation. He didn't exaggerate the dangers the expedition had faced, but he didn't downplay them either (he scarcely mentioned them to Jefferson).

With the report and letters home written and on their way, it was time to begin the celebration. The captains had been invited to take rooms

---

* It may be that Lewis had another motive in drafting the letter for Clark: to get publicity for Clark, again with the thought of compensation in mind.

at the home of Jean-Pierre Chouteau. They did so, and paid visits to other members of the Chouteau family and additional important personages in the town. Apparently they stayed out late; Clark opened his September 24 entry, "I sleped but little last night."

That day, the captains dined with the Chouteaus. They arranged to store their baggage in a room they rented from William Christy, a former neighbor of Clark's in Kentucky and now a tavern keeper in St. Louis. They went to a tailor and got fitted for some clothes. They "payed Some visits of form, to the gentlemen of St. Louis."

Wherever they went, they were all but overwhelmed with questions. First of all, the St. Louis merchants wanted to know about the beaver and the Indians and the distances, but they—like all the other men in town—were keenly aware of the dangers of the unknown wilderness and were adventurers themselves. So they also wanted to know about the close calls, the high mountains, and any anecdotes the captains could tell. The enlisted men, one can assume, were being similarly bombarded with questions from the less exalted citizens of St. Louis.

When Lewis and Clark returned, "their accounts of that wild region, with those of their companions, first excited a spirit of trafficking adventure among the young men of the west," recalled Thomas James, a Missourian who shortly went up the river himself. And a local chronicle recorded, "The daring adventure became the theme of universal conversation in the town."[11]

Arlen Large has captured the essence of oral reporting and its influence: "This kind of unrecorded talk—campfire bull sessions, barroom yarns, refined after dinner conversation over cognac and cigars . . . sparked the initial exploitation of the expedition's findings. The first follow-up wave of fur-business exploration that spread across the west was due more to post-expedition gossip and gab than any written documents."[12]

The early newspaper accounts based on letters sent east by private citizens of St. Louis make the point. A letter printed in Kentucky and picked up across the nation read, "One of the hands, an intelligent man, tells me that Indians are as numerous on [the] Columbia as the whites are in any part of the U States," but they were unarmed and "are represented as being very peaceable. The weather was very mild on the Pacific." Another spoke of "horses without number" among the Indians, but said the Indians were entirely without iron tools—a sentence sure to start the heads of young entrepreneurs spinning, especially since all accounts spoke of "the whole country furnishing valuable furs."[13]

The captains and their men didn't have to stretch in telling their tales of grizzlies and Blackfeet and other dangers to impress their audience. But if they didn't boast, they clearly were not excessively modest. Aside from their justified pride in what they had accomplished, they wanted to tell the American people—and through them their representatives in Congress—how difficult it had been. That they were successful, at least in St. Louis, is evident in the remark of the resident federal surveyor Silas Bent. "All parties," he noted, "have joined here in expressing their high sence of the great merit of these Gentlemen."[14]

The first formal celebration took place on the afternoon and evening of September 25, when the leading men of the town sponsored a dinner and ball at Christy's Inn. It was a long evening. Lewis and Clark joined in a total of seventeen toasts. The first (at their suggestion?) was to Thomas Jefferson, "The friend of science, the polar star of *discovery*, the philosopher and the patriot." There followed toasts to the members of Jefferson's administration, to the expedition, to the enlisted men ("may they be rewarded," a most welcome touch), to the United States (a little politics here: "Whilst they tolerate a spirit of enquiry, may never forget, that *united they stand—but divided they fall*," an obvious reference to Aaron Burr's ongoing conspiracies), to Louisiana, to the memory of Columbus, to the Constitution, to the memory of George Washington, to peace, to commerce, and so on.

That was a lot of toasting for men who had drunk nothing but water for fifteen months, and at that point the captains retired. After they left, there was a final toast, to "Captains Lewis and Clark—Their perilous services endear them to every American heart."[15]

The following day, the captains got back to their writing. Lewis started a letter, intended for publication, that eventually took him four days and thirty-two hundred words to complete. It combined reporting with boosterism. "I consider this Track across the Continent as presenting immense advantages to the Fur Trade," he wrote.

More immediately, Lewis's letter was his most direct bid for an adequate reward from Congress. He had not thought about money for twenty-eight months, but back in St. Louis, that center of get-rich-quick schemes, his friends among the merchants talked of little else, and money became a subject very much on his mind. To become a player in the various schemes, he needed investment capital. His quickest access to it was a generous reward from grateful politicians.

So, although he did not exaggerate, he made certain people knew that he, Clark, and the men had risked their lives for their country. He described in detail the precarious situation the expedition was in at

Cameahwait's village. From there, he wrote, "we attempted with success those unknown formidable snow clad Mountains on the bare word of a Savage [Old Toby], while %⁄₁₀₀th of his Countrymen assured us that a passage was impracticable." In crossing the mountains, "we suffered everything Cold, Hunger & Fatigue could impart, or the Keenest Anxiety excited for the fate of [the] Expedition in which our whole Souls were embarked." Arriving among the Nez Percé, "I suffered a severe Indisposition for 10 or 12 days, sick feeble & emaciated." Descending the Columbia, the men "narrowly escaped with their Lives."

After a description of Fort Clatsop and the return journey over the Lolo Trail, Lewis went into a long account of his side trip to explore the Marias River. He made certain his readers were aware of his purpose, writing that it was of "the highest national importance" to establish the northernmost tributary of the Missouri. "I determined to execute it at every hazard," even though "I was well apprised that the Country thro' which it became necessary for me to pass was inhabited by several large & roving Bands of the Black Foot Indians, who trade at the British Settlements on the Saskoohawan." There followed a stirring account of his encounter with the Blackfeet at Two Medicine River.[16]

Lewis's storytelling was more tantalizing than fulfilling. People wanted to know more. That Lewis was thinking about the value of those journals to himself, as well as to the nation, is hinted at in a comment by an unknown St. Louis resident, written on September 23: "Their journal will no doubt be not only importantly interesting to us all, but a fortune for the worthy and laudable adventurers."[17]

The wording indicates that Lewis expected to get rich from the publication of the journals. Where did he get the idea that they were his—and Clark's—private property? The government had paid for the expedition; Lewis and Clark were on active duty when they wrote their journals; it might have been expected that the maps and journals would be regarded as belonging to the government (indeed, Jefferson later commented, "They are the property of the government, the fruits of the expedition undertaken at such expense of money"), to be published by the government with no royalties to the authors.

Apparently, however, Lewis had discussed this point with Jefferson before he left Washington, and Jefferson had said that Lewis would have the right to publish with a commercial firm and keep the profit. This supposition is based on the contemporary remark about the fortune that would come to the captains from their journals, and Jefferson's statement, ten years later, that "We were willing to give to Lewis and Clarke whatever pecuniary benefits might be derived from the publication, and therefore left the papers in their hands, taking for granted that their interests would produce a speedy publication, which would be better if done under their direction."[18]

Lewis and Clark were not the only ones who kept a journal. All of the sergeants did, as ordered by the captains, and a few of the privates as well. Lewis regarded those journals as subject to his control, making them something considerably short of private property. Private Robert Frazier approached him soon after the arrival in St. Louis, asking permission to publish his journal. Lewis readily gave it, provided Frazier submitted the prospectus for his approval. Frazier did. The prospectus promised a four-hundred-page book that would contain "an accurate description of the Missouri . . . of the Columbia . . . of the face of the Country in general . . . of the several Tribes of Indians . . . of the vegetable, animal and mineral productions discovered," as well as the latitudes and longitudes of the "most remarkable places." Potential subscribers were assured the book would be "Published by Permission of Captn. Meriwether Lewis."[19]

Lewis read the draft and was appalled. He insisted that the publisher would have to "expunge the promise which had been made, that the work should contain certain information in relation to the natural history of the country," because Frazier was "entirely unacquainted with celestial observations, mineralogy, botany, or zoology, and therefore cannot possibly give any accurate information on those subjects, nor on that of geography."

Lewis's objections to the prospectus were well taken. They were also self-serving, in that they were intended to suppress competition for his own book. They further show that Lewis regarded his scientific discoveries as the most valuable part of his journal. (In the event, Frazier's publishers ignored Lewis, but they never brought out the book, and Frazier's journal has never been found—a sad loss to history.)[20]

The Frazier prospectus put added pressure on Lewis to get to Washington as soon as possible, to receive the adulation of his countrymen and his compensation, and to find a publisher—and, he hoped, get an advance. But duty kept him in St. Louis. It took him a month to settle fiscal affairs connected with the expedition. He spent much of his time obtaining hard currency for the enlisted men who wanted an advance on the pay due them; the sums were as large as $400 (for Private John Potts).

The task threw him into the inner circle of money men in St. Louis. Currency was scarce on the frontier; Lewis had to call on sixteen merchants to obtain cash advances ranging from $300 to $19.50. In return, he gave drafts drawn on the War Department.[21] There were supplies to purchase, clothes and provisions for himself, Clark, Big White, and the rest of the party that would soon head off for Washington. He paid with drafts. He easily fell into a habit of paying for whatever he needed or wanted with drafts; why not, since he had an unlimited checking account with the U.S. government?

The riches of Louisiana available for immediate exploitation consisted almost entirely of furs and land; speculation in both was the all-but-consuming activity among St. Louis businessmen. Lewis's men quickly got into the action. He had promised them when they volunteered for the expedition that they would receive "a compensation in Lands equal to that granted to a Soldier of the Revolutionary Army." That unwritten promise, backed by Lewis's word, was considered as good as a land warrant in hand. Private Joseph Whitehouse sold his anticipated warrant to Drouillard for $280, who also bought Private John Collins's. Six months later, Drouillard sold his own warrant and the two he had purchased for $1,300, a handsome profit. The purchasers took a beating; they sold the warrants a year later for $1,100.[22]

The captains held a public auction, in which they sold off the public items that had survived their voyage. These included the rifles, powder horns, shot pouches, kettles, and axes. They brought $408.62.[23]

This was a dreadful disgrace. The artifacts should have been preserved as public treasures rather than sold for a pittance. But apparently the captains had always intended to sell them at the value of their immediate utility rather than preserve them for museums.

As he dealt with these and other matters, Lewis was in constant contact with the St. Louis businessmen. Although there are no contemporary documents revealing what they talked about, it was almost surely land and furs. The merchants certainly bombarded Lewis with questions. Since he was thinking about getting into the fur trade himself, and in any case wanted to get going on his American fur-trade-empire plan, he must have answered in great detail on such subjects as the right size for a party setting off for the Yellowstone country, what trade items were most desired by the Indians on the upper Missouri River, what equipment was needed, and most of all where and in what quantity the beaver were. Manuel Lisa, according to his biographer Richard Oglesby, was "galvanized" by the stories he heard from Lewis and Clark in October 1806. He began raising money for a two-keelboat expedition up the Missouri in the spring.[24] Lewis may have been in on the subscription.

On October 24, Lewis's letter of September 23 arrived in Washington. Jefferson immediately replied. He said he had received it "with unspeakable joy," and allowed himself to express a bit of the terrible anxiety he had felt for his young friend and for the expedition that he had fathered: "The unknown scenes in which you were engaged, & the length of time without hearing of you had begun to be felt awfully." He said he was sending the letter to Charlottesville, where he expected Lewis to arrive shortly, and added that his "only object is to assure you of what you already know, my constant affection for you & the joy with which all your friends here will recieve you."

He suggested that Lewis visit Monticello before coming to Washington, and that he bring Big White with him, to see the Indian Hall that he was building. It included Indian artifacts sent on by Lewis from Fort Mandan in the spring of 1805, plus elk and moose horns (which today hang inside the main entrance at Monticello, with some Mandan artifacts and a portrait of Big White).[25]

Jefferson then talked with his treasury secretary, Albert Gallatin (neither man yet knew that Lewis had named a river for him) about a proper post for Lewis. The president had in mind appointing him governor of Louisiana Territory. Gallatin thought this a good idea, but pointed out it would be necessary to appoint a secretary to govern the territory until Lewis could return to St. Louis from the East, and that would undoubtedly take some time, since Lewis would have to oversee the publication of the journals.[26]

This was a big mistake, easily seen and easily avoidable. Jefferson would have done much better to promote Lewis to higher rank and assign him to duty in the War Department with no other responsibility than working with secretarial help and special advisers in getting the journals published promptly by the government.[27] That would have deprived Lewis of any royalties, and kept him out of St. Louis and thus a nonparticipant in the building of the American fur-trade empire, important objectives to Lewis but surely of no concern to the president. The chief thing—the only thing—was to get those journals published. But, obviously, Jefferson anticipated no difficulty about that.

In early November 1806, Lewis and Clark set off with their entourage. The party included Big White, his translator, and their families, a delegation of Osages led by Pierre Chouteau, Sergeants Gass and Ordway, Privates Labiche and Frazier, plus York. In Louisville on the 9th, they had a visit with George Rogers Clark, and the citizens gave them a banquet and ball and lit bonfires in their honor. On the 13th, they arrived in Frankfort, where they split up. Chouteau took his party of Osage Indians on to Washington. Clark went to Fincastle, Virginia, to see friends—especially Julia Hancock, who had been a child of twelve when he last saw her and after whom he had named the Judith River. Lewis, with Big White and his group, headed out for Charlottesville.

On December 2, Jefferson made his first public comment on the expedition's return. It was a paragraph only, in his annual message to Congress, and it was almost apologetic: "The expedition of Messrs. Lewis and Clarke for exploring the river Missouri, & the best communication from that to the Pacific ocean, has had all the success which could have been expected." Those last four words may have been Jefferson's expression of disappointment about the lack of a Northwest Passage. He gave a one-sentence summary of the voyage, then got to the part that would justify the expenses already incurred and those to come in the form of a compensation for the captains and their men: "In the course of their journey they acquired a knolege of numerous tribes of Indians hitherto unknown; they informed themselves of the trade which may be carried on with them, the best channels & positions for it, & they are enabled to give with accuracy the geography of the line they pursued."

The information obtained, the president assured Congress, was so valuable that "it is but justice to say that Messrs. Lewis & Clarke, & their brave companions, have, by this arduous service, deserved well of their country."[28] To Lewis, the paragraph may have been disappointingly short, but he had to like that last line.

Out in St. Louis, the leading citizens were almost exclusively interested in what Lewis had found with regard to Indians and furs. Back east, his botanical and zoological discoveries excited the members of the American Philosophical Society. They wanted seeds, specimens, descriptions. Jefferson promised Benjamin Smith Barton that Lewis would hurry onto Philadelphia after visiting Washington, bringing with him "much in the lines of botany, & Nat. history." Jefferson kept for himself, to plant at Monticello, seeds of "Missouri hominy corn," of Pawnee corn, nine "nuts from Missouri," and two boxes of unidentified seeds. Over the following years, Jefferson faithfully reported on the Indian corn, which he pronounced excellent.

As Lewis approached Washington, the excitement mounted. Charles Willson Peale, founder of the Philadelphia Museum (and later Peale's Museum) and the leading portrait painter of the day (he did the first portrait of George Washington), wrote Jefferson: "Mr. Lewis is richly entitled to a place amongst the Portraits of the Museum, and I hope he will do me the favor of sitting as soon as he arrives here."[29]

Lewis's progress was slow, at least in part because at every town and village the residents insisted on some sort of dinner and ball to honor him. He arrived at Locust Hill on December 13, for his reunion with his mother and family. Word reached Charlottesville that day; he was expected there on the 15th, and the citizens prepared a reception; despite bad weather and dangerous riding conditions, a local correspondent for the Richmond *Enquirer* reported, "about fifty of the most respectable inhabitants of the county assembled to receive him."

The celebration dinner was held at the Stone Tavern, near the corner of Fifth and Market Streets. Before eating, an unnamed citizen who had been delegated for the task gave a speech. He praised Lewis for "the difficult and dangerous enterprize which you have so successfully achieved." The voyage "has covered with glory, yourself and your gallant little band." He spoke of "this expedition, so wisely planned, so happily executed, the germ of extended civilization, science and liberty." In his view, "Every American, every friend to liberty, to science and to man, participates with us," but stressed that "it is our peculiar felicity to boast, that the man who achieved this interesting and arduous enterprize, is the produce of our soil, was raised from infancy to manhood among us, is our neighbour, *our* friend," and concluded with the hope that the nation would "adequately reward the services you have rendered."

Lewis's reply was taken down verbatim. Because it is the closest account available of his speaking style, it deserves to be quoted at some length. Lewis began by expressing his pleasure at being back in Albemarle County, and at the honor being done him. "This warm and undisguised expression of friendship by those, whom the earliest emotions of my heart compelled me to love, is, in contemplation, not less pleasing than the fond hope, that it may hereafter be believed, that I have discharged my duty to my country on the late expedition to the Pacific Ocean."

His convoluted phraseology may have been a consequence of having to give a formal address to a large audience on such a special occasion. Whatever the cause, he took pains to share the credit: "To have conceived is but little; the merit of having added to the world of science, and of liberty, a large portion of the immense unknown wilds of North America, is equally due to my dear and interesting friend capt. Clark, and to those who were the joint companions of our labours and difficulties in performing that task."

He closed on a political and economic note, expressing the wish that "the discoveries we have made, will not long remain unimproved; and that the same sentiment which dictated to our government, an investigation into the resources so liberally bestowed by nature on this fair portion of the globe, will prompt them to avail themselves of those resources, to promote the cause of liberty and the honour of America, and to relieve distressed humanity."

The company then sat down to an excellent dinner, followed by "many" appropriate toasts. Songs were sung and the party "passed the evening in that spirit of festivity and mirth, which the joyful occasion, and the presence of their friends, safely returned from his perilous expedition, and in the bloom of health, inspired."[30]

Then it was off to Washington, where Lewis arrived late in the day of December 28. "Never did a similar event excite more joy," a Washington observer declared. The Washington *National Intelligencer* reported his arrival with "high satisfaction." It said that few expeditions in human history had been "conducted with more patience, perseverance, or success." The paper added, however, that it would give no further particulars, since Lewis himself had promised one and all to lay an account of it before the public in the form of his published journals. The forthcoming book, the paper declared, "would not merely gratify literary curiosity, but open views of great and immediate objects of national utility."[31]

The following evening, Lewis attended the theater, accompanied by Big White and his entourage. During intermission, some of the Indians danced on the stage. On December 30, Jefferson received the Osage delegation, and on the day of New Year's Eve he entertained Big White and the Mandans. To both groups he gave his usual Indian speech.

Lewis was at the President's House on New Year's Day. Things had worked out exactly as he had hoped; a year earlier, he had written that what kept him going was the anticipation of January 1, 1807, when he would be in the bosom of his friends, participating in the mirth and hilarity of the day. His pleasure in the moment, he wrote, would be all the greater thanks to the memory of Fort Clatsop. He had had nothing but cold water to celebrate with then. If he made up for it with his patron's excellent wines, no one who was present would have denied that he had earned it.

No account has been found of Lewis's first meeting with Jefferson since his departure in July 1803, three and a half years past. It can be taken for granted that Lewis had many questions about the political situation in the capital. But one can suppose that Jefferson overwhelmed Lewis with his curiosity about the natural wonders Lewis had encountered, the adventures he had experienced, the Indians he had seen.

And the tales he had to tell! Of grizzlies and gigantic trees and great storms and the almost paradisiacal quality of the Great Plains and the deserts of the upper Missouri, the fierceness of the Indians of the Plains and the numbers of Indians on the lower Columbia, the astonishing bird and animal life, and so much more. The words must have tumbled out. It is a great pity that Jefferson did not think to have a note-taker present, or to write his own summary of what was said.

It must have been a joyous reunion, each man delighted to see the other in good health and spirits. The conversation would have had its down side, especially the disappointment over the Northwest Passage, but we can assume that Jefferson took the blow without flinching. British explorer Captain George Vancouver had caught the spirit of the era when he exclaimed that "the ardour of the present age is to discover and delineate the true geography of the earth."[32] Jefferson completely agreed.

So that's how it is, he might have said, and told Lewis to go on.

Lewis would have had plenty to say about the promise of Louisiana and his plan for an American fur-trade empire. Jefferson must have been delighted. As James Ronda points out, "Generations of empire builders had used the fur trade to secure Indian allies, forestall potential imperial rivals, and expand territorial domain. . . . The course of empire hung on the trade and Jefferson knew it."[33]

Lewis had the journals with him, and Clark's map covering the western two-thirds of the continent. Surely they discussed publication. As Donald Jackson reminds us, "Literally, the world had been waiting for their return."[34] And as James Ronda points out, "The Enlightenment taught that observation unrecorded was knowledge lost."[35] Jefferson must have been delighted by samples of Lewis's descriptions of new flora and fauna, of landforms and soil conditions; many years earlier, he had explained to a would-be explorer that science required "very exact descriptions of what they see."[36]

On that point, Lewis had carried out Jefferson's orders exactly. Indeed, on almost every point Lewis had accomplished his mission.

How long the debriefing by the commander-in-chief lasted, what subjects came up, what was said, is all conjecture. One fact we do know: they spread the map on the floor, got down on hands and knees, and examined it.[37]

34

WASHINGTON

January–March 1807

On January 2, the House created a committee "to inquire what compensation ought to be made to Messrs. Lewis, and Clarke, and their brave companions." Willis Alston, Jr., of North Carolina was named chairman.[1] Lewis, who was living at the President's House, went to work on the politicians, for himself and for Clark and the men.

Official Washington, meanwhile, wanted to honor the captains in a more immediate way, with a grand testimonial dinner and ball that would allow the politicians to be seen with and talk to the young heroes. Clark, however, was still in Virginia, courting Julia Hancock. (Lewis was doing some courting of his own in Washington, although no details about this are known.) The ball was put off on several occasions; finally, it was decided to wait no more, and a date was set for January 14.

Indicative of the excitement in the capital was a recommendation from Joel Barlow, considered by himself and some others to be the leading poet of the nation, to rename the great river of the West, changing it from "Columbia" to "Lewis."[2]

Pierre Chouteau and Big White accompanied Lewis to the ball. Jefferson was not listed in the newspaper account of the dinner, so it can be assumed he was not among the "several officers of government" who attended. Dumas Malone explains that "Jefferson abominated such occasions, and he may have believed that his presence would distract attention from the returned hero."[3]

Many toasts were drunk—to the Constitution, to Lewis and Clark, and so on. Barlow offered one: "To victory over the wilderness, which is more interesting than that over man."

Lewis offered his own: "May works be the test of patriotism as they ought, of right, to be of religion." After the toasts, the party sat down to what the *National Intelligencer* described as a "well spread board."

Barlow wrote a poem of eight stanzas, full of bombast, bad rhymes, and mixed metaphors, that was read after dinner. An example:

> *Then hear the loud voice of the nation proclaim,*
> *   And all ages resound the decree:*
> Let our Occident stream bear the young hero's name
> Who taught him his path to the sea.

This was too much for Senator John Quincy Adams, who wrote a parody ridiculing Jefferson as a "philosopher" and a man absurdly credulous. Adams wrote about what Lewis did *not* find: mammoth or mammoth bones, Welsh Indians, salt mountain. As far as Adams was concerned, Lewis was extravagant in his storytelling:

> *What marvels on the way he found*
> *He'll tell you, if inclin'd, sir—*

But what really set Adams off was Barlow's proposal to rename the Columbia:

> *Let old Columbus be once more*
> *Degraded from his glory;*
> *And not a river by his name*
> *Remember him in story—*
> *For what is old Discovery*
> *Compar'd to that which new is?*
> *Strike—strike Columbia river out,*
> *And put in—River Lewis!*[4]

As to Barlow's line about Lewis teaching the Columbia its path to the sea, Adams wrote in a footnote, "Here the young HERO is exhibited in the interesting character of school-master to a river." Malone comments that this bit of doggerel "revealed more wit than most observers would have expected of the sober Senator from Massachusetts and a more partisan spirit than his public actions showed."[5]

Jefferson, wisely, never followed up on Barlow's proposal. So Columbus, already defrauded of the name of a hemisphere, kept his river.

Lewis stayed at the President's House through the winter. The debriefing continued. In mid-February, Jefferson wrote Secretary Dearborn that in conversation with Lewis he had discussed the items that any future explorers of Louisiana ought to take with them. At the top of the list was blue beads, preferred by the Indians to all others. Lewis told Jefferson that, if he were to perform his journey again, one-half to two-thirds of his stores would consist of blue beads, brass buttons, knives, battle axes and tomahawks (but not rifles), awls, glover's needles, iron combs, nests of camp kettles, and arrow points.[6]

Lewis also worked on the accounts from the expedition, and talked with the politicians about compensation, seeking more money and land for his men, and justice for Clark. In conversation with Secretary Dearborn, he insisted that, whatever grant of land Congress might give him, Clark's should be the same. He further insisted "there should be no distinction of rank."

Dearborn, who was the cause of this sorry mess about rank, refused. In responding to Congressman Alston's request for a formal recommendation from the War Department on compensation, Dearborn proposed that each of the men receive a warrant for 320 acres (the standard Revolutionary War veteran's bonus), that Clark receive a thousand acres, and Lewis fifteen hundred.[7]

Lewis drew up his own formal recommendation, not for himself or Clark but for the enlisted men. He began with a plea for two enlisted men who did not make the journey past Fort Mandan—Corporal Richard Warfington and Private John Newman. Lewis had discharged Newman from the party for mutinous expression at Fort Mandan, but he had conducted himself admirably since and had been invaluable to Warfington on the voyage back to St. Louis.

Then Lewis listed all the men (except York) who had been to the Pacific and back. He asked for additional compensation for Private "Labuiche," on the grounds that Labiche had served as translator from French to English in addition to his regular duties; for Private John Shields, whose "ingenuity . . . in repairing our guns" was indispensable; for the Field brothers ("Two of the most active and enterprising young men who accompanied us"); and for "George Drulyard" (which was perhaps an improvement on his usual spelling of "Drewyer"), whom Lewis described as "a man of much merit." Drouillard's skills with the sign language and as a hunter and woodsman were performed "with an ardor which deserves the highest commendation." He had signed

Drouillard on at twenty-five dollars a month, but recommended that he receive thirty per month.

Lewis was negative only toward Charbonneau, "a man of no peculiar merit." He had hired Charbonneau on as interpreter at $25 a month, but obviously thought it unjust that he receive the same pay as Drouillard.

Lewis ended his recommendation with a plea for all the men, whose conduct had entitled them "to my warmest approbation and thanks; nor will I suppress the expression of a hope, that the recollection of services thus faithfully performed will meet a just reward in an ample remuneration on the part of our Government."[8]

On January 23, Alston presented his bill for compensation. It called for 1,600 acres each to Lewis and Clark, 320 acres to each of the enlisted men, and double pay for all. That included Warfington, Newman, Drouillard, and Charbonneau. There was no provision for anything extra for Labiche, Shields, or the Field brothers, nor did Drouillard get the extra $5 per month. The appropriation to cover the compensation amounted to $11,000.

The Alston bill was hotly debated in the House. Some representatives contended that the grants were extravagant and beyond precedent. One member declared, "It was the equivalent to taking more than $60,000 out of the Treasury, and might be perhaps three or four times that sum, as the grantees might go over all the Western country and locate their warrants on the best land," worth far more than the standard $2 per acre. It took the House over a month to pass the bill (by a vote of 62 to 23). On the same day they did so, February 28, the bill passed the Senate without amendment and with little debate, and without a recorded vote (perhaps luckily for Senator Adams, whose doggerel attacking Lewis and Jefferson was later used against him politically).[9]

The pay scale ranged from $5 per month for privates, $7 for corporals, and $8 for sergeants, to $30 for Lieutenant Clark and $40 for Captain Lewis (the officers also received reimbursements for rations for themselves and, in Clark's case, for York).

For Lewis, that meant a total of $3,360 in pay for the period April 1, 1803, to October 1807, plus $702 in ration money, plus land warrants worth $3,200 payable at any government land office, or a grand total of $7,262. That hardly made him rich, but it did give him some working capital for the expenses involved in preparing the journals for publication, with enough left over to let him become a player in the St. Louis-based fur trade. For himself, for Clark (except for his pay scale), for the men, it was all Lewis could have hoped for or expected.

There were more expenses to be paid, including the cost of getting Big White back to the Mandans; obviously, when the final settlement was made, the expedition was going to turn out costing a lot more than had been anticipated. Jefferson never complained. He was no more likely to haggle over the costs of the expedition than over his own building operations at Monticello, because he regarded the expenditure as an investment in the future of the country.[10]

In July 1808, the president went on record on the matter. He wrote the French naturalist Bernard Lacépède, "I can assure you that the addition to our knowledge, in every department, resulting from this tour of Messrs. Lewis and Clark has entirely fulfilled my expectations in setting it on foot, and that the world will find that those travellers have well earned its favor."[11]

There was another compensation for the captains, in the form of their new appointments. On February 28, 1807, Jefferson nominated Lewis to be governor of the Territory of Louisiana.* The Senate approved the nomination, and on March 2, Lewis resigned his commission in the army.[12] At the same time, Jefferson wanted to nominate Clark for promotion to lieutenant colonel, but when the list of nominees came through from the War Department, Clark's name was not on it. The president queried his secretary of war, who explained that Clark had been left off through "a misunderstanding of my directions" by a clerk.[13]

The Senate rejected Clark's nomination, but as Clark explained to his brother in a March 5 letter, it was done "on the Grounds of braking through a Principal"—namely, seniority. Clark said he was "truly gratified" nevertheless, for the senators had all told him they would confirm any other nomination, and indeed did so when Jefferson appointed him superintendent of Indian affairs for Louisiana Territory, with the rank of brigadier general of militia.[14]

It was midwinter in Washington, wet and cold. At the President's House, Jefferson's son-in-law Thomas Mann Randolph took ill. His fever rose and fell, leaving Jefferson alternately worried and hopeful. The doctor was bleeding the invalid, which certainly did him no good. Jefferson wrote his daughter Martha progress reports, complaining on one occasion that "the quantity of blood taken from him occasions him

---

* In 1807, Congress split the original Louisiana Purchase lands at the thirty-third parallel, the modern northern boundary of the state of Louisiana. Everything below that was the Territory of Orleans; everything above, the Territory of Louisiana.

to recover strength slowly." On March 6, Jefferson informed Martha that Captain Lewis was constantly with Randolph, attending to his needs.

Whatever Randolph had, Lewis caught. Jefferson also had a bad cold. Between them, Jefferson wrote Martha, "we are but a collection of invalids."[15]

Clark, meanwhile, had made it to Washington, where he was gathering up the land warrants for the men still in St. Louis, and the money due them, and preparing to head west to his new post. He and Lewis had agreed that Lewis would stay behind in the East, to oversee the publication of their journals in Philadelphia.

Clark's first task in St. Louis would be to see to Big White's safe return. To that end, Dearborn gave him a letter authorizing him to spend up to four hundred dollars for presents to the Mandans and to draw on the War Department for expenditures that were "indispensibly necessary in fitting out the party for the Voyage." As an inducement to get an armed party of private traders to join Sergeant Nathaniel Pryor, recently promoted to ensign, who would lead the party returning Big White, Dearborn further authorized Clark to enter into contracts with any St. Louis merchants who were interested in pursuing the Missouri River fur trade, granting them a two-year monopoly on a license to trade with the Indians and furnishing their engagés with rifles and ammunition.[16]

Clark received this authorization on March 9. The following day, he visited Lewis in the President's House and was distressed to see his friend so indisposed by his illness. Lewis roused himself sufficiently to go over the details of the land warrants and the back pay—he handed over the warrants plus $6,896 in coin. They discussed the return of Big White and agreed that Pryor should attempt to enlist any men from the expedition still in St. Louis who were willing to go.

After Clark left, Lewis took some pills—whether Rush's or some others is not known. The next morning, he wrote his friend—already en route to St. Louis—that the pills had provided "considerable relief, and [I] have no doubt of recovering my health perfectly in the course of a few days."[17]

He must have, because three days later he sent an open letter to the *National Intelligencer* condemning "several unauthorised and probably some spurious publications now preparing for the press, on the subject of my late tour to the Pacific Ocean by individuals entirely unknown to me" and warning the public to be "on guard with respect to such publications." He said these spurious works would "depreciate the worth of the work" he was preparing and asked for patience from the public, which was clamoring for the journals, "as much time, labor, and expense are absolutely necessary in order to do Justice to the several subjects."

With the letter he included an announcement of his own work, which would give interested people an opportunity to join the list of subscribers. He promised to have the map published by the end of October, with the first volume (the narrative) following by January 1, 1808, the second (on the geography of the country, the Indians encountered, and the prospects for the fur trade) and the third (on scientific discoveries) coming shortly thereafter.

Lewis said that only Robert Frazier had been given permission to publish his journal, and warned that Frazier, who "was only a private," was "entirely unacquainted" with any scientific matters and could provide "merely a limited detail of our daily transactions." He concluded, "With respect to all unauthorised publications relative to this voyage, I presume that they cannot have stronger pretensions to accuracy of information than that of Robert Frazier."[18]

It was a strange document, mean-spirited in tone and content, so unlike Lewis, who had previously been active in promoting the interests of Clark and the men. It was defensive, even greedy. There were no misspellings, which indicates that someone proofread it for him. It used words Lewis did not ordinarily use, such as "depreciate," "subjoined," and "expunged." Further, Lewis was a man whose reputation for telling the truth was unassailable, but he almost certainly lied when he wrote that he had heard reports to the effect that "individuals entirely unknown" to him were preparing books on the expedition.

What he had heard was that Sergeant Gass was about to issue a prospectus for a book based on the daily journal he had kept—as Captain Lewis had ordered him to do. In fact, the Gass prospectus did appear six days later in the Pittsburgh *Gazette*.

All this leads to the conjecture that, when Jefferson and Lewis heard about the Gass journal, they went into something akin to a panic. Jefferson may have urged Lewis to issue his warning against "spurious publications" and helped him write the letter.*

Whoever was responsible for the letter, it was a mistake. It made Lewis look cheap, ungrateful, pleading for special interests—himself.

---

* The eminent authority Paul Russell Cutright, in his *History of the Lewis and Clark Journals*, pp. 20–26, concludes that Jefferson was directly involved.

It opened him to ridicule. He could be considered guilty of a double cross, for he had given Frazier permission to publish and then denigrated the product, which he had not seen.* And how dare he assert his right to publish for profit while denying it to Frazier and Gass?

The battle in Washington over who got the insiders memoirs out first was under way—a battle Lewis was sure to lose. It would cheapen his product, which infuriated him. It would cut into his profit, which made him so angry he lost his common sense.

Lewis knew how vulnerable he was on the money question; in his prospectus he wrote that the author "declares to the public, that his late voyage was not undertaken with a view to pecuniary advantages," and explained that he was asking for subscribers only because he needed to know how many copies to print.[19]

If Jefferson was party to this sordid stuff, as seems likely, he too was guilty of gross misjudgment.

The Gass prospectus was as bad—from Lewis's point of view—as it could have been. It promised a daily narrative, a description of the country and its flora and fauna, soil and minerals, and more. What really hurt was a paragraph explaining that around the campfire "the several journals were brought together, compared, corrected, and the blanks filled up," meaning that early subscribers would be reading material corrected and approved by the captains. What cut to the bone was the publisher's promise to have the work ready for delivery in two months for a price of one dollar per copy.

There went Lewis's market. To add to the injury, Gass's publisher sent to the newspapers his reply to Lewis's warning to the public. The publisher seized on the vulnerabilities Lewis had created to ridicule him. He wrote of "what you very modestly call *your* late tour." He said Mackenzie had faced greater dangers with one-fourth of the men, and done it first. He attacked Lewis's compensation from the government: "Why, sir, these grants and rewards savor more of the splendid munificence of a Prince than the economy of a republican government."

He raised the question "Where was your journal during the session of Congress? Snug, eh!" He exposed Lewis's double standard: "Every man of sense must agree that these journals are either *private* property

---

* Frazier's journal has been lost, but one reader, decades later, said that Frazier's record "was in many respects more interesting than that of his commanders" (Jackson, *Letters*, vol. I, p. 346). Of course the reader would not have seen the Thwaites edition of the captains' journals.

of the individuals who took them, or *public* property." In one sentence he managed to show he knew what he was talking about while suggesting that Gass's journal would be more readable than Lewis's: "He may in some respects be considered as having the advantage; for while your Excellency was star-gazing, and taking celestial observations, he was taking observations in the world below."[20]

Lewis's work had been insulted and pre-empted. He was a writer; we can assume that his mind never stopped composing his reply. But he had the good sense—finally—to keep quiet. He made no public response.

One of the would-be authors, Robert Frazier, was in Washington. He was planning to join Clark in Fincastle, Virginia, for a return trip to St. Louis, where he had been called to appear in the trial of some of the Burr conspirators.* Despite Lewis's comments about Frazier in the newspapers, the two men maintained a friendly relationship. Lewis loaned him fifty dollars, with the understanding that Clark would deduct that amount from Frazier's compensation and return it to Lewis. He sent via Frazier Clark's commission as brigadier general of militia and instructions for Frederick Bates, appointed by Jefferson to be secretary of the territory, a position equivalent to that of lieutenant governor.[21]

Clark was staying at the home of Colonel George Hancock, Julia's father. In a mid-March letter to Lewis, he reported that he had sent Frazier on to St. Louis, along with Lewis's letter to Bates and one of his own.

Clark was in a fine mood. He had his commission, he was headed west, his friend was arranging for the publication of his map and journal, and he had been successful in his courtship. In reporting on the latter, he wrote with uncommon levity.

"I have made an attacked most vigorously," he began. "We have come to terms, and a delivery is to be made first of January when I shall be in possession highly pleasing to my self. I shall return [to Virginia] at that time eagerly to be in possession of what I have never yet experienced." He hoped Governor Lewis would not object to his absence from St. Louis: "You can hint a little on that subject if you think proper and let me know."

Like most young men in love, Clark wanted a similar happiness for his friend. He made an oblique reference to "F.," a young woman Lewis

---

* What Lewis called Burr's "treasonable practices" rivaled the return of Lewis and Clark as the sensation of the season.

was courting, "but should the thing not take to your wish," he went on, "I have discovered a most lovly girl Butiful rich possessing those acomplishments which is calculated to make a man hapy—inferior to you—but to few others." The only trouble was, her father was a Federalist. But that handicap could be overlooked, Clark said, and he knew because he had done it. He confessed he was surprised to discover that Colonel Hancock "is also a Fed. I took him to be a good plain republican. At all events I will hope to introduce some substtantial sincere republicanism into some branch of the family about January."[22]

The head of the Republican Party was also in a good mood. Jefferson was doing what he liked to do best, distributing new knowledge to his naturalist friends. On March 22, he sent Bernard McMahon some seeds brought back by Lewis, explaining that he would not get to Monticello in time to plant them and thought McMahon might put them in the ground in Philadelphia. Jefferson added that Lewis had some seeds set aside for McMahon and would be handing them over when he arrived in Philadelphia, and advised McMahon to "say nothing of your receiving [the enclosed seeds] lest it might lessen the portion he will be disposed to give you."[23]

In his letter of thanks, McMahon said, "I never saw seeds in a better state of preservation," high praise for Lewis's methods. A couple of weeks later, he reported that he already had a fine showing from the Aricka tobacco, the perennial flax, four varieties of currants, and other seeds. He promised regular reports on "the progress of this precious collection."[24]

Two days later, Jefferson sent seeds to another Philadelphia naturalist, William Hamilton, with a similar covering note. In it, Jefferson summed up the results of the three months Lewis had spent in the President's House, three months of almost daily debriefings on what Lewis had done and found. It was a splendid tribute to his young protégé.

"On the whole," the president wrote of Lewis, "the result confirms me in my first opinion that he was the fittest person in the world for such an expedition."[25]

35

PHILADELPHIA

April–July 1807

At the end of March, Lewis left Washington for Philadelphia, taking with him what Paul Russell Cutright has called "perhaps the most important account of discovery and exploration ever written."[1] His objective was singular: to get the journals and map published and made available to the scientific and lay public as soon as possible.

He went at it with as much determination as he had attacked the Rocky Mountains. He got a room at the boardinghouse of Mrs. Eliza Wood, at Cherry near Tenth, and began making calls on the dozen or more men he was relying on for help.

He started with John Conrad, head of a publishing and bookselling firm located at 30 Chestnut Street. As a first-time author, Lewis knew nothing about the preparation of a manuscript for the printer. There were plates to be prepared for the maps, drawings to be done, calculations from the celestial observations to be made, botanical descriptions to be completed, a prospectus to be written, published, and distributed, and more. Most important of all was the editing of the journals.[2]

Conrad's estimate of the publishing costs came to forty-five hundred dollars.[3] This did not include the drawings, calculations, salary for an editor (who presumably would be going to St. Louis with Lewis), and other expenses, all of which would come from Lewis's pocket. Conrad also wrote—or at least helped Lewis write—a formal prospectus, which was signed by Lewis and published on June 3, 1807.

Lewis had to pay for the marketing. He hired J. B. Varnum, Jr., son of a prominent Massachusetts politician, to do the work at a cost of ten dollars. Varnum sent copies to the newspapers and distributed copies in Philadelphia, Washington, and elsewhere.[4]

The prospectus was well done, nicely designed to excite the greatest interest around the country among entrepreneurs looking to invest in the fur trade, potential settlers in the West, scientists, and the general public.

Lewis promised that the first part, consisting of two volumes, would contain "a narrative of the voyage." The second part, in a single volume, would cover the scientific research, "under the heads of Botany, Mineralogy, and Zoology." Part three would consist of Clark's map along with the latitude and longitude of the important places, based on "a series of several hundred celestial observations, made by Captain Lewis during his tour." The price would be ten dollars for the first part, eleven for the second, and ten for the map.[5]

That was a lot to promise. Lewis plunged into the task of making good on his word. He called on Dr. Barton, at his home at 184 Mulberry Street, depending on Barton for help with the natural-history volume. Barton agreed, eagerly: there was so much to excite him in the collection of pressed plants. Lewis had done the pressing in the field, following directions given him by Barton in the spring of 1803, and had done the demanding, time-consuming, detailed work well. Almost all the plants were new to science, as were most of the animals.

Lewis returned to Barton the copy of Antoine du Pratz's *History of Louisiana* that Barton had loaned him on the eve of his departure. On the flyleaf, Lewis wrote: "Dr. Benjamin Smith Barton was so obliging as to lend me this copy of Monsr. Du Pratz' History of Louisiana in June 1803, it has since been conveyed by me to the Pacific Ocean through the interior of North America on my late tour thither and is now returned to it's proprietor by his Friend and Obt. Servt. Meriwether Lewis, Philadelphia, May 9, 1807."[6]

The inscribed book is today in the Library Company, Philadelphia, a piece of Americana beyond price. The book, along with the others in Lewis's traveling library, was one of the few artifacts to go coast-to-coast and back with Lewis. Aside from the books and the then blank journals, almost everything else he took with him from Philadelphia in 1803—medicines, portable soup, scientific instruments, trade goods, and the rest—was either used up on the voyage or sold at auction in St. Louis when he returned. About the only other item Lewis carried from Pittsburgh to the Pacific and back was his rifle.

Books, the journals, and a rifle—these were Meriwether Lewis's essentials. With them, he had conquered and described a wilderness.

Frederick Pursh was a thirty-three-year-old, German-born and -trained botanist, working with Dr. Barton. On April 5, Jefferson's friend and Philadelphia seed merchant Bernard McMahon wrote to Lewis, to thank him for the seeds, and to recommend Pursh to him as the proper person to make the scientific descriptions of the plants. McMahon said Pursh was "better acquainted with plants, in general, than any man I ever conversed with on the subject. . . . He is a very intelligent and practical Botanist [and] would be well inclined to render you any service in his power."⁷

When Lewis met Pursh, he was as impressed as McMahon had been, especially by Pursh's ability to draw plants and to give them proper scientific descriptions—areas in which Lewis felt himself to be deficient. Pursh was excited by the prospect of assisting in the publication of the botanical part of the journals, as well he might have been, since there were over one hundred plants described by Pursh as "either entirely new or but little known." On May 10, Lewis paid Pursh thirty dollars "for assisting me in preparing drawings and arranging specemines of plants for my work," and two weeks later he paid Pursh an additional forty dollars "in advance."*⁸

Jefferson and Lewis were of one mind in regarding Peale's Museum in Independence Hall as the most logical repository for the zoological and ethnological specimens brought back from the West. As a result, with the exception of a few retained by Jefferson for the great hall at Monticello and two or three fancied by Lewis and Clark themselves, Lewis handed the collection over to Peale, which enhanced the prestige of his museum immeasurably.⁹

In return, Peale went to work drawing the animals (which he mounted himself) for Lewis's book.† He also painted Lewis's portrait; it is today in the Independence National Historical Park, Philadelphia,

---

* The money was well spent. In 1814, Pursh published in London his well-known *Flora*. It included Lewis's plants, credited by Pursh with an abbreviated legend, "*v.s. in Herb* [arium] *Lewis.*" He honored Lewis, and Clark, with several binomials, including *Lewisia rediviva* (bitterroot), *Clarkia pulchella* (ragged robin), *Linum lewisii* (Lewis's wild flax), and *Philadelphus lewisii* (Lewis's syringa). (Cutright, *A History of the Lewis and Clark Journals*, p. 48.)
† Two of the drawings survive: one of Lewis's woodpecker (*Asyndesmus lewis*) and the other of the mountain quail.

hanging in the distinguished company of Peale's portraits of Washington and Jefferson. And he made a wax figure of Lewis, informing Jefferson that his intention was "to give a lesson to the Indians who may visit the Museum, and also to show my sentiments respecting wars." He had Lewis dressed in an elegant Indian robe made of 140 ermine skins (given to Lewis by Cameahwait).[10]

Peale was tremendously excited by the specimens. "I have animals brought from the sea coast," he exulted to Philadelphia musician John Hawkins in a May 5 letter, "also some parts of the dress &c of the Natives of Columbia River, [and] have animals totally unknown."

In 1807, Lewis attended three meetings of the American Philosophical Society (April 17, June 19, and July 17), where it can be assumed he was the center of attention, bombarded with questions from the leading scientific figures of the day. Most of all, they wanted to know publication plans.

"It is a work that seems to excite much attention," Peale told Hawkins, "& will I hope have a great sale & give considerable profit to this bold adventurer."[11]

To help ensure that hoped-for success, Lewis got other artists involved. John James Barralet was a sixty-year-old Irish-born engraver. On July 14, Lewis paid him forty dollars for "two drawings [of] water falls."[12] He engaged the well-known thirty-seven-year-old French-born portrait painter Saint-Mémin to do drawings of the Osage and Mandan Indians who had come east with him, at a cost of $83.50. Saint-Mémin also painted Lewis's portrait. *

Alexander Wilson was a thirty-one-year-old, Scottish-born artist-naturalist, best known today for his beautifully illustrated, multivolumed *American Ornithology*. In that work Wilson wrote, "It was the request and particular wish of Captain Lewis made to me in person that I make drawings of each of the feathered tribe as had been preserved, and were new."[13] Among others from the expedition, the set includes Wilson's painting of Lewis's woodpecker.

Lewis had a journal stuffed with figures—the measurements of the passage of the moon past the stars, taken at every opportunity along the voyage. They had cost him much lost sleep, and considerable frustration when clouds obscured the moon. But with the figures, an expert could establish the longitude of the place where they were made.

---

* The original is in the New-York Historical Society; the Corcoran Art Gallery in Washington and the Missouri Historical Society in St. Louis have engravings.

Ferdinand Hassler, a thirty-seven-year-old, Swiss-born mathematician, was the ideal man for the job. He had just been appointed instructor of mathematics at West Point, but, before leaving Philadelphia, Lewis engaged him to make the calculations; he advanced Hassler $100 on May 3.[14]

Before Clark left for St. Louis in March 1807, the captains had made an oral agreement to split the costs involved in preparing the work. They had also agreed to purchase Sergeant Ordway's journal from him at a price of $300, presumably with the objective of forestalling yet another rival and to incorporate Ordway's writing into their book. On April 18, Lewis paid Ordway a $150 advance.[15]

By July, Lewis had signed up botanists, ornithologists, naturalists, artists, mathematicians, zoologists, and others to help make his work as good as it could possibly be. He had done everything he could to hurry along the publication process—except one thing. He had not hired an editor.

This is inexplicable. He knew Conrad could not simply set type from the journals as they stood. In the first place, there was the daunting task of separating out the scientific material from the narrative flow. Then there was the need to incorporate Ordway's journal. In addition, there was the pressing necessity of correcting the spellings and grammar.

Lewis had neither the skills nor the time to do these jobs himself. He was being pressed on an almost daily basis by Conrad to start turning in manuscript. At the American Philosophical Society, and around Philadelphia, the question he most often heard was, When do we get to see the book? He knew that Jefferson greatly desired as early a publication as possible. He had sufficient funds to hire the work done. Yet, as far as is known, he made no effort whatsoever to find an editor, and he prepared not a single line himself.

Lewis spent considerable time on paperwork. Scarcely had he arrived in Philadelphia when the accountant of the War Department, one William Simmons, began to pester him about the many drafts on the government Lewis had signed. The drafts were coming in for payment, and Simmons wanted more information about them. On June 17, in one of his letters, Simmons wrote the heartstopping lines, "You will therefore do well to bring with you [back to Washington] any papers or documents which may relate to your expenditures on the Expedition, so as to explain such of the charges as may require it." As one example,

Lewis had presented no receipts for the rations or the clothing account for the men. "I mention this Item as the most prominent one . . . [but] others may also require [proof]."[16]

The total number of drafts involved ran to 1,989 items. Like any public servant who has his expense account questioned by the government, Lewis was going to find it somewhere between difficult and impossible to come up with all the receipts. Still, he worked at the task, both in Philadelphia and, later, back in Washington. By early August, he had a "final summation" ready. It came to $38,722.25.

For many of the drafts, the government was simply going to have to take Lewis's word for it. One charming example went back to March 1806, when Lewis had traded his uniform coat ("but little worn") to the Clatsops for a canoe. Of course no receipt existed. Lewis listed it this way: "One Uniform Laced Coat, one silver Epaulet, one Dirk, & belt, one hanger & belt, one pistol & one fowling piece, all private property, given in exchange for Canoe, Horses &c. for public service during the expedition—$135."[17]

It is easy to sympathize with Lewis over this bureaucratic harassment, but he really was playing fast and loose with the government during this time. Though living in Philadelphia engaged in what was essentially a private enterprise, he was governor of Louisiana; beyond writing one letter to Secretary Bates asking information about conditions in St. Louis, he had done absolutely nothing on his job. Yet, on June 28, he presented Secretary of State James Madison with a bill for his salary from March 3 to June 30, totaling $666.66.

"You would much oblige me," he wrote Madison, "by forwarding a check on the bank of the U' States for the amount as early as it may be convenient." The State Department, which ran territorial affairs, deducted $5.55 as an overcharge and paid the remainder.[18]

Jefferson, meanwhile, was torn. He wanted Lewis to get the book out, but he was beginning to have cause to regret appointing him governor, for there was turmoil in St. Louis. More Americans arrived daily, creating squabbles over deeds of land, trading licenses, Indian rights, and the other usual items of contention on the frontier. A firm hand was needed.

On June 4, the president had written Lewis a chatty letter ("Your mother returned from Georgia in good health a little before I left Monticello"), signing off with "friendly salutations & assurances of constant affection & respect."[19]

But in an August 8 letter, written from Monticello, the president expressed a certain anxiety as to when Lewis was going to go to St. Louis to take up his responsibilities. He wanted Lewis to get started on "the restoration of that harmony in the territory so essential to it's happiness & so much desired by me," and indicated that he expected Lewis to be "now proceeding to take" up his post.[20]

In his June letter, the president had the painful task of informing Lewis that he had sent twenty-five boxes of artifacts brought back from the West via a ship from Washington to Richmond, but the ship had been stranded and everything was lost save some horns (probably the moose and wapiti horns now hanging at Monticello). Lewis in reply said he sincerely regretted the loss and commented, in what could be read as an implied criticism of Jefferson's lack of care of the priceless artifacts, "It seems peculiarly unfortunate that those at least, which had passed the continent of America and after their exposure to so many casualties and wrisks should have met such destiny in their passage through a small portion only of the Chesapeak."[21]

Lewis was leading a very heady life. At thirty-three, he was the most celebrated man in Philadelphia, a city world-renowned for its celebrated men. He was the protégé of the president. Balls and testimonials were held in his honor, the biggest in the nation's capital. He had been generously rewarded by Congress, praised by the leading scientists of the day, appointed governor of the biggest territory of the United States, and was the center of attention wherever he went. His prospects could hardly have been better.

It was, perhaps, too much success too early in life. There were, perhaps, too many balls with too many toasts.

Public drunkenness was so commonplace in early-nineteenth-century America that it was seldom commented upon. Certainly no one would have objected to the young hero's celebrating his triumph. Still, he was doing a lot of heavy drinking.

On April 20, he entered into his account book a payment of five dollars to his landlady, Mrs. Wood, for "a douzen of porter." On May 5, it was ten dollars for a dozen of ale.[22] More telling, he was out on the town almost every night.

His companion was Mahlon Dickerson, whom he had first met in 1802. Dickerson, a thirty-seven-year-old lawyer and bachelor who moved in the highest social circles in Philadelphia, later served as governor of New Jersey, senator from New Jersey, and secretary of the navy in President Andrew Jackson's second term. His diary records numerous evenings spent with Lewis in the spring and early summer of 1807.

They dined out regularly, and often went for walks around the Center Square (today's Penn Square), a popular park and parade ground.

On July 2, Dickerson noted in his diary, "rode out with Capt. Lewis to the marshal's. Spent the day very pleasantly in eating drinking and shooting at the trees."

On the Fourth of July, "Dined with a large party at Fouquets—delivd. a flaming speech to them—kept myself very sober—went to the play at evg.—the house very uprorious."

That same day, Lewis also attended a dinner given by the Society of the Friends of the People at the Spring Garden Tavern. To the 160 guests he proposed a political toast: "May the man who has by profession and act, proved his sincere attachment for peace, never quit our national helm at a crisis like this."

The crisis was with the British, who had attacked and seized the U.S. frigate *Chesapeake* off the Virginia Capes on June 22. Jefferson's policy was to avoid war if at all possible, while imposing an embargo on Britain.

On July 7, Lewis and Dickerson "walkd. till 11 at night." These walks were a regular thing with them; it seems likely that they frequented taverns as they moved along. On July 18, Dickerson recorded that they went out together and saw a fight in which a knife was flashed and a man's face cut, which certainly sounds like a barroom brawl.[23]

Jefferson later wrote of "the habit into which he [Lewis] had fallen & the painfull reflections that would necessarily produce in a mind like his."[24] It seems that Lewis's high-mindedness caused him to curse himself every morning, and possibly to swear off drinking, only to go back to another ball, or for another walk with Dickerson, that night.

Lewis had problems beyond coping with his celebrity status and his drinking. His friend Clark had found a wife. Lewis wanted one. That fall, he wrote Dickerson in a bantering tone, recalling some of his adventures with "*the girls*" during the summer. He said he was trying to think of "those bewitching gipsies as *a secondary consideration*," but admitted that "Miss E—— B——y of Philadelphia ... will still remain provokingly *important* in spite of all my philosophy."

Then he fired off a series of questions that had all the marks of coming from a man in love: "Have you heard from her? Have you seen her? How is she? Is she well, sick, dead or married?"

Whatever the answers, quite clearly he had failed in his courtship. He went on, "I am now *a perfect widower with rispect to love.* ... I feel all that restlessness, that inquietude, that certain indiscribable something common to old bachelors, which I cannot avoid thinking my dear fellow, proceeds, from that *void in our hearts,* which might, or ought to be better filled. Whence it comes I know not, but certain it is, that I never felt less like a heroe than at the present moment. What may be my next adventure god knows, but on this I am determined, *to get a wife.*"[25]

Meriwether Lewis was a man who usually got what he was determined to get.

36

VIRGINIA

August 1806–March 1807

Sometime in late July, Lewis journeyed to Washington, where he turned in his records and receipts to Mr. Simmons in the War Department. He then went to Locust Hill in Ivy, to be with his family. He took the journals with him. In August, he visited Jefferson at Monticello. In September, he traveled to Richmond, where he was an observer of Burr's treason trial—perhaps at Jefferson's request, with the duty of writing a report. No Lewis report is known to exist, however, and Jefferson was scrupulous in saving his correspondence.

Back in Ivy, Lewis saw to family business (primarily land speculation in the Ohio Valley). Before setting out for the Pacific in 1803, he had urged his mother to make certain his half-brother, John Marks, got an education. In 1807, he took charge of young Marks's professional training. He arranged for Marks to go to Philadelphia to attend medical lectures, with letters of introduction to the various savants in town.

He told Marks to call on Dickerson frequently, and asked Dickerson to look after him, for "we both know that young men are sometimes in want of a friend." Lewis gave Marks sixty dollars and asked Dickerson to advance him two hundred, which he would repay when he received his salary (on January 15) as governor for the last three months of the year.[1]

Some money was coming in from subscribers to the journals. A William Woods, perhaps a local Baptist minister or perhaps the Woods who was a surveyor of Albemarle County, was his agent.

Woods received the thirty-one-dollar total from a number of local residents; other monies came in by mail.[2]

Lewis had written Clark about one of his courtships. Clark had replied with a recommendation for a "Miss C." Lewis had replied in cryptic fashion: "For god's sake do not whisper my attachment to Miss ——— or I am undone."[3]

Who Miss C and "Miss ———" were, or what happened, is unknown. Lewis and Clark biographer John Bakeless speculates that perhaps they didn't meet Lewis's standards: "What mere girl could approach the grace, the charm, the intelligence, and the tremendous vigor of his fascinating mother?"[4] Perhaps the girls didn't want to get into a competition with Lucy Marks.

Sometime later, in Philadelphia, Lewis had what he described to Dickerson as a "little affair" with "Miss A——n R——sh." The relationship, he reported, "had neither beginning nor end on her part; pr. Contra, on my own, it has had both. The fact is, that on enquiry I found that she was previously engaged, and therefore dismissed every idea of prosecuting my pretentions in that quarter."[5] Then there was Lewis's intense interest in "Miss E—— B——y," which also led nowhere.

In late November, Lewis and his younger brother, Reuben (who was planning to join the governor in St. Louis and get into the fur trade), went to Fincastle, where they stayed in the home of Clark's father-in-law, George Hancock. There the brothers met Letitia and Elizabeth Breckenridge, daughters of General James Breckenridge.

Reuben wrote to the family back home, "We . . . had the pleasure of seeing the accomplished and beautiful Miss Lettissia Breckenridge one of the most beautiful women I have ever seen, both as to form and features. . . . I should like to have her as a sister."

Lewis was smitten at first sight. He expressed his intention of making a formal call on Letitia, but he evidently came on too strong. Miss Breckenridge heard "of the Governours intention of Coarting her" and concluded that "if she remained it would look too much like a challange." She accompanied her father on a trip to Richmond; Reuben reported that "unfortunately for his Excellency [Lewis] she left the neighborhood 2 days after our arrival so that he was disappointed in his design of addressing her."[6]

Letitia's sister, Elizabeth, was still in Fincastle, but Lewis had been so taken with Letitia that he was diffident about approaching her. Sometime later, he wrote to a friend from his early army career, "I consider Miss E[lizabeth] B[reckenridge] a charming girl, but such was my passion for her sister that my soul revolts at the idea of attempting to make her my wife, and I shall not consequently travel that road inquest of matrimony."

Whether he courted other young women in Ivy and Fincastle is unknown. Indeed, what he did, even where he lived, for the winter of 1807–8 is unknown.

For the most part, the eight months between Lewis's departure from Philadelphia and his arrival in St. Louis were a lost period in his life. The only thing productive he did was begin work on a major paper recommending a basic Indian policy for Louisiana, which took him over a year to finish. He courted without success. He took care of some family business. Otherwise, he apparently did nothing at all. He makes no appearance in Jefferson's extensive, often chatty correspondence. William Clark made no mention of him.

Was he drinking to excess? Was he depressed? What caused his courtships to fail? He had the journals with him, but he prepared not one line for the printer, made no arrangements for an editor.

He had promised Jefferson he would set out for St. Louis in mid-July 1807 to take up his duties (and earn his salary), but he didn't actually do so until the late winter of 1808. He didn't even ask for reports from Secretary and Acting Governor Bates on the situation in St. Louis.

Any analysis of his lethargy is speculative: some that have been offered include being unlucky in love, or suffering from a manic-depressive psychosis, alcoholism, malaria, or some other physical illness. My own guess is that some combination of these explanations, especially the first three, was among the causes, but there were others that exacerbated the depressions and the drinking, and perhaps his inability to find a wife.

He had had more success than was good for him. At age thirty-four, he missed the adulation he had become accustomed to receiving. Of course he was honored at home in Charlottesville and Ivy, but that was hardly like being celebrated in Washington and Philadelphia.

He had had too independent a command too early in life. Not that he had botched it; obviously he was a genuinely great company commander. But he had become accustomed to instant obedience from a platoon-size force of the best riflemen, woodsmen, and soldiers in the United States. He no longer held that command. He certainly couldn't get his slaves to respond to his commands as quickly or efficiently as the men of the Corps of Discovery had done. And beyond his slaves, he had no one to order about.

In modern popular psychology, he might be said to have been suffering from postpartum depression. Malaria, alcohol, and a predisposition to melancholy would have made it more severe.

His unluckiness in love may have compounded everything. We have no clue why he was spurned. He had a lot to offer: he was young, extremely good-looking, highly cultured for Fincastle, with a prestigious and powerful position in the government and outstanding prospects. Perhaps it was a vicious circle: he was turned down because he drank too much and made a spectacle of himself. That might have been what shocked Miss Breckenridge and caused her to flee. A simpler explanation might be nearer the mark: perhaps Miss Breckenridge and the others could not abide the thought of going to live in a frontier town, albeit the capital of the territory.

Lewis wanted a wife to fill a void in his heart. He never got one. Also during this period, he was without a close companion. For three years, he and Clark had been intimate friends. In Washington in early 1807, he had lived with Jefferson; in Philadelphia, there was Dickerson. In Virginia, his only close companion seems to have been his younger brother, Reuben.

When Lewis finally arrived in St. Louis, he was extremely active on a number of fronts. And we can assume that his courtships were lively affairs, with lots of balls and dinners and visiting, laughter and music. His policy paper was complex and demanding; the work he did on it was outstanding in many respects.

Lewis worked on the paper from August 1807 until August 1808, when he sent the finished version from St. Louis to Secretary Dearborn. It contained about 10,500 words. He called it "Observations and reflections on the present and future state of Upper Louisiana, in relation to the government of the Indian nations inhabiting that country, and the trade and intercourse with the same."

The plan happily combined two impulses, one to improve the Indians, the other to improve the American fur trade. Or, as Lewis put it, it was "a scheme . . . the most expedient that I can devise for the successful consummation of [our] philanthropic views towards those wretched people of America," and to build an American fur-trade empire.

He began with a history of the fur trade based in St. Louis during the Spanish period. He condemned the Spanish system of ceding exclusive trading rights to individuals who lived with the various tribes on the Missouri and the other western tributaries of the Mississippi. The traders holding monopoly licenses from the Spanish government badly overcharged the Indians, an evil that was exacerbated by the "ruinous custom" of extending credit to the tribes.

So much for the Spanish system. Meanwhile, the British had gotten into the game. The Spanish controlled the mouth of the Missouri, but the various British companies doing business out of Montreal controlled the upper parts of the river. They undersold the Spanish, thus making the Indians their fast friends and allies.

That got Lewis to the heart of the matter. He pointed out that the British traders were now operating in American territory, for the United States "at present, through mere courtesy, permit them to extend their trade to the west side of the Mississippi; or rather they are mere tenants at will."

This he thought mistaken policy. The British had unfair advantages over potential American traders, because through mergers and other devices the North West Company had become a giant, with a "surplus of capital and a surplus of men," which meant the British had it "in their power . . . to break any company of merchants of the United States who might enter into a competition with them" by underselling the competition. The North West Company was already fixing a site for a fortification at the Mandan villages.

Following the seizure of the *Chesapeake* and other British outrages on the high seas and within American waters, war between the United States and Great Britain was everywhere expected. If it came, what was there to prevent an expedition from Canada into the upper-Missouri country, using Indian allies? And what if it were accompanied by a simultaneous expedition to take New Orleans? What was at stake here was the whole of the Louisiana Purchase, the great western empire of the United States.

Under the circumstances, Lewis asked, "Can we begin the work of exclusion too soon?" He wanted the authority and resources to mount a campaign to drive the British out of Louisiana.

Since he intended to be a part of the fur trade, here was a case where there was a happy coincidence between his self-interest and solid public policy. The government would provide the resources to take effective control of Upper Louisiana, the Indians would be made dependent on the United States, Lewis would be in fact as well as name the governor of the territory, and the fur trade would prosper, to the great profit of the St. Louis merchants.

Having shown the evils of the Spanish and British systems, Lewis submitted "for the consideration of our government the outlines of a plan which has been dictated as well by a sentiment of philanthropy towards the aborigines of America [Jefferson would like that], as a just regard to the protection of the lives and property of our citizens [and that]; and with the further view also of securing to the people of the United States, exclusively, the advantages which ought of right to accrue to them from the possession of Louisiana [that most of all]."

Lewis wanted authorization to kick the North West Company out of Louisiana; he further wanted to abolish the "pernicious" custom of giving exclusive licenses to traders and allowing them to extend credit to the tribes. He wanted free trade, in other words, for the Americans, or, as he put it "a fair competition among all our merchants."

His plan to realize these objectives was to establish fortifications at various convenient spots along the rivers, especially the Missouri, built and defended by U.S. soldiers, and make these into trading posts where both the Indians and the traders could gather to do business. No more licenses to individuals to monopolize the trade with a single tribe, but a common mart where the marketplace would rule.

Frontier fortifications and trading posts would bring another great benefit. "The first principle of governing the Indians," Lewis wrote, "is to govern the whites," which was impossible to do without such establishments. By "governing the whites" he meant keeping out settlers.

For the immediate future—say the next ten or twenty years—Lewis envisioned a relationship with the Indians exclusively based on the fur trade, which meant leaving them in exclusive possession of their lands. In other words, Governor Lewis had come down on the side of the merchants, as opposed to the potential settlers. If American frontiersmen began to hunt and clear lands along the Missouri, Osage, Des Moines, and other rivers, settlers would follow and there would be no fur trade, only Indian wars along the frontier.

Lewis had seen more of the tribes west of the Mississippi than any other American, even including Clark, who never met the Blackfeet. Better than most others, he could see things from their point of view. Thus in this case he wrote: "With what constitence of precept and practice can we say to the Indians, whom we wish to civilize, that agriculture and the arts are more productive of ease, wealth, and comfort than the occupation of hunting, while they see distributed over their forests a number of white men engaged in the very occupation which our doctrine would teach them to abandon."

In other words, he wanted the hunters as well as the British banned from Upper Louisiana.

But not quite all of Upper Louisiana. Lewis went on to explain that his system of army-built and -defended trading posts applied only as far up the Missouri as the Mandans. West of those villages, either the government would have to become the merchant, "or present no obstacles to their citizens" who might wish to form companies and prepare expeditions. These citizens could establish trading establishments, at their own cost and risk. They would have to be supported by hunters.

Lewis was proposing to adopt the British system for Louisiana west of the Mandans, only with a St. Louis firm running the show instead of the North West Company. He was going to be, perhaps already was, a member of that St. Louis firm. Nevertheless, he described his motive in establishing an American presence in the farthest reaches of the Purchase as altruistic, writing that he assumed "our government [wishes] that the Indians on the extreme branches of the Missouri to the west, and within the Rocky mountains, should obtain supplies of merchandise equally with those more immediately in their vicinity."

Then the clinching argument for this two-version Indian policy as it applied to the western reaches: if we didn't do it, the North West Company would. It was good national policy to "contravene the machinations preparing by the Northwest company for practice in that quarter."

A major obstacle to any trade on the Missouri was the Sioux tribes. Lewis had a plan to deal with them, based on his view of the Indian character. "The *love of gain* is the Indians' ruling passion," he wrote—underscoring it, as if this were some new insight and applied only to Indians, not all human beings. "The fear of punishment must form the corrective." No "punishment could assume a more terrific shape to them [the Sioux] than that of *withholding every description of merchandise from them.*"

He therefore proposed an embargo on the Sioux. The United States should build trading posts on the river, but forbid the Sioux the right to trade at them. That would have the advantage of enforcing "a compliance with our will without the necessity of bloodshed." Soon the Sioux would crumble. "I am confident," Lewis wrote, that in order to trade "they would sacrifice any individual who may be the object of our displeasure, even should he be their favourite chief, for their thirst for merchandise is paramount to every other consideration."[7]

So there was his plan: drive the British out of Upper Louisiana and use the U.S. Army to promote and protect the fur traders of St. Louis while holding back the squatters. It clearly favored the established elite in St. Louis over the onrushing Americans looking for land. Just as clearly, it was going to require expenditures by the government far in excess of anything yet contemplated in Washington.

In late winter of 1807–8, Lewis set out for St. Louis to see if he could put it into execution.

37

ST. LOUIS
March–December 1808

St. Louis was isolated but vibrant. Washington Irving described the city, as he saw it shortly after Lewis's arrival: "Here to be seen [were] the hectoring, extravagant, bragging boatmen of the Mississippi, with the gay, grimacing, singing, good-humored Canadian *voyageurs*. Vagrant Indians of various tribes, loitered about the streets. Now and then a stark Kentucky hunter, in leather hunting-dress, with rifle on shoulder and knife in belt, trode along. Here and there were new rich houses and ships, just set up by bustling, driving and eager men of traffic from the Atlantic States; while, on the other hand, the old French mansions, with open casements, still retained the easy, indolent air of the original colonists."[1]

The Spanish presence was there too, as were black slaves. This was a mixing of three nationalities from the two Old World continents with the citizens of the nations from the New World. It made for a cosmopolitan city, of about five thousand residents, the most cosmopolitan of any in America west of the Eastern Seaboard port cities.

Irving found it charming, but his eyes didn't see what would be the first thing to strike a modern visitor—horse manure everywhere one walked. Because he was so accustomed to them, Irving also failed to note the muddy (or dusty) streets and the smoke-filled rooms.

The American Irving was struck by the extreme distance between the elite and the common citizenry. The Spanish and French merchants lived lives that could only be called princely. They had huge tracts of land and had enjoyed trading monopolies, lived in elegant homes with superb libraries, excellent wines, extravagantly fashionable clothes, the latest wallpaper from New York, New Orleans, or Europe, the finest in furniture and such comforts as man-made lakes, cool cellars, and a fireplace in almost every room. One observer swore "there was a fiddle in every house."

What Irving called "the happy Gallic turn for gayety and amusement" was most in evidence during the carnival season that preceded Mardi Gras. There was an abundance of cotillions, reels, minuets, with balls every night. The ladies wore silk gloves and stockings, bracelets and earrings. One astonished American declared, "I never saw anywhere greater elegance of dress than I have at a ball in St. Louis." Secretary Bates admired the "inimitable grace" with which the ladies danced, but, being an American and a sour one at that, he added that their dancing was "too much in the style of actresses."[2] Shocking to American eyes were the "kings" and "queens" who presided over the balls and public ceremonies of the carnival season.

The great majority of the population, meanwhile, were illiterate, owned little or nothing, and lived in shacks. The men were mainly boatmen. They were the essential industry of St. Louis. It was their muscle power that made it possible for the merchants to move goods up the Missouri River, to the source of the furs. They were always in debt to their bosses, who treated them almost as badly as Virginia planters treated their black slaves.

Their loyalty was to one another. In 1807, while on an expedition organized by private traders, George Drouillard received orders from his employer, Manuel Lisa, to find the deserter Antoine Bissonnette and bring him back dead or alive. Drouillard brought him back dead. When the party returned to St. Louis, Drouillard was put on trial for murder. The jury found that Bissonnette's desertion was a threat to the entire party and discharged Drouillard.[3]

Now the Americans were coming into this Old World society, bringing with them a new energy. Secretary Bates noted the contrast between the two styles: "While the English Americans are hard at labor and sweat under the burning rays of a meridian sun, [the French and Spanish elite] will be seated in their homes or under some cooling shade, amusing themselves with their pipes and tobacco, drinking coffee." He further noted that "the Old Inhabitants" were "rigid economists."[4]

The American threat to this way of life was very great. The Americans were questioning the validity of land titles acquired under the informal land cessions of the Spanish and French regimes, and of the monopolies granted for the lead mines and the Indian trade. There were not enough courts or judges to make decisions, and not enough soldiers to enforce them. The Americans brought with them a spirit of partisanship that added immeasurably to the difficulties of governing. Worse, some of them at least were Burrites, plotting to break Louisiana away from the United States.

Secretary and Acting Governor Bates was ill-suited to handle the responsibilities of governing, and he knew it. From the time of his arrival in the spring of 1807, he wrote Lewis about the quarreling that marked public affairs and urged him to hurry to St. Louis to set things in order. "I take a pleasure in expressing the opinion," he wrote on April 5, 1807, "that you have a fair opportunity of establishing a lasting reputation in Louisiana, by composing the unhappy divisions of her Inhabitants."[5]

Lewis's predecessor, General Wilkinson, had granted trading licenses with abandon (to his own profit), to foreigners as well as U.S. citizens. There was intense fighting over land titles. Bates was trying to straighten things out, but felt overwhelmed. He told his brother, "The difficulties with which I have to contend in this country are numberless and almost insurmountable."

"I have great cause to lament your absence," Bates wrote Lewis. But he also warned the governor, "contrary to my first expectation you must expect to have some enemies." He further warned, "We have among us a set of men turbulent and ungovernable in their dispositions, which I believe may be accounted for, from that spirit of enterprize and adventure which brought them first into the country."[6]

Through to the end of 1807, Bates's anxiety for Lewis to arrive grew. By 1808, he was almost in a frenzy. In January, he wrote Lewis, "No one feels the want of your superintending presence so much as I do." In early February, he wrote again to say he was "eagerly expecting your arrival every day." Later that month, he was hoping to see Lewis "every hour." By the 26th, it was "every moment."[7]

Bates was an experienced bureaucrat. In 1801, he had hoped for the appointment Meriwether Lewis had received, to be Jefferson's private secretary.[8] He had been postmaster and later receiver of public monies and land commissioner in Detroit. He had held these positions as a Federalist, but in 1804, wanting higher office, he switched parties and had his brother use his influence with a Republican member of Congress to help him obtain an appointment as associate judge of Michigan Territory.

"As for my Politics," he said in support of his candidacy and in direct opposition to the facts, "you all know that I am staunch." He got the job, and was a good-enough Republican to receive, in 1807, the appointment to be the secretary of Louisiana Territory.[9]

If even so adroit and experienced a bureaucrat as Bates found governing Louisiana nearly impossible, obviously the inexperienced Governor Lewis was entering dangerous territory. Nevertheless, as he finally broke away from Virginia and headed west, Lewis was bursting with optimism, plans, and energy. The lethargy that had plagued him since the preceding July was gone. He was eager to start his new life.

Lewis arrived in St. Louis on March 8, 1808. He was in independent command—if not as independent as on the expedition, still generally on his own. The government could not get detailed instructions to or set policy for a governor who was a week's travel from the nearest post office, in Vincennes, Indiana. It was another week to the next post office, in Louisville. Under the most favorable of circumstances and in the best weather, mail to or from Washington took nearly a month; in wintertime, in the severest weather, there was no communication at all with the outside world. It took three months to ascend the Mississippi from New Orleans. So Lewis was more or less on his own, with no practical experience in politics or government, in a capital teeming with plots and ambitious and unscrupulous men, with no set of written laws in the English language, and insufficient judges and courts. This was a challenge of a new kind.

He immediately threw himself into his activities, private as well as public. He began speculating in land and in the fur trade. Simultaneously, he searched for suitable lodgings. He was appalled at the rents being charged. He wrote Clark, who was on his honeymoon in Virginia, that one place he looked at cost five hundred dollars per year. "Such rent I never had calculated on giveing." He settled on one for $250 per year.

The home he selected, on the corner of South Main and Spruce Streets, was quite grand—as it had to be, since Lewis and Clark had agreed that they would share quarters and Clark was expected shortly, accompanied by his wife and two nieces. In a letter of May 29, 1808, Lewis described the house to Clark with the enthusiasm of a real estate agent.

There was a good cellar, four rooms on the first floor, rooms upstairs for slaves, a piazza running across the east and south fronts, a detached kitchen with two fireplaces and an oven, and a garden, a stable, and a new smokehouse. Unfortunately, there was only one facility, and that "a small indifferent out house formerly used for smoking meat."

Lewis planned to live with his friend, but was realistic: "Should we find on experiment that we have not sufficient room in the house, I can obtain an Office elsewhere in the neighborhood and still consider myself your messmate." Not surprisingly, after a few months of "experiment," the two men agreed, most likely at the insistence of Julia Clark, that the house wasn't big enough.

Lewis got an office on Main Street and quarters with Pierre Chouteau, but ate with the Clarks.[10] He had no wife, but he acquired what amounted to an adopted son. He brought René Jessaume's thirteen-year-old boy, Toussaint, under an indenture to St. Louis to raise and educate him.[11] (Eventually, Sacagawea's son, Jean Baptiste, and daughter, Lizette, became boarders in Clark's home and were tutored there.)

Ensign Pryor carried Lewis's May 29 letter to Clark, with instructions to hand it over at the mouth of the Ohio, where Clark and party were expected in late June or early July. Pryor would provide a military escort up the Mississippi.

Clark was traveling with two keelboats, bringing his household furniture and heavy equipment for the Indians, including a horse-power mill and blacksmith's tools. And, of course, his wife and his nieces. He had written Lewis that he would be arriving with "goods" and "merchandize."

In his letter to Clark, Lewis showed what a good humor he was in, writing in a jocular vein, "I must halt here in the middle of my communications and ask you if the matrimonial dictionary affords no term more appropriate than that of *goods*, alise *merchandize*, for that dear and interesting part of the creation? It is very well Genl., I shall tell madam of your want of Gallantry; and the triumph too of detection will be more compleat when it is recollected what a musty, fusty, rusty old bachelor I am."

Lewis went on: "I trust you do not mean merely to tantalize us by the promise you have made of bringing with you some of your Neices, I have already flattered the community of S Louis with this valuable acquisition to our female society."[12]

It turned out that Clark had brought only one niece, "the beautiful and accomplished Miss Anderson," his sister's daughter. She caused a flutter in town A friend wrote to Secretary Bates, "Great agitation in St. Louis among the bachelors, to prevent fatal consequences a Town meeting has been proposed for the purpose of disposing of her by lot."[13]

As had been the case on the expedition, Lewis went through periods of doing little or no writing, followed by periods of extensive composition.* In the summer of 1808, he did a lot of writing—personal, chatty letters sparkling with good humor, as well as his official documents. In a long letter of July 25 to his old army friend (and fellow speculator in Kentucky lands) Major William Preston, Lewis gave a glimpse of his life and emotions.

"How wretchedly you married men arrange the subjects of which you treat," Lewis complained in his opening (Preston had recently married Julia Hancock's older sister). Lewis said that, just because "You have gained that which I have yet to obtain, *a wife*," Preston was not excused from starting off with an entire page about land speculation and "your musty frusty trade," and "a flimsy excuse about the want of money to enable you to come and see us &c &c before you came to the point."

The point was that "*she is off.*" "She" was Letitia Breckenridge, who on June 2 had married Robert Gamble of Richmond. "So be it," a disappointed but resigned Lewis wrote. "May God be with her and her's, and the favored angels of heaven guard her bliss both here and hereafter, is the sincere prayer of her very sincere friend, to whom she has left the noble consolation of scratching his head and biting his nails, with ample leasure to reuminate on the chapter of accidents in matters of love and the folly of castle-building."

Lewis was generous about the man who had won his fair lady: "Gamble is a good tempered, easy honest fellow, I have known him from a boy; both his means and his disposition well fit him for sluming away life with his fair one in the fassionable rounds of a large City." He was also charitable about Letitia: "Such is the life she has celected and in it's pursuit I wish she may meet all the pleasures of which it is susceptable."

Lewis wanted his friend to come to St. Louis to participate in the boom. "In my opinion," he wrote, "Louisiana, and particularly the district of St. Louis, at this moment offers more advantages than any other portion of the U'States ... to the honest adventurer who can command money or negroes." He described the economy, based on corn (shipped to New Orleans in the form of barrels of whiskey), wheat,

---

* This went back some time. In 1801, Lewis's friend Tarleton Bates had complained to his brother Frederick that "Meriwether Lewis is silent though he promised to write weekly," and in 1807, Amos Stoddard complained that although he had written Lewis "several friendly epistles" he had not received any reply. (Jackson, *Letters*, vol. II, p. 445)

lead, and furs. "Were I to dwell on the advantages of this country I might fill a volume."

There would never be a better time to take the plunge: "I will wrisk my existence that you will at some future period regret having chosen any other," Lewis wrote. "You have no time to lose. Lands are rising fast, but are yet very low." Prices had doubled in a year. If Preston would sell his place in Kentucky, even if he got only half value for it, "and bring your money or negroes with you to this country you might purchase a princely fortune."

Lewis backed his boosting with his own money. "I have purchased seven thousand four hundred and 40 Arpents* for five thousand five hundred and thirty dollars," all of it in the St. Louis neighborhood and blessed with springs and sites for mills, and excellent soil and ample rain.

As for the Indians, Lewis admitted that they had been "exceedingly troublesome during the last winter and spring," but insisted that "I have succeeded in managing those on the Mississippi." He added, however, that "the Osage and others on the Missouri are yet in a threatening position." Still, he was confident that the steps he was about to take would soon "reduce them to order."[14]

Lewis had indeed been extremely active on the Indian front, although to what extent the policies he had put into motion would bring the various nations to order remained to be seen. He had sent a veteran Indian agent, Nicholas Boilvin, accompanied by a military escort of twenty-seven men, to bring in two Indians of the Sauks and Foxes accused of murder.[15] And he had initiated drastic measures against one band of the Osage tribe, called the Great Osages.

He explained his actions in a July 1 letter to Secretary Dearborn, his first report as territorial governor to the administration. The Great Osages had "cast off all allegiance to the United States," he wrote, and no longer acknowledged the authority of their former leader, White Hair. According to White Hair and other information Lewis had received, the Great Osage had taken some prisoners, stolen some horses, killed some cattle. They had plundered frontier inhabitants of their clothes and furniture and burned their homes.

If the Great Osages wanted war, Lewis was ready. He held several councils with the Shawnees, Delawares, Kickapoos, Iowas, and others, telling them "that they were at liberty to wage war against" the Great

---

* A French unit of land measure; an arpent was the equivalent of about .85 acre.

Osages. He began preparations in St. Louis, because "War appears to me inevitable with these people; I have taken the last measures for peace, which have been merely laughed at by them as the repetition of an old song."

The problem was that the Great Osages felt themselves independent of the government, because they had a Spanish trader among them. Lewis had therefore suspended *all* trading licenses (which caused an uproar among the traders in St. Louis) "until a sufficient force" could be sent to establish permanent trading posts. He provided General Clark with an escort of eighty men to go up the Missouri to establish a fortification and trading post on the Osage River. This amounted to an expedition against the Great Osages.

Lewis needed more men, and asked for an authorization to pay recruits for the militia. He needed supplies, and asked Dearborn to send him 500 muskets, 300 rifles, 120 swords, 60 pairs of pistols, and a ton of gunpowder. That should take care of the Spanish-influenced southern flank.

The danger on the northern front, on the Missouri beyond the Mandans, came from the British. Lewis gave orders that they should be kept out of U.S. territory, but of course he had no power to enforce them. Indeed, he wasn't sure the War Department would approve.[16]

Dearborn had about lost all his patience with the young hero. From his point of view, Lewis was doing everything wrong. The United States was on the verge of war with Britain; the War Department was woefully unprepared; here was Lewis opening up another front, demanding weapons and men, marching regular troops off to deal with some minor Indian problems that sounded like a squabble between the Little Osages and the Great Osages, fed by wild stories from White Hair and some traders.

Lewis had said not one word about returning Big White to his people, even though the commander-in-chief had ordered him to make this his top priority. And he had taken unauthorized actions without properly reporting—the first Dearborn had heard about Boilvin's expedition to bring back the murderers (in itself a very questionable piece of Indian policy) had come from an army officer reporting the requisition for men and supplies.

In a July 2 letter that crossed Lewis's letter to him, Dearborn set a policy: "Except in cases of the most pressing emergency detachments of the troops should not be made" until approved by the president. The secretary closed with a complaint: "No communication except some Drafts for Money, has, for many Months, been received from the Executive of Louisiana."[17] That was a stinging rebuke, and no doubt surprising to Lewis when he received it, so long had he been accustomed to making decisions without having to seek any approval beyond talking it over with Clark.

A worse rebuke quickly followed. On July 17, Jefferson wrote to Lewis. He opened with a complaint: "Since I parted with you in Albemarle in Sept. last I have never had a line from you." He said he would have written earlier but for his conviction "that something from you must be on it's way to us."

Those were stern words for Jefferson, and he immediately softened them. He realized that the slowness of the mails might have been the cause; he said it was not until February that he had learned that the Arikaras had attacked Ensign Pryor's expedition to return Big White to his people, and turned it back, with casualties (including the loss of George Shannon's leg). This was a severe blow to the president, who had given his word that Big White would be returned home safely and soon.

As to his relations with Lewis, Jefferson had decided to "put an end to this mutual silence" and write himself, to ask for a report from Lewis on what he intended to do to return Big White: "We consider the good faith, & the reputation of the nation as pledged to accomplish this." He hastened to add he did not want "any considerable military expedition" sent up the river "in the present uncertain state of our foreign concerns." But he did authorize Lewis to get the job done "if it can be effected in any other way & at any reasonable expence."

That statement from the president amounted to almost a blank check for Lewis, nearly as good as the letter of credit he had carried with him on the expedition—or so at least Governor Lewis chose to read it.

Jefferson passed on some welcome news: "A powerful company is forming for taking up the Indian commerce on a large scale." It was headed by John Jacob Astor and would have a capital of one million dollars. Jefferson described Astor as "a most excellent man long engaged in the [fur] business & perfectly master of it."

As to the bad news, relations with Britain were worse than ever, and the Congress was debating "whether war will not be preferable to a longer continuance of the embargo." In politics, it looked as if the Republican nominee, Secretary of State James Madison, would easily defeat the Federalist Charles Pinckney, "but with this question it is my duty not to intermeddle." Lewis's friends and family in Albemarle were fine.

Jefferson's closing line cut to the heart: "We have no tidings yet of the forwardness of your printer. I hope the first part will not be delayed much longer."[18]

The journals were in St. Louis, and Lewis had not prepared a single line for the printer, who was in Philadelphia. Jefferson here offered him an opportunity to straighten out his misconception, but Lewis did not take it. He never answered the letter.

Nor did he reply to others. In August, Jefferson told Dearborn, "It is astonishing we get not one word from him."[19]

The cause almost surely was Lewis's chagrin at failing to prepare his manuscript for the printer. He knew how much it meant to Jefferson. He further knew how much it meant to his own financial future and to his reputation. Yet he did nothing.

Clark must have talked to him about publication. Still he did nothing. True, he was terribly busy, but he had an option—a man who could put more than five thousand dollars into land speculation could afford a five-hundred-dollar-per-year editor. Not that an editor could have done the job quickly or accurately, at least without Lewis's active help, but hiring one would have meant some progress was being made. In addition, Lewis might have told Jefferson that it was impossible for the governor of Louisiana to find time to do the work himself. Had Lewis pointed this out and confessed to Jefferson that nothing had been done, the president could have helped, perhaps by getting the journals to Washington and putting some War Department clerks to work on them.

Jefferson must bear some of the responsibility. He could have pushed Lewis much harder. Dumas Malone comments that in this case "Jefferson, who was so tolerant of persons he trusted, may have erred on the side of patience."[20]

Lewis found numerous opportunities to get out of the office, sometimes on horseback trips for land speculation, on other occasions to visit old army friends at Bellefontaine. He visited George Shannon in the hospital. He joined other Masons in St. Louis in establishing a Masonic Lodge in St. Louis, and agreed to serve as the first Master.[21] He helped establish the first newspaper west of the Mississippi by participating in the financing of Joseph Charless's Missouri *Gazette*, which printed its initial issue on July 22, 1808. The governor used it as an outlet for his pronouncements. On August 2, the paper printed the first half of Lewis's long policy statement to Dearborn; he used the nom de plume "Clatsop."

He also wrote occasional pieces for the newspaper. On November 16, 1808, he contributed an essay on "The True Ambitions of an Honest Mind." It read, in full:

"Were I to describe the blessings I desire in life, I would be happy in a few but faithful friends. Might I choose my talent, it should rather be good than learning. I would consult in the choice of my house, convenience rather than state; and, for my circumstances, desire a moderate but independent fortune. Business enough to secure me from indolence, and leisure enough always to have an hour to spare. I would have no master, and I desire few servants. I would not be led away by ambition, nor perplexed with disputes. I would enjoy the blessings of health but rather be beholden for it to a regular life and an easy mind, than to the school of Hippocrates. As to my passions, since we cannot be wholly divested of them, I would hate only those whose manners rendered them odious, and love only where I knew I ought. Thus would I pass cheerfully through that portion of my life which cannot last always, & with resignation wait for that which will last forever."[22]

These are ideals that Polonius would have approved, put in the stilted language the earnest young governor often used when he tried to express feeling. Some of the blessings he described, he enjoyed; others, not. He had a few faithful friends, most of all Jefferson and Clark. He lived in fairly simple accommodations. He was short of an independent fortune, but in sight of one. He often complained about his lack of leisure. He had but one servant, a free black man named John Pernier. His ambition was always in danger of leading him away, and he was cursed with disputes aplenty. His health was dependent on the medicines for malaria he regularly took. As to hatred, he perhaps had Bates in mind when he expressed the hope that he would hate only those who were odious.

"My life is still one continued press of business which scarcely allows me leasire to write to you," Lewis told his mother in a letter of December 1, 1808. Of course he was not quite that busy, but that is the way a young man opens a letter to his mother when he suddenly realizes he has not seen her or written to her in over a year. Lewis's first concern was for her health, but he expressed it with a complaint: "I sincerely hope you are all well tho' it seems I shall not know whether you are dead or alive untill I visit you again." With what can only be called a piece of gall from someone who had not written a letter to his family in a year, he went on: "What is John Marks and Edmund Anderson about that they do not write to me?" He wanted to know whether John Marks was studying in Philadelphia, whether Mary was married, and if so if she had moved to Georgia. "I know your feelings on this subject," he continued. "I hope you will bear the seperation with your usual fortitude."

Then he expressed a fantasy of his, one that he had not put into his Missouri *Gazette* article but nevertheless a blessing of great importance to him, to bring his family together in St. Louis. He already had Reuben with him. Now he told his mother that it was his hope "that I shall have it in my power in the course of a few years to bring you together again." He explained that he would be offering John Marks "such inducements as will determine him to remove to Louisiana," and that he had selected a thousand-acre farm for his mother, "with which I am convinced you will be pleased," and was purchasing other land so that Mary and her husband could join them. He said he had paid out three thousand dollars for the land, with fifteen hundred more due in May 1809 and twelve hundred on May 1, 1810. To get the money, he was putting his inheritance—the farm on Ivy Creek—up for sale.

He closed with a promise to come to Virginia for a visit during the course of the winter.[23]

Through the second half of 1808, Lewis was involved in organizing the St. Louis Missouri River Fur Company. Among the partners were William Clark, Manuel Lisa, Pierre Chouteau, Auguste Chouteau, General Wilkinson's brother Benjamin, and Reuben Lewis. Meriwether Lewis was assumed to be a secret partner. Not many details are known, but the general idea was to send a privately raised, publicly financed, very large expedition up the Missouri in 1809 to return Big White to his people. After the expedition got to the Mandan villages, the fur traders could go on to the mouth of the Yellowstone, where the company would enjoy a monopoly granted by Governor Lewis.

The scheme smacked of nepotism and reeked of conflict of interest, but to Lewis and the partners it made perfect sense. The government could not raise the force necessary to overpower the Arikaris and the Sioux; the partners had insufficient capital to finance the military part of such an expedition; the commander-in-chief had authorized Lewis to use whatever means seemed best to him, at whatever "reasonable" cost, to return Big White. The work of forming the company went forward.

In late July, Boilvin returned with four Indians. They were Iowas, and according to the Sauks and the Foxes they were the men who had committed the murder. Lewis said publicly that three of them would be hanged—after trial.

The trial was held on July 23. "The streets of St. Louis teemed with Indian warriors," an observer reported. They incessantly harassed Governor Lewis and General Clark, beseeching pardon. The Iowa warriors were found guilty, but something must have bothered Lewis about the trial, for he ordered a new one, which was held on August 3. The Indians were again found guilty, but instead of hanging them, Lewis had them put in jail, evidently to await instructions.[24]

Not until mid-August did Lewis receive Dearborn's letter of rebuke dated July 2; nor until then did Dearborn receive Lewis's report of July 1—which was then passed on to Jefferson at Monticello, since Dearborn was in Maine. The maddening slowness of the mails made a difficult situation worse.

On August 20, Lewis replied to Dearborn. He got immediately to the point: "I shall in future ... be as cautious with rispect to my requisitions on the regular troops as you can possibly wish me."

Of course there was an immediate "but": "When you take into view Sir, my great distance from the seat of the general government, surrounded as I am with numerous faithless and savage nations [it is obvious] that many cases will arrise which require my acting before it is possible I can consult." That got him into a convoluted sentence of explanation: "I have ever thought it better not to act at all than to act erroniously, and I shall certainly not lay myself liable hereafter to the censure of the executive under this head, tho' I shall ever feel a pleasure in exercising to the best of my judgment and abilities such discretionary powers as they may think proper to confide to me."

He went on at great length to defend what he had done. After nearly a thousand words on the subject, he concluded: "This has been an extreemly perplexing toilsome & disagreeable business to me throughout and I must candidly confess that it is not rendered less so at this moment in reflection than it was in practice from the seeming disapprobation which you appear to have to the measures pursued."[25]

Jefferson, meanwhile, replied on August 21 to Lewis's July 1 report to Dearborn. Although he had privately expressed fear that Lewis had been too prompt "in committing us with the Osages," he told Lewis only that he regretted "that it has been necessary to come to open rupture with the Osages, but, being so, I approve of the course you have pursued in permitting the other nations to take their own satisfaction for the wrongs they complain of." Indeed, the commander-in-chief was willing to go further and supply the guns and ammunition the Indians attacking the Osages would need, a strange action for a man who wanted peace among all the inhabitants of Louisiana.

But Jefferson did not approve at all of sending the Boilvin expedition to snatch the accused murderers from the Sauks and the Foxes, and hoped that nothing had happened yet. If Boilvin had brought in some accused Indians, Jefferson told Lewis to "give time," for "Indulgence on both sides is just & necessary" in such cases.

Like every nineteenth-century president, Jefferson could not set and hold to a consistent Indian policy. This reflected the pressures he was under. On the one side, there were questions of morality and law and order, and certainly the white frontiersmen committed many an outrage on the Indians before crying for help when retribution came. On the other side, the Indians could not be controlled with good intentions, and American citizens had to be protected. Jefferson hoped it could be done without bloodshed, but controlled they must be. Jefferson told Lewis, "Commerce is the great engine by which we are to coerce them, & not war." The operative verb in the sentence was "coerce."

Thus, in the Boilvin matter, Jefferson approved of Lewis's requisition for arms and militia expenses, but in passing this along to Dearborn he expressed the hope that Lewis would be able to settle with the Sauks and the Foxes without war, "to which he seems too much committed."[26]

From the territorial governor's point of view, that was a lovely sentiment, but too mushy for practical affairs. As Lewis had put it in his report to Dearborn, "I sincerely hope that the general government in their philanthropic feelings towards the indians will not loose sight of the safety of our defenceless and extended frontiers."[27]

Three days later, Jefferson again wrote Lewis. He had just heard of Lewis's statement in early July that three Iowas were to be hanged for murder. He hoped it would not be done, "as we know we cannot punish any murder which shall be committed by us on them even if the murderer can be taken. Our juries have never yet convicted the murderer of an Indian." If a hanging was necessary, he instructed Lewis to limit it to one man, the "most guilty & worst character," because only one white man had been killed. (Lewis kept the Indians in jail, from which they escaped in the summer of 1809.)

Jefferson next turned to a much more important matter, one on which Lewis had been inexcusably lax, as far as Jefferson knew. "I am uneasy," the president wrote, "hearing nothing from you about the Mandan chief, nor the measures for restoring him to his country."

Once more, Jefferson authorized in advance any measures Lewis might consider necessary, saying that the return of Big White "is an object which presses on our justice & our honour. And farther than that

I suppose a severe punishment of the Ricaras indispensable, taking for it our own time & convenience." The president signed off, "I repeat my salutations of affection & respect."[28]

Lewis spent much of his time on the routine business of government. His duties put him in contact with men who had been or would be famous, most notably Daniel Boone and Moses Austin. He appointed Boone justice of the district of Femme Osage. He had various dealings with Austin, who held lands west of St. Louis that were rich in lead. Austin expressed his "confidence" in Lewis but warned him that the bickering parties in the territory would attempt to drive a wedge between the governor and Secretary Bates; Austin later commented that a breach between the two "has already taken place and Governor Lewis has expressed his dissatisfaction of the Secretary's conduct."[29]

Indeed, Lewis had dismissed a number of officeholders, some of them Burr-ites who had been appointed by Wilkinson, others friends of Bates.[30] In the process, he made enemies. The governor created what amounted to an Indian territory, access to which by whites would be controlled by him. His purpose was to prevent claim-jumpers and squatters from taking up lands; there was much grumbling about this. When he issued orders suspending all trading with the Great Osages, he made more enemies.

When Clark established Fort Osage near the river by that name, he negotiated a treaty establishing a boundary line. When the Great Osages learned that the treaty forbade them to cross to the east of the line, they complained that they had never understood the treaty and anyway only the Little Osages had agreed to it. Lewis then commissioned Pierre Chouteau to go to Fort Osage and negotiate a new treaty.

Lewis's instructions to Chouteau were solidly in the tradition of treaty-making with the Indians. A line should be drawn that "assures to them, for their exclusive use, the lands west of the boundary line." That was a backward way of saying the Osages would be selling the land east of the line. Any Osages who refused to make their mark on the treaty "can have no future hopes . . . for it is our unalterable determination, that if they are to be considered our friends and allies, they must *sign* that instrument, and *conform* to its *stipulations*." Those who obeyed would have trade goods aplenty, plus a blacksmith shop and the horse-power mill Clark had brought to St. Louis. Those who resisted would be cut off completely from all trade goods.[31]

The Osages did as they were told, adopting the treaty on November 10, 1808. It was ratified by the U.S. Senate, unanimously, on April 28, 1810.

The governor enacted a law to permit villages to incorporate as towns, and laid out a road from St. Louis to Ste. Genevieve, Cape Girardeau, and New Madrid. He oversaw the construction of a shot tower and arranged for the exploration of nearby saltpeter caves.[32]

Lewis's relations with Clark were excellent, as always. He borrowed money from Clark regularly. On one occasion he recorded in his account book, "Borrowed of Genl. Clrk this sum [$1] at a card party in my room." On another occasion he borrowed $6, which he then loaned to his brother, Reuben. On October 7, it was $50 for an unstated purpose. On October 28, Clark loaned him $49.50 for two barrels of whiskey.[33]

In August, when one of Clark's slaves ran away, Lewis gave York $4 for his expenses as he searched for the man. That indicates a high level of trust in York, but nevertheless Clark was upset with York.

York was demanding his freedom as his reward for his services on the expedition. His wife belonged to someone else and lived in Louisville, Kentucky. When Clark refused to free him, York asked to be allowed to go to Louisville. Clark agreed to send him there, but only for a visit. In a November 9, 1808, letter to his brother Jonathan, Clark explained that he would "send York and premit him to Stay a fiew weeks with his wife, he wishes to Stay there altogether and hire himself [a fairly common practice; York was proposing to hire himself out and send the money his labor earned to Clark] which I have refused. he prefers being Sold to return[ing] here, [but] he is Serviceable to me at this place, and I am determined not to Sell him, to gratify him, and have derected him to return . . . to this place, this fall. if any attempt is made by York to run off, or refuse to proform his duty as a Slave, I wish him Sent to New Orleans and sold, or hired out to Some Sevare Master untill he thinks better of Such Conduct. I do not wish him to know my determination if he conducts himself well."

York continued to argue that he should be set free. Clark lamented to his brother, "I did wish to do well by him [York], but as he has got Such a notion about freedom and his emence Services [on the expedition], that I do not expect he will be of much Service to me again."

Clark fretted over the situation. He discussed it with Lewis. In a late-1808 letter to his brother, Clark wrote, "I do not cear for Yorks being in this Country. I have got a little displeased with him and intended to have punished him but Govr. Lewis has insisted on my only hireing him out in Kentucky which perhaps will be best." Clark hoped that York would learn a lesson from "a Severe Master" and thus "give over that wife of his" to return to St. Louis.

York was not the only slave causing Clark problems. He wrote Jonathan that he was often "much vexed & perplexed with my few negrows," so much so that he had been forced to chastise them and was considering selling all but four, not only to relieve the frustration of dealing with them but to obtain badly needed money. Still, he was troubled by his temptation to sell his slaves. "I wish I was near enough to Council with you a little on this Subject will you write a fiew lines about this inclination of mine to turn negrows into goods & cash."

In May 1809, York returned to St. Louis. "York brought my horse," Clark wrote, "he is here but of very little Service to me, insolent and sukly, I gave him a Severe trouncing the other Day and he has much mended."[34]

No commentary is necessary. Much of the evil of slavery is encapsuled in this little story—not least Jefferson's realism about the effect of slavery on the morals and manners of the slaveholder. York had helped pole Clark's keelboat, paddled his canoe, hunted for his meat, made his fire, had shown he was prepared to sacrifice his life to save Clark's, crossed the continent and returned with his childhood companion, only to be beaten because he was insolent and sulky and denied not only his freedom but his wife and, we may suppose, children.

That Lewis's attitude was somewhat softer is obvious, but it is highly unlikely that he ever told Clark to grant York his freedom. Lewis could no more escape the lord-and-master attitude toward black slaves than Clark could—or, come to that, than Jefferson could (Jefferson also sold slaves and separated families). No wonder Jefferson could write, "I tremble for my country when I reflect that God is just."[35]

In the late fall of 1808, war with Great Britain appeared imminent. To prepare for it, President Jefferson asked the nation to raise a hundred thousand men. Louisiana's quota was a mere 377. Lewis used the pages of the Missouri *Gazette* to appeal to the patriotism of the young men of his territory, mainly relying on the Anglophobia of the French and American inhabitants to get a response. He urged the young men to join in "defending our liberties and our country from the unhallowed grasp of the modern barbarians of Europe, who insatiate with the horrid bucheries of the eastern world, are now bending their course towards our peaceful and happy shore. . . . With them power begets right and justice is laughed to scorn. . . . They are destitute of magnanimity and virtue."

Lewis asked that volunteers sign up for twelve months' service and "thus prove themselves worthy of their fathers of '76 whose bequest, purchased with their blood, are those rights we now enjoy and so justly prize; let us then defend and preserve them, regardless of what it may cost, that they may pass unimpaired to the generation who are to succeed us."[36]

The response, sad to relate, hardly matched Lewis's eloquence. Only a few dozen Americans, and no Frenchmen, rallied to the call to arms.

Still, Lewis's first nine months in St. Louis had been busy and relatively successful. He had avoided, although only barely, an Indian war. He had established some law and order on the frontier. He was putting his own men into office. He was building roads and making other improvements. The St. Louis Missouri River Fur Company was a going concern.

But there was much he had not done, most especially on the two matters that most concerned Jefferson: Big White was still in town. And there the journals sat. Lewis apparently never even opened them.

38

ST. LOUIS

January–August 1809

Great joy in camp. Julia Clark has had a baby. William Clark names him Meriwether Lewis Clark. Clark gives a set of Shakespeare to the teenage mother.

Great excitement in St. Louis. The St. Louis Missouri River Fur Company is preparing to ascend the river. There are job opportunities for *voyagers*, for men willing to join the militia, for Indians looking for employment and a chance to get some revenge on the Arikaras and Sioux. For Lewis there is much planning and packing to supervise. It is reminiscent of the winter of 1803–4, when the city had been all hustle and bustle helping Lewis and Clark get ready for their expedition.

Especially for Lewis, who was almost as busy as in 1804. The terms of the contract he signed with the Missouri River Fur Company and the orders he gave the commander, Pierre Chouteau, show how active and productive he was in the winter and spring of 1809, how much he drew on what he had learned about going up the Missouri, how much attention he paid to detail, how imaginative he was, how much thought he put into the task, and how ruthless he could be.

But there was a dark side to his life. It is barely hinted at in the available contemporary documents, but something was bothering him. His drinking, apparently, was heavy. He was taking "medicine" regularly, medicine laced with opium or morphine. His account book contains many references to those medicines, which he indicated he took to deal with malaria attacks. He swallowed a pill containing a gram of opium every night at bedtime to ward off such attacks, and three a night when suffering a fever. If they "do not operate" he took two more in the morning.[1] He said repeatedly he needed to go back east, wanted to go back east, intended to go back east, that he would be off in a few days—but he didn't go. He was borrowing small sums regularly from the Chouteaus, and on May 17 borrowed twenty dollars from Bates. He did not state the reason for the loans; it is possible that they were for drinking money.

His finances were in a sorry state, as shown by a November 9 entry in his account book: "Borrowed of Genl Clark this sum [forty-nine dollars] to pay Doctor Farrow for his attendance on my servant Pernia, an account which I consider exorbitant, but which my situation in life compells me to pay."

In the orders he gave the expedition carrying Big White about how to handle the Arikaras, he was bloodthirsty to a shocking degree and displayed an alarming lack of common sense.

Meanwhile, Secretary Bates had a public scene with Governor Lewis, and the two top officials in Louisiana broke off relations.

Lewis's behavior had become erratic.

On February 24, Lewis signed the contract with the St. Louis Missouri River Fur Company, in his capacity as governor of the Territory of Louisiana, on behalf of the United States of America.

The terms were explicit. The company promised to raise 125 militiamen, of whom at least forty "shall be Americans and expert Riflemen," for the purpose of returning Big White and his party to the Mandan nation. The company was required to provide the militia with "good and suitable Fire Arms, of which Fifty at least shall be Rifles," the numbers and quality to be approved by Lewis. All other expenses—provisions, utensils, boats, Indian presents, and so on—would be borne by the partners. Governor Lewis would sign drafts for the supplies, as an advance to be deducted from the final payment.

The company pledged to deliver Big White and party safely, to "defend them from all Warlike attacks . . . at the risque of their lives." When the job was done, the United States would pay the company $7,000.

Pierre Chouteau of the company would command the expedition until it reached the Mandans and returned Big White; at that point, the military functions would end and command would go over to another partner, Manuel Lisa, who would push off with the company's men for the Yellowstone and beyond in a commercial operation. It would have a monopoly; Lewis pledged to issue no license to any trader for any part of the Missouri higher than the mouth of the Platte River.

The company "shall without any pretence of delay whatsoever embark, start, and proceed on before the Tenth day of May next, under the penalty for default" in the amount of $3,000. The United States would advance the company up to $3,500 after the expedition was fully formed and equipped. Should Lewis be absent from St. Louis, he authorized General Clark to act in his place.[2]

Both sides were delighted with the contract. For Lewis and for the partners, it made perfect sense to combine the military expedition with the commercial venture. After all, the army had tried in 1807 with Ensign Pryor and been turned back, with the loss of three lives, George Shannon's leg, and seven others wounded. The army could not possibly detach a force of 125 men to do the job. As for the partners, they could not expect to get a trading group past the Arikaras without military escort. Frontier army officers and officials of the government regularly engaged in private ventures on the frontier. And, obviously, it was as much in the government's interest as it was in the company's that the Missouri be opened to American fur traders.

Nevertheless, the contract opened Lewis to severe criticism. He had engaged the services of a private company, paying it with government funds. Any profits made from the commercial venture would be shared by his friend William Clark and Lewis's brother, Reuben, and, apparently, Lewis himself. But on the early-nineteenth-century frontier, these were fairly commonplace arrangements. In fact, Dearborn had set a precedent when he authorized Clark to give an exclusive trading license to private traders willing to accompany the Pryor expedition.

Lewis had an explicit authorization for such expenditures from Jefferson, but in a month Jefferson would be leaving office, and the new president, James Madison, and his secretary of war, William Eustis, were set on saving money, not taking on new obligations. They were not close to Lewis, they were much less interested in the West than Jefferson, and they did not approve of Lewis's free and easy way of signing drafts. They agreed with a former Indian agent who wrote to President Madison to protest the contract, asking, "Is it proper for the public service that the U.S. officers as a Governor or a Super Intendant of Indian Affairs should take any share in Mercantile and private concerns?"[3]

Secretary Bates was raising the same question, and he was furious that Lewis—expected to leave for Washington shortly—had named Clark rather than himself as his agent. Further, Bates was in continual disagreement with the governor over policy matters. Lewis was interested in promoting the fur trade; Bates wanted to promote settlement. Lewis refused to issue licenses for hunters in Indian country; Bates thought it a right of Americans to hunt.

So angry was Bates that in mid-April he said publicly that he had decided to write the president a catalogue of his complaints. But before he could do so, he had an "altercation" with Lewis. He spoke to Lewis "with an extreme freedom" of the "wrongs" Lewis had done him. In an April 15 letter to his brother, Bates explained that Lewis had "aroused my indignation" and caused "a heated resentment." What the specific issue was he didn't say; probably it was Clark's appointment as Lewis's agent.

"We now understand each other much better," Bates wrote. "We differ in every thing; but we will be honest and frank in our intercourse."[4]

Bates was an unlikable character, that type of bureaucrat who cannot for the life of him see any other person's point of view. In a letter to his brother, he confessed that he found this "a strange world." He explained, "My habits are pacific; yet I have had acrimonious differences with almost every person with whom I have been associated in public business." He admitted that this disturbed him and had caused him to examine his actions, but, "before God, I cannot acknowledge that I have been blamable in any one instance."[5]

His jealousy of Lewis was obvious. He told his brother that Lewis "has been spoiled by the elegant praises" of scientists and poets, "and over whelmed by so many flattering caresses of the *high & mighty*, that, like an overgrown baby, he begins to think that everybody about the House must regulate their conduct by his caprices."[6]

It was commonly said in St. Louis that Bates wanted Lewis's job. In his April 15 letter, Bates charged that Lewis had lost public confidence. "I lament the unpopularity of the Governor," he claimed, but "he has brought it on himself by harsh and mistaken measures. He is inflexible in error, and the irresistable Fiat of the People, has, I am fearful, already sealed his condemnation.

"Burn this letter."[7]

Through the late winter and into the spring of 1809, the Missouri River Fur Company recruited men and gathered supplies. Word came downriver that the Sioux had joined the Arikaras and were determined to stop all boats headed upstream. Lewis looked over the supply of presents for the Indians and decided it was insufficient, so on March 7 he signed a draft payable to Pierre Chouteau for $1,500 for additional presents; on May 13 he signed another, for $500, and two days later yet another, in the amount of $450, mainly for 500 pounds of gunpowder and 1,250 pounds of lead.[8]

Meanwhile, he worked on a set of orders for Chouteau. He declared that Chouteau's "principal object" was to return Big White and his family. Paraphrasing what Jefferson had told him, Lewis wrote, "I consider the honour and Good faith of our Government pledged For the success of this enterprize."

Lewis avoided specifics: "I deem it improper to trammil your operations by detailed and Positive Commands as to the plan of procedure." But he had suggestions. The first was to employ up to 300 Indians from the nations living below the Arikaras: "You will Promise them, as a reward for their Services, the plunder which they may acquire from the Aricares." He further advised Chouteau to recruit 100 white hunters and trappers, bringing his total up to 250 whites and 300 Indians.

In other words, should the Arikaras prove still to be hostile, Lewis was declaring all-out war on them. He was explicit on the point; he wanted Chouteau to have "a force sufficient Not Onely to bid defiance to the Aricares, but to exterpate that abandoned Nation if necessary."

This went far beyond Jefferson's recommendation that if the Arikaras tried to stop Big White they should be "punished." It went far beyond burning their property or killing their horses. It called for nothing short of genocide.

If the Arikaras proved to be peaceable, Chouteau should demand of them "the unconditional surrender" of the warriors who had killed any member of Ensign Pryor's party. Should the Arikaras claim they could not say who had fired the fatal bullets, Chouteau should require them to deliver up three warriors (three white men had been killed), chosen from among those "most active in stimulating" the hostilities.

"These murderers when Delivered will be shot in the presence of the nation," and the Arikaras required to give their horses to Chouteau's Indian allies.

If the Arikaras refused to deliver up their warriors, "You will take such measures as you may think best calculated to surprise and cut them off." If Chouteau took any prisoners, "you will either give them to the mandane or minnitare nations."

If the expedition got into an inconclusive fight and passed the Arikaras without destroying them, Chouteau should make an alliance with the Mandans and supply them with the necessary firepower to crush the Arikaras.

Lewis also said that Chouteau would be meeting "with sundry american Citizens" whose licenses to trade on the Missouri had expired. If they had acted in good faith, Chouteau should renew their licenses; had their conduct been improper, he should arrest them and return them to St. Louis by force. As for the competition from the north, "No British agent, Clerk, or engagé can under any Pretence whatever be Permitted to trade or hunt within this territory, the limits of which, are to be conceived to extend to all that Country watered by the Missoury."

Lewis signed off, "I sincerely wish you a Pleasant voyage and a safe Return to your Family and Friends."[9]

In mid-May, the expedition was under way. All together there were thirteen keelboats and barges, the largest flotilla sent up the river to date.

Through June and into July, rumors floated around St. Louis about Bates. He had made it known that he intended to denounce Lewis to the president and was said to be "at the head of a Party whose object it would be to procure his dismissal." So widespread was the talk that Lewis called on Bates to demand an explanation.

"You are greatly mistaken," Bates told him. In a letter of July 14 to his brother, Bates related that "As a Citizen, I told him I entertained opinions very different from his, on the subject of civil government, and that those opinions had, on various occasions been expressed with emphasis; but that they had been unmixed with personal malice or hostility."

"Well," Lewis replied, "do not suffer yourself to be separated from me in the public opinion; When we meet in public, let us, at least address each other with cordiality."

Bates agreed, though he complained to his brother that Lewis had "used me badly."

Then Bates demanded that Clark be brought into the conversation, to settle the business about Lewis's appointment of Clark as his agent. When Clark arrived, Bates told the two men that the laws "expressly provided" that he, Secretary Bates, should be the governor's agent when the governor was traveling.

"I will suffer no interferences &c. &c. &c." he declared. To his brother, Bates remarked, "How unfortunate for this man [Lewis] that he resigned his commission in the army: His habits are altogether military & he never can I think succeed in any other profession."[10]

On July 16, Bates wrote the secretary of the Treasury to complain about Lewis's behavior. It seemed Lewis had ordered Bates to print the laws of the territory and charge it to the secretary's office. Bates had refused, but ultimately relented in response to Lewis's repeated order; now he wanted the Treasury to compensate him.[11]

By July 25, Bates was able to boast to an ally, "Our Gov. Lewis, with the best intentions in the world, is, I am fearful, losing ground. . . . He has talked for these 12 Mos. of leaving the country—Every body thinks now that he will positively go, in a few weeks."[12]

In early August, Lewis received a short note from a clerk in the Department of State named R. S. Smith. It referred to a draft Lewis had signed on February 10 in favor of one Peter Provenchere for $18.50 for translating the laws of the territory into French for publication. Although Lewis had no authorization to pay for such services, he explained, "I did not hesitate to cause the copies of those laws to be made out [for a felony trial]. I was compelled to take the course which I have, or suffer a fellow to escape punishment."

Now the bill came back to him, with a note from clerk Smith: "The bill mentioned in this Letter having been drawn without authority it cannot be paid at this Dept."[13]

Lewis was shaken by the refusal. "This occurrence has given me infinite concern as from it the fate of other bills, drawn for similar purposes, to a considerable amount cannot be mistaken," he wrote. "This rejection cannot fail to impress the public mind unfavourably with respect to me, nor is this consideration more painful than the censure which must arise in the Mind of the Executive from my having drawn public monies without authority. A third, and not less embarrassing circumstance attending the transaction is that my private funds are entirely incompetent to meet these bills, if protested."[14]

Secretary Bates thought of himself as a long-suffering, honest, misunderstood man guarding the public treasury. He sent a series of complaints about Lewis's drafts and orders to Washington. Sometime that summer, Lewis struck back; as Bates put it, "he took it into his head to disavow certain statements which I had made, *by his order*, from the Secretary's Office.

"This was too much—I waited on him,—told him my wrongs—that I could not bear to be treated in such a manner."

"Take your own course," Lewis replied.

"I shall, Sir," Bates fired back. "And I shall come, in future to the Executive Office when I have *business* at it."

Shortly thereafter, a ball was held in St. Louis. Bates was present when Lewis entered. Bates recorded: "He drew his chair close to mine—There was a pause in the conversation—I availed myself of it—arose and walked to the opposite side of the room."

Lewis also rose—according to Bates, "evidently in passion." Lewis retired into an adjoining room and sent a servant for Clark. He told

Clark that Bates had "treated him with contempt & insult and that he could not suffer it to pass." He asked him to call Bates into the room.

Clark refused, according to Bates because "he foresaw that a Battle must have been the consequence of our meeting."

Some days later, Clark called on Bates to ask that he patch things up with Lewis.

"NO!" Bates replied. "The Governor has told me to take my own course and I shall step a *high* and a *proud* Path. He has *injured* me, and he must *undo* that injury.

"You come," Bates told Clark, "as *my* friend, but I cannot separate you from Governor Lewis—You have trodden the *ups* & the *Downs* of life with him and it appears to me that these proposals are made solely for *his* convenience."[15]

This unseemly squabbling certainly did Lewis's mood no good, but it was a minor affair compared with what happened to him on August 18. That day, he received a heart-stopping letter from Secretary of War Eustis.

Dated July 19, it was written in the deadly passive voice of the born bureaucrat. Eustis said that, after his department had reluctantly approved Lewis's contract with the Missouri River Fur Company for seven thousand dollars, "it was not expected that any further advances or any further agency would be required on the part of the United States." Lewis should therefore "not be surprized" that his draft of May 13 for an additional five hundred dollars for presents for the Indians "has not been honored."

That meant Lewis was personally responsible for the money.

Eustis went on, "It has been usual to advise the Government of the United States when expenditures to a considerable amount are contemplated in the Territorial Government." When 125 men are to be enlisted for "a military expedition to a point and purpose not designated, which expedition is stated to combine commercial as well as military objects . . . it is thought the Government might, without injury to the public interests, have been consulted."

In fact, Lewis had been explicit about the purpose of the expedition, although he had not cleared the commercial aspects of it with Washington. Eustis seized on that point: "As the object & destination of this Force [beyond the Mandans] is unknown, and more especially as it combines Commercial purposes, so it cannot be considered as having the sanction of the Government of the United States, or that they are responsible for consequences."

Eustis closed with a chilling remark. "The President has been consulted and the observations herein contained have his approval." The president, of course, was Madison, not Jefferson—now retired at Monticello and unable to protect Lewis.[16]

In any event, Jefferson was unhappy with Lewis. He was slow to censure and ready to give Lewis the benefit of the doubt, but his patience was wearing thin. On August 16, he sent Lewis a letter of introduction for an English botanist coming to St. Louis on a "botanising tour."

Then Jefferson wrote: "I am very often applied to know when your work will begin to appear; and I have so long promised copies to my literary correspondents in France, that I am almost bankrupt in their eyes. I shall be very happy to recieve from yourself information of your expectations on this subject. Every body is impatient for it."

Perhaps to soften the blow, Jefferson added some political gossip and commentary on foreign affairs. He said Lewis's friends in Virginia "are well, & have been long in expectation of seeing you. I shall hope in that case to possess a due portion of you at Monticello, where I am at length enjoying the never before known luxury of employing myself for my own gratification only." He asked Lewis to present his best wishes to Clark "and be assured yourself of my constant & unalterable affections."[17]

Lewis never replied, or made any known mention of the letter; nor did he explain to anyone, even Clark, the cause of the delay in preparing the journals for publication.

Lewis did reply to Eustis, in a letter of August 18, the day he got it. He said Eustis's letter of July 19 "is now before me. The feelings it excites are truly painful." He protested that he had accompanied every draft for a public expenditure with an explicit statement of the purpose and insisted, "I have never received a penny of public Money." He added, "To the correctness of this statement, I call my God to witness.

"I have been informed Representations have been made against me," Lewis went on. What those "Representations" might have been is not known, but can be surmised from his protests against them; nor is the source known, but it can be guessed that it was Bates. Evidently Bates—or someone else—had spread a story that the Missouri River Fur Company intended to go into the Rocky Mountains, beyond the Continental Divide, into territory not belonging to the United States, possibly with the intent of setting up a new country, à la Aaron Burr and General Wilkinson.

Whatever the specifics, Lewis said he could not correct by letter "the impressions which I fear, from the tenor of your letter, the Government entertain with respect to me." Therefore, he would leave St. Louis in a week, going by way of New Orleans to Washington. "I shall take with me my papers, which I trust when examined, will prove my firm and steady attachment to my Country."

The expedition to return Big White had only that object, he went on, "and in a commercial point of view, . . . they [the company] intend only, to hunt and trade on the waters of the Misoury and Columbia Rivers within the rockey Mountains and the Planes bordering those Mountains on the east side—and that they have no intention with which I am acquainted, to enter the Dominions, or do injury to any foreign Power.

"Be assured Sir, that my Country can never make 'A Burr' of me— She may reduce me to Poverty; but she can never sever my Attachment from her."

Word that the government had refused to honor Lewis's drafts had spread round town within hours of the arrival of Eustis's letter (Bates again?). Lewis informed Eustis that the protested bills "have effectually sunk my Credit; brought in all my private debts, amounting to about $4,000." He had handed over to his creditors the deeds to the land he had purchased around St. Louis, as security, and pointed out that "the best proof which I can give of my Integrity, as to the use or expenditure of the public Monies, the Government will find at a future day, by the poverty to which they have now reduced me."[18]

Lewis spent the next few days with Clark. They agreed that both of them should go to Washington. Clark was of course deeply involved in the Missouri River Fur Company and in any case had other governmental matters to take up with the War Department, including protested drafts of his brother George Rogers Clark (which had ruined him). Lewis would go by water, Clark overland.

They spent much time attempting to put Lewis's accounts in order. They made up a list of what Lewis owed; it came to some twenty-nine hundred dollars, exclusive of his land debts.[19] Lewis sent ahead to New Orleans the land warrant for sixteen hundred acres he had been given by Congress, to be sold, he hoped, for two dollars an acre. He wanted the money deposited in a New Orleans bank "for the benefit of my creditors." He returned to Auguste Chouteau much of the land he had bought from him on credit. He looked around for anything he had that could be sold; in Clark's memorandum book, Lewis wrote, "The negroe boy *Tom* belongs to my mother, and therefore cannot be sold on my account."[20]

The most valuable item he possessed, by far, was the journals, worth a thousand times and more what the land warrant would bring. Those he would never sell.

Lewis had told Eustis that he would be departing in a week, but it actually took him three weeks to get going. He packed all his belongings, including the journals, which had been continuously in his possession since the end of the expedition. He told Clark he would go to Philadelphia to get the publication process started.

His baggage contained, among many other items, a sea-otter skin, a pair of red slippers, a silver tumbler, a tomahawk, five vests, two pairs of pantaloons, one pair of black silk breeches, two cotton shirts, one flannel shirt, two pairs of cotton stockings, three pairs of silk stockings, a bundle of medicines, a broadcloth coat, a pistol case, three knives, a sword, a "pike blade" with a broken shaft (his espontoon?), and all his official papers.[21] He got off on September 4.[22]

Some days after Lewis left St. Louis, one of the land commissioners in the territory, Clement Penrose, accused Bates of being responsible for "the mental derangement of the Governor," which Penrose said was due to "the *barbarous conduct of the Secretary*."

Bates confronted Penrose after a meeting of the Board of Commissioners. He charged Penrose with spreading slanders against him and said, "*I pledge my word of Honor, that if you ever again bark at my heels, I will spurn you like a Puppy.*" Later that day, he wrote Penrose a record of the conversation.

"You said that I *have been*, and *am* the enemy of the Governor—and that I would be very willing to fill that office myself. I told you this morning that it was *false*—and I repeat that it is an impudent stupidity in you to persist in the assertion. . . . In return for the personal allusions with which you have honored me, I tender to you, my most hearty contempt."[23]

In another letter that week, Bates wrote that "all feeling minds are, in different degrees, affected by the unhappy situation of Governor Lewis, and would feel a painful reluctance in contributing to his mortifications."[24]

Lewis had borrowed again, enough money to purchase a considerable medical chest. He jotted in his account book that he had bought pills for "billious fever, pills of opium and tartar," and others.

The Missouri *Gazette* had reported that Governor Lewis "set off in good health for New Orleans on his way to the Federal City." The emphasis on his health had more an ominous than a reassuring ring.

The day after Lewis's departure, Clark wrote his brother Jonathan, describing Lewis's situation and mood during his last week in St. Louis:

> Govr. L I may Say is ruined by Some of his Bills being protested for a Considerable Sum which was for Moneys paid for Printing the Laws and Expenses in Carrying the mandan home all of which he has vouchrs for. . . .
>
> I have not Spent Such a day as yesterday for maney years. . . . I took my leave of Govr. Lewis who Set out to Philadelphia to write our Book (but more perticularly to explain Some Matter between him and the Govt.) Several of his Bills have been protested, and his Crediters all flocking in near the time of his Setting out distressed him much, which he expressed to me in Such terms as to Cause a Cempothy which is not yet off—I do not beleve there was ever an honester man in Louisiana nor one who had pureor motives than Govr. Lewis. if his mind had been at ease I Should have parted Cherefuly. . . .
>
> I think all will be right and he will return with flying Colours to this Country—prey do not mention this about the Govr. excupt Some unfavourable or wrong Statement is made—I assure you that he has done nothing dishonourable, and all he has done will Come out to be much to his Credit as I am fully purswaded.[25]

39

LAST VOYAGE

September 3–October 11, 1809

The Mississippi River valley in early September 1809 was hot, humid, buggy. Lewis's boat proceeded slowly, since it was necessary for the crew to rest during the middle part of the day. He was in terrible condition, possibly suffering from a malaria attack, certainly in a deep depression that caused him unbearable pain. Twice he tried to kill himself—whether by jumping overboard or with his pistol is not known—and had to be restrained by the crew.[1]

On September 11, he wrote his last will and testament: "I bequeath all my estate, real and personal, to my Mother, Lucy Marks, after my private debts are paid, of which a statement will be found in a small minute book deposited with Pernia, my servant."[2]

Lewis arrived at Chickasaw Bluffs, then the site of Fort Pickering, today the site of Memphis, Tennessee, on September 15. Captain Gilbert Russell was the commander at the fort. On being informed of Lewis's suicide attempts, he "resolved at once to take possession of him and his papers, and detain them there untill he recovered, or some friend might arrive in whose hands he could depart in safety."[3]

Lewis was drinking heavily, using snuff frequently, taking his pills, talking wildly, telling lies. He told Russell (as reported in the November 15, 1809, Washington *Advertiser*) that all the work on the journals had been completed and they were ready for the press. Apparently that was his way of deflecting embarrassing questions about the project's progress. Russell deprived him of liquor, allowing him only "claret & a little white wine."[4]

The day after his arrival, Lewis wrote President Madison. The letter was garbled, although he managed to make his point. It needs to be quoted in full.*

I arrived here {yesterday} about {2 Ock} P.M. {*yesterday*} very much exhausted from the heat of the climate, but having {taken} medicine feel much better this morning. My apprehension for the heat of the lower country and my fear of the original papers relative to my voyage to the Pacific ocean falling into the hands of the British has induced me to change my rout and proceed by land through the state of Tennisee to the City of washington. I bring with me duplicates of my vouchers for public expenditures &c. which when fully explained, or reather the general view of the circumstances under which they were made I flatter myself {*that*} they {will} receive both {sanction &} approbation {*and*} sanction.

   Provided my health permits no time shall be lost in reaching Washington. My anxiety to pursue and to fullfill the duties incedent to {*the*} internal arangements incedent to the government of Louisiana has prevented my writing you {as} more frequently. {*Mr. Bates is left in charge.*} Inclosed I herewith transmit you a copy of the laws of the territory of Louisiana. I have the honour to be with the most sincere esteem your Obt. {*and very humble*} Obt. and very humble Servt."[5]

Over the following five days, Lewis showed no sign of improvement (Russell apparently had not deprived him of his medicines). Russell maintained a twenty-four-hour suicide watch. Finally, Russell reported, "on the sixth or seventh day all symptoms of derangement disappeared and he was completely in his senses," although he was "considerably reduced and debilitated."[6]

He was also ashamed of himself. Russell reported that "he acknowledged very candidly to me after his recovery" that he had been drinking to excess. Lewis said he was resolved "never to drink any more spirits or use snuff again."[7]

Lewis set about straightening out his affairs. On September 22, he wrote his old friend Major Amos Stoddard, in command at Fort Adams, farther down the river. He began with an apology: "I must acknowledge

---

* Words enclosed in { } were inserted between the lines; italicized words enclosed in { } were crossed out.

myself remiss in not writing you in answer to several friendly epistles which I have received from you since my return from the Pacific Ocean." He said he was on his way to Washington to explain his actions in St. Louis, which he hoped "is all that is necessary . . . to put all matters right." But his creditors were pressing him and had "excessively embarrassed me. I hope you will therefore pardon me for asking you to remit as soon as is convenient the sum of $200 which you have informed me you hold for me. . . .

"You will direct to me at the City of Washington untill the last of December after which I expect I shall be on my return to St. Louis."[8]

Lewis asked Russell to accompany him to Washington, and Russell agreed: he too had some protested bills to explain to the new administration. But he could not get the leave of absence he had requested.[9]

Major James Neelly, the U.S. agent to the Chickasaw nation, had arrived at Fort Pickering on September 18. He later wrote Jefferson that he "found the governor in Very bad health" but that during the week Lewis "recovered his health in some digree."[10]

By September 29, Russell and Neelly were satisfied that Lewis was capable of traveling overland to Washington, if accompanied by Neelly, Pernier, and Neelly's servant. Lewis said he was ready to make the journey. Russell lent him $100 and sold him two horses on credit for the journey; Lewis signed a promissory note for $379.58 payable before January 1, 1810, for the loan and the horses.[11]

Lewis had with him the journals, packed in trunks and carried by packhorse. The Natchez Trace seemed much safer to him than risking a sailboat from New Orleans to Washington, with British warships prowling the Atlantic Coast, stopping American vessels, and impressing American seamen into British service. What the British would give to have those journals! There was no danger of that on the Trace, which was the most heavily traveled road of the Old Southwest. The mail passed over it regularly. No robbery had been reported for years. There were inns along the way.[12]

It took the party three days to cover a hundred miles. Along the way, Lewis repeatedly complained about his protested drafts. Pernier later reported to Clark that Lewis would frequently "Conceipt [conceive] that he herd me [Clark] coming on, and Said that he was certain [I would] over take him. that I had herd of his Situation and would Come to his releaf."[13]

Lewis was drinking again, or, as Russell so heartbreakingly put it, "His resolution [never to drink again] left him."[14] Neelly later reported to Jefferson that, when they arrived at the Chickasaw Agency, some six miles north of present Houston, Mississippi, Lewis "appeared at times deranged in mind."

At Neelly's insistence, the party stayed two days at the agency to rest. Lewis asked Neelly, in the event that "any accident happened to him," to send his trunks with the journals to "the President," by whom Neelly assumed Lewis meant Jefferson, not Madison.

On October 6, Lewis, Neelly, and the servants set out again. On the morning of October 9, they crossed the Tennessee River and camped near the present village of Collinwood, Tennessee.

That night, two of the horses strayed. In the morning, Neelly said he would stay behind to find them. Lewis decided to proceed, Neelly reported, "with a promise to wait for me at the first house he Came to that was inhabited by white people."[15]

Late in the afternoon, Lewis arrived at Grinder's Inn, seventy-two miles short of Nashville. It was a rough-hewn, poorly built log cabin that took in overnight customers. Mr. Grinder was away.

Lewis requested accommodations for the night. Are you alone? Mrs. Grinder asked. No, Lewis replied, two servants would be coming on shortly. Mrs. Grinder said they were welcome. Lewis dismounted, unsaddled his horse, and brought the saddle in the house. He was dressed "in a loose gown, white, striped with blue." He asked for some whiskey, of which he drank but a little.

When Pernier and the other servant arrived, Lewis asked for his gunpowder, saying he was sure he had some in a canister. Pernier "gave no distinct reply," probably because he had been told by Neelly to keep the powder away from Lewis.

Lewis began pacing in front of the cabin. Mrs. Grinder later reported that "sometimes he would seem as if he were walking up to her; and would suddenly wheel round, and walk back as fast as he could."

She prepared a meal. Lewis entered the cabin and sat at the table, but after only a few mouthfuls he started up, "speaking to himself in a violent manner." Mrs. Grinder noted that his face was flushed, "as if it had come on him in a fit."

Lewis lit his pipe, drew a chair to the door, sat down, and remarked to Mrs. Grinder, in a kindly tone, "Madam this is a very pleasant evening."

After finishing the pipe, he rose and paced the yard. He sat again, lit another pipe, seemed composed. He cast his eyes "wishfully towards the west." He spoke again of what "a sweet evening" it was.

As he sat on Mrs. Grinder's porch, looking west while the light faded from the sky, what were his thoughts? Were they of the rivers, the

Missouri and the Columbia and the others? Did he recall the Arikaras, the Sioux, the Mandans? Did he think of the first time he had seen Sacagawea? Did he remember the April day in 1805 when he started out from the Mandan nation on his "darling project," daring to link his name with Columbus and Captain Cook? Did he dwell on the decision at the Marias?

Or were the plants, animals, birds, scenery of the Garden of Eden he had passed through commanding his imagination? If so, surely he thought of cottonwoods, prickly pears, the gigantic trees of the Pacific Coast; of grouse and woodpeckers and condors; of the grizzlies and the unbelievable buffalo herds, the pronghorns, sheep, coyotes, prairie dogs, and the other animals he had discovered and described; of those remarkable white cliffs along the Missouri, the Gates of the Rocky Mountains, the Columbia gorge.

Did Three Forks, that "essential spot" in the geography of the West, spring to his mind? Or was it Cameahwait and the Shoshones? Perhaps it was Old Toby, and that terrible trip across the Bitterroots.

Did he recall the Nez Percé and their fabulous ponies and generosity? Or the journey down the western waters to the sea? Or was it his Christmas and New Year's dinners of water and lean elk at Fort Clatsop?

It may be that he thought of the long waiting period with the Nez Percé, and the one time he had been forced to turn back in the first attempt to force the Bitterroots, in the spring of 1806. Or was it the Blackfeet and the only Indian fight of his life? Or the time he got shot in the ass?

Did he do a roll call of his men? If so, surely there was a special place for Drouillard.

If he thought of the men, surely he thought of his co-commander, the best friend any man ever had. He had told Pernier earlier that day that General Clark had heard of his difficulties and was coming on. As the light faded, was he looking westward along the Trace, expecting to see Clark ride in to set everything right?

Did one of Mrs. Grinder's dogs chase a squirrel and remind him of Seaman?

Could it be that he thought of that moment of triumph when his canoes put in at St. Louis in September 1806?

Or were his thoughts gloomy? Were they about his unsolvable problems? Did he agonize over his speculations and the financial ruin they had brought him? Was that awful Secretary Bates foremost in his thoughts? Did he wonder why he had failed in his courtships and had no wife? Did he curse himself for his drinking?

Did his mind dwell on Thomas Jefferson? Was he ashamed of how he had failed the man he adored? Did he think of the journals, over in the corner in his saddlebags?

Or did his mind avoid the past? Was he rehearsing what he would say to Secretary Eustis and President Madison?

Or was he yearning for more pills? Or more whiskey?

We cannot know. We only know that he was tortured, that his pain was unbearable.

Mrs. Grinder began to prepare a bed for him, but he stopped her and said he would sleep on the floor, explaining that since his journey to the Pacific he could no longer sleep on a feather bed. He had Pernier bring in his bear skins and buffalo robe and spread them on the floor. While Pernier was getting the bedding, Lewis found some powder.

Mrs. Grinder went to the kitchen to sleep, and the servants went to the barn, some two hundred yards distant.

Lewis began pacing in his room. This went on for several hours. Mrs. Grinder, who was frightened and could not sleep, heard him talking aloud, "like a lawyer."

Lewis got out his pistols. He loaded them and at some time during the early hours of October 11 shot himself in the head. The ball only grazed his skull.

He fell heavily to the floor. Mrs. Grinder heard him exclaim, "O Lord!"

Lewis rose, took up his other pistol, and shot himself in his breast. The ball entered and passed downward through his body, to emerge low down on his backbone.

He survived the second shot, staggered to the door of his room, and called out, "O madam! Give me some water, and heal my wounds."

Lewis staggered outside, fell, crawled for some distance, raised himself by the side of a tree, then staggered back to his room. He scraped the bucket with a gourd for water, but the bucket was empty. He collapsed on his robes.

At first light, the terrified Mrs. Grinder sent her children to fetch the servants. When they got to Lewis's room, they found him "busily engaged in cutting himself from head to foot" with his razor.

Lewis saw Pernier and said to him, "I have done the business my good Servant give me some water." Pernier did.

Lewis uncovered his side and showed them the second wound. He said, "I am no coward; but I am so strong, [it is] so hard to die." He said he had tried to kill himself to deprive his enemies of the pleasure and honor of doing it.

He begged the servants to take his rifle and blow out his brains, telling them not to be afraid, for he would not hurt them, and they could have all the money in his trunk.

Shortly after sunrise, his great heart stopped beating.[16]

40

AFTERMATH

On October 28, Clark got the news of Lewis's suicide, from the Frankfort, Kentucky, *Argus of Western America*. He was in Shelbyville, on his way to Washington. George Shannon was with him. Clark wrote his brother Jonathan:

> I fear this report has too much truth. . . . my reason for thinking it possible is found on the letter I received from him at your house. . . .
>   I fear O' I fear the weight of his mind has overcome him, what will be the Consequence?[1]

Two days later, Clark wrote again, to report he had

> herd of the Certainty of the death of Govr. Lewis which givs us much uneasiness. . . .
>   I wish much to get the letter I receved of Govr. Lewis from New Madrid, which you Saw it will be of great Service to me prey send it. . . . I wish I had Some Conversation with you.[2]

Lewis's letter to Clark—written around September 11, the day Lewis wrote his will—has never been found.

Jefferson got the news at Monticello in November, via either the newspapers or Neelly's letter to him. Neelly said he had arrived at Grinder's Inn on the morning of October 11, after Lewis's death, and had buried him as "decently as I could."* He gave a brief account of the suicide and asked instructions on what to do with Lewis's trunks.³ A week or so later, Pernier visited Jefferson and gave him an eyewitness account of Lewis's last day on earth.

Jefferson's first known written comment on Lewis's death is in a letter to Dr. William Dickson, of Nashville, dated April 20, 1810. Dickson had sent on a miniature of Lewis and Lewis's watch chain, which had somehow come into his possession. In acknowledging their receipt, Jefferson said he was sending the items to Lewis's mother. "The deplorable accident which has placed her in the deepest affliction," he wrote, "is a great loss to the world also; as no pen can ever give us so faithful & lively an account of the countries & nations which he saw, as his own would have done, under the guidance of impressions made by the objects themselves."⁴

Eight days later, Jefferson wrote Captain Russell, his first known comment on the cause of the suicide. He said Lewis "was much afflicted & habitually so with hypocondria. This was probably increased by the habit into which he had fallen & the painfull reflections that would necessarily produce in a mind like his."⁵

Some three years later, in a short biography of Lewis, Jefferson went into more detail:

> Governor Lewis had from early life been subject to hypocondriac affections. It was a constitutional disposition in all the nearer branches of the family of his name, & was more immediately inherited by him from his father. . . . While he lived with me in Washington, I observed at times sensible depressions of mind, but knowing their constitutional source, I estimated their course by what I had seen in the family. During his Western expedition the constant exertion which that required of all the faculties of body & mind, suspended these distressing affections; but after his establishment at St. Louis in sedentary occupations they returned upon him with redoubled vigor, and began seriously to alarm his friends. . . .
>
> At about 3 o'clock in the night [of October 10–11] he did the deed which plunged his friends into affliction and deprived his country of one of her most valued citizens.⁶

---

* Lewis is buried today at the site of Grinder's Inn, along the Natchez Trace Alexander Wilson saw to preparing a proper plot and putting a fence around it. A broken shaft, authorized by the Tennessee Legislature in 1849 as symbolic of "the violent and untimely end of a bright and glorious career," marks the spot.

There is a considerable literature on the possibility that Lewis did not commit suicide but was murdered. The first to put forth that claim in any detail was Vardis Fisher.[7] Dr. Chuinard has more recently made the same assertion.[8] The literature is not convincing; the detailed refutation by Paul Russell Cutright is.[9]

A suggestion has been made that Lewis's mental problems stemmed not from hypochondria, as Jefferson would have it, or a manic-depressive syndrome, but from the effects of an advanced case of syphilis.[10] It is more intriguing and speculative than convincing.

What is convincing is the initial reaction of the two men who knew Lewis best and loved him most. William Clark and Thomas Jefferson immediately concluded that the story of Lewis's suicide was entirely believable, Clark on the basis of his intimate knowledge of Lewis's mental state and more explicitly on the never-found Lewis letter of mid-September. Neither Jefferson nor Clark ever doubted that Lewis killed himself.

Those who still hold out for murder need to deal with a "dog that did not bark" aspect of the case. Had William Clark entertained the slightest suspicion that his friend had been murdered, can anyone doubt that he would have gone to Tennessee immediately to find and hang the murderer? Or, if Jefferson had such suspicions, that he would have insisted the government launch an investigation?

Lewis's half-brother, John Marks, did an inventory of Lewis's debts and assets. He had private debts amounting to $4,196.12 and protested drafts totaling $6,956.62. His credits and estate were worth $5,700. He had a further credit of $754.50 for Indian presents and gunpowder sold by Chouteau after he returned from successfully getting Big White back to the Mandan nation. It turned out that the presents and the gunpowder, which had been the cause of such distress to Lewis when the Madison administration refused to honor the draft used to pay for them, were not needed.[11]

Clark visited Washington in December 1809. He recorded in the journal he kept that on December 18 he "Went to see the Secretary of War [Eustis], had a long talk abt. Govr. Lewis, [he] pointed out his intentions & views for the protests. Declaired the Govr had not lost the Confidence of the Government."[12] The statement was two months and seven days too late.

"I do not know what I Shall do about the publication of the Book," Clark wrote Jonathan.[13]

Clark was ignorant of what had been done to get a manuscript ready for the printer. In a memorandum he wrote to himself in late 1809, before going to Philadelphia to see what could be done about publication, he put down questions he needed to ask:

> Enquire what has been done by G[overnor] L[ewis] with Calculations—engraving Printing Botany.
> If a man can be got to go to St. Louis with me to write the journal & price.
> The price of engraving animals Ind[ian]s & Maps Paper & other expences.
> Get some one to write the scientific part & natural history—Botany, Mineralogy & Zoology.
> Praries—muddiness of the Miissouri.
> Natural Phenomena—23 vocabularies & plates & engraving.[14]

Obviously, Clark had discussed none of this with Lewis, who had already taken care of and paid for some of the arrangements Clark thought he needed to make. Amazingly, Lewis had never talked to Clark about publication, except to promise one more time that when he got to Philadelphia he would complete the task.

This is the great mystery of Lewis's life. There is only speculation on what kept him from preparing the journals for the publisher, but no one can know the cause for certain, any more than anyone can know for certain the cause of his suicide.

On learning of Lewis's suicide, the publishers, C. and A. Conrad of Philadelphia, told Jefferson that they had a contract to produce the journals and asked what they should do now. "Govr. Lewis never furnished us with a line of the M.S.," they told Jefferson, "nor indeed could we ever hear any thing from him respecting it tho frequent applications to that effect were made to him."[15]

Jefferson replied that the journals were coming to Monticello, and so was Clark; that they would consult; that Clark would come on to Philadelphia to see what could be done.

When Clark arrived at Monticello, there was apparently some talk about Jefferson's taking over the journals and doing the editing to prepare them for the printer. There was no man alive who had a greater interest in the subject, or one who had better qualifications for the job. But he was sixty-five years old and desired to spend his remaining years at Monticello as a gentleman farmer. In January 1810, Lewis's cousin William Meriwether wrote Clark, "Mr Jefferson would not undertake the work."[16]

Clark took the journals to Philadelphia, where he called on the men who had helped Lewis prepare for the expedition and those whom Lewis had hired to do drawings and calculations. Charles Willson Peale was one of them. On February 3, 1810, Peale wrote his brother: "I would rather Clark had undertaken to have wrote the whole himself and then have put it into the hands of some person of talents to brush it up, but I found that the General was too diffident of his abilities."[17]

After some false starts, Clark persuaded Nicholas Biddle to undertake the work. Biddle was only twenty-six years old, but he was a prodigy. He had been granted admission to the University of Pennsylvania at the age of ten. After three years, he had completed the requirements, but the university, citing his extreme youth, denied him a diploma. He went to Princeton, from which he graduated in 1801 at the age of fifteen. After graduation, he studied law and wrote essays. He married one of the richest women in the country, so he had no money problems and lots of time.

Biddle was the perfect choice. He threw himself into the work and did it magnificently. George Shannon helped him, as did Clark, and finally a young man named Paul Allen did some copyediting (for five hundred dollars; Biddle took nothing for himself for more than two years of full-time labor).

Nothing ever came easy for those star-crossed journals, however. Biddle had persuaded Dr. Barton to do the scientific volume, but Barton's health failed and he could not complete the job. And just when Biddle was ready to turn the narrative volume over to the printer, the War of 1812 began. Worse, the firm of C. and A. Conrad collapsed.

As Biddle expressed his fear, "the work will lose some of its interest by so much delay." It took him more than a year to find a publisher (Bradford and Inskeep of Philadelphia).

In 1814, the book appeared, titled *The History of the Expedition Under the Commands of Captains Lewis and Clark*. It was a narrative and paraphrase of the journals, completely true to the original, retaining some of the more delightful phrases, but with the spelling corrected. Biddle did relatively little with the flora and fauna.

Bradford and Inskeep printed 1,417 copies and priced them at six dollars. They sold slowly—there were already editions of Gass's journal in print, and many counterfeits. Biddle wanted the publisher to pay royalties to Clark, but he never received a penny.

For the next ninety years, Biddle's edition was the only printed account based on the journals. As a result, Lewis and Clark got no credit for most of their discoveries. Plants, rivers, animals, birds that they had described and named were newly discovered by naturalists, and the names that these men gave them were the ones that stuck.

In 1893, the naturalist Elliott Coues published a reprint of the Biddle narrative. He added footnotes on many subjects, including material on birds, animals, and plants, and especially geography.

In 1904, on the hundredth anniversary of the beginning of the expedition, Reuben Gold Thwaites of the Wisconsin State Historical Society published (Dodd, Meade) the complete journals, in eight volumes, including never-before-seen journals from two of the enlisted men. His editorial work was outstanding. Often reprinted, "Thwaites," as the work is known among Lewis and Clark fans, is an American classic.

In 1962, Donald Jackson edited the *Letters of the Lewis and Clark Expedition* (University of Illinois Press, expanded to two volumes in 1978). Together with Jackson's notes, it is a work of scholarship almost unequaled anywhere, and certainly never surpassed.

In the 1980s, Gary Moulton edited an eight-volume set of the captains' journals for the University of Nebraska Press. He added much new material, including Lewis's journal of his trip down the Ohio in 1803 (previously published by Milo Quaife in 1916) and innumerable fascinating footnotes, with a special emphasis on botany and other scientific subjects.

Moulton's edition is the definitive work for our time. But he himself points out (as did Jackson before him) that nothing is ever truly definitive in history. There are always new documents coming to light.

Biddle, Thwaites, Jackson, and Moulton together make the rock on which all Lewis and Clark scholarship stands.

Biddle's name appears nowhere in his narrative, apparently because he insisted on complete anonymity. On the title page, where his name should have appeared, it reads: "Prepared for the press by Paul Allen, Esquire."

Allen can be forgiven, for it was he who induced Jefferson to write a memoir-biography of Lewis. He wrote Jefferson, "I wish very much to enliven the dulness of the Narrative by someing more popular splendid & attractive." (Elliott Coues commented that Allen's letter "exhibited an achievement in impudence that deserves to become historical.") Jefferson wrote a five-thousand-word "letter" on Lewis's life in 1813; the first biography of Lewis, it was written with Jefferson's usual care for accuracy and detail.[18]

Jefferson never allowed his disappointment over his inability to send the scientific parts of the journals to his fellow members of the

Enlightenment, both at home and abroad, or his heartbreak over Lewis's suicide, to sour him on his protégé. The expedition had not fulfilled his hopes in many ways, most of all in not discovering an all-water route to the Pacific, but he did not allow that disappointment to affect his judgment of Lewis.

At the time Jefferson wrote his memoir of Lewis, the Louisiana Purchase did not look like such a great bargain. The Indians were up in arms, the St. Louis Missouri River Fur Company and John Jacob Astor had failed to establish permanent posts in the West, the ultimate fate of the great northwestern empire was still to be determined, and the distances involved appeared to preclude any significant economic activity in Louisiana. Federalists such as John Quincy Adams continued to ridicule the Purchase.

Nevertheless, Jefferson knew what he had achieved. Dumas Malone says it perfectly: "Jefferson's vision extended farther and comprehended more than that of anybody else in public life, and, thinking of himself as working for posterity, he was more concerned that things should be well started than that they be quickly finished. . . . In few things that he did as President was he more in character than as a patron of exploration, and he could well afford to leave his performance in that role to the judgment of posterity. One may doubt if any successor of his ever approached it."[19]

Lewis cut his life off at the midpoint. He never reached an age of maturity. Still, enough is known to allow some generalizations.

He was a good man in a crisis. If I was ever in a desperate situation—caught in a grass fire on the prairie, or sinking in a small boat in a big ocean, or the like—then I would want Meriwether Lewis for my leader. I am as one with Private Windsor, who, when about to slip off the bluff over the Marias River, barely managing to hold on, badly frightened, called out, "God, God, Captain, what shall I do?" I too would instinctively trust Lewis to know what to do.

He knew the wilderness as well as any American alive during his day, including Daniel Boone and William Clark, and was only surpassed later by John Colter and a few other of the most famous Mountain Men. His intense curiosity about everything new he saw around him was infectious. Certainly he would be anyone's first choice for a companion on an extended camping trip. Imagine sitting around the campfire while he talked about what he had seen that day.

He had a short temper and too often acted on it. His proclivity for beating Indians who displeased him, his readiness to burn their villages or even "extrapate" them, recalls to mind Jefferson's point that it would be a prodigy indeed who could grow up as a slave master and keep his humanity. Lewis could not keep his "boisterous passions" in check.

He was a man of high energy and was at times impetuous, but this was tempered by his great self-discipline. He could drive himself to the point of exhaustion, then take an hour to write about the events of the day, and another to make his celestial observations.

His talents and skills ran wider than they did deep. He knew how to do many things, from designing and building a boat to all the necessary wilderness skills. He knew a little about many of the various parts of the natural sciences. He could describe an animal, classify a plant, name the stars, manage the sextant and other instruments, dream of empire. But at none of these things was he an expert, or uniquely gifted.

Where he was unique, truly gifted, and truly great was as an explorer, where all his talents were necessary. The most important was his ability as a leader of men. He was born to leadership, and reared for it, studied it in his army career, then exercised it on the expedition.

How he led is no mystery. His techniques were time-honored. He knew his men. He saw to it that they had dry socks, enough food, sufficient clothing. He pushed them to but never beyond the breaking point. He got out of them more than they knew they had to give. His concern for them was that of a father for his son. He was the head of a family.

He could lose his temper with them, and berate them in front of their fellow soldiers. He could be even sterner: he had a few of them take fifty lashes well laid on. But in the judgment of the enlisted men, he was fair.

He didn't make many mistakes. His orders were clear, concise, and correct. Perhaps the finest tribute to his leadership abilities came at the time of the Marias decision. All the men thought the Marias was the river to follow, but they said to Lewis and Clark "very cheerfully that they were ready to follow us any wher we thought proper to direct."

He shared the work. He cooked for his men, and poled a canoe. He was hunter and fisherman. From crossing the Lolo Trail to running the rapids of the Columbia, he never ordered the men to do what he wouldn't do. When it was appropriate, he shared the decision-making. All of it with Clark, of course, but much of it with the men too, as in deciding where to spend the winter of 1805–6.

These are some of the qualities that make for a good company commander. Lewis had them in abundance, plus some special touches that made him a much-loved commander. He had a sense, a feel, for how his family was doing. He knew exactly when to take a break, when to issue a gill, when to push for more, when to encourage, when to inspire, when to tell a joke, when to be tough.

He knew how to keep a distance between himself and the men, and just how big it should be. He knew his profession and was proud of it and one of the very best at it.

But if he was a near-perfect army officer, Lewis was a lousy politician. He was entirely unsuited to the job. Jefferson's appointment of Lewis to the governorship was a frightful misjudgment. Jefferson should have found him a post in Washington or Philadelphia and given him some War Department clerks to help with the publication process.

As governor, Lewis proved incapable of resisting the temptations of high office, incapable of managing different factions, incapable of compromise. Secretary Bates made some observations that need to be considered, even while discounting the source. Lewis had been in the army too long, just as Bates charged, and was too accustomed to military ways to be a successful governor. Lewis did have a swelled head as a result of the adulation he had received. Lewis did lose his temper too often, also just as Bates said. He would never have been a successful politician.

As a man, he was full of contradictions. He had been a curious, active boy; a hard-drinking, hard-riding army officer; an intensely partisan secretary to the president; an eager explorer; a scientific scholar who paid close attention to detail; a Philadelphia playboy (yet a man who lost Letitia Breckenridge to Robert Gamble, a rich layabout Virginia aristocrat—a life Lewis might have chosen); an overeager governor and speculator in land; a drug taker and an alcoholic.

But he was a great company commander, the greatest of all American explorers, and in the top rank of world explorers.

Lewis's determination to "advance the information of the succeeding generation," the vow he had made on his thirty-first birthday, on the Lemhi Pass in 1805, he fulfilled. Not so completely as he would have liked, in the form of the published journals. But his 1805 report from Fort Mandan, along with Clark's map, were printed and widely distributed and had a major impact.

His successful voyage was an inspiration in itself. As for information, he had filled in the main outlines of the previously blank map of the northwestern part of the current United States.

He may have regarded the expedition as a failure by the time he died. No trade empire had been established, or appeared possible anytime in his generation. The Indians controlled the Missouri River and were at war with one another. British traders still encroached on American territory. Lewis's glowing reports on the soil and climate in present Missouri, Kansas, Iowa, and Nebraska had not set off a land rush; there was still plenty of land to be had in Kentucky, Illinois, Indiana, Ohio. The State Department was making no effort to claim sovereignty north of the forty-ninth parallel. The government was pressing no claim to the Oregon country. These things would come, but only with the steamship and the railroad. Until they did, the Louisiana Purchase—save for New Orleans—was exactly what Lewis called it in his Indian-policy paper, a "barren waste."

Had Lewis lived, he would have seen steamships and railroads.*

Lewis's suicide has hurt his reputation. Had Cruzatte's bullet killed him, he would be honored today far more than he is; perhaps there would be a river named for him. But through most of the nineteenth century, he was relatively ignored and in some danger of being forgotten. In 1889–91, Henry Adams could write a multivolume history of the Jefferson administration and scarcely mention Meriwether Lewis or William Clark (whose reputation at that time rested far more on his accomplishments in St. Louis as superintendent of Indian affairs than on the expedition).

The publication of the Thwaites edition of the journals at the end of the century began a revival. It has continued, and the reputations of the captains have soared. Today, there are statues to Meriwether Lewis and William Clark; some towns, some counties, many high schools, and numerous streets are named for them. There is a Lewis and Clark College.

On July 28, 1805, when he named the Jefferson River, Lewis wrote in his journal that he had done so "in honor [of] that illustrious personage Thomas Jefferson President of the United States [and] the author of our enterprize." In that spirit, it is fitting that Jefferson should get the last word.

In his 1813 letter, Jefferson wrote a one-sentence description of Lewis that is as fine a tribute to a subordinate as any president of the

---

* There is a poignant item in the Missouri *Gazette* of August 31, 1808, a report on "an interesting curiosity," the steamboat, which could proceed upriver "without oars or sails, propelled through the element by invisible agency, at a rate of four miles an hour." It was able to go from New York to Albany, a distance of 160 miles, in thirty-two hours, carrying more than a hundred passengers and great quantities of goods. Lewis must have read it.

United States has ever written. It is impossible to imagine higher praise from a better source:

"Of courage undaunted, possessing a firmness & perseverance of purpose which nothing but impossibilities could divert from it's direction, careful as a father of those committed to his charge, yet steady in the maintenance of order & discipline, intimate with the Indian character, customs & principles, habituated to the hunting life, guarded by exact observation of the vegetables & animals of his own country, against losing time in the description of objects already possessed, honest, disinterested, liberal, of sound understanding and a fidelity to truth so scrupulous that whatever he should report would be as certain as if seen by ourselves, with all these qualifications as if selected and implanted by nature in one body, for this express purpose, I could have no hesitation in confiding the enterprize to him."[20]

NOTES

1: YOUTH

1. Edgar Woods, *Albemarle County in Virginia* (Bridgewater, Va.: Green Bookman, 1932), pp. 22–23.
2. Rochonne Abrams, "The Colonial Childhood of Meriwether Lewis," *Bulletin of the Missouri Historical Society*, vol. XXXIV, no. 4, pt. 1 (July 1978), p. 218.
3. Jefferson's biography of Lewis is reprinted in Donald Jackson, ed., *Letters of the Lewis and Clark Expedition, with Related Documents: 1783–1854*, 2nd ed. (Urbana: University of Illinois Press, 1978), vol. II, p. 586.
4. Dumas Malone, *Jefferson the Virginian*, vol. I of *Jefferson and His Time* (Boston: Little, Brown, 1948), p. 23; Fawn M. Brodie, *Thomas Jefferson: An Intimate History* (New York: W. W. Norton, 1974), p. 36.
5. Abrams, "Colonial Childhood," p. 219.
6. Jackson, *Letters*, vol. II, pp. 591–92.
7. Ibid., p. 587.
8. Ibid.
9. Richard Dillon, *Meriwether Lewis: A Biography* (New York: Coward-McCann, 1965), pp. 8–9; John Bakeless, *Lewis and Clark: Partners in Discovery* (New York: William Morrow, 1947), pp. 8–13.
10. Jackson, *Letters*, vol. II, p. 587.
11. Bakeless, *Lewis and Clark*, p. 13.
12. Jackson, *Letters*, vol. I, p. 225.
13. Bakeless, *Lewis and Clark*, pp. 16–17.
14. Ibid.
15. Malone, *Jefferson the Virginian*, p. 390.
16. Woods, *Albemarle County*, p. 26.
17. Jackson, *Letters*, vol. II, p. 587.
18. Abrams, "Colonial Childhood," p. 224.
19. Dillon, *Lewis*, p. 12.
20. Bakeless, *Lewis and Clark*, p. 14.
21. Abrams, "Colonial Childhood," p. 224.
22. Malone, *Jefferson the Virginian*, p. 40.
23. ML to Lucy Markes [sic], May 12, 1789, Lewis Papers.
24. ML to Lucy Marks, n.d., Lewis Papers.
25. ML to Rheubin [sic], March 7, n.y., Lewis Papers.

26. From "The Autobiography of Peachy R. Gilmer," reprinted in Richard Beale Davis, *Francis Walker Gilmer: Life and Learning in Jefferson's Virginia* (Richmond: Dietz Press, 1939) pp. 360–61.
27. Sarah Travers Lewis Anderson, *Lewises, Meriwethers and Their Kin* (Richmond: Dietz Press, 1938), p. 501.
28. Bakeless, *Lewis and Clark*, p. 24.
29. Dillon, *Lewis*, p. 15.
30. ML to Lucy Marks, Oct. 16, 1791, Lewis Papers.
31. ML to Lucy Marks, April 19, 1792, Lewis Papers.
32. Jackson, *Letters*, vol. I, p. 225.

2: PLANTER

1. Dumas Malone, *Jefferson the Virginian*, vol. I of *Jefferson and His Time* (Boston: Little, Brown, 1948), p. 46.
2. Ibid.
3. Ibid., p. 47.
4. Fawn M. Brodie, *Thomas Jefferson: An Intimate History* (New York: W. W. Norton, 1974), p. 39.
5. Gary Moulton, ed., *The Journals of the Lewis & Clark Expedition*, vol. 5 (Lincoln: University of Nebraska Press, 1988), p. 118.
6. Malone, *Jefferson the Virginian*, p. 86.
7. Edgar Woods, *Albemarle County in Virginia* (Bridgewater, Va.: Green Bookman, 1932), pp. 39–40.
8. Richard Dillon, *Meriwether Lewis: A Biography* (New York: Coward-McCann, 1965), p. 16.
9. Woods, *Albemarle County*, p. 40.
10. Thomas P. Slaughter, *The Whiskey Rebellion: Frontier Epilogue to the American Revolution* (New York: Oxford University Press, 1986), p. 82.
11. Malone, *Jefferson the Virginian*, pp. 439–41.
12. John Hammond Moore, *Albemarle: Jefferson's County, 1727–1976* (Charlottesville: University Press of Virginia, 1976), pp. 16–19.
13. Thomas Jefferson, *Notes on the State of Virginia*, p. 85.
14. Brodie, *Intimate History*, pp. 27, 192, 340.
15. John Chester Miller, *The Wolf by the Ears: Thomas Jefferson and Slavery* (New York: Free Press, 1977), pp. 40–41.
16. Ibid., p. 8.
17. Jefferson, *Notes on Virginia*, p. 162.
18. Miller, *Wolf by the Ears*, p. 90.
19. Ibid., p. 181.
20. Winthrop D. Jordan, *White over Black: American Attitudes Toward the Negro, 1550–1812* (Chapel Hill: University of North Carolina Press, 1968), pp. 474–75.
21. Ibid.
22. Donald Jackson, ed., *Letters of the Lewis and Clark Expedition, with Related Documents: 1783–1854* (Urbana: University of Illinois Press, 1978), vol. II, p. 587.
23. Ibid., p. 589.
24. Ibid., pp. 587–88.

3: SOLDIER

1. For a brilliant discussion, see Thomas P. Slaughter, *The Whiskey Rebellion: Frontier Epilogue to the American Revolution* (New York: Oxford University Press, 1986).
2. ML to Lucy Marks, Oct. 13, 1794, Lewis Papers.
3. Slaughter, *Whiskey Rebellion*, p. 213.
4. Ibid., pp. 215–17.
5. ML to Lucy Marks, Oct. 4, 1794, Lewis Papers.
6. ML to Lucy Marks, Oct. 13, 1794, Lewis Papers.
7. ML to Lucy Marks, Nov. 24, 1794, Lewis Papers.
8. ML to Lucy Marks, Dec. 24, 1794, Lewis Papers.
9. ML to Lucy Marks, April 6, 1795, Lewis Papers.
10. ML to Lucy Marks, May 22, 1795, Lewis Papers.
11. William B. Skelton, *An American Profession of Arms: The Army Officer Corps, 1784–1861* (Lawrence: University Press of Kansas, 1992), p. 40.
12. Ibid., p. 41; see also Norman Caldwell, "The Enlisted Soldier at the Frontier Post, 1790–1814," *Mid-America: An Historical Review*, vol. 37, no. 4 (Oct. 1955), p. 201.
13. Skelton, *American Professional*, pp 38–39.
14. Ibid., p. 44.
15. Ibid., p. 51.
16. Ibid., pp. 57, 59.
17. Ibid., p. 53.
18. ML to Lucy Marks, Nov. 23, 1795, Lewis Papers; on the fever, see Norman Caldwell, "The Frontier Army Officer, 1794–1814," *Mid-America: An Historical Review*, vol. 38, no. 1 (Jan. 1955), p. 121.
19. Eldon G. Chuinard, "The Court-Martial of Ensign Meriwether Lewis," *We Proceeded On*, vol. 8, no. 4 (Nov. 1982), pp. 12–15.
20. ML to Lucy Marks, Nov. 23, 1795, Lewis Papers.
21. Richard Dillon, *Meriwether Lewis: A Biography* (New York: Coward-McCann, 1965), pp. 21–23; John Bakeless, *Lewis and Clark: Partners in Discovery* (New York: William Morrow, 1947), p. 70.
22. Eldon G. Chuinard, "Lewis and Clark, Master Masons," *We Proceeded On*, vol. 15, no. 1 (Feb. 1989), pp. 12–15.
23. See for example ML to Lucy Marks, June 14, 1797, Lewis Papers.
24. Dillon, *Lewis*, p. 23.
25. There is great confusion over the actual numbers; for a discussion, See William Murphy, "John Adams: The Politics of the Additional Army, 1798–1800," *New England Quarterly*, vol. 52 (June 1979), pp. 234–49.
26. Skelton, *American Profession*, p. 24.
27. Bakeless, *Lewis and Clark*, p. 70.
28. Donald Jackson, ed., *Letters of the Lewis and Clark Expedition, with Related Documents: 1783–1854* (Urbana: University of Illinois Press, 1978), vol. II, p. 588.
29. Dumas Malone, *Jefferson the President: First Term, 1801–1805*, vol. IV of *Jefferson and His Time* (Boston: Little, Brown, 1970), p. 9.
30. Skelton, *American Profession*, pp. 24–25.

4: THOMAS JEFFERSON'S AMERICA

1. Henry Adams, *History of the United States of America During the Administrations of Thomas Jefferson* (New York: Library of America Edition, 1986), p. 6.
2. Ibid., p. 13.
3. Ibid., pp. 43–44.
4. Thomas P. Slaughter, *The Whiskey Rebellion: Frontier Epilogue to the American Revolution* (New York: Oxford University Press, 1986), p. 70.
5. John Hammond Moore, *Albemarle: Jefferson's County, 1727–1976* (Charlottesville: University Press of Virginia, 1976), p. 99.
6. Dumas Malone, *Jefferson the President: First Term, 1801–1805*, vol. IV of *Jefferson and His Time* (Boston: Little, Brown, 1970), p. 181.
7. Quoted in Fawn M. Brodie, *Thomas Jefferson: An Intimate History* (New York: W. W. Norton, 1974), p. 487.
8. Adams, *History*, pp. 20, 52.
9. Donald Jackson, *Thomas Jefferson and the Stony Mountains: Exploring the West from Monticello* (Urbana: University of Illinois Press, 1981), p. xi.
10. Winthrop D. Jordan, *White over black: American Attitudes Toward the Negro, 1550–1812* (Chapel Hill: University of North Carolina Press, 1968), pp. 27, 453.
11. John Chester Miller, *The Wolf by the Ears: Thomas Jefferson and Slavery* (New York: Free Press, 1977), p. 226.
12. Adams, *History*, p. 101.
13. Ibid., p. 109.

5: THE PRESIDENT'S SECRETARY

1. Donald Jackson, *Letters of the Lewis and Clark Expedition, with Related Documents: 1783–1854*, 2nd ed. (Urbana: University of Illinois Press, 1978), vol. I, p. 3.
2. Ibid., p. 2.
3. Donald Jackson, *Thomas Jefferson and the Stony Mountains: Exploring the West from Monticello* (Urbana: University of Illinois Press, 1981), p. 118.
4. Jackson, *Letters*, vol. I, p. 3.
5. ML to T. Gilmer, June 18, 1801, Lewis Papers.
6. Jackson, *Letters*, vol. I, p. 1.
7. Donald Jackson, "Jefferson, Meriwether Lewis, and the Reduction of the United States Army," *Proceedings of the American Philosophical Society*, vol. 124, no. 2 (April 1980), pp. 91–95. This article was the result of a brilliant piece of detective work by Dr. Jackson—scholarship at its absolute best. It was matched and possibly preceded by that of Theodore Crackel, but Crackel didn't publish his work until 1987.
8. William B. Skelton, *An American Profession of Arms: The Army Officer Corps, 1784–1861* (Lawrence: University Press of Kansas, 1992), p. 73.

9. Jackson, "Reduction of United States Army," p. 96.

10. Theodore J. Crackel, *Mr. Jefferson's Army: Political and Social Reform of the Military Establishment, 1801–1809* (New York: New York University Press, 1987), p. 38.

11. Jackson, *Jefferson and the Stony Mountains*, p. 121.

12. Dumas Malone, *Jefferson the President: First Term, 1801–1805*, vol. IV of *Jefferson and His Time* (Boston: Little, Brown, 1970), pp. 40–41.

13. Ibid., pp. 38–39.

14. Edwin Morris Betts and James Adam Bear, eds., *The Family Letters of Thomas Jefferson* (Charlottesville: University Press of Virginia, 1986 reprint of 1960 University of Missouri Press ed.), p. 202.

15. Jackson, *Letters*, vol. II, pp. 590, 592.

16. Malone, *Jefferson the President: First Term*, p. xiii.

17. Jackson, *Letters*, vol. II, p. 677.

18. Ibid., pp. 678–81.

19. Henry Adams, *History of the United States of America During the Administrations of Thomas Jefferson* (New York: Library of America Edition, 1975), p. 130.

20. Jackson, *Letters*, vol. II, pp. 679–81.

21. Richard Dillon, *Meriwether Lewis: A Biography* (New York: Coward-McCann, 1965), p. 30.

22. Fawn M. Brodie, *Thomas Jefferson: An Intimate History* (New York: W. W. Norton, 1974), pp. 321–22.

23. Malone, *Jefferson the President: First Term*, pp. 210–12; Adams, *History*, pp. 219–21.

24. Dillon, *Lewis*, p. 28.

6: THE ORIGINS OF THE EXPEDITION

1. Donald Jackson, *Thomas Jefferson and the Stony Mountains: Exploring the West from Monticello* (Urbana: University of Illinois Press, 1981), p. 8.

2. Donald Jackson, ed., *Letters of the Lewis and Clark Expedition, with Related Documents: 1783–1854*, 2nd ed. (Urbana: University of Illinois Press, 1978), vol. II, pp. 654–55.

3. Ibid., pp. 655–56.

4. Jackson, *Jefferson and the Stony Mountains*, pp. 48–49.

5. Ibid., pp. 46–50.

6. Jackson, *Letters*, vol. II, pp. 661–65.

7. Ibid., p. 667.

8. Ibid., p. 671.

9. Alexander Deconde, *This Affair of Louisiana* (New York: Charles Scribner's Sons, 1976), pp. 113–14.

10. Ibid., pp. 114–15.

11. On Mackenzie, see Arlen Large, "North and South of Lewis and Clark," *We Proceeded On*, vol. 10, no. 4 (Nov. 1984), pp. 8–12; on the sextant, see Arlen Large, "Fort Mandan's Dancing Longitude," *We Proceeded On*, vol. 13, no. 1 (Feb. 1987), pp. 12–14.

12. Jackson, *Jefferson and the Stony Mountains*, p. 94.
13. John Logan Allen, *Passage Through the Garden: Lewis and Clark and the Image of the American Northwest* (Urbana: University of Illinois Press, 1975), p. 178.
14. Jackson, *Jefferson and the Stony Mountains*, p. 95.
15. Jackson, *Letters*, vol. I, pp. 16–17.
16. Allen, *Passage Through the Garden*, p. 73.
17. Jackson, *Jefferson and the Stony Mountains*, p. 30.
18. Silvio Bedini, "The Scientific Instruments of the Lewis and Clark Expedition," *Great Plains Quarterly*, Winter 1984, pp. 54–69.
19. Jackson, *Letters*, vol. I, p. 5.
20. Ibid., p. 9.
21. Jackson, *Jefferson and the Stony Mountains*, vol. I, pp. 126–27.
22. Jackson, *Letters*, vol. II, pp. 18–19.

7: PREPARING FOR THE EXPEDITION

1. Donald Jackson, ed., *Letters of the Lewis and Clark Expedition, with Related Documents: 1783–1854* (Urbana: University of Illinois Press, 1978), vol. I, p. 21.
2. Ibid., p. 44.
3. Ibid., p. 40.
4. Paul Russell Cutright, "Contributions of Philadelphia to Lewis and Clark History," special issue, *We Proceeded On*, July 1982.
5. Carl Russell, "The Guns of the Lewis and Clark Expedition," *North Dakota History*, vol. 27 (Winter 1960), pp. 25–33.
6. Jackson, *Letters*, vol. I, p. 42.
7. Ibid., p. 43.
8. Ibid., pp. 39–40.
9. ML to William Irvin, April 15, 1803, Lewis Papers.
10. Donald Jackson, *Thomas Jefferson and the Stony Mountains: Exploring the West from Monticello* (Urbana: University of Illinois Press, 1981), pp. 136–37.
11. Jackson, *Letters*, vol. I, p. 40.
12. Cutright, "Contributions of Philadelphia," p. 3.
13. Ibid., p. 51.
14. Jackson, *Letters*, vol. I, p. 48.
15. Ibid., pp. 48–49.
16. Cutright, "Contributions of Philadelphia," pp. 16–17.
17. Jackson, *Letters*, vol. I, p. 55.
18. Ibid., p. 50.
19. Ibid., p. 54.
20. Ibid., vol. II, pp. 680–81.
21. Ibid., p. 52.
22. Elijah Criswell, *Lewis and Clark: Linguistic Pioneers* (Columbia: University of Missouri Press, 1940).
23. Cutright, "Contributions of Philadelphia," pp. 14–15.
24. Ibid., pp. 6, 12–13.

25. Jackson, *Letters*, vol. I, p. 53.
26. John Logan Allen, *Passage Through the Garden: Lewis and Clark and the Image of the American Northwest* (Urbana: University of Illinois Press, 1975), pp. 97, 87.
27. Jackson, *Letters*, vol. I, p. 54.

8: WASHINGTON TO PITTSBURGH

1. Donald Jackson, ed., *Letters of the Lewis and Clark Expedition, with Related Documents: 1783–1854*, 2nd ed. (Urbana: University of Illinois Press, 1978), vol. I, p. 34.
2. Ibid., p. 35.
3. Ibid., pp. 32–33.
4. Ibid., pp. 61–66.
5. Donald Jackson, *Thomas Jefferson and the Stony Mountains: Exploring the West from Monticello* (Urbana: University of Illinois Press, 1981), p. 139.
6. Jackson, *Letters*, vol. I, pp. 68, 76.
7. Ibid.
8. Ibid., p. 68.
9. Ibid.
10. Jackson, *Jefferson and the Stony Mountains*, p. 138.
11. Jackson, *Letters*, vol. I, pp. 57–60.
12. Ibid., p. 114.
13. Ibid., p. 100.
14. Ibid., pp. 102–3.
15. Ibid., p. 107.
16. Henry Adams, *History of the United States of America During the Administrations of Thomas Jefferson* (New York: Library of America Edition, 1986), pp. 334–35.
17. Quoted in Floyd Shoemaker, "The Louisiana Purchase, 1803," *Missouri Historical Review*, vol. 48 (Oct. 1953), p. 9.
18. Jackson, *Letters*, vol. II, p. 591.
19. Alexander Deconde, *This Affair of Louisiana* (New York: Charles Scribner's Sons, 1976), pp. 178–79.
20. Arlen Large, "Trailing Lewis and Clark: 'The Spirit of Party,'" *We Proceeded On*, vol. 6, no. 1 (Feb. 1990), p. 14.
21. Jackson, *Letters*, vol. I, pp. 108–9.
22. Thomas Maitland Marshall, *A History of the Western Boundaries of the Louisiana Purchase, 1819–1841* (Berkeley: University of California Press, 1914), p. 14.
23. Jackson, *Letters*, vol. I, pp. 106–7.
24. Ibid., p. 110.
25. Ibid., p. 112.
26. Ibid., pp. 110–11.
27. Ibid., p. 113.
28. Ibid., pp. 115–16.
29. Ibid., pp. 121–22.

30. See Richard C. Boss, "Keelboat, Pirogue, and Canoe: Vessels Used by the Lewis and Clark Corps of Discovery," *Nautical Research Journal*, June 1993.
31. Jackson, *Letters*, vol. I, p. 122.

9: DOWN THE OHIO

1. Roy Chatters, "The Not-So-Enigmatic Lewis and Clark Airgun," *We Proceeded On*, vol. 3, no. 2 (May 1977), pp. 4–7.
2. Gary Moulton, ed., *The Journals of the Lewis & Clark Expedition*, vol. 2 (Lincoln, University of Nebraska Press, 1986), p. 261.
3. Quoted in Paul Russell Cutright, *Lewis and Clark: Pioneering Naturalists* (Urbana: University of Illinois Press, 1986), p. 45.
4. Moulton, ed., *Journals*, vol. 2, p. 35.
5. Paul Russell Cutright, "Meriwether Lewis's 'Coloring of Events,'" *We Proceeded On*, vol. 11, no. 1 (Feb. 1985), pp. 10–16.
6. Moulton, ed., *Journals*, vol. 2, p. 34. Paul Russell Cutright, "The Journal of Captain Meriwether Lewis," *We Proceeded On*, vol. 10, no. 1 (Feb. 1984), pp. 8–10, makes a strong case for the proposition that Lewis had long lapses in which he did not keep a journal, without explaining why.
7. Donald Jackson, ed., *Letters of the Lewis and Clark Expedition, with Related Documents: 1783–1854*, 2nd ed. (Urbana: University of Illinois Press, 1978), vol. I, p. 124.
8. Eldon Chuinard, *Only One Man Died: The Medical Aspects of the Lewis and Clark Expedition* (Glendale, Calif.: Arthur Clark Company, 1980), p. 175.
9. Robert Hunt, "The Blood Meal: Mosquitos and Agues on the Lewis and Clark Expedition," *We Proceeded On*, vol. 18, no. 3 (May and Aug. 1992), p. 5.
10. Dr. Joseph DiPalma, quoted in Chuinard, *Only One Man Died*, p. 156.
11. Hunt, "Blood Meal," pp. 7–8.
12. Ibid., p. 7.
13. Jackson, *Letters*, vol. I, pp. 117–18.
14. Ibid., p. 125.
15. Ibid., pp. 125–30.
16. Chuinard, *Only One Man Died*, p. 105.
17. Jackson, *Letters*, vol. I, p. 131.
18. Ibid., pp. 136–38.
19. Roy Appleman, *Lewis and Clark* (Washington, D.C.: National Park Service, 1975), p. 52.
20. Olin D. Wheeler, *The Trail of Lewis and Clark, 1804–1806* (New York, 1904), vol. I, p. 122.
21. Appleman, *Lewis and Clark*, p. 57.
22. Arlen Large, "'Additions to the Party': How an Expedition Grew and Grew," *We Proceeded On*, vol. 16, no. 1 (Feb. 1990), pp. 4–7.
23. Arlen Large, "Lewis and Clark: Part Time Astronomers." *We Proceeded On*, vol. 5, no. 1 (Feb. 1979), pp. 8–10.

10: UP THE MISSISSIPPI TO WINTER CAMP

1. Arlen Large, "'Additions to the Party': How an Expedition Grew and Grew," *We Proceeded On*, vol. 16, no. 1 (Feb. 1990), p. 7.
2. Ibid.
3. Donald Jackson, ed., *Letters of the Lewis and Clark Expedition with Related Documents: 1783–1854*, 2nd ed. (Urbana: University of Illinois Press, 1978), vol. I, p. 142.
4. Ibid., p. 143.
5. Ibid., pp. 148–57.
6. Roy Appleman, *Lewis and Clark* (Washington, D.C.: National Park Service, 1975), p. 73.
7. Samuel W. Thomas, "William Clark's 1795 and 1797 Journals and Their Significance," *Missouri Historical Society Bulletin*, July 1969, pp. 277–95.
8. Richard E. Oglesby, *Manuel Lisa and the Opening of the Missouri Fur Trade* (Norman: University of Oklahoma Press, 1963), p. 30.
9. Jackson, *Letters*, vol. I, pp. 217–18, has the list.
10. Ibid., p. 144.
11. Ibid., p. 163.
12. Ibid., pp. 165–66.
13. Paul Russell Cutright, *Lewis and Clark: Pioneering Naturalists* (Urbana: University of Illinois Press, 1986), pp. 41–42.
14. Donald Jackson, *Thomas Jefferson and the Stony Mountains: Exploring the West from Monticello* (Urbana: University of Illinois Press, 1981), p. 161.
15. Michael Brodhead, "The Military Naturalist: A Lewis and Clark Heritage," *We Proceeded On*, vol. 9, no. 4 (Nov. 1983), p. 6.
16. Jackson, *Letters*, vol. I, p. 173.
17. Appleman, *Lewis and Clark*, pp. 67–68.
18. Jackson, *Letters*, vol. I, pp. 167–68.
19. Appleman, *Lewis and Clark*, p. 73.
20. Patrick Gass, *A Journal of the Voyages and Travels of a Corps of Discovery Under the Command of Capt. Lewis and Capt. Clark*, ed. David McKeehan (Minneapolis: Ross and Haines, 1958), p. 12.
21. Jackson, *Letters*, vol. I, pp. 176–77.

11: READY TO DEPART

1. Donald Jackson, ed., *Letters of the Lewis and Clark Expedition with Related Documents: 1783–1854*, 2nd ed. (Urbana: University of Illinois Press, 1978), vol. I, p. 179.
2. Ibid., p. 173.
3. Ibid., p. 179.
4. Ibid., vol. II, pp. 571–72.
5. Theodore J. Crackel, *Mr. Jefferson's Army: Political and Social Reform of the Military Establishment, 1801–1809* (New York: New York University Press, 1987), pp. 109–10.
6. Jackson, *Letters*, vol. I, pp. 189–90.
7. Ibid., pp. 192–95.

8. Roy Appleman, *Lewis and Clark* (Washington, D.C.: National Park Service, 1975), p. 79.
9. Jackson, *Letters*, vol. I, p. 196.

12: UP THE MISSOURI

1. Donald Jackson, *Thomas Jefferson and the Stony Mountains: Exploring the West from Monticello* (Urbana: University of Illinois Press, 1981), p. 163.
2. Ibid., p. 186.
3. Quoted in Robert Hunt, "Gills and Drams of Consolation: Ardent Spirits on the Lewis and Clark Expedition," *We Proceeded On*, vol. 17, no. 3 (Feb. 1991), p. 19.
4. Ibid., pp. 20–22.
5. Jackson, *Jefferson and the Stony Mountains*, p. 182.
6. Paul Russell Cutright, *Lewis and Clark: Pioneering Naturalists* (Urbana: University of Illinois Press, 1986), p. 70.

13: ENTERING INDIAN COUNTRY

1. For a discussion, see Paul Russell Cutright, *Lewis and Clark: Pioneering Naturalists* (Urbana: University of Illinois Press, 1986).
2. James P. Ronda, *Lewis and Clark Among the Indians* (Lincoln: University of Nebraska Press, 1984), p. 3.
3. Ibid., p. 7.
4. Ibid., p. 9.
5. Ibid.
6. Ibid., p. 189.
7. Donald Jackson, ed., *Letters of the Lewis and Clark Expedition, with Related Documents: 1783–1854*, 2nd ed. (Urbana: University of Illinois Press, 1978), vol. I, pp. 203–8.
8. Ronda, *Lewis and Clark Among the Indians*, p. 19.
9. Eldon G. Chuinard, *Only One Man Died: The Medical Aspects of the Lewis and Clark Expedition* (Glendale, Calif.: Arthur Clark Company, 1980), p. 167.
10. Ronda, *Lewis and Clark Among the Indians*, p. 19.

14: ENCOUNTER WITH THE SIOUX

1. James P. Ronda, *Lewis and Clark Among the Indians* (Lincoln: University of Nebraska Press, 1984), p. 33. Ronda has a brilliant chapter on this event.
2. Ibid., p. 36.
3. Ibid., pp. 39–40.

15: TO THE MANDANS

1. Raymond Darwin Burroughs, *The Natural History of the Lewis and Clark Expedition* (East Lansing: Michigan State University Press, 1961), p. 236.

2. James P. Ronda, *Lewis and Clark Among the Indians* (Lincoln: University of Nebraska Press, 1984), chap. 3, is an excellent description of the Arikara.

3. Ibid., p. 55.

4. Ibid., p. 63.

5. Ibid., chap. 4, is indispensable on the Mandans and Hidatsas.

6. Donald Jackson, ed., *Letters of the Lewis and Clark Expedition, with Related Documents: 1783–1854,* 2nd ed. (Urbana: University of Illinois Press, 1978), vol. I, pp. 213–14.

7. Gary Moulton, ed., *The Journals of the Lewis & Clark Expedition,* vol. 3 (Lincoln: University of Nebraska Press, 1987), p. 241, n. 2, discusses Larocque. Larocque's journal is printed in L. R. Masson, *Les Bourgeois de la Compagnie du Nord-Ouest* (New York: Antiquarian Press, 1960 reprint), pp. 304–11.

8. MacKenzie's journal is reprinted in Masson, *Bourgeois,* pp. 330–39.

9. Quoted in Ronda, *Lewis and Clark Among the Indians,* p. 88.

10. Reuben Gold Thwaites, ed., *Original Journals of the Lewis and Clark Expedition* (New York: Arno Press reprint, 1969), vol. I, p. 227, n. 1; Masson, *Bourgeois,* p. 310.

11. Masson, *Bourgeois,* pp. 336–37.

12. Ibid., p. 330.

13. Thwaites, ed., *Original Journals,* vol. I, p. 227, n. 1.

14. See Lewis's entry of Aug. 24, 1805.

15. Ronda, *Lewis and Clark Among the Indians,* p. 93.

16. Masson, *Bourgeois,* p. 331.

16: WINTER AT FORT MANDAN

1. Arlen J. Large, "'. . . It Thundered and Lightened': The Weather Observations of Lewis and Clark," *We Proceeded On,* vol. 12, no. 2 (May 1986), p. 8.

2. James Ronda, "A Most Perfect Harmony: Life at Fort Mandan," *We Proceeded On,* vol. 14, no. 4 (Nov. 1988), p. 8.

3. James P. Ronda, *Lewis and Clark Among the Indians* (Lincoln: University of Nebraska Press, 1984), p. 109.

4. Ibid., pp. 100–103.

5. Ibid., p. 107.

6. Eldon G. Chuinard, *Only One Man Died: The Medical Aspects of the Lewis and Clark Expedition* (Glendale, Calif.: Arthur Clark Company, 1980), p. 267.

7. Ibid., p. 268.

8. Ibid., p. 264.

9. For a discussion of food intake in the conditions facing the expedition, see Jim Smithers, "Food for Mackenzie," *We Proceeded On,* vol. 15, no. 1 (Feb. 1989).

10. Ronda, *Lewis and Clark Among the Indians,* p. 103.

11. Donald Jackson, ed., *Thomas Jefferson and the Stony Mountains: Exploring the West from Monticello* (Urbana: University of Illinois Press, 1981), p. 172.

12. Donald Jackson, *Letters of the Lewis and Clark Expedition, with Related Documents: 1783–1854*, 2nd ed. (Urbana: University of Illinois Press, 1978), vol. I, p. 218.

17: REPORT FROM FORT MANDAN

1. Gary Moulton, ed., *The Journals of the Lewis & Clark Expedition*, vol. 3 (Lincoln: University of Nebraska Press, 1987), p. 333.
2. L. R. Masson, *Les Bourgeois de la Compagnie du Nord-Ouest* (New York: Antiquarian Press, 1960 reprint), pp. 336–37.
3. James P. Ronda, *Lewis and Clark Among the Indians* (Lincoln: University of Nebraska Press, 1984), p. 121.
4. The text I use here is Moulton, ed., *Journals*, vol. 3, pp. 336–69.
5. Donald Jackson, ed., *Letters of the Lewis and Clark Expedition, with Related Documents: 1783–1854*, 2nd ed. (Urbana: University of Illinois Press, 1978), vol. I, pp. 222–23.
6. Moulton, ed., *Journals*, vol. 3, pp. 386–450.
7. Jackson, *Letters*, vol. I, p. 220.
8. Eldon G. Chuinard, *Only One Man Died: The Medical Aspects of the Lewis and Clark Expedition* (Glendale, Calif.: Arthur Clark Company, 1980), pp. 271–72. Chuinard notes that the plant was widely known for its anti-snakebite properties among frontiersmen.
9. Jackson, *Letters*, vol. I, pp. 232–33.

18: FROM FORT MANDAN TO MARIAS RIVER

1. Eldon G. Chuinard, *Only One Man Died: The Medical Aspects of the Lewis and Clark Expedition* (Glendale, Calif.: Arthur Clark Company, 1980), p. 43.
2. Ibid., pp. 158, 279; Gary Moulton, ed., *The Journals of the Lewis & Clark Expedition* (Lincoln: University of Nebraska Press, 1989), n. for April 24, 1805.
3. Chuinard, *Only One Man Died*, p. 24; Lewis's entry of May 10, 1805.
4. Gary Moulton has an excellent chapter on the question of whether Lewis was a risk-taker, using this incident among others to argue that with Lewis reason won out over impulse, restraint over rashness. See "Lewis and Clark: Meeting the Challenges of the Trail," in Carlos Schwantee, ed., *Encounters with a Distant Land: Exploration and the Great Northwest* (Moscow: University of Idaho Press, 1994), p. 105.
5. Entry of May 30, 1805.
6. Donald Jackson, *Thomas Jefferson and the Stony Mountains: Exploring the West from Monticello* (Urbana: University of Illinois Press, 1981), pp. 194–95.
7. According to Moulton (n. 6 for entry of May 31, 1805), it was not a distinct species, as Lewis supposed, but a cross fox, a color phase of the red fox.

20: THE GREAT PORTAGE

1. Eldon G. Chuinard, *Only One Man Died: The Medical Aspects of the Lewis and Clark Expedition* (Glendale, Calif.: Arthur Clark Company, 1980), p. 291.
2. Ibid., p. 290.
3. Ibid., p. 156.
4. Paul Russell Cutright, *Lewis and Clark: Pioneering Naturalists* (Urbana: University of Illinois Press, 1969), p. 332.

21: LOOKING FOR THE SHOSHONES

1. Donald Jackson, *Thomas Jefferson and the Stony Mountains: Exploring the West from Monticello* (Urbana: University of Illinois Press, 1981), p. 197.
2. Donald Jackson, *Among the Sleeping Giants*, p. 16.
3. James P. Ronda, *Lewis and Clark Among the Indians* (Lincoln: University of Nebraska Press, 1984), p. 140; Roy Appleman, *Lewis and Clark* (Washington, D.C.: National Park Service, 1975), p. 155.
4. Ronda, *Lewis and Clark Among the Indians*, p. 140.
5. John Logan Allen, "Summer of Decision: Lewis and Clark in Montana, 1805," *We Proceeded On*, vol. 8, no. 4 (Fall 1976), p. 10.

22: OVER THE CONTINENTAL DIVIDE

1. James P. Ronda, *Lewis and Clark Among the Indians* (Lincoln: University of Nebraska Press, 1984), p. 143.
2. Gary Moulton, ed., *The Journals of the Lewis & Clark Expedition*, vol. 5 (Lincoln: University of Nebraska Press, 1988), p. 116.
3. Biddle edition of the *Journals*.
4. Ronda, *Lewis and Clark Among the Indians*, p. 147.
5. Ibid., p. 154.

24: OVER THE BITTERROOTS

1. Harry M. Majors, "Lewis and Clark Enter the Rocky Mountains," *Northwest Discovery*, vol. 7 (April and May 1986), pp. 4–120, as quoted in *The Journals of the Lewis & Clark Expedition*, Gary Moulton, ed. (Lincoln: University of Nebraska Press, 1988), vol. 5, p. 186.
2. Quoted in James P. Ronda, *Lewis and Clark Among the Indians* (Lincoln: University of Nebraska Press, 1984), p. 156.
3. Roy Appleman, *Lewis and Clark* (Washington, D.C.: National Park Service, 1975), p. 169. No matter how hungry, the Shoshones and the Salish never ate horsemeat. The Americans preferred not to but would if necessary.
4. Quoted in Ronda, *Lewis and Clark Among the Indians*, p. 157.
5. Lewis made the comment in a letter of Sept. 29, 1806, reprinted in Donald Jackson, ed., *Letters of the Lewis and Clark Expedition, with Related*

Documents: 1783–1854, 2nd ed. (Urbana: University of Illinois Press, 1978), vol. I, p. 339.

6. Ibid.

7. Eldon G. Chuinard, *Only One Man Died: The Medical Aspects of the Lewis and Clark Expedition* (Glendale, Calif.: Arthur Clark Company, 1980), p. 321.

8. Gary Moulton, ed., *The Journals of the Lewis & Clark Expedition*, vol. 5 (Lincoln: University of Nebraska Press, 1989), p. 225; Ronda, *Lewis and Clark Among the Indians*, p. 159.

9. Jackson, *Letters*, vol. I, p. 339.

25: DOWN THE COLUMBIA

1. Verne F. Ray, "Lewis and Clark and the Nez Percé Indians," *The Great Western Series*, no. 10 (Dec. 1971), pp. 1–2.

2. James P. Ronda, *Lewis and Clark Among the Indians* (Lincoln: University of Nebraska Press, 1984), pp. 171–72.

3. Ibid., p. 178.

4. Gary Moulton, ed., *The Journals of the Lewis & Clark Expedition*, vol. 6 (Lincoln: University of Nebraska Press, 1989), p. 104.

26: FORT CLATSOP

1. James P. Ronda, *Lewis and Clark Among the Indians* (Lincoln: University of Nebraska Press, 1984), pp. 202–3, has an extended discussion of this point. He goes further in condemning the captains for their attitude than I would.

2. Ibid.

3. Roy Appleman, *Lewis and Clark* (Washington, D.C.: National Park Service, 1975), p. 197.

4. Paul Russell Cutright, *Lewis and Clark: Pioneering Naturalists* (Urbana: University of Illinois Press, 1986), pp. 258–60.

5. Ibid., p. 261.

6. Donald Jackson, ed., *Letters of the Lewis and Clark Expedition, with Related Documents: 1783–1854*, 2nd ed. (Urbana: University of Illinois Press, 1978), vol. I, p. 218.

7. Cutright, *Lewis and Clark*, p. 398.

8. John Logan Allen, *Passage Through the Garden: Lewis and Clark and the Image of the American Northwest* (Urbana: University of Illinois Press, 1975), p. 324.

9. Ibid., p. 325.

10. Jackson, *Letters*, vol. I, p. 336.

11. Ronda, *Lewis and Clark Among the Indians*, pp. 210–11.

27: LEWIS AS ETHNOGRAPHER: *The Clatsops and the Chinooks*

1. Cutright, *Lewis and Clark: Pioneering Naturalists*, pp. 272–73; for a full discussion of Lewis and Clark with the Chinookans, see chapter six, "Cloth Men Soldiers," in Robert H. Ruby and John A. Brown, *The Chinook Indians:*

Traders of the Lower Columbia River (Norman: University of Oklahoma Press, 1976).

28: JEFFERSON AND THE WEST

1. Donald Jackson, ed., *Letters of the Lewis and Clark Expedition, with Related Documents: 1783–1854*, 2nd ed. (Urbana: University of Illinois Press, 1978), vol. I, pp. 199–200.
2. Ibid., p. 209.
3. Ibid., pp. 201–2.
4. Ibid., p. 215.
5. Ibid., p. 216.
6. Ibid., vol. II, p. 215.
7. Ibid., p. 687.
8. Donald Jackson, *Thomas Jefferson and the Stony Mountains: Exploring the West from Monticello* (Urbana: University of Illinois Press, 1981), p. 153.
9. Ibid.
10. David J. Weber, *The Spanish Frontier in North America* (New Haven: Yale University Press, 1992), p. 294.
11. Jackson, *Letters*, vol. I, pp. 688–89.
12. Ibid., pp. 259, 264–65.
13. Jackson, *Jefferson and the Stony Mountains*, p. 214.
14. Jackson, *Letters*, vol. II, p. 155.
15. Ibid., p. 689.
16. Jackson, *Jefferson and the Stony Mountains*, pp. 216.
17. Ibid., pp. 216–17.
18. Ibid., p. 217.
19. Ibid., p. 214.
20. Jackson, *Letters*, vol. I, p. 245.
21. Ibid., vol. II, p. 691.
22. Edwin Morris Betts and James Adam Bear, eds., *The Family Letters of Thomas Jefferson* (Charlottesville: University Press of Virginia, 1986 reprint of 1960 University of Missouri Press ed.), p. 275.
23. Jackson, *Letters*, vol. I, p. 251.
24. Dumas Malone, *Jefferson the President: Second Term* (Boston: Little, Brown, 1974), p. 189.
25. Ibid., p. 189.
26. Ibid., p. 190.
27. Paul Russell Cutright, *A History of the Lewis and Clark Journals* (Norman: University of Oklahoma Press, 1976), pp. 13–14.
28. Malone, *Jefferson the President: Second Term*, p. 190.
29. Jackson, *Letters*, vol. I, pp. 281–82, 286.
30. Ibid., pp. 290–91.
31. Gary Moulton, ed., *The Journals of the Lewis & Clark Expedition*, vol. 6 (Lincoln: University of Nebraska Press, 1989), p. 86.
32. Arlen Large, "The Empty Anchorage: Why No Ship Came for Lewis and Clark," *We Proceeded On*, vol. 15, no. 1 (Feb. 1989), p. 9.
33. Jackson, *Letters*, vol. II, p. 650.

29: RETURN TO THE NEZ PERCÉ

1. Gary Moulton, ed., *The Journals of the Lewis & Clark Expedition*, vol. 7 (Lincoln: University of Nebraska Press, 1990), p. 186.
2. James P. Ronda, *Lewis and Clark Among the Indians* (Lincoln: University of Nebraska Press, 1984), p. 225.
3. Moulton, ed., *Journals*, vol. 7, p. 348.
4. Ibid., p. 297.
5. Cutright, *Lewis and Clark: Pioneering Naturalists* (Urbana: University of Illinois Press, 1986), pp. 297–99.

30: THE LOLO TRAIL

1. James P. Ronda, *Lewis and Clark Among the Indians* (Lincoln: University of Nebraska Press, 1984), p. 236.
2. The letter, written on July 1 but dated July 20, is in Donald Jackson, ed., *Letters of the Lewis and Clark Expedition, with Related Documents: 1783–1854*, 2nd ed. (Urbana: University of Illinois Press, 1978), vol. I, pp. 309–13.

31: THE MARIAS EXPLORATION

1. Paul Russell Cutright, *Lewis and Clark: Pioneering Naturalists* (Urbana: University of Illinois Press, 1986), p. 313.
2. Arlen Large's comments on the manuscript, in author's file.
3. James P. Ronda, *Lewis and Clark Among the Indians* (Lincoln: University of Nebraska Press, 1984), p. 239.
4. Ibid., p. 241.

32: THE LAST LEG

1. Eldon G. Chuinard, *Only One Man Died: The Medical Aspects of the Lewis and Clark Expedition* (Glendale, Calif.: Arthur Clark Company, 1980), pp. 392–94.
2. Quoted in Reuben Gold Thwaites, ed., *Original Journals of the Lewis and Clark Expedition* (New York: Arno Press reprint, 1969), vol. VII, p. 347.

33: REPORTING TO THE PRESIDENT

1. Verne Ray, "Lewis and Clark and the Nez Percé Indians," *The Great Western Series*, no. 10 (Dec. 1971), has a brilliant discussion of Lewis's plan.
2. David Lavender, *The Way to the Western Sea: Lewis and Clark Across the Continent* (New York: Harper & Row, 1988), p. 374. Lavender provides an excellent discussion of Lewis's publicity program.
3. Donald Jackson, *Letters of the Lewis and Clark Expedition, with Related Documents: 1783–1854*, 2nd ed. (Urbana: University of Illinois Press, 1978), vol. I, p. 361.

4. Allan Nevins, ed., *The Diary of John Quincy Adams, 1794–1845* (New York: Frederick Ungar, 1970), pp. 25, 26.

5. Henry Adams, *History of the United States of America During the Administrations of Thomas Jefferson* (New York: Library of America Edition, 1986), pp. 751–52.

6. Dumas Malone, *Jefferson the President: Second Term* (Boston: Little, Brown, 1974), p. 200.

7. Lewis's report is printed in its first draft and in its final form in Jackson, *Letters*, vol. I, pp. 317–25.

8. Ibid., p. 391.

9. Ibid., p. 369.

10. Ibid., p. 330.

11. Quoted in Arlen Large, "Expedition Aftermath: The Jawbone Journals," *We Proceeded On*, vol. 17, no. 1 (Feb. 1991), p. 13.

12. Ibid.

13. Quoted in Reuben Gold Thwaites, ed., *Original Journals of the Lewis and Clark Expedition* (New York: Arno Press reprint, 1969), vol. VII, pp. 347–48.

14. Ibid.

15. James Ronda discovered this account of the ball at Christy's in the October 11, 1806, Frankfort *Western World* and reprinted it in "St. Louis Welcomes and Toasts the Lewis and Clark Expedition," *We Proceeded On*, vol. 13, no. 1 (Feb. 1987), pp. 19–20.

16. Jackson, *Letters*, vol. I, pp. 336–42.

17. Quoted in Thwaites, ed., *Original Journals*, vol. VII, p. 347.

18. Jefferson's comments appear in Jackson, *Letters*, vol. II, p. 612.

19. Ibid., vol. I, p. 345.

20. Ibid., vol. II, p. 386; vol. I, p. 346.

21. Ibid., vol. I, pp. 348–49.

22. Ibid., p. 345.

23. Ibid., vol. II, p. 424.

24. Richard Oglesby, *Manuel Lisa and the Opening of the Missouri Fur Trade* (Norman: University of Oklahoma Press, 1963), p. 40.

25. Jackson, *Letters*, vol. I, p. 351.

26. Ibid.

27. See Eldon G. Chuinard, "Thomas Jefferson and the Corps of Discovery: Could He Have Done More?," *American West*, vol. 12, no. 6 (1975), pp. 12–13.

28. Jackson, *Letters*, vol. I, p. 352.

29. Ibid., pp. 239, 356–58; vol. II, p. 694.

30. Ibid., vol. II, pp. 692–94.

31. Malone, *Jefferson the President: Second Term*, p. 202.

32. Quoted in James Ronda, "A Knowledge of Distant Parts: The Shaping of the Lewis and Clark Expedition," *Montana: The Magazine of Western History*, vol. 41, no. 4 (Autumn 1991), p. 8. This is a seminal article.

33. Ibid., p. 9.

34. Donald Jackson, "The Public Image of Lewis and Clark," *Pacific Northwest Quarterly*, Jan. 1966, p. 3.

35. Ronda, "Knowledge of Distant Parts," p. 9.

36. Quoted in ibid.
37. We know this from Jefferson's remark in a 1816 letter, in Jackson, *Letters,* vol. II, p. 612.

34: WASHINGTON

1. Donald Jackson, ed., *Letters of the Lewis and Clark Expedition, with Related Documents: 1783–1854,* 2nd ed. (Urbana: University of Illinois Press, 1978), vol. I, p. 361.
2. Ibid.
3. Dumas Malone, *Jefferson the President: Second Term* (Boston: Little, Brown, 1974), p. 203.
4. Richard Dillon, *Meriwether Lewis: A Biography* (New York: Coward-McCann, 1965), p. 276.
5. Malone, *Jefferson the President: Second Term,* p. 204.
6. Jackson, *Letters,* vol. I, p. 375.
7. Ibid., p. 362.
8. Ibid., vol. II, pp. 364–69.
9. Ibid., pp. 377–78; see also Malone, *Jefferson the President: Second Term,* p. 205.
10. Malone, *Jefferson the President: Second Term,* p. 205.
11. Jackson, *Letters,* vol. II, p. 443.
12. Ibid., vol. I, p. 376.
13. Ibid., p. 375.
14. Ibid.
15. Edwin Morris Betts and James Adam Bear, eds., *The Family Letters of Thomas Jefferson* (Charlottesville: University Press of Virginia, 1986 reprint of 1960 University of Missouri Press ed.), pp. 298, 300.
16. Jackson, *Letters,* vol. II, p. 382.
17. Ibid., p. 385.
18. Ibid., p. 386.
19. Ibid., p. 396.
20. Ibid., pp. 399–407.
21. Ibid., p. 387.
22. Ibid., pp. 387–88.
23. Ibid., p. 389.
24. Ibid., pp. 391–92.
25. Ibid., p. 389.

35: PHILADELPHIA

1. Paul Russell Cutright, "Contributions of Philadelphia to Lewis and Clark History," *We Proceeded On,* suppl. no. 6 (July 1982), p. 32.
2. Reuben Gold Thwaites, ed., *Original Journals of the Lewis and Clark Expedition* (New York: Arno Press reprint, 1969), vol. VII, p. 363.
3. Donald Jackson, ed., *Letters of the Lewis and Clark Expedition, with Related Documents: 1783–1854,* 2nd ed. (Urbana: University of Illinois Press, 1978), vol. II, pp. 392–93.

4. Ibid., p. 463.
5. Ibid., pp. 394–97; Thwaites, ed., *Original Journals*, vol. VII, p. 366.
6. Jackson, *Letters*, vol. II, p. 695.
7. Ibid., p. 398.
8. Ibid., p. 463.
9. Cutright, "Contributions of Philadelphia," pp. 23–24.
10. Jackson, *Letters*, vol. II, p. 439.
11. Ibid., p. 411.
12. Ibid., p. 463.
13. Alexander Wilson, *American Ornithology*, 9 vols. (Philadelphia: Bradford & Inskeep, 1808–14), vol. III, pp. 31–32.
14. Jackson, *Letters*, vol. II, p. 463.
15. Ibid., p. 462.
16. Ibid., pp. 408, 417.
17. Ibid., p. 428.
18. Clarence E. Carter, ed., *The Territorial Papers of the United States*, vol. XIV, *The Territory of Louisiana-Missouri 1806–1814* (Washington, D.C.: Government Printing Office, 1949), p. 131.
19. Jackson, *Letters*, vol. II, p. 415.
20. Carter, ed., *Territorial Papers*, vol. XIV, p. 139.
21. Jackson, *Letters*, vol. II, p. 418.
22. Ibid., pp. 393, 463.
23. Ibid., pp. 683–84.
24. Ibid., p. 575.
25. Ibid., p. 720.

36: VIRGINIA

1. Donald Jackson, ed., *Letters of the Lewis and Clark Expedition, with Related Documents: 1783–1854*, 2nd ed. (Urbana: University of Illinois Press, 1978), vol. II, p. 721.
2. Ibid., pp. 431, 439.
3. Quoted in John Bakeless, *Lewis and Clark: Partners in Discovery* (New York: William Morrow, 1947), p. 384.
4. Ibid., p. 385.
5. Jackson, *Letters*, vol. II, p. 720.
6. Bakeless, *Lewis and Clark*, pp. 384–85; Jackson, *Letters*, vol. II, p. 721.
7. Jackson, *Letters*, vol. II, pp. 725–32.

37: ST. LOUIS: *March–December 1808*

1. Washington Irving, *Astoria* (New York, 1868), pp. 154–55, quoted in Harvey Wish, "The French of Old Missouri (1801–1821): A Study in Assimilation," *Mid-America: An Historical Review*, vol. XII, no. 3 (July 1941), p. 173. See also William Foley, "St. Louis: The First Hundred Years," *Bulletin of the Missouri Historical Society*, July 1978, p. 193.
2. Wish, "The French of Old Missouri," p. 186.
3. Ibid., p. 174.

4. Thomas Maitland Marshall, *The Life and Papers of Frederick Bates*, 2 vols. (St. Louis: Missouri Historical Society, 1926), vol. I, p. 241.

5. Ibid., p. 99.

6. Ibid., pp. 108, 114, 135.

7. Ibid., p. 300.

8. Donald Jackson, ed., *Letters of the Lewis and Clark Expedition, with Related Documents: 1783–1854*, 2nd ed. (Urbana: University of Illinois Press, 1978), vol. I, p. 134.

9. Marshall, *Bates*, vol. I, p. 9.

10. Grace Lewis, "The First Home of Governor Lewis in Louisiana Territory," *Missouri Historical Society Bulletin*, vol. XIV (July 1958), pp. 363–64.

11. There is a copy of the indenture, dated May 13, 1809, in the Grace Lewis Miller Papers, National Park Service, Jefferson National Expansion Memorial Archives, St. Louis.

12. Quoted in John Bakeless, *Lewis and Clark: Partners in Discovery* (New York: William Morrow, 1947), p. 391.

13. Marshall, *Bates*, vol. I, p. 301.

14. James Bentley, ed., "Two Letters from Meriwether Lewis to Major William Preston," *Filson Club History Quarterly*, vol. 44 (April 1970), pp. 170–75.

15. Clarence E. Carter, ed., *The Territorial Papers of the United States*, vol. XIV, *The Territory of Louisiana-Missouri 1806–1814* (Washington, D.C.: Government Printing Office, 1949), p. 189.

16. Carter, ed., *Territorial Papers*, vol. XIV, pp. 196–202.

17. Ibid., p. 204.

18. Jackson, *Letters*, vol. II, pp. 444–45.

19. Ibid.

20. Dumas Malone, *Jefferson the President: Second Term* (Boston: Little, Brown, 1974), p. 209.

21. There is a copy of his application in the Grace Lewis Miller Papers.

22. Missouri *Gazette*, Nov. 16, 1808.

23. ML to Lucy Marks, Dec. 1, 1808, copy in Grace Lewis Miller Papers.

24. Marshall, *Bates*, vol. I, p. 84.

25. Carter, ed. *Territorial Papers*, vol. XIV, pp. 212–16.

26. Ibid., pp. 219–21.

27. Ibid., p. 200.

28. Ibid., p. 222.

29. Richard Dillon, *Meriwether Lewis: A Biography* (New York: Coward-McCann, 1965), p. 298.

30. Carter, ed., *Territorial Papers*, vol. XIV, pp. 34–39.

31. Ibid., pp. 229–30.

32. Dillon, *Lewis*, p. 313.

33. Lewis's account book is in the Missouri State Historical Society; there is a copy in the Grace Lewis Miller Papers.

34. James J. Holmberg, "'I Wish You to See & Know All': The Recently Discovered Letters of William Clark to Jonathan Clark," *We Proceeded On*, vol. 18, no. 4 (Nov. 1992), pp. 7–9.

35. Jefferson, *Notes on the State of Virginia*, p. 163.

36. Carter, ed., *Territorial Papers*, vol. XIV, pp. 240–41.

38: ST. LOUIS: *January–August 1809*

1. See Lewis's 1808 book, in the Missouri Historical Society, for his descriptions of the pills and his practice in taking them.
2. Donald Jackson, ed., *Letters of the Lewis and Clark Expedition, with Related Documents: 1783–1854*, 2nd ed. (Urbana: University of Illinois Press, 1978), vol. II, pp. 446–50.
3. Donald Jackson, "A Footnote to the Lewis and Clark Expedition," *Manuscripts*, vol. 24 (Winter 1972), p. 9.
4. Thomas Maitland Marshall, *The Life and Papers of Frederick Bates* (St. Louis: Missouri Historical Society, 1926), p. 64.
5. Ibid., p. 112.
6. Ibid., pp. 108–9.
7. Ibid., p. 64.
8. Jackson, *Letters*, vol. II, pp. 450–51; there is a copy of the receipt from Pierre Chouteau in the Grace Lewis Miller Papers.
9. Jackson, *Letters*, vol. II, pp. 451–56.
10. Marshall, *Bates*, pp. 68–69.
1. Ibid., p. 73.
12. Ibid., p. 75.
13. Jackson, *Letters*, vol. II, p. 722.
14. Richard Dillon, *Meriwether Lewis: A Biography* (New York: Coward-McCann, 1965), pp. 323–24.
15. Marshall, *Bates*, pp. 108–11.
16. Clarence E. Carter, ed., *The Territorial Papers of the United States*, vol. XIV, *The Territory of Louisiana-Missouri 1806–1814* (Washington, D.C.: Government Printing Office, 1949), pp. 285–86.
17. Jackson, *Letters*, vol. II, p. 458.
18. Ibid., pp. 459–61.
19. Ibid., pp. 723–24.
20. Jackson, "Footnote," pp. 11–12.
21. Jackson, *Letters*, vol. II, pp. 470–73.
22. Marshall, *Bates*, p. 86.
23. Ibid., pp. 99, 111.
24. Ibid., pp. 101, 111.
25. James J. Holmberg, "'I Wish You to See & Know All': The Recently Discovered Letters of William Clark to Jonathan Clark," *We Proceeded On*, vol. 18, no. 4 (Nov. 1992), p. 10.

39: LAST VOYAGE

1. See Captain Gilbert Russell's statement of Nov. 26, 1811, in Donald Jackson, ed., *Letters of the Lewis and Clark Expedition, with Related Documents: 1783–1854*, 2nd ed. (Urbana: University of Illinois Press, 1978), vol. II, p. 573.
2. Richard Dillon, *Meriwether Lewis: A Biography* (New York: Coward-McCann, 1965), p. 328.
3. Jackson, *Letters*, vol. II, p. 573.

4. Ibid., p. 748.
5. Ibid., p. 464.
6. Ibid., p. 573.
7. Ibid., p. 748.
8. Ibid., p. 466.
9. Dawson A. Phelps, "The Tragic Death of Meriwether Lewis," *William and Mary Quarterly*, vol. XIII, no. 3 (1956), p. 317.
10. Clarence E. Carter, ed., *The Territorial Papers of the United States*, vol. XIV, *The Territory of Louisiana-Missouri 1806–1814* (Washington, D.C.: Government Printing Office, 1949), pp. 332–33.
11. Gary Moulton, "New Documents of Meriwether Lewis," *We Proceeded On*, vol. 13, no. 4 (Nov. 1987), p. 7.
12. Phelps, "Tragic Death," p. 317.
13. James J. Holmberg, "'I Wish You to See & Know All': The Recently Discovered Letters of William Clark to Jonathan Clark," *We Proceeded On*, vol. 18. no. 4 (Nov. 1992), p. 11.
14. Jackson, *Letters*, vol. II, p. 748.
15. Carter, ed., *Territorial Papers*, vol. XIV, p. 333.
16. This account is taken from Russell's statement, in Jackson, *Letters*, vol. II, p. 574, and from Alexander Wilson's interview with Mrs. Grinder, May 28, 1811, in Elliott Coues, ed., *The History of the Lewis and Clark Expedition*, 3 vols. (New York: Dover ed., 1987; reprint of 1893 Francis P. Harper 4-vol. ed.), vol. I, pp. xliv–xlvi.

40: AFTERMATH

1. James J. Holmberg, "'I Wish You to See & Know All': The Recently Discovered Letters of William Clark to Jonathan Clark," *We Proceeded On*, vol. 18, no. 4 (Nov. 1992), p. 10.
2. Ibid.
3. Clarence E. Carter, ed., *The Territorial Papers of the United States*, vol. XIV, *The Territory of Louisiana-Missouri 1806–1814* (Washington, D.C.: Government Printing Office, 1949), p. 333.
4. Donald Jackson, ed., *Letters of the Lewis and Clark Expedition, with Related Documents: 1783–1854*, 2nd ed. (Urbana: University of Illinois Press, 1978), vol. II, p. 474.
5. Ibid., p. 575.
6. Ibid., pp. 591–92.
7. Vardes Fisher, *Suicide or Murder? The Strange Death of Governor Meriwether Lewis* (Chicago: Swallow Press, 1962).
8. Eldon G. Chuinard, "How Did Meriwether Lewis Die? It Was Murder," *We Proceeded On*, vol. 18, nos. 1 and 2 (Jan. and May 1992).
9. "Rest, Rest, Perturbed Spirit," *We Proceeded On*, vol. 12, no. 1 (March 1986).
10. Reimert Thorolf Ravenholt, "Triumph Then Despair: The Tragic Death of Meriwether Lewis," *Epidemiology*, vol. 5, no. 3 (May 1994), pp. 366–79.
11. Jackson, *Letters*, vol. II, pp. 730–31.
12. Donald Jackson, "A Footnote to the Lewis and Clark Expedition," *Manuscripts*, vol. 24 (Winter 1972), p. 19.

13. Holmberg, "'I Wish You to See & Know All,'" p. 11.
14. Jackson, *Letters*, vol. II, p. 486.
15. Ibid., p. 469.
16. Paul Russell Cutright, *A History of the Lewis and Clark Journals* (Norman: University of Oklahoma Press, 1976), pp. 55–56.
17. Jackson, *Letters*, vol. II, p. 493.
18. Cutright, *Journals*, p. 63.
19. Dumas Malone, *Jefferson the President: Second Term* (Boston: Little, Brown, 1974), p. 212.
20. Jackson, *Letters*, vol. II, p. 590.

BIBLIOGRAPHY

Abrams, Rochonne. "The Colonial Childhood of Meriwether Lewis." *Bulletin of the Missouri Historical Society*, vol. xxxiv (July 1978).

Adams, Henry. *History of the United States of America During the Administrations of Thomas Jefferson*. New York: Library of America Edition, 1986.

Allen, John Logan. *Passage Through the Garden: Lewis and Clark and the Image of the American Northwest*. Urbana: University of Illinois Press, 1975.

———. "Summer of Decision: Lewis and Clark in Montana, 1805." *We Proceeded On*, Fall 1976.

Anderson, Sarah Lewis Travers. *Lewises, Meriwethers and Their Kin*. Richmond: Dietz Press, 1938.

Appleman, Roy. *Lewis and Clark*. Washington, D.C.: National Park Service, 1975.

Bakeless, John. *Lewis and Clark: Partners in Discovery*. New York: William Morrow, 1947.

Bedini, Silvio. "The Scientific Instruments of the Lewis and Clark Expedition." *Great Plains Quarterly*, Winter 1984.

Bentley, James, ed. "Two Letters from Meriwether Lewis to Major William Preston." *Filson Club History Quarterly*, April 1970.

Betts, Edwin Morris, and James Adam Bear, eds. *The Family Letters of Thomas Jefferson*. Charlottesville: University Press of Virginia 1986 reprint of 1960 University of Missouri Press ed.

Boss, Richard C. "Keelboat, Pirogue, and Canoe: Vessels Used by the Lewis and Clark Corps of Discovery." *Nautical Research Journal*, June 1993.

Botkin, Daniel. *Our Natural History: The Lessons of Lewis and Clark*. New York, G. P. Putnam's Sons, 1995.

Brodhead, Micheal. "The Military Naturalist: A Lewis and Clark Heritage." *We Proceeded On*, vol. 9, no. 4 (November 1983).

Brodie, Fawn M. *Thomas Jefferson: An Intimate History*. New York: W. W. Norton, 1974.

Burroughs, Raymond Darwin. *The Natural History of the Lewis and Clark Expedition*. East Lansing: Michigan State University Press, 1961.

Caldwell, Norman. "The Enlisted Soldier at the Frontier Post, 1790–1814." *Mid-America: An Historical Review*, vol. 37, no. 4 (October 1955).

Carter, Clarence E., ed. *The Territorial Papers of the United States*, vol. XIV, *The Territory of Louisiana-Missouri 1806–1814*. (Washington: Government Printing Office, 1949).

Chatters, Roy. "The Not-So-Enigmatic Lewis and Clark Airgun." *We Proceeded On*, vol. 3, no. 2 (May 1977).

Chuinard, Eldon G. "The Court-Martial of Ensign Meriwether Lewis." *We Proceeded On*, vol. 8, no. 4 (Nov. 1982).

———. "Lewis and Clark, Master Masons." *We Proceeded On*, vol. 15, no. 1 (February 1989).

———. *Only One Man Died: The Medical Aspects of the Lewis and Clark Expedition*. Glendale, Calif.: Arthur Clark Company, 1980.

———. "Thomas Jefferson and the Corps of Discovery: Could He Have Done More?" *American West*, vol. 12, no. 6 (1975).

———. "How Did Meriwether Lewis Die? It Was Murder." *We Proceeded On*, vol. 18, nos. 1 and 2 (January and May 1992).

Coues, Elliot, ed. *The History of the Lewis and Clark Expedition*. New York: Dover ed., 1987; reprint of 1893 Francis P. Harper 4-vol. ed., 1893.

Crackel, Theodore J. *Mr. Jefferson's Army: Political and Social Reform of the Military Establishment, 1801–1809*. New York: New York University Press, 1987.

Criswell, Elijah. *Lewis and Clark: Linguistic Pioneers*. Columbia: University of Missouri Press, 1940.

Cutright, Paul Russell. "Contributions of Philadelphia to Lewis and Clark History." *We Proceeded On*, special issue, July 1982.

———. *Lewis and Clark: Pioneering Naturalists*. Urbana: University of Illinois Press, 1969 (reprinted by University of Nebraska, 1989).

———. "Meriwether Lewis's 'Coloring of Events.'" *We Proceeded On*, vol. 11, no. 1 (February 1985).

———. "The Journal of Captain Meriwether Lewis." *We Proceeded On*, vol. 10, no. 1 (February 1984).

———. *A History of the Lewis and Clark Journals*. Norman: University of Oklahoma Press, 1976.

———. "Rest, Rest, Perturbed Spirit." *We Proceeded On*, vol. 12, no. 1 (March 1986).

Davis, Richard Beale, *Francis Walker Gilmer: Life and Learning in Jefferson's Virginia*. Richmond: Dietz Press, 1939.

Deconde, Alexander. *This Affair of Louisiana*. New York: Charles Scribner's Sons, 1976.

DeVoto, Bernard. *Journals of Lewis and Clark*. Houghton Mifflin, 1953.

Dillon, Richard. *Meriwether Lewis: A Biography*. New York: Coward-McCann, 1965.

Fanselow, Julie. *The Traveler's Guide to the Lewis and Clark Trail*. Helena, Montana: Falcon Press, 1994.

Fisher, Vardis. *Suicide or Murder! The Strange Death of Governor Meriwether Lewis*. Chicago: Swallow Press, 1962.

Foley, William. "St. Louis: The First Hundred Years." *Bulletin of the Missouri Historical Society*, vol. XXXIV, no. 4, pt. 1 (July 1978).

Gass, Patrick. *A Journal of the Voyages and Travels of a Corps of Discovery Under the Command of Capt. Lewis and Capt. Clark*. Minneapolis: Ross and Haines, 1958.

Holmberg, James J. "'I Wish You to See & Know All': The Recently Discovered Letters of William Clark to Jonathan Clark." *We Proceeded On*, vol. 18, no. 4 (November 1992).

Hunt, Robert. "The Blood Meal: Mosquitos and Agues on the Lewis and Clark Expedition." *We Proceeded On*, vol. 18, no. 3 (May and August 1992).

———. "Gills and Drams of Consolation: Ardent Spirits on the Lewis and Clark Expedition." *We Proceeded On*, vol. 17, no. 3 (February 1991).

Jackson, Donald. ed., *Letters of the Lewis and Clark Expedition, with Related Documents: 1783–1854*, 2nd ed. Urbana: University of Illinois Press, 1978.

———. "Jefferson, Meriwether Lewis, and the Reduction of the United States Army." *Proceedings of the American Philosophical Society*, vol. 124, no. 2 (April 1980).

———. *Thomas Jefferson and the Stony Mountains; Exploring the West from Monticello*. Urbana: University of Illinois Press, 1981.

———. "The Public Image of Lewis and Clark." *Pacific Northwest Quarterly*, January 1966.

———. "A Footnote to the Lewis and Clark Expedition." *Manuscripts*, vol. 24 (Winter 1972).

Jefferson, Thomas. *Notes on the State of Virginia*. Paris, 1794.

Jordan, Winthrop D. *White over Black: American Attitudes Toward the Negro, 1550–1812*. Chapel Hill: University of North Carolina Press, 1968.

Large, Arlen. "North and South of Lewis and Clark." *We Proceeded On*, vol. 12, no. 4 (November 1984).

———. "Fort Mandan's Dancing Longitude." *We Proceeded On*, vol. 13, no. 1 (February 1987).

———. "Trailing Lewis and Clark: 'The Spirit of Party.'" *We Proceeded On*, vol. 6, no. 1 (February 1990).

———. "'Additions to the Party': How an Expedition Grew and Grew." *We Proceeded On*, vol. 16, no. 1 (February 1990).

———. "Lewis and Clark: Part Time Astronomers." *We Proceeded On*, vol. 5, no. 1 (February 1979).

———. "'. . . It Thundered and Lightened': The Weather Observations of Lewis and Clark." *We Proceeded On*, vol. 12, no. 2 (May 1986).

———. "The Empty Anchorage: Why No Ship Came for Lewis and Clark." *We Proceeded On*, vol. 15, no. 1 (February 1989).

———. "Expedition Aftermath: The Jawbone Journals." *We Proceeded On*, vol. 17, no. 1 (February 1991).

Lavender, David. *The Way to the Western Sea: Lewis and Clark Across the Continent*. New York: Harper & Row, 1988.

Lewis, Grace. "The First Home of Governor Lewis in Louisiana Territory." *Missouri Historical Society Bulletin*, vol. XIV (July 1958).

Malone, Dumas. *Jefferson the Virginian*. Vol. I. Boston: Little, Brown, 1948.

———. *Jefferson the President: First Term, 1801–1805.* Vol. IV. Boston: Little, Brown, 1970.

———. *Jefferson the President: Second Term.* Boston: Little, Brown, 1974.

Marshall, Thomas Maitland. *A History of the Western Boundaries of the Louisiana Purchase, 1819–1841.* Berkeley: University of California Press, 1914.

———. *The Life and Papers of Frederick Bates.* St. Louis: Missouri Historical Society, 1926.

Masson, L. R. *Les Bourgeois de la Compagnie du Nord-Ouest.* New York: Antiquarian Press, 1960 reprint.

Miller, John Chester. *The Wolf by the Ears: Thomas Jefferson and Slavery.* New York: Free Press, 1977.

Moore, John Hammond. *Albemarle: Jefferson's County, 1727–1976.* Charlottesville: University Press of Virginia, 1976.

Moulton, Gary, ed. *The Journals of the Lewis & Clark Expedition.* Lincoln: University of Nebraska Press, 1988.

———. "New Documents of Meriwether Lewis." *We Proceeded On,* vol. 13, no. 4 (November 1987).

Murphy, William. "John Adams: The Politics of the Additional Army, 1798–1800." *New England Quarterly,* vol. 52 (June 1979).

Nevins, Allen, ed. *The Diary of John Quincy Adams, 1794–1845.* New York: Frederick Ungar, 1970.

Oglesby, Richard E. *Manuel Lisa and the Opening of the Missouri Fur Trade.* Norman: University of Oklahoma Press, 1963.

Phelps, Dawson A. "The Tragic Death of Meriwether Lewis." *William and Mary Quarterly,* vol. XIII, no. 3 (1956).

Ravenholt, Reimert Thorolf. "Triumph Then Despair: The Tragic Death of Meriwether Lewis." *Epidemiology,* vol. 5, no. 3 (May 1994), pp. 366–79.

Ray, Verne F. "Lewis and Clark and the Nez Percé Indians." *The Great Western Series.* No. 10. Washington, D.C.: Westerners.

Ronda, James P. *Lewis and Clark Among the Indians.* Lincoln: University of Nebraska Press, 1984.

———. "A Most Perfect Harmony: Life at Fort Mandan." *We Proceeded On,* vol. 14, no. 4 (November 1988).

———. "St. Louis Welcomes and Toasts the Lewis and Clark Expedition." *We Proceeded On,* vol. 13, no. 1 (February 1987).

———. "A Knowledge of Distant Parts: The Shaping of the Lewis and Clark Expedition." *Montana: The Magazine of Western History,* vol. 41, no. 4 (Autumn 1991).

Ruby, Robert H., and John A. Brown. *The Chinook Indians: Traders of the Lower Columbia River.* Norman: University of Oklahoma Press, 1976.

Russell, Carl. "The Guns of the Lewis and Clark Expedition." *North Dakota History,* vol. 27 (Winter 1960).

Schwantee, Carlos, ed. *Encounters with a Distant Land: Exploration and the Great Northwest.* Moscow: University of Idaho Press, 1994.

Shoemaker, Floyd. "The Louisiana Purchase, 1803." *Missouri Historical Review,* vol. 48 (October 1953).

Skelton, William B. *An American Profession of Arms: The Army Officer Corps, 1784–1861.* Lawrence: University Press of Kansas, 1992.

Slaughter, Thomas P. *The Whiskey Rebellion: Frontier Epilogue to the American Revolution.* New York: Oxford University Press, 1986.

Smithers, Jim. "Food for Mackenzie." *We Proceeded On*, vol. 15, no. 1 (February 1989).

Thomas, Samuel W. "William Clark's 1795 and 1797 Journals and Their Significance." *Missouri Historical Society Bulletin*, July 1969.

Thwaites, Reuben Gold, ed. *Original Journals of the Lewis and Clark Expedition.* New York: Arno Press reprint, 1969.

Van Wormer, Joe. *The World of the Pronghorn.* Philadelphia: Lippincott, 1969.

Weber, David J. *The Spanish Frontier in North America.* New Haven: Yale University Press, 1992.

Wheeler, Olin D. *The Trail of Lewis and Clark, 1804–1806.* New York, 1904. Two volumes.

Wilson, Alexander. *American Ornithology.* Philadelphia: Bradford & Inskeep, 1808–1814.

Wish, Harvey. "The French of the Old Missouri (1801–1821): A Study in Assimilation." *Mid-America: An Historical Review*, vol. XII, no. 3 (July 1941).

Woods, Edgar. *Albemarle County in Virginia.* Bridgewater, Va.: Green Bookman, 1932.

MANUSCRIPTS

Meriwether Lewis Anderson Papers, Missouri State Historical Society.

William Clark Papers, Missouri State Historical Society.

Meriwether Lewis Papers, Missouri State Historical Society.

Grace Lewis Miller Papers, National Park Service, Jefferson National Expansion Memorial Archives, St. Louis.

INDEX

Adams, Abigail 18, 50, 51
Adams, Henry 38–41, 45, 52, 95, 446
Adams, John 24, 34–7, 48, 50, 53
Adams, John Quincy 17–18, 96, 446, 460,
    462, 528
Adams, Samuel 24
Aird, James 435
Alabama 19
Alaska 66
Albemarle County, Va. 1–12, 32–4, 53
Alien Act 35, 54
Allen, John Logan 65, 67, 84, 281, 353–4
Allen, Paul 526–7
Alston, Willis, Jr. 459, 461
American Ornithology (Wilson) 472
American Philosophical Society 21, 52,
    59, 60, 81, 84, 115, 124, 375, 455,
    472–3
    ML's election to 124–5, 445
    natural-history specimens sent to 125,
        212, 375
*American Profession of Arms, An: The
    Army Officer Corps, 1784–1861*
    (Skelton) 29
American Revolution 19, 24, 44–5, 48, 57,
    63, 93, 100, 119, 123, 146, 188, 232,
    368
    Conway Cabal and 368
    cultural and social life after 13–22
    political background of 1–2, 23, 24
    veterans of 25, 27, 32, 35–6, 63, 93, 100
Anderson, Edmund 8, 495
Anderson, Jane Lewis 8, 9, 10, 11
Anderson, Miss 489
Appalachian Mountains 29, 38, 42, 43, 57,
    65, 76, 122, 277, 355, 443
Appleman, Roy 123
Arapaho Indians 187
Arcawechar (chief) 166
Arctic Ocean 63
Arikara Indians 182–9, 193–5, 198, 205,
    209, 432–4, 436–7, 493, 503–7, 519
Arkansas River 373, 436
Armstrong, John 59
Army, U.S. 55, 76, 112, 137–8, 148, 181,
    197, 342, 368, 371, 384, 390, 429, 438,
    484
    Chosen Rifle Company of 32
    Corps of Artillerists of 133
    Corps of Engineers of 133
    discipline problems and desertion in
        26–30
    duels in 30–32
    expansion and reduction of 35–6
    Federalist officers in 31, 34–7, 48–9
    First Infantry Regiment of 33, 37, 128,
        376
    frontier defense by 23–5, 29, 333, 342,
        347, 483
    Indian wars of 57, 384
    ML's career in 22–9, 31–4, 36–7, 46–8, 91
    officers vs. enlisted men in 26, 30
    politics and 34–6, 48–50, 55
    Second Sub-Legion of 31
    Spanish spying within 368
    WC's career in 32, 91, 92, 108, 133–4
    see also Corps of Discovery
Assiniboine Indians 187
Assiniboine River 189
Astor, John Jacob 368n, 493
Atlantic Ocean 38, 39, 63, 66, 119, 215,
    442, 443, 444
Atsina Indians 290, 418, 419
Audubon, John James 152
Austin, Moses 499
Australia 41, 59

Bache, William 52
Badlands 42
Bakeless, John 479
Bald Mountain 403
Barlow, Joel 52, 459–61
Barralet, John James 472
Barton, Benjamin Smith 83–4, 455, 470–1,
    526
Bates, Frederick 467, 474, 480, 486–9,
    490n
    ML's relations with 495, 499, 504–13,
        516, 519, 530
    political background of 487–8

Bates, Tarleton 490n
Benoit, Francis132
Bent, Silas 450
Bering Sea 58
Biddle, Nicholas 134, 262, 526–7
Big Horse (chief) 161
Big White (chief) 187–8, 192, 432–3, 438, 445, 453–5
  Washington, D.C., visit of 457–9, 463–4, 492–3, 496, 498, 502, 504, 507, 512, 524
Bismarck, N.Dak 71, 182, 187
Bissell, Russell 95, 120
Bissonnette, Antoine 486
Bitterroot Mountains 281, 308–11, 317, 323n, 354, 387
Bitterroot River 313, 404, 408, 410
Black Buffalo (chief) 172, 174–8
Black Cat (chief) 187, 189–90, 193, 205, 219–20
Blackfeet Indians 242, 266, 270, 278–9, 285, 289, 291–2, 300–2, 310, 320, 390, 393, 395, 405–6, 408, 416, 418–22, 423–7, 430, 432, 440, 444, 450–1, 483, 519
Blackfoot River 266n, 411
Black Hills 210
Black Moccasin (chief) 187
Blue Ridge Mountains 1, 42, 251
Boilvin, Nicholas 491, 492, 496–8
Boley, John 127
Boone, Daniel 2, 141, 144, 499
Boone's Settlement 141, 430
Boston, Mass. 39, 363
Boston Tea Party 1
Botany Bay 59
Braddock, Edward 3
Bradford and Inskeep 526
Bratton, William 100, 162, 233, 383, 391
Breckenridge, Elizabeth 479
Breckenridge, James 479
Breckenridge, Letitia 479, 481, 490, 530
Broad River 6
Brodhead, Michael 125
Broken Arm (chief) 388–90
Broughton, William 330n, 338
Bruff, James 367–8, 369–70
Buffalo Medicine (chief) 172
Burke, Edmund 18
Burr, Aaron 450, 499, 511–12
  conspiracy charges against 467, 478
  Hamilton's fatal duel with 365, 436
  vice-presidency of 37, 44
Burroughs, Raymond 182n

Cahokia, Ill. 120, 121, 123, 131, 440
California 42, 58

Callender, James Thomson 53–5
Cameahwait (chief) 285–95, 297–9, 301–5, 308, 323, 432, 451, 472, 519
Camp Disappointment 419
Camp Fortunate 143, 294n
Canada 2, 42, 63–6, 88, 113, 145, 151, 173, 189–90, 211, 214, 231, 320, 330, 355, 406, 443, 482, 485
C. and A. Conrad 525
Canton 442–3
Cape Girardeau 119, 500
Cape of Good Hope 443
Cascade Mountains 325, 328, 380
Catherine the Great, Empress of Russia 58
Charbonneau, Jean Baptiste "Pomp" 209, 219, 220, 252, 340, 391, 405
  WC's sponsorship of 433n
Charbonneau, Lizette 489
Charbonneau, Toussaint 192–3, 202–3, 228, 231, 233–5, 239, 268–9, 274, 387
  as interpreter 209, 294, 298, 385, 462
  Sacagawea and 202–3, 209, 219–20, 246, 294, 297–8, 302, 340, 385, 405, 433
Charles, Joseph 494
Charlottesville, Va. 3, 32, 36, 57, 342, 454–6, 480
Chase, Samuel 53
Cherokee Indians 4
Chesapeake 476
Cheyenne Indians 187
Chickasaw Agency 515
Chinook Indians 326–8, 334–7, 346–8, 359, 361–4, 378, 380, 383–4, 389, 399, 406,
Chouteau, Auguste, Sr. 135–6, 436–7, 496, 512, 524
Chouteau, Lorimier 119
Chouteau, Pierre 123–5, 126, 128, 366, 369, 377, 435, 440, 449, 454, 459, 489, 496
Christy, William 499, 450
Chuinard, Eldon G. "Frenchy" 201, 232, 253, 391n, 524
Cincinnati, Ohio 36, 110, 111
Civil War, U.S.23
Claiborne, Ferdinand 34, 36, 47
Clark, George Rogers 32, 45, 57, 92, 113, 114, 119, 123, 138, 146, 187, 368
Clark, Jonathan 500, 501, 514, 522
Clark, Julia Hancock 237, 454, 459, 467, 489, 490, 503
Clark, Meriwether Lewis 503
Clark, William:
  Army career of 32, 91, 92, 108, 133–4
  birth of 91
  business affairs of 92, 97, 123, 496, 512–13

captain's commission withheld from 133–4, 376, 447
compensation and reward of 462–3
courtship and marriage of 459, 467, 476
expeditionary co-command proposed by ML to 91–3
illness and injury of 108–9, 268, 272–4, 275, 276, 321
journals of 104–5, 128, 132, 141, 147, 149, 151, 162, 165, 174, 177–8, 207, 252, 256, 262, 268–9, 272, 302, 307, 321, 331–4
as judge of men 100, 126
mapmaking of 91, 136, 213, 353, 357, 375, 431, 441, 446–7, 458, 470
medical practices of 386, 392
ML's correspondence with 91–3, 479, 489
political appointment of 463, 489, 492, 524–5
politics of 114
son born to 503
TJ and 19, 32, 92
as woodsman and waterman 126, 168–70, 201, 203, 219n, 245, 400
writing style of 141, 269
see also Lewis and Clark
Clarksville, Indiana Territory 92, 99, 113, 114, 115, 138
Clatsop Indians 334, 336–8, 340–1, 346–58, 359, 361, 363–4, 375, 399, 406, 474
Clearwater River 318, 320, 322, 395, 404, 442
Cloverfields 4, 8, 9
Coboway (chief) 340, 357–8
Collins, John 148–50, 453
Colorado River 42, 87
Colter, John 100, 111, 127–9, 162, 167, 171, 299, 310, 334–5, 338, 380, 433, 528
Columbia 21, 41, 59
Columbia River 59–66, 73, 87, 92, 212, 215, 217, 230, 240, 263, 266n, 273, 276–7, 282, 309, 318, 323, 377
ascent of 379–81
The Dalles of 326, 379, 381–2, 388, 442
descent of 60, 325–36, 354
estuary of 21, 41, 59, 71, 245, 246n, 286, 360, 362
portage 326–7, 355
rapids and falls of 325–8, 332, 356
Columbus, Christopher 138, 219, 221, 368, 446, 450, 460, 461, 519
Committee of Correspondence 1
Congress, U.S. 34–6, 46, 50, 53, 63, 68–71, 73, 90, 111, 210, 235, 370, 375–6, 447,

448, 450, 455, 461, 463n, 466, 475, 487, 493, 512
Conrad, John 469, 473
Constitution, U.S. 44, 68, 90, 95, 444, 450, 460
Continental Army 29
Continental Congress 2, 52
Continental Divide 63, 96, 97, 117, 118, 241, 263, 289, 307, 309, 310, 390, 410, 417, 439n, 511
Conway Cabal 368
Cook, James 11, 41, 58–9, 64, 67, 138, 219, 221, 446, 519
Coon, Enos 33
Corcoran Art Gallery 472n
Corps of Discovery 128–34, 188, 197, 208, 364, 480
celebrations of 150, 152, 161, 199, 259, 300
compensation and rewards of 130, 453, 461–3, 464
drinking and disciplinary problems of 117, 127, 129, 135, 148–50, 186–7, 197, 461
early deaths among 348n
hunting for food by 145, 154, 161, 167–8, 181–2, 195, 198, 203, 217, 225, 229, 232, 248, 290–2, 314, 349–51, 400
illnesses and injuries of 147, 149, 162, 201–2, 232, 246, 254, 268, 272–5, 314, 318–19, 339–40, 347–8
journals of 130, 141, 159, 236, 356, 429, 452, 465, 466–8, 473, 526
officers and men engaged for 92, 93–5, 99–100, 110, 114–16, 120, 124, 126, 129–30, 137, 203, 439
permanent party completed for 203
rations of food and whiskey for 132, 145, 146, 147–8, 149, 167, 195, 204, 217, 232
sexual relations with Indian women by 185, 199, 200, 303–4, 314
spirit and morale of 237–8, 245, 246, 257–8, 259, 268, 275, 312, 315–18, 325, 334
cotton gin 19
Coues, Elliott 377, 527
Crackel, Theodore 134
Criswell, Elijah 84
Croghan, William 138
Crow at Rest (chief) 184
Crow Indians 187, 305, 406
Cruzatte, Pierre (Peter) 137, 146, 171, 172, 174, 175–6, 182, 199, 234, 235, 260, 325, 328, 331, 385, 395, 429–30
Cumberland Gap 2, 38, 57

Cumberland River 76
Cuscalah (chief) 340
Cushing, Thomas 95
Cut Bank Creek 417, 422
Cut Nose (chief) 387–9, 397, 402
Cutright, Paul Russell 81, 105, 263, 352, 395, 415, 465n, 469, 524

Dakota Territory 141, 163, 172, 180, 211
Dalles, The 326, 328, 379, 381–2, 388, 442
Dearborn, Henry 49, 52, 76, 90, 91, 93, 94–5, 120, 125, 133–4, 138, 266, 287, 310, 365, 369, 371, 373, 448, 461, 464, 481, 491–2, 494, 497–8, 505
Dearborn River 287, 411, 415
Declaration of Independence 18, 44, 52, 81, 95, 373
Delassus, Carlos Dehault 120, 128
Delaware Indians 491
Department of Upper Louisiana 367
DeSoto, Hernando 357
De Voto, Bernard 377
Dickerson, Mahlon 51, 52, 83, 475–6, 478–9, 481, 509
Dickinson, John 52
Dickson, Joseph 420–3
Dickson, William 523
Dillon, Richard 55
Dorion, Pierre, Sr. 146–7, 163–6, 436–7
Drouillard, George 160, 203, 219, 220, 258, 275, 283–98, 394, 448, 453
    as interpreter 115, 171–2, 192, 284–7, 304, 327, 385, 388, 420, 461–2
    ML and 115, 124, 129, 229–31, 242, 246, 265, 274, 335, 338, 356, 416
    murder trial of 486
    as woodsman and guide 115, 124, 135, 145, 162, 198, 229, 239, 248, 254, 258, 278–80, 291–8, 338, 349, 393, 400–1, 405, 414–24, 461–2
Dunbar, William 374, 376
Dunmore, Lord 1–2

East India Company 443
Eisenhower, Dwight D. 72
Elections:
    of 1801 36–7
    of 1804 55
Electoral College 36
electricity 391
Elements of Botany (Barton) 84
Elements of Mineralogy (Kirwan) 84
Eliott, Lieutenant 31
Ellicott, Andrew 79–80
Enlightenment 18, 61, 125, 202, 208, 297, 306, 355

Eustis, William 505, 510, 511–12, 513, 520, 524
Evans, John 123, 136
Everitt, Charles 10

Fallen Timbers, Battle of 24, 27, 29, 32
Federalist Party 31, 34–7, 48, 49, 53–5, 69, 70, 86, 96, 111, 124
Ffirth, S. 109
Field, Joseph 100, 149, 151, 154, 229–30, 232, 246, 248, 251, 255, 268, 339, 340, 414, 416, 418–20
Field, Reubin 100, 127, 129, 168, 254, 268, 315, 318, 358, 394, 411, 418–20, 422–5, 461–2
First Continental Congress 1–2
Fisher, Vardis 524
Flathead Indians 212, 215, 286, 299, 308, 310, 395
Flathead River 246
Flora (Pursh) 471n
Florida 97, 153
Floyd, Charles 100, 114, 129, 162
Forest Service, U.S. 281n, 403n
Fort Adams 95, 516
Fort Bellefontaine 438, 494
Fort Benton 238n, 240n, 281n
Fort Chipewyan 63, 64
Fort Clatsop 338–58, 359, 375, 378–9, 391n, 393, 405, 451, 457, 519
Fort Defiance 29–30
Fort Fork 63
Fort Kaskaskia 94, 95, 119, 128
Fort Mandan 5, 12, 191–230, 257, 306, 329, 348, 353, 376, 441, 454, 461, 530
Fort Massac 115, 116
Fort Mountain 265
Fort Osage 499
Fort Pickering 515, 517
Fort Wayne 36
Fox Indians 491, 496–8
France 17, 34, 44, 48, 61, 62, 70, 86, 96, 97, 121, 128
    Jefferson as foreign minister to 58
    see also Louisiana Purchase; Paris
Frankfort *Argus of Western America* 522
Frankfort *Western World* 448
Franklin, Benjamin 52, 391
Fraser River 64, 66
Frazier, Robert 198, 268, 406, 452, 454, 465–7
Frederick the Great, King of Prussia 148
Freemasonry 33–4, 494
French and Indian War 57
French Revolution 31
Freneau, Philip 52
Fulton, Robert 118, 446

fur trade 58, 61, 63, 65, 66, 69, 71, 80, 120,
    123, 145, 154, 184, 209, 211, 214,
    267–8, 324, 330, 355, 360n, 370, 375,
    408, 442–4, 453–4, 458, 462, 464–5,
    470, 479, 481–4, 488, 496, 505

Gallatin, Albert 52, 69, 71, 84, 87, 272,
    366, 454
Gamble, Robert 490, 530
Gass, Patrick 95, 130, 159, 162, 185, 241,
    255, 274, 275, 309, 346, 401–2, 406,
    429–30, 447–8, 454, 465–7, 526
George III, King of England 41
Georgia 3, 6–11, 19, 34, 64
Gibson, George 100, 162, 246, 339
Gilmer, George R. 3, 6
Gilmer, "Peachy" 9, 10, 12, 53
Gilmer, Thomas 10
Gilmer, Thornton 48
Glacier National Park 231, 246n, 417
Goforth, William 111
Goodrich, Silas 198, 246–7, 248, 340, 347,
    348n
Grand River 183
Gratiot, Charles 123, 134, 137
Gravelines, Joseph 183–4, 187–8, 203, 216,
    436–7
Gray, Robert 21, 41, 59
Great Britain 19, 23, 24, 83
    exploration and trade development by
        59, 63–8, 87, 97, 443, 482–4
    U.S. relations with 34, 45, 48, 97, 435,
        476, 482–4, 492, 493, 501
Great Lakes 38
Great Osage Indians 206, 365–7, 454, 457,
    472, 483, 491–2, 497, 499, 500
Great Plains 42, 154, 156, 173, 180, 190,
    256, 332, 355, 411, 414, 436, 457
Great Slave Lake 63
Greece, ancient 40–1
Greene, Griffin 108
Greenville, Treaty of 31, 157
Greenwich 64, 116–17, 229, 418
Grinder, Mr. 518
Grinder, Mrs. 518–20
Grinder's Inn 518–20, 522, 523n
Gulf of Mexico 38, 97, 153, 277

Hall, Hugh 148–9
Hamilton, Alexander 21, 23–4, 26, 31,
    34–7, 54–5, 60, 96
    fatal duel of 365, 436
Hamilton, William 468
Hancock, Forrest 430–3
Hancock, George 467, 479
Hancock, Julia, *see* Clark, Julia Hancock
Harmar, Josiah 24, 59

Harpers Ferry, Va. 76–9, 81, 83, 90, 92,
    97–9, 238, 261, 262n
Harrison, John 64
Harrison, William Henry 371, 372
Harvard University 394
Harvie, Lewis 77
Hassler, Ferdinand 473
Hawaiian Islands 362
Hawkins, John 472
Hawk's Feather (chief) 184, 186
Hay (chief) 184–6
Hay, John 354n
Hemmings, Sally "Black Sally" 55
Heney, Hugh 406–8, 430
Henry, Patrick 24
Hidatsa Indians 187, 192–4, 197–9, 205,
    209, 214–15, 220–1, 230–1, 237–9,
    240, 248, 249, 260, 263, 273, 277–9,
    294, 301–2, 306, 389, 406, 410–11, 432
High Federalists 34–5, 70
History of the Expedition Under the
    Commands of Captains Lewis and
    Clark, The (Biddle) 526
History of the Lewis and Clark Journals,
    A (Cutright) 465n, 471n
History of Louisiana, or of the Western
    Parts of Virginia and Carolina, The
    (Pratz) 67, 84, 470
History of the United States in the
    Administration of Thomas Jefferson
    (Adams) 96
Hooke, Moses 93–4, 133
Horned Weasel (chief) 193
House of Representatives, U.S. 37, 459,
    462, 506
Howard, Thomas 197
Hudson's Bay Company 187, 189, 197, 421

Idaho Territory 281, 285, 308, 318, 320, 323
Illinois Territory 115, 118, 120–2, 146,
    184, 197, 371, 430, 435, 440, 448, 531
Independence Hall 83, 471
Independence National Historical Park
    471
Indiana Territory 92, 113, 122, 371
Indians:
    "civilizing" of 371, 372–3
    communication with 115, 137, 146–7,
        156–7, 171, 174, 175, 183–6,
        187–90, 191–5, 202, 209, 269, 279,
        384–6, 283–90, 323, 359
    councils with 156–66, 171–9, 183–6,
        187–90, 293–6, 389–92
    culture and customs of 82, 86, 88,
        164–5, 175–6, 183, 187–8, 195, 196,
        199–201, 209, 284–7, 302–6,
        359–64, 392–4

Indians – *continued*
  diseases contracted by 182, 185, 188,
    303, 314, 359, 360, 363–4, 376
  frontier business trade with 88, 301,
    304, 306, 366, 370–1, 372, 406–8;
    see also fur trade
  gift-giving and trade with 73, 80, 132,
    136, 145, 148, 155, 159, 161, 172,
    184–5, 187, 191–2, 204, 268, 279,
    284, 295, 297–300, 318, 335–6,
    356–7, 361, 389, 392–3, 461
  guidance and help from 307–10, 311,
    313–15, 322, 364, 401–5, 408–10
  hostile encounters with 173–8, 198,
    418–27, 519
  Jefferson's policy toward 122, 154–6,
    173–5, 189, 306, 346, 365–7, 370–4,
    376, 430, 497–9
  Lewis's diplomacy with 183–90, 194–5,
    199–205, 211–19, 283–300, 303–4,
    324, 343, 346–7, 367, 370–2,
    380–92, 430, 440, 491–2
  as "noble savages" 42–3
  petty theft by 328, 330, 335, 343, 360,
    380–3, 414, 430, 431
  status of women among 303, 360, 363
  warfare among 175, 183–6, 193–5, 198,
    301–3, 432
  Washington, D.C., delegations of 124,
    128, 131, 135, 136, 206, 365–7, 369,
    374, 376–7, 390, 394, 407–8, 432,
    434, 436, 454
  see also specific tribes
Internal Provinces of New Spain 369
Iowa Indians 491, 496–8
Irvin, William 78
Irving, Washington 485–6

Jackson, Andrew 475
Jackson, Donald 42, 89, 91, 136, 139, 236,
    267–8, 353, 354n, 367n, 368, 373,
    433n, 448, 458, 466n, 490n, 527
James, Thomas 449
James River 163, 289
Jarrot, Nicholas 120, 121
Jay, John 24
Jay's Treaty 24, 27, 29, 34
Jefferson, Martha, *see* Randolph, Martha
    Jefferson
Jefferson, Peter 3, 14, 57
Jefferson, Thomas 9, 24, 295, 352–5
  charm and erudition of 11, 17, 42–3, 51
  childhood and adolescence of 13–14
  coast to coast "Empire of Liberty"
    vision of 16, 43–5, 68, 97, 373–4
  congressional reports of 210, 370, 375,
    447, 455

  contemporary opinion on 18, 51, 52
  correspondence of ML and 46–8,
    112–13, 121, 124, 440, 453–4,
    474–5, 493–4
  criticism of 377, 446, 460
  cross-continental water route sought by
    42–3, 60, 87–8, 230, 354, 442
  expeditions sponsored by 21, 57–61, 63,
    65–93, 94–9, 372, 373–5
  as foreign minister to France 58
  foreign policy of 61–3, 68–70, 95–7, 476
  Indian-language interest of 43, 209
  Indian policy of 122, 154–6, 173–5, 189,
    306, 346, 365–7, 370–4, 376, 430,
    497–9
  inventions of 40
  as landowner and host 16–19, 44–5,
    50–2
  on Lewis family 2–5, 51, 523
  Louisiana Purchase and 62–3, 69–70, 90
  marriage and family of 16, 20, 50, 463
  memoir-biography of ML by 527
  on ML 7, 10, 13, 15, 21, 36, 50–1, 66, 70,
    72, 140, 206, 332, 366, 523, 532
  ML as private secretary to 46–56, 65–70,
    77, 342, 446, 487
  ML's relationship with 8, 14, 19, 21,
    45–56, 60, 65–70, 77–80, 154–5,
    206, 221–2, 332, 342, 453–8, 464–5,
    481, 493–4, 511
  ML's reports to 84, 98, 108, 111–12,
    122–5, 201, 206, 208–17, 218, 302,
    354–5, 367, 374–6, 440–8
  ML's studies with 55, 66–8, 70–2,
    116–17, 124, 151, 267, 277
  presidency of 19, 38–56, 61–3, 66–97,
    111–13, 134, 186, 206, 272, 435–7,
    443–8, 501, 527–8
  Republican Party and 31, 35, 36, 63, 444
  retirement of 511, 522–5
  sexual misconduct and miscegenation
    charged to 53–5
  slavery and 18–21, 44, 55, 501
  State of the Union Address of 53
  visits of Indian chiefs to 124, 128, 131,
    135, 136, 206, 365–7, 369, 374,
    376–7, 390, 394, 407–8, 432, 434,
    436, 454
  writings of 18–19, 44, 210, 297
Jefferson River 273–4, 289, 310, 398, 405,
    531
Jessaume, René 188–9, 191, 192–3, 202,
    209, 432–3, 489
Jessaume, Toussaint 489
Johnson, Samuel 18
Jones, John Paul 58
Jordan, Winthrop 21

Joseph (chief) 308
Journals of the Lewis & Clark Expedition, The (Moulton, ed.) 104n
Judith River 237, 455
Jumping Fish 294, 296

Kansas 112, 531
Kansas Indians 149
Kansas River 111, 141, 147, 221, 437
Karsmizki, Ken 260n
Kentucky 2, 21, 27–8, 34, 38, 42, 54, 61, 76, 91, 110, 111, 113, 119, 128, 144, 347, 371, 448, 449, 490–1, 500–1, 522, 531
Kickapoo Indians 126, 491
Kiowa Indians 187
Kirwan, Richard 84
Knife River 187
Knox, Henry 59
Knoxville, Tenn. 38

Labiche, Francis 137, 146, 160, 294, 338, 385, 454, 461–2
Lacépède, Bernard 463
Lake Athabaska 63
Lake of the Woods 113n
Lancaster 79, 81
La Pérouse, Jean-François de Galaup, Comte de 58–9, 68
Large, Arlen 118–20, 262, 377, 417, 449
Larocque, François-Antoine 190–1, 194, 197
Lavender, David 377
Leander 435
Le Borgne (One Eye) (chief) 187, 432
Ledyard, John 58
Lemhi Pass 281n, 286, 287, 289–90, 295–6, 298, 398, 405, 530
Lemhi River 285, 286, 287, 289, 295–6, 299, 323
Lepage, Baptiste 221, 242, 314
Letters from a Farmer in Pennsylvania (Dickinson) 52
Letters of the Lewis and Clark Expedition (Jackson, ed.) 527
Lewis, Colonel Robert 2
Lewis, Fielding 3
Lewis, Meriwether:
    accidental shooting of 429–32, 433–4, 531
    anger of 381, 384, 423–4
    Army career of 22–9, 31–4, 36–7, 46–8, 91
    birth of 1, 2, 4
    botanical and wildlife knowledge of 4, 16, 21, 56, 66–8, 70, 83–4, 125, 140, 150–1, 152–4, 246, 283n, 352–3,

445–6
    burial place of 523n
    celestial observations of 79, 113, 116–17, 148, 169, 189, 229, 265, 273, 297, 310, 328, 347, 417, 452, 467, 470, 472, 529
    childhood and adolescence of 4–12
    compensation and reward of 462–3
    courage of 7, 10, 532
    courtships of 459, 467, 476–7, 479–80, 481, 490
    debts incurred by 453, 474, 478, 500, 504, 509–10, 512–14, 517, 524
    depressions of 51, 331–3, 480–1, 515–21, 523
    Detachment Orders of 127, 141, 144–6
    drinking habits of 15, 333, 475–6, 480, 481, 503, 515, 517, 530
    education and training of 8–12, 55, 66–8, 70–2, 76, 79–80, 81–5, 94, 117, 124–5
    elite political connections of 51–2, 55–6, 83
    ethnology of 301–6, 359–64
    failed iron-frame boat experiment of 73–8, 216, 238, 253–63
    family background of 2–7
    financial accounting of 215, 473–4, 478
    frontier skills and hunting of 7, 13, 36, 66, 72, 83, 124, 168–71, 181
    fur trade plan of 407–8, 442–44, 450, 453, 462, 481–4, 496, 502, 503–5
    as governor of Louisiana Territory 463, 467, 474, 479–514, 530
    horsemanship of 13, 36, 110, 120, 193, 195
    horses acquired from Indians by 296, 298–300, 308, 377, 379, 382, 387–9, 392, 397
    idealism of 14, 296–7
    illnesses of 116, 246, 319–22, 384, 464, 480, 495, 503–4
    impact of success and idleness on 475–7, 480–1
    Indian diplomacy of 183–90, 194–5, 199–205, 211–19, 283–300, 303–4, 324, 343, 346–7, 367, 370–2, 380–92, 430, 440, 491–2
    introspection and self-criticism of 296
    journals of 56, 67, 103–5, 116, 137, 151, 168–71, 201, 202, 205, 219, 220, 221, 224–5, 234, 237, 238, 250, 255, 257, 259–63, 268–9, 272, 296–7, 301–6, 312–13, 314–15, 341, 350–3, 357–8, 360–4, 378, 394–5, 399–401, 408, 450–4, 458, 464, 469–71, 494, 511, 513, 515, 517, 525–7

Lewis, Meriwether – *continued*
  land speculation of 27, 34, 478, 488, 491, 496, 531
  last will and testament of 515
  leadership qualities of 9, 140, 141–6, 197–8, 243–4, 288–9, 314–18, 425, 447, 480, 528–30
  as Mason 33–4, 494
  medical practices of 201–2, 232, 246–7, 253, 254, 272, 274, 347–8
  natural-history specimens collected by 125, 136, 140, 151, 152–4, 182, 209–10, 212–13, 226, 236, 283, 352, 368, 374, 394, 445, 454, 468, 471
  new species of plants and animals discovered by 151, 167, 168, 314, 439n, 471
  perseverance and self-possession of 10, 12, 288, 532
  physical appearance of 10, 113–14
  as planter and head of household 11–16, 21, 33–4, 94, 137, 210–11, 380
  politics of 31, 36–7, 47–9, 111, 114
  portraits and wax figure of 455, 471–2
  as presidential secretary 45–56, 65–70, 77, 342, 446, 487
  roving penchant of 10, 21, 25, 29, 33, 36
  scant attention to mineral deposits by 267
  suicide of 520–4, 525, 528
  suicide attempts of 515–16
  TJ's letter of credit for 327, 335, 493
  traveling library of 84, 236, 470
  wild animal encounters of 249–51
  writing style of 55, 103–5, 169–71, 247–8
  see also Lewis and Clark
Lewis, Nicholas 3, 4, 8
Lewis, Reuben 4, 9, 10, 11, 28, 34, 206, 367, 374, 377, 479, 481, 496, 500, 505
Lewis, Robert (Lewis's ancestor) 2
Lewis, Robert (Lewis's cousin) 9
Lewis, Thomas 3
Lewis, William 2–4
Lewis and Clark:
  co-command of 93–4, 133, 134
  complementary qualities of 91
  decision making of 240–6, 255, 257–8, 269, 274–5, 336–7, 399–401
  differences of opinion between 262, 269, 274–5, 336–7, 350
  early Army association of 32, 91
  friendship and trust of 91, 92, 99, 111, 132, 314–15, 447, 481, 489, 500
  joyful return and reception of 438, 448–50, 453–61
  naming of rivers by 149, 162, 172n, 231,

237, 239, 254, 265, 272, 307, 314, 455, 531
  plants named for 471n
  separations risked by 313–18, 325, 334–5, 339, 381–2, 405–6
  traders encountered by 431–33, 436–8
Lewis and Clark College 531
Lewis and Clark Expedition:
  arms and ammunition on 76–7, 81, 126, 144, 155, 156, 165, 257, 300, 319, 327, 355
  auction of artifacts from 453, 470
  canoes of 216, 218, 262–3, 264, 320
  costs of 86, 90–1, 128, 473–4
  flora and fauna seen on 128, 131, 139, 149–51, 152–4, 167–70, 180–2, 208, 224–8, 232–3, 238, 242, 249–51, 256, 264–5, 298, 315
  horses killed for food on 311–12, 315
  Indian guides used on 307–10, 311, 315–16, 402–5, 408–10
  Indian policy of 154–66, 173–5
  justice and punishment on 129, 148–9, 160, 186–7, 197
  keelboat and pirogues of 92, 98–102, 105–6, 115, 129, 135, 138–40, 141–6, 153, 163, 168, 172, 196, 207, 216, 218
  maps produced on 136, 213, 353, 357, 368, 374, 375, 415, 441, 446–7, 458, 470
  ML offered command of 66–8, 70, 71
  newspaper accounts of 374, 448–9, 457, 464–6
  notes lost from 140, 169, 171
  oral accounts of 448–50, 453
  origins of 57–70
  political consequences of 365–77
  preparation for 66–102
  published maps and documents of 375–6, 441, 525–7
  purposes of 72–3, 87, 88–90, 112, 144, 189–91, 404
  rumors about loss of 437
  scientific observations and notes of 150–1, 152–4, 168–9, 196, 208–17, 236, 298, 352–4, 439, 458
  security measures on 144–5, 150, 154–5, 171–5, 176–7, 188, 191, 198–9
  Spanish plot against 368–9
  supplying of 73–83, 85, 93, 109, 119–20, 121, 123–4, 125–7, 128, 132, 135, 217
  TJ's instructions for 72, 79, 81, 86–90, 92, 97, 112–13, 121, 124, 154, 163, 174, 230–1, 267, 310–11, 352–3, 397

WC offered co-command of 91–4
  winter of 1804–5 and 195–207, 329–30
  winter of 1805–6 and 338–58
  see also Corps of Discovery
Lewis and Clark Pass 266n, 310, 411n
Lewis and Clark: Pioneering Naturalists
  (Cutright) 352, 439n
Lewis and Clark River 338
Lewis, Fielding 3
Library Company 470
Lincoln, Abraham 41
Lincoln, Levi 52
Linnaean system 67
Linnaeus 84, 236
Lisa, Manuel 123–4, 226–7, 132, 135n,
  366, 453, 486, 496, 504
Little Osage Indians 492, 499
Little Raven (chief) 187
Little Thief (chief) 157, 159–61, 367
Livingston, Robert 63, 70
Locust Hill 3, 5–6, 11–12, 15–16, 21–2,
  27–8, 33, 52, 456, 478
Logan, George 52, 83
Lolo Hot Springs 311, 404
Lolo Trail 281n, 311, 323, 385, 395, 399,
  401–2, 404n, 408, 410, 439, 451, 529
London 24, 64, 225, 355, 363, 443
Lord Dunmore's War 2
Lorimier, Louis 119
Lost Tribe of Israel 82, 154
Louisiana Purchase 96–7, 110, 113, 121,
  122, 134, 144, 372, 373, 390, 444,
  463n, 482, 531
  formal transfer of power in 121, 127–8
  negotiation for 62–3, 69–70, 90
  political opposition to 69–70, 96–7, 121,
  528
  price of 69–70
Louisiana Territory 42–5, 60–3, 369, 435,
  528
  ML as governor of 463, 467, 474,
  480–514, 530
  Spain and 27, 42–5, 60–3, 68, 86–7, 97,
  128
  WC as superintendent of Indian affairs
  for 464, 491, 531
  see also New Orleans; Territory of
  Orleans; Upper Louisiana
Louisville, Ky. 99, 110, 113, 115, 119, 370,
  454, 488, 500
Louis XVI, king of France 58, 68
Loyal Land Company 57
Lukens, Isaiah 103

McClallen, John 437
McClellan, Robert 436–7
McCracken, Hugh 189

Mackay, Alexander 63
Mackay, James 123
McKean, Thomas 52, 68, 83
Mackenzie, Alexander 63–7, 466
MacKenzie, Charles 190, 191–3, 195, 197,
  209
McMahon, Bernard 468, 471
McNeal, Hugh 278–81, 290–1, 293, 348n
Madison, Dolley 50, 271
Madison, James 50, 52, 86, 271, 272, 474,
  493, 505, 511, 516, 518, 520, 524
Madoc, Prince 308
Magellan, Ferdinand 138
Majors, Harry 317
Malone, Dumas 8, 51, 375, 459–60, 494,
  528
Mandan Indians 71, 72, 97, 101, 120, 121,
  123, 141, 154, 156, 168, 183–6,
  187–206, 302, 329, 367, 375, 406, 407,
  428, 431–3, 463
  Arikara Indians and 183–9, 194–5, 432
  ceremonial and social life of 187, 188,
  199–201, 209, 364
  horsemanship of 188, 195, 200–1
  Lewis and Clark relations with 183–6,
  188–9, 194–5, 199–205, 212, 214,
  217–18, 364
  trading customs of 168, 187, 189, 204
Mardi Gras 486
Marias Pass 246n
Marias River 245, 246n, 259, 262, 313,
  398, 405, 407, 415–17, 421, 426–7,
  439, 451, 519, 528
Marietta, Ohio 108, 110
Marks, John 4–5, 6, 10, 11, 16, 27, 34
Marks, John Hastings 5, 6, 10, 94, 478,
  495–6, 524
Marks, Lucy Meriwether Lewis 3–6, 33,
  479, 515
  character and personality of 4–6, 479
  family background of 3
  herbal knowledge of 5, 7
  ML's correspondence with 5, 8, 10–11,
  26, 27–9, 31, 32–4, 94, 208, 495
  ML's relationship with 5, 7–8, 34, 52,
  456, 478
Marks, Mary Garland 6, 12, 94, 495
Marquette, Jacques 354
Marshall, Thomas Maitland 97
Martínez de Yrujo, Carlos 87
Maryland 24, 98
Massachusetts 1
Matthews, John 6
Maury, James 57
Maury, Matthew 9, 13, 33, 57
Medicine River 215, 249–50, 254, 417–18,
  422, 451

Memphis, Tenn. 128, 471
Meriwether, Colonel Nicholas 3, 8
Meriwether, Nicholas, II 3
Meriwether, William D. 9
Michaux, André 21
Mississippi 22, 38, 39, 41–5
Mississippi River 38–9, 41–2, 43, 55, 57–61,
    63, 67, 69, 71, 76–7, 89, 91–2, 94–7,
    112, 113n, 115–17, 122, 125–6, 129–31,
    135–6, 139–40, 150–1, 162, 196, 199,
    206, 208, 213, 226, 265, 278, 305, 319,
    366, 368, 371–4, 406, 408, 431, 438,
    442, 448, 481–3, 485, 491, 494, 515
  ascent of 101, 117–20, 321, 488, 489
  confluence of rivers with 76, 115, 129,
    210
Missouri Gazette 494, 496, 501, 514, 531n
Missouri Historical Society 472n
Missouri Indians 156, 210, 367
Missouri River 5, 12, 42–3, 48, 56–7,
    59–61, 66–9, 71, 73, 76, 84, 87–9,
    91–3, 95, 97–8, 100–1, 108, 442–4
  ascent of 107, 110, 112, 129, 135–95,
    221–82, 286, 354, 288, 368
  breaks area of 235, 240n
  confluence of rivers with 129, 150, 192,
    210, 214, 230, 240–1, 257
  descent of 379, 398, 405
  Great Bend of 71, 84, 434
  Great Falls of 240, 244–50, 253, 257,
    259, 263–5, 288, 333, 354, 377, 394,
    398, 405, 411
  portage 240, 251, 252–7, 288, 405, 415
  source of 281, 297, 376
  Three Forks area of 192, 215, 230, 268,
    271, 273, 308, 333, 398, 518–19
  White Cliffs area of 235–9, 240n, 333
Monongahela River 27, 38
Monroe, James 54, 63, 69, 70
Montana Territory 230–1, 235, 259,
    410–11
Montana, University of 411
Monticello 3, 11, 17, 39–40, 50, 52–3, 65,
    67, 116, 374–7, 454–5, 463, 468, 471,
    474–5, 478, 497, 511, 522, 525
  expedition plants and artifacts at
    Indian Hall of
  library of
  TJ's retirement at
Montreal 63, 184, 407, 443
Morgan, Daniel 27
Morris, Robert 21, 60
Moulton, Gary 104, 105, 192n, 208, 232,
    243n, 245n, 283n, 288n, 304n, 348n,
    389n, 410n, 527
Mountain Men 433, 528
Mount Vernon 35, 53

Museum of the Rockies 260n

Napoleon I, Emperor of France 61–3, 69,
    95–7, 122, 144
Nashville, Tenn. 76, 78, 85
Natchez, Miss. 91, 376
Natchez Trace 517, 123n
National Park Service 340n
*Nautical Almanac and Astronomical
    Ephemeris, The* 84
Navy, U.S. 377
Nebraska Territory 151, 165–7
Neely, James 517, 518, 222
*New and Complete Dictionary of the Arts
    and Sciences, A* 236
New Jersey 24–5, 51, 475
Newman, John 186–7, 198, 216, 461–2
New Mexico 111, 112, 121, 124, 210, 368,
    369, 437
New Orleans 41–4, 61–3, 69–70, 85, 90,
    95, 123–4, 136, 368, 374–5, 482, 486,
    488, 490, 500, 512, 514, 517, 531
New York, N.Y. 37, 39, 146, 225, 366, 376,
    435, 443n, 486, 531
New York *Evening Post* 54
New-York Historical Society 472n
Nez Percé Indians 204n, 212, 288, 289,
    294, 298, 300, 303, 310–11, 315,
    318–20, 322–4, 331, 353–5, 379,
    383–4, 386–400, 404–6, 409–11, 416,
    421, 435, 439, 442–3, 451, 519
Northern Pacific Railroad 246n
North West Company 63, 66, 173, 187,
    189, 191–2, 197, 406–7, 421, 430, 443,
    482–4
Northwest Ordinance 44
Northwest Passage 58, 352, 373, 442, 455,
    458
Northwest Territory 24, 52, 45, 57, 59, 66,
    72
Notes on the State of Virginia (Jefferson)
    18–19, 210

Oglesby, Richard 123, 453
Ohio River 2, 27, 33, 36, 44–5, 76, 87, 92,
    98–9, 101–2, 126
  descent of 94–5, 101, 103–112, 114–16,
    321, 527
  portage 103, 105–6, 107
Ohio Territory 2, 24, 29, 31, 33, 42–4, 91,
    122, 347
Old Toby (Indian guide) 307–11, 313, 315,
    322, 404, 439, 451, 519
Omaha Indians 123, 137, 156, 161, 175–7
One Eye (Le Borgne) (chief) 188, 432
Only One Man Died (Chuinard) 253n,
    391n

Ordway, John 127–31, 145, 148, 150, 159, 165, 173, 176, 185–6, 197, 199, 229, 357, 405, 426–7, 429, 454, 470, 473
Oregon Historical Society Museum 245n
Oregon River 112, 173
Oregon Territory 43, 56, 97, 144, 368n, 407, 440
Osage Indians 124–6, 128, 454, 472, 491–2
  visits of, to Washington, D.C. 131, 132, 135, 136, 206, 365–7, 457
  see also Great Osage Indians; Little Osage Indians
Osage River 122, 137, 140, 367, 483, 492
Oto Indians 153, 156–61, 210, 367, 369, 377
Ottawa Indians 2

Pacific Ocean 5, 21, 56, 57–8, 60–1, 63–8, 73, 76, 87, 98, 120, 123–5
  coastal areas of 43, 59, 71, 89
Paine, Thomas 52
Paris 58, 60, 63, 70, 446
Paris, Treaty of 60
Parker, Thomas 79
Partisan, the (chief) 172–4, 176–8
Passage Through the Garden: Lewis and Clark and the Image of the American Northwest (Allen) 65
Patterson, Robert 72, 79–80, 84, 106
Patterson, William 106
Pawnee Indians 367
Peace River 63
Peale, Charles Willson 52, 375, 455, 471, 526
Peale's Museum 455, 471
Pennsylvania 24–7, 52, 68
  University of 83, 84, 109, 526
Penrose, Clement 513
Pernier, John 495, 517–20, 523
Philadelphia, Pa. 2, 38, 39, 51, 52, 55, 70, 72, 76, 77–85, 89, 92, 94, 96–8, 103, 342, 375, 445, 468–81
  Museum of 455
Piegan Indians 420–7
Pike, Zebulon 436
Pinckney, Charles 493
Pittsburgh, Pa. 27, 33, 38, 47, 76, 85, 92, 94, 97–100, 107, 370
Pittsburgh *Gazette* 448, 465
Pizarro, Francisco 357
Platte River 141, 146, 150–1, 156, 159, 206, 210, 230, 436–7, 504
Poland 58
Ponca Indians 156, 452
Potomac River 3, 38
Potts, John 148, 452
Practical Introduction to Spherics and

Nautical Astronomy, A 84
Pratz, Antoine Simor Le Page du 67, 84, 470
President 435
President's House 46, 50–5, 68, 71, 116, 332, 342, 355, 366, 375, 446, 457, 459, 461, 463–4, 468
Preston, William 490–1
Princeton College 527
Prospect Before Us, The (Callender) 53
Provenchere, Peter 509
Pryor, Nathaniel 100, 114, 129, 148, 163–4, 241–2, 339, 405–6, 430, 464, 489, 493, 505, 507
Pursh, Frederick 471

Quaife, Milo 527
Quebec 184, 190
Quebec Act of 1774 2

railroads 41, 431
Randolph, Martha Jefferson 26, 40, 50, 463–4
Randolph, Thomas Mann 463
Rannie 52
Raven Man (chief) 187
Red River 365, 373, 436
Reed, Moses B. 160, 162, 186, 216
Regulations for the Order and Discipline of the Troops of the United States (Steuben) 30, 31–2
Republican Party 35–7, 50–1, 53, 55, 70, 114, 444, 468
  TJ and 31, 35, 48, 49, 50, 63, 444
Richard 435
Richmond *Enquirer* 456
Richmond *Recorder* 54
Rio Grande River 42, 437
Rivanna River 4
Robidoux, Joseph 366
Robinson, John 127
Rockfish River 1
Rocky Mountains 42, 56, 73, 114, 188, 192, 193, 204n, 214, 230, 236, 240, 245, 247, 257, 267, 281, 283–4, 301, 305–6, 309, 315, 319, 355, 370, 379, 390, 417, 422, 442, 444, 469, 484, 511, 519
Roman Catholic Church 2, 137
Roman legions 147, 346
Ronda, James 155, 156, 164, 183, 205, 209, 294, 300, 329, 437, 357, 390, 419, 422, 458
Roosevelt, Theodore 104
Rosa, Salvator 248
Rush, Benjamin 70, 81–3, 109
Rush's Pills 82, 116, 154, 202, 272, 319

Russell, Charley, 144, 181n, 265
Russell, Gilbert 515–17, 523
Russia 42–3, 58, 66

Sacagawea 192, 219–20, 241, 246, 257,
    265, 336–7, 340, 349, 351, 391, 405,
    431, 489, 519
  character and fortitude of 235, 273, 294,
    433n
  Charbonneau and 192, 202–3, 212,
    219–20, 231, 252, 254–5, 294, 295,
    297, 298, 302, 340, 405, 433
  food gathered by 220, 231–2, 255
  Hidatsa capture of 192, 215, 273, 294
  illness and treatment of 252–3, 254, 269
  as interpreter 192, 203, 209, 241, 252–3,
    269, 294, 298, 359, 385
  nickname of 337
  pregnancy and childbirth of 192, 202–3
  Shoshone Indians and 192, 215, 257, 268,
    273–8, 286, 293, 294, 297–8, 301–3,
    385
  WC on 433n
St. Charles, Mo. 145–6, 156, 206, 210, 327,
    438
St. Clair, Arthur 24, 59
St. Lawrence River 65, 355, 443
St. Louis 34, 43, 60, 71, 73, 76, 77, 89, 95,
    100, 112, 115, 117, 119–21, 123,
    126–9, 131–3, 135–8, 145–6, 151, 155,
    160, 163, 165, 187, 189, 191, 206, 208,
    212–13, 215, 216n, 218, 225, 257, 273,
    276, 289, 333, 354n, 366–70, 374,
    376–7, 393, 398, 406, 419, 421, 432–3,
    435–6, 438, 440–55, 461, 469, 473–4,
    479–514, 517, 519, 523, 525
St. Louis Missouri River Fur Company
    496, 502–3, 504, 528, 531
Saint-Mémin, Charles B. J. Févret de 472
Salcedo, Nemesio 379
Salish Indians 308
Salmon River 286–7, 388n, 295, 299, 307
salt making 339, 341, 342, 350, 351
Santa Fe 111, 112, 121, 124, 210, 368–9,
    437
Santo Domingo 62
Sauk Indians 372, 491, 496, 498
Seaman (dog) 101, 107, 117, 129, 181, 229,
    256, 381, 519
Sedition Act 35, 54
Senate, U.S. 133, 462–3, 500
Shahaptian language 324
Shakespeare, William 11, 40, 503
Shannon, George 100, 111, 129, 162, 226,
    254, 493, 494, 505, 522, 526
Shawnee Indians 2, 30, 115, 119, 491
Sheaff, Henry 52

Shields, John 100, 127–9, 167–8, 203–5,
    242, 255, 278–80, 291–3, 337, 343,
    356, 381, 391, 461–2
Shoshone Indians (Snake Indians) 192,
    193, 202, 203, 212, 215, 217, 241, 253,
    257, 269, 272, 301–6, 354, 389
  contact and communication with
    283–300, 301
  customs and clothing of 301–2, 303–4
  demeanor of 302
  diseases of 303
  economics and politics of 301, 314–5
  geographical information conveyed by
    307–10, 312, 315–18
  Hidatsa Indians' warfare with 192, 215,
    273, 278, 289, 294, 411, 429
  horsemanship of 202, 217, 273, 279–80,
    284, 286, 289–91, 294–6, 298–300,
    301, 312–3, 304, 355
  hunting of 304
  personal and sexual relations among
    301, 302–3, 304–5
  physical appearance and stature of
    301–2
  Sacagawea and 192, 215, 257, 268,
    273–8, 286, 293, 294, 297–81, 302,
    303, 385
  search for 263–70, 313
  tribes hostile to 192, 193, 215, 266, 273,
    278, 285, 289–93, 300, 301–2,
    304–5, 313
Simmons, William 473, 478
Sioux Indians 126, 136, 147, 150, 154–5,
    160–4, 166, 167, 171, 173, 175–9,
    183–4, 189, 192–4, 198–9, 205,
    210–12, 216, 218, 357, 301, 354, 365,
    373, 398, 406–7, 430, 432, 434, 435,
    440, 444, 484, 496, 503, 506, 519
  see also Teton Sioux Indians; Yankton
    Sioux Indians
Skelton, William 29, 30
Slaughter, Thomas 25–6
slavery 2, 5, 6, 8, 11, 12, 15–21, 122
  ML and 8, 11, 12, 15–21, 242, 380, 480,
    500
  TJ and 18–22, 45, 500–2
  WC and, *see* York
smallpox 9, 28, 111, 161, 182, 188, 304,
    348, 359
Smith, Adam 123
Smith, Robert 265
Smith, R. S. 509
Smith's River 265
Snake Indians, *see* Shoshone Indians
    (Snake Indians)
Snake River 322–3, 337, 342, 384–5, 388
Soulard, Antoine 121, 122

South West Post 76, 77, 85, 115
Spain 25, 43, 44, 60–2, 86, 97, 121, 128, 368–9, 435
Spring Mountain 403
Square Butte 242, 265, 411
State Department, U.S. 474, 509, 531
Statute for Religious Freedom, Virginia 18
steam engine 19, 40, 118, 446, 531
Steuben, Baron Frederick William von 30
Steubenville, Ohio 106
Stoddard, Amos 120, 128, 131–2, 134, 136, 138, 146, 365, 367, 369–70, 376, 490n, 516
Struck by the Pana (chief) 165

Tabeau, Pierre-Antoine 184
Talleyrand, Charles Maurice de 34
Tarleton, Banastre 6
Tennessee 38, 42, 76, 78, 114
Territory of Orleans 463n
Tetoharsky (chief) 323, 236, 327, 328, 386
Teton Sioux Indians 164, 171–9, 212, 434, 437
Texas 97, 435–6
Thames River 64
Thompson, David 84
Thompson, James 248
Thwaites, Reuben Gold 104n, 446n, 466
Tiber Dam 242
tobacco 6, 11, 16, 19, 44, 80, 155, 371n
Transylvania Company 2
Travellers Rest 391, 395, 398, 403
Treasury Department, U.S. 90
Treaty of Greenville 31, 157
Treaty of Paris 60
Tripoli 377
Twisted Hair (chief) 318, 310, 322–4, 326, 327–8, 379, 386, 388–9, 395
Two Medicine River 417, 418, 422, 451

United States:
    agriculture in 6, 16–17, 19, 40, 87
    1801 population of 38
    foreign colonization feared in 58, 61–6
    immigration and emigration in 371–4
    mail service in 76, 492
    political parties in 31, 34–7
    secessionist threats in 24, 31, 41
    travel and commerce in 39–42, 43, 62, 63, 69, 76, 87–9
United States Military Academy 134
University of Nebraska Press 527
Upper Louisiana 43, 120–2, 127–8, 136, 173, 190, 208, 210–11, 367, 370–1, 373, 431, 440, 442, 481–4

Vancouver, George 59, 84, 325, 330, 338, 458
Van Wormer, Joe 171n
Varnum, J. B., Jr. 470
venereal disease 185, 232, 303, 304, 314, 347–8, 360
Vietnam War 384
Virginia 1–22, 24, 25, 210
    Albemarle County in 1–12, 31–4, 48
    Piedmont and Tidewater areas of 1, 16
    plantation life in 1–8, 11–22, 33, 45, 380
    University of 125
voyagers, French Canadian 63, 135–6, 140, 146, 154, 157, 160, 163, 168, 183, 221, 503
Voyages from Montreal, on the River St. Lawrence, Through the Continent of North America, to the Frozen and Pacific (Mackenzie) 65
Voyage to the Pacific Ocean, A (Cook) 67

Waddell, James 9, 10
Walker, Thomas 57
Wallawalla Indians 324, 384–5
Wanapam Indians 324
War Department, U.S. 31, 49, 57, 90, 134, 216, 369, 447, 452, 454, 461, 463–4, 473, 478, 492, 494, 512, 530
War of 1812 469, 173, 232, 526
Warfington, Richard 129, 135, 140, 191, 216, 218, 219n, 236n, 367, 374, 433, 461–2
Washington, D.C. 39, 41, 46–56, 86
    Indian delegations to 124, 128, 131, 135, 136, 206, 365–7, 369, 374, 376–7, 390, 394, 407–8, 432, 434, 436, 454, 457
Washington, George 2, 3, 16, 21, 40, 60, 295, 450, 455
    land speculation of 2, 16, 23
    military career of 4, 22, 25, 35
    presidency of 21–5, 34–5, 50, 60
Washington *Advertiser* 515
Washington *National Intelligencer* 95, 448, 457, 460, 464
Watkuweis 320
Watt, James 19
Wayne, Anthony 24, 31–3, 36, 157, 368
Weippe Prairie 395–7, 404n
Weiser, Peter 127
"Welsh Indians" 67, 154, 192n, 308, 460
Werner, William 339, 406
Weuche (chief) 164, 165
Wheeling, Va. 36, 102, 106, 107, 108, 370
When the Land Belonged to God (Russell) 181n
Whiskey Rebellion 22–9, 39

White Bear Islands 255–6, 261
White Crane Man (chief) 165
White Hair (chief) 491–2
White House 46n, 51 52
Whitehouse, Joseph 191, 236, 308, 340
White Over Black: American Attitudes Toward the Negro (Jordan) 21
Whitney, Eli 19
Wilkinson, Benjamin 496
Wilkinson, James 48–9, 368–71, 374, 435–8, 487, 496, 499, 510
Willamette River 330, 380
Willard, Alexander 114, 150, 267, 313, 334–5, 382
William and Mary, College of 12, 94
Williamsburg, Va. 94
Wilson, Alexander 20–1, 152, 472, 523n
Wilson, Woodrow 53n
Winchester, Va. 26
Windsor, Private 242, 243–4, 528
Wisconsin 435

State Historical Society of 537
Wistar, Caspar 84, 96
Wood, Eliza 469
Wood, Maria 244
Wood River 120–1, 124, 126–7, 128, 132, 133, 135, 150, 184, 197, 373, 438
Woods, Edgar 6
Woods, William 478–9
World of the Pronghorns, The (Van Wormer) 171n
Wyandot Indians 33

Yakima Indians 324, 385
Yankton Sioux Indians 146, 163–6, 435
Yellept (chief) 324, 384–5
Yellowstone National Park 230, 271, 433
Yellowstone River 214, 228–30, 257, 259, 398, 405, 409, 419, 428, 430, 431
York (slave) 114, 115, 129, 131, 168, 185, 199, 203, 219, 246, 295, 328, 336–7, 339, 405, 454, 451–2, 500–1